Good Housekeeping

COOKERY BOOK

Good Housekeeping

COOKERY BOOK

THE COOK'S CLASSIC COMPANION

This edition published in Great Britain in 2011
by Collins & Brown
10 Southcombe Street
London W14 0RA

An imprint of Anova Books Company Ltd

The Good Housekeeping website is
www.allaboutyou.com/goodhousekeeping

10 9 8 7 6 5 4 3 2

ISBN 978-1-84340-592-4

A catalogue record for this book is available from the
British Library.

Reproduction by Dot Gradations Ltd, UK
Printed and bound by 1010 Printing Ltd, China

This book can be ordered direct from the publisher at
www.anovabooks.com

NOTES

— Both metric and imperial measures are given for the
recipes. Follow either set of measures, not a mixture
of both, as they are not interchangeable.

— All spoon measures are level.
1 tsp = 5ml spoon; 1 tbsp = 15ml spoon.

— Ovens and grills must be preheated to the specified
temperature.

— Use sea salt and freshly ground black pepper unless
otherwise suggested.

— Fresh herbs should be used unless dried herbs are
specified in a recipe.

— Medium eggs should be used except where otherwise
specified. Free-range eggs are recommended.

— Note that some recipes contain raw or lightly cooked
eggs. The young, elderly, pregnant women and anyone
with an immune-deficiency disease should avoid these
because of the slight risk of salmonella.

Picture Credits
Photographers: Marie-Louise Avery (pages 409, 452, 453, 454, 457 and 459);
Neil Barclay (pages 55, 79, 147T, 236B, 264 and 265); Steve Baxter (pages 99,
243, 248 and 443); Martin Brigdale (pages 129, 147B, 151, 262B, 269, 355,
369, 423 and 445); Nicki Dowey (pages 45, 46, 47, 49, 50, 52, 65, 66, 69, 70T,
74, 77, 80, 115, 120T, 141, 142, 143, 144, 145, 146, 148, 149, 154, 167, 179, 182,
184, 185, 189, 190, 200T, 202, 209T, 213, 222B, 230T, 232, 233T, 237B, 247B,
250, 225 1T, 262T, 263, 266, 268B, 273, 284, 285, 286B, 290T, 292B, 298T, 310,
311, 312B, 313T, 314T, 315, 316, 318B, 319B, 320B, 321T, 333, 334, 337, 342B,
350B, 351, 353T, 357B, 358, 363, 364, 366, 367, 368, 391, 402, 406, 408, 410,
420, 442, 444B, 447, 448, 456T, 465B and 473); Will Heap (pages 62, 233B,
286T and 407); Emma Lee (pages 214 and 414); William Lingwood (page
419); Gareth Morgans (page 169); Myles New (page 341); Craig Robertson
(pages 51B, 53T, 54, 58B, 85, 95, 98, 108, 120B, 136, 137, 139, 153, 155, 162B,
165, 166, 176, 177, 180, 183, 197,198, 203, 206, 208, 209B, 211B, 242, 268T,
270, 277, 296, 299T, 321B, 325-6, 330, 331, 332, 336, 338, 340, 342T, 347, 348,
352, 356, 359, 360, 361, 362, 365, 379B, 394, 404 and 464); Clive Streeter
(page 138); Brett Stevens (page 335); Roger Stowell (page 164B); Lucinda
Symons (pages 28, 32-9, 43, 44, 48, 51T, 53B, 57, 58T, 59, 67, 68, 70B, 71, 75,
76, 81, 86-9, 90, 92, 93, 94, 96, 97, 102-7, 109, 110, 111, 112, 113, 114, 116,
117, 119, 121, 122, 123, 124, 125, 126, 127, 128T, 134-5, 150, 152, 160-1,
162T, 163, 164T, 168, 174-5, 181, 187, 188, 191, 192, 193, 194-5, 199, 200B,
201, 204-5, 207, 210, 211T, 212, 215, 216, 218-9, 220, 221, 222T, 223, 226, 229,
230B, 231, 234, 235, 236T, 237T, 244, 245, 246, 247T, 249, 251, 256-7, 259-61,
267, 271, 272, 278-83, 287, 288, 289, 290B, 291, 292T, 293, 294, 295, 297, 298B,
299B, 300B, 301, 302, 303,304, 305, 309, 312T, 313B, 314B, 317, 318T, 319T,
320T, 339, 345, 346, 348, 350T, 353B, 354, 357T, 370, 372, 373, 374, 375, 376,
377, 378, 379T, 380, 381, 382, 383, 384385, 387, 388, 389, 392, 395, 398, 399,
401, 403, 405, 411, 413, 415, 416, 418, 421, 422, 424430, 433, 440, 444t, 446,
455, 456b, 468 and 470); Martin Thompson (pages 412 and 427); Philip Webb
(pages 196, 300T, 429 and 441); Kate Whitaker (pages 390, 417 and 449)

Home Economists: Joanna Farrow, Emma Jane Frost, Teresa Goldfinch, Alice
Hart, Lucy McKelvie, Kim Morphew, Aya Nishimura, Bridget Sargeson, Kate
Trend and Mari Mererid Williams

Stylists: Wei Tang, Helen Trent and Fanny Ward

CONTENTS

FOREWORD

Cooking occupies a lot of my time. It is literally a labour of love: I work with food and I love it. Judging by the many reader letters we get at Good Housekeeping, I know that there are others who, like me, cook to relax, to show they care, to exercise creativity, to chat and, of course, to feed. Naturally, there are nights when cooking is more of a rushed duty than the cerebral experience I had hoped it to be, but that's to be expected with the busy lives we lead.

Whenever I have a spare few hours, I'll dive into my cookery books. Admittedly, with a collection of hundreds this can take some dedication and determination (and lots of cups of tea!), but the forthcoming inspiration and increased understanding is always worth the effort. Occasionally, a tidying bug will get hold of me and I'll set forth with keen vigour. The aim? To put my collection on a diet, thin out the stragglers and use the remaining books more efficiently. But just at the critical recycling moment, a little chef on my shoulder always pipes up by whispering that a day might come when I'll want to learn how to make Hungarian cakes … and back into the collection it goes.

To make a great cookery book, and one you'll turn to time and again, you need a mix of inspiring recipes, helpful tips, truthful photography and a user-friendly index. This book ticks all these boxes and offers so much more on top. It really will become your first port of call to answer all your culinary queries, and each and every recipe has been developed and triple tested in our dedicated test kitchens, so they're guaranteed to work.

It's a fantastic book and I hope you enjoy it.

Meike.

Meike Beck
Cookery Editor
Good Housekeeping

THE GOOD HOUSEKEEPING INSTITUTE AND THE COOKERY BOOK

The Good Housekeeping Institute was created in 1924 to provide readers of Good Housekeeping magazine with expert consumer advice and delicious easy-to-follow recipes. These ideals still hold true today. The Good Housekeeping *Cookery Book* is the Institute's famous classic cookbook. Since its first publication in 1948 it has served four generations of cooks and sold more than 2 million copies, firmly establishing it as the ultimate cook's bible. This edition has been completely revised and updated for the 21st-century cook, while keeping faith with the traditions and precision of the original book. Every recipe published in this book has been rigorously triple-tested by the Good Housekeeping Institute experts so that you can cook any dish with confidence.

STOCKS AND STUFFINGS

STOCKS

Well-flavoured stocks form the basis of soups, sauces, stews and many other savoury dishes. You will find an extensive range of ready-made stock products in most supermarkets and these have improved significantly in recent years, but the flavour of a good home-made stock is incomparable. Stocks are easy to make.

Fishmongers are usually only too happy to let you have fish bones and trimmings; similarly poulterers and butchers will generally supply chicken carcasses and other bones. Freeze any stock that is not required for immediate use, in manageable quantities. To save freezer space, you can boil the stock to reduce by half and concentrate prior to freezing.

The characteristics of a good stock are clarity and a fine flavour. Guard against over-seasoning, as boiling concentrates the flavour and saltiness. Fat and impurities will make a stock cloudy, so these should always be removed by skimming the surface from time to time during cooking. If possible, use a conical sieve to strain the stock and allow the liquid to drip through; avoid pressing the vegetables in the sieve or you will lose clarity.

Once strained, cool the stock quickly, ideally over a bowl of chilled water, then chill. A thin, solid layer of fat will form on the surface of most stocks; this can easily be removed. Bring the stock up to the boil before use.

If you haven't the time to make your own stock, opt for one of the better ready-made alternatives. Fresh stocks available in cartons from the chilled cabinet, liquid stock concentrates and vegetable bouillon powder are preferable to powdered stock cubes. These are still inclined to be strong and salty so, if you use them, do so sparingly, or opt for a low-salt variety.

VEGETABLE STOCK

Makes 1.1 litres (2 pints)
Preparation 10 minutes
Cooking time 35 minutes

225g (8oz) onions, roughly chopped
225g (8oz) celery sticks, roughly chopped
225g (8oz) trimmed leeks, roughly chopped
225g (8oz) carrots, roughly chopped
2 bay leaves
a few fresh thyme sprigs
1 small bunch of parsley
10 black peppercorns
$^1/_2$ tsp sea salt

1 Put the onions, celery sticks, leeks and carrots into a large pan.
2 Add 1.7 litres (3 pints) cold water, the herbs, black peppercorns and salt. Bring slowly to the boil and skim the surface. Partially cover the pan and simmer for 30 minutes; check the seasoning.
3 Strain the stock through a fine sieve into a bowl and allow to cool. Cover and keep in the fridge for up to three days. Use as required.

NUTRITION PER 100ml (3$^1/_2$fl oz)
5 cals | trace fat (trace sats) | 1g carbs | 0.2g salt Ⓥ

BASIC BONE STOCK

Makes about 900ml–1.1 litres (1$^1/_2$–2 pints)
Preparation 10 minutes
Cooking time about 3 hours

900g (2lb) meat bones, fresh or from cooked meat
2 onions, chopped
2 celery sticks, chopped
2 carrots, chopped
1 tsp salt
3 black peppercorns
bouquet garni (1 bay leaf, a few fresh parsley and thyme sprigs)

1 Chop the bones. Put in a pan with 2 litres (3$^1/_2$ pints) water, the vegetables, salt, peppercorns and herbs. Bring to the boil and skim off any scum. Cover and simmer for about 3 hours. Strain the stock and, when cold, remove all traces of fat.

COOK'S TIP
If using a pressure cooker, add the bones and 1.4 litres (2$^1/_2$ pints) water, bring to the boil and skim. Add the vegetables, salt, peppercorns and herbs. Bring to High 6.8kg (15lb) pressure and cook for 1–1$^1/_4$ hours. If you are using marrow bones, increase the water to 1.7 litres (3 pints) and cook for 2 hours. Reduce the pressure at room temperature.

NUTRITION PER 100ml (3$^1/_2$fl oz)
12 cals | 1g fat (trace sats) | 1g carbs | 0.5g salt

CHICKEN STOCK

Makes 1.1 litres (2 pints)
Preparation 10 minutes
Cooking time about 2 hours

225g (8oz) onions, roughly chopped
150g (5oz) trimmed leeks, roughly chopped
225g (8oz) celery sticks, roughly chopped
1.6kg (3½ lb) raw chicken bones
bouquet garni (2 bay leaves, a few fresh parsley and
    thyme sprigs)
1 tsp black peppercorns
½ tsp sea salt

1 Put the vegetables into a large pan with the chicken
bones, 3 litres (5¼ pints) cold water, the bouquet garni,
peppercorns and salt. Bring slowly to the boil and skim
the surface. Partially cover the pan and simmer gently for
2 hours; check the seasoning.
2 Strain the stock through a fine sieve into a bowl and cool
quickly. Cover and keep in the fridge for up to three days.
Remove the fat from the surface and use the stock as required.

COOK'S TIP
Instead of chicken bones, you can use a large boiling
chicken – obtainable from selected butchers and
poulterers. Or use the poultry giblets, if they are available.

NUTRITION PER 100ml (3½ fl oz)
10 cals | 1g fat (trace sats) | 1g carbs | 0.2g salt

FISH STOCK

Makes 900ml (1½ pints)
Preparation 10 minutes
Cooking time 35 minutes

900g (2lb) fish bones and trimmings
2 carrots, chopped
1 onion, chopped
2 celery sticks, sliced
bouquet garni (1 bay leaf, a few fresh parsley and
    thyme sprigs)
6 white peppercorns
½ tsp sea salt

1 Wash and dry the fish trimmings and put into a large pan.
2 Add the vegetables to the pan together with 900ml
(1½ pints) cold water, the bouquet garni, peppercorns and
salt. Bring slowly to the boil and skim the surface. Cover and
simmer gently for about 30 minutes.
3 Strain the stock through a fine sieve into a bowl and check
the seasoning. Cool quickly, cover and keep in the fridge for
up to two days. Use as required.

TRY SOMETHING DIFFERENT
For court bouillon, an enriched fish stock, add 150ml (¼ pint)
dry white wine and 3 tbsp white wine vinegar at step 2.

NUTRITION PER 100ml (3½ fl oz)
5 cals | trace fat (trace sats) | 1g carbs | 0.2g salt

BASIC GRAVY

Makes about 300ml (½ pint)
Preparation 2 minutes
Cooking time 2–3 minutes

1 Carefully pour (or skim) off the fat from a corner of the
roasting tin, leaving the sediment behind. Put the tin on the
hob over a medium heat and pour in 300–450ml (½–¾
pint) vegetable water, or chicken, vegetable or meat stock
as appropriate.
2 Stir thoroughly, scraping up the sediment, and boil steadily
until the gravy is a rich brown colour.

TRY SOMETHING DIFFERENT
Rich Wine Gravy Deglaze the roasting tin with about
150ml (¼ pint) red or white wine, or 90ml (3fl oz) fortified
wine such as sherry or Madeira, and allow to bubble for a
minute or two before adding the stock or water. For a
sweeter flavour, add 2 tbsp redcurrant jelly with the wine.

Thick Gravy Sprinkle 1–2 tbsp flour into the roasting tin
and cook, stirring, until browned, then gradually stir in the
liquid and cook, stirring, for 2–3 minutes until smooth and
slightly thickened.

COOK'S TIPS
- Gravy is traditionally served with roast meat
  and poultry.
- If possible, make the gravy in the roasting tin while
  the joint (or bird) is resting. This will incorporate
  the meat juices that have escaped during roasting.
- A little gravy browning can be added to intensify
  the flavour and colour.

NUTRITION PER 100ml (3½ fl oz)
10 cals | 2g fat (1g sats) | 1g carbs | 0.2g salt

STUFFINGS

A moist, tasty stuffing will enhance the flavour of poultry and game birds; it will also improve their appearance by helping to plump the bird into a neat shape. Boned joints of meat, whole boned fish, and vegetables such as peppers, aubergines and large tomatoes, lend themselves perfectly to stuffing, too.

Most stuffings are based on breadcrumbs, rice, sausage meat, oatmeal or suet, with added flavouring ingredients and beaten egg or other liquid to bind the stuffing together. If required, the dry ingredients can be mixed together in advance, but the liquid should be added shortly before use. Stuff the bird (or meat or fish) just before cooking, and weigh after stuffing in order to calculate the cooking time.

When stuffing poultry, stuff the neck end only to ensure sufficient heat penetration through to the body cavity. The stuffing swells during cooking as it absorbs juices from the meat, poultry or fish, so don't pack it in too tightly or it may spill out. Cook any surplus stuffing in a separate baking dish.

HERB AND LEMON STUFFING

Serves 4
Preparation 10 minutes
Cooking time 10 minutes, plus cooling
Sufficient for a 1.4kg (3lb) oven-ready chicken

40g (1½ oz) butter
1 small onion, chopped
1 garlic clove, crushed
75g (3oz) white breadcrumbs
2 tbsp freshly chopped flat-leafed parsley
2 tbsp freshly chopped tarragon or thyme
finely grated zest and juice of 1 small lemon
1 medium egg yolk
salt and ground black pepper

1 Melt the butter in a small pan, add the onion and garlic, and fry gently for 7–10 minutes to soften. Tip into a bowl and leave to cool.
2 Add the breadcrumbs, chopped herbs, lemon zest and juice, then stir in the egg yolk to bind the stuffing. Season well with salt and ground black pepper.

CHESTNUT STUFFING

Serves 10
Preparation 15 minutes
Cooking time about 50 minutes
Sufficient for a 4.5–5.4kg (10–12lb) oven-ready turkey

450g (1lb) fresh chestnuts or 225g (8oz) can whole
    chestnuts (unsweetened), drained and roughly chopped
25g (1oz) butter
2 onions, chopped
350g (12oz) fresh breadcrumbs
75g (3oz) shredded suet
3 tbsp creamed horseradish
1 tsp lemon juice
salt and ground black pepper

1 If using fresh chestnuts, make a small cut along the flat side of each. Bake in the oven at 200°C (180°C fan oven) mark 6 for 10 minutes or until the skins crack. Peel when cool. Simmer in salted water for 20 minutes or until tender. Drain and chop.
2 Melt the butter in a frying pan and fry the onions until soft but not coloured. Remove from the heat, stir in the chestnuts, breadcrumbs, suet, horseradish, lemon juice and seasoning.
3 Fry slowly, stirring occasionally, for 15–20 minutes, or spoon into an ovenproof dish, cover and bake in the oven at 200°C (180°C fan oven) mark 6 for 30–35 minutes. Uncover and bake for a further 15 minutes. Cool before use.

TRY SOMETHING DIFFERENT
Sausage Meat and Chestnut Stuffing Put 225g (8oz) fresh breadcrumbs, 450g (1lb) pork sausage meat, finely grated zest of 1 orange, 1 tsp dried sage, and salt and pepper in a large bowl. Stir well to mix. Drain and roughly chop a 400g (14oz) can whole chestnuts in water. Add to the bowl with the juice of 1 orange and gently bind.

COOK'S TIP
Keep the spent lemon halves to put into
the cavity of the bird for flavour.

NUTRITION PER 100ml (3½fl oz)
150 cals | 10g fat (6g sats) | 12g carbs | 1.1g salt **V**

NUTRITION PER 100ml (3½fl oz)
285 cals | 11g fat (5g sats) | 45g carbs | 1g salt

SPICY SAUSAGE STUFFING

Serves 8
Preparation 10 minutes
Cooking time 10 minutes, plus cooling
Sufficient for a 4.5kg (10lb) oven-ready turkey

350g (12oz) spicy Italian-style pork sausages
125g (4oz) butter
2 onions, chopped
225g (8oz) oatmeal
1 tsp finely chopped fresh thyme
salt and ground black pepper

1 Skin the sausages and break up the sausage meat in a bowl.
2 Melt the butter in a pan, add the onions and cook gently for 7–10 minutes until soft and golden, then mix in the oatmeal and thyme. Leave to cool.
3 Add the mixture to the sausage meat and mix well, seasoning generously with salt and pepper.

NUTRITION PER 100ml (3^1/$_2$fl oz)
400 cals | 29g fat (12g sats) | 28g carbs | 1.5g salt

MUSHROOM AND CASHEW NUT STUFFING

Serves 10
Preparation 15 minutes
Cooking time 15 minutes, plus cooling
Sufficient for a 4.5kg (10lb) oven-ready turkey.

50g (2oz) butter
2 onions, finely chopped
450g (1lb) brown-cap mushrooms, roughly chopped
4 tbsp freshly chopped parsley
75g (3oz) salted cashew nuts, toasted and roughly chopped
125g (4oz) fresh white breadcrumbs
2 large eggs, beaten
salt and ground black pepper

1 Melt the butter in a pan, add the onions and cook gently for 7–10 minutes until soft and golden. Add the mushrooms and fry briskly for 4–5 minutes until softened and the moisture has evaporated. Turn into a bowl. Mix in the parsley, cashew nuts and breadcrumbs. Leave to cool.
2 Add the beaten eggs and mix well to bind the stuffing, seasoning with salt and pepper.

NUTRITION PER 100ml (3^1/$_2$fl oz)
140 cals | 9g fat (4g sats) | 11g carbs | 0.7g salt ✔

SAGE AND ONION STUFFING

Serves 4
Preparation 10 minutes
Cooking time 10 minutes, plus cooling
Sufficient for a 1.4kg (3lb) oven-ready chicken

1 tbsp oil
75g (3oz) onion, chopped
125g (4oz) pork sausage meat
1 tbsp finely chopped fresh sage
salt and ground black pepper

1 Heat the oil in a pan, add the onion and cook gently for 7–10 minutes until soft and golden. Turn into a bowl and leave to cool.
2 Add the sausage meat and sage to the cooled onion mixture and season with salt and pepper.

NUTRITION PER 100ml (3^1/$_2$fl oz)
150 cals | 13g fat (4g sats) 4g carbs | 1.3g salt

WILD RICE AND CRANBERRY STUFFING

Serves 10
Preparation 5 minutes
Cooking time 45 minutes
Sufficient for a 5kg (11lb) oven-ready goose

125g (4oz) wild rice
^{1}/$_4$ tsp salt
225g (8oz) rindless streaky bacon, cut into strips
2 red onions (about 225g/8oz), peeled and finely chopped
75g (3oz) dried cranberries
1 medium egg, beaten

1 Put the rice and salt into a pan, add 900ml (1^1/$_2$ pints) cold water and bring to the boil. Simmer, partially covered, for 45 minutes or until the rice is cooked. Drain and cool.

NUTRITION PER 100ml (3^1/$_2$fl oz)
146 cals | 6g fat (2g sats) | 18g carbs | 0.9g salt

SAUCES AND DRESSINGS

SAUCES

A certain mystique is attached to sauce-making, but all that is required is a little time, patience and your undivided attention. Essentially, a sauce should complement and enhance the dish it is served with. It must never be so overpowering that it masks the intrinsic flavours of the dish it is accompanying.

Roux-based sauces, such as béchamel, are probably the most familiar of all. These are based on equal quantities of butter and flour, which are cooked together. First the butter is melted, then the flour is mixed in and the resultant roux is cooked before the liquid is added. For a classic white béchamel sauce the roux is cooked but not coloured; for a blond sauce, such as velouté, the roux is cooked until biscuit-coloured; for a brown sauce, such as espagnole, the roux is cooked until brown.

The classic French emulsified sauces, such as hollandaise, Béarnaise and beurre blanc, rely on the reduction of liquids to give an intense flavour, and the addition of either butter or eggs to enrich and thicken. These sauces are a little more difficult to make because of their tendency to separate, but using a blender or food processor simplifies the process and is relatively foolproof.

Emulsified sauces are best made shortly before serving and kept warm over a pan of hot water.

Some sauces are thickened towards the end of preparation. Last-minute thickeners include arrowroot, cornflour and beurre manié (butter and flour kneaded together in equal quantities).

Other popular sauces included in this chapter are tomato sauces, pesto, salsa verde and classic British favourites, such as apple sauce, mint sauce and cranberry sauce; also gravies, savoury butters, custard and other sweet sauces to accompany desserts.

Allow yourself sufficient time to make a sauce – it is invariably working in haste that results in a lumpy or curdled sauce. If a roux-based sauce becomes lumpy, just whisk or beat vigorously; if this doesn't work, pass through a sieve, or whiz in a blender or food processor. An emulsified sauce that shows signs of curdling can often be rescued by adding an ice cube and whisking thoroughly.

Most sauces can be prepared in advance and reheated carefully when required. Cover the surface closely with damp greaseproof paper as soon as the sauce is made, to prevent a skin from forming on standing.

BÉCHAMEL SAUCE

Makes 300ml (^{1}/$_2$ pint)
Preparation 5 minutes, plus infusing
Cooking time 5 minutes

300ml (^{1}/$_2$ pint) semi-skimmed milk
1 onion slice
6 peppercorns
1 mace blade
1 bay leaf
15g (^{1}/$_2$ oz) butter
15g (^{1}/$_2$ oz) plain flour
salt and ground black pepper
freshly grated nutmeg

1 Pour the milk into a pan. Add the onion slice, peppercorns, mace and bay leaf. Bring almost to the boil, remove from the heat, and cover and leave to infuse for about 20 minutes, then strain.

2 To make the roux, melt the butter in a pan, stir in the flour and cook, stirring, for 1 minute until cooked but not coloured.

3 Remove from the heat and gradually pour on the infused milk, whisking constantly. Season lightly with salt, pepper and grated nutmeg.

4 Return to the heat and cook, stirring constantly, until the sauce is thickened and smooth. Simmer gently for 2 minutes.

TRY SOMETHING DIFFERENT

Simple White Sauce Omit the flavouring ingredients and infusing stage, and just stir the cold milk into the roux.
Thick (Binding) Sauce Increase the butter and flour to 25g (1oz) each.
Cheese (Mornay) Sauce Off the heat, stir 50g (2oz) finely grated Gruyère or mature Cheddar cheese and a large pinch of mustard powder or cayenne pepper into the finished sauce. Heat gently to melt the cheese, if necessary.
Parsley Sauce Stir in 2 tbsp freshly chopped parsley at step 4.
Onion (Soubise) Sauce Sauté 1 large, finely diced onion in a little butter over a low heat for 10–15 minutes until softened. Stir the sautéed onion into the sauce at step 4.

NUTRITION PER 75ML (5 TBSP)
75 cals | 4g fat (3g sats) | 7g carbs | 0.8g salt Ⓥ

HOLLANDAISE

Serves 6
Preparation 20 minutes
Cooking time 8 minutes

4 tbsp white wine vinegar
6 black peppercorns
1 mace blade
1 onion slice
1 bay leaf
3 medium egg yolks
150g (5oz) unsalted butter, at room temperature,
   cut into pieces
2 tbsp single cream (optional)
lemon juice, to taste
salt and ground white pepper

1 Put the vinegar into a small pan with the peppercorns, mace, onion slice and bay leaf. Bring to the boil and reduce to 1 tbsp liquid. Dip the base of the pan in cold water to stop further evaporation; set aside.
2 Put the egg yolks into a heatproof bowl with 15g (½oz) butter and a pinch of salt. Beat until well combined, then strain in the reduced vinegar.
3 Put the bowl over a pan of barely simmering water and whisk for 3–4 minutes until the mixture is pale and beginning to thicken.
4 Beat in the remaining butter, a piece at a time, until the mixture begins to thicken and emulsify. Ensure each addition of butter is incorporated before adding the next. Do not allow the mixture to overheat or the eggs will scramble and split. Remove from the heat.
5 Whisk in the cream, if using. Season the sauce with salt and pepper, and add a little lemon juice to taste. Serve at once.

COOK'S TIPS
—➤ Hollandaise is a wonderfully rich sauce to serve with hot or cold vegetables, such as asparagus and globe artichokes, poached fish and shellfish.
—➤ If the sauce shows signs of curdling, add an ice cube and whisk thoroughly; the hollandaise should re-combine.
—➤ To make hollandaise in a food processor, melt the butter and allow it to cool until tepid. Put the strained reduced vinegar, egg yolks and salt in the processor bowl and process for 10 seconds. With the motor running, add the melted butter in a thin steady stream through the feeder tube and process until emulsified. Finish the sauce as in step 5, above.

NUTRITION PER SERVING
230 cals | 24g fat (14g sats) | trace carbs | 0.8g salt Ⓥ

BÉARNAISE SAUCE

Serves 4
Preparation 20 minutes
Cooking time 8–10 minutes

4 tbsp white wine vinegar or tarragon vinegar
2 shallots, finely chopped
6 black peppercorns
a few fresh tarragon sprigs, chopped
2 medium egg yolks
75g (3oz) butter, at room temperature, cut into pieces
2 tsp freshly chopped flat-leafed parsley or chervil (optional)
salt and ground white pepper

1 Put the vinegar, shallots, peppercorns and tarragon into a very small pan. Bring to the boil and reduce to 1 tbsp. Dip the base of the pan in cold water to stop further evaporation; allow to cool, then strain.
2 Beat the egg yolks and reduced vinegar together in a heatproof bowl.
3 Put the bowl over a pan of barely simmering water and whisk for 3–4 minutes until the mixture is pale and beginning to thicken.
4 Beat in the butter a piece at a time, until the mixture begins to thicken and emulsify. Ensure each addition of butter is incorporated before adding the next. Do not allow the mixture to overheat or the eggs will scramble and split. Take off the heat.
5 Season with salt and pepper to taste. Stir in the chopped herbs if using.

COOK'S TIPS
—➤ If the sauce shows signs of curdling, add an ice cube and whisk thoroughly; the sauce should re-combine.
—➤ Serve this classic butter sauce with grilled beef and lamb steaks.

NUTRITION PER SERVING
180 cals | 18g fat (11g sats) | 2g carbs | 0.9g salt Ⓥ

BEURRE BLANC

Serves 4
Preparation 5 minutes
Cooking time 5 minutes

3 tbsp white wine vinegar
3 tbsp white wine
2 shallots, finely chopped
225g (8oz) butter, chilled and cut into small cubes
salt and ground black pepper

1 Put the vinegar, white wine and shallots into a very small pan. Bring to the boil and reduce to 1 tbsp.
2 Over a low heat, whisk in the butter, a piece at a time, until the sauce begins to thicken as the butter melts. Move the pan on and off heat to avoid overheating.
3 If you like a smooth sauce, pass the sauce through a sieve. Season with salt and pepper to taste.

TRY SOMETHING DIFFERENT
Herb Beurre Blanc Add 2 tbsp freshly chopped herbs, such as tarragon, chives or chervil, to the finished sauce.
Red Wine Sauce Use 6 tbsp red wine instead of the white wine and vinegar.

COOK'S TIPS
- If the sauce shows signs of curdling, add an ice cube and whisk thoroughly; the sauce should re-combine.
- Serve with poached or grilled fish and poultry.

NUTRITION PER SERVING
420 cals | 46g fat (29g sats) | 2g carbs | 1.5g salt Ⓥ

MILD CURRY SAUCE

Serves 4
Preparation 5 minutes
Cooking time 20 minutes

50g (2oz) butter
1 medium onion, finely chopped
3–4 tsp mild curry powder
3 tbsp flour
450ml (¾ pint) milk or half stock and half milk
2 tbsp mango or apple chutney, roughly chopped
salt and ground black pepper

1 Melt the butter in a pan, add the onion and fry until golden.
2 Stir in the curry powder and cook for 3–4 minutes. Add the flour and cook gently for 2–3 minutes.
3 Remove the pan from the heat and gradually stir in the milk or stock and milk mixture. Bring to the boil slowly and continue to cook, stirring, until the sauce thickens.
4 Add the chutney and seasoning. Reheat the sauce gently before serving.

COOK'S TIP
Curry sauce is useful when you want to make a curry in a hurry, and it makes good use of leftovers of meat, poultry and fish.

NUTRITION PER SERVING
245 cals | 13g fat (8g sats) | 28g carbs | 1.5g salt Ⓥ

BARBECUE SAUCE

Serves 4
Preparation 5 minutes
Cooking time about 25 minutes

50g (2oz) butter
1 large onion, chopped
1 tsp tomato purée
2 tbsp wine vinegar
2 tbsp Worcestershire sauce
2 tsp mustard powder
salt and ground black pepper

1 Melt the butter in a pan, add the onion and sauté gently for 10 minutes or until softened. Stir in the tomato purée and cook, stirring, for 2 minutes.
2 Mix together the wine vinegar, Worcestershire sauce, mustard powder, salt and pepper in a bowl, stir in 150ml (¼ pint) water, then add to the pan. Bring to the boil and let it bubble for 10 minutes.

COOK'S TIP
Serve with barbecued or grilled chicken, sausages, burgers or chops.

NUTRITION PER SERVING
110 cals | 10g fat (7g sats) | 4g carbs | 1g salt

BREAD SAUCE

Serves 8
Preparation 10 minutes
Cooking time 15 minutes

1 onion, quartered
4 cloves
2 bay leaves
450ml (³/₄ pint) milk
150g (5oz) fresh white breadcrumbs
¹/₂ tsp freshly grated nutmeg, or to taste
50g (2oz) butter
200ml (7fl oz) crème fraîche
salt and ground black pepper

1 Stud each onion quarter with a clove. Put the onion, bay leaves and milk into a pan. Heat very gently on the lowest possible heat for 15 minutes.
2 Remove the onion and bay leaves, then add the breadcrumbs, nutmeg and butter, and stir to combine. Add the crème fraîche and season with salt and pepper to taste. Serve warm.

NUTRITION PER SERVING
210 cals | 16g fat (11g sats) | 13g carbs | 0.8g salt Ⓥ

APPLE SAUCE

Serves 4
Preparation 10 minutes
Cooking time 10 minutes

450g (1lb) cooking apples, such as Bramleys
2 tbsp sugar, or to taste
25g (1oz) butter

1 Peel, core and slice the apples and put into a pan with 2–3 tbsp water. Cover and cook gently for 10 minutes, stirring occasionally, or until soft and reduced to a pulp.
2 Beat with a wooden spoon until smooth, then pass through a sieve, if you like a smooth sauce. Stir in sugar to taste and the butter. Serve warm.

COOK'S TIP
This sauce is traditionally served with roast pork and goose, to cut the richness of the meats.

NUTRITION PER SERVING
110 cals | 5g fat (3g sats) | 17g carbs | 0.1g salt Ⓥ

CREAMY MUSHROOM AND WINE SAUCE

Serves 6
Preparation 10 minutes
Cooking time 20 minutes

2 tbsp oil
2 shallots or 1 onion, finely diced
175g (6oz) button or cup mushrooms, sliced
150g (5oz) mixed wild mushrooms, sliced
2 garlic cloves, crushed
150ml (¹/₄ pint) white wine
200ml (7fl oz) crème fraîche
2 tsp freshly chopped thyme
salt and ground black pepper

1 Heat the oil in a pan, add the shallots or onion and cook gently for 10 minutes. Add the mushrooms and garlic, and cook over a high heat for 4–5 minutes until tender and all the moisture has been driven off.
2 Pour in the wine, bring to the boil and let it bubble until reduced by half.

3 Add the crème fraîche, 100ml (3¹/₂fl oz) water and the seasoning. Bring to the boil and bubble for 5 minutes or until the liquid is slightly thickened and syrupy.
4 Add the chopped thyme, adjust the seasoning and serve the sauce immediately.

TRY SOMETHING DIFFERENT
Replace the crème fraîche with red wine for a lighter sauce.

COOK'S TIP
This sauce is particularly good with pan-fried steak or chicken.

NUTRITION PER SERVING
190 cals | 18g fat (10g sats) | 3g carbs | 0.4g salt Ⓥ

CRANBERRY SAUCE

Serves 8
Preparation 30 minutes
Cooking time 1 hour 5 minutes, plus chilling

2 tbsp olive oil
450g (1lb) red onions, thinly sliced
grated zest and juice of 1 large orange
1 tsp coriander seeds, lightly crushed
1/4 tsp ground cloves
1 bay leaf
150g (5oz) dark muscovado sugar
150ml (1/4 pint) red wine
450g (1lb) cranberries

1 Heat the oil in a medium pan, add the onions and cook gently for 5 minutes. Add the orange zest and juice, coriander seeds, ground cloves, bay leaf, sugar and red wine. Simmer gently for 40 minutes.
2 Add the cranberries, bring back to the boil and simmer for 20 minutes. Cool and chill until required. Bring to room temperature before serving.

COOK'S TIP
Serve this tangy relish with a traditional Christmas turkey.

NUTRITION PER SERVING
140 cals | 3g fat (0.4g sats) | 26g carbs | 0g salt Ⓥ

CUMBERLAND SAUCE

Serves 4
Preparation 10 minutes
Cooking time 10 minutes, plus cooling

finely pared zest and juice of 1 orange
finely pared zest and juice of 1 lemon
4 tbsp redcurrant jelly
1 tsp Dijon mustard
4 tbsp port
pinch of ground ginger (optional)
salt and ground black pepper

1 Cut the citrus zests into fine julienne strips and put into a small pan. Add cold water to cover and simmer for 5 minutes; drain.
2 Put the orange and lemon juices, citrus zests, redcurrant jelly and mustard into a pan and heat gently, stirring, until the sugar has dissolved. Simmer for 5 minutes, then add the port.
3 Allow to cool. Season with salt and pepper to taste, and add a little ginger if you like.

COOK'S TIP
Serve this sauce cold, with gammon.

NUTRITION PER SERVING
70 cals | 0g fat (0g sats) | 15g carbs | 0.7g salt Ⓥ

FRESH TOMATO SAUCE

Serves 4
Preparation 10 minutes
Cooking time about 30 minutes

900g (2lb) vine-ripened tomatoes, roughly chopped
2 tbsp extra virgin olive oil
2 garlic cloves, crushed
grated zest of 1 lemon
1 tsp dried oregano
2 tbsp freshly chopped basil
pinch of sugar, or to taste (optional)
salt and ground black pepper

1 Put the tomatoes into a pan with the olive oil, garlic, lemon zest and oregano. Bring to the boil, cover and simmer gently for 20 minutes.
2 Add the chopped basil, salt and pepper to taste and a little sugar if required. Simmer, uncovered, for a further 10 minutes or until the sauce is slightly thickened. If you like a smooth sauce, pass through a sieve and reheat before serving.

COOK'S TIP
This sauce is good with meat loaf.

NUTRITION PER SERVING
100 cals | 7g fat (1g sats) | 8g carbs | 0.6g salt Ⓥ

ANCHOVY SAUCE

Serves 4
Makes 300ml (¹/₂ pint)
Preparation 5 minutes
Cooking time about 10 minutes

15g (¹/₂ oz) butter
15g (¹/₂ oz) flour
150ml (¹/₄ pint) milk
150ml (¹/₄ pint) fish stock
1–2 tsp anchovy essence
a squeeze of lemon juice
red food colouring (optional)
salt and ground black pepper

1 Melt the butter in a pan, stir in the flour and cook gently for 1 minute, stirring.
2 Remove the pan from the heat and gradually stir in the milk and fish stock. Bring to the boil slowly and continue cooking, stirring all the time, until the sauce comes to the boil and thickens.
3 Simmer very gently for a further 2–3 minutes. Stir in anchovy essence to taste, the lemon juice and a few drops of red food colouring to tint it a pale pink, if you like. Season with salt and pepper.

COOK'S TIP
Serve hot with plaice, brill or turbot.

NUTRITION PER SERVING
58 cals | 4g fat (2g sats) | 5g carbs | 0.7g salt

MINT SAUCE

Serves 4
Preparation 10 minutes, plus standing

1 small bunch of mint, stalks removed
1–2 tsp golden caster sugar, to taste
1–2 tbsp wine vinegar, to taste

1 Finely chop the mint leaves and put into a bowl with the sugar. Stir in 1 tbsp boiling water and set aside for about 5 minutes to dissolve the sugar.
2 Add the wine vinegar to taste. Leave to stand for about 1 hour before serving.

COOK'S TIP
The classic accompaniment to roast lamb.

NUTRITION PER SERVING
10 cals | trace fat (0g sats) | 2g carbs | 0g salt Ⓥ

HORSERADISH CREAM

Serves 4
Preparation 5 minutes

2 tbsp grated fresh horseradish
2 tsp lemon juice
2 tsp sugar
a pinch of mustard powder (optional)
150ml (¹/₄ pint) double cream

1 Mix together the horseradish, lemon juice, sugar and mustard, if using.
2 Whip the double cream to soft peaks, then fold in the horseradish mixture.

COOK'S TIP
The classic accompaniment to roast beef.

NUTRITION PER SERVING
198 cals | 20g fat (13g sats) | 3g carbs | trace salt Ⓥ

TARTARE SAUCE

Makes 150ml (¹/₄ pint)
Preparation 5 minutes, plus standing

150ml (¹/₄ pint) mayonnaise (see page 29)
1 tsp freshly chopped tarragon or snipped chives
2 tsp chopped capers
2 tsp chopped gherkins
2 tsp freshly chopped parsley
1 tbsp lemon juice or tarragon vinegar

1 Put all the ingredients into a bowl and mix well. Allow to stand for at least 1 hour before serving, to allow the flavours to blend.

COOK'S TIP
Traditionally served with fried or poached fish.

NUTRITION PER TEASPOON
1 cal | 0g fat (0g sats) | trace carbs | trace salt Ⓥ

PESTO

Serves 4
Preparation 10 minutes

50g (2oz) fresh basil leaves
1–2 garlic cloves, peeled
25g (1oz) pinenuts
6 tbsp extra virgin olive oil
2 tbsp freshly grated Parmesan (see Cook's Tip, page 228)
squeeze of lemon juice (optional)
salt and ground black pepper

1 Roughly tear the basil and put it into a mortar with the garlic, pinenuts and a little of the olive oil. Pound with a pestle to a paste. Alternatively, work in a food processor to a fairly smooth paste.
2 Gradually work in the rest of the oil and season with salt and pepper to taste. Transfer to a bowl.
3 Stir in the Parmesan, check the seasoning and add a squeeze of lemon juice, if you like.
4 Store in a screw-topped jar, covered with a thin layer of oil, in the fridge for up to three days.

TOMATO KETCHUP

Makes 1.1 litres (2 pints)
Preparation 30 minutes
Cooking time 1 hour

2.7kg (6lb) ripe tomatoes
225g (8oz) sugar
300ml (¹/₂ pint) spiced vinegar (see Pickled Onions, page 482)
1 tbsp tarragon vinegar (optional)
a pinch of cayenne pepper
1 tsp paprika
1 tsp salt

1 Slice the tomatoes and cook over a very low heat for about 45 minutes, stirring frequently, until they cook down to a pulp. Bring to the boil and cook rapidly, stirring frequently, until the pulp thickens.
2 Press the pulp through a nylon or stainless steel sieve, then return to the pan and stir in the remaining ingredients. Simmer gently until the mixture thickens.
3 Pour the ketchup into warm, sterilised bottles. Seal and label, and store in a cool, dark place for up to one year.

NUTRITION PER TEASPOON
24 cals | 0.1g fat (trace sats) | 6g carbs | 0.1g salt Ⓥ

TRY SOMETHING DIFFERENT
Sun-dried Tomato Pesto Replace half the basil with 50g (2oz) sun-dried tomatoes in oil, drained and roughly chopped. Use a blender or food processor to work the ingredients together to a paste.
Coriander Pesto Replace the basil with coriander leaves. Add 1 seeded and chopped chilli (see Cook's Tips, page 69) with the garlic if you like. Omit the Parmesan.
Rocket Pesto Replace the basil with rocket leaves. Add 1 tbsp freshly chopped parsley at step 3.

NUTRITION PER SERVING
250 cals | 26g fat (4g sats) | 1g carbs | 0.7g salt Ⓥ

SALSA VERDE

Serves 4
Preparation 5 minutes

a small handful of fresh parsley, about 40g (1½ oz)
6 tbsp fresh white breadcrumbs
5 tbsp olive oil
1 tsp capers
1 gherkin
2 tbsp lemon juice
1 tbsp chopped chives
salt and ground black pepper

1 Put all the ingredients, except the seasoning, into a blender or food processor and process until thoroughly combined.
2 Turn into a bowl and season with salt and pepper to taste. Store in the fridge for up to five days.

COOK'S TIP
This piquant, fresh-tasting sauce is good with pork schnitzel and grilled meats.

NUTRITION PER SERVING
190 cals | 17g fat (2g sats) | 8g carbs | 1g salt Ⓥ

FLAVOURED BUTTERS

These are excellent quick alternatives to sauces for serving with grilled meats, fish and all kinds of vegetables. They need to be prepared several hours in advance to allow time to chill and become firm enough to slice.

Use unsalted butter at room temperature. Beat in the flavouring(s) by hand or using a food processor. Turn on to clingfilm, shape into a log, wrap tightly and chill in the fridge for at least 1 hour. Allow about 25g (1oz) savoury butter per person.

Add the following flavourings to 125g (4oz) butter, at room temperature:

Anchovy Butter Add 6 mashed anchovy fillets.
Blue Cheese Butter Add 50g (2oz) blue cheese.
Citrus Butter Add the finely grated zest of 1 lemon, or 1 orange or 1 lime. Season to taste.
Herb Butter Add 2 tbsp freshly chopped mixed fresh herbs, such as flat-leafed parsley, chervil and tarragon, plus a squeeze of lemon juice.
Garlic Butter Add 1 crushed garlic clove and 2 tsp chopped parsley or chervil.
Horseradish Butter Mix in 2 tbsp creamed horseradish.

FRESH VANILLA CUSTARD

Serves 8
Preparation 20 minutes
Cooking time 10 minutes, plus cooling if needed

600ml (1 pint) whole milk
1 vanilla pod or 1 tsp vanilla extract
6 large egg yolks
2 tbsp golden caster sugar
2 tbsp cornflour

1 Pour the milk into a pan. Slit the vanilla pod lengthways and scrape out the seeds, adding them to the milk with the pod, or add the vanilla extract. Slowly bring to the boil. Turn off the heat immediately and set aside to infuse for 5 minutes.
2 Put the egg yolks, sugar and cornflour into a bowl and whisk together. Gradually whisk in the warm milk, leaving the vanilla pod behind if using.
3 Rinse the pan and pour the mixture back in. Heat gently, whisking or stirring constantly for 2–3 minutes or until the custard thickens – it should just coat the back of a wooden spoon in a thin layer. Serve immediately or cover the surface closely with a round of wet greaseproof paper, then cover with clingfilm and chill until needed.

> ### COOK'S TIP
> If prepared ahead, to serve warm, microwave on medium for 2 minutes, stir, and then microwave for a further 2 minutes.

NUTRITION PER SERVING
120 cals | 8g fat (3g sats) | 10g carbs | 0.1g salt Ⓥ

BUTTERSCOTCH SAUCE

Serves 8
Preparation 5 minutes
Cooking time 10 minutes

50g (2oz) butter
75g (3oz) light muscovado sugar
50g (2oz) golden caster sugar
150g (5oz) golden syrup
125ml (4fl oz) double cream
a few drops of vanilla extract
juice of 1/2 lemon

SABAYON SAUCE

Serves 6
Preparation 15 minutes
Cooking time about 10 minutes, plus chilling

75g (3oz) golden caster sugar
3 medium egg yolks
125ml (4fl oz) double cream
grated zest and juice of 1 lemon

1 Put the sugar and 125ml (4fl oz) water into a small pan over a low heat until dissolved. Increase the heat to high and boil for 7–8 minutes or until the syrup registers 105°C on a sugar thermometer (and looks very syrupy with large pea-size bubbles).
2 Meanwhile, whisk the egg yolks in a small bowl. Gradually pour in the hot syrup in a thin stream, whisking all the time. Continue to whisk until the mixture is thick, mousse-like and cool.
3 In a separate bowl, whisk the cream until it forms stiff peaks, then add the lemon zest and juice, and whip again to form soft peaks. Fold the citrus cream into the mousse mixture.
4 Cover and chill in the fridge until required. Whisk well before serving.

> ### COOK'S TIP
> Serve as an alternative to vanilla custard, with grilled fruit and other desserts.

NUTRITION PER SERVING
170 cals, | 12g fat (6g sats) | 14g carbs | trace salt

1 Put the butter, sugars and golden syrup in a medium heavy-based pan over a low heat and stir occasionally until melted together and smooth. Cook gently, stirring, for 5 minutes.
2 Off the heat, slowly stir in the double cream. Add the vanilla extract and lemon juice. Stir over a low heat for 1–2 minutes until smooth. Serve hot or cold.

> ### COOK'S TIP
> Serve poured over ice cream or steamed or baked puddings.

NUTRITION PER SERVING
230 cals | 12g fat (8g sats) | 32g carbs | 0.1g salt Ⓥ

CARAMEL SAUCE

Serves 6
Preparation 5 minutes
Cooking time 10 minutes

50g (2oz) golden caster sugar
150ml (¼ pint) double cream

1 Melt the sugar in a small heavy-based pan over a low heat until liquid and golden in colour. Increase the heat to medium and cook to a rich, dark caramel.
2 Immediately take off the heat and pour in the cream in a slow steady stream, taking care, as the hot caramel will cause the cream to boil up in the pan.
3 Stir over a gentle heat until the caramel has melted and the sauce is smooth. Serve hot or cold.

COOK'S TIP
Serve poured over ice cream
or steamed or baked puddings.

NUTRITION PER SERVING
150 cals | 12g fat (8g sats) | 9g carbs | trace salt V

COFFEE SAUCE

Serves 4
Preparation 5 minutes
Cooking time 3 minutes

5 tsp instant coffee powder
1½ tsp arrowroot
175g (6oz) can evaporated milk
2 tbsp soft light brown sugar

RICH CHOCOLATE SAUCE

Serves 6
Preparation 5 minutes
Cooking time 5 minutes

125g (4oz) plain, dark chocolate
    (at least 70% cocoa solids), in pieces
2 tbsp light muscovado sugar
25g (1oz) unsalted butter

1 Put the chocolate into a small pan with the sugar and 150ml (¼ pint) water. Stir over a low heat until the chocolate has melted and the sugar has dissolved, then bring to the boil, stirring.
2 Let it bubble for 1 minute, then remove from the heat and stir in the butter.

TRY SOMETHING DIFFERENT
Chocolate and Grand Marnier Sauce Omit the sugar. Add 2 tbsp Grand Marnier (or other liqueur of your choice) to the sauce with the butter.

COOK'S TIP
Serve poured over ice cream, profiteroles,
or steamed or baked puddings.

NUTRITION PER SERVING
150 cals, | 12g fat (6g sats) | 10g carbs | trace salt V

---

1 Mix the coffee powder and arrowroot to a smooth paste with a little water, then make up to 150ml (¼ pint) with more water.
2 Pour into a pan, add the evaporated milk and brown sugar, and slowly bring to the boil, stirring. Simmer for 1 minute.

COOK'S TIP
Serve poured over ice cream, plain cakes,
or steamed or baked puddings.

NUTRITION PER SERVING
102 cals | 4g fat (3g sats) | 14g carbs | 0.2g salt V

LEMON OR ORANGE SAUCE

Serves 4
Preparation 10 minutes
Cooking time 15 minutes, plus cooling

grated zest and juice of 1 large lemon or orange
1 tbsp cornflour
2 tbsp sugar
a knob of butter
1 medium egg yolk (optional)

1 Put the fruit zest and juice in a bowl and make up to 300ml (½ pint) with water. Blend the cornflour and sugar with a little of the liquid to make a smooth cream.
2 Heat the remaining liquid until boiling, then pour on to the blended mixture, stirring all the time. Put back in the pan and bring to the boil, stirring until the sauce thickens and clears. Add the butter.
3 Cool, then beat in the egg yolk, if using, and reheat, stirring, without boiling.

> **COOK'S TIP**
> Serve with pancakes, plain cakes or steamed or baked puddings.

NUTRITION PER SERVING
91 cals | 3g fat (2g sats) | 15g carbs | trace salt Ⓥ

RASPBERRY COULIS

Serves 4
Preparation 10 minutes, plus chilling

225g (8oz) raspberries
2 tbsp Kirsch or framboise eau de vie (optional)
icing sugar to taste.

1 Put the raspberries into a blender or food processor with the Kirsch or eau de vie, if using. Whiz until they are completely puréed.
2 Transfer the purée to a fine sieve, and press and scrape it through the sieve until nothing is left but the pips.
3 Sweeten with icing sugar to taste and chill until needed.

TRY SOMETHING DIFFERENT

Use different soft fruits and liqueurs; for example, try crème de cassis with blackcurrants or Amaretto with apricots.

> **COOK'S TIP**
> Serve with ice cream or meringues.

NUTRITION PER SERVING
32 cals | trace fat (trace sats) | 6g carbs | trace salt Ⓥ

CHANTILLY CREAM

Serves 8
Preparation 10 minutes, plus chilling

285ml (10fl oz) double cream
1 tbsp golden caster sugar
finely grated zest of 1 orange (optional)

1 Whip the cream with the sugar until it forms soft peaks. Fold in half the grated orange zest, if using. Cover and chill until needed.
2 Serve the Chantilly Cream sprinkled with the remaining orange zest if you like.

> **COOK'S TIPS**
> ⌐ Use to sandwich meringues or serve with fruit and jelly.
> ⌐ Flavour the Chantilly Cream with 2 tbsp Grand Marnier to serve with Christmas pudding.

NUTRITION PER SERVING
180 cals | 17g fat (12g sats) | 4g carbs | trace salt

CRÈME PÂTISSIÈRE

Makes 450ml ($^3/_4$ pint)
Preparation 15 minutes, plus infusing
Cooking time 5 minutes, plus cooling

300ml ($^1/_2$ pint) milk
1 vanilla pod, split, or 1 tsp vanilla extract
3 medium egg yolks, beaten
50g (2oz) golden caster sugar
2 tbsp plain flour
2 tbsp cornflour

1 Pour the milk into a heavy-based pan. Scrape the vanilla seeds into the milk and add the pod, or add the vanilla extract. Slowly bring to the boil, take off the heat and leave to infuse for 10 minutes. Discard the pod.
2 Meanwhile, whisk the egg yolks and sugar together in a bowl until thick and creamy, then whisk in the flour and cornflour until smooth. Gradually whisk in the hot milk, then strain back into the pan.
3 Slowly bring to the boil, whisking constantly. Cook, stirring, for 2–3 minutes until thickened and smooth.
4 Pour into a bowl, cover the surface with a round of wet greaseproof paper and allow to cool.

> ### COOK'S TIP
> Use as a filling for fruit flans and other pastries.

> NUTRITION PER SERVING
> 120 cals | 4g fat (2g sats) | 8g carbs | trace salt Ⓥ

BRANDY BUTTER

Serves 8
Preparation 10 minutes, plus chilling

150g (5oz) unsalted butter, at room temperature
150g (5oz) golden icing sugar, sifted
3 tbsp brandy

1 Put the butter into a bowl and whisk to soften. Gradually whisk in the icing sugar, pouring in the brandy just before the final addition. Continue whisking until the mixture is pale and fluffy, then spoon into a serving dish.
2 Cover and chill until needed. Remove from the fridge 30 minutes before serving.

TRY SOMETHING DIFFERENT
Rum Butter Cream 75g (3oz) butter until pale and soft. Gradually beat 75g (3oz) soft brown sugar into the butter, then add 4 tbsp rum a few drops at a time, taking care not to allow the mixture to curdle, then stir in the grated zest of $^1/_2$ lemon and a squeeze of lemon juice. The finished sauce should be pale and frothy.

> ### COOK'S TIPS
> ⌐ Serve with Christmas pudding.
> ⌐ For a light, fluffy texture, whisk the brandy butter using an electric mixer just before serving.

> NUTRITION PER SERVING
> 230 cals | 16g fat (10g sats) | 20g carbs | 0.3g salt Ⓥ

DRESSINGS

A salad is rarely complete without a dressing. Whether it's a piquant vinaigrette, a creamy mayonnaise or just a squeeze of lemon or lime juice, it is invariably the dressing that pulls all the ingredients together.

There are two main types of salad dressings: oil and vinegar or citrus dressings, and creamy dressings, which are usually mayonnaise-based. The proportion of oil to vinegar in the former is largely a matter of personal taste. In general, about six parts oil to one part vinegar works best, but if you prefer a more acidic dressing, perhaps four parts oil to one part vinegar.

Oils and vinegars form the basis of most salad dressings. For best results, use the correct oil, and/or vinegar, for the particular dressing.

OILS AND VINEGARS

 **Olive oil** comes in a range of flavours and styles, from zingy, pungent extra virgin to light, mild olive oil. Extra virgin olive oil – cold pressed and from a single estate – is the premium type. A good extra virgin olive oil can be used with great effect in salads. It is particularly good drizzled liberally over raw vegetables, tomatoes or salad leaves, with just a little lemon juice or balsamic vinegar. Light or mild olive oil is the best choice for making mayonnaise, where extra virgin oil would be too overpowering.

 **Flavoured oils** These add character to salad dressings. You can buy ready-made flavoured oils or make your own. Try the following simple ideas:
Fresh herb oil needs to be used within a day. To make this, put 15g (1/2 oz) mixed chopped fresh herbs – such as basil, chervil, chives and parsley – in a bowl, pour on 150ml (1/4 pint) extra virgin olive oil and set aside to infuse for 2–3 hours.
Chilli and garlic oil will spike up a salad. To prepare, put the peeled cloves from a whole head of garlic into a small pan with 300ml (1/2 pint) mild olive oil and 1 small red chilli, seeded and very finely chopped (see page 69). Heat gently for 5–6 minutes until the garlic is golden. Cool, then strain the oil into a clean bottle. Use as required.

 **Nut oils** These are excellent in salads. Ranging from mild to strong, these include groundnut or peanut, hazelnut, walnut, almond and sesame oils. Sesame oil is used in very small amounts, often blended with groundnut or even vegetable oil. Nut oils combine particularly well with fruit-flavoured vinegars and sherry vinegar.

 **Balsamic vinegar** Dark and aromatic, this Italian vinegar has an exquisite mellow, sweet–sour flavour and lends a good depth and character to salad dressings. Traditionally matured in oak casks for anything between five to 20 years, balsamic vinegar is expensive, but a little goes a long way – a few drops can transform a salad.

 **Wine vinegar** This is the strongest natural vinegar with an average acidity of 6.5 per cent and no preservatives. Special varieties include pale yellow Champagne vinegar, Rioja red wine vinegar with a deep mellow flavour, and full-bodied, nutty brown sherry vinegar.

 **Cider vinegar** This is milder than wine vinegar and works well in salad dressings where a subtle acidity is required.

 **Flavoured vinegar** Wine vinegars can be flavoured with aromatic herbs, fruits, spices, and even flower petals. Better wine vinegars, such as Champagne and sherry vinegars, need nothing to enhance their natural flavours. Of the fruit vinegars, raspberry vinegar is the most popular. Strawberry, blackberry and peach vinegars are also obtainable. To make your own herb vinegar, immerse a few herb sprigs, such as rosemary or thyme, in a bottle of red or white wine vinegar, or cider vinegar. Leave in a cool, dark place to infuse for two to three weeks. Strain and re-bottle, adding a fresh herb sprig if you like.

FRENCH DRESSING

Makes 100ml (3¹/₂ fl oz)
Preparation 10 minutes

1 tsp Dijon mustard
a pinch of sugar
1 tbsp white or red wine vinegar
90ml (6 tbsp) extra virgin olive oil
salt and ground black pepper

1 Whisk the mustard, sugar, vinegar and seasoning together in a bowl, then gradually whisk in the olive oil until the dressing is amalgamated and thickened.

TRY SOMETHING DIFFERENT
Herb Dressing Use ¹/₂ tsp mustard. Replace the vinegar with lemon juice and add 2 tbsp freshly chopped mixed herbs, such as parsley, chervil and chives.
Balsamic Dressing Omit the mustard and sugar. Use balsamic vinegar instead of wine vinegar.
Garlic Dressing Whisk 1 crushed garlic clove into the dressing.
Honey and Lemon Dressing Use lemon juice instead of vinegar, 1 tsp clear honey in place of the sugar, and wholegrain rather than Dijon mustard.

> ### COOK'S TIP
> Alternatively, put all the ingredients in a screw-topped jar and shake well to combine.

NUTRITION PER SERVING
110 cals | 11g fat (2g sats) trace carbs | 0.4g salt Ⓥ

MAYONNAISE

Makes 300ml (¹/₂ pint)
Preparation 10 minutes

2 medium egg yolks, at room temperature
2 tsp lemon juice or white wine vinegar
1 tsp Dijon mustard
a pinch of sugar
300ml (¹/₂ pint) light olive oil
salt and ground black pepper

1 Put all the ingredients except the oil and seasoning into a food processor. Season and blend briefly until pale and creamy.
2 With the blade motor running, pour in the olive oil through the feeder tube, in a steady stream, until the mayonnaise is thick. Thin to the required consistency, if necessary, with a little hot water.
3 Store the mayonnaise in a screw-topped jar in the fridge for up to three days.

TRY SOMETHING DIFFERENT
Herb Mayonnaise Fold in 2 tbsp freshly chopped herbs, such as chives, chervil, basil, tarragon or coriander.
Lemon Mayonnaise Use lemon juice. Add 1 tsp grated lemon zest and an extra 1 tbsp lemon juice at the end.
Aïoli Put 4 crushed garlic cloves into the processor with the egg yolks, 1 tbsp lemon juice and ¹/₂ tsp salt; process as in step 1, until evenly combined. Continue as step 2.
Garlic and Basil Mayonnaise Add 1 crushed garlic clove at step 1. Fold 2 tbsp freshly shredded basil into the mayonnaise at the end.
Mustard Mayonnaise Stir in 4 tbsp Dijon mustard at the end.
Thousand Island Dressing Add 2 tsp tomato purée, 2 tbsp chopped stuffed olives, 2 tsp finely chopped onion, 1 chopped hard-boiled egg and 1 tbsp chopped parsley to the finished mayonnaise.

> ### COOK'S TIPS
> ⌐ The ingredients must be at room temperature. If eggs are used straight from the fridge the mayonnaise is liable to curdle.
> ⌐ To make mayonnaise by hand, mix the egg yolks, mustard, sugar and seasoning in a bowl, then whisk in the oil, drop by drop to begin with, then in a slow, steady stream. Finally, add the lemon juice or vinegar.

NUTRITION PER SERVING
110 cals | 12g fat (2g sats) trace carbs | 0.2g salt

HERBS, SPICES AND FLAVOURINGS

HERBS

Fresh herbs lend a superb flavour to all kinds of dishes. Their flavour is derived from essential oils in the leaves and stems, which are released when the herb is heated, crushed or chopped. Herbs may be chopped before they are added to a dish, or used whole. The more delicate herbs, such as parsley, chervil and tarragon, should be added towards the end of cooking, while tougher varieties, such as rosemary and thyme, are added at the start. Ideally, pick fresh herbs just before using, or use soon after purchase.

Dried herbs work well in cooked dishes, such as casseroles, but they are generally not suitable for use in salads. Dried herbs have a stronger flavour than fresh ones and should be used more sparingly: if substituting dried for fresh herbs, use one-third of the amount specified. Dried herbs keep best in airtight jars away from the light. They will retain their flavour for about six months.

Angelica
All parts of this tall plant are used for flavouring, although only the young candied stem is available commercially. Crystallised angelica stems are used to decorate cakes, pastries and desserts. The root is good for stewing with acid fruits such as rhubarb. Angelica leaves can be chopped and used to flavour salads or fish dishes.

Basil
This popular Italian herb has a distinctive aroma and flavour. The delicate leaves are easily bruised by chopping, so it's better to tear or shred them with your fingers. Basil has a natural affinity with tomatoes, but goes well with most salads, grilled meat and green vegetables. It also forms the basis of the classic Italian sauce – pesto. This herb has a short growing period during the summer and needs plenty of sun, but it is sold fresh all year round.

Bay leaves
Shiny and smooth, bay leaves are highly aromatic, so one or two leaves are sufficient to flavour a dish. Bay leaves are used in marinades, casseroles, soups and stocks, and to flavour infusions of milk for use in sauces such as béchamel. Bay is one of the classic ingredients of a bouquet garni. You can buy sprigs, freeze them in a plastic bag and use straight from the freezer.

Chervil
A delicate, sweet-flavoured herb with attractive leaves, used in a similar way to parsley. It will enhance many vegetables, especially new potatoes, as well as salads, and egg, cheese, fish and chicken dishes. Chervil is one of the classic components of the French *fines herbes*. It is also an excellent flavouring for butter sauces, such as hollandaise, and makes a pretty garnish.

Chive
This member of the onion family has long narrow, green leaves and purple flowers. The leaves are used to flavour salads, sauces and dressings, and as a garnish. A hardy perennial, this herb is easy to grow in the garden and in containers. To use, snip the chives into short lengths with scissors.

Coriander
Pungent and intensely flavoured, this herb is an important flavour-ing, especially in Indian and Thai dishes. It is sold in pots, bunches and packs. It resembles flat-leafed parsley, with more rounded leaves. The plant is also commercially grown for its seeds, which taste quite different and are used as a spice. Aromatic coriander leaves are often used with spices, especially in Middle Eastern, Asian and Mexican dishes, as well as in salads and soups.

Curry leaves

These shiny, spiky leaves have a fresh-tasting flavour akin to curry powder. They are used as a herb in cooking, most often added whole, but sometimes chopped first. Curry leaves often feature in curries from southern India, and the fresh or dried leaves can be used sparingly to flavour soups and stews. Sold fresh in bunches, curry leaves can be frozen in a plastic bag, and added to dishes as and when required.

Dill

This fragrant hardy annual is grown for its feathery leaves (also known as dill weed) and for its seeds, which are dried and used as a spice. Dill leaves have a slightly sharp, yet sweet flavour, which complements fish and shellfish dishes perfectly, and it is the classic flavouring in gravad lax (Scandinavian smoked salmon). Dill is also added to salads, omelettes, chicken dishes and used as a garnish.

Fennel

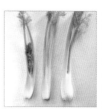

This herb resembles dill and is a member of the same family, but it has a sweet anise flavour, which is quite different. Both the feathery leaves and seeds are used. Fennel is a classical flavouring for fish – especially oily fish, as it counteracts the richness. It also works well in marinades, soups and vegetable dishes.

Lemongrass

A tall, hard grass with pale green leaves, lemongrass has a distinctive lemony aroma and taste. It is used in Thai and other South-east Asian dishes to flavour soups, chicken, fish and meat dishes, and can be used to flavour puddings. The stems are usually bruised to release their flavour and added whole before cooking, then removed. Or, the tough outer leaves are removed and the rest chopped. Dried and powdered lemongrass is also available.

Lime leaves, kaffir

The leaves of the kaffir lime tree have a highly aromatic lime flavour and are frequently used in Thai and Malaysian dishes. They are available from selected supermarkets and Asian food stores, and freeze successfully.

Lovage

This herb has an intense peppery flavour, akin to celery. Lovage leaves are best used sparingly to enhance the flavour of robust soups and meat stews. A little chopped lovage will add an unusual tang to salads and cold roast beef sandwiches.

Marjoram

There are three forms of this aromatic herb: sweet marjoram, pot marjoram and wild marjoram, which is better known as oregano. Pot marjoram has a more powerful flavour than sweet marjoram but it is used in a similar way: to flavour pizzas, savoury flans, sausages, marinades, stuffings and roasts, such as game and pork. It is also good to add flavour to vegetables.

Mint

Among the many mints available are peppermint, spearmint, pineapple mint, lemon mint and apple mint. Most varieties have a powerful flavour and should be used sparingly. Mint is the perfect partner to potatoes, peas and many other vegetables, and fresh mint sauce or jelly is the classic accompaniment to lamb. The leaves are used to embellish wine and fruit cups, fruit salads and other desserts. It is widely available and very easy to grow.

Mixed herbs, dried

Sold in jars, mixed dried herbs are used for seasoning soups and casseroles. The combination usually includes parsley, sage, thyme, marjoram and tarragon.

Oregano (wild marjoram)
Also called wild marjoram, the herb oregano and its close relative, marjoram, are largely interchangeable in dishes, although oregano is more aromatic and strongly flavoured. It is used with meat, sausages, soups, pizzas, pasta sauces and other Italian dishes, tomatoes, in salads, with cooked vegetables, and in egg and cheese dishes.

Parsley
Both the flat-leafed and curly leafed varieties of this common herb are widely available. Flat-leafed parsley has a more pronounced flavour and is generally preferred. Parsley stalks are always included in a bouquet garni and chopped parsley is a classic ingredient of *fines herbes*. Chopped parsley leaves are used in all kinds of savoury dishes, including sauces, soups, salads, stuffings and herb butters, with vegetables, chicken, ham, fish and shellfish, and as a garnish.

Rosemary
This pungent herb with its spiky leaves is the classic partner to lamb. Rosemary sprigs are usually added whole to a dish and taken out before serving, for a more subtle flavour. Finely chopped leaves are used sparingly, and more often as the sole herb. Rosemary sprigs are used in marinades for meat, fish and poultry, and to flavour roast and barbecued meats. Finely chopped rosemary can be added to pizza and bread doughs, stuffings, cakes and biscuits.

Sage
This soft-leafed herb has a strong, distinctive taste. Garden sage has pale grey-green leaves, but there are many other varieties, including purple sage and variegated sage. It is the classic flavouring for roast pork, and is used to enhance other meat dishes, especially liver and sausages, casseroles, stuffings, salads, egg and cheese dishes. As it is powerful, sage should be used sparingly. Melted butter flavoured with fresh sage leaves is delicious on pasta, gnocchi and vegetables.

Tarragon
Of the two main species of this herb, French tarragon is far superior in flavour and texture to the Russian variety. Tarragon is a strongly flavoured herb with important culinary uses. It is a component of *fines herbes* and is often added to tartare, hollandaise and béarnaise sauces. Tarragon is also used to flavour wine vinegar, marinades, fish and chicken dishes, savoury butters and sauces.

Thyme
Of the many varieties of this important herb, garden and lemon thyme are the most common. Thyme has a distinctive flavour and is one of the classic ingredients in a bouquet garni. It can be rubbed over beef and lamb before roasting, and used to flavour casseroles, soups, stuffings, bread sauce, carrots, onions and mushrooms. Lemon thyme is especially good in stuffings, and in fish dishes. Thyme is also used to flavour oils and vinegars.

AROMATICS

Garlic
Although not a herb, garlic is an important aromatic flavouring, often used in conjunction with fresh herbs. It is the most pungent member of the onion family. There are three main varieties: white, red and pinkish-purple. Garlic is widely used to enhance the flavour of savoury dishes. Raw garlic is used in marinades, salads and dressings. During cooking, the flavour of garlic becomes mellow and sweet. Choose firm garlic bulbs and pull off individual cloves as required.

SPICES

Most spices come from hot countries. They are the dried parts of aromatic plants and may be the fruit, bark, seed, root or flower bud. Once rare and expensive commodities, they are now everyday flavouring ingredients. Most spices are sold dried, either whole or ground.

For optimum flavour, buy whole spices and grind them yourself – using a pestle and mortar, or an electric spice grinder – rather than buying ready-ground spices. If possible, grind the spice just before use. An electric coffee grinder can be used, but should then be reserved for this purpose. An electric blender is suitable for larger quantities. Ground spices may be fried in oil before adding other ingredients such as vegetables and meat.

Buy spices in small quantities, as their flavour deteriorates relatively quickly. Keep them in small, airtight glass jars, coloured if possible, and away from light, as this adversely affects their flavour. Discard any that are not used within a year of purchase.

DRY-FRYING SPICES

Spices are often toasted in a dry heavy-based frying pan to mellow their flavour and lose any raw taste. They can be dry-fried individually or as mixtures. Put the hardest ones, such as fenugreek, into the pan first and add softer ones, like coriander and cumin, after a minute or so. Stir until evenly browned. Cool, then grind, or crush.

Allspice
Also called Jamaica pepper, allspice is sold as small dried berries or ready ground. The whole spice is an ingredient of pickling spice. It tastes like a mixture of cloves, cinnamon and nutmeg. Allspice can be used whole in marinades, meat dishes, pickles, chutneys and with poached fish. Ground allspice is added to meat and vegetable dishes, cakes, milk puddings and fruit pies.

Aniseed (anise)
These small seeds have a strong, distinctive flavour – used mainly to flavour cakes and biscuits, but also in salad dressings, with red cabbage, in cheese, fish and shellfish dishes. Aniseed is the main flavouring in Pernod, anisette and ouzo.

Caraway seeds
These small brown seeds have a sharp, liquorice-like taste that is widely appreciated in central European and Jewish cookery. Caraway seeds are primarily used for flavouring cakes, biscuits and breads; they also add flavour to sauerkraut, vegetables, cheese dishes, sausages and pork.

Cardamom
Available both as small green and large black pods containing seeds, cardamom has a strong aromatic quality and should be used sparingly. Add cardamom pods whole and remove before serving, or extract the seeds and use these whole or grind them to a powder just before use. Cardamom is a component of most curry powders. It is also used in pickles, beef and pork dishes; with roasted vegetables; to infuse custards and rice puddings and in baking.

Cayenne
This spice is made from small, hot, dried red chillies. It is always sold ground as cayenne pepper and is sweet, pungent and very hot. Use it sparingly to flavour meats, barbecue sauces, eggs, fish, vegetables, cheese sauces, pastry and vegetable soups. Unlike paprika, cayenne pepper cannot be used for colouring as its flavour is too pronounced.

Chilli powder/ chilli seasoning
Fiery hot chilli powder is a spice that is used cautiously in Mexican dishes, Indian curries, pickles, chutneys, ketchups, soups, tomato dishes, casseroles, spaghetti and meat sauces. Some brands, often called mild chilli powder or chilli seasoning, are a mixture of chilli and other flavourings, such as cumin, oregano, salt and garlic; these are therefore considerably less fiery than hot chilli powder. Adjust the quantity you add to dishes accordingly.

SPICES

Cinnamon

The dried, rolled bark of a tropical evergreen tree, cinnamon is available as sticks and powdered. It has a sweet, pungent flavour. Cinnamon sticks have a more pronounced flavour than the powder, but they are difficult to grind at home, so buy ready-ground cinnamon for use in sweet, spicy baking. Use cinnamon sticks to flavour meat casseroles, vegetable dishes, chutneys and pickles, with chocolate and to infuse fruit compotes, custards, hot drinks, mulled wine and fruit punches.

Cloves

Sold whole and ground, cloves have a distinctive, pungent flavour. They are used mainly to flavour apple dishes, Christmas pudding, mincemeat, bread sauce, pumpkin, mulled wine, and to stud whole baked gammon and onions. In general, whole cloves are best removed from a dish before serving.

Coriander seeds

The mild, sweet, orangey flavour of coriander seeds tastes quite different from the herb. Sold whole or ground, coriander is an ingredient of most curry powders and of pickling spice. It is a typical flavouring in many spicy Moroccan, Middle Eastern and Indian meat and vegetable dishes. It is also very good in home-made chutneys and pickles.

Cumin seeds

The strong, slightly bitter taste of cumin is improved by toasting. Sold whole as seeds, or ground, cumin is an ingredient of curry powders and some chilli powder mixtures. Cumin is also used to flavour pickles, chutneys, cheese dishes, soups, cabbage, rice, Middle Eastern dishes, marinades and fruit pies.

Curry pastes

These ready-made mixtures contain spices, fresh chillies, onion, ginger and oil. Many different varieties of curry pastes are available, including Thai red curry paste and special Indian curry pastes.

Curry powder

Bought curry powders are readily available, but for optimum flavour make your own. Put the following spices into an electric blender or grinder: 1 tbsp each cumin and fenugreek seeds; 1/2 tsp mustard seeds; 1 1/2 tsp each black peppercorns, poppy seeds and ground ginger; 4 tbsp coriander seeds; 1/2 tsp hot chilli powder and 2 tbsp ground turmeric. Grind to a fine powder. Store the curry powder in an airtight container and use within one month.

Fenugreek seeds

Small, hard fenugreek seeds have a distinctive aroma and slightly harsh, hot flavour. An ingredient of commercial curry powders, fenugreek is also used in chutneys, pickles and sauces, but rarely as the only spice.

Five-spice powder

A powerful, pungent ground mixture of star anise, Szechuan pepper, fennel seeds, cloves and cinnamon or cassia, five-spice powder is used sparingly in Chinese cooking. It is added to Chinese red-cooked meats, roast meat and poultry, marinades and stir-fries.

Garam masala

Sold ready prepared, this Indian spice mix is aromatic rather than hot. To make your own garam masala, grind together 10 green cardamom pods, 1 tbsp black peppercorns and 2 tsp cumin seeds.

Ginger

The root of ginger has a hot, fairly sweet taste and is sold in various forms as fresh root ginger or dried, and in dried ground form. Root ginger needs to be cooked to release its true flavour – peel, slice and use in curries, sauces, chutneys and in Chinese cooking. Ground ginger is used in curries, sauces, preserves, cakes as well as sprinkled on melon. Stem ginger is also preserved in syrup or crystallised and used to flavour sweet dishes.

Harissa

A hot mixture of chilli and up to 20 spices, harissa can be bought in powder and paste form. To make harissa: grill 2 red peppers until charred, cool, then skin, core and seed. Put 4 seeded, roughly chopped red chillies into a food processor with 6 peeled garlic cloves, 1 tbsp ground coriander and 1 tbsp caraway seeds. Process to a rough paste. Add the grilled peppers, 2 tsp salt and 4 tbsp olive oil. Whiz until smooth. Store in a screw-topped jar, covered with a thin layer of olive oil. Use within two weeks.

Horseradish

A root of the mustard family, horseradish has a hot, biting, pungent taste and is used raw, but sparingly. It is sold ready-grated in jars. Creamed horseradish is the classic relish for roast beef and is excellent with oily fish; it is sold in jars or you can make it.

Juniper berries

These small purple-black berries have a distinctive scent, with a hint of pine. They should be crushed before being added to a dish to release their maximum flavour. Use juniper berries with game, venison, pork, in marinades and casseroles with those ingredients, and in pâtés and sauerkraut. Juniper is also a flavouring agent in gin.

Mace

The outer covering of the nutmeg, mace is bright red when harvested and dries to a deep orange colour. It is sold as blades (useful for infusing) or ground. It has a sweeter, more delicate flavour than nutmeg but it is more expensive. Use mace in mulled wine and punches, potted meat, fish dishes, béchamel sauce, soups, meat stews, milk puddings and fruit compotes.

Mustard seeds

There are three types of mustard seed: black, brown and white (or yellow). The darker seeds are the more pungent. Most ready-prepared mustards are a combination of the three. The seeds are either left whole (as in wholegrain mustard) or ground, then mixed with liquid such as wine, vinegar or cider. English mustard is sold dry as well as ready-mixed. As a condiment, mustard is served with sausages, steaks, ham, gammon and cheese; it is also used to flavour dressings and sauces.

Nutmeg

This seed of the nutmeg fruit has a distinctive, nutty flavour. It is sold whole or ground, but is best bought whole, as the flavour of freshly grated nutmeg is far superior. Use it in creamy soups; sprinkled on buttered corn, spinach, carrots and beans; in cheese dishes; with chicken and veal; in custards, milk puddings, Christmas pudding, biscuits and cakes.

Paprika

A sweet mild spice, paprika is always sold ground to a red powder. It is good for adding colour to pale egg and cheese dishes. Some varieties, particularly Hungarian, are hotter than others. Use it in salads, fish, meat and chicken dishes, with vegetables, on canapés and in goulash. Produced from oak-smoked red peppers, smoked paprika has an intense flavour and a wonderful smoky aroma, which lends an authentic flavour to paella; it is also excellent with potatoes, fish and chicken dishes.

Pepper

There are several forms: green, black and white. Green or unripe berries have a mild flavour and are used whole in pâtés, with duck and other rich meats, in casseroles and sauces. They are sometimes lightly crushed. Black pepper has a strong, pungent, hot flavour and is best used freshly ground to season dishes. White pepper is more aromatic and less hot in flavour. Its main use is in light-coloured dishes and sauces whose appearance could be marred by dark flecks.

Pink peppercorns

Unrelated to the pepper plant, pink peppercorns are the dried berries of a shrub from South America. These attractive, peppery berries are used in small quantities to flavour pâtés, poultry and game dishes. If consumed in large quantities, they are mildly toxic.

Poppy seeds

The small hard, black seeds from the opium poppy, poppy seeds have a nutty flavour and no narcotic effect. Poppy seeds are used to add flavour and enhance the appearance of breads, biscuits and cakes; dips and spreads; salads and dressings; they are also used in curry powder. Creamy-coloured poppy seeds are also available.

Saffron

The most expensive of all spices, saffron is the dried stigma of the saffron crocus flower. It has a subtle flavour and aroma, and imparts a hint of yellow to foods. Powdered saffron is available, but it is the whole stigmas, called saffron strands or threads, which give the best results. A generous pinch is all that is needed to flavour and colour dishes such as bouillabaisse, chicken soup, rice, paella, fish sauces, breads and cakes.

Star anise

Attractive, dried, star-shaped fruit of an evergreen tree native to China, star anise is red-brown in colour with a pungent aniseed flavour. It is used whole to flavour Chinese meat stews and steamed fish. One star anise is sufficient to flavour a large quantity. Ground star anise should be used sparingly; it is a component of Chinese five-spice powder.

Szechuan pepper

Also called anise pepper, this hot aromatic spice is made from the dried red berries of a Chinese tree. It is one of the ingredients of Chinese five-spice powder.

Tamarind

Dark brown, with a fresh, acidic flavour, tamarind is the pulp that surrounds the seeds within the large pods of the Indian tamarind tree. It is sold dried and compressed into blocks. To use, break off pieces and soak 1 tbsp dried tamarind pulp in 4 tbsp warm water for 20 minutes, then strain the liquid through a sieve, pressing to extract the juice. Use to add a sour flavour to chutneys, sauces and curries. Ready-made tamarind paste is available in jars from larger supermarkets.

Turmeric

This bright spice resembles ginger and is a member of the same family, although it is rarely available fresh. The orange flesh is commonly dried, then ground and sold in powdered form. Turmeric powder has an aromatic, slightly bitter flavour and should be used sparingly in curry powder, pickles, relishes and rice dishes.

Vanilla

These pods are the long, thin, dried, black seed pods of a climbing orchid, which are sold whole. Natural vanilla extract is also obtainable. You can also buy vanilla bean paste: pure vanilla with natural vanilla seeds in a paste form. To release the seeds from the pod, slit the pod in half lengthways, then run the point of a knife along the central core to extract the seeds. To make vanilla sugar, leave a vanilla pod in a jar of caster sugar to impart its flavour. To flavour custards, sweet sauces, ice creams and other creamy desserts, put a whole or split pod in the milk or cream to infuse. The vanilla pod can be rinsed, dried and used again.

FLAVOURINGS AND ESSENCES

Included here are a selection of common bottled flavourings and essences, although wines and other alcoholic drinks also have a culinary role. True essences are made by naturally extracting the flavour from the food itself; flavourings are synthetic and tend to be cheaper and more potent. Both flavourings and essences are intensely flavoured and frequently only a few drops are needed in a recipe.

Almond essence
Made from bitter almonds, this essence is used in baking, usually to reinforce the flavour of almonds in the recipe. Synthetic almond flavouring is widely available, but most larger supermarkets stock real almond essence, which is far superior.

Angostura bitters
This is made from a secret formula, which includes cloves, cinnamon, citrus peel, nutmeg, prunes, quinine and rum. Used to flavour aperitifs, such as Pimm's and other drinks, angostura bitters may also be added to casseroles, fruit salads, puddings and cakes.

Orange flower water
This potent, colourless flavouring liquid is distilled from the flowers of the Seville orange. Orange flower water is used sparingly to flavour cakes, biscuits, pastries and desserts.

Oyster sauce
A thick, dark brown Chinese sauce, which is both sweet and salty. It is widely used in Asian dishes, especially stir-fries, and is available from supermarkets.

Plum sauce
Chinese plum sauce is made from plums, vinegar, salt and sugar. It has a sweet, salty and fruity flavour and is traditionally served with Peking duck, or as a dipping sauce with crispy deep-fried snacks.

Peppermint oil
Similar to peppermint essence, peppermint oil is made from the concentrated oil from the natural plant. The oil is mostly used for making sweets.

Rose water
A highly fragrant rose-flavoured water, which is either distilled from rose petals or prepared from rose oil. It is used sparingly in baking and desserts, Turkish delight, and other Middle Eastern recipes.

Soy sauce
A light or dark brown sauce with a salty, sweetish taste, made from boiled and fermented soya beans. Light soy sauce has a delicate flavour and is not as salty or strong as the dark variety. Japanese soy sauce is light and refined. Soy sauce is used in Asian cookery.

Tabasco
This fiery hot sauce is based on red chillies, spirit vinegar and salt, and prepared to a secret recipe. A dash of Tabasco may be used to add a kick to soups, casseroles, sauces, rice dishes and tomato-based drinks.

Tahini
A creamy-textured paste, tahini is made from finely ground sesame seeds. It is widely used in Middle Eastern dishes and is sold in jars in larger supermarkets and delicatessens.

Thai fish sauce
Known as nam pla in Thailand, this highly pungent sauce adds a distinctive taste to Asian dishes. It is obtainable from most supermarkets, although light soy sauce can be substituted if necessary.

Vanilla extract
True vanilla extract is extracted from vanilla pods. Vanilla flavouring is made from an ingredient in clove oil; it is widely available but inferior. Vanilla is used to enhance many sweet dishes, sometimes to bring out the flavour of chocolate.

SOUPS

SOUPS

There is nothing quite as comforting as a flavourful home-made soup that makes the most of seasonal ingredients. The secret of a great-tasting soup is invariably a well-flavoured home-made stock, but if you are short of time, use one of the fresh stock products available from supermarkets. Chunky hot soups are the obvious choice for winter starters, and several of the recipes in this chapter are substantial enough to serve as a meal in themselves – especially if you increase the quantities and serve them with lots of warm, crusty bread. For summer starters, choose lighter soups – a chilled soup is the perfect refreshing choice for a hot day. For best results, use really fresh ingredients in prime condition. A blender or a food processor is a great help when making creamy soups.

GARNISHES AND ACCOMPANIMENTS

Adding a complementary finishing touch will enhance the flavour as well as the appearance of a fresh soup. Smooth soups, in particular, benefit from a contrasting swirl of cream or crème fraîche and, perhaps, a sprinkling of pepper or paprika.

Top robust soups with Parmesan shavings or a sprinkling of freshly grated Gruyère, Parmesan, Pecorino or Cheddar cheese. Try stirring a spoonful of pesto (page 22) into hearty vegetable potages; this also works well with tomato soups. Use classic, sun-dried tomato, coriander or rocket pesto.

Citrus butters make a tasty garnish (see page 23). Thinly slice the butter and top each portion of soup with a few slices – it will melt deliciously into the soup as you serve it.

CROUTONS
This classic garnish for soups is very easy to make. Remove the crusts from 3 or 4 thick slices of day-old white bread, then cut into 2.5cm (1in) squares. Heat a 2.5cm (1in) depth of oil in a frying pan, then fry the bread cubes, turning constantly, until crisp and golden. Remove and drain on kitchen paper.

Use flavoured bread, such as walnut or sun-dried tomato bread, to make savoury croutons. Toss the flavoured bread cubes in oil – such as walnut or sun-dried tomato (from a jar of sun-dried tomatoes). Put into a shallow roasting tin and bake in the oven at 200°C (180°C fan oven) mark 6 for 15 minutes or until golden; drain on kitchen paper.

Chunky bread slices can also be just toasted and then cut into cubes. Croutons can be prepared ahead, allowed to cool, then stored in an airtight tin. To serve, warm through in the oven.

FRESH HERBS
A simple sprinkling of fresh herbs will enliven most soups. Fresh herb flowers can also make a pretty and unusual garnish. Chop the herbs just before serving, and choose a herb that complements that flavour of soup – for example, basil with tomato, chives with creamy soups, or coriander with Asian-style soups.

MELBA TOAST
This wafer-thin, brittle toast is traditionally served with soups and pâtés. Toast 3 or 4 slices of soft-grain bread lightly on both sides. Quickly cut off the crusts, split each slice horizontally in two and scrape off any doughy bits. Sprinkle with Parmesan and paprika, if you like. Lay on a baking sheet and bake at 180°C (160°C fan oven) mark 4 for about 10 minutes or until golden and curled. Melba toast can be prepared ahead, cooled then stored in an airtight tin. To serve, warm through in the oven.

BRUSCHETTA
This Italian favourite goes well with most soups. Grill thick slices of day-old rustic bread lightly on both sides. Immediately rub all over with a peeled garlic clove, drizzle with a little extra virgin olive oil and serve.

PARMESAN CRISPS
These complement fresh-tasting creamed soups. See Cook's Tip page 45 for the recipe.

CHICKEN SOUP WITH DUMPLINGS

Serves 4 as a main course
Preparation 15 minutes
Cooking time 1 hour 20 minutes

1.1–1.4kg (2¹/₂–3lb) oven-ready
    chicken, skinned
1 onion, chopped
1 litre (1³/₄ pints) chicken stock
350g (12oz) carrots, peeled and sliced
125g (4oz) celery sticks with leaves,
    chopped
salt and ground black pepper

For the dumplings
75g (3oz) matzo meal
1 medium egg, beaten

1 Put the chicken, onion, stock, carrots and seasoning into a large pan and bring to the boil. Reduce the heat, cover and simmer for about 1 hour or until the chicken is tender. Remove the chicken and leave to stand for a few minutes. Strain the stock into a pan and heat to just simmering while you make the dumplings.

2 To make the dumplings, mix together the matzo meal, 125ml (4fl oz) boiling water, the beaten egg and salt to taste. Shape the mixture into small marble-sized dumplings with your hands.

3 Add the dumplings and celery to the simmering soup and cook gently for about 20 minutes.

4 Carve the chicken off the bones. Cut the meat into small chunks, stir into the soup and heat through. Taste and adjust the seasoning, and serve immediately.

TRY SOMETHING DIFFERENT

Chicken Consommé Heat 1.7 litres (3 pints) well-flavoured fat-free chicken stock in a pan. Put 350g (12oz) minced skinless chicken breast in another large pan and add 2 thinly sliced leeks, 2 thinly sliced celery sticks, 2 thinly sliced carrots and 2 diced shallots. Mix in 2 medium egg whites, lightly whisked, and the crushed egg shells. Gradually whisk in the hot stock, then bring to the boil, whisking. When it comes to the boil, stop whisking, reduce the heat and simmer gently for 1 hour. A crust will have formed on the surface and the stock underneath should be clear. Make a hole in the crust and ladle the clear stock into a muslin-lined sieve over a large bowl. Allow to drain through slowly, then reheat in the cleaned pan. Season and add a dash of sherry or Madeira, if you like.

NUTRITION PER SERVING 323 cals |
6g fat (2g sats) | 24g carbs |1.1g salt

CLASSIC SOUP DUMPLINGS

Serves 4
Preparation 10 minutes
Cooking time 15–20 minutes

125g (4oz) self-raising flour
50g (2oz) shredded suet
salt and ground black pepper

1 In a bowl, mix the flour, suet and seasoning with sufficient cold water to make an elastic dough.

2 Divide into about 16 portions and, with lightly floured hands, roll into small balls.

3 Add to the soup and simmer for 15–20 minutes.

TRY SOMETHING DIFFERENT

Flavour these dumplings with any of the following ingredients:

- 25g (1oz) finely grated Cheddar cheese
- ¹/₂ finely chopped small onion
- 1 tbsp freshly grated Parmesan
- ¹/₂ tsp mild curry powder
- 1 tbsp chopped watercress
- 1¹/₂ tsp freshly chopped parsley
- 1¹/₂ tsp snipped fresh chives
- 1 tsp freshly chopped tarragon
- ¹/₂ tsp mixed dried herbs
- ¹/₂ tsp paprika
- 1 tbsp canned sweetcorn, drained
- 1 tsp caraway seeds

CREAM OF MUSHROOM SOUP

Serves 4
Preparation 15 minutes, plus soaking
Cooking time 40 minutes

15g ($^{1}/_{2}$ oz) dried porcini mushrooms
50g (2oz) butter
1 large onion, chopped
1 garlic clove, crushed
1 tbsp freshly chopped sage
700g (1$^{1}/_{2}$ lb) chestnut mushrooms, or mixed
    chestnut and flat mushrooms, chopped
750ml (1$^{1}/_{4}$ pints) vegetable stock
150ml ($^{1}/_{4}$ pint) crème fraîche
a pinch of freshly grated nutmeg
salt and ground black pepper
snipped chives, to serve

1 Put the dried mushrooms into a bowl, pour on 150ml ($^{1}/_{4}$ pint) boiling water and set aside to soak for 20 minutes. Remove the porcini with a slotted spoon; strain the liquid and keep to one side. Chop the mushrooms and set aside.
2 Melt half the butter in a pan, add the onion, porcini, garlic and sage, and fry for 10 minutes or until softened and lightly golden. Add the remaining butter, then add the fresh mushrooms and increase the heat. Stir-fry for 5 minutes or until the mushrooms are browned.
3 Stir in the reserved porcini liquid and stock. Bring to the boil, cover and simmer gently for 20 minutes. Transfer to a blender or food processor and whiz until smooth. Return to the pan.
4 Stir in most of the crème fraîche and salt, pepper and nutmeg to taste. Reheat the soup gently. Spoon into warmed bowls and add a swirl of crème fraîche and a sprinkling of snipped chives to each portion. Serve at once.

NUTRITION PER SERVING
290 cals | 26g fat (11g sats) | 8g carbs | 0.8g salt **V**

CREAM OF WATERCRESS SOUP

Serves 6
Preparation 15 minutes
Cooking time 30 minutes

250g (9oz) watercress
50g (2oz) butter
1 onion, finely chopped
700g (1½lb) potatoes, cut into small pieces
900ml (1½ pints) milk
900ml (1½ pints) vegetable stock
6 tbsp single cream
salt and ground black pepper
Parmesan Crisps (see Cook's Tip below and vegetarian
    cheeses on page 228) to serve (optional)

1 Trim the watercress and discard the coarse stalks. Reserve
a few sprigs to garnish, then roughly chop the rest.
2 Melt the butter in a large pan, add the onion and cook
gently for 8–10 minutes until soft. Add the potatoes and cook
for 1 minute, then pour in the milk and stock, and bring to
the boil. Reduce the heat and simmer for 15–20 minutes
until tender.
3 Take the pan off the heat. Stir in the chopped watercress,
then transfer to a blender and whiz, in batches, until smooth.
Pour the soup into a clean pan, then add the cream and
season with salt and pepper. Heat through, then serve
garnished with the reserved watercress sprigs and a Parmesan
crisp, if you like, and serve with the remaining Parmesan crisps
on the side.

COOK'S TIP

Parmesan Crisps Preheat the oven to 200°C
(180°C fan oven) mark 6 and line two baking sheets
with baking parchment. Put heaped tablespoonfuls of
freshly grated Parmesan on to the sheets, spacing them
well apart, and spread each one out. Sprinkle with
poppy seeds and bake for 5–10 minutes until lacy and
golden. Leave on the baking sheet for 2–3 minutes to
firm up slightly, then transfer to a wire rack to cool.

NUTRITION PER SERVING
251 cals | 13g fat (8g sats) | 26g carbs | 0.4g salt **V**

FRENCH ONION SOUP

Serves 4
Preparation 30 minutes
Cooking time about 1 hour

75g (3oz) butter
700g (1½lb) small onions, finely chopped
3 garlic cloves, crushed
1 tbsp plain flour
200ml (7fl oz) dry white wine (optional)
1.4 litres (2½ pints) vegetable stock
bouquet garni (1 bay leaf, a few fresh parsley
    and thyme sprigs)
salt and ground black pepper

To serve
1 small baguette, cut into slices 1cm (½ in) thick
50g (2oz) Gruyère or Cheddar cheese, grated

1 Melt the butter in a large heavy-based pan. Add the onions and cook slowly over a very low heat, stirring frequently, until very soft and golden brown; this should take at least 30 minutes. Add the garlic and flour and cook, stirring, for 1 minute.
2 Pour in the wine, if using, and let it bubble until reduced by half. Add the stock, bouquet garni and seasoning. Bring to the boil, then reduce the heat and simmer gently, uncovered, for 20–30 minutes.
3 Discard the bouquet garni and let the soup cool a little. Whiz one-third in a food processor or blender until smooth, then stir this back into the soup in the pan.
4 Preheat the grill. Lightly toast the baguette slices on both sides. Reheat the soup and adjust the seasoning.
5 Divide the soup among four ovenproof soup bowls. Float two or three slices of toast on each portion and sprinkle thickly with the grated cheese. Stand the bowls under the hot grill until the cheese has melted and turned golden brown. Serve at once.

NUTRITION PER SERVING
438 cals | 21g fat (13g sats) | 45g carbs | 1.3g salt **V**

BROCCOLI AND GOAT'S CHEESE SOUP

Serves 6
Preparation 10 minutes
Cooking time 20 minutes

50g (2oz) butter
2 medium onions, chopped
1 litre (1³/₄ pints) vegetable, chicken or turkey stock
700g (1¹/₂ lb) broccoli, broken into florets, stout stalks
    peeled and chopped
1 head of garlic, separated into cloves, unpeeled
1 tbsp olive oil
150g (5oz) goat's cheese
salt and ground black pepper

1 Preheat the oven to 200°C (180°C fan oven) mark 6. Melt the butter in a pan over a gentle heat. Add the onions, then cover the pan and cook for 4–5 minutes until translucent. Add half the stock and bring to the boil. Add the broccoli and return to the boil, then cover the pan, reduce the heat and simmer for 15–20 minutes until the broccoli is tender.

2 Meanwhile, toss the cloves of garlic in the oil and tip into a roasting tin. Roast in the oven for 15 minutes or until soft when squeezed.

3 Leave the soup to cool a little, then add the goat's cheese and whiz in batches in a blender or food processor until smooth. Return the soup to the pan and add the remaining stock. Reheat gently on the hob and season to taste with salt and pepper.

4 Ladle the soup into warmed bowls, squeeze the garlic out of their skins and scatter over the soup, add a sprinkling of black pepper and serve.

TRY SOMETHING DIFFERENT
- Double the quantity of goat's cheese, if you prefer a stronger taste.
- Instead of goat's cheese, substitute a soft garlic cheese for a really garlicky flavour.

NUTRITION PER SERVING
220 cals | 16g fat (10g sats) | 8g carbs | 0.5g salt Ⓥ

FRESH TOMATO SOUP WITH BASIL

Serves 6
Preparation 15 minutes
Cooking time 40 minutes

50g (2oz) butter
2 onions, thinly sliced
900g (2lb) tomatoes
3 tbsp flour
900ml (1$\frac{1}{2}$ pints) chicken stock
2 tbsp tomato purée
1$\frac{1}{2}$ tsp freshly chopped basil
    or $\frac{1}{2}$ tsp dried
150ml ($\frac{1}{4}$ pint) single cream (optional)
salt and ground black pepper

1 Melt the butter in a pan, add the sliced onions and fry gently until golden brown.
2 Meanwhile, halve the tomatoes, scoop out the seeds into a sieve placed over a bowl. Press the seeds to remove all the tomato pulp and juice; discard the seeds and put the juice aside.
3 Remove the pan from the heat. Stir in the flour and cook gently for 1 minute, stirring. Remove the pan from the heat and gradually stir in the stock. Bring to the boil slowly and continue to cook, stirring, until thickened.
4 Stir in the tomato purée, herbs and the tomatoes with the reserved juice, and season. Cover the pan and simmer gently for about 30 minutes.
5 Leave the soup to cool slightly, then sieve or purée in a blender or food processor. Strain through a sieve into a clean pan and reheat gently. Taste and adjust the seasoning if necessary.
6 Ladle the soup into individual soup bowls and, if you like, swirl a little cream through each bowl just before serving.

NUTRITION PER SERVING
193 cals | 12g fat (8g sats) | 18g carbs | 0.6g salt

CARROT AND CORIANDER SOUP

Serves 6
Preparation 15 minutes
Cooking time about 30 minutes

40g (1½ oz) butter
175g (6oz) trimmed leeks, sliced
450g (1lb) carrots, sliced
2 tsp ground coriander
1 tsp plain flour
1.1 litres (2 pints) vegetable stock
150ml (¼ pint) single cream
salt and ground black pepper
coriander leaves, roughly torn,
    to serve

1   Melt the butter in a large pan. Add the sliced leeks and carrots, stir, then cover the pan and cook gently for 7–10 minutes until the vegetables begin to soften but not colour.

2   Stir in the ground coriander and flour and cook, stirring, for 1 minute.
3   Add the stock and bring to the boil, stirring. Season with salt and pepper, then reduce the heat, cover the pan and simmer for about 20 minutes, until the vegetables are tender.
4   Leave the soup to cool a little, then whiz in batches in a blender or food processor until quite smooth. Return to the pan and stir in the cream. Adjust the seasoning and reheat gently; do not boil.
5   Ladle into warmed bowls, scatter with torn coriander leaves and serve.

NUTRITION PER SERVING 140 cals | 11g fat (7g sats) | 10g carbs | 0.2g salt ⓥ

MINESTRONE WITH PESTO

Serves 4
Preparation 10 minutes
Cooking time 45 minutes

2 tbsp olive oil
1 small onion, finely chopped
1 carrot, chopped
1 celery stick, chopped
1 garlic clove, crushed
2 tbsp freshly chopped thyme
1 litre (1¾ pints) hot vegetable stock
400g can chopped tomatoes
400g can borlotti beans, drained and
    rinsed
125g (4oz) minestrone pasta
175g (6oz) Savoy cabbage, shredded
salt and ground black pepper
fresh pesto (see page 22), toasted
    ciabatta and extra virgin olive oil
    to serve

1   Heat the oil in a large pan and add the onion, carrot and celery. Cook for 8–10 minutes until softened, then add the garlic and thyme and fry for another 2–3 minutes.
2   Add the hot stock, tomatoes and half the borlotti beans to the pan and bring to the boil. Mash the remaining beans and stir into the soup, then reduce the heat and simmer for 30 minutes, adding the minestrone pasta and cabbage for the last 10 minutes of cooking time.
3   Check the seasoning, then ladle the soup into four warmed bowls and serve with a dollop of fresh pesto on top and with slices of toasted ciabatta drizzled with extra virgin olive oil on the side.

NUTRITION PER SERVING 334 cals | 11g fat (3g sats) | 47g carbs | 1.5g salt ⓥ

MULLIGATAWNY SOUP

Serves 4
Preparation 10 minutes
Cooking time 40 minutes

3 streaky bacon rashers, rinded and
    finely chopped
550g (1¼ lb) chicken portions
600ml (1 pint) chicken stock
1 carrot, sliced
1 celery stick, chopped
1 apple, cored and chopped
2 tsp curry powder
4 peppercorns, crushed
1 clove and 1 bay leaf
1 tbsp plain flour
150ml (¼ pint) milk
50g (2oz) long-grain rice, cooked, and
    crusty bread to serve

1 Fry the bacon in a large pan until the
fat begins to run. Do not allow the
bacon to become brown.

2 Add the chicken and brown well.
Drain the meat on kitchen paper and
pour off the fat.
3 Return the bacon and chicken to
the pan and add the stock, the carrot,
celery, apple, and flavourings. Cover the
pan and simmer for about 30 minutes
or until the chicken is tender.
4 Remove the chicken and allow to
cool a little. Cut off the meat and return
it to the soup. Discard the clove and
bay leaf, and reheat the soup gently.
5 Mix the flour with a little cold water.
Add to the soup with the milk and
reheat without boiling.
6 Ladle the soup into warmed bowls,
spoon a mound of rice into each one
and serve immediately with chunks of
crusty bread.

NUTRITION PER SERVING 252 cals |
13g fat (4g sats) | 7.3g carbs | 0.9g salt

CURRIED PARSNIP SOUP

Serves 6
Preparation 20 minutes
Cooking time 50 minutes

40g (1½ oz) butter
1 onion, sliced
700g (1½ lb) parsnips, peeled, cored
    and finely diced
1 tsp curry powder
½ tsp ground cumin
1.1 litres (2 pints) chicken or vegetable
    stock
150ml (¼ pint) single cream, plus extra
    to garnish
salt and ground black pepper
paprika to serve

1 Melt the butter in a large pan,
add the onion and fry gently for
5–7 minutes. Add the parsnips and
fry gently for about 3 minutes.

2 Stir in the curry powder and cumin,
and cook for a further 2 minutes.
3 Add the stock, season to taste with
salt and pepper and bring to the boil.
Reduce the heat, cover the pan and
simmer for 35 minutes or until the
vegetables are tender.
4 Leave the soup to cool a little, then
whiz in batches in a blender or food
processor until smooth. Return the
soup to the pan and adjust the
seasoning. Add the cream and reheat
but do not boil.
5 Ladle the soup into warmed bowls,
swirl in a little cream, then sprinkle with
paprika and serve.

NUTRITION PER SERVING 184 cals |
12g fat (7g sats) | 17g carbs | 0.2g salt

BORSCHT

Serves 4
Preparation 10 minutes
Cooking time 45 minutes, plus chilling

6 small raw beetroot, about 1kg
  (2¼ lb), peeled
2 medium onions, chopped
1.1 litres (2 pints) beef stock
2 tbsp lemon juice
6 tbsp dry sherry
salt and ground black pepper
150ml (¼ pint) soured cream or
  natural yogurt and snipped fresh
  chives or dill to garnish

1 Grate the beetroot coarsely and put into a pan with the onions, stock and seasoning. Bring to the boil, cover and simmer for about 45 minutes.
2 Strain, discarding the vegetables, then add the lemon juice and sherry to the liquid and adjust the seasoning. Leave to cool, then chill in the fridge.
3 Serve well chilled, garnished with a whirl of soured cream or yogurt and snipped chives or dill.

NUTRITION PER SERVING 220 cals |
8g fat (5g sats) | 27g carbs | 2.4g salt

EASY PEA SOUP

Serves 4
Preparation 3 minutes, plus thawing
Cooking time 25 minutes

1 small baguette, thinly sliced
2 tbsp basil-infused olive oil, plus extra
  to drizzle
450g (1lb) frozen peas, thawed
600ml (1 pint) vegetable stock
salt and ground black pepper

1 Preheat the oven to 220°C (200°C fan oven) mark 7. To make the croutons, put the baguette slices on a baking sheet, drizzle with 2 tbsp oil and bake for 10–15 minutes until golden.
2 Meanwhile, put the peas in a food processor, add the stock and season with salt and pepper. Whiz for 2–3 minutes.
3 Pour the soup into a pan and bring to the boil, then reduce the heat and simmer for 10 minutes. Spoon into warmed bowls, add the croutons, drizzle with extra oil and sprinkle with salt and pepper. Serve immediately.

NUTRITION PER SERVING 408 cals |
9g fat | (2g sats) | 69g carbs | 1.8g salt ⓥ

MEXICAN BEAN SOUP

Serves 6
Preparation 15 minutes
Cooking time 25 minutes

4 tbsp olive oil
1 onion, chopped
2 garlic cloves, chopped
a pinch of dried chilli flakes
1 tsp ground coriander
1 tsp ground cumin
$^1/_2$ tsp ground cinnamon
900ml (1$^1/_2$ pints) vegetable stock
300ml ($^1/_2$ pint) tomato juice
1–2 tsp chilli sauce
2 × 400g cans red kidney beans
2 tbsp freshly chopped coriander
salt and ground black pepper
lime butter to serve (optional, see Citrus Butter, page 23)
coriander leaves, roughly torn, to garnish

1 Heat the oil in a large pan, add the onion, garlic, chillies and spices and fry gently for 5 minutes or until lightly golden.
2 Add the stock, tomato juice, chilli sauce and beans with their liquid. Bring to the boil, then reduce the heat, cover the pan and simmer gently for 20 minutes.
3 Leave the soup to cool a little, then whiz in batches in a blender or food processor until very smooth. Return the soup to the pan. Stir in the chopped coriander and heat through, then season to taste with salt and pepper.
4 Ladle the soup into warmed bowls. Top each portion with a few slices of lime butter, if you like, and scatter with torn coriander leaves.

NUTRITION PER SERVING without lime butter
184 cals | 8g fat (1.2g sats) 21g carbs | 1.3g salt Ⓥ

SIMPLE VEGETABLE SOUP

Serves 4
Preparation 10 minutes
Cooking time 40 minutes

1 or 2 onions, finely chopped
2 tbsp oil, or 1 tbsp oil and 25g (1oz) butter
1 or 2 garlic cloves, crushed (optional)
450g (1lb) chopped mixed vegetables, such as leeks, potatoes, celery, fennel, canned tomatoes and parsnips (chopped finely or into larger dice for a chunky soup)
1.1 litres (2 pints) vegetable stock

1 Fry the onions in the oil, or oil and butter, until soft and add the garlic, if you like.
2 Add the chopped mixed vegetables and the stock. Bring to the boil and simmer for 20–30 minutes until the vegetables are tender.
3 Leave chunky, partially purée or blend until smooth, if you like. Reheat and serve.

NUTRITION PER SERVING   114 cals | 6g fat (1g sats) | 13g carbs | 1.5g salt Ⓥ

LENTIL AND BACON SOUP

Serves 6 as a main course
Preparation 10 minutes
Cooking time 1 hour 40 minutes

175g (6oz) red lentils
1.7 litres (3 pints) chicken stock
1 garlic clove, crushed
1 clove
200g (7oz) lean bacon rashers, rinded and diced
225g (8oz) can tomatoes
1 onion, chopped
450g (1lb) potatoes, diced
2 tbsp lemon juice
salt and ground black pepper
crisply fried bacon strips, freshly chopped parsley, grated cheese or croutons to garnish

1 Put the lentils in a pan with the stock. Add the garlic, clove, bacon, tomatoes, onion and seasoning.
2 Bring to the boil, cover and simmer for about 1 hour or until the lentils are soft.
3 Add the potatoes and cook for a further 20 minutes or until tender.
4 Remove the clove. Allow the soup to cool slightly, then sieve or purée in a blender or food processor until smooth.
5 Return the soup to the pan, add the lemon juice and reheat gently. Adjust the seasoning and garnish with bacon strips, chopped parsley, grated cheese or croutons just before serving.

NUTRITION PER SERVING 209 cals | 3g fat (1g sats) | 32g carbs | 1.6g salt

SCOTCH BROTH

Serves 8
Preparation 15 minutes
Cooking time 2 hours

1 piece marrow bone, about 350g (12oz)
1.4kg (3lb) piece beef skirt (ask your butcher for this)
300g (11oz) broth mix (to include pearl barley, red lentils, split peas and green peas), soaked according to the pack instructions
2 carrots, finely chopped
1 parsnip, finely chopped
2 onions, finely chopped
$^1/_4$ white cabbage, finely chopped
1 leek, trimmed and finely chopped
$^1/_2$ tbsp salt
ground black pepper
2 tbsp freshly chopped parsley to serve

1 Put the marrow bone and beef skirt into a 5.7 litre (10 pint) stock pot and add 2.6 litres (4$^1/_2$ pints) cold water – there should be enough to cover the meat.
2 Bring the water to the boil. Remove any scum from the surface with a spoon and discard. Reduce the heat to low, add the broth mix and simmer, partially covered, for 1$^1/_2$ hours, skimming the surface occasionally.
3 Add the carrots, parsnip, onions, cabbage, leek and another 600ml (1 pint) cold water. Cover to bring to the boil quickly, then reduce the heat and simmer for 30 minutes.
4 Remove the marrow bone and piece of beef from the broth. Add a few shreds of beef to the broth, if you like. Season the broth well with the salt and some pepper, and stir in the chopped parsley. Ladle into warmed bowls and serve hot.

COOK'S TIP
This is really two meals in one: a starter and a main course. The beef flavours the stock and is removed before serving. Later, you divide up the meat and serve it with mashed potatoes, swedes or turnips.

NUTRITION PER SERVING
173 cals | 2g fat (trace sats) | 35g carbs | 2.3g salt

COCK-A-LEEKIE SOUP

Serves 8
Preparation 30–40 minutes
Cooking time 1 hour 20 minutes

1.4kg (3lb) oven-ready chicken, including giblets if available
2 onions, roughly chopped
2 carrots, roughly chopped
2 celery sticks, roughly chopped
1 bay leaf
25g (1oz) butter
900g (2lb) trimmed leeks, sliced
125g (4oz) ready-to-eat dried prunes, sliced
Classic Soup Dumplings (see page 43), made with the
    addition of 2 tbsp freshly chopped parsley and 2 tbsp
    freshly chopped thyme
salt and ground black pepper
freshly chopped parsley to garnish

1 Put the chicken into a pan in which it fits quite snugly, then add the chopped vegetables, bay leaf and chicken giblets. Pour in 1.7 litres (3 pints) water and bring to the boil, then reduce the heat, cover and simmer gently for 1 hour.
2 Meanwhile, melt the butter in a large pan. Add the leeks and fry gently for 10 minutes or until softened.
3 Remove the chicken from the pan and leave until cool enough to handle. Strain the stock and put to one side. Strip the chicken from the bones and shred roughly. Add to the stock with the prunes and softened leeks.
4 Make the dumplings and lightly shape the dough into 2.5cm (1in) balls. Bring the soup just to the boil and season well. Reduce the heat, add the dumplings and cover the pan with a lid. Simmer for about 15–20 minutes until the dumplings are light and fluffy. Serve the soup sprinkled with chopped parsley.

COOK'S TIP
Make the stock a day ahead, if possible,
then cool overnight. The following day,
remove any fat from the surface.

NUTRITION PER SERVING
280 cals | 4g fat (1g sats) | 40g carbs | 0.2g salt

BOUILLABAISSE

Serves 4
Preparation 15 minutes
Cooking time 45 minutes

1kg (2¼lb) mixed fish fillets and shellfish, such as red mullet, John Dory, monkfish, red snapper, whiting, cleaned mussels in shells (see Cook's Tips, page 95), cooked large prawns and crab claw meat
pinch of saffron
3 tbsp olive oil
1 onion, sliced
1 leek, trimmed and sliced
2 celery sticks, sliced
2 garlic cloves, crushed
400g can plum tomatoes, or skinned, seeded flavourful fresh ones, chopped (see page 277)
bouquet garni (1 bay leaf, a few fresh parsley and thyme sprigs)
1 strip of orange zest
1 tbsp sun-dried tomato paste
½ tsp fennel seeds
1.1 litres (2 pints) fish stock
2 tbsp freshly chopped parsley
1 tbsp freshly chopped thyme
salt and ground black pepper
crusty bread to serve

1 Cut the fish fillets into bite-sized pieces.
2 Put the saffron into a bowl, pour on 150ml (¼ pint) boiling water and leave to soak.
3 Heat the olive oil in a large pan, add the onion, leek, celery and garlic, and cook until softened. Add the tomatoes, bouquet garni, orange zest, sun-dried tomato paste and fennel seeds; cook for 1–2 minutes.
4 Add the fish stock together with the saffron and its soaking liquid. Season with pepper and a little salt and bring to the boil. Lower the heat and simmer for about 30 minutes.
5 Add the fish pieces and mussels (not the prawns or crab claws) and cook for about 5–6 minutes until the fish is just cooked and the mussels have opened; discard any mussels that remain closed.
6 Stir in the chopped herbs, prawns and crab claw meat. Heat through and serve in warmed bowls with plenty of crusty bread.

COOK'S TIP
This classic French fish soup originates from Marseilles. If possible, buy whole fish and fillet them yourself, using the bones and trimmings to make a flavourful stock (see page 11).

NUTRITION PER SERVING
330 cals | 13g fat (1g sats) | 9g carbs | 1.5g salt

SMOKED HADDOCK CHOWDER

Serves 4
Preparation 15 minutes
Cooking time 25 minutes

25g (1oz) butter
2 onions, chopped
125g (4oz) rindless smoked streaky
    bacon rashers, chopped
600ml (1 pint) whole milk
225g (8oz) potatoes, cut into 1cm
    (1/2in) cubes
3 celery sticks, thinly sliced
198g can sweetcorn, drained
450g (1lb) skinless smoked haddock
    fillet, cut into 8 pieces
salt and ground black pepper
crusty bread to serve

1 Heat the butter in a large, wide pan, add the onions and fry for 3 minutes. Add the bacon and cook for a further 5 minutes or until it is no longer pink.
2 Add the milk and 600ml (1 pint) boiling water, then season with 1 tsp salt and plenty of pepper. Add the potatoes and celery, and cook for 5 minutes.
3 Stir in the drained sweetcorn and lower in the haddock gently. Cover and cook for 10 minutes or until the fish is just cooked. Serve in individual bowls, with plenty of crusty bread.

TRY SOMETHING DIFFERENT
Serve the chowder topped with croutons (see page 59) and plenty of chopped parsley.

NUTRITION PER SERVING 410 cals | 20g fat (10g sats) | 26g carbs | 4.2g salt

VICHYSSOISE

Serves 4
Preparation 10 minutes
Cooking time 45 minutes

25g (1oz) butter
1 onion, finely chopped
1 garlic clove, crushed
550g (1 1/4 lb) trimmed leeks, chopped
200g (7oz) floury potatoes, sliced
1.3 litres (2 1/4 pints) hot vegetable
    stock
crème fraîche and chopped chives to
    garnish

1 Melt the butter in a pan over a gentle heat, then cook the onion for 10–15 minutes until soft. Add the garlic and cook for a further 1 minute. Add the leeks and cook for 5–10 minutes until softened. Add the potatoes and toss together with the leeks.
2 Pour in the hot stock and bring to the boil, then reduce the heat and simmer the soup for 20 minutes or until the potatoes are tender.
3 Leave the soup to cool a little, then whiz in batches in a blender or food processor until smooth.
4 To serve, reheat the soup gently. Ladle into warmed bowls and garnish with crème fraîche and chives.

NUTRITION PER SERVING 117 cals | 6g fat (4g sats) | 13g carbs | 0.1g salt ⓥ

GAZPACHO

Serves 6
Preparation 20 minutes, plus chilling
Cooking time 10 minutes

1 medium cucumber, peeled, seeded and coarsely chopped
450g (1lb) fully ripened tomatoes, skinned, deseeded and
    chopped (see page 277)
100g (3$^{1}/_{2}$ oz) green pepper, cored, seeded and chopped
50–100g (2–3$^{1}/_{2}$ oz) onions, chopped
2 garlic cloves, chopped
3 tbsp olive oil
3 tbsp white wine vinegar
450ml ($^{3}/_{4}$ pint) tomato juice
2 tbsp tomato purée
salt and ground black pepper
ice cubes and 1 green pepper, cored, seeded and finely
    diced to serve

For the croutons
4 thick slices of white bread, crusts removed
50g (2oz) butter

1 Mix all the gazpacho ingredients together in a large bowl,
seasoning with $^{1}/_{4}$ tsp salt. Purée the mixture in batches in a
blender or food processor until smooth.
2 Return the soup to the bowl, cover and chill for at least
2 hours.
3 To make croutons, cut the bread into cubes. Heat the
butter in a large frying pan and sauté the bread cubes over
a medium heat, stirring frequently, until golden on all sides.
Remove and drain the croutons on kitchen paper.
4 Just before serving, add a few ice cubes to the soup.
Serve each portion garnished with diced green pepper and
the croutons.

COOK'S TIP
This Spanish iced soup is wonderfully refreshing in hot
weather. Drop in a few ice cubes just before serving
to make it as cold as possible.

NUTRITION PER SERVING
220 cals | 14g fat (5g sats) | 21g carbs | 1.4g salt ⓥ

DIPS, CANAPÉS AND NIBBLES

DIPS

Serve these dips with warm pitta bread fingers, corn chips, breadsticks or an assortment of crudités (vegetable sticks), such as strips of celery, fennel, cucumber, courgette, peppers and carrots, blanched asparagus tips and cauliflower florets, and cherry or baby plum tomatoes.

TZATZIKI

Serves 8 • Preparation 10 minutes

1 cucumber
300g (11oz) Greek-style yogurt
2 tsp olive oil
2 tbsp freshly chopped mint
1 large garlic clove, crushed
salt and ground black pepper
pitta bread and vegetable sticks to serve

1 Halve, seed and dice the cucumber and put into a bowl.
2 Add the yogurt and olive oil. Stir in the chopped mint and garlic, and season with salt and pepper to taste. Cover and chill in the fridge until ready to serve.
3 Serve with warm pitta bread and vegetable sticks.

NUTRITION PER SERVING
50 cals | 4g fat (2g sats) | 1g carbs | 0.4g salt ⓥ

HUMMUS

Serves 6 • Preparation 15 minutes

400g can chickpeas, drained and rinsed
juice of 1 lemon
4 tbsp tahini
1 garlic clove, crushed
5 tbsp extra virgin olive oil
salt and ground black pepper
pitta bread or toasted flatbreads to serve

1 Put the chickpeas, lemon juice, tahini, garlic and olive oil in a blender or food processor. Season generously with salt and pepper, then whiz to a paste.
2 Spoon the hummus into a bowl, then cover and chill until needed.
3 Serve with warm pitta bread or toasted flatbreads.

TRY SOMETHING DIFFERENT
Black Olive Hummus (pictured) Stir 25g (1oz) roughly chopped pitted black olives and 1 tsp paprika into the hummus paste. Sprinkle with a little extra paprika and oil, if you like.

NUTRITION PER SERVING
170 cals | 14g fat (2g sats) | 7g carbs | 0.7g salt ⓥ

TARAMASALATA

Serves 6 • Preparation 15 minutes

100g (3¹/₂ oz) country-style bread, crusts removed
75g (3oz) smoked cod roe
2 tbsp lemon juice
100ml (3¹/₂ fl oz) light olive oil
ground black pepper
pitta bread or toasted flatbreads to serve

1 Put the bread into a bowl, cover with cold water and leave to soak for 10 minutes. Drain and squeeze out most of the water.
2 Soak the smoked cod roe in cold water to cover for 10 minutes, then drain and remove the skin.
3 Put the roe in a blender or food processor with the bread and whiz for 30 seconds. With the motor running, add the lemon juice and olive oil, and whiz briefly to combine. Season with pepper to taste.
4 Spoon into a bowl, cover and chill until needed. Serve with warm pitta bread or toasted flatbreads.

NUTRITION PER SERVING
180 cals | 15g fat (2g sats) | 7g carbs | 0.3g salt

BLUE CHEESE DIP

Serves 6 • Preparation 5 minutes

150ml (¹/₄ pint) soured cream
1 garlic clove, crushed
175g (6oz) blue Stilton cheese
juice of 1 lemon
salt and ground black pepper
snipped chives to garnish
vegetable sticks to serve

1 Put all the ingredients into a blender or food processor and work to a smooth paste.
2 Transfer to a serving dish and chill until required. Check the seasoning, sprinkle with chives and serve with a selection of vegetable sticks.

TRY SOMETHING DIFFERENT
Use Dolcelatte instead of Stilton cheese.

NUTRITION PER SERVING
170 cals | 15g fat (7g sats) | 1g carbs | 1g salt Ⓥ

GUACAMOLE

Serves 6 • Preparation 10 minutes

2 ripe avocados
2 small tomatoes, seeded and chopped
    (see page 277)
juice of 2 limes
2 tbsp extra virgin olive oil
2 tbsp freshly chopped coriander
salt and ground black pepper
tortilla chips, or pitta bread and
    vegetable sticks to serve

1 Cut the avocados in half, remove the stones and peel away the skin. Tip the flesh into a bowl and mash with a fork.
2 Quickly add the tomatoes, lime juice, olive oil and chopped coriander. Mix well and season with salt and pepper to taste. Cover and chill until ready to serve.
3 Serve the guacamole with tortilla chips or warm pitta bread and vegetable sticks.

NUTRITION PER SERVING
160 cals | 16g fat (3g sats) | 2g carbs | 0.4g salt Ⓥ

TAPENADE

Serves 4 • Preparation 5 minutes

3 tbsp capers, rinsed and drained
75g (3oz) pitted black olives
50g can anchovy fillets in oil, drained
100ml (3¹/₂ fl oz) olive oil
2 tbsp brandy
ground black pepper
vegetable sticks or grilled vegetables and toasted French
    bread to serve

1 Put the capers into a blender or food processor with the olives and anchovies. Process briefly to chop.
2 With the motor running, add the olive oil in a steady stream. Stir in the brandy and season with pepper to taste. Transfer to a serving bowl.
3 Serve the tapenade with raw vegetable sticks and/or grilled vegetables and toasted French bread.

NUTRITION PER SERVING
270 cals | 26g fat (2g sats) | trace carbs | 2.3g salt

SUN-DRIED TOMATO PESTO

Makes about 12 tbsp • Preparation 10 minutes

100g (3¹/₂ oz) sun-dried tomatoes in oil, drained weight
20g pack basil
1 small garlic clove, roughly chopped
25g (1oz) pinenuts toasted (see Cook's Tip, page 312)
4–6 tbsp olive oil, plus extra to store
25g (1oz) freshly grated Pecorino (see page 238)

1 Drain the sun-dried tomatoes. Put into a blender or food processor with the basil, garlic and pinenuts. Whiz to a rough purée.
2 Gradually add enough of the oil to make a loose but not too sloppy paste. Stir in the cheese. Check the seasoning.

> **COOK'S TIP**
> This will store in the fridge for up to one month in a sterilised jar – cover the top with a layer of olive oil.

NUTRITION PER SERVING
84 cals | 8.3g fat (1.3g sats) | 8g carbs | 0.3g salt ⓥ

RED PEPPER AND FETA DIP

Makes about 375g (13oz) (25 tbsp) • Preparation 5 minutes

290g jar roasted red peppers, drained
200g (7oz) feta cheese (see page 238), crumbled
1 small garlic clove
1 tbsp natural yogurt
toasted pitta bread to serve

1 Put all the ingredients into a blender or food processor and whiz until smooth. Serve the dip with strips of toasted pitta bread.

NUTRITION PER SERVING
32 cals | 3g fat (1g sats) | 1g carbs | 0.3g salt ⓥ

CANAPÉS AND NIBBLES

Dips, canapés and savoury finger foods, such as spiced nuts and marinated olives, are perfect for drinks parties, as they can be made ahead. Simply warm canapés through prior to serving. Allow about 10 canapés per person, with nuts, olives, dips and 'dunks' as extras. A colourful platter of crudités with a selection of dips always looks attractive.

LEMON AND ROSEMARY OLIVES

Serves 6
Preparation Time 15 minutes, plus at least 24 hours chilling

a few fresh rosemary sprigs, plus extra to decorate
1 garlic clove
175g (6oz) mixed black and green Greek olives
pared zest of 1 lemon
2 tbsp vodka (optional)
300ml (¹/₂ pint) extra virgin olive oil

1 Put the rosemary and garlic in a small heatproof bowl and pour over enough boiling water to cover. Leave for 1–2 minutes, then drain well.
2 Put the olives, lemon zest and vodka, if using, in a glass jar and add the rosemary and garlic. Pour over enough olive oil to cover the olives. Cover and chill for at least 24 hours before using.
3 To serve, remove the olives from the oil and decorate with sprigs of fresh rosemary. Use within one week.

> **COOK'S TIP**
> Don't waste the flavoured oil left over from the olives. It's perfect for using in salad dressings and marinades.

NUTRITION PER SERVING
300 cals | 36g fat (5g sats) | 0g carbs | 1.2g salt ⓥ

COCKTAIL ROLLS

Serves 10
Preparation 20 minutes

200g (7oz) smoked salmon slices
100g (3½oz) cream cheese or goat's
   cheese
1 tbsp dill-flavoured mustard or
   creamed horseradish
1 large courgette
about 2 tbsp hummus
200g (7oz) prosciutto (see Cook's Tip)
about 2 tbsp fruity chutney, such as
   mango
1 small bunch of chives, finely chopped
1 roasted red pepper, finely chopped
ground black pepper

1 Lay the smoked salmon on a sheet
of greaseproof paper. Spread with a thin
layer of cheese, then a layer of mustard
or horseradish, and roll up.
2 Using a vegetable peeler, pare the
courgette into long, wafer-thin strips.
Lay the strips on a board, spread with
cheese, then hummus, and roll up.

3 Lay the prosciutto on a board.
Spread thinly with cheese, then with
the chutney, and roll up.
4 Stand the rolls on a greaseproof
paper-lined baking sheet (trimming the
bases if necessary), cover with clingfilm
and chill for up to 8 hours.
5 About 2 minutes before serving, top
each roll with a little cheese. Dip the
salmon rolls into the chopped chives,
the prosciutto rolls into the red pepper
and the courgette rolls into coarsely
ground black pepper.

COOK'S TIP
Prosciutto is Italian dry-cured ham.
It is available from Italian delis and
most supermarkets. Parma ham is a
type of prosciutto, but other types
are less expensive.

NUTRITION PER SERVING 117 cals |
7g fat (3g sats) | 4g carbs | 1.7g salt

RED PEPPER PESTO CROÛTES

Serves 24
Preparation 20 minutes
Cooking time 15–20 minutes

1 thin French stick, sliced into
   24 rounds
olive oil to brush
fresh pesto (see page 22)
4 pepper pieces (from a jar of
   marinated peppers), each sliced
   into 6 strips
pinenuts to garnish

1 Preheat the oven to 200°C (180°C
fan oven) mark 6. Brush both sides of
the bread slices with oil and put on a
baking sheet. Cook in the oven for
15–20 minutes.
2 Spread 1 tsp pesto on each croûte,
top with a pepper strip and pinenuts,
and serve.

NUTRITION PER SERVING 90 cals |
5g fat (1g sats) | 10g carbs | 0.3g salt

MOZZARELLA NIBBLES

Makes 30
Preparation 15 minutes

2 ×125g tubs mozzarella bocconcini, drained (see Cook's Tips)
75g (3oz) thinly sliced Parma ham, cut into strips (see Cook's Tip, page 65)
400g (14oz) pitted black and green olives, halved
125g (4oz) roasted artichokes, cut into small pieces
125g (4oz) roasted peppers, cut into small pieces
1 bunch of basil leaves

1 Wrap each mozzarella ball in a piece of Parma ham. Push a halved olive on to a cocktail stick, then add a piece of artichoke, a piece of pepper, a basil leaf, then a wrapped mozzarella ball.

Repeat to make about 30 nibbles. Serve immediately or cover and chill for up to 1 hour.

COOK'S TIPS
~ Bocconcini are mini mozzarella balls – the perfect bite-size nibble. They are available from Italian delis and good supermarkets. Alternatively, replace with two regular mozzarella balls, cubed.
~ For vegetarians, omit the ham.
~ Instead of artichokes use halved cherry tomatoes.

NUTRITION PER SERVING 41 cals | 3g fat (1g sats) | 1g carbs | 0.9g salt

SWEET CHILLI PRAWNS

Makes 30
Preparation 20 minutes, plus overnight marinating

30 cooked peeled large prawns, about 250g (9oz)
150ml bottle sweet chilli sauce
grated zest and juice of ¹/₂ lime
3 tbsp freshly chopped basil
¹/₂ cucumber, about 15cm (6in) long
2 tbsp clear honey

1 The night before you want to serve this recipe, put the prawns, 2 tbsp of the chilli sauce, the lime zest and juice, and the basil into a small bowl. Stir gently to mix, then cover the bowl with clingfilm and chill overnight.
2 Up to three hours before serving, use a vegetable peeler to pare along the length of the cucumber to make 15 thin strips. Cut each cucumber strip in half widthways.

3 Thread each piece of cucumber on to a cocktail stick in a concertina shape, then add a marinated prawn. Cover the skewers with clingfilm and chill until ready to serve.
4 To serve, spoon the remaining chilli sauce into a small serving bowl and stir in the honey. Pile the prawn and cucumber skewers on to a large serving plate and serve with the chilli sauce for dipping.

TRY SOMETHING DIFFERENT
~ Use fresh coriander instead of basil.
~ Instead of prawns, use cooked and peeled crayfish tails.

NUTRITION PER CANAPÉ 16 cals | trace fat (0g sats) | 1g carbs | 0.1g salt

CHEESE STRAWS

Makes 24
Preparation 10 minutes, plus chilling
Cooking time 18–20 minutes, plus cooling

200g (7oz) self-raising flour, sifted, plus extra to dust
pinch of cayenne pepper
125g (4oz) unsalted butter, diced and chilled, plus extra
    to grease
125g (4oz) Parmesan (see page 228), finely grated
2 medium eggs
1 tsp ready-made English mustard
sesame and poppy seeds to sprinkle

1 Put the flour, cayenne and butter into a food processor and pulse until the mixture resembles breadcrumbs. (Alternatively, rub the butter into the flour and cayenne in a large bowl by hand, until it resembles fine crumbs.) Add the Parmesan and mix in.
2 Crack one egg into a bowl. Separate the other egg, put the white to one side and add the egg yolk to the bowl with the whole egg. Mix in the mustard. Add to the flour mixture and mix together. Tip on to a board and knead lightly for 30 seconds, then wrap in clingfilm and chill for 30 minutes.
3 Preheat the oven to 180°C (160°C fan oven) mark 4. Grease two baking sheets. Roll out the pastry on a lightly floured surface to a 23 x 30.5cm (9 x 12in) rectangle, cut out 24 straws and carefully twist each straw twice. Put on the baking sheets.
4 Beat the reserved egg white with a fork until frothy, and brush over the cheese straws, then sprinkle with the sesame and poppy seeds. Bake for 18–20 minutes until golden. Remove from the oven and cool for 5 minutes, then transfer to a wire rack and leave to cool completely.

NUTRITION PER SERVING
96 cals | 6.5g fat (4g sats) | 6.3g carbs | 0.3g salt

DEVILS ON HORSEBACK

Makes 8
Preparation 10 minutes
Cooking time 15 minutes

8 blanched almonds
olive oil
8 large ready-to-eat prunes, stoned
4 thin streaky bacon rashers, rinded
8 rounds of bread, about 5cm (2in)
    in diameter
50g (2oz) butter
salt and cayenne pepper
watercress to garnish

1   Preheat the grill. Fry the almonds for 2–3 minutes in a little oil, until they are golden brown, then toss in a little salt and cayenne pepper. Put an almond in the cavity of each prune.
2   Stretch the bacon rashers with the back of a knife, cut in half and roll around the prunes. Secure with a wooden cocktail stick or small skewer and cook under a medium grill, turning, until all the bacon is golden brown.
3   Meanwhile, fry the bread for 2–3 minutes in the butter, until golden. Put a prune on each piece, garnish with watercress and serve at once.

TRY SOMETHING DIFFERENT

Angels on Horseback Omit the almonds and prunes and replace with 8 oysters sprinkled with cayenne pepper and lemon juice. Put one roll on top of each croûte of bread and bake in the oven at 200°C (180°C fan oven) mark 6 for 15 minutes or until the bacon is lightly cooked. Serve at once, garnished with watercress.

NUTRITION PER SERVING
128 cals | 9g fat (4g sats) | 9g carbs | 0.5g salt

CHICKEN SATAY SKEWERS

Serves 4
Preparation 30 minutes, plus chilling and soaking
Cooking time 8–10 minutes

1 tbsp each coriander and cumin seeds
2 tsp ground turmeric
4 garlic cloves, roughly chopped
grated zest and juice of 1 lemon
2 bird's eye chillies, finely chopped (see Cook's Tips)
3 tbsp vegetable oil
4 boneless, skinless chicken breasts, about 550g (1 1/4 lb),
    cut into finger-length strips
salt and ground black pepper
1/2 cucumber, cut into sticks to serve

For the satay sauce
200g (7oz) salted peanuts
1 tbsp molasses sugar
1/2 lemongrass stalk, chopped
2 tbsp dark soy sauce
juice of 1/2 lime
200ml (7fl oz) coconut cream

1 Put the coriander and cumin seeds and the turmeric into a
dry frying pan and heat for 30 seconds. Tip into a blender and
add the garlic, lemon zest and juice, chillies, 1 tbsp oil and
1 tsp salt. Whiz for 1–2 minutes.
2 Put the paste into a large shallow dish, add the chicken and
toss everything together. Cover and chill in the fridge for at
least 20 minutes or up to 12 hours.
3 To make the satay sauce, put the peanuts, sugar,
lemongrass, soy sauce, lime juice and coconut cream into a
food processor and add 2 tbsp water. Whiz to make a thick
chunky sauce, then spoon into a dish. Cover and chill.
4 Preheat the barbecue or grill until hot. Soak 24 bamboo
skewers in water for 20 minutes. Thread the chicken on to
the skewers, drizzle with the remaining oil and cook for
4–5 minutes on each side until cooked through. Serve with
the satay sauce and the cucumber.

TRY SOMETHING DIFFERENT

Replace the chicken with strips of pork tenderloin or
beef rump.

COOK'S TIPS

⁓ Chillies vary enormously in strength, from quite
mild to blisteringly hot, depending on the type of
chilli and its ripeness. Taste a small piece first to
check it's not too hot for you.
⁓ Be extremely careful when handling chillies not to
touch or rub your eyes with your fingers, as they
will sting. Wash knives immediately after handling
chillies for the same reason. As a precaution, use
rubber gloves when preparing them, if you like.

NUTRITION PER SERVING
687 cals | 51g fat (21g sats) | 11g carbs | 2.1g salt

TANGY CHICKEN BITES

Makes 48
Preparation 10 minutes

2 × 50g packs mini croustades
about 275g (10oz) fruity chutney, such
    as mango
2 roast chicken breasts, skinned, torn
    into small pieces
250g carton crème fraîche
a few fresh thyme sprigs

1 Put the croustades on a board.
Spoon about 1/2 tsp chutney into each
one. Top with a few shreds of chicken, a
small dollop of crème fraîche and a few
thyme leaves. Transfer the croustades
to a large serving plate and serve
them immediately.

TRY SOMETHING DIFFERENT
- Use mini poppadoms instead of croustades.
- Replace the chutney with cranberry sauce.
- Instead of roast chicken, use turkey.

NUTRITION PER SERVING 43 cals |
2g fat (1g sats) | 4g carbs | 0.1g salt

SMOKED SALMON BLINIS

Makes 16
Preparation 5 minutes

3 tbsp crème fraîche
16 small blinis or 125g pack
    (see Cook's Tips)
125g (4oz) thinly sliced smoked
    salmon
1 tbsp freshly snipped chives
lemon wedges to serve

1 Spread crème fraîche on to the
blinis, then fold the salmon loosely on
top. Sprinkle with chives and serve
with lemon wedges to squeeze over.

NUTRITION PER BLINI 43 cals |
3g fat (1g sats) | 2g carbs | 0.3g salt

COOK'S TIPS
- Originally from Russia, blinis are bite-size pancakes made with a yeast batter; they can be topped with a variety of ingredients to make perfect party canapés. Available from most supermarkets.
- Instead of blinis, use small pieces of pumpernickel or rye bread.
- Instead of smoked salmon, use hot-smoked salmon flakes. Put the salmon flakes, crème fraîche and a little ground black pepper into a bowl and mix gently. Put 1 tsp of the mixture on to each blini, sprinkle with chopped chives and serve immediately.

BUCKWHEAT BLINIS

Makes 30
Preparation 15 minutes
Cooking time 30 minutes

225g (8oz) buckwheat flour, sifted (see Cook's Tip)
225g (8oz) plain flour, sifted
2 tsp caster sugar
a large pinch of salt
2 × 7g packs fast-action dried yeast
3 medium eggs
700ml (24 fl oz) warm milk
1 tbsp sunflower oil, plus extra for frying
lumpfish roe and dill to garnish
pickled herring and soured cream
    to serve

1   Put the flours in a large bowl with the sugar and salt. Stir in the yeast. Make a well in the centre and add 2 whole eggs and 1 yolk, putting the white aside for later.
2   Gradually blend in the milk to make a smooth batter. Stir in the oil. Cover with clingfilm and leave for an hour.
3   Heat a large heavy-based frying pan over a medium–low heat. Put the egg whites into a clean, grease-free bowl and whisk until they form stiff peaks. Fold into the yeast mixture.
4   When the pan is hot, add a splash of oil and wipe around the base with a thickness of folded kitchen paper. Pour in a couple of spoonfuls of mixture to make a 7.5–8cm (3–3¼in) circle. When bubbles come to the surface, turn and cook the other side until golden. Continue with the remaining mixture, putting the cooked blinis into a warmed oven between sheets of greaseproof paper as you go.
5   Serve topped with pickled herring and soured cream, and garnished with lumpfish roe and dill.

COOK'S TIP
You can find buckwheat in major supermarkets, delis and health-food shops. Alternatively, swap wholemeal flour for the buckwheat.

NUTRITION PER BLINI
80 cals | 2g fat (0.5g sats) | 14g carbs | 0.1g salt

STARTERS

MIXED ITALIAN BRUSCHETTA

Serves 6
Preparation 25 minutes

1 long thin French stick
400g can butter beans, drained and rinsed
a small handful of fresh mint, shredded
zest and juice of $^1/_2$ lemon
2 tbsp extra virgin olive oil, plus extra to garnish
seeds from $^1/_2$ pomegranate
150g (5oz) cherry tomatoes, quartered
200g (7oz) mozzarella bocconcini, halved (see Cook's Tips,
    page 66)
1 tbsp fresh basil pesto (see page 22)
2 tbsp freshly chopped basil, plus extra leaves to garnish
a small handful of rocket
6 slices bresaola
15g ($^1/_2$ oz) freshly shaved Parmesan
75g (3oz) roasted red pepper, sliced
2 tbsp black olive tapenade (see page 63)
salt and ground black pepper

1 Cut the bread diagonally into 24 slices and toast in batches.
Mash together the butter beans, mint, lemon zest and juice
and oil. Season to taste with salt and pepper and stir through
most of the pomegranate seeds. Set aside.
2 In a separate bowl, stir together the cherry tomatoes,
mozzarella bocconcini, pesto and basil.
3 To assemble, spoon the bean mixture on to six toasts and
garnish with the remaining pomegranate seeds. Top a further
six with the mozzarella mixture and six with rocket, bresaola
and Parmesan. Drizzle with the oil. For the final six bruschetta,
put a few slices of roasted pepper on each toast. Add a little
tapenade and garnish with a basil leaf.

NUTRITION PER SERVING
398 cals | 15g fat (7g sats) | 47g carbs | 2.5g salt

STUFFED MUSHROOMS

Serves 4
Preparation 5 minutes
Cooking time about 12 minutes

125g (4oz) couscous
20g pack fresh flat-leafed parsley,
    roughly chopped, plus extra
    to garnish
280g jar mixed antipasti in oil, drained
    and oil put to one side
8 large flat portabellini mushrooms
25g (1oz) butter
25g (1oz) plain flour
300ml ($^{1}/_{2}$ pint) skimmed milk
75g (3oz) mature Cheddar cheese
    (see page 228), grated, plus extra
    to sprinkle
salt and ground black pepper
green salad to serve

1 Preheat the oven to 220°C (200°C
fan oven) mark 7. Put the couscous into
a bowl with 200ml (7fl oz) boiling water,
the parsley, antipasti and 1 tbsp of the
reserved oil. Stir well.
2 Put the mushrooms on a non-stick
baking tray and spoon a little of the
couscous mixture into the centre of
each. Cook in the oven while you make
the sauce.
3 Whisk together the butter, flour and
milk in a small pan over a high heat until
the mixture comes to the boil. Reduce
the heat as soon as it starts to thicken,
then whisk constantly until smooth. Take
off the heat and stir in the cheese.
4 Spoon the sauce over the
mushrooms and sprinkle with the
remaining cheese. Put back into the
oven for a further 7–10 minutes until
golden. Sprinkle with some parsley and
serve with a green salad.

NUTRITION PER SERVING 290 cals |
26g fat (6g sats) | 8g carbs | 1.5g salt ⓥ

SEAFOOD COCKTAIL

Serves 4
Preparation 15 minutes

$^{1}/_{2}$ iceberg lettuce, shredded
175g (6oz) cooked peeled prawns or
    shrimps, flaked white crab meat or
    lobster meat, thawed if frozen
cucumber slices, capers or lemon
    wedges to garnish

For the dressing
2 tbsp mayonnaise (see page 29)
2 tbsp tomato ketchup (see page 22)
2 tbsp yogurt
squeeze of lemon juice, or a dash of
    Worcestershire sauce
salt and ground black pepper

1 Line four small glasses with the
shredded lettuce.
2 To make the dressing, put the
mayonnaise in a bowl and mix with the
tomato ketchup, yogurt and lemon juice
or Worcestershire sauce. Season with
salt and pepper to taste.
3 Combine the shellfish and dressing,
and pile the mixture into the glasses.
4 Garnish each glass with cucumber
slices, capers or lemon wedges and
serve immediately.

COOK'S TIP
This dish can be as simple or as
exotic as you like, depending on
which shellfish you choose.

NUTRITION PER SERVING 110 cals |
7g fat (1g sat) | 3g carbs | 2.5g salt

GRIDDLED SCALLOPS WITH BACON AND PEA PURÉE

Serves 4
Preparation 15 minutes
Cooking time 5 minutes

8 smoked streaky bacon rashers
300g (11oz) frozen peas
1 tbsp basil oil
12 scallops, cleaned and halved
    horizontally if large
    (see Cook's Tips page 96)
sunflower oil
salt and ground black pepper

1 Heat the grill to high. Put a griddle over a high heat. Bring a pan of lightly salted water to the boil.
2 Cook the bacon under the grill for 3–4 minutes until crispy and golden. Keep warm.

3 Meanwhile, add the peas to the boiling water and cook for 4–5 minutes until tender. Drain and return to the pan. Add the basil oil and whiz in a blender until roughly puréed – or you can use a fork or potato masher if you like. Keep warm.
4 Brush the scallops with oil and season, then sear on the griddle for 30 seconds per side. Serve immediately on a bed of pea purée with the streaky bacon on top.

TRY SOMETHING DIFFERENT
Omit the basil oil, cook the peas with a mint stalk and add 1 tbsp roughly chopped mint leaves before blitzing.

NUTRITION PER SERVING 284 cals | 15g fat (5g sats) | 9g carbs | 1.8g salt

MELON AND PARMA HAM

Serves 4
Preparation 10 minutes

900g (2lb) cantaloupe melon, chilled
8 thin slices Parma ham (see Cook's
    Tip page 65)
juice of 1 lemon
ground black pepper

1 Cut the melon in half lengthways and scoop out the seeds. Cut each half into four wedges.
2 With a sharp knife and a sawing action, separate the flesh from the skin, keeping it in position on the skin.
3 Cut across the flesh into bite-sized slices, then push each in opposite directions to make an attractive pattern.
4 Roll up each slice of ham into a cigar shape. Put on serving dishes with the melon wedges, and sprinkle with lemon juice and pepper.

NUTRITION PER SERVING 83 cals | 1g fat (0.4g sats) | 12g carbs | 0.7g salt

SMOKED SALMON PARCELS

Serves 8
Preparation 35 minutes
Cooking time 5–6 minutes

8 large scallops or 16 small queen scallops with corals
    attached, about 300g (11oz) total weight
2 large ripe avocados, peeled and stones removed
1 large garlic clove, crushed
6 small spring onions, finely chopped
1 green chilli, seeded and chopped (see Cook's Tips
    page 69)
1½ tbsp grapeseed oil
grated zest and juice of 1 lime, plus extra to squeeze
8 large slices smoked salmon, about 400g (14oz) total
    weight and 23cm (9in) in length
salt and ground black pepper
rocket leaves and lime wedges to garnish

For the coriander dressing
25g (1oz) fresh coriander sprigs
1 small garlic clove, crushed
50ml (2fl oz) grapeseed oil
1 tbsp lime juice

1 To make the coriander dressing, put all the ingredients in a
blender and process until smooth.
2 To make the parcels, remove any tough membranes from
the scallops and season with salt and pepper. Put them in a
steamer and cook for about 5 minutes or until the flesh is
just white. Alternatively, put the scallops on a heatproof plate,
cover with another plate and steam over a pan of simmering
water for about 3 minutes on each side. Drain and set on
kitchen paper to cool.
3 Put the avocados, garlic, spring onions, chilli, oil and lime
zest and juice in a bowl. Mash the avocado with a fork, mix
well and season with salt and pepper.
4 Lay the salmon on a worksurface, put a large scallop or
two small ones on each slice and spoon some avocado
mixture on top. Roll the salmon around the filling. Put the
parcels on serving plates and squeeze over a little lime juice.
Drizzle with the coriander dressing and serve with rocket
and lime wedges.

> NUTRITION PER SERVING
> 209 cals | 12g fat (2g sats) | 3g carbs | 2.3g salt

POTTED PRAWN PÂTÉ

Serves 4
Preparation 15 minutes, plus chilling

225g (8oz) peeled prawns
75g (3oz) butter, softened
2 tsp lemon juice
4 tsp freshly chopped parsley
salt and ground black pepper
peeled prawns and lemon slices to garnish
French bread to serve

1 Finely chop the prawns. Beat them into 50g (2oz) butter with the lemon juice, parsley and seasoning.
2 Spoon into a serving dish and level the surface. Melt the remaining butter and pour over the prawn mixture. Chill in the fridge for 1 hour. Garnish with prawns and lemon slices. Serve with French bread.

> NUTRITION PER SERVING
> 195 cals | 16g fat (10g sats) | 0.1g carbs | 3.1g salt

CHICKEN LIVER PÂTÉ

Serves 4
Preparation 15 minutes
Cooking time 10 minutes, plus chilling

700g (1½lb) chicken livers
75g (3oz) butter
1 onion, finely chopped
1 large garlic clove, crushed
1 tbsp double cream
2 tbsp tomato purée
3 tbsp dry sherry or brandy
4 bay leaves, to garnish (optional)
hot toast fingers or French bread to serve

1 Trim away any sinews and fat from the chicken livers, then rinse and pat dry on kitchen paper. Melt the butter in a frying pan over a low heat, then increase the heat to medium and fry the chicken livers for about 5 minutes or until they change colour; do not overcook or they will toughen.
2 Reduce the heat and add the onion and garlic. Cover the pan and cook the mixture for 5 minutes. Tip the contents of the pan into a bowl and cool.
3 Add the cream, tomato purée and sherry or brandy. Transfer the mixture to a food processor or blender and whiz until smooth.
4 Pack the pâté into four 150ml (¼ pint) individual dishes and cool until firm. Top with bay leaves, if you like. Chill the pâté for at least 2 hours or overnight.
5 Serve the chicken liver pâté with hot toast fingers or French bread.

TRY SOMETHING DIFFERENT
Pack the pâté into a 450g (1lb) loaf tin. After chilling, cut it into chunky slices to serve.

> NUTRITION PER SERVING
> 420 cals | 28g fat (14g sats) | 6g carbs | 0.7g salt

SMOKED MACKEREL PÂTÉ

Serves 6
Preparation 10 minutes, plus chilling

275g (10oz) smoked mackerel
50g (2oz) butter, softened
3 tbsp creamed horseradish sauce
2 tbsp single cream
ground black pepper
fresh parsley sprig to garnish

1 The day before, skin the mackerel and discard the bones. Mash the flesh in a bowl.
2 Mix the butter with the fish and add the horseradish sauce and cream. Season with pepper. Salt is not usually needed.
3 Spoon the mixture into a serving dish, cover tightly and chill until required.
4 Leave the pâté at room temperature for 30 minutes before serving. Decorate the surface of the pâté with indentations made using a blunt-edged knife and garnish with a parsley sprig.

TRY SOMETHING DIFFERENT
Herby Mackerel Pâté Cream together 125g (4oz) butter, 2 tbsp freshly chopped parsley and 1 tsp lemon juice and beat well. In a 600ml (1 pint) dish, layer the mackerel mixture and parsley butter, beginning and ending with a thick layer of mackerel.

> NUTRITION PER SERVING
> 249 cals | 23g fat (8g sats) | 2g carbs | 1.2g salt

CHUNKY PÂTÉ WITH PORT

Serves 8
Preparation 25 minutes, plus setting
Cooking time about 1¹/₂ hours, plus cooling

350g (12oz) boneless belly pork, rind removed, roughly chopped
1 large skinless chicken breast, about 150g (5oz)
225g (8oz) chicken livers, trimmed
1 large duck breast, about 200g (7oz), skinned and chopped into small pieces
125g (4oz) rindless streaky bacon rashers, diced
3 tbsp port or brandy
1 tbsp freshly chopped rosemary
2 tbsp green peppercorns
salt and ground black pepper
crusty bread to serve

To finish
a few bay leaves
2 tsp powdered gelatine
150ml (¹/₄ pint) white port or sherry

1 Preheat the oven to 170°C (150°C fan oven) mark 3. Coarsely mince the belly pork in a food processor, retaining some small chunks. Mince the chicken breast in the processor, then mince the chicken livers.
2 Mix all the meats together in a large bowl with the port or brandy, 1 tsp salt, some pepper, the chopped rosemary and green peppercorns.
3 Pack the mixture into a 1.1 litre (2 pint) terrine and stand in a roasting tin containing 2.5cm (1in) boiling water. Cover with foil and cook in the oven for 1 hour.
4 Remove the foil and arrange a few bay leaves on top of the pâté. Cook for a further 30 minutes or until the juices run clear when the pâté is pierced in the centre with a sharp knife or skewer.
5 Drain the meat juices into a small bowl and leave to cool. Skim off any fat, then sprinkle over the gelatine and leave until softened. Stand the bowl in a pan of gently simmering water until the gelatine has dissolved. Stir in the port or sherry. Make up to 450ml (³/₄ pint) with water, if necessary.
6 Pour the jellied liquid over the pâté and chill until set. Store the pâté in the fridge for up to two days. Serve with crusty bread.

NUTRITION PER SERVING
344 cals | 22g fat (8g sats) | 3g carbs | 0.7g salt

SALMON AND ASPARAGUS TERRINE

Serves 10
Preparation 40 minutes
Cooking time about 1 hour, plus overnight chilling

75g (3oz) butter, plus extra to grease
1 garlic clove, chopped
1 medium red chilli, seeded and finely chopped
    (see Cook's Tips, page 69)
½ lemongrass stalk, finely chopped
250g (9oz) asparagus spears
250g (9oz) sliced smoked salmon
3 tbsp freshly chopped dill, plus extra sprigs to garnish
1kg (2¼ lb) salmon fillet, skinned and boned
salt and ground black pepper

1 Put the butter in a pan and melt over a low heat. Bring to the boil and skim off any impurities until clear. Pour into a bowl and add the garlic, chilli and lemongrass. Leave to infuse.
2 Cook the asparagus in a pan of salted boiling water for 2–3 minutes until just tender. Drain and refresh under cold water. Drain well.
3 Grease and line a 900g (2lb) loaf tin with foil, then grease the foil. Line the bottom and sides of the tin with smoked salmon, reserving some for the top. Sprinkle over 1 tbsp chopped dill, drizzle with a little of the infused butter and season with salt and pepper.
4 Preheat the oven to 180°C (160°C fan oven) mark 4. Cut the salmon fillet in half lengthways to fit it into the loaf tin and put one of the pieces inside. Sprinkle over 1 tbsp of the chopped dill and drizzle with a little of the infused butter. Layer up the terrine with the asparagus spears and the other salmon half, sprinkling the remaining dill, infused butter and salt and pepper on top of the salmon. Finish with a layer of smoked salmon, then cover with foil.
5 Put the loaf tin in a roasting tin and half-fill the roasting tin with hot water. Cook the terrine in the preheated oven for 50 minutes–1 hour or until a skewer inserted into the middle for 30 seconds comes out warm. Leave to cool, then weigh the terrine down with two food cans and chill overnight. To serve, turn out the terrine, decorate with dill sprigs and slice.

NUTRITION PER SERVING
278 cals | 18g fat (6g sats) | 1g carbs | 1.4g salt

CHICKEN AND VEGETABLE TERRINE

Serves 8
Preparation 40 minutes, plus chilling
Cooking time 1 hour 2 minutes, plus chilling

900g (2lb) chicken joints
1 small slice of white bread, crusts removed
450ml (³/₄ pint) double cream, chilled
1 small bunch of watercress
125g (4oz) small young carrots
125g (4oz) French beans, trimmed and stringed
275g (10oz) peas in the pod, shelled
75g (3oz) small even-sized button mushrooms
200g (7oz) can artichoke hearts, drained
butter to grease
salt and ground black pepper
rocket leaves to garnish (optional)

For the sauce
225g (8oz) ripe tomatoes, skinned and quartered
    (see page 277)
125ml (4fl oz) vegetable oil
50ml (2fl oz) white wine vinegar
75ml (2¹/₂ fl oz) tomato purée

1 Cut all the chicken flesh away from the chicken bones; discard the skin and any fat. Finely mince the chicken and the bread. Chill for 30 minutes. Stir the cream, a little at a time, into the chicken mixture with salt and pepper to taste.
2 Trim the watercress and discard the coarse stalks. Stir one-third of the chicken mixture into the watercress. Cover both bowls and chill for 2 hours.
3 Preheat the oven to 170°C (150°C fan oven) mark 3. The careful preparation of vegetables is essential to the final presentation. Cut the carrots into neat matchstick pieces, 2.5cm (1in) by 3mm (¹/₈ in). Cut the beans into similar-length pieces. Blanch the carrots, beans and peas for 2 minutes in separate pans of boiling water. Drain.
4 Trim the mushroom stalks level with the caps. Cut the mushrooms across into slices 5mm (¹/₄ in) thick. Dice the artichoke hearts into 5mm (¹/₄ in) pieces.
5 Grease a 1.1 litre (2 pint) lidded terrine dish and base line with a rectangular piece of paper, grease the top of the paper. Take half the watercress and chicken mixture and spread it evenly over the base of the terrine. Arrange the carrots in neat crossways lines over the top, then spread one-quarter of the chicken mixture carefully over the carrots.
6 Lightly seasoning the vegetables as they are layered, sprinkle the peas over the chicken mixture in the dish and put another thin layer of chicken mixture on top. Next, put the mushrooms in crossways lines and top with the remaining

watercress and chicken mixture. Arrange the artichokes on top, cover with half the remaining chicken mixture, arrange the beans in crossways lines, and cover with the remaining chicken mixture.
7 Put a double sheet of greased greaseproof paper on top and cover tightly with the lid. Put the terrine in a roasting tin with water to come halfway up the side. Cook in the oven for 1 hour or until firm.
8 Cool a little, drain off any juices, then invert the terrine on to a serving plate. Cool, then chill for 1 hour before serving.
9 Meanwhile, to make the sauce. Purée the tomatoes in a blender or food processor with the oil, vinegar, tomato purée and seasoning. Rub through a sieve. Chill lightly before serving, then garnish with some rocket leaves, if you like.

NUTRITION PER SERVING
616 cals | 54g fat (23g sats) | 8g carbs | 0.6g salt

SHELLFISH
AND FISH

SHELLFISH

Shellfish are prized for their delicate flavours and textures, especially the excellent species that are caught off our coastline – including lobsters, crabs and scallops. Shellfish can be divided into three main categories: crustaceans, molluscs and cephalopods. Crustaceans – lobsters, crabs, crayfish, prawns, shrimps and so on – have hard external skeletons, which are segmented to allow for movement. Molluscs live inside one or two hard shells (valves). Cockles, winkles and whelks are univalves. The bivalves include mussels, clams, oysters and scallops. Cephalopods, namely squid, octopus and cuttlefish, belong to the mollusc family, but they do not have external shells; the clear plastic-like quill inside squid is effectively an internal shell.

CHOOSING SHELLFISH

Always buy shellfish from a reputable fishmonger or supermarket fresh fish counter with a high turnover of stock and prepare it within 24 hours. Most seafood from supermarkets has been previously frozen, so don't re-freeze it. It is unwise to gather shellfish yourself, unless you are sure the area is free from pollution; molluscs are particularly susceptible to pollution and can carry diseases.

When choosing molluscs, select those with tightly closed, undamaged shells. Mussels, clams, scallops and oysters that are sold fresh are still alive and an open shell may indicate that the shellfish is far from fresh. A sharp tap on the shell should persuade it to close up if it's alive, if not discard it. Similarly, univalves should withdraw back into their shell when prodded.

When buying cooked shellfish, such as lobster, crab and prawns, make sure the shells are intact. Lobsters and crabs should feel heavy for their size and have a fresh aroma. Any unpleasant smell is an indication that the shellfish is past its best. When choosing cephalopods, such as octopus and squid, look for those with firm flesh and a smell of the sea.

Crustacea
A large family of shellfish, crustacea are characterised by an external skeleton and jointed limbs. They include crabs, lobsters and shrimps.

Molluscs
These are a highly diverse group of shellfish including bivalves, gastropods and cephalopods:

Bivalves With a hinged, two-piece external shell, this group of shellfish includes mussels and oysters.

Gastropods have snail-like shells and include whelks, winkles, conch, abalone and limpets.

Cephalopods are classed as shellfish, although most do not have an obviously external skeleton and have a modified body that includes tentacles or arms, such as squid, cuttlefish and octopus. The 'shell' is in the form of a hard, transparent internal quill.

BUYING SHELLFISH

Shellfish have seasons and although some are available all year round, others are harder to find. Weather conditions can affect availability and therefore cost. When buying crustaceans they should smell sweet and fresh and be moist. Crabs, lobsters and langoustines are best when sold live for home cooking and should feel heavy for their size.

When buying molluscs, look for those with shells that are smooth and shiny. The shells of oysters, scallops, clams and mussels should be shut, or should close when tapped. Some shellfish are always sold live. This includes all the bivalves except scallops, which are sometimes removed from their shells and cleaned. Live crabs, lobsters and crayfish should display plenty of movement, with snapping claws or pincers. When buying precooked shellfish, such as langoustines, prawns and crab, buy from a reputable supplier. Use all shellfish on the day of purchase.

FROZEN SHELLFISH
Apart from scallops, prawns and other frozen shellfish, are sold raw or cooked. Shellfish can be cooked from frozen.

PREPARING AND COOKING SHELLFISH

Stir-fry This method is best suited to pieces of firm shellfish, prawns or squid. Toss the prepared fish in a little oil, with spices and aromatics, in a wok for 1–2 minutes until just cooked through. Prawns are cooked when they turn pink. Do not overcook them.

Sear Use for firm-fleshed shellfish such as scallops. Heat a little oil in a frying pan until very hot, then cook briefly for about 1 minute on each side, to give it a flavourful crust on the outside while the centre remains tender.

Deep-fry Use for all shellfish. Prepare the fish and a coating (which can be batter, seasoned flour, or flour, egg and breadcrumbs). Heat vegetable oil in a deep-fryer to 180°C, or until a cube of bread browns in 40 seconds.

Coat the shellfish, then carefully lower into the oil a few pieces at a time and cook until crisp and golden. Remove using a slotted spoon. Drain on kitchen paper.

Grill Marinate the shellfish, or season and brush with oil, then grill on both sides until just cooked through.

Braise Best suited to shellfish such as prawns. Prepare a tomato sauce, then add the prepared shellfish. Spoon the sauce over to cover and simmer gently for 5–10 minutes until just cooked through. It will need only a few minutes.

Steam Season and/or marinate the shellfish, then put into a dish that will fit into a bamboo steamer. Put the steamer into a pan or wok over boiling water. Steam for 10–15 minutes until firm and just cooked through. Shellfish will require just a few minutes.

Preparing prawns

1 To shell prawns, pull off the head and put to one side. Using pointed scissors, cut through the soft shell on the belly side.
2 Prise the shell off, leaving the tail attached. (Add to the head; it can be used later for making stock.)
3 Using a small sharp knife, make a shallow cut along the length of the back of the prawn. Using the point of the knife, carefully remove and discard the black vein (the intestinal tract) that runs along the back of the prawn.

4 To 'butterfly' the prawn, cut halfway through the flesh lengthways from the head end to the base of the tail, and open up the prawn.

Preparing crabs

1 Live crabs must be humanely killed before cooking. Put it into the freezer for 5 minutes, then on to a board, with the belly facing up. Take a large chef's knife and plunge it straight down into the crab's head, right between or just below the eyes. Put into a pan of boiling water and cook for 5 minutes per 450g (1lb), or steam for 8 minutes per 450g (1lb).

2 To serve whole, simply set on the table with crackers and crab picks for diners to use themselves.
3 To remove the cooked meat for a recipe, put the crab on a board, with the belly facing up. Twist off the legs and claws. Lift off and discard the 'apron' (tail) – long and pointed in a male, short and broad in a female. Pull the body out of the shell and remove and discard the feathery gills and grey stomach sac. Cut the body into pieces and pick out the meat using your fingers and a crab pick or small knife. Scrape the brown meat from the shell, keeping it separate from the white meat. If there is roe in a female, keep that separate, too.
4 Crack the claws with the back of a large knife, and pull out the meat in a single piece or in large chunks.
5 Cut through the shells of the legs with scissors, then cut through the opposite side. Pull off the shell halves to expose the meat and remove.

Preparing lobsters

1 To kill a lobster humanely before grilling, boiling or baking, put it into the freezer for 5 minutes. Then put it on a chopping board and hold the body firmly. Take a large chef's knife and plunge it straight down into the lobster's head, right between or just below the eyes. (It is inhumane to simply plunge it into boiling water or to put it into cold water and then bring it up to the boil.)
2 To cook the lobster whole, put it into a pot of boiling water and cook for 15–20 minutes (see Cook's Tip page 92).
3 If you are going to split the raw lobster for grilling or baking, cut the freshly killed lobster right through the head, then cut all the way down the length of the tail to split it in two. Remove the head sac, which lies just behind the eyes, and discard. If you wish, you can remove the black coral (tomalley) and the green intestine, which lie inside the back of the shell just behind the head sac, or they may be left in place for cooking.
4 If you want the tail meat in one piece, split the head to where the tail begins, then use scissors to cut through the soft shell of the belly, down to the tail.
5 Pull the tail meat out with your fingers. Clean the head as in step 3. Cut off the claws and spiny legs. Crack the claws with a hammer or lobster cracker and remove the meat. Save the shells to make stock.

1 **Squid: all year**
Squid are often sold ready prepared, either as whole tubes or sliced into rings. Small squid can be sautéed, poached, grilled or deep-fried; larger ones require stewing.

2 **Octopus: May–Dec**
Octopus can grow up to 3m (10ft). Small specimens are better for eating, as large ones are usually tough. All but the smallest need long, slow braising or stewing.

3 **Crayfish: all year**
Crayfish are sold both live and ready cooked. Use small crayfish to garnish fish dishes or in soups; larger ones are best served cold with a salad or hot with a creamy sauce.

4 **Tiger prawn: all year**
A translucent grey colour with dark stripes when raw, tiger prawns turn pink on cooking and have tender, juicy flesh. Sold either raw or cooked, peeled or unpeeled; sometimes partially shelled with just the tail left on. Raw prawns should be deveined, and can be peeled or cooked in the shell: grill, barbecue, stir-fry, pan-fry, braise, coat and deep-fry; add to fish stews and curries.

5 **Shrimp: Feb–Oct**
Greyish-brown when alive, shrimps become pink or brown when cooked. Fresh shrimps are invariably sold cooked, either peeled or whole, and have a delicate flavour; frozen and canned shrimps are also available.

6 **Langoustine**
Pink-shelled langoustines are a relative of the lobster. They are sometimes referred to as Norwegian lobster and Dublin Bay prawns. They have tender flesh that is sweet and succulent. They go well with Mediterranean flavours such as tomatoes, garlic, white wine and fresh herbs. Poach, grill or add to recipes such as paella and risotto.

7 **(Common) Prawn: all year**
Prawns are available in a variety of sizes and most are sold ready-cooked, but raw prawns – especially king prawns and tiger prawns – are increasingly available. Buy fresh ones if possible, as these tend to have a superior flavour and texture. Cook just until they turn pink and opaque: 3–8 minutes depending on size. Do not overcook or they will toughen. Heat ready-cooked prawns through for a few minutes only. Deep-sea and Mediterranean prawns are similar in appearance; treat in the same way.

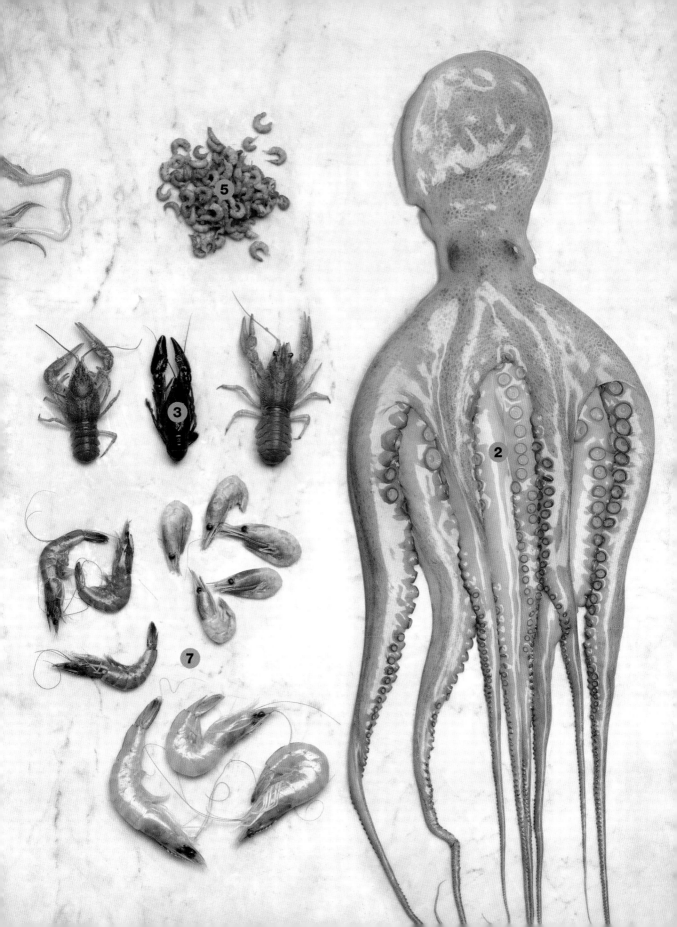

1 Common crab: all year
The common crab has firm, sweet and well-flavoured flesh. Boil raw crabs. Serve cooked crabmeat with mayonnaise in salads; toss into stir-fries, soups or crab cakes.

2 Soft-shell crab: all year
These crabs are caught after they have shed their hard shell and before they have grown a new one, so the whole crab can be eaten, shell and all. They are usually only available frozen in the UK. Flour and pan- or deep-fry; eat whole.

3 Lobster: April–Nov
Sold either live, ready-cooked or ready-dressed, lobsters have a fine, delicate flavour. Serve with a simple accompaniment, such as good mayonnaise or a warm butter sauce.

4 Mussel: Sept–March
With tender, smooth, sweet-tasting flesh, mussels can be steamed, stuffed and baked, or grilled.

5 Cockle: May–Dec
These molluscs are invariably sold cooked and shelled, and they are typically eaten plain or with vinegar.

6 Clam: all year, best in autumn
There are many varieties of this bivalve, varying considerably in size. Clams are sold live in their shells and smaller ones are eaten raw; larger ones are cooked before they are eaten. If eating raw, open as for oysters. Otherwise cook and shell clams as for mussels. Clams are available frozen, canned and smoked.

7 Razor clam: all year
Razor clams, a variety of the clam, have a fragile shell with open ends.

8 Oyster: Sept–April
With the exception of the large varieties, oysters are considered at their best eaten raw. Frozen and smoked oysters are also available. Oysters can be used sparingly to enhance the flavour of some cooked dishes.

9 Scallop: Sept–March
Fresh scallops are sold both in the shell and ready-shelled; they are also available frozen. Scallops may be pan-fried, lightly poached or grilled, but care must be taken to avoid overcooking or their delicate texture will be ruined.

GRILLED LOBSTER

Serves 2
Preparation 20 minutes
Cooking time 15 minutes

1 killed fresh lobster, about 700g (1½lb) (see page 85)
25g (1oz) butter, softened, plus melted butter to brush |
and serve
salt and cayenne pepper

1 Split the lobster lengthways. Remove the head sac, which lies just behind the eyes, and discard. Remove the black coral (tomalley) and the green intestine, which lie inside the back of the shell just behind the head sac.

2 Brush the shell and flesh with melted butter and grill the flesh side for 8–10 minutes, then turn the lobster and grill the shell side for 5 minutes.

3 Dot the flesh with small pieces of softened butter, sprinkle with a little salt and cayenne pepper and serve immediately, with melted butter.

COOK'S TIP
If you are able to buy a live lobster from your fishmonger, choose one that has all claws and legs intact. Prepare as page 85.

NUTRITION PER SERVING
186 cals | 120g fat (7g sats) | 0g carbs | 1.6g salt

LOBSTER THERMIDOR

Serves 4
Preparation 30 minutes
Cooking time about 15 minutes

4 cooked lobsters, about 450g (1lb) each
25g (1oz) butter
1 shallot, finely chopped
150ml (¼ pint) dry white wine
300ml (½ pint) béchamel sauce (see page 16)
1½ tbsp freshly chopped parsley
2 tsp freshly chopped tarragon
6 tbsp freshly grated Parmesan
pinch of mustard powder
salt
pinch of paprika

1 Lay the lobsters, back upwards, on a board. Using a sharp knife, split each lobster lengthways cleanly in two, piercing through the cross at the centre of the head, then prepare them according to the instructions for raw lobster on page 85, steps 3–5. Cut the tail meat into thick slices. Scrub the body shell under cold running water and dry well.
2 Melt the butter in a pan, add the shallot and fry gently for 5 minutes to soften. Add the wine and let it bubble until reduced by half. Add the béchamel sauce and simmer until reduced to a creamy consistency.
3 Add the lobster meat with the herbs, 4 tbsp of the Parmesan, and mustard, salt and paprika to taste.
4 Spoon the mixture into the cleaned shells, sprinkle with the remaining cheese and pop under a hot grill briefly, to brown the top. Serve at once.

COOK'S TIP
To cook a lobster, put into a pan of boiling water. Boil steadily, allowing 10 minutes for the first 450g (1lb) and a further 5 minutes for each additional 450g (1lb). Leave to cool in the liquid.

NUTRITION PER SERVING
400 cals | 19g fat (8g sats) | 8g carbs | 3g salt

CLASSIC DRESSED CRAB

Serves 2
Preparation 30 minutes

1 medium cooked crab, about
    900g (2lb), cleaned (see page 85)
1 tbsp lemon juice
2 tbsp fresh white breadcrumbs
1 egg, hard-boiled
1 tbsp freshly chopped parsley
salt and ground black pepper
salad leaves, and brown bread
    and butter to serve

1 Flake the white crab meat into a bowl, removing any shell
or membrane, then add 1 tsp lemon juice and season to taste.
Mix lightly with a fork.
2 Pound the brown crab meat in another bowl and work in
the breadcrumbs and remaining lemon juice. Season with salt
and pepper to taste.
3 Using a small spoon, put the white crab meat into the
cleaned crab shell, arranging it down either side and piling it
up well. Spoon the brown meat into the middle between the
sections of white meat.
4 Chop the egg white; press the yolk through a sieve. To
garnish the crab, spoon lines of chopped parsley, sieved egg
yolk and chopped egg white along the 'joins' between the
white and brown crab meat. Serve on a bed of salad leaves,
with brown bread and butter.

COOK'S TIP
Crab is available cooked or live, but it is better to buy
a live crab and cook it at home to ensure it is
perfectly fresh (see page 85).

NUTRITION PER SERVING
180 cals | 8g fat (1g sats) | 5g carbs | 3g salt

PRAWNS FRIED IN GARLIC

Serves 2
Preparation 10 minutes
Cooking time 5 minutes

50g (2oz) unsalted butter
2 tbsp olive oil
12 raw Dublin Bay prawns in their
  shells
3 garlic cloves, crushed
4 tbsp brandy
salt and ground black pepper
flat-leafed parsley sprigs to garnish
lemon wedges and crusty bread to
  serve

1 Heat the butter with the olive oil
in a large heavy-based frying pan.
2 Add the prawns and garlic and fry
over a high heat for about 5 minutes,
tossing the prawns constantly, until the
shells have turned pink.
3 Sprinkle the brandy over the prawns
and let it bubble rapidly to reduce right
down. Season with salt and pepper.
4 Serve immediately, garnished with
parsley and with lemon wedges and
plenty of crusty bread. Remember to
provide everyone with finger bowls
and napkins.

NUTRITION PER SERVING 360 cals |
32g fat (15g sats) | 0.1g carbs | 1.4g salt

OYSTERS

Serves 2
Preparation 20 minutes

12 oysters
salt and ground black pepper
lemon wedges and Tabasco sauce to
  serve

1 Scrub the oysters with a stiff
scrubbing brush, then prise open.
2 Remove the beard from each and
loosen the oysters, leaving them in
the deeper half-shell. Season lightly
and serve with lemon wedges and
Tabasco sauce.

NUTRITION PER SERVING 40 cals |
0.8g fat (0.2g sats) | 2g carbs | 2g salt

FRIED SQUID AND CHORIZO

Serves 4 as tapas
Preparation 5 minutes
Cooking time 5 minutes

$^{1}/_{2}$ tbsp olive oil
250g (9oz) baby squid, sliced
1 garlic clove, crushed
75g (3oz) chorizo, skinned and sliced
420g can butter beans, drained and rinsed
a squeeze of lemon juice
a small handful of freshly chopped mint
salt and ground black pepper

1 Heat the oil in a frying pan and cook the squid and garlic for 30 seconds or until the squid is cooked. Put into a warmed serving dish.
2 Return the pan to the heat and cook the chorizo for 2 minutes or until golden. Toss through the butter beans and add to the squid. Quickly stir in the lemon juice, seasoning and mint, and then serve.

NUTRITION PER SERVING
205 cals | 8g fat (2g sats) | 15g carbs | 2.3g salt

FISH

Fish is classified into two main categories: white fish or demersal, which have their oil concentrated in the liver; and oily fish or pelagic, where the oil is dispersed throughout the flesh. There are two types of white fish: round species, such as cod, and flat species, such as plaice. White fish have a more delicate flavour and texture than oily fish.

Fish is tasty, satisfying and highly nutritious. It is high in protein and rich in B vitamins, minerals and natural oils. White fish are low in calories, whereas oil-rich fish are an important source of vitamins A and D, and omega-3 fatty acids that help to lower blood cholesterol levels.

Some fish are available fresh all year round, whereas others have a close period when they cannot be fished, which is usually the spawning time. General availability is given in the individual entries, but it can vary depending on the region and weather conditions. There is increasing concern about the impact of over-fishing, in the North Sea in particular. Stocks of favourite fish, including cod, haddock, skate and tuna, have been depleted in recent years and consumers are being encouraged to buy farmed fish and less vulnerable species, such as hoki, witch and tilapia.

In addition to fresh fish, some varieties are sold preserved by salting, marinating or smoking. There are two methods of smoking fish: hot and cold. Most cold-smoked fish, like kippers, have a strong smoky flavour and must be cooked before they are eaten. The most notable exception is salmon, which is cold-smoked for a long time and eaten raw. Hot-smoked fish, such as trout, doesn't need further cooking. Both hot- and cold-smoked mackerel are available, although the former is more common.

BUYING FISH

Freshness is of prime importance when it comes to choosing and buying fish. Fresh fish should be evaluated with both your eyes and your nose. The smell of truly fresh fish is, somewhat surprisingly, not a 'fishy' smell. It is a fresh sea smell or, in fact, hardly any smell at all – and you shouldn't be able to detect it until you get quite close to the fish. Whole fish must have bright eyes standing proud of the head rather than sunk into it, glossy, moist, firm skin, tight-fitting scales and vivid pink or red gills. The fish should feel stiff to the touch and smell like a whiff of sea air. Fillets, steaks and cutlets must have translucent flesh and show no signs of discoloration. Avoid any that look wet, shiny or slimy. Smoked fish should appear glossy with a fresh smoky aroma. Ideally, fish should be cooked on the day you purchase it, but it can be stored, well wrapped, in the fridge for up to 24 hours. If you are buying frozen fish, make sure it is frozen hard with no sign of partial thawing, freezer burn or damaged packaging. Frozen fish is best thawed in the fridge overnight before cooking.

PREPARING FISH

Your supplier can gut and clean fish for you, if you don't want to do it. Ask for heads, bones and trimmings to make into stock, either for your chosen recipe, or to freeze for future use. Prepare and cook fish as soon as possible after purchase. Note that once fish has been cut into pieces it is liable to deteriorate more rapidly.

STORING FISH

Fish is always best eaten fresh. So store it in the fridge when you get home, and cook it that day.

Frozen fish is usually snap-frozen shortly after it is caught, and is generally of good quality. It is usually prepared as fillets and is used in processed products, such as fish fingers and fish cakes. Many types of fish and processed foods can be cooked directly from frozen. Other frozen fish should be thawed according to the pack instructions and cooked as for fresh fish.

FREEZING AND THAWING FISH

Fish can be frozen whole or in fillets, cutlets or steaks. Freeze as soon as possible after purchase.

1 Gut and clean the fish. Pat dry on kitchen paper, then snip off any sharp fins or spikes.
2 Wrap fish or fillets individually in clingfilm or a freezer bag, making sure the wrapping is airtight. Label with the date and store in the freezer. Use within two to three months.
3 To thaw, put the fish in the fridge until completely thawed. This may take 24 hours for a large fish.
4 Do not refreeze thawed raw fish. You can, however, freeze it again after you have cooked it.

COOKING FISH

Fish is relatively quick to cook, whichever method you use. To check when fish is cooked, insert a thin skewer into the thickest part of the flesh. It should pass through easily and the flesh should begin to flake. White fish loses its translucency when it is cooked, turning white and opaque.

Bake This is suitable for most whole fish, steaks, cutlets and fillets. Put the fish into an ovenproof dish, season with salt and pepper, then add herbs, a knob of butter and a little stock or white wine. Or wrap the fish in greased foil with herbs, seasoning, lemon slices and a knob of butter or a little liquid. Bake at 180°C (160°C fan oven) mark 4, allowing 30–40 minutes for large whole fish, 15–25 minutes for steaks, cutlets and small fish.

Barbecue This is suitable for many types of fish, especially firm-textured varieties and oily fish including trout, red mullet and sardines. Special fish-shaped racks can be used to prevent whole fish from breaking up; or fish can be threaded on to long skewers.

Braise Cooking fish on a bed of sautéed vegetables in a sealed pan is another good method, especially suited to firm, meaty fish, such as monkfish or tuna. Lay the fish on top of the vegetables, add some stock, court bouillon or wine, cover and cook for 10–20 minutes over a low heat or in the oven at 180°C (160°C fan oven) mark 4.

Cook 'en papillote' Small whole fish, cutlets and fillets cook well in a sealed paper or foil parcel with flavourings such as herbs, spices, a flavoured butter or citrus juice.

Deep-fry Small whole fish, such as whitebait and squid, as well as cutlets and fillets are suited to deep-frying. Normally the fish is first coated with seasoned flour, beaten egg and breadcrumbs, or batter, which forms a crisp, protective coating.

To make a suitable coating batter, sift 125g (4oz) plain flour with a large pinch of salt into a bowl, add 1 egg, then gradually beat in 150ml (1/4 pint) milk, or milk and water mixed, until smooth.

Heat the oil in a deep-fryer to 190°C (test by frying a small cube of bread; it should brown in 20 seconds), dip the fish into the batter, or flour, egg and breadcrumbs, then lower into the oil in the basket and deep-fry for 4–5 minutes until the batter is crisp and golden brown and the fish is cooked. Drain on kitchen paper.

Griddle cook
Cooking fish on a ridged cast-iron or non-stick griddle pan is an excellent quick method. It's best applied to firmer fish, such as monkfish, tuna, swordfish and squid, which will hold together over the high heat. This method produces attractive criss-cross markings on the fish.

Grill This method is ideal for cooking small whole fish, thin fillets and thicker cuts. Make two or three slashes through the skin on each side of whole fish to allow the heat to penetrate through to the flesh. Brush with oil or melted butter and grill under a medium heat, basting frequently and turning thicker cuts halfway through. Allow 4–5 minutes for thin fillets; 8–10 minutes for thicker cuts and small whole fish.

Pan-fry A good technique for small oily fish, such as sardines, herring and red mullet, all need the merest lick of oil or butter. White fish should be coated in seasoned flour or egg and breadcrumbs before shallow-frying in a little hot oil, clarified butter, or oil and butter. Allow 3–4 minutes to pan-fry small whole fish, fillets and steaks, 8–10 minutes for larger cuts, which will need turning halfway through.

Poach This method is perfect for larger whole fish such as salmon and sea bass, as well as smaller whole fish, cutlets and fillets. The fish is gently cooked in a court bouillon, flavoured broth or milk. Heat the liquid in a shallow pan, or fish kettle if cooking large whole fish, then add the fish and simmer very gently, until just cooked. Cooking times vary considerably, depending on size and thickness. The cooking liquor can be used to make a sauce.

To poach a whole salmon to serve cold: put the cleaned fish into a fish kettle, add sufficient court bouillon to cover, put on a tight-fitting lid and slowly bring to a simmer; simmer for about 2 minutes, then turn off the heat and leave the fish to cool completely; it will slowly cook in the residual heat.

Microwave cooking This is ideal for small whole fish, and fish fillets and steaks of uniform thickness. Cook in a covered container with a little butter or liquid and season after cooking. Cooking time is determined by the thickness of the fish and the quantity; for example, 450g (1lb) fish fillets would take about 4–5 minutes, plus 2 minutes standing time.

Steam This is a simple, healthy technique, suitable for whole fish, steaks and fillets. The fish cooks in its own juices, so much of the original flavour is retained. Season the fish, put in the steamer over boiling water and cover with a tight-fitting lid. Allow 5–10 minutes for fillets; 15–20 minutes for steaks and whole fish.

ROUND SEA FISH

1. Haddock: May–Feb
A grey-skinned fish with firm white flesh, usually sold as fillets or steaks. Suited to most cooking methods. Smoked haddock is pale yellow; a bright yellow-orange colour indicates it has been artificially dyed as well. Finnan haddock are split, lightly salted and smoked. Arbroath smokies are hot-smoked haddock, which don't need further cooking.

2. Bream (sea), red: June–Feb
With firm, delicately flavoured white flesh, whole bream may be stuffed and baked, poached or braised. Fry or grill fillets.

3. Coley (saithe): Aug–Feb
The pinkish-grey flesh of coley turns white when cooked. Sold as fillets. Cook as cod, with some liquid, as the flesh can be dry.

4. Hake: June–March
A member of the cod family and similar in shape, but with a closer-textured white flesh and a finer flavour. Hake is sold whole, and as steaks, cutlets and fillets. Cook as for cod.

5. Bass: Aug–March
Delicate white or pale pink flesh. Bass is sold whole (up to 4.5kg (10lb) or as steaks or fillets. Small whole fish can be grilled; steaks and fillets are usually poached or baked.

6. Cod: June–Feb
Popular for its close-textured white flesh, cod is usually sold as steaks or fillets; smaller fish may be sold whole. Suitable for most cooking methods. Smoked cod, salt cod and cod's roe are also available.

7. Mullet, red: May–Nov
Unrelated to the grey mullet, this small bright red fish has firm flesh with a unique, delicate flavour. Sold whole and suitable for pan-frying, grilling, barbecuing and baking.

8. Mullet, grey: Sept–Feb
Similar to sea bass but with an inferior flavour and texture, grey mullet is sold whole or as fillets. Suitable for baking, grilling, steaming or poaching.

9. Whiting: June–Feb
A fairly small fish with soft and white flesh with a delicate flavour. Sold whole or as fillets; best poached, steamed or pan-fried.

1 Sole: May–Feb

This name is applied to several species, including Dover sole (1a), lemon sole (1b) and witch, or Torbay sole. The Dover sole is one of the finest flat fish, with a delicious flavour. Lemon sole is lighter in colour, slightly longer and its head is more pointed than Dover sole. Witch is shaped like Dover sole, but it has slightly pinkish skin and its flesh tastes more like that of lemon sole. Sold whole or as fillets; sole can be grilled, fried, baked or steamed.

2 Halibut: June–March

A very large flat fish, halibut is prized for its fine flavoured flesh. Sold as fillets or steaks; cook as for turbot or cod.

3 Turbot: April–Feb

A diamond-shaped fish with very small scales, turbot has delicious, creamy-white flesh and it is considered to be the finest of the flat fish. Usually sold as steaks, which can be grilled, baked or poached.

4 Plaice: May–Feb

A popular variety with soft, white delicately flavoured flesh. Sold whole or as fillets; suitable for most cooking methods, including steaming, frying, baking and grilling.

5 Skate: May–Feb

This is a ray-shaped fish. Only the wings are sold for cooking. They may be fried, grilled or poached.

1 **Sea trout: all year, best March–July**
The flesh has a flavour and colour rather like salmon, but the texture is coarser and less succulent. Prepare and cook as for salmon.

2 **Herring: May–Dec**
A fairly small, round fish with creamy-coloured flesh that has a distinctive flavour. Usually grilled, fried or stuffed and baked. Cured herrings are also available.

3 **Eel: all year, best Sept–Dec**
Dense, fatty flesh. Eels must be eaten very fresh and are therefore often sold live. They are also sold as fillets, and jellied. Fresh eels are best sautéed or stewed.

4 **Sardine: Nov–Feb**
These are immature pilchards. Most are sold canned in olive oil or tomato sauce, but fresh are increasingly available. Grill, fry or bake.

5 **Whitebait: all year, best Feb–June**
Tiny silvery young of the sprat or herring, whitebait are eaten whole, typically coated in flour and deep-fried.

6 **Salmon: all year**
The deep pink flesh turns pale pink when cooked. Fresh 'wild' Scottish salmon is the best; in season from February to August. Farmed and imported salmon are always available. Sold whole, and as steaks and fillets. Bake or poach whole salmon; grill, pan-fry, poach or bake steaks and cutlets.

7 **Sprat: Oct; March**
Small member of the herring family. Clean through the gills, then grill or fry.

8 **Anchovy: all year**
Small fish with a strong flavour, usually filleted and cured, by salting or brining. Fresh anchovies are sometimes obtainable.

9 **Tuna: all year; fresh or frozen**
The meaty flesh is deep reddish-pink and is sold in steaks or slices. Braise, poach, grill or pan-fry. Canned tuna is popular.

10 **Mackerel: all year, best May–June**
In plentiful supply and inexpensive. The average mackerel weighs about 450g (1lb). Its beige-pink flesh has a meaty texture and rich flavour. Whole fish and fillets can be grilled, baked, pan-fried or braised.

NAVARIN OF COD

Serves 6
Preparation 15 minutes
Cooking time 25 minutes

175g (6oz) podded broad beans, skinned (see page 278)
25g (1oz) butter
2 tbsp sunflower oil
1 onion, sliced
225g (8oz) baby carrots, trimmed and halved
225g (8oz) courgettes, cut into 2cm ($^3/_4$ in) chunks
1 garlic clove, crushed
1.1kg (2$^1/_2$ lb) thick cod fillet, skinned
4 tbsp plain flour
150ml ($^1/_4$ pint) dry white wine
300ml ($^1/_2$ pint) fish stock
1 tbsp lemon juice
3 tbsp double cream
2 tbsp freshly chopped flat-leafed parsley, plus extra to
    garnish
salt and ground black pepper
baby new potatoes to serve (optional)

1 If the beans are large, blanch them in boiling water for
1–2 minutes, then drain and refresh in cold water.
2 Heat half the butter and half the oil in a large sauté pan.
Add the onion, carrots, courgettes and garlic, and cook gently
until softened and just beginning to brown. Remove from the
pan and put to one side.
3 Season the fish with salt and pepper, then dust lightly with
the flour. Heat the remaining butter and oil in the pan, add the
fish and brown on all sides. Remove from the pan and put to
one side.
4 Add the wine to the pan, scraping up any sediment from
the base. Simmer for 1–2 minutes, then put the carrot mixture
and fish back in the pan. Add the beans and stock. Bring to a
simmer, cover and simmer gently for 10 minutes or until the
fish is opaque and flakes easily. Stir in the lemon juice, cream
and parsley. Divide among six bowls, garnish with parsley, and
serve with baby new potatoes, if you like.

COOK'S TIP
With the depletion of North Sea cod stocks, try to
buy Icelandic or Norwegian cod instead. You can also
cook it with other white fish.

NUTRITION PER SERVING
346 cals | 13g fat (5g sats) | 16g carbs | 0.4g salt

COD FILLETS WITH A HERBY CHEESE CRUST

Serves 4
Preparation 30 minutes, plus chilling
Cooking time 15 minutes

4 long skinless cod fillets, about 175g (6oz) each
plain flour, to coat
50g (2oz) fresh white breadcrumbs
50g (2oz) freshly grated Pecorino or Parmesan
2 tbsp freshly chopped parsley
2 tbsp freshly chopped chervil or dill
1 large egg, beaten
oil to grease
salt and ground black pepper
peas and grilled tomatoes to serve

1 Season the fish with salt and pepper and toss in flour to coat, shaking off the excess.
2 Mix the breadcrumbs with the cheese, herbs and salt and pepper.
3 Dip the floured cod fillets into the beaten egg, then immediately roll in the breadcrumb mixture to coat thoroughly. Put on a baking sheet, cover lightly and chill for 1 hour.
4 Put the fish in a lightly oiled grill pan and cook under a medium-hot grill for 12–14 minutes or until cooked through, turning halfway through. Serve with tomatoes and peas.

NUTRITION PER SERVING
260 cals | 7g fat (3g sats) | 11g carbs | 1.4g salt

OLD-FASHIONED FISH PIE

Serves 4
Preparation 20 minutes
Cooking time 50 minutes

450g (1lb) haddock, cod or coley fillets
300ml (½ pint) milk
1 bay leaf
6 black peppercorns
2 onion slices for flavouring
65g (2½ oz) butter
3 tbsp flour
150ml (¼ pint) single cream
2 medium eggs, hard-boiled, shelled and chopped
2 tbsp freshly chopped parsley
6 tbsp milk
900g (2lb) potatoes, cooked and mashed
1 medium egg
salt and ground black pepper

1 Put the fish in a frying pan, pour over the milk and add the bay leaf, peppercorns, onion slices and a good pinch of salt. Bring slowly to the boil, cover and simmer for 8–10 minutes until the fish flakes when tested with a fork.

2 Lift the fish out of the pan using a fish slice and put on a plate. Flake the fish, discarding the skin and bone. Strain and put the milk to one side. Preheat the oven to 200°C (180°C fan oven) mark 6.

3 Melt 40g (1½ oz) butter in a pan, stir in the flour and cook gently for 1 minute, stirring. Remove the pan from the heat and gradually stir in the reserved milk. Bring to the boil slowly and continue to cook, stirring until the sauce thickens. Season.

4 Stir in the cream and fish, together with any juices. Add the chopped eggs and parsley, and adjust the seasoning. Spoon the mixture into a 1.1 litre (2 pint) pie dish or similar ovenproof dish.

5 Heat the 6 tbsp milk and remaining butter in a pan, then beat into the potatoes. Season and leave to cool slightly.

6 Spoon the cooled potato into a large piping bag fitted with a large star nozzle. Pipe shell-shaped lines of potato across the fish mixture. Alternatively, spoon potato on top and roughen the surface with a fork.

7 Put the dish on a baking sheet and cook in the oven for 10–15 minutes until the potato is set.

8 Beat the egg with a good pinch of salt then brush over the pie. Return to the oven for 15 minutes or until golden brown.

TRY SOMETHING DIFFERENT

- Stir 125g (4oz) grated Cheddar cheese into the sauce.
- Beat 125g (4oz) grated Cheddar or Red Leicester cheese into the mashed potatoes.
- Stir 175g (6oz) canned sweetcorn, drained, and ¼ tsp cayenne pepper into the fish mixture.
- Fry 125g (4oz) sliced button mushrooms in 25g (1oz) butter for 3 minutes. Stir into the fish mixture.
- Sprinkle the potato topping with 50g (2oz) mixed grated Parmesan and fresh breadcrumbs after the first 10–15 minutes.
- Cover the pie with puff pastry instead of the potatoes.

NUTRITION PER SERVING
610 cals | 28g fat (15g sats) | 56g carbs | 1.4g salt

CEVICHE

Serves 4
Preparation 20 minutes, plus overnight chilling
Cooking time 7 minutes, plus cooling and chilling

450g (1lb) haddock fillets, skinned and
    cut diagonally into thin strips
1 tsp coriander seeds
1 tsp black peppercorns
juice of 6 limes
1 tsp salt
2 tbsp olive oil
1 bunch of spring onions, sliced
4 tomatoes, peeled and chopped
    (see page 277)
a dash of Tabasco sauce, or to taste
2 tbsp freshly chopped coriander
1 avocado
lime slices (optional) and fresh coriander to garnish

1 Put the fish strips into a bowl. Using a pestle and mortar, crush the coriander seeds and peppercorns to a fine powder, mix with the lime juice and salt, then pour over the fish. Cover and chill in the fridge for 24 hours, turning the fish over occasionally.

2 The next day, heat the oil in a frying pan, add the spring onions and fry gently for 5 minutes. Add the tomatoes and Tabasco sauce to taste and toss together over brisk heat for 1–2 minutes. Remove from the heat and cool for 20–30 minutes.

3 To serve, drain the fish from the marinade, discarding the marinade, and mix with the spring onion and tomatoes and the chopped coriander.

4 Halve the avocado, peel and remove the stone. Slice the flesh crossways. Arrange the slices around the inside of a serving bowl and pile the fish mixture in the centre. Garnish and serve immediately.

NUTRITION PER SERVING
227 cals | 14g fat (3g sats) | 4g carbs | 1.4g salt

DOVER SOLE WITH PARSLEY BUTTER

Serves 2
Preparation 5 minutes
Cooking time 20 minutes

2 Dover soles, about 275g (10oz) each, gutted and descaled
3 tbsp plain flour
2 tbsp sunflower oil
25g (1oz) unsalted butter
2 tbsp chopped flat-leafed parsley
juice of ½ lemon
salt and ground black pepper
lemon wedges to serve

1 Rinse the fish under cold water, then gently pat them dry with kitchen paper. Put the flour on a large plate and season with salt and pepper. Dip the fish into the seasoned flour, to coat both sides, gently shaking off the excess.
2 Heat 1 tbsp oil in a large sauté pan or frying pan and fry one fish for 4–5 minutes on each side until golden. Transfer to a warmed plate and keep warm in a low oven. Add the remaining oil to the pan and cook the other fish in the same way; put on a plate in the oven to keep warm.
3 Add the butter to the pan and melt. Turn up the heat slightly until it turns golden, then take off the heat. Add the parsley and lemon juice, then season well. Put one fish on each warmed dinner plate and pour over the parsley butter. Serve with lemon wedges.

NUTRITION PER SERVING
450 cals | 25g fat (8g sats) | 16g carbs | 1.5g salt

SKATE WITH BLACK BUTTER AND ROCKET MASH

Serves 6
Preparation 40 minutes
Cooking time 40 minutes

6 skate wings, about 175g (6oz) each
125g (4oz) plain flour, to dust
125g (4oz) butter
salt and ground black pepper
a handful of rocket leaves and lemon wedges to serve

For the rocket mash
1.8kg (4lb) floury potatoes, such as Maris Piper,
    cut into chunks
3 garlic cloves, peeled
200ml carton crème fraîche
100g (3¹/₂ oz) rocket leaves

For the black butter
175g (6oz) butter
30 capers
6 tbsp white wine vinegar

1 To make the rocket mash, put the potatoes and garlic into
a large pan of cold salted water. Cover, bring to the boil and
cook for 15 minutes or until tender.
2 Meanwhile, trim the skate wings if necessary. Put the flour
on a plate and season well with salt and pepper. Dip each
skate wing in the seasoned flour to cover both sides evenly
and shake off the excess.
3 Melt the 125g (4oz) butter in a large frying pan over a low
heat, then fry the skate over a medium heat, in two or three
batches, for 5 minutes on each side, taking care that the butter
doesn't burn. Put the skate wings on a baking sheet and keep
them warm in a low oven while you cook the rest. Don't throw
away the butter in the frying pan when you have finished.
4 Drain the potatoes and garlic, then return to the pan.
Add the crème fraîche and mash until smooth. Season well
with salt and pepper. Chop the rocket leaves and stir them
into the mash. Put the lid on to keep the potatoes warm.
5 For the black butter, add the butter to the frying pan and
melt over a low heat. Add the capers and wine vinegar, and
stir until heated through. Season well with salt and pepper.
6 Transfer the skate wings to warmed plates, drizzle with the
black butter and top with rocket leaves. Serve with lemon
wedges and the rocket mash.

NUTRITION PER SERVING
830 cals | 56g fat (35g sats) | 6g carbs | 1.7g salt

BRAISED MONKFISH IN PARMA HAM WITH LENTILS

Serves 4
Preparation 15 minutes, plus marinating
Cooking time 40 minutes

1kg (2¼ lb) monkfish tail, filleted and skinned
1 tbsp freshly chopped marjoram
1 small lemon, peel and pith removed, thinly sliced
4–6 thin slices Parma ham (see Cook's Tip page 65)
3 tbsp olive oil
1 small onion, finely diced
1 carrot, finely diced
1 celery stick, finely diced
1 garlic clove, finely chopped
350g (12oz) Puy lentils
150ml (¼ pint) red wine
2 tbsp freshly chopped coriander
salt and ground black pepper

1 Lay the fish, cut side up, on a board and sprinkle with the marjoram. Season with salt and pepper. Lay the lemon slices over one fillet, then sandwich together with the other monkfish fillet.
2 Wrap the fish in the Parma ham, making sure it is completely covered. Tie at 5cm (2in) intervals with fine cotton string. Cover and leave in a cool place for 1–2 hours to allow the flavours to develop.
3 Heat 2 tbsp olive oil in a medium pan, then add the onion, carrot, celery and garlic. Cook, stirring, for about 8 minutes until golden. Stir in the lentils and wine. Add sufficient water to cover, bring to the boil and cook for 10 minutes.
4 Heat the remaining oil in a large frying pan. Add the monkfish parcel and fry, turning, until the Parma ham is browned all over. Carefully take out the fish parcel and transfer the lentils to the frying pan. Put the fish on top, partially burying it in the lentils. Cover and cook on a medium-low heat for 20 minutes or until the juices from the fish run clear, when tested with a knife.
5 Remove the string and cut the fish into thick slices. Serve on the lentils, sprinkled with the coriander.

NUTRITION PER SERVING
610 cals | 15g fat (2g sats) | 47g carbs | 1.1g salt

ROASTED SALMON

Serves 20
Preparation 20 minutes
Cooking time about 30 minutes, plus cooling and chilling

2 lemons, sliced, and the juice of $\frac{1}{2}$ lemon,
    plus extra lemon slices to garnish
2 salmon sides, filleted, each 1.4kg (3lb),
    skin on, boned and trimmed
2 tbsp dry white wine
salt and ground black pepper
cucumber slices and 2 large bunches
    of watercress to garnish

For the dressing
500g (1lb) carton crème fraîche
500g (1lb) carton natural yogurt
2 tbsp horseradish sauce
3 tbsp freshly chopped tarragon
4 tbsp capers, roughly chopped, plus extra to garnish
$\frac{1}{4}$ cucumber, seeded and finely chopped

1 Preheat the oven to 190°C (170°C fan oven) mark 5. Take two pieces of foil, each large enough to wrap one side of salmon, and put a piece of greaseproof paper on top. Divide the lemon slices between each piece of greaseproof paper and lay the salmon on top, skin side up. Season with salt and pepper, then pour over the lemon juice and wine.
2 Score the skin of each salmon fillet at 4cm (1½in) intervals to mark 10 portions. Scrunch the foil around each fillet, keeping it loose so the fish doesn't stick. Cook for 25 minutes until the flesh is just opaque. Unwrap the foil and cook for a further 5 minutes until the skin is crisp. Leave the fish to cool quickly in a cold place. Re-wrap and chill.
3 Put all the dressing ingredients in a bowl and season with salt and pepper. Mix well, then cover and chill.
4 Serve the salmon on a serving plate garnished with lemon, cucumber and watercress. Garnish the dressing with capers and chopped cucumber.

GET AHEAD
Complete the recipe to the end of step 3, then keep the salmon wrapped and chilled for up to one day.

COOK'S TIPS
- There'll be a lot of hot liquid in the parcel of salmon, so ask someone to help you lift it out of the oven.
- To check the fish is cooked, ease a knife into one of the slashes in the skin. The flesh should look opaque and the knife should come out hot.

NUTRITION PER SERVING
347 cals | 25g fat (9g sats) | 3g carbs | 0.2g salt

POACHED SALMON

Serves 8
Preparation 15 minutes
Cooking time see below

1 salmon
wine or Court Bouillon (see Try Something Different,
    page 11) (optional)
salt and ground black pepper
lemon slices and chervil or parsley sprigs to garnish

1 To prepare the salmon, slit the fish along the underside
between the head and rear gill opening. Cut out the entrails
and discard. Rinse the fish to remove all the blood.
2 Snip off the fins and trim the tail into a neat 'V' shape.
Leave on the head, if you like. Pat dry with kitchen paper
and weigh the fish before cooking.
3 Fill a fish kettle or large pan with water, or a mixture of
water and wine or Court Bouillon. Bring to the boil, then
lower the fish into the kettle or pan. (A piece of muslin
wrapped around the salmon will enable it to be lifted out.)
4 Bring the liquid back to the boil, then simmer for
7–8 minutes per 450g (1lb) if eating hot.
5 If eating cold, bring the liquid back to the boil, then cook
for 5 minutes for fish under 3.2kg (7lb), 10–15 minutes for fish
over 3.2kg (7lb), allow to cool completely in the liquid, then lift
out and remove the skin and bones. Garnish with lemon slices
and chervil or parsley sprigs.

TRY SOMETHING DIFFERENT
Salmon can also be poached in the oven. Put the fish into
a deep roasting tin – it must fit snugly. Preheat the oven to
150°C (130°C fan oven) mark 2. Pour over enough water, or
water and wine or Court Bouillon to three-quarters cover it.
Cover tightly with buttered foil. Cook in the oven allowing
10 minutes per 450g (1lb). If serving the fish hot, allow an
extra 10 minutes at the end of the cooking time.

NUTRITION PER SERVING
675 cals | 41g fat (7g sats) | 0g carbs | 0.4g salt

TERIYAKI TUNA WITH SESAME NOODLES

Serves 2
Preparation 20 minutes, plus marinating
Cooking time 10 minutes

2 tuna steaks
2 nests medium egg noodles
75g (3oz) green beans, trimmed and halved
1 tsp toasted sesame oil
4 spring onions, sliced
1 tbsp freshly chopped coriander
2 tsp sesame seeds
lime wedges to serve

For the marinade
1 small garlic clove, crushed
2.5cm (1in) piece fresh root ginger, peeled
    and grated
3 tbsp teriyaki sauce
1 tbsp clear honey
1 tsp oil

1 Mix together the marinade ingredients in a non-metallic dish and add the tuna steaks. Leave to marinate in the fridge for 2 hours.
2 Preheat the grill to high. Cook the egg noodles according to the pack instructions with the green beans. Drain and cool under running water.
3 Meanwhile, put the tuna on a grill rack and cook for 3 minutes per side, brushing with the marinade, until firm but still moist.
4 Gently heat the sesame oil in a pan and toss in the noodles and green beans to reheat. Add the spring onions, coriander and sesame seeds.
5 To serve, divide the noodles between two plates, top with the tuna and garnish with lime wedges.

NUTRITION PER SERVING
508 cals | 17g fat (4g sats) | 48g carbs | 5.1g salt

SEA BASS WITH SAFFRON AND ORANGE SAUCE

Serves 6
Preparation 25 minutes
Cooking time 40 minutes

75g (3oz) butter, plus extra to grease
1 large sea bass, about 1.4kg (3lb)
a handful of mixed fresh herb sprigs, such as tarragon,
     parsley and chervil, plus chopped herbs to garnish
salt and ground black pepper
orange wedges to garnish

For the saffron and orange sauce
$^1/_2$ tsp saffron
1 tsp cornflour
300ml ($^1/_2$ pint) double cream
finely grated zest of 1 orange

1 Preheat the oven to 220°C (200°C fan oven) mark 7. Line a roasting tin large enough to hold the fish with a lightly buttered sheet of foil. Rub the fish inside and out with salt and pepper and put in the foil-lined tin. Tuck the herbs into the cavity and dot the butter over the fish.
2 Cover the sea bass with foil and bake for 40 minutes or until the thickest part flakes easily when tested with a knife.
3 Meanwhile make the sauce. Crumble the saffron into a bowl, add 2 tbsp hot water and set aside. Blend the cornflour with a little cold water in a small pan, then stir in the cream, orange zest and a little seasoning. Add the saffron and liquid to the pan and cook, stirring, until slightly thickened. Simmer gently for 3 minutes.
4 Carefully lift the cooked sea bass on to a board and peel away the skin from the upper surface, then turn the bass on to a warmed serving serving plate. Remove the skin from the other side. Garnish the fish lavishly with herbs and with the orange wedges, and serve with the warm saffron and orange sauce.

TRY SOMETHING DIFFERENT
Use a sea trout instead of bass.

COOK'S TIP
If the bass won't fit comfortably in the tin, cut off the head and bake it beside the fish. Reposition the head as you serve the fish.

NUTRITION PER SERVING
520 cals | 38g fat (24g sats) | 2g carbs | 1g salt

RED MULLET WITH CHERRY TOMATOES AND BASIL OIL

Serves 6
Preparation 10 minutes
Cooking Time about 40 minutes

50g (1lb) cherry tomatoes, mixture of
    red and yellow
2 tbsp green peppercorns in brine,
    drained
8 garlic cloves, bruised not peeled
zest and juice of 1 small lemon
75ml (2½fl oz) basil oil
12 × 50g (2oz) red mullet fillets,
    descaled
a small handful of fresh basil leaves,
    sliced
salt and ground black pepper
new potatoes, to serve

1 Preheat the oven to 180°C (160°C fan oven) mark 4. Halve the larger tomatoes, then put them all into a shallow roasting tin. Add the peppercorns, garlic and lemon zest, drizzle with half the oil and cook in the oven for 20 minutes.
2 Add the fish to the tin and drizzle with the remaining oil. Cook for a further 15–20 minutes until golden and cooked through.
3 Pour the lemon juice over the fish and sprinkle with basil leaves, salt and pepper. Serve with the mullet with steamed new potatoes.

NUTRITION PER SERVING 282 cals |
17g fat (2g sats) | 4g carbs | 0.4g salt

QUICK FISH AND CHIPS

Serves 2
Preparation 15 minutes
Cooking time 12 minutes

4 litres (7 pints) sunflower oil for
    deep-frying
125g (4oz) self-raising flour
¼ tsp baking powder
¼ tsp salt
1 medium egg
150ml (¼ pint) sparkling mineral
    water
2 hake fillets, about 125g (4oz) each
450g (1lb) Desirée potatoes, cut into
    1cm (½ in) chips
salt, vinegar and lemon mayonnaise
    (see page 29) to serve

1 Heat the oil in a deep-fryer to 190°C (test by frying a small cube of bread – it should brown in 20 seconds).
2 Whiz the flour, baking powder, salt, egg and water in a food processor or blender until combined into a batter. Remove the blade from the food processor. (Alternatively, put the ingredients into a bowl and beat everything together until smooth.) Drop one of the fish fillets into the batter to coat it.
3 Put half the chips into the deep-fryer, then add the battered fish. Fry for 6 minutes or until just cooked, then remove and drain well on kitchen paper. Keep warm if not serving immediately.
4 Drop the remaining fillet into the batter to coat, then repeat step 3 with the remaining chips. Serve with salt, vinegar and garlic mayonnaise.

NUTRITION PER SERVING 1186 cals |
79g fat (18g sats) | 73g carbs | 3.2g salt

SOUSED HERRINGS

Serves 4
Preparation 10 minutes
Cooking time 45 minutes, plus cooling

4 large or 6–8 small herrings, cleaned,
    boned, and heads and tails
    removed
1 small onion, sliced into rings
6 black peppercorns
1–2 bay leaves
fresh parsley sprigs
150ml (¼ pint) malt vinegar
salt and ground black pepper
salad to serve (optional)

1 Preheat the oven to 180°C
(160°C fan oven) mark 4. Season
the fish and divide into fillets. Roll up
and secure. Arrange in a shallow
ovenproof dish with the onion rings,
peppercorns and herbs.
2 Pour in the vinegar and enough
water to almost cover the fish. Cover
with greaseproof paper or foil and
cook in the oven for 45 minutes or
until tender.
3 Leave the herrings to cool in the
cooking liquid before serving as an
appetiser or with salad.

NUTRITION PER SERVING 215 cals |
13g fat (3g sats) | trace carbs | 1.1g salt

SARDINES WITH HERBS

Serves 4
Preparation 10–30 minutes
Cooking time about 10 minutes

900g (2lb) sardines (at least 12), gutted
125ml (4fl oz) olive oil
3 tbsp lemon juice
2 tsp grated lemon zest
4 tbsp freshly chopped mixed herbs,
    such as parsley, chervil and thyme
salt and ground black pepper
crusty bread to serve

1 If you like, bone the sardines (see
Cook's Tip), leaving the heads and tails
intact. Rinse the sardines and pat dry
with kitchen paper.
2 In a bowl, mix together the olive
oil, lemon juice, lemon zest, herbs
and seasoning.
3 Lay the sardines on a grill rack,
drizzle the herb dressing over them
and grill under a medium-high heat
for 5–7 minutes each side, basting
frequently with the dressing. Serve hot
or cold, with plenty of crusty bread.

COOK'S TIP
To remove the backbones from
small fish, such as sardines, make
sure the cut along the belly (used
for gutting) extends along to the
tail. Put the fish, slit-side down, on a
board and open it out. Press firmly
along the length of the backbone
with your thumbs to loosen it from
the flesh. Turn the fish over and pull
out the backbone through the slit
in the belly. Use scissors to snip the
end of the backbone free inside the
fish if necessary.

NUTRITION PER SERVING 340 cals |
25g fat (7g sats) | 0g carbs | 1.3g salt

TROUT WITH ALMONDS

Serves 4
Preparation 5 minutes
Cooking time 10–15 minutes

4 trout, gutted, with heads and tails intact
2 tbsp plain flour
65g (2½oz) butter
50g (2oz) flaked almonds
juice of ½ lemon, or to taste
1–2 tbsp freshly chopped parsley
salt and ground black pepper

1 Rinse the trout and pat dry with kitchen paper. Put the flour on a plate and season with salt and pepper. Dust the fish with the seasoned flour to coat lightly. Melt 50g (2oz) of the butter in a large frying pan. Fry the trout, two at a time, for 5–7 minutes on each side, turning once, until golden on both sides and cooked.
2 Remove the fish from the pan, drain on kitchen paper and put on a warmed serving plate; keep warm. Wipe out the pan.
3 Melt the remaining butter in the pan and fry the almonds until lightly browned. Add the lemon juice and spoon over the trout. Scatter with chopped parsley and serve immediately.

NUTRITION PER SERVING
450 cals | 28g fat (11g sats) | 6g carbs | 1.1g salt

MARINATED MACKEREL

Serves 4
Preparation 20 minutes, plus marinating
Cooking time 25 minutes

4 mackerel, about 350g (12oz) each, cleaned
3 onions, 1 finely chopped, 2 finely sliced
3 garlic cloves, peeled and crushed
1 lemon, sliced, and the juice of 1 lemon
3 tbsp olive oil
1 red pepper, seeded and finely sliced into rings
5 black peppercorns
2 bay leaves
150ml (¼ pint) white wine vinegar
salt and ground black pepper

1 Rinse the mackerel and pat dry with kitchen paper. Put into a large, shallow container and sprinkle inside and out with the chopped onion, a little salt and one-third of the garlic. Scatter over the lemon slices, pour over the lemon juice and season generously with pepper. Cover and leave to marinate in the fridge for at least 2 hours.
2 Heat 1 tbsp of the olive oil in a frying pan, add the sliced onions and fry over a low heat for 5 minutes to soften, stirring regularly. Add the remaining garlic and the red pepper, and cook for a further 3 minutes.
3 Add the peppercorns, bay leaves, wine vinegar and 150ml (¼ pint) water. Bring to the boil, then lower the heat and simmer for 10 minutes or until the liquid is reduced by one-third. Set aside.
4 Drain the mackerel. Heat the remaining 2 tbsp of oil in a large heavy-based frying pan. Add the mackerel and fry for 8–10 minutes, turning as needed, until the fish is tender and lightly browned.
5 Return the mackerel to a shallow dish and pour over the vinegar and pepper mixture. Serve warm, or cool and chill.

COOK'S TIP
This dish is best prepared a day ahead to allow the flavours to mingle. To serve warm the next day, microwave on full power for about 3 minutes.

NUTRITION PER SERVING
560 cals | 39g fat (13g sats) | 12g carbs | 1.2g salt

TRADITIONAL KIPPERS

Serves 2
Preparation 0 minutes
Cooking time 5–15 minutes

2 kippers
butter, freshly chopped parsley and toast to serve

Three ways to cook kippers:

1 Grill the kippers for 5 minutes.
2 Alternatively, put into a jug of boiling water and leave in a warm place for 5–10 minutes.
3 You can also wrap them in foil and cook them in the oven at 190°C (170°C fan oven) mark 5 for 10–15 minutes.
4 Serve with butter, parsley and toast.

COOK'S TIP
Kippers are whole herrings that have been split and opened out flat. They are lightly brined, then cold-smoked, which gives them a rich flavour.

NUTRITION PER SERVING
331 cals | 25g fat (4g sats) | 38g carbs | 3.1g salt

SMOKED HADDOCK KEDGEREE

Serves 4
Preparation 10 minutes
Cooking time 20 minutes

175g (6oz) long-grain rice
450g (1lb) smoked haddock fillets
2 medium eggs, hard-boiled and shelled
75g (3oz) butter
salt and cayenne pepper
freshly chopped parsley to garnish

1 Cook the rice in a pan of fast-boiling salted water until tender. Drain well and rinse under cold water.
2 Meanwhile, put the haddock in a large frying pan with just enough water to cover. Bring to simmering point, then simmer for 10–15 minutes until tender. Drain, skin and flake the fish, discarding the bones.
3 Chop one egg and slice the other into rings. Melt the butter in a pan, add the cooked rice, fish, chopped egg, salt and cayenne pepper, and stir over a medium heat for 5 minutes or until hot. Pile on to a warmed serving dish and garnish with parsley and the sliced egg.

NUTRITION PER SERVING
429 cals | 20g fat (11g sats) | 38g carbs | 3.1g salt

DEEP-FRIED WHITEBAIT

Serves 4
Preparation 5 minutes
Cooking time about 15 minutes

700g (1½ lb) whitebait
4 tbsp plain flour
oil, to deep-fry
lime or lemon wedges (optional) to serve
salt and ground black pepper

For the flavoured mayonnaise
150ml (¼ pint) mayonnaise (see Cook's Tip)
grated zest of 1 lime
1 tbsp chopped basil

1 Rinse the whitebait and pat thoroughly dry with
kitchen paper.
2 To make the flavoured mayonnaise, mix the ingredients
together in a bowl and season with salt and pepper.
3 Put the flour into a large plastic bag and season with salt
and pepper to taste. Add the whitebait and toss to coat in
the seasoned flour.
4 Heat the oil in a deep-fryer to 190°C (test by frying a
small cube of bread; it should brown in 20 seconds). Deep-fry
the whitebait in batches in the hot oil for 3 minutes or until
golden brown. Drain on crumpled kitchen paper and keep hot
in a low oven while cooking the rest of the fish.
5 Serve the hot whitebait with lime or lemon wedges, if you
like, and the flavoured mayonnaise.

> ## COOK'S TIP
> Use either homemade mayonnaise (see page 29)
> or a good, thick ready-made alternative.

NUTRITION PER SERVING
800 cals | 77g fat (4g sats) | 5g carbs | 2g salt

FRITTO MISTO DI MARE

Serves 6
Preparation 20 minutes
Cooking time 10 minutes

450g (1lb) squid, cleaned
225g (8oz) whitebait
4 small red mullet, boned, cleaned and heads and tails
    removed, sliced
225g (8oz) firm white fish fillets, such as cod, haddock or
    sole, skinned, and cut into long, thin strips
8–12 large prawns, peeled with tails intact
4 tbsp seasoned flour
vegetable oil for deep-frying
fresh parsley sprigs and lemon wedges to garnish

1 Slice the body of the squid into rings 5mm (¹/₄in) thick
and the tentacles into 1cm (¹/₂in) pieces. Toss all the fish in
seasoned flour to coat.
2 Heat the oil in a deep-fat fryer to 190°C (test by frying a
small cube of bread; it should brown in 20 seconds). Add the
fish pieces a few at a time and fry until crisp and golden. Drain
on absorbent kitchen paper and keep each batch warm while
frying the rest.
3 Divide the fish between six warmed plates and garnish
with lemon wedges and sprigs of parsley.

TRY SOMETHING DIFFERENT
Dip the fish in Fritter Batter before frying. Sift 125g (4oz) plain
flour with a pinch of salt into a bowl and make a well in the
centre. Break in 1 medium egg and beat well with a wooden
spoon, then gradually beat in 150ml (¹/₄ pint) milk, or milk and
water mixed, drawing in the flour from the sides to make a
smooth batter.

NUTRITION PER SERVING
512 cals | 33g fat (2g sats) | 11g carbs | 0.8g salt

FISH GOUJONS

Serves 4
Preparation 15 minutes
Cooking time 10 minutes

450g (1lb) hake fillets, skinned, boned
    and cut into 20 even-sized pieces
1 medium egg, beaten
50g (2oz) fresh breadcrumbs
vegetable oil for deep-frying
Tartare Sauce to serve (see page 22)

1 Coat the fish pieces in egg, then in the breadcrumbs.
2 Heat the oil in a deep-fat fryer to 180°C (test by frying a small cube of bread; it should brown in 40 seconds), add the fish and fry until golden. Drain on kitchen paper.
3 Serve the goujons on cocktail sticks with the sauce handed separately.

TRY SOMETHING DIFFERENT

Other firm fish such as haddock, coley, cod, monkfish and huss can be cooked in the same way.

NUTRITION PER SERVING 267 cals | 15g fat (2g sats) | 10g carbs | 0.6g salt

FISH CAKES

Serves 4
Preparation 15 minutes
Cooking time 20 minutes

350g (12oz) fish, such as cod, haddock
    or coley, cooked and flaked
350g (12oz) potatoes, cooked and
    mashed
25g (1oz) butter
1 tbsp freshly chopped parsley
a few drops of anchovy essence
    (optional)
milk, if needed
1 medium egg, beaten
125g (4oz) fresh breadcrumbs
vegetable oil for shallow frying
salt and ground black pepper
basil leaves to garnish
lemon wedges and salad to serve

1 Mix the fish with the potatoes, butter, parsley, seasoning and anchovy essence, if using, binding if necessary with a little milk or beaten egg.
2 On a lightly floured board, form the mixture into a roll, then cut into eight slices and shape into flat cakes. Coat them with egg and breadcrumbs.
3 Heat the oil in a frying pan, add the fishcakes and fry, turning once, until crisp and golden. Drain well on kitchen paper. Garnish with basil and serve with lemon wedges and salad.

TRY SOMETHING DIFFERENT

Replace the cod, haddock or coley with smoked haddock, herrings, canned tuna or salmon.

NUTRITION PER SERVING 412 cals | 19g fat (5g sats) | 39g carbs | 1.5g salt

THAI RED FISH CURRY

Serves 4
Preparation 10 minutes
Cooking time 8–10 minutes

1 tbsp vegetable oil
3 tbsp Thai red curry paste
450g (1lb) monkfish tail, boned to make 350g (12oz) fillet, sliced into rounds
350g (12oz) large raw peeled prawns, deveined (see page 85)
400ml can half-fat coconut milk (see Cook's Tip)
200ml (7fl oz) fish stock
juice of 1 lime
1–2 tbsp Thai fish sauce (nam pla)
125g (4oz) mangetouts
3 tbsp fresh coriander, roughly torn
salt and ground black pepper
fine chilli strips and coriander leaves to garnish

1 Heat the oil in a wok or large non-stick frying pan. Add the curry paste and cook for 1–2 minutes.
2 Add the monkfish and prawns, and stir well to coat in the curry paste. Add the coconut milk, stock, lime juice and fish sauce. Stir all the ingredients together and bring just to the boil.
3 Add the mangetouts and simmer for 5 minutes or until the mangetouts and fish are tender. Stir in the coriander and check the seasoning, adding salt and pepper to taste. Serve garnished with fine chilli strips and coriander leaves.

COOK'S TIP
If you can't find half-fat coconut milk, use half a can of full-fat coconut milk and make up the difference with water or stock. Freeze the remaining milk for up to one month.

NUTRITION PER SERVING
252 cals | 8g fat (1g sats) | 9g carbs | 2.2g salt

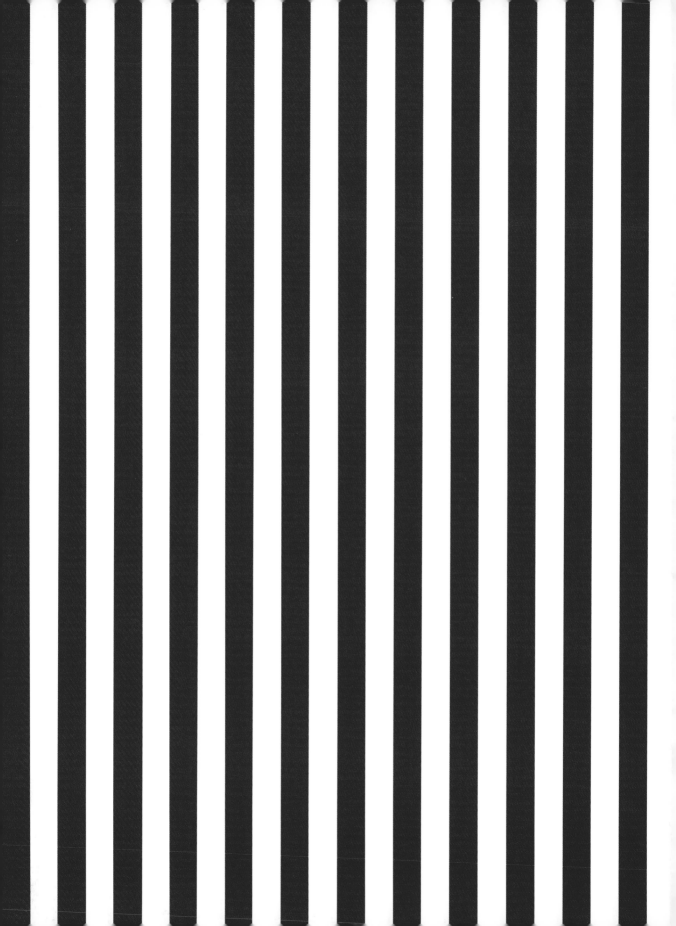

POULTRY

POULTRY

Domesticated birds that are bred for the table – including chicken, turkey, duckling, guinea fowl and goose – are classified as poultry (wild birds that are hunted for food, are referred to as game). Chicken, in particular, has become increasingly popular in recent years as a less expensive and healthier option to red meat. From a nutritional angle, it is an excellent food – high in protein and vitamins, yet low in fat (once the skin has been removed).

CHOOSING POULTRY

Whichever type of bird you are buying, freshness is of the utmost importance, so check the 'use-by' date. Look for a bird with a good plump breast and firm, unblemished skin. If you are buying from a farm, refuse a bird that's been carelessly plucked and singed. A young chicken will have a pliable breastbone, and a young duckling a pliable beak.

BREEDING AND REARING

How poultry is bred and reared has a significant effect on its health and welfare, and on taste and texture. The issues arise mainly in connection with chickens and turkeys, as these are often intensively reared. Other birds, such as ducks and geese, are usually farmed in a more humane way because they do not adapt well to intensive rearing.

Selective breeding and intensive rearing methods have changed the way chicken and turkey are farmed in recent decades leading to a huge increase in production and a drop in the price paid by consumers. Whereas chicken was once a luxury, today it is one of the cheapest forms of animal protein, but this has had serious consequences for birds and consumers.

The greatest changes are in maturation and in housing. Intensively reared chickens have been bred to take just six weeks to become fully grown (about 2kg/4½lb) and ready for slaughter. A naturally reared chicken will reach that weight in about 14 weeks. Intensively reared birds can suffer from health problems such as weak, under-developed legs that are not strong enough to carry the bird's ever-growing body. Because thousands of birds are packed into a single shed, antibiotics and other chemicals are routinely used to protect them from disease and infection. Traces of these chemicals will remain in the poultry flesh after slaughter.

Dubious hygiene is a natural part of intensive rearing. Excrement-filled sheds containing dead birds cannot be cleaned adequately until the flock is removed for slaughter. Disease and bacterial infection such as salmonella spread quickly, and as these infections remain in the meat after slaughter they pose risks for the consumer.

CATEGORIES FOR POULTRY

Organic chickens and other organic birds can roam freely and are reared without drugs. They can feed on organic pasture and are fed at least 80 per cent organic, non-GM (genetically modified) feed. Synthetic drugs and pesticides are avoided wherever possible. There's also a limit to the number of birds that can be reared in one space. All this helps to make a good, well-flavoured bird. Organic chickens cost about twice as much as intensively reared birds, but invariably have a superior flavour and texture.

Free-range birds are raised predominantly on a grain diet and allowed access to open-air runs, although they do not necessarily get as much exercise as organic chickens. Drugs may be used routinely. In the UK there are three categories of free-range bird: free range, traditional free range, and free range – total freedom. The last category is regarded as the best, and these birds are likely to cost more than the other two. Free-range birds are usually tastier than intensively reared chickens, but less so than organic birds.

Intensively reared poultry is raised in overcrowded huts. As the birds cannot move around easily, they end up fatter. The use of drugs and undesirable farming practices, such as beak trimming, are routine.

HANDLING AND STORING POULTRY

All poultry contains low levels of salmonella and campylo-bacter, which can cause food poisoning if they multiply. Always get poultry home and into a fridge as soon as possible after buying. If the bird contains giblets, remove them and store in a separate container, since these will deteriorate most rapidly. To avoid spreading bacteria, always wash your hands (and the tap) immediately after handling raw poultry. Never use the same utensils for preparing raw poultry and cooked foods. Thoroughly scrub chopping boards, knives and other utensils used for preparing raw poultry.

FREEZING POULTRY

Fresh chicken and poultry can be frozen successfully and safely:
- Always freeze poultry before its 'use by' date, even better on the day of purchase.
- Follow any freezing or thawing instructions given.
- Wrap portions in individual freezer bags, seal tightly

and label with the date of freezing. They can be stored in the freezer for up to three months.

→ To thaw, put the poultry in a dish (to catch dripping juices) and leave overnight in the fridge until completely thawed, then cook within 24 hours.

→ Do not refreeze thawed poultry. You can, however, freeze it again after you have cooked it.

Frozen poultry can be kept in the freezer for up to three months. Check that it is well wrapped to prevent the skin from being damaged by freezer burn. Defrost poultry at cool room temperature rather than in the fridge and make sure you allow sufficient time. A large turkey, weighing 6.8–9kg (15–20lb) for example, will take 24–30 hours to thaw thoroughly at cool room temperature. Even a 3.6–5kg (8–11lb) turkey will take 18–20 hours. It is essential that frozen poultry is fully thawed before cooking. Check that there are no ice crystals in the body cavity. A fully thawed bird will be flexible, too – try moving the leg joints. Once fully thawed, poultry can be stored in the fridge for a short time but it should be cooked within 24 hours.

CLEANING AND TRUSSING

1 Before stuffing a bird for roasting, clean it thoroughly. Put the bird in the sink and pull out any loose fat with your fingers. Run cold water through the cavity and dry the bird well using kitchen paper.

2 Trussing poultry before roasting gives it a neater shape for serving at the table. Cut the wishbone out by pulling back the flap of skin at the neck end. Run a sharp knife along the inside of the bone on both sides. Use poultry shears to snip the tip of the bone from the breastbone, and pull away. Snip or pull out the two ends.

3 Put the wing tips under the breast and fold the neck flap on to the back of the bird. Thread a trussing needle and use it to secure the neck flap.

4 Push a metal skewer through the legs, at the joint between thigh and drumstick. Twist some string around both ends of the skewer and pull firmly to tighten. Turn the bird over. Bring the string over the ends of the drumsticks, pull tight and tie to secure the legs in place.

JOINTING

1 Using a sharp meat knife with a curved blade, cut out the wishbone. Remove the wings in one piece. Remove wing tips.

2 With the tail pointing towards you and breast side up, pull one leg away and cut through the skin between the leg and breast. Pull the leg down until you crack the joint between the thigh bone and ribcage. Cut through that joint, then cut through the remaining leg meat. Repeat on the other side.

3 To remove the breast without any bone, make a cut along the length of the breastbone. Gently teasing the flesh away from the ribs with the knife, work the blade down between the flesh and ribs of one breast and cut it off neatly. (Always cut in, towards the bone.) Repeat on the other side.

4 To remove the breast with bone in, cut down the length of the breastbone. Using poultry shears, cut through the breastbone, then cut through the ribcage following the outline of the breast meat. Repeat on the other side. Trim off any flaps of skin or fat.

COOKING POULTRY

Ensure poultry is cooked thoroughly. To test, pierce the thickest part of the thigh with a skewer. Only when the juices run clear – with no trace of pink – is the poultry cooked. Chill leftover meat as soon as possible and eat within two days.

ROASTING TIMES FOR POULTRY

Bird	Oven temperature	Cooking time	Quantities for roasting
Poussin	200°C (180°C fan oven) mark 6	Allow 25–40 minutes total roasting time	Allow 1 bird per person
Chicken	200°C (180°C fan oven) mark 6	Allow 20 mins per 450g (1lb)	A 2kg (4$\frac{1}{2}$lb) bird will serve about 5 people
Capon	200°C (180°C fan oven) mark 6	Allow 20 mins per 450g (1lb)	A 3kg (6$\frac{1}{2}$lb) bird will serve 6–8 people
Duck	200°C (180°C fan oven) mark 6	Allow 20 mins per 450g (1lb)	Allow 450g (1lb) per person
Goose	220°C (200°C fan oven) mark 7	Allow 35 minutes per 1kg (2$\frac{1}{4}$lb)	A 4.5kg (10lb) goose will serve 6–8 people
Guinea fowl	200°C (180°C fan oven) mark 6	Allow 35 minutes per 1kg (2$\frac{1}{4}$lb), plus 15 minutes	1 bird will serve 2–4 people
Turkey	180°C (160°C fan oven) mark 4	Allow 45 minutes per 1kg (2$\frac{1}{4}$lb), plus 20 minutes	A 3.5kg (7$\frac{3}{4}$lb) turkey will serve about 10 people

CHICKEN AND OTHER BIRDS

Duck
Domesticated duck has rich, dark, meaty flesh. It can also be very fatty. Roast whole birds; portions can be pan-fried, braised, casseroled or cut into strips and stir-fried. Wild duck has a stronger, more gamey flavour. Prepare and cook in the same way.

Capon
Strictly speaking, capons are cocks that were castrated when young, then fattened up. The practice is now illegal in the UK, but the term is used for larger birds. Cook as for chicken.

Guinea fowl
With darker flesh than chicken and a slightly gamey flavour, guinea fowl can be used in most chicken or pheasant recipes. Look for birds with a plump breast and smooth-skinned legs; one bird will feed 2–4 people. Bard with strips of bacon to roast or spatchcock.

Chicken
The breast is fine-textured, lean and white; leg meat is darker and more flavoursome. Chicken is available fresh and frozen. Whole birds can be roasted, casseroled or pot-roasted, or spatchcocked and grilled or barbecued. Portions can be pan-fried, coated and deep-fried, grilled, steamed, baked, braised, casseroled or cut into strips and stir-fried. **Boiling** chickens are usually older and are better suited to long, slow cooking. **Corn-fed** chickens have bright yellow flesh and, often, an improved flavour.

Poussin
These small, tender birds, 4–8 weeks old, weigh only about 450g (1lb) and have a mild flavour. Usually sold whole, oven ready; one bird will feed one person. Cook in the same way as chicken, but for a shorter time.

Turkey
Oven-ready turkeys are available from 2.3kg (5lb) to 9kg (20lb). The flavour of a fresh turkey is superior to that of frozen. Also available are self-basting turkeys, turkey steaks, escalopes and mince. Similar cuts of chicken and turkey can be cooked in the same way.

Goose
Look for a young goose that is less than a year old (older geese have dark yellow fat.) A 'green goose' is less than 3–4 months old; a 'gosling' is less than 6 months old. The flesh is dark, rich, meaty and fatty, and suits a sharp, acidic sauce such as gooseberry.

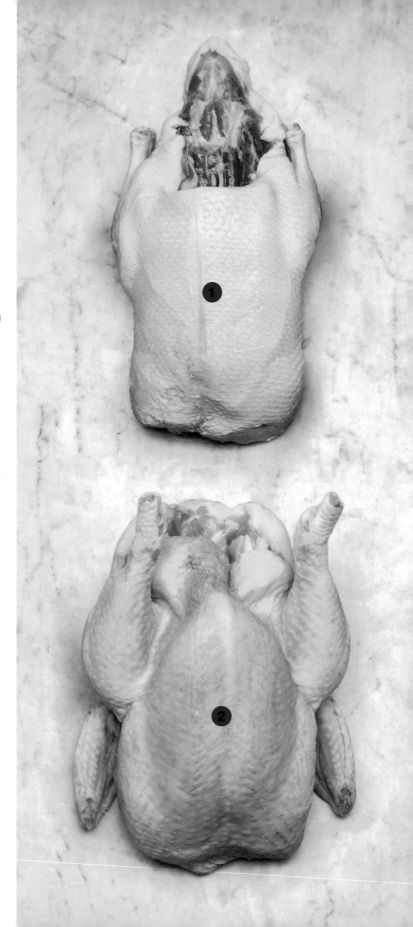

CLASSIC ROAST CHICKEN

Serves 5
Preparation 30 minutes
Cooking time about 1 hour 20 minutes, plus resting

1.4kg (3lb) chicken
2 garlic cloves
1 onion, cut into wedges
2 tsp sea salt
2 tsp ground black pepper
4 fresh parsley sprigs
4 fresh tarragon sprigs
2 bay leaves
50g (2oz) butter, cut into cubes
salt and ground black pepper

For the stuffing
40g (1½oz) butter
1 small onion, chopped
1 garlic clove, crushed
75g (3oz) fresh white breadcrumbs
finely grated zest and juice of 1 small lemon, halves reserved
    for the chicken
2 tbsp each freshly chopped flat-leafed parsley and tarragon
1 medium egg yolk

For the gravy
200ml (7fl oz) white wine
1 tbsp Dijon mustard
450ml (¾ pint) hot chicken stock
25g (1oz) butter, mixed with 25g (1oz) plain flour
    (beurre manié, see Cook's Tip)

1 Preheat the oven to 190°C (170°C fan oven) mark 5. To make the stuffing, melt the butter in a pan, add the onion and garlic, and fry for 5–10 minutes until soft. Cool, then add the remaining ingredients, stirring in the egg yolk last. Season well.
2 Put the chicken on a board, breast upwards, then put the garlic, onion, reserved lemon halves and half the salt, pepper and herb sprigs into the body cavity.
3 Lift the loose skin at the neck and fill the cavity with stuffing. Turn the bird on to its breast and pull the neck flap over the opening to cover the stuffing. Rest the wing tips across it and truss the chicken (see page 133). Weigh the stuffed bird to calculate the cooking time, and allow 20 minutes per 450g (1lb), plus an extra 20 minutes.
4 Put the chicken on a rack in a roasting tin. Season with the remaining salt and pepper, then top with the remaining herbs and the bay leaves. Dot with the butter and roast, basting halfway through, until cooked and the juices run clear when the thickest part of the thigh is pierced with a skewer.

5 Put the chicken on a serving dish and cover with foil. Leave to rest while you make the gravy. Pour off all but about 3 tbsp fat from the tin, put the tin over a high heat, add the wine and boil for 2 minutes. Add the mustard and hot stock and bring back to the boil. Gradually whisk in knobs of the butter mixture until smooth, then season with salt and pepper. Carve the chicken and serve with the stuffing and gravy.

COOK'S TIP
Beurre Manié A beurre manié is a mixture of equal parts of softened butter and flour that has been kneaded together to form a paste. It is used to thicken sauces and stews and is whisked in towards the end of cooking, then boiled briefly to allow it to thicken.

NUTRITION PER SERVING
682 cals | 49g fat (21g sats) | 17g carbs | 1g salt

MEDITERRANEAN ROAST CHICKEN

Serves 4
Preparation 40 minutes
Cooking time about 1½ hours

900g (2lb) floury potatoes, such as Maris Piper,
  cut into chunks
125g (4oz) butter, softened
4 tbsp freshly chopped sage leaves, stalks reserved,
  plus extra leaves
4 tbsp freshly chopped thyme, stalks reserved,
  plus extra sprigs
1.4kg (3lb) chicken
juice of 1 lemon, halves reserved
2 fennel bulbs, cut into wedges
1 red onion, cut into wedges
salt and ground black pepper

1 Preheat the oven to 190°C (170°C fan oven) mark 5. Put the potatoes into a large pan of lightly salted cold water and bring to the boil. Cook for 5 minutes.

2 Meanwhile, put the butter into a bowl and mix in the chopped sage and thyme. Season well.

3 Put the chicken on a board and push the lemon halves and herb stalks into the cavity. Ease your fingers under the skin of the neck end to separate the breast skin from the flesh, then push the herby butter up under the skin, reserving a little. Season well.

4 Put the chicken into a large roasting tin, pour the lemon juice over it, then top with the extra sage and thyme and the reserved butter. Drain the potatoes and shake in a colander to roughen their edges.

5 Put the potatoes around the chicken with the fennel and red onion. Roast in the oven for 1 hour 20 minutes or until the juices run clear when the thickest part of the thigh is pierced with a skewer. Carve and serve with the vegetables.

NUTRITION PER SERVING
843 cals | 58g fat (26g sats) | 42g carbs | 0.9g salt

CHICKEN IN A POT

Serves 6
Preparation 20 minutes
Cooking time 1 hour 40 minutes

2 tbsp olive oil
1 large onion, cut into wedges
2 rindless streaky bacon rashers, chopped
1 chicken, about 1.6kg (3½ lb)
6 carrots
2 small turnips, cut into wedges
1 garlic clove, crushed
bouquet garni (1 bay leaf, a few fresh parsley and thyme
    sprigs)
600ml (1 pint) hot chicken stock
100ml (3½ fl oz) dry white wine
12 button mushrooms
3 tbsp freshly chopped flat-leafed parsley
salt and ground black pepper
mashed potatoes to serve (optional)

1 Heat the oil in a non-stick flameproof casserole. Add the onion and bacon, and fry for 5 minutes or until golden. Remove and put to one side.
2 Add the whole chicken to the casserole and fry for 10 minutes, turning carefully to brown all over. Remove and put to one side.
3 Preheat the oven to 200°C (180°C fan oven) mark 6. Add the carrots, turnips and garlic to the casserole and fry for 5 minutes, then add the onion and bacon. Put the chicken back into the casserole, add the bouquet garni, hot stock and wine, and season with salt and pepper. Bring to a simmer, then cover the casserole and cook in the oven for 30 minutes.
4 Remove the casserole from the oven and add the mushrooms. Baste the chicken, then re-cover and cook for a further 50 minutes.
5 Lift out the chicken, then stir the parsley into the cooking liquid. Carve the chicken and serve with the vegetables and cooking liquid, and mashed potatoes, if you like.

TRY SOMETHING DIFFERENT
Use chicken pieces such as drumsticks or thighs, reducing the cooking time in step 4 to 20 minutes.

NUTRITION PER SERVING
474 cals | 33g fat (9g sats) | 6g carbs | 0.6g salt

CHICKEN AND MUSHROOM PIES

Serves 4
Preparation 20 minutes, plus chilling
Cooking time 55 minutes–1 hour 5 minutes

2 tbsp olive oil
1 trimmed leek, about 200g (7oz), finely sliced
2–3 garlic cloves, crushed
350g (12oz) boneless, skinless chicken thighs, cut into
    2.5cm (1in) cubes
200g (7oz) chestnut mushrooms, sliced
150ml (¼ pint) double cream
2 tbsp freshly chopped thyme
500g pack puff pastry, thawed if frozen
plain flour to dust
1 medium egg, beaten
salt and ground black pepper

1 Heat the oil in a pan. Add the leek and fry over a medium heat for 5 minutes. Add the garlic and cook for 1 minute. Add the chicken and continue to cook for 8–10 minutes. Add the mushrooms and cook for 5 minutes or until all the juices have disappeared.
2 Pour the cream into the pan and bring to the boil. Cook for 5 minutes to make a thick sauce. Add the thyme, then season well with salt and pepper. Tip into a bowl and leave to cool.
3 Roll out the pastry on a lightly floured surface until it measures 33cm (13in) square. Cut into four squares. Brush the edges with water and spoon the chicken mixture into the middle of each square. Bring each corner of the square up to the middle to make a parcel. Crimp the edges to seal, leaving a small hole in the middle. Brush the pies with beaten egg, put on a baking sheet and chill for 20 minutes.
4 Preheat the oven to 200°C (180°C fan oven) mark 6. Cook the pies for 30–40 minutes until golden.

TRY SOMETHING DIFFERENT
For a vegetarian alternative, replace the chicken with 200g (7oz) cooked, peeled (or vacuum-packed) chestnuts, roughly chopped. Add another finely sliced leek and increase the quantity of mushrooms to 300g (11oz).

NUTRITION PER SERVING
805 cals | 58g fat (14g sats) | 49g carbs | 1.2g salt

COQ AU VIN

Serves 6
Preparation 15 minutes
Cooking time 2 hours

1 large chicken, jointed
 or 6–8 chicken joints
2 tbsp well-seasoned flour
100g (3½oz) butter
125g (4oz) lean bacon, diced
1 onion, quartered
1 carrot, quartered
4 tbsp brandy
600ml (1 pint) red wine
1 garlic clove, crushed
1 bouquet garni (1 bay leaf, a few
 fresh parsley and thyme sprigs)
1 sugar lump
2 tbsp vegetable oil
450g (1lb) button onions
a pinch of sugar
1 tsp wine vinegar
225g (8oz) button mushrooms
6 slices white bread, crusts removed
salt and ground black pepper

1 Coat the chicken pieces with 1 tbsp seasoned flour. Melt 25g (1oz) butter in a flameproof casserole. Add the chicken and fry gently until golden brown on all sides. Add the bacon, onion and carrot, and fry until softened.

2 Heat the brandy in a small pan, pour over the chicken and ignite, shaking the pan so that all the chicken pieces are covered in flames. Pour in the wine and stir to dislodge any sediment from the base of the casserole. Add the garlic, bouquet garni and sugar lump, and bring to the boil. Reduce the heat, cover and simmer for 1–1½ hours until the chicken is cooked through.

3 Meanwhile, melt 25g (1oz) butter with 1 tsp oil in a frying pan. Add the button onions and fry until they begin to brown. Add the pinch of sugar and the vinegar together with 1 tbsp water. Cover and simmer for 10–15 minutes until just tender. Keep warm.

4 Melt 25g (1oz) butter with 2 tsp oil in a pan. Add the mushrooms and cook for a few minutes, then turn off the heat and keep warm.

5 Remove the chicken from the casserole and put in a dish. Surround with the onions and mushrooms and keep hot.

6 Discard the bouquet garni. Skim the excess fat from the cooking liquid, then boil the liquid in the casserole briskly for 3–5 minutes to reduce it.

7 Add the remaining oil to the fat in the frying pan and fry the pieces of bread until golden brown on both sides. Cut each slice into triangles.

8 Work the remaining butter and flour to make a beurre manié (see Cook's Tip page 136). Remove the casserole from the heat and add small pieces of the beurre manié to the cooking liquid. Stir until smooth, then put back on to the heat and bring just to the boil. The sauce should be thick and shiny. Take off the heat and adjust the seasoning. Return the chicken, onions and mushrooms to the casserole and stir to combine. Garnish with the fried bread and serve.

NUTRITION PER SERVING
740 cals | 44g fat (17g sats) | 26g carbs | 1.8g salt

CHICKEN CASSEROLE

Serves 6
Preparation 15 minutes
Cooking time 50 minutes

1 fresh rosemary sprig
2 bay leaves
1.4kg (3lb) chicken
1 red onion, cut into wedges
2 carrots, cut into chunks
2 leeks, trimmed and cut into chunks
2 celery sticks, cut into chunks
12 baby new potatoes
900ml (1½ pints) hot chicken stock
200g (7oz) green beans
salt and ground black pepper

1 Preheat the oven to 180°C (160°C fan oven) mark 4. Put the herbs and chicken into a large, flameproof casserole. Add the onion, carrots, leeks, celery, potatoes, hot stock and seasoning. Bring to the boil, then cook in the oven for 45 minutes or until the chicken is cooked through. To test the chicken, pierce the thickest part of the leg with a knife; the juices should run clear.

2 Add the beans and cook for 5 minutes. Remove the chicken and spoon the vegetables into six bowls. Carve the chicken and divide among the bowls, then ladle the cooking liquid over the top.

TRY SOMETHING DIFFERENT
Omit the baby new potatoes and serve with mashed potatoes.

NUTRITION PER SERVING 323 cals | 18g fat (5g sats) | 17g carbs | 0.9g salt

STUFFED CHICKEN BREASTS

Serves 4
Preparation 5 minutes
Cooking time 20 minutes

vegetable oil to grease
150g (5oz) ball mozzarella
4 skinless chicken breasts, about 125g (4oz) each
4 sage leaves
8 slices Parma ham (see Cook's Tip page 65)
ground black pepper
new potatoes and spinach to serve

1 Preheat the oven to 200°C (180°C fan oven) mark 6. Lightly oil a baking tray. Slice the ball mozzarella into eight, then put two slices on top of each chicken breast. Top each one with a sage leaf.

2 Wrap each piece of chicken in two slices of Parma ham, covering the mozzarella. Season with pepper.

3 Put on the prepared baking sheet and cook in the oven for 20 minutes or until the chicken is cooked through. Serve with new potatoes and spinach.

COOK'S TIP
Sage has a strong, pungent taste, so you need only a little to flavour the chicken. Don't be tempted to add more than just one leaf to each chicken breast or it will overpower the finished dish.

NUTRITION PER SERVING 297 cals | 13g fat (7g sats) | trace carbs | 1.4g salt

TARRAGON CHICKEN

Serves 4
Preparation 10 minutes
Cooking time 45–55 minutes

1 tbsp olive oil
4 chicken thighs
1 onion, finely chopped
1 fennel bulb, finely chopped
juice of ½ lemon
200ml (7fl oz) hot chicken stock
200ml (7fl oz) crème fraîche
1 small bunch of tarragon,
    roughly chopped
salt and ground black pepper
new potatoes and broccoli
    to serve

1 Preheat the oven to 200°C (180°C fan oven) mark 6. Heat the oil in a large flameproof casserole over a medium-high heat. Add the chicken thighs and fry for 5 minutes or until browned, then remove and put them to one side to keep warm.
2 Add the onion to the casserole and fry for 5 minutes, then add the fennel and cook for 5–10 minutes until the vegetables are softened.
3 Add the lemon juice to the casserole, followed by the hot stock. Bring to a simmer and cook until the sauce is reduced by half.
4 Stir in the crème fraîche and put the chicken back into the casserole. Stir once to mix, then cover and cook in the oven for 25–30 minutes. Stir the tarragon into the sauce, season with salt and pepper and serve with potatoes and broccoli.

NUTRITION PER SERVING 334 cals |
26g fat (15g sats) | 3g carbs | 0.5g salt

LEMON CHICKEN

Serves 4
Preparation 2 minutes
Cooking time 6–8 minutes

4 small skinless chicken breasts, about
    125g (4oz) each
juice of 2 lemons
2 tbsp olive oil
4–6 tbsp demerara sugar
salt
green salad and lemon wedges
    to serve

1 Put the chicken into a large bowl and season with salt. Add the lemon juice and oil and stir to mix.
2 Preheat the grill to medium. Spread the chicken out on a large baking sheet and sprinkle over 2–3 tbsp demerara sugar. Grill for about 3–4 minutes or until caramelised, then turn the chicken over, sprinkle with the remaining sugar and grill until the chicken is golden and cooked through.
3 Divide the chicken among four plates and serve with a green salad and lemon wedges.

NUTRITION PER SERVING 231 cals |
7g fat (1g sats) | 13g carbs | 0.2g salt

CHICKEN KIEV

Serves 6
Preparation 15 minutes, plus chilling
Cooking time 45 minutes

175g (6oz) butter, softened
grated zest of ½ lemon
1 tbsp lemon juice
1 tbsp freshly chopped parsley
1 garlic clove, crushed
6 large boneless, skinless chicken breasts
25g (1oz) seasoned flour
1 medium egg, beaten
125g (4oz) fresh breadcrumbs
vegetable oil for deep-frying
salt and ground black pepper
potato wedges and peas to serve

1 Put the butter, lemon zest and juice, parsley, garlic and salt and pepper to taste into a bowl and beat well to combine. (Alternatively, whiz in a food processor.) Form into a roll, cover and chill for at least 1 hour.

2 Put the chicken breasts on a flat surface and, using a meat mallet or rolling pin, pound them to an even thickness. Cut the butter into six pieces and put one piece on the centre of each chicken breast. Roll up, folding the ends in to enclose the butter completely. Secure the rolls with wooden cocktail sticks.

3 Put the seasoned flour, beaten egg and breadcrumbs in three separate flat dishes. Coat each chicken roll with the flour, then turn them in the beaten egg and coat them with breadcrumbs, patting the crumbs firmly on to the chicken.

4 Put the rolls on to a baking sheet, cover lightly with non-stick or greaseproof paper and chill in the fridge for 2 hours or until required, to allow the coating to dry.

5 Heat the oil in a deep-fryer to 160°C (test by frying a small cube of bread; it should brown in 60 seconds). Put two chicken rolls into a frying basket and lower into the oil. Fry for 15 minutes – the chicken is cooked when it is browned and firm when pressed with a fork. Do not pierce.

6 Remove the rolls from the fryer, drain on kitchen paper and keep them warm while you cook the remaining chicken. Remove the cocktail sticks before serving.

7 Serve with potato wedges and peas.

TRY SOMETHING DIFFERENT
Spicy Chicken Kiev To make a spicy butter filling, sauté 1 finely chopped shallot with 2 tsp cayenne pepper in 1 tbsp butter until soft but not brown. Cool. Stir in 1 tbsp freshly chopped parsley. Combine with 175g (6oz) softened butter and season. Form into a roll, cover and chill for at least 1 hour as step 1, then continue with the recipe.

NUTRITION PER SERVING
594 cals **|** 41g fat (19g sats) **|** 20g carbs **|** 1.2g salt

CLASSIC FRIED CHICKEN

Serves 4
Preparation 5 minutes
Cooking time 35–45 minutes

4 chicken joints or pieces
3 tbsp plain flour
50g (2oz) butter or 3 tbsp
    vegetable oil
salt and ground black pepper
green salad to serve

1 Wipe the chicken joints and pat dry with kitchen paper. Season with salt and pepper.
2 Toss the chicken in the flour until completely coated.
3 Heat the butter or oil in a large frying pan or flameproof casserole over a high heat. Add the chicken and cook until golden brown on both sides. Reduce the heat and cook for 30–40 minutes until tender. Drain on kitchen paper. Serve with a green salad.

> **COOK'S TIP**
> To ensure that the chicken pieces remain moist, the surface should be browned at a high temperature to seal in all the juices and give a good colour; the heat should then be reduced for the remaining cooking time.

NUTRITION PER SERVING   565 cals |
41.7g fat (9.9g sats) | 8.8g carbs | 0.5g salt

STICKY CHICKEN THIGHS

Serves 4
Preparation time 5 minutes
Cooking time 20 minutes

1 garlic clove, crushed
1 tbsp clear honey
1 tbsp Thai sweet chilli sauce
4 chicken thighs
rice (optional) and green salad
    to serve

1 Preheat the oven to 200°C (180°C fan oven) mark 6. Put the garlic into a bowl with the honey and chilli sauce and stir to mix. Add the chicken thighs and toss to coat.
2 Put the chicken into a roasting tin and roast in the oven for 15–20 minutes until golden and cooked through and the juices run clear when the thighs are pierced with a skewer. Serve with rice, if you like, and a crisp green salad.

TRY SOMETHING DIFFERENT

- **Italian Marinade** Mix 1 crushed garlic clove with 4 tbsp olive oil, the juice of 1 lemon and 1 tsp dried oregano. If you like, leave to marinate for 1–2 hours before cooking.
- **Oriental Marinade** Mix together 2 tbsp soy sauce, 1 tsp demerara sugar, 2 tbsp dry sherry or apple juice, 1 tsp finely chopped fresh root ginger and 1 crushed garlic clove.
- **Honey and Mustard Marinade** Mix 2 tbsp grain mustard, 3 tbsp clear honey and the zest and juice of 1 lemon.
- Use sausages instead of chicken, if you like.

NUTRITION PER SERVING   218 cals |
12g fat (3g sats) | 5g carbs | 0.4g salt

TANDOORI CHICKEN WITH CUCUMBER RAITA

Serves 4
Preparation 45 minutes, plus marinating
Cooking time 20 minutes

4 tbsp groundnut oil, plus extra to grease
3 × 150g cartons natural yogurt
juice of ½ lemon
4 boneless, skinless chicken breasts, about 600g (1lb 5oz),
    cut into finger-width pieces
½ cucumber
salt and ground black pepper
fresh mint leaves to garnish

For the tandoori paste
24 garlic cloves, about 125g (4oz), crushed
5cm (2in) piece fresh root ginger, peeled and chopped
3 tbsp each coriander seeds, cumin seeds, ground fenugreek
    and paprika
3 red chillies, seeded and chopped (see Cook's Tip, page 69)
3 tsp English mustard
2 tbsp tomato purée
1 tsp salt

1 Put all the ingredients for the tandoori paste into a food
processor or blender with 8 tbsp water and blend to a paste.
Divide the paste into three equal portions, freeze two (see
Freezing Tip) and put the other in a large bowl.
2 To make the tandoori chicken, add 2 tbsp oil, 2 cartons of
yogurt and the lemon juice to the tandoori paste. Add the
chicken and stir well to coat. Cover the bowl, chill and leave
to marinate for at least 4 hours.
3 Preheat the oven to 220°C (200°C fan oven) mark 7.
Oil a roasting tin. Put the chicken in it, drizzle the remaining
oil over the chicken and roast in the oven for 20 minutes or
until cooked through.
4 Meanwhile, prepare the raita. Whisk the remaining carton
of yogurt. Using a vegetable peeler, scrape the cucumber into
very thin strips. Put the strips in a bowl and pour the whisked
yogurt over them. Season, then chill until ready to serve.
Garnish the cucumber raita with mint. Sprinkle the chicken
with mint and serve with the raita.

FREEZING TIP
➤ To freeze the paste, at the end of step 1, put two of the
   portions of tandoori paste into separate freezer bags and
   freeze. They will keep for up to three months.
➤ To use the frozen paste, put the paste in a microwave and
   cook on Defrost for 1 minute 20 seconds (based on a
   900W oven), or thaw at a cool room temperature for
   1 hour.

NUTRITION PER SERVING
399 cals | 20g fat (4g sats) | 15g carbs | 2g salt

CHICKEN TIKKA MASALA

Serves 4
Preparation 15 minutes
Cooking time 30 minutes

2 tbsp vegetable oil
1 onion, finely sliced
2 garlic cloves, crushed
6 boneless, skinless chicken thighs, cut
    into strips
2 tbsp tikka masala curry paste
200g can chopped tomatoes
450ml (³/₄ pint) hot vegetable stock
225g (8oz) baby spinach leaves
fresh coriander leaves to garnish
basmati rice, Sweet Mango Chutney
    (see page 485) and poppadoms to
    serve

1 Heat the oil in a large pan. Add the onion and fry over a medium heat for 5–7 minutes until golden. Add the garlic and chicken strips, and stir-fry for about 5 minutes or until golden.
2 Stir in the curry paste, then add the tomatoes and hot stock. Bring to the boil, then reduce the heat, cover the pan and simmer over a low heat for 15 minutes or until the chicken is cooked through.
3 Add the spinach to the curry, stir and cook until the leaves have just wilted. Garnish with coriander and serve with rice, mango chutney and poppadoms.

NUTRITION PER SERVING 297 cals |
17g fat (4g sats) | 4g carbs | 0.6g salt

THAI GREEN CHICKEN CURRY

Serves 6
Preparation 10 minutes
Cooking time 15 minutes

2 tsp vegetable oil
1 green chilli, seeded and finely
    chopped (see Cook's Tips, page 69)
4cm (1¹/₂ in) piece fresh root ginger,
    peeled and finely grated
1 lemongrass stalk, trimmed and cut
    into three pieces
225g (8oz) brown-cap or oyster
    mushrooms
1 tbsp Thai green curry paste
300ml (¹/₂ pint) coconut milk
150ml (¹/₄ pint) chicken stock
1 tbsp Thai fish sauce
1 tsp light soy sauce
350g (12oz) boneless, skinless chicken
    breasts, cut into bite-size pieces
350g (12oz) cooked peeled
    large prawns (optional)

fresh coriander sprigs to garnish
rice to serve

1 Heat the oil in a wok or large frying pan. Add the chilli, ginger, lemongrass and mushrooms and stir-fry for about 3 minutes or until the mushrooms begin to turn golden. Add the curry paste and fry for a further 1 minute.
2 Pour in the coconut milk, stock, fish sauce and soy sauce and bring to the boil. Stir in the chicken, then reduce the heat and simmer for about 8 minutes or until the chicken is cooked.
3 Add the prawns, if using, and cook for a further 1 minute. Garnish with coriander sprigs and serve immediately with rice.

NUTRITION PER SERVING 132 cals |
2g fat (0g sats) | 4g carbs | 1.4g salt

CORONATION CHICKEN

Serves 6
Preparation 20 minutes
Cooking time about 50 minutes, plus chilling

1 tbsp vegetable oil
1 onion, chopped
1 tbsp each ground coriander and ground cumin
1½ tsp ground turmeric
1½ tsp paprika
150ml (¼ pint) dry white wine
500ml (18fl oz) chicken stock
6 boneless, skinless chicken breasts or thighs
2 bay leaves
2 fresh thyme sprigs
2 fresh parsley sprigs
salt and ground black pepper
3–4 tbsp freshly chopped flat-leafed parsley to garnish
mixed leaf salad and French bread to serve

For the dressing
150ml (¼ pint) mayonnaise (see page 29)
5 tbsp natural yogurt
2 tbsp mango chutney
125g (4oz) ready-to-eat dried apricots, chopped
juice of ½ lemon

1 Heat the oil in a large, heavy-based pan, add the onion and fry for 5–10 minutes until softened and golden. Add the spices and cook, stirring, for 1–2 minutes.

2 Pour in the wine, bring to the boil and let it bubble for 5 minutes to reduce right down. Add the stock and bring to the boil again.

3 Season the chicken with salt and pepper, then add to the pan with the bay leaves and herb sprigs. Cover and bring to the boil. Reduce the heat to low and poach the chicken for 25 minutes or until cooked through. Cool quickly by plunging the base of the pan into a sink of cold water, replacing the water as it warms up.

4 Meanwhile, to make the dressing, mix the mayonnaise, yogurt and mango chutney together in a bowl. Drain the cooled stock from the chicken and whisk 200ml (7fl oz) into the mayonnaise mixture. Add the apricots and lemon juice, and season well.

5 Roughly chop the chicken into bite-size pieces, then stir into the curried mayonnaise. Cover and chill until required. Garnish with chopped parsley and serve with a mixed leaf salad and French bread.

NUTRITION PER SERVING
425 cals | 26g fat (4g sats) | 14g carbs | 0.6g salt

ROAST TURKEY WITH PARSLEY, SAGE AND THYME

Serves 16
Preparation 40 minutes, plus chilling
Cooking time 3³/₄ hours

6.3kg (14lb) turkey
2 small red onions, cut into wedges
2 lemons, cut into wedges
6 whole garlic cloves
8 fresh thyme sprigs
8 fresh sage leaves
8 fresh flat-leafed parsley sprigs
250ml (9fl oz) olive oil
roast vegetables to serve

For the seasoning
1 tbsp whole pink peppercorns
2 tsp sea salt
2 tbsp paprika
2 tbsp celery salt

For the stuffing
4 tbsp olive oil
2 large onions, finely chopped
4 garlic cloves, crushed
150g (5oz) fresh white breadcrumbs
75g (3oz) medium cornmeal or polenta
100g (3¹/₂oz) hazelnuts, toasted and chopped
finely grated zest of 2 lemons and juice of 1 lemon
4 tbsp freshly chopped flat-leafed parsley
4 tbsp freshly chopped sage
2 medium eggs, lightly beaten
salt and ground black pepper

1 To make the stuffing, heat the oil in a pan. Add the onions and garlic, and fry gently for 10 minutes to soften but not brown. Tip into a bowl to cool. Meanwhile, put the breadcrumbs, cornmeal or polenta, hazelnuts, lemon zest, parsley, sage and eggs into a large bowl and squeeze over the lemon juice. Add the cooled onion and garlic, and season with salt and pepper. Stir to bind together and leave to cool.

2 To make the seasoning, put the peppercorns, sea salt, paprika and celery salt into a pestle and mortar and pound to crush, or whiz in a mini processor. Stand the turkey upright on a board, with the parson's nose (the rear end) facing upwards. Sprinkle the inside cavity with 1 tbsp of the peppercorn seasoning, then pack the cavity with half the onions and lemon wedges, garlic cloves, thyme and sage and all the parsley sprigs.

3 Sit the turkey with the parson's nose facing away from you. Lift up the loose skin at the neck end with one hand and, using the other, fill the cavity with handfuls of cold stuffing. Turn the turkey over on to its breast, then lift the neck flap up and over the stuffing to cover and bring the wing tips round on top.

4 Thread a trussing needle with 2m (6ft) fine string and sew the neck flap to the turkey. Push the skewer firmly through the wings, twist the string around the ends and pull to tighten so that both wings are snug against the breast. Turn the turkey over, tuck in the parson's nose, cross the legs together, then bring the string up and over the legs and wrap around tightly, finishing with a double knot to secure. Cut off any excess.

5 Pour the olive oil into a large roasting tin. Immerse a piece of muslin, about 60cm (24in), in it to coat completely, then stretch it out, with the edges overhanging the tin. Sit the turkey on top and sprinkle with the remaining peppercorn seasoning. Scatter over the remaining thyme and sage, then arrange the remaining lemon and onion wedges and the garlic cloves around the bird. Bring the muslin up and over the turkey to wrap completely, then turn it over so that it's breast side down in the tin. Over-wrap with clingfilm and leave to chill overnight in the bottom of the fridge. Remember to take it out 30 minutes before cooking so that it has time to come to room temperature.

6 Remove the muslin and keep the turkey breast side down. Preheat the oven to 180°C (160°C fan oven) mark 4. Roast the turkey for about 3³/₄ hours, basting occasionally to keep the flesh moist. Turn the turkey over after cooking for 1 hour 50 minutes. To check that the turkey is cooked, pierce the thickest part of the thigh with a skewer; the juices should run clear. Serve with roasted vegetables.

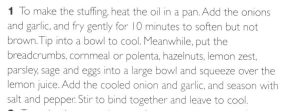

NUTRITION PER SERVING
280 cals | 10g fat (2g sats) | 11g carbs | 2.2g salt

TURKEY CURRY

Serves 4
Preparation 15 minutes
Cooking time 35 minutes

2 tbsp oil
1 large onion, chopped
2 garlic cloves, finely chopped
1 tsp ground turmeric
$^1/_2$ tsp chilli powder
1$^1/_2$ tsp ground cumin
1$^1/_2$ tsp ground coriander
400g can chopped tomatoes
$^1/_2$ tsp salt
600g (1lb 5oz) cooked turkey
1 tsp garam masala
150ml ($^1/_4$ pint) thick yogurt
coriander to garnish
rice to serve

1 Heat the oil in a heavy-based pan, add the onion and garlic, and fry gently until softened and golden. Add the turmeric, chilli powder, cumin and coriander, and cook, stirring, for 1 minute.
2 Add the tomatoes and salt. Bring to the boil, cover and simmer for 20 minutes.
3 Remove any skin from the turkey, then cut into chunks. Add to the pan with the garam masala and 4 tbsp yogurt. Cover and cook gently for 10 minutes, then stir in the remaining yogurt. Garnish with coriander and serve with rice.

TRY SOMETHING DIFFERENT
- For a more intense flavour, fry 1 tsp black mustard seeds with the spices.
- Scatter over 2–3 tbsp chopped coriander to serve.

COOK'S TIP
This is an ideal recipe for using up turkey leftover from your Christmas meal.

NUTRITION PER SERVING
330 cals | 12g fat (4 sats) | 8g carbs | 0.4g salt

ROAST DUCK WITH ORANGE SAUCE

Serves 4
Preparation 50 minutes
Cooking time I hour 40 minutes, plus resting

2 large oranges
2 large fresh thyme sprigs
2.3kg (5lb) duck, with giblets if possible
4 tbsp vegetable oil
2 shallots, chopped
I tsp plain flour
600ml (1 pint) chicken stock
25g (1oz) caster sugar
2 tbsp red wine vinegar
100ml (3¹/₂ fl oz) fresh orange juice
100ml (3¹/₂ fl oz) fruity German white wine
2 tbsp orange liqueur, such as Grand Marnier (optional)
I tbsp lemon juice
salt and ground black pepper
glazed orange wedges (see Cook's Tip) to garnish
mangetouts and broccoli to serve

1 Preheat the oven to 200°C (180°C fan oven) mark 6. Using a zester, remove strips of zest from the oranges. Put half the zest into a pan of cold water, bring to the boil, then drain and put to one side. Remove the pith from both oranges and cut the flesh into segments.

2 Put the thyme and unblanched orange zest inside the duck and season. Rub the skin with 2 tbsp oil, sprinkle with salt and put, breast side up, on a rack over a roasting tin. Roast, basting every 20 minutes, for 1¹/₄–1¹/₂ hours until just cooked and the juices run clear when the thickest part of the thigh is pierced with a skewer. After 30 minutes, turn breast side down, then breast side up for the last 10 minutes.

3 Meanwhile, cut the gizzard, heart and neck into pieces. Heat the remaining 2 tbsp oil in a heavy-based pan. Add the giblets and fry until dark brown. Add the chopped shallots and flour, and cook for I minute. Pour in the stock, bring to the boil and bubble until reduced by half, then strain.

4 Put the sugar and vinegar into a heavy-based pan over a low heat until the sugar dissolves. Turn up the heat and cook until it forms a dark caramel. Pour in the orange juice and stir. Cool, cover and put to one side.

5 Lift the duck off the rack and keep warm. Skim all the fat off the juices to leave about 3 tbsp sediment. Stir the wine into the sediment, bring to the boil and bubble for 5 minutes or until syrupy. Add the stock mixture and orange mixture. Bring back to the boil and bubble until syrupy, skimming if necessary. To serve the sauce, add the blanched orange zest and segments. Add Grand Marnier, if using, and lemon juice to taste.

6 Carve the duck and garnish with the glazed orange wedges. Serve with the orange sauce, and steamed mangetouts and broccoli.

COOK'S TIPS

Glazed Oranges Preheat the grill. Quarter the oranges or cut into wedges. Dust with a little caster sugar and grill until caramelised.

— Some fat may be in the cavity of the duck, and should be pulled out before cooking. Most of the fat is under the skin and will melt out during cooking. Save it and use for roasting root vegetables.
— Whole ducks look large because they have a large cavity and carcass. They don't feed as many people as the size might suggest.

NUTRITION PER SERVING
561 cals | 38g fat (9g sats) | 20g carbs | 0.5g salt

PEKING-STYLE DUCK

Serves 4
Preparation 10 minutes, plus overnight drying
Cooking time about 1 hour

1.5–2kg (3lb 4oz–4¹/₂ lb) duck
1 tsp palm sugar or dark brown sugar
2 tbsp dark soy sauce

To serve
ready-made Chinese pancakes
8 tbsp plum sauce
8 tbsp hoisin sauce
1 bunch spring onions, sliced into thin 5cm (2in) strips
¹/₂ cucumber, seeded and cut into thin 5cm (2in) sticks

1 Put the duck into a very large bowl. Pour a kettleful of boiling water over it, ensuring the whole bird is doused. Remove and dry inside and out with plenty of kitchen paper. Prick the skin all over with a fork, taking care not to pierce the flesh. Hang it up somewhere cool and airy to dry overnight, putting a bowl underneath to catch any drips.
2 Heat the oven to 190°C (170°C fan oven) gas mark 5. Mix the sugar with the soy sauce and rub over the duck. Leave to dry for 10 minutes. Put the duck on a wire rack set in a roasting tin and roast for 1 hour – do not baste.
3 Reheat the Chinese pancakes according to the pack instructions. Strip the skin and meat from the duck and put on a warmed serving plate. Put the remaining ingredients into separate bowls.
4 To assemble, spread a spoonful of plum or hoisin sauce on to a pancake, followed by strips of spring onion and cucumber and a layer of duck meat and skin. Roll up and enjoy.

COOK'S TIP
Chinese pancakes can be found in the ready-meal chiller aisle or freezer aisles of major supermarkets or at specialist Asian stores.

NUTRITION PER SERVING
761 cals | 42g fat (11g sats) | 11g carbs | 1.2g salt

ROAST GUINEA FOWL

Serves 4
Preparation 20 minutes, plus marinating
Cooking time 1 hour 10 minutes, plus resting

1 guinea fowl
grated zest and juice of 1 lemon, and
    1 lemon quartered lengthways
3 bay leaves
5 fresh thyme sprigs
1 tbsp black peppercorns, lightly crushed
25g (1oz) butter
150ml (¼ pint) hot chicken stock
roast potatoes and green beans to serve

For the gravy
2 tbsp redcurrant jelly
100ml (3½ fl oz) dry white wine
salt and ground black pepper

1 Put the guinea fowl into a bowl and add the lemon zest and juice, bay leaves, thyme sprigs and peppercorns. Cover, chill and leave to marinate for 1 hour. Preheat the oven to 200°C (180°C fan oven) mark 6.
2 Put the bird into a roasting tin, breast side down, put the lemon quarters and the butter into the cavity, pour the hot stock over and roast in the oven for 50 minutes.
3 Turn the guinea fowl breast side up and continue to roast for about 20 minutes or until cooked and the juices run clear when the thigh is pierced with a skewer.
4 Put the guinea fowl on a board, cover with foil and leave to rest for 10 minutes.
5 To make the gravy, put the roasting tin on the hob and scrape up the juices. Add the redcurrant jelly, wine and 50ml (2fl oz) water and bring to the boil. Reduce the heat and simmer for 3–5 minutes. Season well. Carve the guinea fowl and serve with the gravy, roast potatoes and green beans.

NUTRITION PER SERVING
585 cals | 27g fat (11g sats) | 5g carbs | 0.7g salt

ROAST GOOSE WITH WILD RICE AND CRANBERRY STUFFING

Serves 6
Preparation 45 minutes
Cooking time about 3 hours, plus resting

5kg (11lb) goose (with giblets for stock)
Wild Rice and Cranberry Stuffing, thawed if frozen
    (see page 13)
25g (1oz) butter, plus extra to grease
3 red-skinned apples
4 fresh sage sprigs, plus extra to garnish
2 tbsp golden caster sugar
salt and ground black pepper

For the gravy
2 tbsp plain flour
150ml (¼ pint) red wine
600ml (1 pint) giblet stock (see Cook's Tip, page 11)
2 tbsp redcurrant jelly

1 To make the goose easier to carve, remove the wishbone from the neck by lifting the flap and cutting around the bone with a small knife. Remove the wishbone. Using your fingers, ease the skin away from the flesh to make room for the stuffing, then put the goose on a tray in the sink and pour a generous amount of freshly boiled water over, then pat dry with kitchen paper.

2 Preheat the oven to 230°C (210°C fan oven) mark 8. Pack the neck of the goose with half the stuffing and secure the neck shut with skewers or by using a trussing needle with fine string. Put any remaining stuffing on to a buttered sheet of foil and wrap it up. Season the cavity of the bird with salt and pepper, then put 1 whole apple and the sage sprigs inside.

3 Put the goose on a rack in a roasting tin and season well with salt and pepper. Roast in the oven for 30 minutes, basting occasionally, then remove and set aside any excess fat. Reduce the oven temperature to 190°C (170°C fan oven) mark 5 and cook for a further 2½ hours, removing any excess fat every 20 minutes. Thirty minutes before the end of cooking, put the parcel of stuffing into the oven.

4 Test whether the goose is cooked by piercing the thigh with a skewer – the juices should run clear. Remove the goose from the oven and put it on a board. Cover with foil and leave to rest for at least 20 minutes.

5 Meanwhile, cut the remaining apples into thick wedges. Heat the butter in a heavy-based frying pan until it is no longer foaming. Add the apples and the sugar, and stir-fry over a high heat for 4–5 minutes until caramelised, then put to one side.

6 To make the gravy, drain all but 3 tbsp fat from the roasting tin. Add the flour and stir to make a smooth paste. Add the wine and boil for 5 minutes, then add the stock and redcurrant jelly, and mix well. Bring to the boil, then reduce the heat and simmer for 5 minutes. Strain before serving. Serve the goose, garnished with sage sprigs, with the stuffing and caramelised apples.

COOK'S TIP

→ Like ducks, geese have a large cavity and large carcass, so even a large bird will not feed as many people as a turkey of comparable size.

→ Try to collect the fat and use it, as you would duck fat, for roasting potatoes. The best way to collect the fat is to spoon it out of the roasting tin regularly during cooking and put it to one side.

NUTRITION PER SERVING
820 cals | 51g fat (18g sats) | 32g carbs | 1.7g salt

POUSSINS WITH PANCETTA, ARTICHOKE AND POTATO SALAD

Serves 6
Preparation 20 minutes, plus overnight marinating
Cooking time 1 hour 40 minutes, plus resting

grated zest of 1 lemon
5 large fresh rosemary sprigs, leaves stripped
4 tbsp white wine vinegar
150ml (¼ pint) fruity white wine
4 garlic cloves, crushed
3 tbsp freshly chopped oregano or a pinch of dried oregano
290g jar marinated artichokes, drained, oil reserved
3 poussins, about 450g (1lb) each
½ tsp cayenne pepper
450g (1lb) new potatoes, quartered
225g (8oz) pancetta, prosciutto or streaky bacon, roughly chopped
350g (12oz) peppery salad leaves, such as watercress, mustard leaf and rocket
salt and ground black pepper

1 Put the lemon zest and rosemary leaves into a large bowl with the vinegar, wine, garlic, oregano and 4 tbsp oil from the artichokes. Stir well. Using a fork, pierce the skin of the poussins in five or six places, then season well with black pepper and the cayenne pepper. Put the birds, breast side down, in the bowl and spoon the marinade over them. Cover and chill overnight.
2 Cook the potatoes in lightly salted boiling water for 2 minutes. Drain. Preheat the oven to 200°C (180°C fan oven) mark 6.
3 Lift the poussins from the marinade and put, breast side up, into a large roasting tin. Scatter the potatoes, pancetta or bacon and artichokes around them and pour the marinade over. Cook for 1½ hours, basting occasionally, or until golden and cooked through.
4 Cut each poussin in half lengthways and keep warm. Toss the salad leaves with about 5 tbsp warm cooking juices. Arrange the leaves on warmed plates, then top with the potatoes, pancetta, artichokes and poussins.

COOK'S TIP
Use the oil drained from the artichokes to make a salad dressing for another meal.

NUTRITION PER SERVING
442 cals | 27g fat (8g sats) | 13g carbs | 1.5g salt

GAME

GAME

Wild animals or birds that are hunted for food are classified as game, although nowadays many types of game, including rabbit, pheasant, pigeon and quail, are farmed. Farmed game birds are available all year round, but true game birds are available only seasonally – usually in autumn and winter, and not during their breeding season in spring and early summer. Most game is protected by law and can only be hunted at certain times of the year; quail is now a protected species that cannot be hunted.

Fresh wild game meat is only available during the hunting season, but farmed varieties are usually obtainable all year round from specialist suppliers and some supermarkets. Farmed game is usually milder than its hunted counterpart. Most game birds and meat need to be hung to develop the flavour and tenderise the flesh. Game meats include venison, wild boar, rabbit and hare, and there are also the more unusual 'new meats' such as alligator and llama. All are good sources of protein but some can also be high in fats, particularly saturated fats, which everyone should aim to limit for health reasons.

CHOOSING GAME

Game birds are best eaten young. The feathers are a good guide, as young birds tend to have soft, even feathers. Young pheasants and partridges tend to have long, V-shaped wing feathers, whereas in older birds the same feathers tend to be rounded. Also look for a plump breast, smooth legs and pliable spurs. Look for birds that have not been extensively damaged by shot: telltale signs are red/black entrance wounds on the breast and/or broken legs. Game should be well cut and neatly trimmed.

You need smaller quantities when buying cuts of meat off the bone: allow 100–150g (3¹/₂–5oz) per person. For meat on the bone, allow slightly more, anything from 175–350g (6–12oz) per person depending on the cut.

Both wild and farmed rabbit are available. Farmed rabbit is often likened to chicken in flavour and texture while wild is much tougher.

Hare has darker, more strongly flavoured flesh and is not farmed. Young hare (leveret) is best and can be cooked quickly. Young animals have white fat, whereas that of older animals tends to be more yellow. Older hare requires long, slow cooking.

Boar is sold in various cuts, as well as minced and processed into products such as sausages. Meat from older deer has a better flavour than that from young but requires longer cooking.

BREEDING AND REARING

How farmed game is bred and reared has a significant effect on its health and welfare, and on taste and texture.

CATEGORIES FOR GAME MEATS

For game birds, see the details for poultry on page 132. Many game meats are now farmed, but as a general rule animals that have been allowed to grow naturally produce meat with a better flavour and texture.

The two main alternatives to intensively reared game are free-range and organic:

Free-range Different countries have their own guidelines as to what constitutes free-range rearing but, broadly speaking, the animals are allowed to roam and graze freely.

Organic Once again, different countries have their own guidelines but, generally, these animals are not intensively reared and are bred without artificial intervention. They are allowed to feed on organic pasture and are fed 80 per cent organic, non-GM (genetically modified) feed. Synthetic medicines and pesticides are avoided wherever possible. The organic label means that the animal should have been raised in accordance with the laws of the certifying body for the country of origin.

HANDLING AND STORING GAME

Game meats As for other meat (see page 172), game should be wrapped and stored in the fridge, placed in a dish so that if any juices escape they cannot drip and contaminate other foods. Do not allow the meat to touch any other foods.

Game birds are traditionally hung for several days to deepen their gamey flavour and tenderise the flesh – an unhung bird will be tough and tasteless. Most game from a butcher or supermarket will have been hung, but if you have a freshly shot bird, hang it yourself in a cool, airy place for the periods listed below.

Hanging Times for Birds

Grouse	2–4 days
Partridge	3–5 days
Pheasant	3–10 days
Wood pigeon	Requires no hanging
Woodcock	3–5 days

A prepared bird can be stored in the fridge for one to two days. But birds that have been significantly damaged by shot will not keep as well, so cook as soon as possible.

FREEZING GAME
• Freeze meat before its 'use-by' date, even better on the day of purchase.
• Wrap portions in individual freezer bags, seal tightly and label with the date of freezing. Meat can be stored in the freezer for up to three months.
• To thaw, put the meat in a dish to catch any juices and put in the fridge until completely thawed. Use within two days.
• Do not refreeze raw meat that has thawed. You can, however, freeze dishes made from thawed meat that you have then cooked.

For game birds, check the advice given on page 132.

FOOD SAFETY
Although raw meat does not carry the same food poisoning risks as poultry, it may still contain harmful bacteria (see Food Storage and Hygiene, page 498).

CLEANING, TRUSSING AND JOINTING
Prepare game birds as for poultry (see page 133).

COOKING GAME
When preparing game birds, follow the guidelines for poultry given on page 133 and see the roasting chart below. Game birds become dry and tough if overcooked; there should still be a trace of pinkness in the flesh and juices.

Grill Best suited to cuts such as steaks, chops, cutlets, cubed meat made into kebabs, and burgers and sausages. Season or marinate, then cook under a preheated grill.

Griddle Best suited to cuts such as steaks, chops and cutlets. Preheat the griddle for about 3 minutes or until smoking hot, then brush the meat with oil and cook for a few minutes on each side until cooked to your liking.

Stir-fry Best suited to tender, lean cuts such as fillet. Slice the meat into strips no thicker than 5mm ($^1/_4$ in). Heat a wok or large heavy pan until hot, then add oil to coat the inside. Add the meat and stir-fry, moving the pan contents constantly. Remove, then cook the remaining ingredients. Return the meat to the pan to warm through.

Pan-fry Best suited to cuts such as steaks, chops and cutlets. Preheat a frying pan and season the meat. Add enough oil to coat the base of the pan, then add the meat and brown on one side, not moving it for at least 1 minute, before turning to cook on the other side.

Braise and pot-roast Suited to tougher cuts that require long, slow cooking. Preheat the oven to 170°C (150°C fan oven) mark 3. Heat some oil in a large, flameproof casserole and brown the meat all over, working in batches if necessary. Remove from the pan and fry onions and garlic for a few minutes until beginning to colour, then return the meat to the pan with tomatoes or vegetables, and wine or stock. Stir well and season, then cover and cook in the oven for 2 hours or until tender.

Roast Suited to larger and more tender joints of meat. Different cuts need different treatment, so follow the recipe and also see the general tips for roasting meat on page 173.

ROASTING TIMES FOR GAME BIRDS

Bird	Oven temperature	Cooking time	Quantities for roasting
Grouse	200°C (180°C fan oven) mark 6	Allow about 40 minutes total roasting time	Allow 1 bird per person
Partridge	200°C (180°C fan oven) mark 6	Allow about 40 minutes total roasting time	Allow 1 bird per person
Pheasant	230°C (210°C fan oven) mark 8	Roast for 10 minutes, then reduce the temperature to 200°C (180°C fan oven) mark 6 and roast for a further 30–50 minutes	1 bird will serve 2–3 people
Pigeon	200°C (180°C fan oven) mark 6	Allow 20–30 minutes total roasting time	Allow 1 bird per person
Quail	220°C (200°C fan oven) mark 7	Allow about 25 minutes total roasting time	Allow 2 birds per person
Woodcock	190°C (170°C fan oven) mark 5	Allow 15–25 minutes total roasting time	Allow 1 bird per person

1 Grouse: 12 Aug –10 Dec
One of these small birds will serve 1–2 people. The young birds are best for eating; roast or grill. Braise or casserole older birds.

2 Quail: all year
Quail are tiny birds with a mild flavour; serve 2 per person. Roast – whole or spatchcocked, or split and grill or pan-fry.

3 Partridge: all year
The pale flesh has a delicate flavour and fine texture. Young partridge, 2–4 months old, are best: bard with bacon, and roast; braise, pot-roast or stew older birds.

4 Pigeon: all year
Wild wood pigeon has very dark meat with a full flavour. Available fresh or frozen, usually plucked and oven ready. Cook as partridge.

5 Pheasant: 1 Oct–1 Feb
The hen pheasant is smaller than the cock pheasant and has more tender flesh. Roast only young pheasant; both young and older pheasants make good casseroles.

6 Rabbit: all year
Farmed rabbit has pale, tender meat; wild rabbit has darker, tougher flesh. Both can be bought whole or in pieces. The meat is lean: baste with oil, don't overcook. Wild: braise, casserole, stew or add to pie fillings. Farmed: grill, sauté, roast.

7 Boar: all year
A dark and strongly flavoured meat, with lean flesh. Roast tender cuts; braise, stew or casserole tougher cuts or use in pie fillings, sauces, patties, meatballs and meat loaves.

8 Venison: all year
Has lean, dark, close-textured meat with a good flavour. Roast loin, saddle, fillet and leg; pan-fry escalopes and medallions; casserole neck and breast. Marinate before cooking.

9 Hare: all year
Hare has dark, strongly flavoured flesh. Roast young hare; braise, casserole or stew older hare, or add to pie fillings.

10 Goat: all year
The meat has a distinctive and pungent aroma. Braise, stew or casserole. Roast or barbecue young goat.

11 Woodcock: 1 Oct–31 Jan
These small birds are generally roasted whole (undrawn) and served on toast.

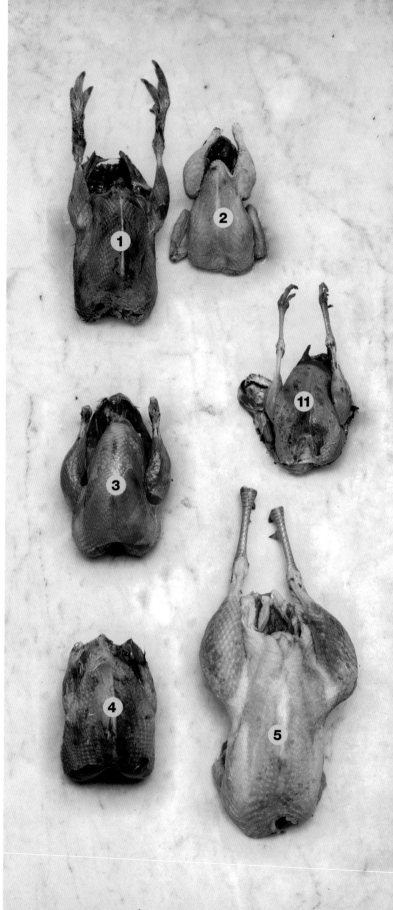

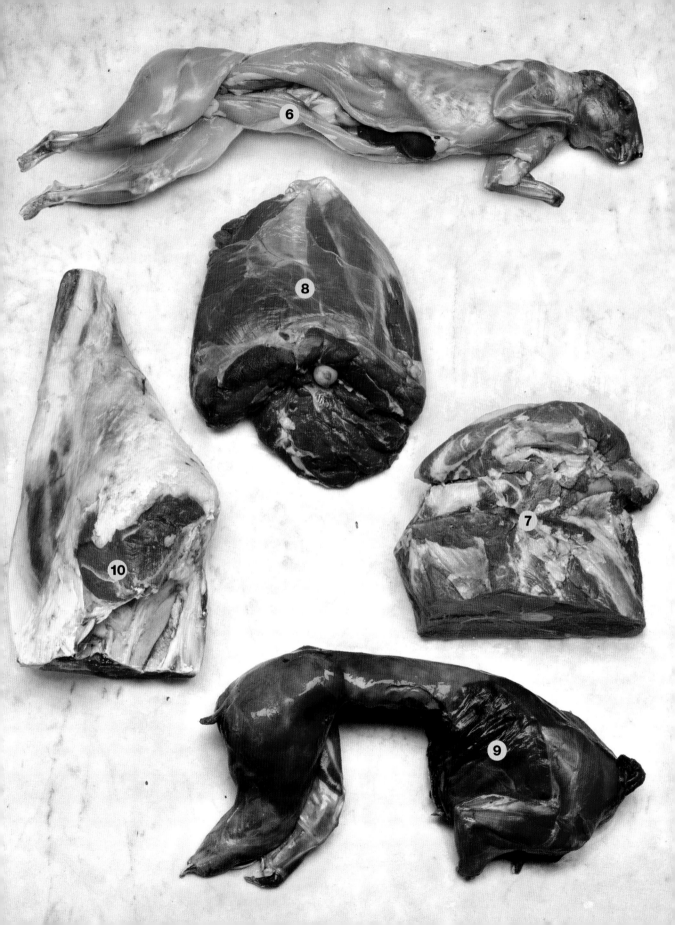

ROAST QUAIL IN RED PEPPERS

Serves 4
Preparation 20 minutes
Cooking time 35–40 minutes

4 quails
4 tbsp olive oil
2 large red peppers, halved lengthways, cored and seeded
4 slices Parma ham (see Cook's Tip page 65)
125ml (4fl oz) chicken stock
2 tbsp balsamic vinegar
salt and ground black pepper
Soft Herb Polenta to serve (see Try Something Different, page 266)

1 Preheat the oven to 200°C (180°C fan oven) mark 6. Season the quails inside and out with salt and pepper, rubbing well into the skin. Heat the olive oil in a heavy-based frying pan and quickly fry the quails over a high heat until browned on all sides; remove with a slotted spoon.

2 Fry the pepper halves in the oil remaining in the pan until slightly softened. Line each pepper cavity with a slice of Parma ham and sit a quail in each one. Put into a flameproof casserole and sprinkle with half the stock and vinegar.

3 Cook in the oven, basting regularly, for 25–30 minutes until the quails are cooked. Remove and keep warm.

4 Put the casserole over a high heat and add the remaining stock and vinegar, stirring to deglaze. Bubble until reduced and slightly syrupy. Pour over the quails and serve, with piping hot herb polenta.

NUTRITION PER SERVING (without polenta) 480 cals | 35g fat (8g sats) | 3g carbs | 0.4g salt

ROAST GROUSE

Serves 4
Preparation 10 minutes
Cooking time 40 minutes, plus resting

2 oven-ready grouse
6 streaky bacon rashers
2 tbsp vegetable oil
2 tbsp freshly chopped rosemary or thyme (optional)
salt and ground black pepper
deep-fried thinly sliced potatoes and parsnips or hand-cooked salted crisps and watercress to serve

1 Preheat the oven to 200°C (180°C fan oven) mark 6. Put the grouse into a large roasting tin, with enough space between them so that they can brown evenly. Cover the breast of each with bacon, then drizzle with 1 tbsp oil. Season with salt and pepper and sprinkle with herbs, if using.

2 Roast in the oven for 40 minutes or until the juices run clear when the thigh is pierced with a skewer.

3 Leave to rest in a warm place for 10 minutes before serving.

4 Serve with crisp deep-fried slices of potato and parsnip or ready-made hand-cooked crisps, plus watercress to contrast with the richness of the meat.

NUTRITION PER SERVING 320 cals | 18g fat | (4g sats), trace carbs | 0.3g salt

PIGEON ON CRISP POLENTA WITH TOMATO SALSA

Serves 4
Preparation 40 minutes
Cooking time 25 minutes

4 wood pigeons, plucked and drawn
25g (1oz) butter
1 garlic clove, crushed
4 chicken livers, trimmed
a pinch of powdered mace
oil to brush
salt and ground black pepper
freshly chopped herbs, to garnish
Fried Herb Polenta to serve (see Try Something Different,
    page 266)

For the tomato salsa
4 large ripe tomatoes, skinned, seeded and diced
    (see page 277)
2 garlic cloves, finely chopped
4 tbsp freshly chopped mixed herbs, such as basil,
    oregano and parsley
5 tbsp olive oil

1 Mix together the ingredients for the tomato salsa in a bowl
and season with salt and pepper to taste.
2 Cut the legs from the pigeons and set aside. Using a sharp
knife, cut down the breastbone on each side and ease off the
pigeon breasts; cover and set aside.
3 Melt the butter in a frying pan, add the garlic and fry gently
for 2 minutes until golden. Add the chicken livers and cook
over a high heat for 5 minutes until browned and cooked
through. Season with the mace, salt and pepper. Transfer to a
bowl and set aside.
4 Lay the pigeon legs on the grill rack, brush with oil and grill
under a medium-high heat for 2 minutes. Turn the legs over.
Add the pigeon breasts to the rack, skin side up, brush with oil
and grill for 4 minutes. Turn the pigeon legs and breasts and
cook for a further 2 minutes.
5 Meanwhile, warm the tomato salsa. Mash the chicken livers
and spread on the hot fried polenta slices, or serve on the
side. Put the polenta on warmed plates and top with the
pigeon. Garnish with herbs and serve with the tomato salsa.

NUTRITION PER SERVING
980 cals | 62g fat (12g sats) | 36g carbs | 0.7g salt

ROAST VENISON WITH MUSTARD AND MUSHROOMS

Serves 4
Preparation 15 minutes
Cooking time 30 minutes, plus resting

600g (1lb 5oz) piece loin of venison, about 6.5cm (2¹/₂ in) in diameter
1 tbsp wholegrain mustard
2 small onions, thinly sliced
350g (12oz) small shiitake or brown-cap mushrooms, halved
150ml (¹/₄ pint) olive oil
1 tbsp freshly chopped thyme
1 tbsp freshly chopped parsley
5 tsp balsamic vinegar
lemon juice, to taste
salt and ground black pepper

1 Preheat the oven to 230°C (210°C fan oven) mark 8. Rub the venison with the mustard and put into a roasting tin. Scatter the onions and mushrooms around the meat and drizzle over half the olive oil. Roast, allowing 30–35 minutes for medium-rare or 40 minutes for well-done meat.

2 Scatter the chopped thyme and parsley on a board. Roll the hot venison in the chopped herbs to coat and put on a warmed serving dish with the mushrooms and onions. Cover with foil and leave to rest in a warm place while preparing the dressing.

3 Add the remaining olive oil and the balsamic vinegar to the roasting tin and warm on the hob, stirring. Season with salt and pepper and add lemon juice to taste.

4 Carve the venison into thick slices and serve with the hot dressing.

NUTRITION PER SERVING 600 cals | 42g fat (7g sats) | 6g carbs | 1g salt

VENISON SAUSAGES WITH RED ONION MARMALADE

Serves 6
Preparation 15 minutes
Cooking time 35 minutes

12 gluten-free (100% meat) venison sausages
6 tsp redcurrant jelly

For the red onion marmalade
400g (14oz) red onions, chopped
2 tbsp olive oil
4 tbsp red wine vinegar
2 tbsp demerara sugar
1 tsp juniper berries, crushed
Colcannon (see page 295) or mashed potatoes to serve

1 Preheat the oven to 220°C (200°C fan oven) mark 7. Put the sausages into a small roasting tin. Roast in the oven for 35 minutes, turning once.

2 After 25 minutes, spoon the redcurrant jelly over and continue to cook.

3 Meanwhile, make the red onion marmalade. Gently fry the red onions in the olive oil for 15–20 minutes. Add the vinegar, sugar and juniper berries, and cook for a further 5 minutes or until the onions are very tender. Serve the sausages with the red onion marmalade and Colcannon or mashed potatoes.

NUTRITION PER SERVING 390 cals | 25g fat (10g sats) | 14g carbs | 0.3g salt

PEPPERED VENISON STEW

Serves 6
Preparation 20 minutes
Cooking time 2¾ hours

25g (1oz) plain flour
900g (2lb) stewing venison, beef or lamb,
    cut into 4cm (1½ in) cubes
5 tbsp oil
225g (8oz) button onions or shallots,
    peeled with root end intact
225g (8oz) onion, finely chopped
4 garlic cloves, crushed
2 tbsp tomato purée
125ml (4fl oz) red wine vinegar
75cl bottle red wine
2 tbsp redcurrant jelly
1 small bunch of fresh thyme, plus extra
    sprigs to garnish (optional)
4 bay leaves
1 tbsp coarsely ground black pepper
6 cloves
900g (2lb) mixed root vegetables, such as carrots, parsnips,
    turnips and celeriac, cut into 4cm (1½ in) chunks;
    carrots cut a little smaller
600–900ml (1–1½ pints) beef stock
salt and ground black pepper

1   Preheat the oven to 180°C (160°C fan oven) mark 4. Put the flour into a plastic bag, season with salt and pepper, then toss the meat in it.
2   Heat 3 tbsp of the oil in a large flameproof casserole over a medium heat and brown the meat well in small batches. Remove and put to one side.
3   Heat the remaining oil and fry the button onions or shallots for 5 minutes or until golden. Add the chopped onion and the garlic, and cook, stirring, until soft and golden. Add the tomato purée and cook for a further 2 minutes, then add the vinegar and wine, and bring to the boil. Bubble for 10 minutes.
4   Add the redcurrant jelly, thyme, bay leaves, 1 tbsp pepper, cloves and meat to the pan, together with the vegetables and enough stock to barely cover the meat and vegetables. Bring to the boil, cover and cook in the oven for 1¾–2¼ hours until the meat is very tender. Serve hot, garnished with thyme sprigs if you like.

NUTRITION PER SERVING
540 cals | 24g fat (7g sats) | 24g carbs | 1.5g salt

FREEZING TIP

⌐ To freeze, complete the recipe to the end of step 4, without the garnish. Cool quickly and put into a freezerproof container. Seal and freeze for up to one month.

⌐ To use, thaw overnight at cool room temperature. Preheat the oven to 180°C (160°C fan oven) mark 4. Put in a flameproof casserole, and add an extra 150ml (¼ pint) beef stock. Bring to the boil. Cover and reheat for 30 minutes

POT-ROASTED PHEASANT WITH RED CABBAGE

Serves 4
Preparation 15 minutes
Cooking time about 1 hour

25g (1oz) butter
1 tbsp oil
2 oven-ready young pheasants, halved
2 onions, peeled and sliced
450g (1lb) red cabbage, cored and finely shredded
1 tsp cornflour
250ml (9fl oz) red wine
2 tbsp redcurrant jelly
1 tbsp balsamic vinegar
4 rindless smoked streaky bacon rashers, halved
salt and ground black pepper

1 Preheat the oven to 200°C (180°C fan oven) mark 6. Melt the butter with the oil in a large flameproof casserole over a medium to high heat. Add the pheasant halves and brown on all sides, then remove and put to one side. Add the onions and cabbage to the casserole and fry for 5 minutes, stirring frequently, until softened.

2 Blend the cornflour with a little water to make a paste. Add to the casserole with the wine, redcurrant jelly and vinegar. Season with salt and pepper, and bring to the boil, stirring.

3 Arrange the pheasant halves, skin side up, on the cabbage. Put the halved bacon rashers on top. Cover the casserole and cook in the oven for 30 minutes or until the birds are tender (older pheasants will take an extra 10–20 minutes).

4 Serve the pot-roasted pheasants and red cabbage with the cooking juices spooned over them.

TRY SOMETHING DIFFERENT

Instead of the pheasants, use oven-ready poussins, small corn-fed chickens or small guinea fowl; put an onion wedge inside each bird before browning to impart extra flavour.

NUTRITION PER SERVING
659 cals | 21g fat (12g sats) | 11g carbs | 1.4g salt

PHEASANT WITH CIDER AND APPLES

Serves 8
Preparation 1 hour
Cooking time 1–1½ hours

2 pheasants, each weighing about 700g (1½lb),
    each cut into four portions
2 tbsp plain flour, plus extra to dust
50g (2oz) butter
4 streaky bacon rashers
225g (8oz) onions, roughly chopped
275g (10oz) celery, roughly chopped
4 eating apples, such as Granny Smith, cored,
    cut into large pieces and tossed in
      1 tbsp lemon juice
1 tbsp dried juniper berries, lightly crushed
2.5cm (1in) piece fresh root ginger, peeled
    and finely chopped
300ml (½ pint) chicken stock
2 × 440ml cans dry cider
140ml (4½fl oz) double cream
salt and ground black pepper
fried apple wedges, thyme sprigs and juniper
    berries to garnish

1 Preheat the oven to 170°C (150°C fan) mark 3. Season
each pheasant portion and dust lightly with flour. Melt the
butter in a large flameproof casserole and brown the
pheasant pieces in batches until deep golden brown.
Remove and keep warm.
2 Put the bacon into the casserole and cook for 2–3 minutes
until golden. Add the onions, celery, apples, lemon juice,
juniper and ginger, and cook for 8–10 minutes. Stir the flour
into the vegetables and cook for 2 minutes, then add the
stock and cider and bring to the boil. Return the pheasant to
the casserole, cover and cook in the oven for 45 minutes–
1 hour until tender.
3 Lift the pheasant out of the sauce and keep it warm. Strain
the sauce through a sieve and return it to the casserole with
the cream. Bring to the boil and bubble for 10–15 minutes
until syrupy. Return the pheasant to the sauce and season.
4 To serve, garnish the pheasant with the fried apple wedges,
thyme sprigs and juniper berries.

GET AHEAD
— Complete the recipe to the end of step 3, cool quickly,
   cover and chill for up to two days.
— To use, Bring the pheasant to the boil and reheat in the
   oven at 180°C (160°C fan) mark 4 for 20–25 minutes.

NUTRITION PER SERVING
463 cals | 27g fat (13g sats) | 13g carbs | 0.7g salt

RABBIT CASSEROLE WITH GRAINY MUSTARD

Serves 4
Preparation 15 minutes
Cooking time 1–1½ hours

4–6 rabbit joints, about 700–900g (1½–2lb) in total
2 tbsp plain flour, plus extra to dust
2 tbsp oil
15g (½oz) butter
2 garlic cloves, crushed
300g (11oz) shallots, halved if large
225g (8oz) carrots, thickly sliced
150ml (¼ pint) white wine
300ml (½ pint) chicken stock
3–4 tbsp wholegrain mustard
4 tbsp crème fraîche
salt and ground black pepper
chopped herbs, to garnish

1 Preheat the oven to 170°C (150°C fan oven) mark 3.
Season the rabbit joints with salt and pepper, and toss in flour
to coat lightly, shaking off the excess.
2 Heat the oil and butter in a large flameproof casserole and
brown the rabbit joints on all sides over a high heat, in batches
if necessary. Remove and set aside.
3 Reduce the heat and add the garlic, shallots and carrots to
the casserole; cook for 5 minutes. Stir in the flour and cook for
2 minutes.
4 Add the wine, stock and mustard, stir well and bring to
the boil. Return the rabbit to the casserole, then put the lid
on and cook in the oven for 1–1½ hours until the rabbit is
very tender.
5 Transfer the rabbit and vegetables to a warmed serving
dish, using a slotted spoon; keep warm.
6 If necessary, put the casserole over a high heat for a few
minutes to reduce the sauce a little. Stir in the crème fraîche
and check the seasoning. Pour the creamy mustard sauce over
the rabbit and garnish with herbs to serve.

COOK'S TIP
Rabbit meat is low in fat and cholesterol, making
it a healthy option.

NUTRITION PER SERVING
410 cals | 24g fat (12g sats) | 16g carbs | 1.3g salt

GAMEKEEPER'S PIE

Serves 8
Preparation 20 minutes
Cooking time 1 hour 15 minutes

2 tbsp sunflower oil
800g (1lb 12oz) minced venison
1 onion, finely chopped
1 celery stick, finely chopped
1 large carrot, grated
1 garlic clove, crushed
1¹/₂ tbsp plain flour
150ml (¹/₄ pint) full-fat milk
2 tbsp port
150ml (¹/₄ pint) red wine
350ml (12fl oz) hot beef or game stock
1 tbsp Worcestershire sauce
2 tsp dried juniper berries, roughly crushed
¹/₂ tbsp fresh thyme leaves
1 bay leaf
1.3kg (2lb 14oz) Desirée or similar waxy potatoes,
    cut into chunks
50g (2oz) butter
50–75ml (2–2¹/₂ fl oz) double cream
salt and ground black pepper
seasonal vegetables to serve

1 Heat 1 tbsp oil in a large pan and brown the mince over a medium heat in batches. Remove from the pan using a slotted spoon and set aside.

2 Using the same pan, turn the heat down to low, add the remaining oil and gently fry the onion, celery and carrot for 15 minutes or until softened but not coloured. Add the garlic and fry for 1 minute. Sprinkle the flour over and cook, stirring, for 1 minute.

3 Turn the heat to medium and add the milk, 2 tbsp at a time, stirring until it is absorbed. Stir in the port and wine, and simmer until thickened. Add the hot stock, Worcestershire sauce, juniper berries, thyme and bay leaf, and bring to the boil. Return the mince to the pan, cover and simmer for 45 minutes, stirring occasionally.

4 Meanwhile, bring a large pan of lightly salted water to the boil and cook the potatoes for about 15 minutes or until tender. Drain and leave to steam dry in the colander. Heat the butter and cream in a small pan. Push the potato through a potato ricer or sieve into the rinsed potato pan. Stir in enough cream and butter to make a smooth but not sloppy mash. Check the seasoning.

5 Preheat the grill to medium. Tip the hot venison into an ovenproof dish about 30.5 × 20.5cm (12 × 8in). Spread the mash on top and grill for 3–4 minutes until golden. Serve with seasonal vegetables.

GET AHEAD

→ Assemble the pie up to two days ahead, wrap the dish in clingfilm and chill. Alternatively, wrap in clingfilm and freeze for up to three months.

→ To use, if frozen, thaw overnight in the fridge. Reheat at 200°C (180°C fan) mark 6 for 25 minutes.

NUTRITION PER SERVING
403 cals | 17g fat (8g sats) | 34g carbs | 1g salt

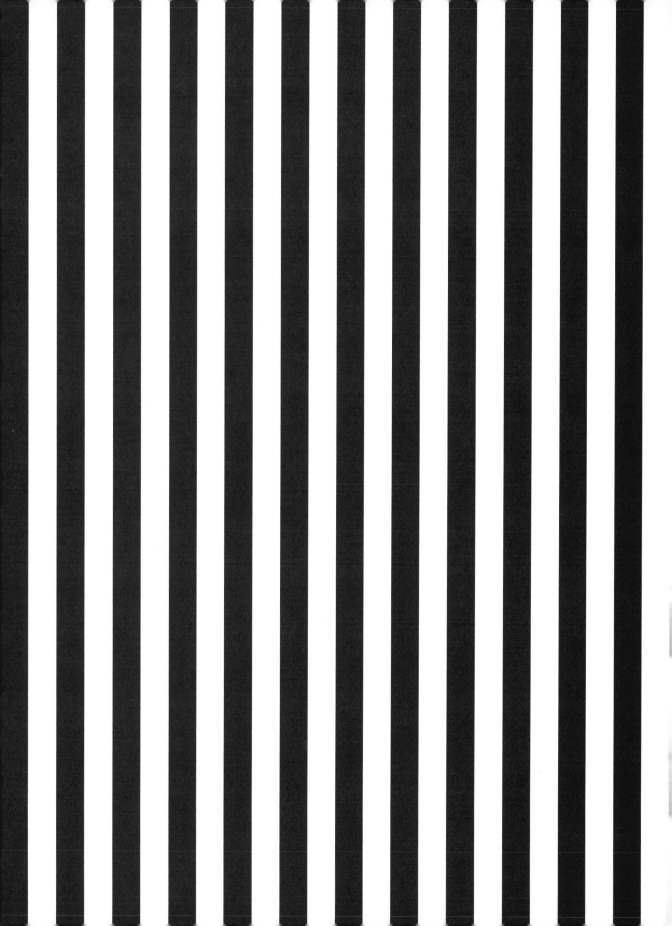

MEAT

MEAT

Meat is a valuable source of high-quality protein, B vitamins and iron, and has an important role in a healthy balanced diet; however, it is also a source of saturated fatty acids, which are associated with raised blood cholesterol levels – a risk factor in coronary heart disease. For this reason, it is wise to avoid eating too much red meat, perhaps limiting it to a maximum of three main meals per week.

In the UK beef, lamb and pork are the most popular red meats, whereas veal is eaten to a much lesser extent. The flavour and texture of meat is determined by the breed of the animal, its environment and its feed. Meat from cattle raised on lush pastures will taste far superior to that from corn-fed animals. Organic meat is derived from animals that have been reared on a natural diet, and is therefore an endorsement of quality. With the exception of veal, meat is hung before it is sold to improve the texture and develop its flavour. The most expensive cuts – suitable for roasting, grilling and frying – are from those parts of the animal that are the least exercised – rump, tenderloin, and so on. Cheaper, tougher cuts from those parts of the animal that move the most need slow, gentle cooking with liquid to tenderise them. If you prefer to cut down on red meat, make a little go further by serving it with lots of vegetables or by combining it with pulses in casseroles and stews.

CHOOSING MEAT

Always buy your meat from a reliable source. Quality butchers and supermarkets sell a wide range of cuts, and a helpful butcher should be able to offer you advice and also be willing to bone meat, cut steaks to a certain thickness and prepare meat in other ways to your specific requirements. For categories of meat see Game, page 158.

Meat should look and smell fresh, but colour is not an obvious indicator. Bright red, for example, doesn't necessarily indicate quality. Instead, look for a good clear colour, which will darken naturally on exposure to the air. A greyish tinge is a bad sign. A little fat is essential to prevent meat drying out during cooking, but look for relatively lean cuts without too much visible fat. Any fat should be creamy white. With the exception of some specialist breeds, such as Jersey and Guernsey beef, creamy yellow fat suggests that the meat is probably past its prime. Look for a smooth outer layer of fat, if appropriate to the cut, and a fine marbling of fat distributed throughout the meat; this will keep it moist during cooking and add flavour.

Always choose a neat, fairly well-trimmed piece of meat. Splinters of bone and ragged edges indicate poor butchery. Cuts should be trimmed of sinew. Joints and steaks should be of uniform thickness so that they cook evenly. Offal should look fresh and moist, and it should not smell.

HANDLING AND STORING MEAT

Once you've made your purchase, get the meat home and into the fridge as soon as possible. It should be stored in the coolest part of the fridge, loosely wrapped and well away from cooked foods to prevent cross-contamination.

If you've bought pre-packed meat from a supermarket, stick to the 'use-by' date. Offal, minced meat and small cuts of veal are best eaten on the day of purchase. Larger joints, chops and steaks will keep in the fridge for two to three days. If meat is past its best, the fat will begin to turn rancid. 'Off' or bad meat will have an unpleasant smell, a slimy surface and possibly a greenish tinge. Because of the risk of food poisoning, it's not worth the risk if you have any doubt about freshness.

For freezing meat, see the advice given for Game on page 159. (See also Food Storage and Hygiene, page 498.)

MARINATING MEAT

A good marinade tenderises tougher cuts of meat and lends a subtle aroma and flavour. Oil, fruit juice and wine-based marinades tend to permeate the meat adding moisture to dry cuts, whereas yogurt will tenderise and form a soft crust on the food as it cooks. Aromatics – lemon zest, thyme, bay, garlic and onion – add fragrance and flavour.

Put the meat into a shallow non-metallic dish and pour over the marinade. Leave in a cool place for at least 1 hour or overnight. Remove the meat from the marinade and cook as the recipe, basting with marinade regularly if you are cooking on a barbecue or under the grill.

COOKING MEAT

Lean, fine-grained cuts can be cooked quickly whereas tougher cuts need long, slow cooking to make them tender.

Stew and casserole A stew is cooked on the hob whereas a casserole is cooked in the oven – both at a gentle simmer. Brown the meat before adding any liquid. Choose a heavy-based pan or casserole with a tight-fitting lid. Meat labelled 'stewing' will take longer to cook than meat labelled 'braising'. Skim off the excess fat before serving.

Braise involves less liquid than stewing or casseroling, and slightly more tender cuts are used. The browned meat is set on a bed of vegetables with sufficient liquid to create steam, covered tightly and cooked very gently.

Boil Meat for 'boiling' is usually salted and must be soaked overnight in several changes of cold water before cooking. Cover the meat with fresh cold water and bring to a simmer. Cover with a tightly fitting lid and simmer gently for 25 minutes per 450g (1lb) plus 30 minutes for large joints; 1½ hours minimum for small joints; do not boil. Add aromatics if you intend using the liquid as stock.

Fry, grill and barbecue These methods are suitable for tender cuts. The pan, grill or barbecue must be hot before cooking so that the meat is sealed and browned. If cooking thicker pieces, or pork or sausages, reduce the heat once the meat has browned, or move it further from the heat source if barbecuing, so that it cooks right through.

Stir-fry Cut the meat into small even-sized pieces across the grain; marinate first if you like. Heat a little vegetable oil in a preheated wok until very hot. Add the meat and stir as it cooks.

Cooking steaks to perfection can be difficult. The most reliable way is to cut the steak open and look at it. Timing depends on the thickness of the meat. As a rough guide, a 2cm (³⁄₄ in) thick steak will take about 2½ minutes' grilling or frying on each side for rare; 3–4 minutes each side for medium; 6 minutes for well-done.

Roast Only good-quality tender joints are suitable for roasting. Roasting at a constant high temperature of 230°C (210°C fan oven) mark 8, is only suitable for prime cuts, such as beef fillet. Bring the meat to room temperature. Put it, fat side up, on a roasting rack and smear with mustard or stud with slivers of garlic. Pork should be rubbed with oil and salt to make crackling. Except for pork with crackling, baste roasts during cooking to keep them moist; if the joint is very lean, add dripping or oil.

Use a meat thermometer to check that the joint is cooked. Or insert a skewer into the thickest part, press the surface and watch the colour of the juices: slightly red for rare meat; pink for medium; clear for well done.

ROASTING TIMES FOR MEAT
Roast meat at 230°C (210°C fan oven) mark 8 for the first 20 minutes, then reduce the temperature to 180°C (160°C fan oven) mark 4 and cook for the times as shown belowl.

CARVING MEAT
Use a large, sharp knife and a carving fork. Rest the joint, loosely covered with foil, for 5–15 minutes before carving. Loosen the meat from any exposed bones. Cut across the grain of the meat (usually at right angles to the main bone). Lay boned and rolled joints on their side and carve through.

Leg of lamb Cut a narrow wedge-shaped piece of meat from the top (middle) of the joint, cutting down to the bone. Carve slices from either side of the cut then turn over and repeat.

Shoulder of lamb Hold the shank end with the crisp skin uppermost. Cut a wedge-shaped slice through the middle of the joint. Carve slices from the cut as before.

Pork loin Ask the butcher to chine the bone. When you carve, sever the chined bone from the ribs. Cut off the crackling. Cut down between the rib bones to divide the joint into chops, or cut along the length between the meat and rib bones and carve off slices.

Leg of pork For a shank end, remove some crackling. Cut thin slices down to the bone. Carve at an angle over the top of the shank bone. Turn and cut down towards the thin end of the bone at an angle. For a fillet end, carve slices through to the bone on either side of it.

ROASTING TIMES FOR MEAT

Meat		Cooking time	Internal temperature
Beef	Rare	20 minutes per 450g (1lb), plus 20 minutes	60°C
	Medium	25 minutes per 450g (1lb), plus 25 minutes	70°C
	Well done	30 minutes per 450g (1lb), plus 30 minutes	80°C
Veal	Well Done	25 minutes per 450g (1lb), plus 25 minutes	70°C
Lamb	Medium	25 minutes per 450g (1lb), plus 25 minutes	70–75°C
	Well done	30 minutes per 450g (1lb), plus 30 minutes	75–80°C
Pork	Well done	35 minutes per 450g (1lb), plus 35 minutes	80–85°C

1 Topside
A very lean cut with little fat, topside is usually sold with a layer of fat tied around it. Roast, braise or use sliced for beef roulades.

2 Fillet or tenderloin
A lean tender cut. Cook in a large piece or as steaks. Filet mignon, chateaubriand and tournedos are also cut from the fillet.

3 Rump steak
A lean, tender cut from the hind quarter. Suitable for grilling and frying.

4 Silverside
A lean, boneless joint from the hind quarter, traditionally salted and boiled.

5 Sirloin
Sold boned and rolled for roasting, or cut into sirloin steaks. Porterhouse, bone-in T-bone steaks and minute steaks are also cut from the sirloin.

6 Rib
Sold both as a roasting joint on the bone, and boned and rolled; sometimes called rib eye. Rib has more fat than topside, but its flavour is superb. Strictly speaking, entrecôte is, literally, the meat between the ribs.

7 Skirt
Cut from the belly, this is a well-flavoured, fairly tough cut that is lean but with quite a coarse texture. Stew, braise or pot-roast.

8 Thick flank (top rump)
A lean cut from the top of the leg for pot roasting and braising. **Thin flank** Braise or stew. Slice thinly and stir-fry.

9 Chuck and blade steak
Lean shoulder meat, usually sold sliced or cubed for braising, stewing and pie fillings. Look for some marbling of fat throughout.

10 Brisket
A shoulder joint. It has a good flavour but is inclined to be fatty. Sold boned and rolled, it may also be salted. Brisket is best braised or pot roasted, but it can be roasted.

11 Neck and clod
Economical cuts, used for stewing or mince.

12 Shin and leg
Relatively lean cuts with lots of connective tissue; stew or casserole.

CLASSIC ROAST BEEF WITH YORKSHIRE PUDDINGS

Serves 8
Preparation 20 minutes
Cooking time about 1½ hours, plus resting

1 boned and rolled rib, sirloin, rump or topside of beef,
    about 1.8kg (4lb)
1 tbsp plain flour
1 tbsp mustard powder
salt and ground black pepper
fresh thyme sprigs to garnish
vegetables to serve

For the Yorkshire pudding
125g (4oz) plain flour
½ tsp salt
300ml (½ pint) milk
2 eggs

For the gravy
150ml (¼ pint) red wine
600ml (1 pint) beef stock

1 Preheat the oven to 230°C (210°C fan oven) mark 8. Put the beef in a roasting tin, thickest part of the fat uppermost. Mix the flour with the mustard powder and salt and pepper. Rub the mixture over the beef.
2 Roast the beef in the centre of the oven for 30 minutes.
3 Baste the beef and reduce the oven temperature to 190°C (170°C fan oven) mark 5. Cook for a further 1 hour, basting occasionally.
4 Meanwhile, prepare the Yorkshire pudding batter. Sift the flour and salt into a bowl. Mix in half the milk, then add the eggs and season with pepper. Beat until smooth, then whisk in the remaining milk.
5 Put the beef on a warmed carving dish, cover loosely with foil and leave to rest in a warm place. Increase the oven temperature to 220°C (200°C fan oven) mark 7.
6 Pour off about 3 tbsp fat from the roasting tin and use to grease 8–12 individual Yorkshire pudding tins. Heat in the oven for 5 minutes or until the fat is almost smoking. Pour the Yorkshire batter into the tins. Bake for 15–20 minutes until well risen, golden and crisp.
7 Meanwhile, make the gravy. Skim off any remaining fat from the roasting tin. Put the tin on the hob, add the wine and boil until syrupy. Pour in the stock and, again, boil until syrupy – there should be about 450ml (¾ pint) gravy. Taste and adjust the seasoning.
8 Carve the beef into slices. Garnish with thyme, serve with the gravy, Yorkshire puddings and vegetables of your choice.

NUTRITION PER SERVING
510 cals | 24g fat (9g sats) | 16g carbs | 0.5g salt

STUFFED TOPSIDE OF BEEF

Serves 6
Preparation 35 minutes, plus marinating
Cooking time 1–1¼ hours, plus resting

1.4kg (3lb) topside or top rump of beef
1 tbsp balsamic vinegar
2 tbsp white wine vinegar
3 tbsp olive oil
3 tbsp freshly chopped marjoram or thyme
2 red peppers, cored, seeded and quartered
75g (3oz) fresh spinach, cooked and well drained
75g (3oz) pitted black olives, chopped
50g (2oz) smoked ham, chopped
75g (3oz) raisins or sultanas
salt and ground black pepper
roast potatoes and vegetables to serve

1 Make a deep cut along the beef to create a pocket and put the joint into a dish. Combine the vinegars, oil, marjoram or thyme and some black pepper. Pour over the beef and into the pocket. Marinate in a cool place for 4–6 hours, or overnight.

2 Grill the peppers, skin side up, under a hot grill until the skins are charred. Cool in a covered bowl, then remove the skins.

3 Squeeze the excess water from the spinach, then chop and put into a bowl with the olives, ham and raisins or sultanas. Mix well and season with salt and pepper.

4 Preheat the oven to 190°C (170°C fan oven) mark 5. Line the pocket of the beef with the peppers, keeping back two pepper quarters for the gravy. Spoon the spinach mixture into the pocket and spread evenly. Reshape the meat and tie at intervals with string. Put the beef into a roasting tin just large enough to hold it and pour the marinade over it.

5 Roast for 1 hour for rare beef, or 1¼ hours for medium-rare, basting from time to time. Put the beef on a board, cover with foil and leave to rest in a warm place while you make the gravy.

6 Skim off the excess fat from the roasting tin. Put the tin on the hob and bring the pan juices to the boil. Add 125ml (4fl oz) water and bubble for 2–3 minutes. Finely chop the remaining pepper pieces and add to the gravy.

7 Carve the beef and serve with the gravy, roast potatoes and vegetables of your choice.

NUTRITION PER SERVING
535 cals | 29g fat (10g sats) | 13g carbs | 1.4g salt

FILLET OF BEEF EN CROÛTE

Serves 6
Preparation 1 hour, plus soaking and chilling
Cooking time about 1 hour 20 minutes, plus resting

1–1.4kg (2¼–3lb) fillet of beef, trimmed
50g (2oz) butter
2 shallots, chopped
15g (½oz) dried porcini mushrooms, soaked in
    100ml (3½fl oz) boiling water
2 garlic cloves, chopped
225g (8oz) flat mushrooms, finely chopped
2 tsp freshly chopped thyme, plus extra sprigs to garnish
175g (6oz) chicken liver pâté
175g (6oz) thinly sliced Parma ham (see Cook's Tip, page 65)
375g ready-rolled puff pastry
plain flour to dust
1 medium egg, beaten
salt and ground black pepper
Rich Red Wine Sauce (see Cook's Tip) to serve

1 Season the beef with salt and pepper. Melt 25g (1oz) butter in a large frying pan and, when foaming, add the beef and cook for 4–5 minutes to brown all over. Transfer to a plate and leave to cool.
2 Melt the remaining butter in a pan, add the shallots and cook for 1 minute. Drain the porcini mushrooms, saving the liquid, and chop them. Add them to the pan with the garlic, the reserved liquid and the fresh mushrooms. Increase the heat and cook until the liquid has evaporated, then season with salt and pepper and add the thyme. Leave to cool.
3 Put the pâté into a bowl and beat until smooth. Add the mushroom mixture and stir well until thoroughly combined. Check the seasoning. Spread half the mushroom mixture evenly over one side of the beef. Lay half the Parma ham on a length of clingfilm, overlapping the slices. Invert the mushroom-topped beef on to the ham. Spread the remaining mushroom mixture on the other side of the beef, then lay the remaining Parma ham, also overlapping, on top of the mushroom mixture. Wrap the beef in the clingfilm to form a firm sausage shape and chill for 30 minutes. Preheat the oven to 220°C (200°C fan oven) mark 7.
4 Cut off one-third of the pastry and roll out on a lightly floured surface to 3mm (⅛in) thick and 2.5cm (1in) larger all around than the beef. Prick all over with a fork. Transfer to a baking sheet and bake for 12–15 minutes until brown and crisp. Cool on a wire rack, then trim to the size of the beef and place on a baking sheet. Remove the clingfilm from the beef, brush with the egg and place on the cooked pastry.
5 Roll out the remaining pastry to a 25.5 × 30.5cm (10 × 12in) rectangle. Roll a lattice pastry cutter over it and gently ease the lattice open. Cover the beef with the lattice, tuck the ends under and seal the edges. Brush with the beaten egg, then cook for 40 minutes for rare to medium-rare, 45 minutes for medium. Leave to rest for 10 minutes before carving. Garnish with thyme and serve with Red Wine Sauce.

COOK'S TIP
Rich Red Wine Sauce Soften 350g (12oz) finely chopped shallots in 2 tbsp olive oil for 5 minutes. Add 3 chopped garlic cloves and 3 tbsp tomato purée and cook for 1 minute, then add 2 tbsp balsamic vinegar. Simmer briskly until reduced to almost nothing, then add 200ml (7fl oz) red wine and reduce by half. Pour in 600ml (1 pint) beef stock and simmer until reduced by one-third.

NUTRITION PER SERVING
802 cals | 53g fat (15g sats) | 27g carbs | 2.4g salt

ROAST RIB

Serves 8
Preparation 5 minutes
Cooking time 2¹/₂ hours, plus resting

2-bone rib of beef, about 2.5–2.7kg (5¹/₂–6lb)
1 tbsp plain flour
1 tbsp mustard powder
150ml (¹/₄ pint) red wine
600ml (1 pint) beef stock
600ml (1 pint) water from parboiled potatoes
salt and ground black pepper
thyme sprigs to garnish
Yorkshire Puddings (see page 176), roasted root vegetables
and a green vegetable to serve

1 Preheat the oven to 230°C (210°C fan oven) mark 8. Put the beef, fat side up, in a roasting tin just large enough to hold the joint. Mix the flour and mustard together in a small bowl and season with salt and pepper, then rub the mixture over the beef. Roast in the centre of the oven for 30 minutes.
2 Move the beef to a lower shelf, near the bottom of the oven. Turn the oven down to 220°C (200°C fan oven) mark 7 and continue to roast the beef for a further 2 hours, basting occasionally.
3 Put the beef on a carving dish, cover loosely with foil and leave to rest while you make the gravy. Skim off most of the fat from the roasting tin. Put the roasting tin on the hob, pour in the wine and boil vigorously until very syrupy. Pour in the stock and, again, boil until syrupy. Add the vegetable water and boil until syrupy. There should be about 450ml (³/₄ pint) gravy. Taste and adjust the seasoning.
4 Remove the rib bone and carve the beef. Garnish with thyme. Serve with gravy, Yorkshire puddings and vegetables.

NUTRITION PER SERVING
807 cals | 53g fat (24g sats) | 2g carbs | 0.5g salt

STEAK AU POIVRE

Serves 4
Preparation 10 minutes
Cooking time 4–12 minutes

2 tbsp black or green peppercorns
4 rump or sirloin steaks, 200g (7oz) each
25g (1oz) butter
1 tbsp oil
2 tbsp brandy
150ml (¼ pint) double cream or crème fraîche
salt
herbed roast potatoes and green beans to serve

1 Crush the peppercorns coarsely using a pestle and mortar or a rolling pin. Scatter the peppercorns on a board, lay the steaks on top and press hard to encrust the surface of the meat; repeat with the other side.

2 Heat the butter and oil in a frying pan and quickly sear the steaks over a high heat. Lower the heat to medium and cook for a further 3–12 minutes, according to taste, turning every 2 minutes (see Cook's Tip). Season with salt.

3 Remove the steaks from the pan; keep warm. Add the brandy to the pan, take off the heat and set alight. When the flame dies, stir in the cream or crème fraîche, season and reheat gently. Pour the sauce over the steaks to serve.

TRY SOMETHING DIFFERENT

Steak Diane Trim 4 pieces of fillet steak, 5mm (¼ in) thick, of excess fat. Fry the steaks in 25g (1oz) butter and 2 tbsp vegetable oil for 1–2 minutes on each side. Remove with a slotted spoon and keep warm. Stir 2 tbsp Worcestershire sauce and 1 tbsp lemon juice into the pan juices. Warm through, then add 1 small onion, skinned and grated and 2 tsp freshly chopped parsley, and cook gently for 1 minute. Serve the sauce spooned over the steaks.

COOK'S TIP
Allow 4 minutes (one turn) for rare steaks; 8 minutes (three turns) for medium. For well-done, 12 minutes, increasing the time between turns to 3 minutes.

NUTRITION PER SERVING
480 cals | 35g fat (19g sats) | 1g carbs | 1g salt

SESAME BEEF

Serves 4
Preparation 20 minutes
Cooking time 10 minutes

2 tbsp soy sauce
2 tbsp Worcestershire sauce
2 tsp tomato purée
juice of $^1/_2$ lemon
1 tbsp sesame seeds
1 garlic clove, crushed
400g (14oz) rump steak, sliced
1 tbsp vegetable oil
3 small pak choi, chopped
1 bunch of spring onions, thickly sliced
egg noodles or tagliatelle to serve

1 Put the soy and Worcestershire sauces, tomato purée,
lemon juice, sesame seeds and garlic into a bowl
and mix well. Add the steak and toss to coat.
2 Heat the oil in a large wok or non-stick frying pan until hot.
Add the steak and sear well. Remove from the wok and put
to one side.
3 Add any sauce from the bowl to the wok and heat for 1
minute. Add the pak choi, spring onions and steak and stir-fry
for 5 minutes. Add freshly cooked and drained noodles or
tagliatelle, toss and serve immediately.

TRY SOMETHING DIFFERENT
Use 400g (14oz) pork escalope cut into strips instead of beef.
Cook for 5 minutes before removing from the pan at step 2.

NUTRITION PER SERVING
207 cals | 10g fat (3g sats) | 4g carbs | 2g salt

BEEF STROGANOFF

Serves 4
Preparation 10 minutes
Cooking time about 20 minutes

700g (1½lb) rump or fillet steak, trimmed
50g (2oz) unsalted butter or 4 tbsp olive oil
1 onion, thinly sliced
225g (8oz) brown-cap mushrooms, sliced
3 tbsp brandy
1 tsp French mustard
200ml (7fl oz) crème fraîche
100ml (3½fl oz) double cream
3 tbsp freshly chopped flat-leafed parsley
salt and ground black pepper
rice or noodles to serve

1 Cut the steak into strips about 5mm (¼in) wide and
5cm (2in) long.
2 Heat half the butter or oil in a large heavy frying pan over
a medium heat. Add the onion and cook gently for 10 minutes
or until soft and golden. Remove with a slotted spoon and
put to one side. Add the mushrooms to the pan and cook,
stirring, for 2–3 minutes until golden brown; remove and put
to one side.
3 Increase the heat and add the remaining butter or oil to
the pan. Quickly fry the meat, in two or three batches, for
2–3 minutes, stirring constantly to ensure even browning.
Remove from the pan. Add the brandy to the pan and allow
it to bubble to reduce.
4 Put all the meat, onion and mushrooms back into the pan.
Reduce the heat and stir in the mustard, crème fraîche and
cream. Heat through, stir in most of the parsley and season
with salt and pepper. Serve with rice or noodles, with the
remaining parsley scattered over the top.

FREEZING TIP
➤ To freeze, complete the recipe, transfer to a freezerproof
container, cool, label and freeze for up to three months.
➤ To use, thaw overnight in the fridge. Put in a pan, cover
and bring to the boil; reduce the heat to low and simmer
until piping hot.

NUTRITION PER SERVING
750 cals | 60g fat (35g sats) | 3g carbs | 0.5g salt

SMOKY PIMENTO GOULASH

Serves 8
Preparation 20 minutes
Cooking time about 3 hours

1.1kg (2½ lb) braising steak
3 tbsp olive oil
16 shallots or button onions
225g (8oz) piece chorizo sausage, roughly chopped
1 red chilli, seeded and finely chopped (see Cook's Tips, page 69)
3 bay leaves
3 garlic cloves, crushed
2 tbsp plain flour
2 tbsp smoked paprika
700g jar tomato passata
100ml (3½ fl oz) hot beef stock
salt and ground black pepper
mashed potatoes and green vegetables to serve

For the minted soured cream
284ml carton soured cream
1 tbsp finely chopped fresh mint
1 tbsp extra virgin olive oil, plus extra to drizzle

1 Mix together all the ingredients for the minted soured cream and season with a little salt and plenty of coarsely ground black pepper. Cover and chill until needed.
2 Preheat the oven to 170°C (150°C fan oven) mark 3. Cut the braising steak into large cubes, slightly larger than bite-size.
3 Heat the olive oil in a 4 litre (7 pint) flameproof casserole until really hot. Brown the beef, a few cubes at a time, over a high heat until it is deep brown all over. Remove with a slotted spoon and set aside. Repeat with the remaining beef until all the pieces have been browned.
4 Reduce the heat under the casserole, then add the onions, chorizo, chilli, bay leaves and garlic. Fry for 7–10 minutes until the onions are golden brown and beginning to soften. Return the meat to the casserole and stir in the flour and paprika. Cook, stirring, for 1–2 minutes, then add the passata. Season, cover and cook in the oven for 2½ hours or until the beef is meltingly tender. Check halfway through cooking – if the beef looks dry, add the hot beef stock. Serve with the minted soured cream, drizzled with a little olive oil and a grinding of black pepper, and some creamy mashed potatoes and green vegetables.

GET AHEAD
➥ To prepare ahead, complete the recipe. Cool and chill (it will keep for up to three days) or freeze (it will keep for up to one month).
➥ To use, if frozen, thaw overnight at a cool room temperature. Return the goulash to the casserole, bring to the boil and simmer gently for 15–20 minutes until piping hot, adding 100ml (3½ fl oz) hot beef stock if it looks dry.

NUTRITION PER SERVING
515 cals | 35g fat (14g sats) | 13g carbs | 1.3g salt

COTTAGE PIE

Serves 4
Preparation 15 minutes
Cooking time about 1 hour

1 tbsp olive oil
1 onion, peeled and finely chopped
2 garlic cloves, peeled and crushed
450g (1lb) minced beef
1 tbsp plain flour
450ml (¾ pint) beef stock
2 tbsp Worcestershire sauce
1 medium carrot, peeled and diced
125g (4oz) button mushrooms, sliced
1kg (2¼ lb) potatoes, roughly chopped
25g (1oz) butter
60ml (2¼fl oz) milk
salt and ground black pepper

1 Heat the oil in a large pan, add the onion and fry over a medium heat for 15 minutes until softened and golden, stirring occasionally. Add the garlic and cook for 1 minute.
2 Preheat the oven to 200°C (180°C fan oven) mark 6. Add minced beef to the onion and garlic and, as it browns, use a wooden spoon to break up the pieces. Once it's brown, stir in the flour. Stir in the stock to the browned mince, cover the pan with a lid and bring to the boil. Add the Worcestershire sauce, carrot and mushrooms and season well with salt and pepper. Reduce the heat, cover and cook for 15 minutes.
3 Meanwhile, put the potatoes into a large pan of salted water. Bring to the boil and cook for about 20–25 minutes until very soft. Drain and put back into the pan over a low heat to dry off. Mash until smooth, and then beat in the butter and milk. Season with salt and pepper to taste.
4 Spoon the sauce into a 1.7 litre (3 pint) ovenproof dish, cover with the mashed potato, then cook in the oven for 20–25 minutes or until piping hot and the topping is golden brown.

TRY SOMETHING DIFFERENT
To make individual pies, use four 450ml (¾ pint) shallow ovenproof dishes.

NUTRITION PER SERVING
581 cals | 28g fat (12g sats) | 55g carbs | 1.8g salt

BOEUF BOURGUIGNONNE

Serves 6
Preparation 30 minutes
Cooking time 3 hours

1kg (2¼ lb) topside, rump or lean braising steak
50g (2oz) butter
2 tbsp oil
125g (4oz) bacon lardons
1 garlic clove, crushed
3 tbsp plain flour
bouquet garni (1 bay leaf, a few fresh parsley and thyme
    sprigs)
150ml (¼ pint) beef stock
300ml (½ pint) Burgundy or other full-bodied red wine
12 baby onions, peeled
175g (6oz) button mushrooms
salt and ground black pepper
freshly chopped parsley, to garnish

1 Cut the meat into 3cm (1¼ in) cubes.
2 Melt half the butter with 1 tbsp oil in a large flameproof casserole. Add the bacon and brown quickly, then remove with a slotted spoon.
3 Reheat the fat in the casserole and brown the meat in batches. Return the bacon to the casserole and add the garlic. Sprinkle in the flour and stir well.
4 Add salt and pepper, the bouquet garni, stock and wine. Bring to the boil, stirring, then cover and cook in the oven at 170°C (150°C fan oven) mark 3 for about 2½ hours.
5 Meanwhile, heat the remaining butter and oil in a frying pan and fry the onions until glazed and golden brown. Remove with a slotted spoon and set aside. Sauté the mushrooms in the pan for 2–3 minutes until slightly softened.
6 Add the sautéed mushrooms and onions to the casserole and cook for a further 30 minutes. Discard the bouquet garni, check the seasoning and serve sprinkled with chopped parsley.

NUTRITION PER SERVING
470 cals | 27g fat (9g sats) | 14g carbs | 1.8g salt

MEAT LOAF

Serves 4
Preparation 10 minutes
Cooking time 1 hour 40 minutes

25g (1oz) butter
1 onion, finely chopped
1 tsp paprika
450g (1lb) minced beef
50g (2oz) fresh breadcrumbs
3 tbsp natural wheatgerm
1 garlic clove, crushed
1 tbsp freshly chopped herbs or 1 tsp dried mixed herbs,
    plus fresh herbs to garnish
4 tbsp tomato purée
1 medium egg, beaten
salt and ground black pepper
Fresh Tomato Sauce to serve (see page 20)

1 Preheat the oven to 180°C (160°C fan oven) mark 4.
Grease and base line a 450g (1lb), capacity 900ml (1½ pint),
loaf tin.
2 Melt the butter in a frying pan, add the onion and cook
until softened. Add the paprika and cook for 1 minute, stirring,
then turn the mixture into a large bowl.
3 Add all the remaining ingredients and stir thoroughly until
evenly mixed. Spoon the mixture into the loaf tin, level the
surface and cover tightly with foil.
4 Stand the loaf tin in a roasting tin and pour in water to a
depth of 2.5cm (1in). Cook in the oven for 1½ hours. Turn
out and serve with the sauce.

NUTRITION PER SERVING
406 cals | 26g fat (12g sats) | 17gcarbs | 1.4g salt

CHILLI CON CARNE

Serves 4
Preparation 5 minutes
Cooking time about 1 hour

2 tbsp olive oil
450g (1lb) minced beef
1 large onion, finely chopped
1 tsp each hot chilli powder and ground cumin
3 tbsp tomato purée
300ml (1/2 pint) hot vegetable stock
400g can chopped tomatoes with garlic (see Cook's Tips)
25g (1oz) dark chocolate (see Cook's Tips)
400g can red kidney beans, drained and rinsed
2 × 20g packs coriander, chopped
salt and ground black pepper
guacamole, salsa, soured cream, grated cheese, tortilla chips
   and pickled chillies to serve

1 Heat 1 tbsp oil in a large non-stick pan and fry the beef
for 10 minutes or until well browned, stirring to break up
any lumps. Remove from the pan with a slotted spoon and
set aside.
2 Add the remaining oil to the pan, then fry the onion,
stirring, for 10 minutes or until soft and golden.
3 Add the spices and fry for 1 minute, then return the beef
to the pan. Add the tomato purée, hot stock and tomatoes.
Bring to the boil, then reduce to a simmer. Continue to bubble
gently, uncovered, for 35–40 minutes, or until the sauce is well
reduced and the mixture is quite thick.
4 Stir in the chocolate, kidney beans and coriander, season
with salt and pepper, then simmer for 5 minutes.
5 Serve with guacamole, salsa, soured cream, grated cheese,
tortilla chips and pickled chillies.

COOK'S TIPS

- Instead of a can of tomatoes with garlic, use a can
  of chopped tomatoes and 1 crushed garlic clove.
- Adding a little dark chocolate to chilli con carne
  brings out the flavours of this tasty dish.

NUTRITION PER SERVING
408 cals | 19g fat (7g sats) | 28g carbs | 1.1g salt

HAMBURGERS

Serves 6
Preparation 20 minutes, plus chilling
Cooking time 10 minutes

1kg (2¼ lb) extra-lean minced beef
2 tsp salt
2 tbsp steak seasoning
sunflower oil to brush
6 large soft rolls, halved
6 thin-cut slices havarti or raclette cheese
4 small cocktail gherkins, sliced lengthways
6 tbsp mustard mayonnaise (see page 29)
6 lettuce leaves, such as frisée
4 large vine-ripened tomatoes, sliced thickly
2 large shallots, sliced into thin rings
ground black pepper

1 Put the minced beef into a large bowl and add the salt, steak seasoning and plenty of pepper. Use your hands to mix the ingredients together thoroughly. Lightly oil the inside of six 10cm (4in) rosti rings and put on a foil-lined baking sheet. Press the meat firmly into the rings, or use your hands to shape the mixture into six even-sized patties. Cover with clingfilm and chill for at least 1 hour.
2 Heat a large griddle pan until it's really hot. Put the rolls, cut sides down, on the griddle and toast.
3 Lightly oil the griddle, ease the burgers out of the moulds and brush with oil. Griddle over a medium heat for about 3 minutes, then turn the burgers over carefully. Put a slice of cheese and a few slices of gherkin on top of each and cook for another 3 minutes. While the burgers are cooking, spread the mustard mayonnaise on the toasted side of the rolls. Add the lettuce, tomatoes and shallots. Put the burgers on top and sandwich with the other half-rolls.

TRY SOMETHING DIFFERENT
For a more sophisticated burger, replace the cheese and gherkins with thick slices of ripe avocado and use a generous handful of fresh rocket instead of the lettuce.

NUTRITION PER SERVING
645 cals | 45g fat (17g sats) | 19g carbs | 2.3g salt

VEAL TONNATO

Serves 6
Preparation 30 minutes, plus chilling
Cooking time 1¼–1½ hours

1 boned loin of veal, about 900g (2lb)
225g (8oz) frozen leaf spinach, thawed
1 tbsp extra virgin olive oil
finely grated zest of 1 lemon
6–8 thin slices Parma ham (see Cook's Tip, page 65)
300ml (½ pint) dry white wine
1 carrot, sliced
1 celery stick, sliced
1 onion, quartered
2 bay leaves
4–6 juniper berries, crushed
salt and ground black pepper
black olives to garnish

For the dressing
200g can tuna chunks in oil, drained
4 anchovy fillets in oil, drained
300ml (½ pint) good thick mayonnaise (see page 29)
3 tbsp chopped basil
1 tbsp capers in brine, rinsed, drained and roughly chopped

1 Lay the meat on a clean surface and season the inside well. Squeeze the spinach to remove as much moisture as possible, then toss in the olive oil, lemon zest and season. Spread this over the meat, bringing the flap over the spinach to cover.
2 Carefully wrap the meat in the Parma ham and tie at intervals with string. Place in a flameproof casserole. Add the wine, carrot, celery, onion, bay leaves, juniper berries and seasoning. Add enough water to just cover the veal and bring slowly to the boil. Lower the heat and barely simmer for 1¼–1½ hours until tender. Leave the veal to cool in the liquid.
3 When cold, take out the veal, drain and pat dry. Strain the liquid and keep to one side. Cover the veal and chill.
4 To make the dressing, mash the tuna and anchovy fillets together or pound with a pestle and mortar. Stir in the mayonnaise, basil and capers. Thin to a pouring consistency with a little of the reserved liquid and check the seasoning.
5 To serve, thinly slice the veal and arrange on a plate. Spoon the dressing over the meat and serve with black olives.

NUTRITION PER SERVING
730 cals | 56g fat (9g sats) | 4g carbs | 2.4g salt

VEAL SCHNITZEL WITH SALSA VERDE

Serves 4
Preparation 30 minutes
Cooking time 15 minutes

4 veal escalopes, about 100g (3¹/₂ oz) each
175g (6oz) dried breadcrumbs
125g (4oz) ground almonds
flour to coat
1 egg, beaten
6 tbsp oil
salt and ground black pepper
Salsa Verde (see page 23) and lemon wedges to serve

1 Lay the veal escalopes between two pieces of greaseproof paper and beat with a rolling pin to flatten. If too large for the frying pan, cut in half.
2 Mix the dried breadcrumbs and ground almonds together on a plate. Season the veal, then coat lightly with flour. Dip each piece in beaten egg, then into the breadcrumb mixture to coat, patting to adhere.
3 Heat 2 tbsp oil in a large heavy-based frying pan, add one-third of the veal and fry for 1–2 minutes on each side until deep golden brown. Transfer to a heatproof plate and keep warm in a low oven. Wipe out the frying pan with kitchen paper and cook the remaining veal in the same way, using fresh oil for each batch.
4 Serve the schnitzel as soon as it is all cooked, with the Salsa Verde and lemon wedges.

NUTRITION PER SERVING (without salsa verde)
650 cals | 41g fat (22g sats) | 39g carbs | 1.4g salt

SALTIMBOCCA ALLA ROMANA

Serves 8
Preparation 10 minutes
Cooking time about 10 minutes

8 veal escalopes, about 125g (4oz)
    each
1–2 tbsp lemon juice
8 thin slices Parma ham (see Cook's
    Tip, page 65)
8 fresh sage leaves
50g (2oz) butter
1 tbsp oil
2 tbsp Marsala
ground black pepper
fried sage leaves to garnish
bread to serve

1 Put the veal escalopes between two sheets of greaseproof paper and pound with a rolling pin to flatten. Sprinkle with lemon juice and pepper.
2 Wrap each escalope in a slice of Parma ham. Place a sage leaf on top and secure with a wooden cocktail stick.
3 Heat the butter and oil in a frying pan, then add the veal and fry gently until golden brown. Stir in the Marsala, bring to simmering point, then cover the pan and simmer gently for 8–10 minutes.
4 Serve the veal with the pan juices poured over, and garnished with fried sage leaves. Serve with bread.

NUTRITION PER SERVING 220 cals |
11g fat (5 sats) | trace carbs | 1.3g salt

OSSO BUCO

Serves 4
Preparation 15 minutes
Cooking time 1 hour 50 minutes–
2 hours 20 minutes

50g (2oz) butter
1 tbsp olive oil
1 onion, finely chopped
4 large or 8 small ossi buchi (veal shin,
    hind cut), weighing about 1.7kg
    (3³/₄ lb), sawn into 5cm (2in)
    lengths
3 tbsp seasoned flour
300ml (¹/₂ pint) dry white wine
300ml (¹/₂ pint) veal or chicken stock
finely grated zest of 1 lemon
1 garlic clove, finely chopped
3 tbsp freshly chopped parsley
Risotto Milanese (see page 263)
    to serve

1 Melt the butter with the oil in a flameproof casserole, add the onion and fry gently for 5 minutes or until soft but not coloured.
2 Coat the veal in the flour, add to the casserole and fry for about 10 minutes or until browned.
3 Pour over the wine and boil rapidly for 5 minutes, then add the stock.
4 Cover the pan tightly and simmer for 1¹/₂–2 hours, basting and turning the meat occasionally.
5 Transfer the meat to a warmed serving dish, cover and keep warm. If necessary, boil the sauce rapidly to thicken, then pour it over the meat.
6 Mix together the lemon zest, garlic and parsley, and sprinkle over the dish. Serve with the risotto.

NUTRITION PER SERVING 559 cals |
26g fat (8g sats) | 22g carbs | 1.3g salt

1 Loin
The loin comprises both chump and loin chops. Chump chops (1b) have a small round bone in the centre, and loin chops (1a) a small T-bone. Loin steaks are boneless loin chops. The whole loin can also be roasted.

2 Fillet of lamb
A lean cut from the middle neck; roast, fry or cook en croûte.

3 Scrag (3a) and middle neck (3b)
Cuts on the bone for stewing and braising.

4 Saddle of lamb or double loin
The whole loin. It is sometimes sold sliced into butterfly or Barnsley chops.

5 Leg of lamb
A lean cut, good for roasting. Traditionally sold with the bone in (5a), either whole or as a half leg – fillet end or knuckle/shank end. Boned and rolled leg is also available. Boned, it can also be 'butterflied' – flattened for grilling or barbecuing. Leg steaks (5b) are prime cuts for grilling and pan-frying.

6 Rack of lamb
Also known as best end of neck, this is a whole roasting joint of 6–8 chops or cutlets. Usually chined to make serving easier, the tips of the cutlet bones are then scraped of all fat and meat to look neat. This cut is used for 'crown roast' and 'guard of honour'.

7 Shoulder
Sold whole or as a half shoulder – knuckle or blade end – for roasting, or as chops or steaks for grilling or braising.

8 Lamb cutlets
Boned and rolled cutlets are called noisettes; these neat lean portions are excellent grilled or pan-fried.

9 Breast of lamb
Sold ready boned and rolled, this is best cooked slowly and thoroughly. If braised, it must be well trimmed, as it is a fatty cut.

10 Shank
Taken from the lower part of the hind leg, the shank is usually cooked on the bone. Braise, casserole or pot-roast.

11 Mince
Look for mince with a low proportion of fat. Use in stuffings, sauces, burgers, meat loaf, kebabs, and so on.

ROAST LEG OF LAMB WITH ROSEMARY

Serves 8
Preparation 15 minutes
Cooking time 1 hour 29 minutes, plus resting

2.5kg (5¹/₂lb) leg of lamb
4 rosemary sprigs
¹/₂ tbsp oil
4 garlic cloves, cut into slivers
4 anchovy fillets, roughly chopped
4 oregano sprigs
1 large onion, thickly sliced
1 lemon, cut into 6 wedges
salt and ground black pepper
vegetables to serve

1 Take the lamb out of the fridge an hour before roasting. Pat the skin dry with kitchen paper.
2 Preheat the oven to 220°C (200°C fan) mark 7. Cut the rosemary into smaller sprigs. Rub the oil over the lamb. Cut small slits all over the meat and insert the garlic slivers, rosemary sprigs, anchovy pieces and the leaves from two oregano sprigs into the gaps. Season well.
3 Put the onion slices into the base of a roasting tin just large enough to hold the lamb. Top with the remaining oregano, then put in the meat, fat side up (the onions must be covered to prevent them burning). Tuck lemon wedges around the meat.
4 Put the lamb into the oven and turn down the heat to 190°C (170°C fan) mark 5. Roast for 15 minutes per 450lb (1lb) for pink meat, or longer if you like it more cooked.
5 Transfer the lamb to a board and cover with foil, reserving the roasting tin and its contents to make gravy (see page 11). Rest for 30 minutes before carving (see page 173). Serve with vegetables.

GET AHEAD
→ Prepare the lamb to the end of step 3 up to 2 hours ahead
→ To use, complete the recipe.

COOK'S TIP
Buy the best meat you can to ensure great flavour and texture. The lamb is served pink here, but allow an extra 20–30 minutes if you prefer your meat more cooked.

NUTRITION PER SERVING
601 cals | 39g fat (17g sats) | 1g carbs | 1.3g salt

LANCASHIRE HOTPOT

Serves 4
Preparation 20 minutes
Cooking time 2¹/₂ hours

12 lamb cutlets
2 medium onions, sliced
2 large carrots, sliced
leaves from 2 sprigs of thyme
750ml (1¹/₄ pints) hot lamb stock
450g (1lb) potatoes, sliced
25g (1oz) butter
salt and ground black pepper
Pickled Red Cabbage (see page 483)
    to serve

1 Heat the oven to 180°C (160°C fan oven) mark 4. Put a layer of cutlets into a large lidded casserole. Cover with a layer of onions and carrots and a sprinkling of thyme. Season well with salt and ground black pepper. Repeat with the remaining lamb, onions, carrots and thyme.

2 Pour in enough hot stock to almost cover the meat. Top with an overlapping layer of potatoes. Season, cover and cook in the oven for 2 hours.

3 Increase the oven temperature to 230°C (210°C fan oven) gas mark 8. Remove the lid and dot the top of the casserole with knobs of butter. Continue cooking for 30 minutes, uncovered, until the potatoes are golden brown. Serve with Pickled Red Cabbage.

NUTRITION PER SERVING 653 cals |
48g fat (24g sats) | 29g carbs | 1.4g salt

LAMB NOISETTES WITH TARRAGON SAUCE

Serves 4
Preparation 25 minutes
Cooking time 25 minutes

2 tbsp olive oil
8 lamb noisettes, about 125g (4oz)
    each
175g (6oz) onion, finely chopped
1 tbsp tarragon vinegar
150ml (¹/₄ pint) white wine
150ml (¹/₄ pint) double cream
300ml (¹/₂ pint) lamb or chicken stock
1 tbsp freshly chopped tarragon, plus
    extra sprigs to garnish
salt and ground black pepper
vegetables to serve

1 Heat 1 tbsp olive oil in a frying pan and brown the lamb noisettes, in batches, for 2 minutes on each side or until the fat is crisp.

2 Put the lamb in a roasting tin and cook at 200°C (180°C fan oven) mark 6 for 10 minutes for medium-rare; 15 minutes for well done.

3 Meanwhile, heat the remaining oil in the frying pan, add the onion and cook for 5–7 minutes until softened but not coloured. Add the tarragon vinegar and wine, bring to the boil and bubble for 2 minutes. Add the cream and stock; let it bubble for 10 minutes or until syrupy. Check the seasoning.

4 Remove the string from the lamb. Add the chopped tarragon and roasting juices to the sauce and warm through.

5 Serve the lamb with the sauce poured over, garnished with tarragon sprigs. Serve with vegetables.

NUTRITION PER SERVING 743 cals |
60g fat (29g sats) | 1g carbs | 1g salt

MOUSSAKA

Serves 6
Preparation 20 minutes
Cooking time 1 hour 20 minutes, plus standing

1kg (2¼ lb) aubergines, trimmed
5 tbsp olive oil
450g (1lb) onions, finely sliced
3 garlic cloves, crushed
700g (1½ lb) minced lamb
2 tbsp sun-dried tomato paste
400g can chopped tomatoes
1 cinnamon stick, slightly crushed
2 bay leaves
1 tbsp freshly chopped oregano
salt and ground black pepper
green salad to serve

For the topping
200g carton Greek-style yogurt
1 large egg
50g (2oz) Parmesan, freshly grated
freshly grated nutmeg
75g (3oz) feta cheese, roughly crumbled

1 Preheat the oven to 200°C (180°C fan oven) mark 6. Cut the aubergines into 5mm (¼ in) thick slices, brush both sides with a little olive oil and lay on four baking sheets. Season and roast for 35–40 minutes, turning halfway through.
2 Meanwhile, heat the remaining olive oil in a large pan. Add the onions and cook over a low heat for about 10 minutes or until soft. Add the garlic and cook for 2 minutes. Tip into a bowl and set aside while you cook the mince.
3 Put the mince in the pan and brown, stirring, over a high heat. Return the onions and garlic to the pan. Add the tomato paste, chopped tomatoes, cinnamon, bay leaves and oregano. Bring to a simmer and add seasoning. Simmer, half-covered, for 20 minutes.
4 To make the topping, put the yogurt, egg and half the grated Parmesan into a bowl and season with salt, pepper and a little nutmeg. Mix together, using a balloon whisk, until combined.
5 Spoon half the lamb mixture into a 2 litre (3½ pint) ovenproof dish. Cover with half the aubergine slices, overlapping them as necessary. Season well and repeat the layers, finishing with aubergine slices.
6 Scatter the crumbled feta on top, then pour the yogurt mixture over and sprinkle with the remaining Parmesan. Bake for 35–40 minutes until golden brown. Leave the moussaka to stand for 10–15 minutes, then serve with a green salad.

NUTRITION PER SERVING
470 cals | 31g fat (12g sats) | 12g carbs | 1.4g salt

LAMB, PRUNE AND ALMOND TAGINE

Serves 6
Preparation 20 minutes, plus marinating
Cooking time 2¹/₂ hours

2 tsp coriander seeds
2 tsp cumin seeds
2 tsp chilli powder
1 tbsp paprika
1 tbsp ground turmeric
5 garlic cloves, chopped
6 tbsp olive oil
1.4kg (3lb) lamb leg steaks
75g (3oz) ghee or clarified butter (see Cook's Tip)
2 large onions, finely chopped
1 carrot, roughly chopped
900ml (1¹/₂ pints) lamb stock
300g (11oz) ready-to-eat prunes
4 cinnamon sticks
4 bay leaves
50g (2oz) ground almonds
12 shallots
1 tbsp honey
salt and ground black pepper
toasted blanched almonds and freshly chopped
     flat-leafed parsley to garnish
couscous to serve

1 Using a pestle and mortar or a blender, combine the coriander and cumin seeds, chilli powder, paprika, turmeric, garlic and 4 tbsp oil. Coat the lamb with the paste, then cover and chill for at least 5 hours.
2 Preheat the oven to 170°C (150°C fan oven) mark 3. Melt 25g (1oz) ghee or butter in a large flameproof casserole. Add the onions and carrot, and cook until soft. Remove and put to one side. Fry the paste-coated lamb on both sides in the remaining ghee or butter. Add a little of the stock and bring to the boil, scraping up the sediment from the base. Put the onions and carrot back in the casserole and add 100g (3¹/₂ oz) prunes. Add the remaining stock with the cinnamon sticks, bay leaves and ground almonds. Season, cover and cook in the oven for 2 hours or until the meat is really tender.
3 Meanwhile, fry the shallots in the remaining oil and the honey until they turn a deep golden brown. Add to the casserole 30–40 minutes before the end of the cooking time.
4 Take the lamb out of the sauce and put to one side. Put the casserole over the heat and bring the sauce to the boil, then reduce to a thick consistency. Put the lamb back in the casserole, add the remaining prunes and bubble for 3–4 minutes. Garnish with the almonds and parsley. Serve hot with couscous.

COOK'S TIP
Clarified Butter Heat butter in a pan without allowing it to colour. Skim off the foam; the solids will sink. Pour the clear butter into a bowl through a lined sieve. Leave for 10 minutes. Pour into a bowl, leaving any sediment behind. Cool. Store in a jar in the fridge for up to six months.

NUTRITION PER SERVING
652 cals | 44g fat (16g sats) | 31g carbs | 0.6g salt

1 Chump
A roasting cut from the hindquarters. Cook the joint whole to feed 2–4 people.

2 Chump chop
A cut from between the loin and leg. Grill, pan-fry, braise or casserole.

3 Loin chop
This cut from the hind loin, gives tender, well-flavoured chops. Grill, pan-fry, braise or casserole; slice into strips and stir-fry.

4 Loin
Consists of the hind loin, for roasting, and the foreloin, which is the rib end. Roast, either on the bone or boned, stuffed and rolled. Loin steaks are boned loin chops.

5 Shoulder steak
These steaks are sweet and succulent. Remove the rind before cooking. Grill, pan-fry or braise; cut into strips and stir-fry.

6 Blade bone
A fatty joint, cut from the neck end of the shoulder and sold off the bone. Whole: roast, pot-roast or braise; cut into cubes, thread on to skewers and grill, or casserole.

7 Leg
Comprises fillet end (7a) and knuckle or shank end (7b); both good for roasting. The fillet end is sometimes cut into leg steaks. Roast, or split, stuff and roll. Grill, pan-fry or braise steaks or escalopes.

8 Tenderloin or pork fillet
A lean cut from the hind loin. Split, stuff and roast; pan-fry or grill medallions or escalopes; pan-fry or braise cubes; stir-fry strips.

9 Belly
A long, thin cut streaked with fat. Roast whole or boned as a rolled joint. Grill or fry slices; add pieces to casseroles and stews; mince for sausages. **Spare ribs (9a):** Cut from the belly or the ribs. Spare rib chops can be casseroled or braised; trimmed American or Chinese spare ribs are typically cooked in barbecue sauce.

10 Hand and spring
Cut from the lower part of the forequarter; often divided into two: the hand and shank. Pot-roast, casserole or braise; cut into cubes and stew; roast. **Knuckle (10a):** bone, stuff, roll and roast; pot-roast, braise or casserole; cut into cubes and stew.

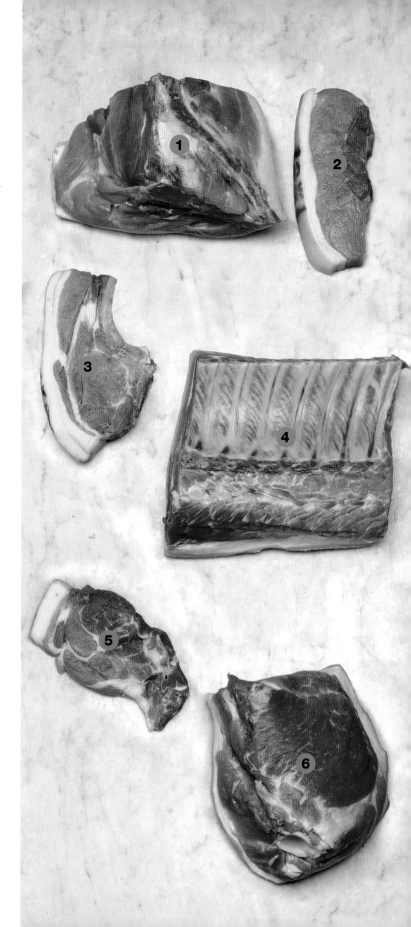

CRISP ROAST PORK WITH APPLE SAUCE

Serves 6
Preparation 30 minutes, plus standing
Cooking time 2 hours, plus resting

1.6kg (3¹/₂ lb) boned rolled loin of pork
olive oil
1kg (2¹/₄ lb) cooking apples
1–2 tbsp granulated sugar
1 tbsp plain flour
600ml (1 pint) chicken stock or dry cider
salt and ground black pepper
roast potatoes and green vegetables to serve (optional)

1 Score the pork skin, sprinkle generously with salt and leave at room temperature for 1–2 hours.
2 Preheat the oven to 220°C (200°C fan oven) mark 7. Wipe the salt off the skin, rub with oil and sprinkle again with salt. Core and roughly chop the apples, then put half in a small roasting tin, sit the pork on top and roast for 30 minutes. Turn the oven down to 190°C (170°C fan oven) mark 5 and roast for a further 1¹/₂ hours or until cooked.
3 Meanwhile, put the remaining apples in a pan with the sugar and 2 tbsp water, cover with a tight-fitting lid and cook until just soft. Put this sauce into a small serving dish.
4 Remove the pork from the tin and leave to rest. Skim off most of the fat, leaving about 1 tbsp and the apples in the tin. Stir in the flour until smooth, stir in the stock and bring to the boil. Bubble gently for 2–3 minutes, skimming if necessary. Strain the sauce through a sieve into a jug, pushing through as much of the apple as possible. Slice the pork and serve with the sauce, gravy, roast potatoes and green vegetables, if you like.

NUTRITION PER SERVING
769 cals | 50g fat (18g sats) | 22g carbs | 0.4g salt

STUFFED PORK TENDERLOINS

Serves 6
Preparation 25 minutes, plus cooling
Cooking time 1 hour, plus resting

25g (1oz) butter
1 onion, finely chopped
1 tbsp freshly chopped thyme
grated zest of ½ orange
50g (2oz) fresh white breadcrumbs
2 pork fillets (tenderloins)
2 tbsp olive oil
200ml (7fl oz) hot chicken stock
50ml (2fl oz) red wine
salt and ground black pepper
herby mashed potato and carrots to serve

1 Melt the butter in a pan, add the onion and cook for 3–4 minutes until softened. Add the thyme and orange zest, and cook for a further 1 minute. Add the breadcrumbs, stir and season with salt and pepper. Allow to cool.

2 Preheat the oven to 190°C (170°C fan oven) mark 5. Trim any fat from the pork, then cut each fillet lengthways down the middle, almost but not quite through. Season well, then open out and spoon half the breadcrumb mixture along each fillet. Bring the sides over the filling to enclose and carefully tie with string at intervals to secure.

3 Heat the olive oil in a heavy-based roasting tin on the hob, add the pork fillets and brown all over, then transfer to the oven and roast for 40–45 minutes until cooked through.

4 Lift the pork on to a warmed plate, cover with foil and leave to rest. Add the hot stock and red wine to the roasting tin and bring to the boil, scraping up the sediment from the base. Season with salt and pepper to taste and simmer for 5–6 minutes until syrupy. Slice the pork and serve with the sauce, mashed potato and carrots.

NUTRITION PER SERVING
280 cals | 16g fat (3g sats) | 7g carbs | 0.3g salt

BELLY OF PORK WITH CIDER AND ROSEMARY

Serves 8
Preparation 30 minutes, plus cooling and chilling
Cooking time about 4¹/₂ hours

2kg (4¹/₂ lb) piece pork belly roast, on the bone
500ml bottle medium cider
600ml (1 pint) hot chicken stock
6–8 fresh rosemary sprigs
3 fat garlic cloves, halved
2 tbsp olive oil
grated zest and juice of 1 large orange and 1 lemon
3 tbsp light muscovado sugar
25g (1oz) softened butter, mixed with 1 tbsp plain flour as beurre manié (see Cook's Tip page 136)
salt and ground black pepper
mixed vegetables to serve

1 Preheat the oven to 150°C (130°C fan oven) mark 2. Put the pork, skin side up, in a roasting tin just large enough to hold it. Add the cider, hot stock and half the rosemary. Bring to the boil on the hob, then cover with foil and cook in the oven for 4 hours. Leave to cool in the cooking liquid.
2 Strip the leaves from the remaining rosemary and chop. Put into a pestle and mortar with the garlic, oil, orange and lemon zest, 1 tsp salt and 1 tbsp sugar. Pound for 3–4 minutes to make a rough paste.
3 Remove the pork from the tin (keep the cooking liquid) and slice off the rind from the top layer of fat. Set aside. Score the fat into a diamond pattern and rub in the rosemary paste. Cover loosely with clingfilm and chill until required.
4 Pat the rind dry with kitchen paper and put it fat side up on a foil-lined baking sheet. Cook under a hot grill, about 10cm (4in) away from the heat, for 5 minutes. Turn over, sprinkle lightly with salt, then grill for 7–10 minutes until crisp. Cool, then cut the crackling into rough pieces.
5 Make the gravy. Strain the cooking liquid into a pan. Add the orange and lemon juice and the remaining 2 tbsp sugar, bring to the boil and bubble until reduced by half. Whisk the butter mixture into the liquid and boil for 4–5 minutes until thickened. Set aside.
6 When almost ready to serve, preheat the oven to 220°C (200°C fan oven) mark 7. Cook the pork, uncovered, in a roasting tin for 20 minutes or until piping hot. Wrap the crackling in foil and warm in the oven for the last 5 minutes of the cooking time. Heat the gravy on the hob. Carve the pork into slices and serve with the crackling, gravy and vegetables.

COOK'S TIP
The best cut of belly pork is the thicker part of the belly, as it is leaner and sometimes more tender.

NUTRITION PER SERVING
694 cals | 52g fat (19g sats) | 9g carbs | 0.5g salt

ITALIAN MEATBALLS

Serves 4
Preparation 15 minutes
Cooking time 50 minutes

50g (2oz) fresh breadcrumbs
450g (1lb) lean minced pork
1 tsp fennel seeds, crushed
1/4 tsp dried chilli flakes, or to taste
3 garlic cloves, crushed
4 tbsp freshly chopped flat-leafed parsley
3 tbsp red wine
oil–water spray (see Cook's Tip)
freshly chopped oregano to garnish
spaghetti to serve

For the tomato sauce
oil–water spray
2 large shallots, finely chopped
3 pitted black olives, shredded
2 garlic cloves, crushed
2 pinches of dried chilli flakes
250ml (9fl oz) vegetable or chicken stock
500g carton passata
2 tbsp each freshly chopped flat-leafed parsley,
    basil and oregano
salt and ground black pepper

1 To make the tomato sauce, spray a pan with the oil–water spray and add the shallots. Cook gently for 5 minutes. Add the olives, garlic, chilli flakes and stock, and bring to the boil, then reduce the heat, cover and simmer for 3–4 minutes.
2 Uncover and simmer for 10 minutes or until the shallots and garlic are soft and the liquid syrupy. Stir in the passata and season with salt and pepper. Bring to the boil, then reduce the heat and simmer for 10–15 minutes. Stir in the herbs.
3 Meanwhile, put the breadcrumbs into a large bowl and add the pork, fennel seeds, chilli flakes, garlic, parsley and wine, Season and mix together, using your hands, until thoroughly combined. (If you wish to check the seasoning, fry a little mixture, taste and adjust if necessary.)
4 With wet hands, roll the mixture into balls. Line a grill pan with foil, shiny side up, and spray with the oil–water spray. Cook the meatballs under a preheated grill for 3–4 minutes on each side. Serve with the tomato sauce and spaghetti, garnished with oregano.

COOK'S TIP
Oil–water spray is far lower in calories than oil alone and, as it sprays on thinly and evenly, you'll use less. Fill one-eighth of a travel-sized spray bottle with oil such as sunflower, light olive or vegetable (rapeseed) oil, then top up with water. To use, shake well before spraying. Store in the fridge.

NUTRITION PER SERVING
275 cals | 12g fat (4g sats) | 16g carbs | 1.8g salt

FENNEL AND LEMON RACK OF PORK

Serves 8
Preparation 20 minutes, plus resting
Cooking time about 2½ hours

For the pork
large handful fresh curly parsley
1 garlic clove, roughly chopped
finely grated zest of 1 lemon
2 tsp fennel seeds
1 fresh bay leaf
3 tbsp olive oil
8-rib pork rack – around 2kg (4½lb); ask your butcher
    to scrape the bones and remove the fat
1 medium onion, sliced thickly into rings
sea salt

For the gravy
1 tbsp plain flour
200ml (7fl oz) cider
500ml (18fl oz) hot chicken stock
1 tbsp quince redcurrant jelly
1 tsp Dijon mustard

1 Preheat the oven to 240°C (220°C fan) mark 9. Put the parsley, garlic, lemon zest, fennel seeds, bay leaf and 2 tbsp oil into a food processor and whiz to make a paste.
2 Remove the butcher's string from the pork rack and, using a sharp knife, carefully cut away the rind in one piece, leaving behind the fat on the pork. Set aside. Rub the fennel paste over the fat, then replace the rind. Tie in place with six to eight pieces of string. Weigh the pork and calculate the cooking time, allowing 25 minutes per 450g (1lb).
3 Keeping the onion rings intact, arrange them in the base of a roasting dish just large enough to hold the meat. Put the pork on top. Rub the rind with the remaining oil and sprinkle generously with sea salt. Roast for 30 minutes, then reduce the oven temperature to 180°C (160°C fan) mark 4. Continue cooking for the calculated time until the juices run clear when you pierce the meat with a knife. Put the pork on a board, cover loosely with foil and set aside to rest – it will keep warm for up to an hour.
4 To make the gravy, discard the onion from the pan. Tip away all but 1 tbsp of the fat and put the pan on the hob over a medium heat. Sprinkle in the flour and stir, scraping up all the meaty bits stuck to the bottom – they contain lots of flavour. Take off the heat and slowly blend in the cider. Return to the heat and bubble for 2 minutes, then add the stock. Simmer for 15 minutes.
5 Stir in the jelly, mustard and any meat juices from the resting pork, then strain and check the seasoning. Pour into a

warmed jug and take to the table. Remove the string from the pork and slice between the bones with the crackling still attached. Divide among eight plates and serve.

COOK'S TIPS
- ➥ If the crackling softens under the foil, pop under a high grill for a minute or two to crisp up – but watch it closely to make sure it doesn't burn.
- ➥ If you don't want to rest the pork for more than half an hour, you can still make a gravy ahead of time. Transfer the joint to a clean pan 30 minutes before the end of its cooking time, then put it back in the oven. There will be enough juices in the original pan to make the gravy while the joint carries on cooking.

NUTRITION PER SERVING
431cals | 33g fat (11g sats) | 4g carbs | 5.4g salt

CUMBERLAND GLAZED BAKED GAMMON

Serves 16
Preparation 30 minutes
Cooking time 3½–4¼ hours

4.5kg (10lb) smoked gammon joint, on the bone
2 celery sticks, roughly chopped
1 onion, quartered
1 carrot, roughly chopped
1 tsp black peppercorns
1 tbsp cloves
75g (3oz) redcurrant sprigs

For the Cumberland glaze
grated zest and juice of ½ lemon and ½ orange
4 tbsp redcurrant jelly
1 tsp Dijon mustard
2 tbsp port
salt and ground black pepper

1 Put the gammon into a large pan. Add the celery, onion, carrot and peppercorns. Cover the meat and vegetables with cold water and bring to the boil. Simmer, covered, for 2¾ hours–3½ hours, or allowing 15–20 minutes per 450g (1lb) plus 15 minutes. Lift the gammon out of the pan. Preheat the oven to 200°C (180°C fan oven) mark 6.
2 Meanwhile, make the glaze. Heat the lemon and orange zests and juices, redcurrant jelly, mustard and port in a pan to dissolve the jelly. Bring to the boil and bubble for 5 minutes or until syrupy. Season with salt and pepper to taste.
3 Remove the gammon rind and score the fat in a diamond pattern. Put the gammon into a roasting tin, then stud the fat with cloves. Spoon the glaze evenly over the gammon joint.
4 Roast the gammon for 40 minutes, basting the meat with any juices. Add the redcurrant sprigs 10 minutes before the end of the cooking time. Serve the gammon hot or cold, carved into thin slices with the redcurrant sprigs.

> **NUTRITION PER SERVING**
> 406 cals | 21g fat (7g sats) | 4g carbs | 6.3g salt

RAISED PORK PIE

Serves 8
Preparation 45 minutes, plus cooling and chilling
Cooking time about 3½ hours, plus cooling and chilling

3 or 4 small veal bones
1 small onion, peeled
1 bay leaf
4 black peppercorns
900g (2lb) boneless leg or shoulder of pork, cubed
¼ tsp cayenne pepper
¼ tsp ground ginger
¼ tsp ground mace
¼ tsp dried sage
¼ tsp dried marjoram
1 tbsp salt
½ tsp pepper
300ml (½ pint) milk and water mixed
150g (5oz) lard
450g (1lb) plain flour
1 medium egg, beaten
salad to serve

1 Put the bones, onion, bay leaf and peppercorns in a pan and cover with water. Simmer for 20 minutes, then boil to reduce the liquid to 150ml (¼ pint). Strain and cool.
2 Mix the pork with the spices and herbs, 1 tsp salt and the pepper.
3 Bring the milk, water and lard to the boil in a pan, then gradually beat it into the flour and remaining salt in a bowl. Knead for 3–4 minutes.
4 Roll out two-thirds of the pastry on a lightly floured surface and mould into a 20.5cm (8in) base-lined, springform cake tin. Cover and chill for 30 minutes. Keep the remaining pastry covered. Preheat the oven to 220°C (200°C fan oven) mark 7.
5 Spoon the meat mixture and 4 tbsp cold stock into the pastry case. Roll out the remaining pastry to make a lid and put on top of the meat mixture, sealing the pastry edges well. Decorate with pastry trimmings and make a hole in the centre. Glaze with the beaten egg.
6 Bake for 30 minutes. Cover loosely with foil, reduce the heat to 180°C (160°C fan oven) mark 4 and bake for a further 2½ hours. Cool.
7 Warm the remaining jellied stock until liquid, then pour into the centre hole of the pie. Chill and serve with salad.

TRY SOMETHING DIFFERENT

Raised Veal and Ham Pie Mix together 700g (1½lb) diced pie veal and 225g (8oz) diced cooked ham, 1 tbsp freshly chopped parsley, grated zest and juice of 1 lemon and seasoning, and use to half-fill the pie. Put one hard-boiled egg in the centre and cover with the remaining veal mixture. Proceed as above.

COOK'S TIP
If you have no bones available for stock, use
2 tsp gelatine to 300ml (½ pint) stock.

NUTRITION PER SERVING
617 cals | 37g fat (14g sats) | 45g carbs | 2g salt

1 Liver
Chicken (1), duck and turkey livers are similar in taste. Make into pâtés, or sauté in butter and/or oil. Goose liver (2) in the form of foie gras is produced by intensive feeding of geese to enlarge their livers (also comes from ducks fed in the same way). Calf's liver (3) has a delicate flavour and is usually pan-fried. Lamb's liver (4) is slightly stronger in flavour than calf's. Pig's (5) and ox liver are strongly flavoured, with a coarser texture.

6 Oxtail
A tough but flavourful cut, usually sold jointed. Casserole larger pieces; smaller pieces are better for making stocks and soups. Braise, stew or casserole.

7 Lamb's hearts
These have a tender texture and mild flavour. Pig's and ox hearts are larger and coarser. All suit long, slow cooking. Soak in salted water for 1 hour, then rinse and slice or stuff. Braise, casserole or stew.

8 Kidney
Veal kidneys (8a) are mild. Lamb's kidneys (8b) have a 'lamby' taste. Pig's and ox kidneys (8c) have a stronger flavour and suit long, slow cooking. Grill, pan-fry, or add to casseroles, stews, pies and savoury puddings.

9 Sweetbreads
Sweetbreads require precooking in stock or water and can then be pan-fried, roasted or braised. Soak in lightly salted water, rinse, blanch and remove the outer membrane.

10 Tripe
The stomach lining of the cow. Tripe is sold bleached, and par-boiled to varying degrees. Casserole or stew.

11 Ox tongue
Sold fresh or brined, pressed and served cold, cut into thin slices, or hot. Soak fresh tongue for about 2 hours, and brined ox tongue overnight. Boil with spices until tender; drain and peel.

12 Trotter
Pig's feet release gelatine when cooked. Boil for stock; boil to pickle; or boil, then grill or bake, with or without a filling.

13 Brain
Usually taken from the heads of lambs and calves, brains need soaking and par-boiling before pan-frying or braising.

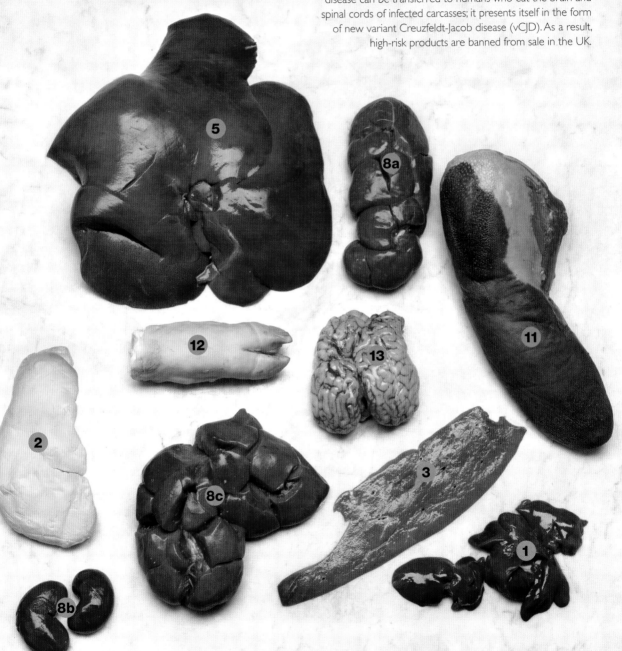

Bovine Spongiform Encephalopathy

More commonly known as BSE, or mad cow disease, bovine spongiform encephalopathy is a fatal neurodegenerative disease found in cattle. It is thought to have arisen as a result of feeding ground-up sheep carcasses infected with a similar disease that affects sheep – scrapie – to cattle. Cattle in the UK have been the most widely affected and any animals suspected of having the disease are slaughtered. It is widely believed that the disease can be transferred to humans who eat the brain and spinal cords of infected carcasses; it presents itself in the form of new variant Creuzfeldt-Jacob disease (vCJD). As a result, high-risk products are banned from sale in the UK.

BRAISED OXTAIL

Serves 6
Preparation 20 minutes
Cooking time about 4 hours

2 oxtails, about 1.6kg (3¹/₂ lb) in total, trimmed
2 tbsp plain flour
4 tbsp oil
2 large onions, sliced
900ml (1¹/₂ pints) beef stock
150ml (¹/₄ pint) red wine
1 tbsp tomato purée
finely grated zest of ¹/₂ lemon
2 bay leaves
2 medium carrots, chopped
450g (1lb) parsnips, chopped
salt and ground black pepper
freshly chopped parsley, to garnish

1 Cut the oxtails into large pieces. Season the flour with
salt and pepper and use to coat the pieces. Heat the oil in
a large flameproof casserole and brown the oxtail pieces,
a few at a time. Remove from the casserole with a slotted
spoon and set aside.
2 Add the onions to the casserole and fry over a medium
heat for about 10 minutes or until softened and lightly
browned. Stir in any remaining flour.
3 Stir in the stock, red wine, tomato purée, lemon zest and
bay leaves. Season with salt and pepper. Bring to the boil, then
return the oxtail and lower the heat. Cover and simmer very
gently for 2 hours.
4 Skim off the fat from the surface, then stir in the carrots
and parsnips. Re-cover the casserole and simmer very gently
for a further 2 hours or until the oxtail is very tender.
5 Skim off all the fat from the surface, then check the
seasoning. Serve scattered with chopped parsley.

COOK'S TIP
Oxtail contains a modest amount of meat and often
plenty of firm white fat, although the fat can be
trimmed before cooking. It also releases generous
amounts of gelatine, which helps to enrich dishes.

NUTRITION PER SERVING
616 cals | 35g fat (12g sats) | 16g carbs | 1.2g salt

LANCASHIRE TRIPE AND ONIONS

Serves 4
Preparation 20 minutes
Cooking time about 2¼ hours

450g (1lb) dressed tripe, washed
225g (8oz) shallots, peeled
600ml (1 pint) milk
a pinch of freshly grated nutmeg
1 bay leaf
25g (1oz) butter
3 tbsp plain flour
salt and ground black pepper
freshly chopped parsley, to garnish
crusty bread to serve

1 Put the tripe into a pan and cover with cold water. Bring to the boil, then drain and rinse under cold running water. Cut into 2.5cm (1in) pieces.
2 Put the tripe, shallots, milk, seasoning, nutmeg and bay leaf into the rinsed-out pan. Bring to the boil, cover and simmer for about 2 hours or until tender. Strain and keep to one side 600ml (1 pint) of the liquid. Discard the bay leaf.
3 Melt the butter in a pan, stir in the flour and cook gently for 1 minute, stirring. Remove the pan from the heat and gradually stir in the reserved cooking liquid. Bring to the boil and continue to cook, stirring, until the sauce thickens.
4 Add the tripe and shallots and reheat. Check the seasoning and sprinkle with chopped parsley. Serve with bread.

NUTRITION PER SERVING
240 cals | 10g fat (5g sats) | 20g carbs | 1g salt

LIVER AND ONIONS

Serves 4
Preparation 10 minutes
Cooking time 20–25 minutes

25g (1oz) butter
450g (1lb) onions, sliced or chopped
1/2 tsp freshly chopped sage (optional)
450g (1lb) calf's or lamb's liver, cut into thin strips
salt and ground black pepper

1 Melt the butter in a frying pan, add the onions and fry gently until they begin to colour, then add the seasoning and the sage, if using. Cover the frying pan and simmer very gently for 10 minutes or until the onions are soft.
2 Add the liver strips to the onions, increase the heat slightly and continue cooking for 5–10 minutes, stirring all the time, until the liver is just cooked. Transfer to a warmed serving dish.

NUTRITION PER SERVING 204 cals | 9g fat (4g sats) | 9g carbs | 0.9g salt

CALF'S LIVER WITH SAGE AND BALSAMIC

Serves 4
Preparation 5 minutes
Cooking time 5 minutes

15g (1/2 oz) butter plus a little olive oil for frying
12 sage leaves
4 thin slices of calf's liver
1–2 tbsp balsamic vinegar
rice, with freshly chopped parsley stirred through, or grilled polenta to serve

1 Preheat the oven to 110°C (90°C fan oven) mark 1/4. Melt the butter with a little oil in a heavy-based frying pan and when hot add the sage leaves. Cook briefly for 1 minute or so until crisp. Remove, put in a single layer in a shallow dish and keep hot in the oven.
2 Add a little extra oil to the pan, put in two slices of calf's liver and cook quickly for 30 seconds on each side over a high heat. Remove and place on a plate while you quickly cook the remaining two slices.
3 Return all four slices to the pan, splash the balsamic vinegar over the top and cook for another minute or so. Serve immediately with the sage leaves, rice or grilled polenta.

NUTRITION PER SERVING 88 cals | 6g fat (3g sats) | trace carbs | 0.1g salt

SAUTÉED LAMB'S KIDNEYS AND BABY ONIONS

Serves 4
Preparation 10 minutes
Cooking time 30 minutes

8 lamb's kidneys, membrane removed
225g (8oz) baby onions, peeled
25g (1oz) unsalted butter
3 tbsp balsamic vinegar
1 tbsp plain flour
300ml (¹/₂ pint) well-flavoured lamb stock
3 tbsp Madeira
salt and ground black pepper
freshly chopped parsley, to garnish
rice to serve

1   Halve the lamb's kidneys lengthways and snip out the white cores with kitchen scissors. Add the baby onions to a pan of boiling water and blanch for 3–5 minutes; drain well.
2   Melt the butter in a sauté pan, add the onions and cook gently for 10–15 minutes until soft and browned. Increase the heat and add the lamb's kidneys, stirring and turning them for about 2 minutes or until browned. Lift out the kidneys and onions and put on to a plate.
3   Deglaze the pan with the balsamic vinegar, scraping up any sediment from the base of the pan, and allow almost all of the liquid to evaporate. Sprinkle in the flour and cook, stirring, over a medium heat until it begins to colour. Whisk in the stock and Madeira. Bring the sauce to the boil, then turn down the heat and simmer until reduced and slightly syrupy. Check the seasoning.
4   Return the kidneys and baby onions to the sauce and reheat gently for 5 minutes. Scatter with plenty of chopped parsley and serve with rice.

NUTRITION PER SERVING
180 cals | 8g fat (4g sats) | 8g carbs | 1.6g salt

EGGS AND CHEESE

EGGS

Eggs are a concentrated source of protein and vitamins, including A, B$_{12}$, D, E and K; they also contain iron. Although not high in calories, eggs are relatively high in cholesterol; however, this dietary cholesterol does not have a marked affect on the cholesterol in our blood. Providing you are eating a healthy, balanced diet there should be no reason to limit the number of eggs you eat in week. Eggs are a wonderfully useful fast food and have special culinary properties: they are invaluable for thickening, binding, emulsifying, raising and glazing.

BUYING AND STORING EGGS

Most supermarkets stock a range of eggs produced by different farming methods, including organic, free-range, eggs from hens fed only with grain, and barn eggs. Free-range eggs are produced by hens that have easy access to open pasture and are fed a natural cereal diet; however, the majority of eggs sold in this country are still produced by 'battery hens', which are raised entirely indoors using intensive farming methods.

Always refer to the 'use-by' date on the pack. The familiar lion – displayed on egg boxes – is a symbol of quality. Never buy cracked or damaged eggs; open the box before buying and check that all the eggs are sound.

Store eggs in the fridge, pointed-end down to centre the yolk within the white. Bring to room temperature before use.

There is no intrinsic difference in flavour or value between white or brown eggs. Eggs are now graded into four categories according to weight: very large, large, medium and small. It is important to use the correct size of egg for a recipe. Unless otherwise stated, medium eggs should be used for the recipes in this book.

EGG SAFETY

Eggs are susceptible to salmonella, one of the bacteria responsible for food poisoning. This is because their shells are porous and can absorb the bacteria if they come into contact with it. Thorough cooking will destroy salmonella, so it isn't generally a problem; however, raw or lightly cooked eggs are used in many classic recipes, including mayonnaise, cold soufflés, meringues, ice creams and sorbets, lemon curd and scrambled eggs. Although the risk is small, those who are particularly vulnerable – including the young, the elderly, pregnant women and anyone with an immune-deficiency disease – should avoid eating raw or lightly cooked eggs.

TYPES OF EGGS

Hen's eggs are the most frequently used and any general culinary reference to eggs implies these, although other types are available.

Duck's eggs are larger and richer (higher in fat) than hen's eggs, and they have a smooth shell, which is stronger and less porous. The yolk is a deep yellow and the white is more gelatinous.

Quail's eggs are tiny and attractively speckled; they are usually soft-boiled for 1–2 minutes and often used as a garnish or as or canapé. They have a light-textured pale yolk and very thin shells, which are laborious to peel.

A goose egg weighs about the same as three hens' eggs. They have a slightly stronger taste and make excellent scrambled egg and omelettes. Allow about 7 minutes for a soft-boiled egg.

Because duck and goose eggs are often sold loose rather than in labelled cartons, you may have to ask what the 'use-by' date is. Duck and goose eggs are particularly vulnerable to salmonella and, therefore, should always be cooked thoroughly.

COOKING EGGS

In addition to being poached, fried, baked, boiled, scrambled or turned into omelettes, eggs are used to lighten soufflés and cakes; thicken mousses; bind stuffings; set baked custards; glaze pastry and breads; and emulsify sauces and dressings, such as hollandaise and mayonnaise.

Whisked egg whites incorporate air and dramatically increase their volume, giving soufflés, meringues and whisked cakes their characteristic light, airy texture.

To separate an egg

Crack the egg against the rim of a clean, dry bowl and open the two halves, allowing some of the white to run into the bowl. Carefully pass the egg yolk back and forth between the two half-shells without breaking it, allowing the egg white to fall into the bowl. Put the yolk into another bowl. Don't let the yolk break and mingle with the white, because egg whites will not whisk satisfactorily if a trace of yolk is present.

To whisk egg whites

Use a large balloon whisk or a hand-held electric whisk. Make sure the bowl and whisk are scrupulously clean and dry with no trace of grease, water or egg yolk, which will adversely affect the whisking.

Whisk the egg whites until they stand in soft or stiff peaks (as specified in the recipe). Do not over-whisk or you will have dry powdery whites, which will be impossible to fold into a mixture evenly.

Fold in egg whites as soon as you have whisked them or they will collapse. Make sure the mixture you are folding into is neither too hot nor too cold, otherwise much of the volume will be lost. To lighten the mixture, quickly fold in a spoonful of whisked egg white, then lightly fold in the remaining whites, using a large metal spoon and a cutting and folding action.

Cooking methods

Baked Put a knob of butter into each ramekin and heat in the oven until melted. Break a large egg into each ramekin and bake at 170°C (150°C fan oven) mark 3 for 10 minutes.

Boiled Lower the egg(s) into a small pan of simmering water, using a spoon, making sure there is sufficient water to cover. If the egg cracks, add a little salt or vinegar to coagulate the white. For soft-boiled eggs, allow 3¹/₂–5 minutes, according to size and whether you prefer a very soft or slightly firmer set.

Eggs mollet are soft-boiled eggs with firm whites. Simmer for about 6 minutes, then plunge into cold water and peel.
For lightly set coddled eggs, put into a pan of boiling water, cover with a lid, take off the heat and leave to stand in a warm place for 8–10 minutes.
For hard-boiled eggs, allow 10–12 minutes. Once cooked, drain and cool quickly under cold running water, then crack the shell to prevent a black rim forming around the yolk.

Poached Take a wide shallow pan and two-thirds fill it with boiling water, adding 1 tbsp vinegar to each 600ml (1 pint) water. Carefully break an egg into a saucer, make a whirlpool in the water using a spoon and lower in the egg. Reduce the heat and cook for 3 minutes or until the white is just set and the yolk soft. Using a slotted spoon, lift the egg out of the pan. (Alternatively, cook the eggs in a poacher. Half-fill the lower container with water and boil. Put a small knob of butter into each cup. Break an egg into each cup and cook gently for 3 minutes or until set.)

Fried Heat a little butter or oil in a frying pan. Break an egg into a cup and add to the hot fat. Fry over a medium heat until lightly set, spooning the hot fat on top of the yolk as it cooks. The eggs can also be fried on both sides.

Scrambled Beat the eggs well with seasoning. Melt a knob of butter in a heavy non-stick pan and add the eggs. Stir over a very gentle heat until just beginning to thicken. Add another knob of butter and continue stirring over the heat until the eggs start to scramble. Take off the heat and continue to stir; the eggs will continue to cook in the residual heat.

Omelette You will need a good heavy-based non-stick omelette pan or frying pan. Use an 18–20.5cm (7–8in) pan for a two- or three-egg omelette, or a 23–25.5cm (9–10in) pan for a six-egg omelette. Lightly beat the eggs in a bowl with 1–2 tbsp water, using a fork or balloon whisk. Heat a large knob of butter in the pan, then pour in the eggs. Stir with a fork or wooden spatula until the mixture is three-quarters set to ensure an even, creamy texture, then cook without stirring for a further 30 seconds or until set; do not overcook. Serve immediately.

CHEESE

For culinary purposes, most cheeses can be categorised as follows: hard cheeses, such as Parmesan and Pecorino; semi-hard cheeses, such as Cheddar, Gruyère and Stilton; soft ripened cheeses, such as Brie and Camembert; and fresh soft cheeses, such as mozzarella, mascarpone and soft goat's cheeses. Most cheeses have a high fat content and should be consumed in moderate quantities, although low-fat varieties are available. In the cheese-making process, rennet (or a vegetarian alternative) is used to curdle milk and separate it into firm curds and liquid whey. The curds are then processed, shaped and matured as necessary to create a wide range of cheeses. The method varies according to the type of cheese. Very hard cheeses, such as Parmesan, take up to three years to develop their full flavour, whereas soft cheeses, such as Brie, are ready to eat within a month or two. Fresh soft goat's cheeses, mozzarella and cream cheeses are not matured in this way and most can be eaten within a few days of being made.

BUYING AND STORING CHEESE

Probably the best place to buy cheese is from a specialist cheese shop if you are lucky enough to have access to one, otherwise many supermarkets have a fresh cheese counter offering a good variety of farmhouse and factory-made cheeses.

Try to taste first before you commit to buying a cheese, as artisan cheeses will vary within, as well as across, varieties – some cheeses differ according to the time of year, and certain varieties are seasonal. Once you have made your choice, make sure the cheese is freshly sliced to your requirements. Buy only as much or as little as you think you need – central heating and refrigeration will dry out the cheese once you get it home.

The best way to store cheese is to wrap it in waxed paper then to put into an unsealed plastic food bag or cheese box. Keep in the fridge in the least cold area away from the freezer compartment. If you have a whole, rinded cheese, cover the cut surface with clingfilm.

To enjoy cheese at its best, you should always remove it from the fridge at least 2 hours before serving to bring it to room temperature. Loosen the wrapping and remove it just before serving. Provide at least two knives for cutting, so that there is a separate one for blue cheese.

Buying cheese for vegetarians Some vegetarians prefer to avoid cheeses that have been produced by the traditional method, because this uses animal-derived rennet (see opposite); however, most supermarkets and cheese shops now stock an excellent range of vegetarian cheeses, produced using vegetarian rennet. The recipes marked as vegetarian in this book assume that you will choose a suitable cheese if cooking for vegetarians. Always check the label when buying.

SELECTING FOR A CHEESEBOARD

Choosing cheeses for a cheeseboard is a matter of satisfying everyone's taste, so a range of flavours from mild to strong, and a variety of textures, is important. Think about shapes and colours, too. If you are serving four cheeses, choose one hard, one soft, one blue and one goat's cheese. If you are buying from a specialist cheese shop or a supermarket cheese counter, ask to try a piece first so that you know what you are getting and can balance the flavours. It is a question of quality rather than quantity, as a few excellent cheeses are more appealing than five or six with competing flavours.

To accompany your cheeses, choose crisp apples, juicy pears, grapes or figs. Very mild, soft goat's cheeses can be eaten with strawberries; slightly harder ones go well with cherry tomatoes or olives. Salad leaves should be bitter – try some chicory, frisée or rocket. Walnuts and celery are excellent with blue cheese. Oatcakes, wheat wafers and digestive biscuits go well with most cheeses, and if you want to serve bread, make sure it is fresh and crusty. Butter should be unsalted.

As for when you serve cheese, rounding off the meal with the cheeseboard is the norm in this country, but the French custom of moving from main course to cheese course is worth considering. It enables you to savour the cheeses before you are too full to enjoy them, and you can carry on with the same wine.

Hard and semi-hard cheeses are produced by removing as much of the whey as possible from the curds, then moulding and ripening the cheese. Hard cheeses undergo a further process which involves heating the curd so that it shrinks and hardens. Semi-hard cheeses include Cheddar and Edam, and the most familiar hard cheeses are Parmesan and Pecorino.

Vegetarian cheeses produced using vegetarian rennet are becoming increasingly available from supermarkets and specialist cheese shops. If you are cooking for vegetarians always check that the cheese you are using for your recipe is suitable.

Soft ripened cheeses are generally made by coagulating milk with rennet; the addition of a starter ensures a clean, acidic flavour. Some varieties of soft cheese, such as Brie, Camembert and the blue-veined cheeses are mould-ripened. It is these cheeses that are susceptible to listeria contamination.

Fresh cheeses are soft and light, with a refreshing tang. There are many different types of fresh cheeses, with different fat contents, depending on whether they are made from whole or skimmed milk. These cheeses have a relatively short shelf life.

Cream cheese is a fresh, bland cheese made from pasteurised milk. Its fat content varies, depending on the type. Cream cheese has many uses, including dips, nibbles and cheesecakes.

Fromage frais is a soft cheese produced from skimmed milk and rennet. The curd is stirred and the whey drained off. Fromage frais can be used as an alternative to cream.

Curd cheese has a clean, acidic flavour and a soft, slightly granular texture. It is made solely by the action of lactic acid; rennet is not used. There are several varieties of this soft, fresh cheese, including quark, which has a very low fat content.

Cottage cheese is made from the curds of skimmed milk, which are heated to make them firm and dense. The resulting curd cheese is then broken up and finished with a little cream. Cottage cheese is low in fat.

Goat's cheeses are increasingly popular, as reflected in the infinite variety now available, most of which are just termed chèvres. British-made goat's cheeses are now widely produced, in response to the demand. Young, soft goat's cheese is rindless with a mild, clean flavour – ideal for recipes using soft cheeses. Harder, rinded varieties are often sliced and grilled, then served on salads or bread.

CLASSIC OMELETTE

Serves 1
Preparation 5 minutes
Cooking time 5 minutes

2–3 medium eggs
1 tbsp milk or water
25g (1oz) unsalted butter
salt and ground black pepper
sliced or grilled tomatoes and
    freshly chopped flat-leafed
    parsley to serve

1 Whisk the eggs in a bowl, just enough to break them down – over-beating spoils the texture of the omelette. Season with salt and pepper, and add the milk or water.

2 Heat the butter in an 18cm (7in) omelette pan or non-stick frying pan until it is foaming, but not brown. Add the eggs and stir gently with a fork or wooden spatula, drawing the mixture from the sides to the centre as it sets and letting the liquid egg in the centre run to the sides. When set, stop stirring and cook for 30 seconds or until the omelette is golden brown underneath and still creamy on top: don't overcook. If you are making a filled omelette, add the filling at this point.

3 Tilt the pan away from you slightly and use a palette knife to fold over one-third of the omelette to the centre, then fold over the opposite third. Slide the omelette out on to a warmed plate, letting it flip over so that the folded sides are underneath. Serve immediately, with tomatoes sprinkled with parsley.

NUTRITION PER SERVING 449 cals |
40g fat (19g sats) | 1g carbs | 1g salt Ⓥ

OMELETTE ARNOLD BENNETT

Serves 2
Preparation 15 minutes
Cooking time about 20 minutes

125g (4oz) smoked haddock
50g (2oz) butter
150ml (¼ pint) double or single cream
3 medium eggs, separated
50g (2oz) Cheddar cheese, grated
salt and ground black pepper
rocket salad to serve

1 Put the fish in a pan and cover with water. Bring to the boil and simmer gently for 10 minutes. Drain and flake the fish, discarding the skin and bones.

2 Put the fish in a pan with half the butter and 2 tbsp cream. Toss over a high heat until the butter melts. Leave to cool.

3 Beat the egg yolks in a bowl with 1 tbsp cream and seasoning. Stir in the fish mixture. Put the egg whites into a clean, grease-free bowl and whisk until they form stiff peaks; fold into the yolks.

4 Heat the remaining butter in an omelette pan. Fry the egg mixture, but make sure it remains fairly fluid. Do not fold over. Slide it on to a flameproof serving dish.

5 Blend together the cheese and remaining fresh cream, then spread on top of the omelette and brown under the grill. Serve with a rocket salad.

NUTRITION PER SERVING 835 cals |
79g fat (46g sats) | 1g carbs | 2.8g salt

SPANISH OMELETTE

Serves 4
Preparation 15 minutes
Cooking time 30–45 minutes

900g (2lb) potatoes, peeled and left whole
3–4 tbsp vegetable oil
1 onion, finely sliced
8 medium eggs
3 tbsp chopped flat-leafed parsley
3 streaky bacon rashers
salt and ground black pepper
green salad to serve

1 Add the potatoes to a pan of cold salted water, bring to the boil and simmer for 15–20 minutes or until almost cooked. Drain and leave until cool enough to handle, then slice thickly.
2 Heat 1 tbsp oil in an 18cm (7in) non-stick frying pan (suitable for use under the grill). Add the onion and fry gently for 7–10 minutes until softened; remove and set aside.
3 Lightly beat the eggs in a bowl and season well with salt and pepper.
4 Heat the remaining oil in the frying pan, then layer the potato slices, onion and 2 tbsp chopped parsley in the pan. Pour in the beaten eggs and cook for 5–10 minutes until the omelette is firm underneath. Meanwhile, grill the bacon until golden and crisp, then break into pieces.
5 Put the omelette in the pan under the grill for 2–3 minutes until the top is just set. Scatter the bacon and remaining chopped parsley over the surface. Serve cut into wedges, with a green salad.

NUTRITION PER SERVING
453 cals | 25g fat (6g sats) | 38g carbs | 1.6g salt

EGGS BENEDICT

Serves 4
Preparation 15 minutes
Cooking time 10 minutes

4 slices bread
4 medium eggs
150ml (¼ pint) hollandaise sauce (see page 17)
4 thin slices lean ham
parsley sprigs to garnish

1 Toast the bread on both sides. Poach the eggs (see page 221). Gently warm the hollandaise sauce.
2 Top each slice of toast with a folded slice of ham, then with a poached egg. Finally, coat with hollandaise sauce.
3 Garnish each with a sprig of parsley and serve.

TRY SOMETHING DIFFERENT

Eggs Florentine Cook 900g (2lb) washed spinach in a pan with a little salt until tender. Drain well, chop and reheat with 15g (½oz) butter. Melt 25g (1oz) butter, stir in 3 tbsp plain flour and cook gently for 1 minute, stirring. Remove from the heat and gradually stir in 300ml (½ pint) milk. Bring to the boil and cook, stirring, until thickened. Add 50g (2oz) grated Gruyère or Cheddar cheese and season. Do not allow to boil. Poach the eggs. Put the spinach in an ovenproof dish, arrange the eggs on top and pour the cheese sauce over them. Sprinkle with 25g (1oz) grated cheese and brown under the grill.

NUTRITION PER SERVING
402 cals | 33g fat (18g sats) | 14g carbs | 1.6g salt

CHEESE FONDUE

Serves 4
Preparation 10 minutes
Cooking time about 10 minutes

1 large garlic clove, halved
2 tsp cornflour
3 tbsp Kirsch
200ml (7fl oz) dry white wine
1 tbsp lemon juice
200g (7oz) Gruyère cheese, grated
200g (7oz) Emmental cheese, grated
ground black pepper
bite-sized chunks of crusty bread
    to serve

1 Rub the halved garlic clove around the inside of a fondue pan (or heavy-based pan). Blend the cornflour to a smooth paste with the Kirsch.
2 Put the wine, lemon juice and cheeses in the pan with the blended cornflour and slowly bring to the boil over a very low heat, stirring all the time. Simmer gently for 3–4 minutes, stirring frequently. Season with pepper to taste.
3 Set the pan over the fondue burner (or over a heated serving tray) at the table. Serve with plenty of chunks of crusty bread for dipping into the fondue using long-handled forks.

NUTRITION PER SERVING (without bread) 460 cals | 32g fat (20g sats) | 6g carbs | 1.4g salt Ⓥ

CAULIFLOWER CHEESE

Serves 2
Preparation 5 minutes
Cooking time 20 minutes

1 cauliflower
1 quantity cheese (mornay) sauce
    (see béchamel sauce, page 16)
extra grated cheese to sprinkle
salt
jacket potato to serve (optional)

1 Preheat the grill. Remove the coarse outer leaves from the cauliflower, cut a cross in the stalk end and wash the whole cauliflower under the tap.
2 Put the cauliflower into a medium pan, with the stem side down, then pour over enough boiling water to come halfway up it. Add a pinch of salt and cover the pan. Bring to the boil and cook for 10–15 minutes. Stick a sharp knife into the florets – they should be tender but not mushy.
3 Drain the cauliflower and put it into an ovenproof dish. Pour the cheese sauce over it, sprinkle with a little grated cheese, then grill for 2–3 minutes until golden on top. Serve on its own or with a jacket potato.

TRY SOMETHING DIFFERENT
Make this with ½ head of cauliflower and ½ head of broccoli. Cut the stems off the florets, then peel and chop them into pieces the same size as the cauliflower and broccoli florets. They will take only about 4 minutes to cook until just tender. Make as above.

NUTRITION PER SERVING 383 cals | 24g fat (14g sats) | 20g carbs | 2.2g salt Ⓥ

PASTA AND GNOCCHI

PASTA

Endlessly versatile, inexpensive and quick to cook, pasta is incredibly popular. It is primarily a carbohydrate food, but it also provides protein, useful vitamins and some minerals. Certain types of pasta, notably those made with eggs, may contain as much as 13 per cent protein. Contrary to popular belief, pasta isn't particularly high in calories – it's the rich, creamy accompanying sauces that give some pasta dishes a high calorie value.

FRESH PASTA

Pasta is surprisingly easy and very satisfying to make. Good homemade pasta has an excellent light texture and incomparable flavour – almost melting in the mouth. You need very little basic equipment – a rolling pin, metal pastry cutters, a sharp knife and a pastry wheel will suffice – but, if you intend to make pasta regularly, it is worth buying a pasta machine to take all the hard work out of rolling and cutting the dough.

Pasta dough can be made either by hand, in a food processor with a dough attachment, or in a large mixer with a dough hook. Initially, it is probably best to make it by hand to learn how the dough should feel at each stage. The more you make fresh pasta the easier it will be to judge the correct texture of the dough – it should be soft, not at all sticky, and with a good elasticity.

The best type of flour to use for making pasta is '00' or 'farino tipo 00'. This very fine-textured soft wheat flour is available from larger supermarkets and delicatessens. Once you have mastered the basic pasta recipe, try making flavoured pastas; these are just as easy and taste especially good.

If you want to buy fresh pasta rather than making your own, find a good Italian delicatessen where it is freshly prepared on the premises. Commercially produced fresh pasta can be stodgy and disappointing – quite unlike homemade pasta.

DRIED PASTA

There is an extensive range of shapes, sizes and flavours available for dried pasta. The best are made from 100 per cent durum wheat (pasta di semola grano duro); some varieties include eggs (all'uova). Dried pasta is suitable for using with all of the recipes in this chapter.

The choice of pasta is largely a matter of personal taste, but you will find that some shapes are more suited to particular sauces than others. Smooth-textured, slippery sauces are generally better served with long, fine pastas, such as spaghetti or linguine, whereas chunky sauces are better with short-shaped varieties. Shapes such as conchiglie (shells) and penne are ideal because they hold the sauce, and larger pasta shapes can be stuffed.

The names of shapes often vary from one region of Italy to another, and new ones are constantly being introduced. Note that the suffix gives an indication of the size of the pasta: -oni suggests large, as in conchiglioni (large shells); -ette or -etti denotes small, as in spaghetti and cappelletti (small hats); while -ine or -ini means tiny, as in pastina (tiny soup pasta) and spaghettini, the finer version of spaghetti.

STORING PASTA

Pasta is arguably the world's greatest industrial food product, and one of the few manufactured ingredients that are often better when made commercially than at home. Furthermore, fresh pasta is not 'better' than dried. It is just different. And most commercial fresh pasta is vastly inferior to dried. Many Italian cooks choose dried pasta over fresh – and the best dried pasta still comes from Italy.

Dried pasta has a long shelf life. Stored in an airtight container in a cool, dry place, it will keep for many months (or even years). Fresh pasta should be stored in the fridge and used within a few days.

COOKING PASTA

All pasta should be cooked until al dente – tender yet firm to the bite, definitely not soft, and without a hard, uncooked centre. It is essential to cook pasta in plenty of fast-boiling water. If there is too little water, the pasta will cook unevenly and become stodgy. Allow 4 litres (7 pints) water and 1 tbsp salt to 500g (1lb 2oz) pasta. There's no need to add any oil. Bring the salted water to the boil in a large pan. Add the pasta to the fast-boiling water and stir once to prevent sticking. Cook until al dente.

Fresh pasta needs only the briefest of cooking, so watch it carefully. Fresh tagliatelle or spaghetti will take only about 1–2 minutes to cook. Stuffed pasta shapes, such as ravioli or tortelloni, need about 3 minutes to cook the filling through. Most dried pasta takes around 8–12 minutes. Use the pack instructions as a guideline, but the only way to determine when pasta is cooked is by tasting. Avoid overcooking at all costs.

As soon as the pasta is cooked, drain it in a colander or large strainer, then immediately add to the sauce, or it may start to stick together. When combining pasta with an oily sauce, hold back a few tablespoons of the cooking water; this helps to make a glossy coating sauce.

QUANTITIES

It is difficult to give specific quantity guidelines for pasta, because there are so many factors, including the nature of the sauce and whether you are serving the pasta as a starter, lunch or main meal. Individual appetites for pasta seem to vary enormously too. As a very approximate guide, allow about 100–125g (3½–4oz) uncooked weight per person.

It's not easy to weigh spaghetti to calculate the correct quantity to cook, but a spaghetti tool is a handy way of measuring it. Made of wood, plastic or metal it is a gauge with holes that correspond to different portion sizes. You line up the tool with the open end of the spaghetti pack and drop the spaghetti through the relevant hole. Alternatively, you can use the spaghetti gauge on this page by holding a small or large handful of strands against the portion circle. Once you have an idea of how much you need for the portions you regularly use, you'll soon be able to estimate the quantity just by holding the spaghetti in your hand.

SERVING PASTA

Pasta quickly loses its heat once drained, so have warmed serving plates or bowls ready. Toss the pasta with the sauce, butter or olive oil as soon as it is cooked, then transfer to the serving bowls. If Parmesan is the finishing touch, either grate it over the finished dish or shave off thin flakes, using a swivel potato peeler.

GNOCCHI

Not actually a type of pasta, but often grouped with it, these little Italian potato dumplings are usually boiled for a few minutes, then served with butter or a sauce, or they can be coated in sauce and baked. Gnocchi are usually made from mashed potato and flour, rolled into ridged ovals. Other varieties include spinach and ricotta or Parmesan, semolina and pumpkin. Store in a plastic bag in the fridge. Use within a few days.

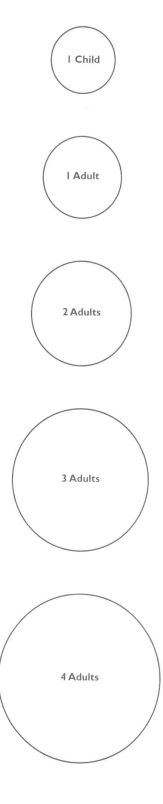

1 Child

1 Adult

2 Adults

3 Adults

4 Adults

BASIC PASTA DOUGH

Serves 4
Preparation 5 minutes, plus resting
Cooking time 1–2 minutes

225g (8oz) '00' pasta flour, plus extra to dust
1 tsp salt
2 medium eggs, plus 1 egg yolk, beaten
1 tbsp extra virgin olive oil
1–2 tbsp cold water

1 Sift the flour and salt into a mound on a clean surface. Make a well in the centre and add the eggs, egg yolk, olive oil and 1 tbsp water.
2 Gently beat the eggs together with a fork, then gradually work in the flour, adding a little extra water if needed to form a soft but not sticky dough.
3 Transfer to a lightly floured surface and knead for about 5 minutes or until firm, smooth and elastic.
4 Form the dough into a flattish ball, wrap in clingfilm and leave to rest for at least 30 minutes.

TRY SOMETHING DIFFERENT

Flavoured pastas are easy to make and have a delicious flavour. Vegetable purées and flavoured pastas, such as sun-dried tomato and olive, make vibrant coloured pastas – note that some of the colour will be lost during cooking, without detriment to the flavour.
Herb Pasta Sift the flour and salt into the bowl and stir in 3 tbsp freshly chopped mixed herbs, such as basil, marjoram and parsley. Continue as for the basic pasta dough.
Olive Pasta Beat the eggs with 2 tbsp black olive paste before adding to the flour. Reduce the water to about 2 tsp.
Sun-dried Tomato Pasta Beat the eggs with 2 tbsp sun-dried tomato paste before adding to the flour. Reduce the water to about 2 tsp.
Spinach Pasta Blanch 50g (2oz) spinach leaves in a little boiling water until just wilted. Refresh under cold running water, then drain thoroughly and squeeze out all the excess water. Finely chop the spinach and add to the flour and salt, together with the remaining ingredients. Continue as for the basic pasta dough.

Rolling and Shaping Pasta

To use a pasta machine, feed small pieces of dough through the rollers two or three times, narrowing the space until the pasta is the correct thickness, then cut as required. If you do not have a pasta machine you can roll the dough out very thinly by hand on a clean surface. Keep lifting and rotating the dough as you roll to prevent it from sticking. For lasagne, trim the pasta sheets to neaten and cut into lengths. For tagliatelle,

fold the sheet of dough to make a cigar shape, then cut into strips. For stuffed pastas, roll out the dough to form a long thin sheet. Lay on a clean surface dusted with semolina flour, cut in two and cover with a damp cloth. Dust the surface with semolina flour. Brush one sheet of pasta with beaten egg. Top with heaped teaspoons of filling, set 1cm (½in) apart. Cover this with a second pasta sheet. Starting at the middle, press down gently around the mounds of filling to expel any air trapped inside. Cut around each mound with a pastry wheel. Lay them on trays dusted with semolina flour and leave for 30 minutes to dry. Don't chill or the pasta will become sticky.

COOK'S TIP
To make pasta in a food processor, sift the flour and salt into the bowl and add the eggs, egg yolk, olive oil and 1 tbsp water (together with any flavourings). Whiz until the dough just begins to come together, adding the extra water if necessary to form a soft but not sticky dough. Wrap in clingfilm and rest (as above).

NUTRITION PER SERVING
280 cals | 9g fat (2g sats) | 42g carbs | 1.3g salt

SPAGHETTI ALLA CARBONARA

Serves 4
Preparation 10 minutes
Cooking time 10 minutes

2 tbsp olive oil
25g (1oz) butter
125–150g (4–5oz) smoked pancetta (see Cook's Tips),
    rind removed, cut into strips
1 garlic clove, halved
3 medium eggs
2 tbsp dry white wine
40g (1½oz) freshly grated Parmesan
40g (1½oz) freshly grated Pecorino cheese
400g (14oz) dried spaghetti
salt and ground black pepper
2 tbsp freshly chopped parsley to garnish

1 Heat the olive oil and butter in a heavy-based pan.
Add the pancetta and garlic, and cook over a medium heat
for 3–4 minutes until the pancetta begins to crisp. Turn off
the heat; discard the garlic.
2 Meanwhile, in a bowl, beat the eggs with the white wine
and half each of the cheeses. Season with salt and pepper.
3 Cook the spaghetti in a large pan of boiling salted water
according to the pack instructions until al dente.
4 When the spaghetti is almost cooked, gently reheat the
pancetta in the pan.
5 Drain the spaghetti thoroughly, then return to the
pan. Immediately add the egg mixture together with the
pancetta. Take the pan off the heat and toss well; the eggs
will cook in the residual heat to form a light creamy sauce.
Add the remaining cheeses, toss lightly and serve garnished
with parsley.

COOK'S TIPS
- If smoked pancetta is unobtainable, use
  smoked bacon instead, increasing the quantity
  to 175–225g (6–8oz).
- If Pecorino is unobtainable, just double the
  quantity of Parmesan.

NUTRITION PER SERVING
750 cals | 38g fat (12g sats) | 74g carbs | 2.2g salt

SPAGHETTI BOLOGNESE

Serves 6
Preparation 15 minutes
Cooking time 40 minutes

500g (1lb 2oz) dried spaghetti
50g (2oz) Parmesan, freshly grated

For the Bolognese sauce
2 tbsp olive oil
1 onion, finely chopped
2 garlic cloves, crushed
450g (1lb) extra-lean minced beef
2 tbsp sun-dried tomato paste
300ml (1/2 pint) red wine
400g can chopped tomatoes
125g (4oz) chestnut mushrooms, sliced
2 tbsp Worcestershire sauce
salt and ground black pepper

1 To make the Bolognese sauce, heat the olive oil in a large pan, add the onion and fry over a medium heat for 10 minutes or until softened and golden. Add the garlic and cook for 1 minute.
2 Add the minced beef and brown evenly, using a wooden spoon to break up the pieces. Stir in the tomato paste and the red wine, cover and bring to the boil. Add the tomatoes, mushrooms and Worcestershire sauce, and season well with salt and pepper. Bring back to the boil, lower the heat and simmer for 20 minutes.
3 Cook the spaghetti in a large pan of boiling salted water according to the pack instructions until al dente. Drain the pasta well, then return to the pan. Add the Bolognese sauce and toss to mix together. Check the seasoning.
4 Divide among warmed plates and sprinkle with the Parmesan to serve.

TRY SOMETHING DIFFERENT
Add 125g (4oz) chopped rinded smoked streaky bacon with the mince, brown, then stir in 200g (7oz) chopped chicken livers. Cook for 3 minutes before adding the tomato paste, then continue as above.

> NUTRITION PER SERVING
> 510 cals | 12g fat (4g sats) | 67g carbs | 1.5g salt

SPAGHETTI WITH CLAMS

Serves 4
Preparation 10 mins
Cooking time 25 minutes

2 tbsp olive oil
2 shallots, finely sliced
3 garlic cloves, thinly sliced
150ml (¼ pint) dry white wine
400g can chopped tomatoes
350g (12oz) spaghetti
1kg (2¼lb) fresh clams, scrubbed
salt and ground black pepper
1 tbsp freshly chopped parsley to garnish

1 Heat the oil in a very large pan and gently fry the shallots for 5 minutes. Add the garlic and cook for 1 minute.
2 Add the wine and bubble until reduced by half, then add the tomatoes along with half a can of water. Season with salt and pepper. Bring to the boil, then reduce the heat and simmer for 15 minutes until reduced slightly.
3 Meanwhile, cook the spaghetti according to the pack instructions until al dente.
4 Add the clams to the tomato sauce, cover and simmer for 1–2 minutes until they have opened – discard any that stay closed. Check the seasoning.
5 Drain the pasta and toss into the clam sauce. Serve garnished with parsley.

> NUTRITION PER SERVING
> 488 cals | 8g fat (1g sats) | 71g carbs | 4.4g salt

PASTA WITH ANCHOVIES, TOMATOES AND OLIVES

Serves 4
Preparation 15 minutes
Cooking time 20–25 minutes

50g can anchovy fillets in oil
2 garlic cloves, crushed
4 sun-dried tomatoes, drained and roughly chopped
400g can chopped tomatoes
500g (1lb 2oz) dried spaghetti
200g (7oz) pitted black olives, roughly chopped
2 tbsp capers, drained
2–3 tbsp freshly chopped flat-leafed parsley
salt and ground black pepper

1 Drain the oil from the anchovies into a large pan. Heat the oil, then add the garlic and cook for 1 minute. Add the anchovies and sun-dried tomatoes and cook, stirring, for a further 1 minute. Add the canned tomatoes and bring to the boil. Season well with salt and pepper and simmer for 10–15 minutes.

2 Meanwhile, cook the spaghetti in a large pan of boiling salted water according to the pack instructions until al dente.

3 Stir the olives and capers into the tomato sauce. Drain the spaghetti thoroughly, reserving about 4 tbsp of the cooking water, then return to the pan.

4 Add the tomato sauce and chopped parsley to the pasta and toss well to mix, thinning the sauce with the reserved cooking water, if necessary. Serve at once.

COOK'S TIP
Spaghetti takes its name from the Italian word *spago*, meaning string.

NUTRITION PER SERVING
620 cals | 12g fat (2g sats) | 96g carbs | 4.5g salt

TUNA PASTA

Serves 4
Preparation 10 minutes
Cooking time 30 minutes

225g can tuna steak in olive oil
1 onion, finely sliced
1 garlic clove, chopped
2 × 400g cans chopped tomatoes
500g (1lb 2oz) dried penne or other
    pasta
50g can anchovy fillets in oil, drained
    and chopped
2 tbsp small capers
2 tbsp basil leaves, roughly torn
    (optional)
salt and ground black pepper

1 Drain the oil from the tuna into a
pan and put the tuna to one side.
2 Heat the tuna oil, then add the sliced
onion and fry over a low heat for
10 minutes or until softened but not
browned. Add the chopped garlic and
cook for 1 minute.
3 Add the tomatoes and stir well.
Season generously with salt and pepper,
then simmer over a medium heat for
15 minutes to reduce and thicken
the sauce.
4 Meanwhile, cook the pasta in a large
pan of boiling salted water according to
the pack instructions until al dente.
5 Flake the tuna and add to the
tomato sauce with the anchovies,
capers and basil leaves, if using. Stir to
mix well.
6 Drain the pasta well, return to the
pan and add the tuna sauce. Toss
everything together to mix and serve
immediately in warmed bowls.

NUTRITION PER SERVING 650 cals |
16g fat (2g sats) | 102g carbs | 2.3g salt

PENNE WITH SMOKED SALMON

Serves 4
Preparation 5 minutes
Cooking time 10–15 minutes

350g (12oz) penne or other short
    tubular pasta
200ml (7fl oz) half-fat crème fraîche
150g (5oz) smoked salmon, roughly
    chopped
20g (³/₄ oz) fresh dill, finely chopped
salt and ground black pepper
lemon wedges to serve (optional)

1 Cook the pasta in a large pan of
lightly salted boiling water according
to the pack instructions until al dente,
then drain.
2 Meanwhile, put the crème fraîche
into a large bowl. Add the smoked
salmon and chopped dill, season well
with salt and pepper and mix together.
Gently stir into the drained penne and
serve immediately with lemon wedges,
if you like, to squeeze over the salmon
and pasta.

COOK'S TIP
The name 'penne' means quill,
and reflects the shape of this
pasta. Varieties include smooth,
ridged and flavoured.

NUTRITION PER SERVING 432 cals |
11g fat (6g sats) | 67g carbs | 1.7g salt

MACARONI CHEESE

Serves 4
Preparation 10 minutes
Cooking time 15 minutes

225g (8oz) short-cut macaroni
50g (2oz) butter
50g (2oz) plain flour
900ml (1 1/2 pints) milk
1/2 tsp grated nutmeg or mustard powder
225g (8oz) mature Cheddar cheese
   (see page 228), grated
3 tbsp fresh white or wholemeal breadcrumbs
salt and ground black pepper

1 Cook the macaroni in a large pan of boiling salted water according to the pack instructions until al dente.
2 Meanwhile, melt the butter in a pan, stir in the flour and cook, stirring, for 1 minute. Remove from the heat and gradually stir in the milk. Bring to the boil and cook, stirring, until the sauce thickens. Remove from the heat. Season with salt and pepper, and add the nutmeg or mustard.
3 Drain the macaroni and add to the sauce, together with three-quarters of the cheese. Mix well, then turn into an ovenproof dish.
4 Preheat the grill to high. Sprinkle the breadcrumbs and remaining cheese over the macaroni. Put under the grill for 2–3 minutes until golden brown on top and bubbling. Serve.

NUTRITION PER SERVING
680 cals | 34g fat (21g sats) | 67g carbs | 2g salt V

SPINACH AND RICOTTA CANNELLONI

Serves 4
Preparation 25 minutes
Cooking time 1 hour 10 minutes

1 tbsp olive oil
1 small onion, chopped
1 bay leaf
1 garlic clove, crushed
400g can chopped tomatoes
300g (11oz) spinach, coarse stalks removed
2 × 250g tubs ricotta cheese
1 large egg
25g (1oz) freshly grated Parmesan (see page 228)
freshly grated nutmeg
15 cannelloni tubes
125g mozzarella ball, roughly torn
salt and ground black pepper
fresh basil leaves to garnish

1 Heat the oil in a pan and gently fry the onion with the bay leaf for 10 minutes or until softened. Add the garlic and fry for 1 minute. Pour in the tomatoes along with half a can of cold water, bring to the boil, then simmer for 20 minutes or until slightly thickened.

2 Meanwhile, wash the spinach and put into a large pan set over a low heat. Cover the pan and cook the spinach for 2 minutes or until just wilted. Drain and cool under running water. When cool enough to handle, squeeze out the excess moisture and roughly chop.

3 Preheat the oven to 180°C (160°C fan oven) mark 4 and lightly oil a baking dish. Mix together the ricotta, egg, Parmesan and spinach with a grating of nutmeg and season with plenty of salt and ground black pepper. Spoon or pipe into the cannelloni tubes and put into the dish in one layer.

4 Pour the tomato sauce over the pasta, then dot with the mozzarella. Bake for 30–40 minutes until golden and bubbling. Scatter with the basil and serve.

COOK'S TIP
Usually made from egg pasta, cannelloni are large, broad tubes designed to be stuffed, coated in sauce and baked.

NUTRITION PER SERVING
409 cals | 14g fat (7g sats) | 53g carbs | 1.5g salt **V**

BUTTERNUT SQUASH AND SPINACH LASAGNE

Serves 6
Preparation 30 minutes
Cooking time about 1 hour

1 butternut squash
2 tbsp olive oil
1 medium onion, sliced
salt and ground black pepper

For the sauce
25g (1oz) butter
25g (1oz) plain flour
600ml (1 pint) milk

To assemble
225g bag baby leaf spinach
250g carton ricotta cheese
1 tsp freshly grated nutmeg
6 'no need to pre-cook' lasagne sheets, about 100g (3½ oz)
50g (2oz) Pecorino or Parmesan (see page 228), freshly
    grated

1 Preheat the oven to 200°C (180°C fan oven) mark 6.
Peel, halve and seed the butternut squash, then cut into 3cm
(1¼ in) cubes. Put into a large roasting tin with the olive oil,
onion and 1 tbsp water. Toss everything together and season
well with salt and ground black pepper. Roast for 25 minutes,
tossing halfway through.
2 To make the sauce, melt the butter in a pan, then stir in
the flour and cook over a medium heat for 1–2 minutes.
Gradually add the milk over the heat, stirring constantly.
Reduce the heat to a simmer and cook, stirring, for 5 minutes
or until the sauce has thickened.
3 Heat 1 tbsp water in another pan. Add the spinach, cover
and cook until the leaves are just wilted. Season generously.
4 Crumble the ricotta into the sauce and add the nutmeg.
Mix together thoroughly and season with salt and pepper
to taste.
5 Spoon the squash and onion mixture into a 1.7 litre
(3 pint) ovenproof dish. Layer the spinach on top, then
cover with a third of the sauce, then the lasagne. Spoon
the remaining sauce on top, season and sprinkle with the
grated cheese. Bake for 30–35 minutes or until the cheese
topping is golden and the pasta is cooked.

NUTRITION PER SERVING
320 cals | 17g fat (8g sats) | 30g carbs | 1g salt

CLASSIC LASAGNE

Serves 6
Preparation 40 minutes
Cooking time 45 minutes (without the Bolognese Sauce)

1 quantity Bolognese Sauce (see page 244)
butter to grease
350g (12oz) fresh lasagne, or 225g (8oz) 'no need to pre-cook' dried lasagne (see Cook's Tip) (12–15 sheets)
1 quantity of béchamel sauce (see page 16)
3 tbsp freshly grated Parmesan
salad leaves to serve

1 Preheat the oven to 180°C (160°C fan oven) mark 4. Spoon one-third of the Bolognese Sauce over the base of a greased 2.3 litre (4 pint) ovenproof dish. Cover with a layer of lasagne sheets, then a layer of béchamel sauce. Repeat these layers twice more, finishing with a layer of béchamel to cover the lasagne.
2 Sprinkle the Parmesan over the top and stand the dish on a baking sheet. Cook in the oven for 45 minutes or until well browned and bubbling. Serve with salad leaves.

> **COOK'S TIP**
> If using 'no need to pre-cook' dried lasagne, add a little extra stock or water to the sauce.

NUTRITION PER SERVING 367 cals | 14g fat (5g sats) | 36g carbs | 1.9g salt

VERY EASY FOUR-CHEESE GNOCCHI

Serves 2
Preparation 3 minutes
Cooking time 10 minutes

350g pack fresh gnocchi
300g tub fresh four-cheese sauce (see page 228)
240g pack sunblush tomatoes
2 tbsp freshly torn basil leaves, plus basil sprigs to garnish
1 tbsp freshly grated Parmesan
15g (½ oz) butter, chopped
salt and ground black pepper
salad to serve

1 Cook the gnocchi in a large pan of lightly salted boiling water according to the pack instructions or until all the gnocchi have floated to the surface. Drain well and put the gnocchi back into the pan.
2 Preheat the grill. Add the four-cheese sauce and tomatoes to the gnocchi and heat gently, stirring, for 2 minutes.
3 Season with salt and pepper, then add the basil and stir again. Spoon into individual heatproof bowls, sprinkle a little Parmesan over each one and dot with butter.
4 Cook under the grill for 3–5 minutes until golden and bubbling. Garnish with basil sprigs and serve with salad.

NUTRITION PER SERVING 630 cals | 28g fat (15g sats) | 77g carbs | 1g salt **V**

RICE, GRAINS AND PULSES

RICE AND GRAINS

In many countries, rice and grains are staple foods. They provide energy and useful amounts of protein, fibre, B vitamins, calcium and iron. There are many varieties of rice and grains, each with its own characteristics, and it is important to choose the correct type for a particular dish. Most grains can be stored for several years, making them the perfect standby storecupboard ingredients.

RICE

Some rice varieties cook to a separate firm texture, some to a creamy consistency, whereas others cook to a sticky mass. Brown rice is the whole rice grain with only the tough outer husk removed. Like other unrefined grains, it is richer in fibre, protein and B vitamins than refined rice. Because the bran is retained, brown rice has a good chewy texture and nutty flavour, and it takes longer to cook than white rice.

Long-grain white rice is the most common general-purpose rice and there are many varieties, including Patna and Carolina. The rice grains, once cooked, are separate, dry and fluffy and suitable as an accompaniment to many dishes. Other rices are used for their special qualities, such as Arborio, a short-grained rice that is used to make creamy risottos, and glutinous rice, which is cooked to make sticky rice used in Chinese and South-east Asian cuisines.

COOKING RICE

Some of the speciality rices are cooked in specific ways: hot liquid is added gradually to Arborio when making a risotto, for example; pudding rice is usually baked slowly in the oven; glutinous rice is steamed; but in general all long-grain varieties can be cooked in the same way – either by the absorption method or by boiling in plenty of water. In general, the absorption method works better. Always check the pack instructions for suggested cooking times and methods.

Most rice is bought pre-packed and does not require washing, but if you do buy it loose, wash thoroughly. With some varieties, such as basmati, rinsing is advisable to remove the excess starch. To rinse rice, put it into a sieve and hold under cold running water until the water runs clear, picking out any tiny bits of grit. Don't wash risotto rice, as it is the starch that lends its essential creamy texture.

To cook rice by the absorption method, measure it in a measuring jug and note the volume. Tip the rice into a heavy-based pan and add twice its volume of cold water. Add salt, bring to the boil, cover with a tight-fitting lid and turn the heat down to low. Cook until the water is absorbed and the rice is tender – allow 15–20 minutes for white rice, 40–45 minutes for brown rice. Don't lift the pan lid during cooking. (Alternatively, just add rice to a large pan of fast boiling salted water, return to the boil, stir once and cook, uncovered, until tender. White rice generally takes 10–12 minutes; brown rice usually cooks in 35–40 minutes. Drain the rice in a sieve and rinse with a kettleful of boiling water.)

To impart extra flavour, cook rice with herbs or spices. For saffron rice, add a large pinch of saffron to the cooking water. For spiced rice, add a cinnamon stick, 1 clove, a blade of mace and a bay leaf to the pan; discard the spices once the rice is cooked. For herb-flavoured rice, add 1–2 tbsp freshly chopped parsley, coriander, thyme or mixed herbs to the cooking liquid. Rice can also be cooked in stock rather than water for extra flavour.

GRAINS

Wheat, barley, corn, oats and rye are the edible seeds of different grasses. Probably the most familiar grains are those from wheat, corn and rye that are ground into flours, but other grains are becoming popular to cook as wholesome and sustaining side dishes, such as barley, wheat berries and quinoa (a seed-like grain with a high protein content). Buckwheat is sold as a grain, although it is actually the seed of a plant related to rhubarb. Oats are one of the more commonly eaten grains used in breakfast cereals such as muesli and cooked into porridge. Some grains are high in the protein gluten, and a significant number of the population are sensitive to this so need to avoid foods that contain it. Wheat is especially high in gluten and lower levels are found in barley and rye; very low levels are also present in oats.

STORING RICE AND GRAINS

Direct sunlight and high temperatures can cause the grains to become stale, thereby losing their flavour and nutritional value. Keep grains in a cool, dark and dry cupboard in a sealed packet or airtight container and always use within the 'use-by' date.

FLOUR

There are numerous types of flour, all made by finely grinding grains to make a fine or medium-fine powder. Flours may be white or brown, depending on whether the husk and germ have been removed before grinding.

PULSES AND SEEDS

The term 'pulse' is used to describe all of the various beans, peas and lentils that have been preserved by drying. They are highly nutritious, especially when eaten with grains, such as couscous, pasta, rice or bread. Pulses and seeds are rich in nutrients and are a good source of vegetarian protein. However, most do not constitute a whole protein (containing all eight amino acids) and need to be combined with grains or cereals to make up full protein. They are a good source of fibre, B vitamins, potassium and iron.

STORING PULSES

Pulses should be stored in airtight containers in a cool, dry cupboard. They keep well, but after about six months their skins start to toughen, and they take progressively longer to cook the longer they are stored.

PREPARING AND COOKING PULSES

The weight of dried beans approximately doubles during soaking and cooking, so if a recipe calls for 225g (8oz) cooked beans, you would need to start with 125g (4oz) dried weight. Once cooked, pulses keep well in the fridge for two to three days.

With the exception of lentils and split peas, pulses need to be soaked overnight in plenty of cold water. The following day, drain off the water prior to cooking.

Cooking pulses is quite a lengthy process. For some pulses, notably red kidney beans, aduki beans, black-eyed beans, black beans and borlotti beans, it is essential to cover with plenty of fresh cold water, bring to the boil and boil vigorously for 10 minutes to destroy any toxins present on the skins. Although pre-boiling isn't mandatory for other dried pulses, it does no harm and saves the need to remember which ones require it.

After the initial fast-boiling, lower the heat, then cover and simmer until tender. To enhance the flavour, a bouquet garni (1 bay leaf, a few fresh parsley and thyme sprigs) and/or 1 or 2 garlic cloves can be added to the cooking water. Salt should only be added 10–15 minutes before the end of the cooking time; if added at the start, it will toughen the skins.

The cooking time is determined by the type of pulse, soaking time and, above all, by the length of time it has been stored. As an approximate guide: red lentils cook in 20 minutes; green lentils take 30–45 minutes; split peas require 45–60 minutes; aduki, black-eyed, borlotti, butter, pinto, flageolet and haricot beans need 1–1½ hours; black beans and red kidney beans take 1½–2 hours; chickpeas require 2–3 hours; while soya beans need 3–4 hours. (Note that soya beans must always be pre-boiled for 1 hour, to destroy a substance they contain that prevents the body from absorbing protein.)

USING CANNED PULSES

Canned pulses are a convenient, quick alternative to cooking your own, and most supermarkets stock a wide range. A 400g can is roughly equivalent to 75g (3oz) dried beans and contains about 150ml (¼ pint) liquid. Always drain canned pulses, then rinse and drain again before using.

SEEDS

Seeds are an excellent, highly nutritious vegetarian ingredient, adding texture, flavour and interest to a variety of foods, including breads, cakes and salads. Sunflower seeds, poppy seeds, sesame seeds and pumpkin seeds are especially popular. To enhance their flavour, toast in a dry frying pan for a few minutes, shaking the pan constantly.

SPROUTED BEANS AND SEEDS

These are rich in nutrients and lend a nutty taste and crunchy texture to salads and stir-fries. Fresh bean sprouts are available from most supermarkets. Many beans and seeds can be sprouted at home, though it is important to buy ones which are specifically produced for sprouting – from a healthfood shop or other reliable source. Mung beans, aduki beans, alfalfa seeds and fenugreek are all suitable. (See also Bean Sprout on page 278.)

Long-grain rice

These long, narrow grains may be white or brown. Brown rice contains the husk and bran and has a distinctive nutty flavour and chewy texture. White rice has been milled to remove the husk. It is tender and delicately flavoured, but lacks the fibre and nutritional benefits of brown rice. Serve long-grain rice as an accompaniment to curries and stews, or in pilaus, salads and stuffings for meat and vegetables. Easy-cook rice is long-grain rice that has been steam-treated to harden the grain, which prevents the cooked grains from sticking together.

Basmati rice

Slender and fragrant basmati rice has a good flavour and texture and is available as white and brown. Serve as an accompaniment to curries and other dishes or in pilaus. Rinse the grains well in cold water, then add two-and-a-half times its volume of boiling water and a pinch of salt. Cover the pan tightly and simmer for 12 minutes for white rice and 20–25 minutes for brown until all the water has been absorbed, then leave to stand for 5 minutes.

Thai fragrant rice

Also known as jasmine rice, this white rice is highly prized in Thailand for its fragrance, flavour and tender, slightly sticky texture. It is cooked in water or coconut milk, and served as an accompaniment to South-east Asian dishes, and can also be cooked in milk or coconut milk with spices and sugar to make a rice pudding. Cook with double the volume of boiling water; cover the pan tightly and simmer for 12 minutes or until all the water has been absorbed. Leave to stand for 5 minutes.

Risotto rice

There are three main varieties of the fat, high-starch rice used to make Italian risotto: Arborio, carnaroli and vialone nano. The grains are simmered and stirred frequently during cooking to release their starches into the cooking liquid and to produce a rich, creamy-textured risotto. It is often cooked with garlic, onions, white wine and stock, then flavoured with Parmesan or a variety of other additions.

Paella rice

Sometimes referred to as Valencia rice, paella rice is fat and starchy. There are three main varieties: bomba, bahia and grano largo. It is usually cooked gently in a large, flat paella pan with additional ingredients, including onions, garlic, saffron, tomatoes, stock, sausage, chicken and rabbit and/or shellfish. A traditional paella is not stirred during cooking but shaken occasionally. It is ready when the grains have plumped up and are slightly sticky and all the liquid has been absorbed.

Glutinous rice

Short, fat glutinous rice is used in Chinese and South-east Asian cooking. It is often referred to as sticky or sweet rice because the grains become sticky when cooked. It may be black or white and is often sweetened and served with fruit as a dessert. In Japan, glutinous rice is a favoured accompaniment to savoury dishes because it can be eaten easily with chopsticks. Wash the rice well in cold water, then leave to stand for 1 hour. Simmer in an equal volume of boiling water in a covered pan until all the liquid has been absorbed.

Wild rice

Not actually a rice, but the grain of a wild marsh grass, wild rice is dark brown-black with a rich, complex, nutty flavour and firm texture. It is costly to buy and is often sold in mixes with long-grain or basmati rice. Most wild rice is now farmed and is a delightful and luxurious treat. Red rice is a natural hybrid of wild rice and has a red-brown colour and nutty flavour. Boil in salted water for 30 minutes, or until tender.

Cornmeal

The colour of cornmeal – white or yellow – is dependent on the colour of the corn (maize) from which it is ground; but there is no other difference. Cornmeal can be coarse, medium or fine and is used to make a quick bread that doesn't require yeast, and occasionally cakes, muffins and biscuits or added to flour for leavened baking. Mexican tortillas can be made solely with cornmeal. Most cornmeal is ground to remove all the bran and germ. Cornmeal can be used to coat foods before deep-frying, to give a crunchy crust.

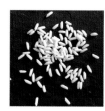

Polenta

Italian cooks prepare polenta by boiling cornmeal (usually fine) in water with salt to make a thick purée. It is served both as a staple and an accompaniment. Polenta may be served plain or with cheese stirred through it. It may also be left to cool until firm, then sliced and pan-fried, griddled or baked. Traditional polenta should be stirred into boiling salted water, then stirred constantly for 45 minutes or until thick and tender. Quickcook varieties can be cooked in only a few minutes.

Grits

Popular in the southern states of the US, hominy grits, or grits, are the American version of polenta. They are made from coarsely ground white or yellow maize, boiled in water to make a thin, pale porridge. Grits is usually served as a savoury breakfast food, often with eggs and sausage. They may also be flavoured with cheese and baked to make the dish, cheese grits. Boil grits in water with a pinch of salt.

Popcorn

Golden popcorn is a type of corn kernel specially bred to make the snack. When the kernels are heated, the starch inside expands rapidly, creating a white, fluffy ball. Popcorn is eaten as a snack food, and can be sprinkled with salt, tossed in butter or drizzled with honey, syrup or caramel. The unpopped kernels are also referred to as popping corn. Heat a little oil in a pan with enough popcorn to cover the base in a single layer. Cover tightly with a lid and cook at medium-high heat until all sounds of popping have stopped.

Whole wheat

Also known as wheat berries, these small, golden-brown grains of husked wheat have a chewy texture and a wholesome, nutty taste when cooked. They are good added to soups, stews, casseroles and pilaus, and can be sprinkled over bread before baking. Soak overnight in cold water, then boil in salted water for 1 hour or until tender. The processed form requires no presoaking and has a much shorter cooking time. Wheat germ is the tiny embryo of a whole-wheat grain from which the grain will sprout. It is highly nutritious.

Cracked wheat

Uncooked wheat berries are crushed to produce cracked wheat. It has a nutty flavour and chewy texture similar to whole wheat, and can be served as an accompaniment or used in salads and added to soups, stews and casseroles. Boil cracked wheat in salted water until tender.

Bulgur wheat

Although sometimes referred to as cracked wheat, bulgur is a completely different product. It has a pleasantly chewy texture and nutty taste, and is available in various grades, from fine to coarse. Popular in Middle Eastern cooking, bulgur wheat is used in tabbouleh and several other herby salads. It can also be used in pilaus or as an accompaniment. Soak in boiling, salted water for 20 minutes or until tender, then drain and use as required.

Wheat flakes

Whole grains are steamed to soften them and then flattened by rollers to produce wheat flakes. They are added to breakfast cereals, such as muesli, and can be sprinkled over loaves before baking or added to fruit crumble mixtures. Malted wheat flakes, made from grains that have briefly germinated, have a darker colour and richer, slightly sweeter, fruitier flavour. Also known as rolled wheat.

Couscous

Couscous consists of tiny, pasta-like pellets made from moistened, rolled grains of semolina. It is served as an accompaniment to spicy stews and to make salads. It is available as fine, medium and giant. The giant variety is known as Israeli couscous, pearl couscous and moghrabieh. You may also find barley and maize varieties, and flavoured brands. Traditionally, the grains are soaked and then steamed in a perforated pot set over a pan of stew. Quick-cook varieties can just be soaked in boiling water for 5 minutes.

Semolina

Pale yellow semolina is made from durum wheat, ground either coarsely or finely. It is used to make sweet milk puddings and is added to cake and biscuit mixtures and some breads.

Wheat bran

Bran is the thin, brown, papery outer layer of the wheat grain. Wheat bran is not nutritious, but it provides a valuable source of fibre. Added in small quantities to breads, cereals and some cakes and biscuits, it adds a rich brown colour and wholesome, slightly nutty flavour. Bran contains phytates, which can prevent minerals, such as calcium and iron, being absorbed into the body, so should not be consumed in excess or routinely added to food. Use in very small quantities.

WHEAT FLOUR

The most widely used type of flour, wheat flour has a high gluten content, making it ideal for baking breads, cakes and biscuits. It is also used for pastry, pasta, crumbles and batters, to thicken sauces and soups and to coat meat and fish before frying.

White flour

By far the most versatile of all wheat flours, white flour can be used for most cooking purposes (apart from bread-making or pasta).

Wholemeal flour

Made from whole-wheat grains, this flour is pale brown with a slightly coarse texture and a nutty flavour. It is denser than white flour.

Self-raising flour

Usually made from white flour with the addition of baking powder. Self-raising flour is used primarily for cakes and biscuits.

Strong bread flour

Specifically produced for making bread. Strong flour contains high levels of gluten, which improve the elasticity of the dough so that air is trapped inside as it rises. The flour may be white, brown (a mixture of white and wholemeal), wholemeal or Granary (with malted wheat flakes).

Tipo 00

Also known as farina bianca, this fine white Italian flour is used to make pasta.

Chapati flour

Also known as ata, this fine wholemeal wheat flour is used to make Indian flatbreads.

OTHER FLOURS

Rice flour

This flour is gluten-free and can be used as a thickener. Finely ground rice flour is used in Asia to make doughs, dumpling wrappers, cakes and sweets.

Rye flour

This greyish-brown flour has a distinctive, slightly sharp flavour. It is widely used in Russia, Scandinavia and Germany to make dense, dark, rye breads.

Buckwheat flour

This grey-brown flour has a distinctively earthy taste and is traditionally used to make blini and pancakes.

Barley flour

A pale, mildly flavoured flour, barley flour has a low gluten content and is usually combined with wheat flour to make soft-textured breads.

Millet flour

Pale yellow millet flour has a mild, slightly sweet flavour. Low in gluten, it is best combined with wheat flour to make crumbly breads and cakes.

Spelt flour

Ground from a type of wheat that has been cultivated since the Bronze Age, spelt flour has a slightly nuttier flavour than ordinary wheat flour. Use alone or blend with wheat flour in cakes and breads.

Potato flour

This fine, white, soft flour is gluten-free and favoured by those on a gluten-free diet for making cakes. It gives a spongy result. Potato flour is best used with other flours.

Chestnut flour

Made from ground sweet chestnuts, this pale, sweet and nutty flour is used in cakes, such as Italian castagnaccio, biscuits and bread.

Soya flour

This fine white flour, ground from partially cooked soya beans, is gluten-free with a high protein content. It can be used with other flours to make cakes, biscuits and bread.

Chickpea flour

Also known as gram flour and besan, chickpea flour is a pale, creamy yellow flour with a nutty and slightly bitter flavour. It is used to make batter for Indian-style fritters such as pakora, or to thicken savoury sauces.

Cornflour

Pure white, and much finer than wheat flour, cornflour is ground from the white part of the corn kernel. It is used to thicken soups, sauces and gravies, and added in small quantities to desserts such as pavlova to give the meringue a slightly chewy consistency. As a thickener, cornflour is blended with a small amount of cold liquid, then added towards the end of cooking. It is wheat- and gluten-free (although gluten-intolerant people should always check the packaging to ensure there are no traces).

Arrowroot

A white starch powder from the maranta plant, arrowroot becomes clear when dissolved in liquid. It is used as a thickener for desserts and fruit sauces.

Oats

Oats are widely sold in the form of rolled oats and oatmeal. Pinhead oatmeal is the coarsest grade and is used in haggis and for making Scottish porridge, although many people now use rolled oats instead. Finer grades of oatmeal are often combined with wheat flour to make breads, cakes such as parkin and biscuits, or for coating herring and other oily fish before frying. Rolled oats are the main ingredient in flapjacks and can also be added to breads, cakes, biscuits and cereals such as muesli.

Barley

Pearl barley, whose grains have been husked, steamed and polished, is most commonly used in cooking. The grains have a delicate, sweet flavour and a slightly chewy texture. Add to soups, salads and stews, or serve as a side dish. Barley can also be cooked like risotto. Pot barley, which has less of the husk removed, can be used in the same way but it requires a longer cooking time. Add pearl barley to soups and stews, or boil in salted water for 45 minutes–1 hour, until tender. Soak pot barley overnight, then cook for 1–2 hours.

Quinoa

This South American grain is the only grain to contain all eight amino acids and thus to be considered a complete protein. The tiny round grains swell up when cooked and have a mildly nutty taste with a firm, slightly slippery texture. Quinoa can be used in pilaus, salads and baked dishes, as well as in stuffings for vegetables. Rinse before using. Simmer in boiling water for 20 minutes, or until tender.

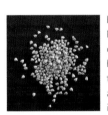

Buckwheat

Not in fact a cereal or grass, buckwheat has triangular seeds and is widely used in Eastern European and Ashkenazi Jewish cooking. It is available toasted or plain and has a nutty, wholesome flavour and soft texture when cooked. It is traditionally cooked into a porridge known as kasha, and served as an accompaniment to lamb and beef pot roasts and stews, with onions and brown gravy. Toast plain buckwheat in a dry frying pan for a few minutes, then simmer in stock or salted water for 10–20 minutes, until tender.

Spelt

A type of wheat that has been cultivated since the Bronze Age, spelt has slender golden grains. It is often more readily tolerated by those who cannot eat wheat or gluten due to a food intolerance. With a slightly chewy and firm texture, spelt can be cooked and used in the same way as whole wheat, in soups, stews and pilaus.

Millet

This small, round, mildly flavoured pale-brown grain is widely eaten in some European countries. Millet can be cooked with milk and sugar into a sweet 'porridge' rather like rice pudding, or added to soups, stews and pilaus. Millet flakes can be used in place of millet, or added to muesli or multigrain breads. Toast millet grains in a dry frying pan for a few minutes before simmering in liquid until tender.

Tapioca

Derived from the vegetable root cassava, this starchy product consists of small, round, pearly white granules. Tapioca is used in South-east Asia, India and Brazil to make sweet desserts, cooked with milk and sugar rather like rice pudding. The pearls become extremely soft with cooking. Some recipes recommend soaking the grains first, but others simmer tapioca in milk with sugar, and often spices, until tender.

Chickpea

These hazelnut-sized peas are also known as chana and garbanzo beans. They have a slightly knobbly surface, a rich, nutty flavour and a firm but tender texture. The cooked beans can be puréed to make hummus, and the raw, soaked beans can be ground to make falafel. They make a good addition to mixed bean and couscous salads. Soak dried chickpeas overnight in cold water. Drain, then boil in fresh, unsalted water for 2 hours or until tender.

Kidney bean

These beans have a pale flesh, a smooth, firm texture and sweetish, earthy flavour. They are good in any spicy stew or soup, and in mixed bean salads. Soak dried kidney beans overnight in cold water. Drain, boil rapidly in fresh, unsalted water for 10 minutes, then simmer for 1–1½ hours until just tender. Note: kidney beans contain toxic substances that can only be removed by boiling rapidly for 10 minutes. They should be added to stews only if they have been pre-boiled.

Cannellini bean

These beans have a tender, buttery texture and a very mild flavour. A good addition to tomato-based and meat stews, they suit robust flavours with plenty of herbs and aromatics. Cannellini beans can be tossed in a little dressing with salad vegetables or in the classic Italian bean salad with tuna fish, tonno e fagioli. Soissons is a dried haricot bean used in France, particularly in the classic goose (or duck) and sausage stew, cassoulet. Soak dried cannellini beans overnight in cold water. Drain, then boil in fresh, unsalted water for 1½ hours or until tender.

Flageolet bean

Flageolet beans are small, young haricot beans harvested and dried before they are fully ripe. They have a deliciously subtle, fresh flavour and a smooth, buttery texture. Although they go well in robust, tomato-based and meat stews, they can also be served on their own or combined with other beans, such as mixed bean salads, with fresh herbs and olive oil, or tossed with garlic and olive oil and served as an accompaniment to roast lamb. Soak dried flageolet beans overnight in cold water. Drain, then boil in fresh, unsalted water for 1–1½ hours or until tender.

Butter bean

One of the largest of the dried beans, butter beans are flat and kidney shaped with a creamy and mild flavour, and a floury texture. This versatile bean is added to vegetable and meat stews, and goes well with strong flavours such as tomatoes and spices. It is also often used in traditional Greek dishes and in other Mediterranean recipes. Butter beans taste good in mixed bean and couscous salads, and added to soups. Soak dried butter beans overnight in cold water. Drain, then boil in fresh, unsalted water for 1 hour or until tender.

Broad bean

This dried version of the fresh broad bean is pale brown and flat. When bought whole, the skins can be tough, but they are also sold pre-skinned, when the beans are usually off-white, thin and 'split'. Popular in Middle Eastern cooking, broad beans are the favoured bean used to make the golden fritter falafel, and for a number of spiced bean purées. They have a distinctive flavour and a tender texture, and can also be added to meat and vegetable stews. Soak dried broad beans overnight in cold water. Drain, then boil in fresh, unsalted water for 30–50 minutes or until tender.

Borlotti bean

Borlotti beans have a pale, tender and buttery flesh with a sweetish, earthy flavour. They are good used in soups, stews and salads, and feature in the classic pasta and bean soup, pasta e fagioli. They lose a bit of their colour when cooked, but retain enough to make them still attractive. Soak dried borlotti beans overnight in cold water. Drain, then boil rapidly in fresh, unsalted water for 10 minutes. Simmer for 1½ hours or until tender. Note: borlotti beans contain toxic substances (see Kidney Bean above).

Pinto bean

A type of kidney bean that is popular in both Spain and Mexico, pinto beans have a pinky-beige skin with dark orange-red streaks and a tender pale flesh with a nutty flavour. Good used in soups, stews and salads, they were the original bean used to make Mexican refried beans, where tender-cooked beans are fried and roughly mashed with garlic, tomatoes and spices. Pinto beans are also a popular addition to Spanish stews. Soak dried pinto beans overnight in cold water. Drain, then boil in fresh, unsalted water for 1–1½ hours or until tender.

Lima bean

As lima beans are similar in appearance, taste and texture to butter beans, they can be used in the same way. The pale, flat bean is found in the US, where it is often added to soups, stews and salads. Cook as for butter beans. Soak dried lima beans overnight in cold water. Drain, then boil in fresh, unsalted water for 1–1½ hours or until tender.

Haricot bean

Known as navy beans in the US, haricot beans are small, oval and creamy white, and are the classic ingredient in Boston baked beans (cooked with cured pork, tomato and spices). With a mild flavour and smooth, buttery texture, they are good used in robust, well-flavoured soups and stews, such as cassoulet, or made into purées flavoured with spices, herbs and aromatics. Soak dried haricot beans overnight in cold water. Drain, then boil in fresh, unsalted water for 1–1½ hours or until tender.

Soya bean

As well as being rich in nutrients, soya beans are an excellent source of protein. They are rather bland and are best added to spicy soups and stews where they will absorb the flavours. Soak dried soya beans overnight in cold water. Drain, then boil rapidly in fresh, unsalted water for 1 hour. Drain, then boil in fresh, unsalted water for 2 hours or until tender. Note: soya beans contain toxic substances (see Kidney Bean, page 260).

Tofu is made from pressed soya beans.

Black-eyed bean

Also known as black-eyed peas and cow peas, these creamy white beans have a distinctive black mark where the bean was once attached to the pod. With a tender texture and mild flavour, they are good added to soups, stews, curries and salads, and go particularly well with pork and ham. Soak dried black-eyed beans overnight in cold water. Drain, then boil in fresh, unsalted water for 1½ hours or until tender.

Black bean

Black beans have a distinctive, slightly sweet, earthy flavour, they are good added to soups, stews and salads, and can be cooked with spices to make purées. Soak dried black beans overnight in cold water. Drain, then boil rapidly in fresh, unsalted water for 15 minutes. Drain, then boil in fresh, unsalted water for 1 hour or until tender. Note: black beans contain toxic substances (see Kidney Bean, page 260).

Mung bean

Also known as green gram and moong dal, these small beans are widely used in India to make curries. They are available both whole and split. With a tender texture and fresh, slightly sweet flavour, mung beans are also good added to soups, stews and salads. They are also the most popular bean for sprouting. Mung beans require no soaking and can be boiled in unsalted water for 40 minutes or until tender. If soaked overnight, the cooking time can be reduced to 25 minutes.

Aduki bean

These beans have a smooth texture and distinctive, slightly sweet flavour. Popular in Japanese cooking, aduki beans are most often used to make sweet dishes, such as cooked to a purée with sugar and used as a filling for pancakes, or wrapped around rice balls to make the Japanese sweet rice cakes known as ohagi. They may also be used in savoury dishes, added to stews, stir-fries and salads. Soak dried black-eyed beans overnight in cold water. Drain, then boil in fresh, unsalted water for 1½ hours or until tender.

Green lentil (pictured), brown lentil

Grey-green lentils have a mild flavour and soft texture. They retain their shape well (unless overcooked) and are a good addition to soups and stews, but can also be used to stuff vegetables or added to salads. Cook without soaking in boiling unsalted water for 30 minutes or until tender. Brown lentils are similar to green lentils and can be used in the same way in soups, stews and rice dishes. Their colour is sadly unexciting, but they have good flavour and a solid skin that holds up well.

Red split lentil (pictured), yellow lentil

These tiny lentils both disintegrate as they cook, producing a thick purée. As they have a mild flavour, they benefit from the addition of spices and strong flavours. They are used to make spicy Indian dhal but they can also be used to thicken soups and casseroles. Cook without soaking in boiling unsalted water for 20 minutes (red lentils), 30 minutes (yellow lentils) or until tender.

Split peas are similar – cook as above for 45 minutes or until tender.

Puy lentil

These lentils are highly prized for their excellent taste and texture. Grown in France, they are often boiled until tender, then cooked briefly with a little stock, fried onion or garlic and fresh herbs, and served as an accompaniment to meats and fish, or tossed in salads. They can also be used in soups and stews in the same way as green and brown lentils. Puy lentils hold their shape better than any other lentil, even when fully cooked. Cook without soaking in boiling unsalted water for 30 minutes or until tender.

BASIC PILAU RICE

Serves 4
Preparation 5 minutes
Cooking time 20 minutes, plus standing

50g (2oz) butter
225g (8oz) long-grain white rice
750ml (1¼ pints) chicken stock
salt and ground black pepper
generous knob of butter, to serve

1 Melt the butter in a pan, add the rice and fry gently for 3–4 minutes until translucent.
2 Slowly pour in the stock, season, stir and cover with a tight-fitting lid. Leave, undisturbed, over a very low heat for about 15 minutes or until the water has been absorbed and the rice is just tender.
3 Remove the lid and cover the surface of the rice with a clean cloth. Replace the lid and leave to stand in a warm place for about 15 minutes to dry the rice before serving.
4 Fork through and add a knob of butter to serve

NUTRITION PER SERVING 320 cals |
13g fat (8g sats) | 45g carbs | 0.8g salt

SPECIAL FRIED RICE

Preparation 5 minutes
Cooking time 10–15 minutes
Serves 4

2 × 250g packs of microwavable rice or 200g (7oz) long-grain rice, cooked, rinsed and drained
1 tbsp sesame oil
6 tbsp nasi goreng paste (see Cook's Tips)
200g (7oz) green cabbage, shredded
250g (9oz) cooked and peeled large prawns
2 tbsp light soy sauce
1 tbsp sunflower oil
2 medium eggs, beaten
2 spring onions, thinly sliced
1 lime, cut into wedges, to serve

1 Cook the rice according to the pack instructions.
2 Heat the sesame oil in a wok or large pan and fry the nasi goreng paste for 1–2 minutes. Add the cabbage and stir-fry for 2–3 minutes. Add the prawns and stir briefly, then add the rice and soy sauce and cook for a further 5 minutes, stirring occasionally.
3 Heat the sunflower oil in a non-stick frying pan, about 25.5cm (10in) in diameter, and add the eggs. Swirl around to cover the base of the pan in a thin layer and cook for 2–3 minutes until set.
4 Roll up the omelette and cut it into strips. Serve the rice scattered with strips of omelette and spring onions, and pass round the lime wedges to squeeze over it.

COOK'S TIP
Nasi goreng paste can be bought at large supermarkets and Asian food shops.

NUTRITION PER SERVING 412 cals |
18g fat (3g sats) | 46g carbs | 1.9g salt

RISOTTO MILANESE

Preparation 15 minutes
Cooking time about 30 minutes

50g (2oz) butter
1 onion, finely chopped
150ml (1/4 pint) dry white wine
300g (11oz) Arborio rice
1 litre (1³/4 pints) chicken stock
large pinch of saffron
50g (2oz) Parmesan, freshly grated,
    plus shavings to serve
salt and ground black pepper

1 Melt half the butter in a heavy-based pan. Add the onion and cook gently for 5 minutes to soften, then add the wine and boil rapidly until almost totally reduced. Add the rice and cook, stirring, for 1 minute or until the grains are coated with the butter and glossy.

2 Meanwhile, heat the stock in a separate pan to a steady, low simmer.
3 Add the saffron and a ladleful of the stock to the rice and simmer, stirring, until absorbed. Continue adding the stock, a ladleful at a time, until the rice is tender but still has some bite to it. This will take about 25 minutes and you may not need to add all the stock.
4 Add the remaining butter and the grated Parmesan. Season with salt and pepper to taste, garnish with shavings of Parmesan and serve.

> NUTRITION PER SERVING 461 cals |
> 15g fat (9g sats) | 64g carbs | 0.6g salt

WILD MUSHROOM RISOTTO

Serves 6
Preparation 10 minutes
Cooking time 30 minutes

6 tbsp olive oil
2 shallots, finely chopped
2 garlic cloves, finely chopped
2 tsp freshly chopped thyme,
    plus sprigs to garnish
1 tsp grated lemon zest
350g (12oz) Arborio rice
150ml (1/4 pint) dry white wine
900ml (1¹/2 pints) vegetable stock
450g (1lb) mixed fresh mushrooms,
    such as oyster, shiitake and cep,
    sliced if large
1 tbsp freshly chopped flat-leafed
    parsley
salt and ground black pepper

1 Heat half the oil in a heavy-based pan. Add the finely chopped shallots and garlic, chopped thyme and lemon zest, and fry gently for 5 minutes or until the shallots are softened. Add the rice and stir for 1 minute until the grains are glossy. Add the wine, bring to the boil and let it bubble until almost totally evaporated. Heat the stock in a separate pan to a steady, low simmer.
2 Gradually add the stock to the rice, a ladleful at a time, stirring with each addition and allowing it to be absorbed before adding more. Continue adding the stock slowly until the rice is tender. This should take about 25 minutes.
3 About 5 minutes before the rice is ready, heat the remaining oil in a large frying pan and stir-fry the mushrooms over a high heat for 4–5 minutes. Add to the rice with the parsley. The risotto should still be moist: if necessary add a little more stock. Check the seasoning and serve at once, garnished with thyme.

> NUTRITION PER SERVING 347 cals |
> 12g fat (2g sats) | 50g carbs | 0.6g salt Ⓥ

SIMPLE PAELLA

Serves 6
Preparation 15 minutes, plus infusing
Cooking time 50 minutes

1 litre (1³/₄ pints) chicken stock
¹/₂ tsp saffron
5 tbsp extra virgin olive oil
6 boneless, skinless chicken thighs, each cut into
    three pieces
1 large onion, chopped
4 large garlic cloves, crushed
1 tsp paprika
2 red peppers, seeded and sliced
400g can chopped tomatoes
350g (12oz) long-grain rice
200ml (7fl oz) dry sherry
500g (1lb 2oz) cooked mussels
200g (7oz) cooked and peeled tiger prawns
juice of ¹/₂ lemon
salt and ground black pepper
lemon wedges and fresh flat-leafed parsley to serve

1 Heat the stock, then add the saffron and leave to infuse
for 30 minutes.
2 Heat half the oil in a frying pan and fry the chicken in
batches for 3–5 minutes until golden brown. Set the chicken
aside. Lower the heat slightly. Add the remaining oil. Fry the
onion for 5 minutes or until soft. Add the garlic and paprika,
and stir for 1 minute. Add the chicken, red peppers and
tomatoes. Stir in the rice. Add one-third of the stock and
bring to the boil. Season with salt and pepper. Reduce the
heat to a simmer. Cook, uncovered, stirring continuously,
until most of the liquid has been absorbed.
3 Add the remaining stock a little at a time, letting the
rice absorb it before adding more. (This should take about
25 minutes.) Add the sherry and cook for 2 minutes – the
rice should be quite wet, as it will continue to absorb liquid.
Add the mussels and prawns, with their juices, and the lemon
juice. Stir in and cook for 5 minutes to heat through. Adjust
the seasoning and serve with lemon wedges and parsley.

COOK'S TIP
Ready-cooked mussels are available vacuum-packed
from supermarkets. Alternatively, to cook from
fresh, follow the preparation instructions in Cook's
Tips, page 95, then put them in a large pan and
add 50ml (2fl oz) water. Cover with a tight-fitting lid
and cook for 3–4 minutes, shaking the pan
occasionally, until the mussels open. Transfer to a
bowl, discard any unopened mussels, and keep
the cooking liquid to one side.

NUTRITION PER SERVING
554 cals | 16g fat (3g sats) | 58g carbs | 0.5g salt

JAMBALAYA

Serves 4
Preparation 15 minutes
Cooking time about 50 minutes, plus standing

2 tbsp olive oil
300g (11oz) boneless, skinless chicken thighs, cut
    into chunks
75g (3oz) French sausage, such as saucisse sèche, chopped
2 celery sticks, chopped
1 large onion, finely chopped
225g (8oz) long-grain rice
1 tbsp tomato purée
2 tsp Cajun spice mix
500ml (18fl oz) hot chicken stock
1 bay leaf
4 large tomatoes, roughly chopped
200g (7oz) raw tiger prawns, deveined (see page 85)

1 Heat 1 tbsp oil in a large pan and fry the chicken and
sausage over a medium heat until browned. Remove with a
slotted spoon and set aside.
2 Add the remaining oil to the pan with the celery and
onion. Fry gently for 15 minutes or until the vegetables are
softened but not coloured. Tip in the rice and stir for 1 minute
to coat in the oil. Add the tomato purée and spice mix, and
cook for another 2 minutes.
3 Pour in the hot stock and return the browned chicken and
sausage to the pan with the bay leaf and tomatoes. Simmer
for 20–25 minutes until the stock has been fully absorbed and
the rice is cooked.
4 Stir in the prawns and cover the pan. Leave to stand
for 10 minutes or until the prawns have turned pink.
Serve immediately.

NUTRITION PER SERVING
558 cals | 25g fat (6g sats) | 49g carbs | 04g salt

CHEESE POLENTA WITH TOMATO SAUCE

Serves 6
Preparation 15 minutes, plus cooling
Cooking time 45 minutes

oil to grease
225g (8oz) polenta
4 tbsp freshly chopped herbs, such as oregano, chives and
    flat-leafed parsley
100g (3¹/₂ oz) freshly grated Parmesan, plus fresh Parmesan
    shavings to serve (see page 228)
salt and ground black pepper

For the tomato and basil sauce
1 tbsp vegetable oil
3 garlic cloves, crushed
500g carton creamed tomatoes or passata
1 bay leaf
1 fresh thyme sprig
a large pinch of caster sugar
3 tbsp freshly chopped basil, plus extra to garnish

1 Lightly oil a 25.5 × 18cm (10 × 7in) dish. Bring 1.1 litres
(2 pints) water and ¹/₄ tsp salt to the boil in a large pan.
Sprinkle in the polenta, whisking constantly. Reduce the heat
and simmer, stirring frequently, for 10–15 minutes until the
mixture leaves the sides of the pan.
2 Stir in the herbs and Parmesan, and season to taste with
salt and pepper. Turn into the prepared dish and leave to cool.
3 Next, make the tomato and basil sauce. Heat the oil in a
pan and fry the garlic for 30 seconds (do not brown). Add the
creamed tomatoes or passata, the bay leaf, thyme and sugar.
Season with salt and pepper and bring to the boil, then reduce
the heat and simmer, uncovered, for 5–10 minutes. Remove
the bay leaf and thyme sprig and add the chopped basil.
4 To serve, cut the polenta into pieces and lightly brush with
oil. Preheat a griddle and fry for 3–4 minutes on each side, or
grill under a preheated grill for 7–8 minutes on each side.
Serve with the tomato and basil sauce, fresh Parmesan
shavings and chopped basil.

GET AHEAD
Complete the recipe to the end of step 3. Cover and chill
separately for up to two days. To use, complete the recipe.

TRY SOMETHING DIFFERENT
Fried Herb Polenta Bring 900ml (1¹/₂ pints) water to the
boil in a large pan with a good pinch of salt added. Sprinkle
in 175g (6oz) coarse polenta, whisking constantly. Lower the
heat and simmer, stirring frequently, for 20 minutes or until

the polenta leaves the sides of the pan; it will be very thick.
Stir in 2 tbsp freshly chopped sage and 1 tbsp freshly chopped
rosemary and plenty of salt and pepper. Turn out on to a
board and shape the polenta into a thick oblong mound.
Leave for about 1 hour until set, then cut into slices. Melt
the butter in a frying pan. When foaming, fry the polenta
slices on both sides until golden. Serve with meat, poultry
or vegetarian dishes.
Soft Herb Polenta Serve the Fried Herb Polenta after
you've stirred in the fresh sage and rosemary, as you would
mashed potato.

NUTRITION PER SERVING
249 cals | 9g fat (4g sats) | 31g carbs | 0.9g salt

MEDITERRANEAN VEGETABLE COUSCOUS WITH FETA

Serves 4
Preparation 20 minutes, plus soaking
Cooking time 1 hour

2 red onions, roughly chopped
2 courgettes, roughly chopped
1 aubergine, roughly chopped
2 red peppers, seeded and roughly chopped
2 garlic cloves, sliced
4 tbsp olive oil
350g (12oz) tomatoes, quartered
225g (8oz) couscous
300ml (½ pint) hot vegetable stock
4 tbsp roughly chopped fresh flat-leafed parsley
2 tbsp balsamic vinegar
200g (7oz) feta cheese, cubed (see page 228)
salt and ground black pepper

1 Preheat the oven to 200°C (180°C fan oven) mark 6. Put the red onions, courgettes, aubergine, peppers and garlic into a roasting tin and drizzle with the olive oil. Season with salt and pepper, then toss together and roast for 30 minutes.
2 Add the tomatoes to the tin. Toss together and roast for a further 30 minutes.
3 Meanwhile, put the couscous into a large bowl. Pour in the hot stock, stir and cover. Set aside to soak for 10 minutes.
4 Fluff up the warm couscous with a fork, then add the chopped parsley, balsamic vinegar, and roasted vegetables. Toss together, then spoon into warmed bowls, scatter over the feta cheese and serve.

NUTRITION PER SERVING
580 cals | 25g fat (8g sats) | 73g carbs | 2.3g salt

LENTIL CHILLI

Serves 6
Preparation 10 minutes
Cooking time 30 minutes

oil–water spray (see Cook's Tip, page 213)
2 red onions, chopped
1 1/2 tsp each ground coriander and ground cumin
1/2 tsp ground paprika
2 garlic cloves, crushed
2 sun-dried tomatoes, chopped
1/4 tsp crushed dried chilli flakes
125ml (4fl oz) red wine
300ml (1/2 pint) hot vegetable stock
2 × 400g cans brown or green lentils, drained and rinsed
2 × 400g cans chopped tomatoes
sugar to taste
salt and ground black pepper
natural low-fat yogurt, or soya yogurt, and rice to serve

1 Spray a pan with the oil–water spray and cook the onions for 5 minutes or until softened. Add the coriander, cumin and paprika. Combine the garlic, sun-dried tomatoes, chilli, wine and hot stock, and add to the pan. Cover and simmer for 5–7 minutes. Uncover and simmer until the onions are very tender and the liquid has almost gone.
2 Stir in the lentils and canned tomatoes, and season with salt and pepper to taste. Simmer, uncovered, for 15 minutes or until thick. Stir in sugar to taste. Remove from the heat.
3 Ladle out a quarter of the mixture and whiz in a food processor or blender. Combine the puréed and unpuréed portions. Serve with yogurt and rice.

NUTRITION PER SERVING 195 cals | 2g fat (trace sats) | 32g carbs | 0.1g salt **V**

CHICKPEAS WITH SPINACH

Serves 6
Preparation 10 minutes
Cooking time 12–15 minutes

3 tbsp olive oil
2.5cm (1in) piece fresh root ginger, finely chopped
3 garlic cloves, chopped
2 tsp each ground coriander and paprika
1 tsp ground cumin
2 × 400g cans chickpeas, drained and rinsed
4 tomatoes, roughly chopped
a handful of coriander leaves
450g (1lb) fresh spinach
salt and ground black pepper
rice and grated carrots with lemon juice to serve

1 Heat the oil in a large heavy-based pan, add the ginger, garlic and spices, and cook for 2 minutes, stirring. Stir in the chickpeas.
2 Add the tomatoes to the pan with the coriander leaves and spinach, and cook gently for 10 minutes. Season to taste with salt and pepper, and serve immediately, with rice and a salad of grated carrots tossed in a little lemon juice to taste.

NUTRITION PER SERVING 204 cals | 10g fat (1g sats) | 21g carbs | 0.8g salt **V**

SWEET CHILLI TOFU STIR-FRY

Serves 4
Preparation 5 minutes, plus marinating
Cooking time 12 minutes

200g (7oz) firm tofu (see Cook's Tips)
4 tbsp sweet chilli sauce
2 tbsp light soy sauce
1 tbsp sesame seeds
2 tbsp toasted sesame oil
600g (1lb 5oz) ready-prepared mixed stir-fry vegetables,
    such as carrots, broccoli, mangetouts and bean sprouts
a handful of pea shoots or young salad leaves to garnish

1 Drain the tofu, pat it dry and cut it into large cubes. Put the tofu in a shallow container and pour over 1 tbsp sweet chilli sauce and 1 tbsp light soy sauce. Cover and marinate for 10 minutes.
2 Meanwhile, toast the sesame seeds in a hot wok or large frying pan until golden. Tip on to a plate.
3 Return the wok or frying pan to the heat and add 1 tbsp sesame oil. Add the marinated tofu and stir-fry for 5 minutes or until golden. Remove and set aside.
4 Heat the remaining 1 tbsp oil in the pan, add the vegetables and stir-fry for 3–4 minutes until just tender. Stir in the cooked tofu.
5 Pour the remaining sweet chilli sauce and soy sauce into the pan, toss well and cook for a further 1 minute until heated through. Sprinkle with the toasted sesame seeds and pea shoots or salad leaves and serve immediately.

NUTRITION PER SERVING
290 cals | 26g fat (6g sats) | 8g carbs | 1.5g salt

COOK'S TIPS
→ Tofu is highly nutritious and readily absorbs other flavours on marinating. It is sold as a chilled product and should be stored in the fridge. Once the packet is opened, the tofu should be kept immersed in a bowl of water in the fridge and eaten within four days.
→ Firm tofu is usually cut into chunks, then immersed in tasty marinades and dressings prior to grilling, stir-frying, deep-frying, adding to stews, or tossing raw into salads. It can also be chopped and made into burgers and nut roasts.
→ Smoked tofu has more flavour than firm tofu; it is used in the same way.
→ Silken tofu is softer and creamier than firm tofu and is useful for sauces and dressings.

MUSHROOM AND BEAN HOTPOT

Serves 6
Preparation 15 minutes
Cooking time 45 minutes

3 tbsp olive oil
700g (1½lb) chestnut mushrooms, roughly chopped
1 large onion, finely chopped
2 tbsp plain flour
2 tbsp mild curry paste (see Cook's Tip)
150ml (¼ pint) dry white wine
400g can chopped tomatoes
2 tbsp sun-dried tomato paste
2 × 400g cans mixed beans, drained and rinsed
3 tbsp Mango Chutney (see page 485)
3 tbsp roughly freshly chopped coriander and mint

1 Heat the oil in a large pan over a low heat, then fry the mushrooms and onion until the onion is soft and dark golden. Stir in the flour and curry paste, and cook for 1–2 minutes.
2 Add the wine, tomatoes, sun-dried tomato paste and beans. Bring to the boil, then reduce the heat and simmer gently for 30 minutes or until most of the liquid has reduced. Stir in the chutney and herbs before serving.

COOK'S TIP
If cooking for vegetarians, check the ingredients in the curry paste: some brands may not be suitable.

NUTRITION PER SERVING
280 cals | 10g fat (1g sats) | 34g carbs | 1.3g salt

BOSTON BAKED BEANS

Serves 4
Preparation 10 minutes, plus overnight soaking
Cooking time 2–2¹/₂ hours

225g (8oz) dried black-eyed beans, soaked overnight
    in cold water
2 tbsp olive oil
1 large onion, chopped
1 large garlic clove, finely chopped
600ml (1 pint) dry cider
150g (5oz) passata
2 tbsp sun-dried tomato paste or tomato purée
1 tbsp black treacle
1 tbsp demerara sugar
1 tsp French mustard
sea salt and ground black pepper
parsley sprigs, to garnish
garlic bread or jacket potatoes and salad to serve

1 Drain the beans, rinse under cold running water, then put into a large pan. Cover with plenty of fresh cold water, bring to the boil and boil steadily for 10 minutes. Remove any scum from the surface with a slotted spoon. Lower the heat, cover and simmer for a further 20 minutes. Preheat the oven to 170°C (150°C fan oven) mark 3.

2 Heat the olive oil in another pan, add the onion and garlic, and fry gently until tender. Add the cider, passata, tomato paste, black treacle, demerara sugar and mustard. Bring to the boil.

3 Drain the beans and transfer to a casserole. Stir in the tomato mixture. Cover and cook in the oven for 1¹/₂–2 hours or until the beans are tender. Check and stir the beans occasionally during cooking and add a little extra cider or water if necessary to prevent them drying out; the finished sauce should be thick and syrupy.

4 Season with salt and pepper to taste. Serve garnished with parsley and with hot crusty garlic bread or jacket potatoes and a salad.

TRY SOMETHING DIFFERENT
Use haricot beans instead of black-eyed beans, adjusting the cooking time accordingly.

NUTRITION PER SERVING
310 cals | 8g fat (1g sats) | 45g carbs | 0.9g salt

NUTTY BEAN BURGERS

Serves 6
Preparation 20 minutes, plus standing
Cooking time 25 minutes

2 tbsp olive oil
1 small onion, chopped
1 garlic clove, crushed
2 tsp freshly chopped thyme
400g can red kidney beans, rinsed and drained
400g can butter beans, rinsed and drained
50g (2oz) chopped mixed nuts
40g (1 1/2 oz) fresh white breadcrumbs
1 tbsp dark soy sauce
1 tbsp lemon juice
oil to shallow-fry
6 soft burger buns, split
salt and ground black pepper
selection of relishes and mixed salad to serve

1 Heat the olive oil in a frying pan, add the onion, garlic and thyme, and fry for 10 minutes or until softened and golden.
2 Add the canned beans to the pan. Fry gently for a further 5 minutes, then transfer to a food processor and process briefly to form a rough paste; turn into a bowl.
3 Add the nuts, breadcrumbs, soy sauce and lemon juice, stir until evenly combined and season generously with salt and pepper. Cover and set aside for several hours to allow the flavours to develop.
4 Divide the bean mixture into six equal portions and shape into burgers.
5 Heat a little oil in a heavy-based frying pan and fry the burgers in batches for 2–3 minutes on each side until golden and cooked through. Drain on kitchen paper and keep warm while frying the rest.
6 Serve in burger buns, with your favourite relishes and a mixed salad.

NUTRITION PER SERVING
450 cals | 13g fat (2g sats) | 70g carbs | 3.5g salt

SPICY BEAN AND TOMATO FAJITAS

Serves 4
Preparation 15 minutes
Cooking time 25 minutes

2 tbsp sunflower oil
1 medium onion, sliced
2 garlic cloves, crushed
$\frac{1}{2}$ tsp hot chilli powder
1 tsp ground coriander
1 tsp ground cumin
1 tbsp tomato purée
400g can chopped tomatoes
220g can red kidney beans, drained and rinsed
300g can borlotti beans, drained and rinsed
300g can flageolet beans, drained and rinsed
150ml ($\frac{1}{4}$ pint) hot vegetable stock
2 ripe avocados, quartered, chopped
juice of $\frac{1}{2}$ lime
1 tbsp chopped coriander, plus sprigs to garnish
pack of 8 ready-made flour tortillas
142ml carton soured cream
salt and ground black pepper
lime wedges, to serve

1 Heat the oil in a large pan, add the onion and cook gently for 5 minutes. Add the garlic and spices and cook for a further 2 minutes.

2 Add the tomato purée and cook for 1 minute, then add the tomatoes, beans and hot stock. Season well with salt and pepper, bring to the boil and simmer for 15 minutes, stirring occasionally.

3 Put the avocados into a bowl, add the lime juice and the chopped coriander, and mash together. Season well with salt and pepper.

4 Warm the tortillas: either wrap them in foil and heat in the oven at 180°C (160°C fan oven) mark 4 for 10 minutes or put on a plate and microwave on high for 45 seconds.

5 Spoon the beans down the centre of each tortilla. Fold up one edge to keep the filling inside, then wrap the two sides in so that they overlap. Dollop on the avocado and top with soured cream. Garnish with coriander sprigs and serve with lime wedges.

NUTRITION PER SERVING
620 cals | 28g fat (8g sats) | 74g carbs | 1.8g salt Ⓥ

VEGETABLES

VEGETABLES

Low in fat and cholesterol, yet high in fibre, vegetables are an important source of roughage and are highly nutritious. In particular, they are an excellent source of vitamins and minerals. Starchy varieties, such as potatoes, are also a good source of energy, but most vegetables are low in calories. Many varieties provide some protein too. Frozen vegetables are as nutritious as fresh, because they will have been snap frozen soon after picking.

Most supermarkets now stock a wide range of organic vegetables – grown without the use of chemical pesticides and artificial fertilisers – although they do tend to be more expensive.

Vegetables can be classified into categories:

Brassicas, otherwise known as the cabbage family, include broccoli, Brussels sprouts, cauliflower and curly kale, as well as the many different types of cabbage.

Roots and tubers are vegetables that grow underground, such as carrots, potatoes, parsnips, turnips, swede, celeriac, Jerusalem artichokes, beetroot and the lesser-known salsify and eddoes.

Pods, peas and beans take in the many varieties of fresh beans, along with peas, mangetouts, okra and sweetcorn.

Stalks and shoots encompass such prized delicacies as asparagus, globe artichokes and fennel, along with celery.

The onion family comprises red, white and brown-skinned onions, as well as leeks, garlic, shallots and spring onions.

Mushrooms are a type of fungus. A number of cultivated varieties are available, and seasonal fresh wild mushrooms, such as chanterelles and ceps, are now easier to obtain.

Leafy vegetables include the array of salad leaves – baby spinach, rocket, lamb's lettuce, frisée, radicchio, chicory and all kinds of lettuces.

Vegetable fruits is a diverse category in which the vegetables are more correctly the fruits of their plants. Aubergines, avocado, peppers, tomatoes, cucumbers, courgettes and the other varieties of squash are all included.

BUYING AND STORING VEGETABLES

Look for bright, firm vegetables. Avoid any that look shrivelled or bruised. Resist buying the largest specimens, particularly when choosing roots. In general, the younger and smaller the vegetable, the sweeter and more tender it will be, although some of the baby vegetables may lack flavour because they are so immature.

To enjoy them at their best and most nutritious, vegetables should be eaten as soon as possible after picking or buying, but most will keep for a few days in a cool, dark place. Store green vegetables and salad ingredients in the salad drawer of the fridge. Root vegetables can be stored in a cool, dark place, such as a wire rack in a cool larder, for up to one week. Exposure to light turns potatoes green, so they must be kept in the dark.

PREPARING AND COOKING VEGETABLES

Clean all vegetables thoroughly before cooking. Brush or shake off any loose dirt, then wash thoroughly (except mushrooms which are best wiped). As soon as vegetables are peeled they begin to lose vitamins so, where possible, prepare at the last minute. If the produce is organic and the skins are edible, there is no need to peel. Non-organic produce is better peeled; washing alone is not enough to remove all traces of residual chemicals. Never prepare vegetables hours in advance and leave them immersed in cold water, as water-soluble vitamins will be lost.

Vegetables can be cooked by a variety of methods, including steaming, boiling, sautéeing, stir-frying, roasting, braising and grilling. To minimise the loss of water-soluble vitamins, cook in the minimum amount of water (if boiling), and use the cooking water as vegetable stock or to make a sauce. Avoid overcooking, whichever method you are using. In general, vegetables are at their best cooked until al dente – tender but still retaining some bite.

Potatoes
Most of the nutrients in a potato are stored just beneath the skin so, where possible, leave the skin on. New potatoes

can be scrubbed, or scraped with a knife, although you may need to peel maincrop potatoes if you are planning to boil and mash or roast them. Use a vegetable peeler that removes the skin in a thin, even layer.

Boil Cut peeled maincrop potatoes into large chunks. Put in cold salted water, bring to the boil, then cook for 10–20 minutes until tender. To mash, drain and allow to steam dry. Mash with plenty of butter and milk until smooth, then season.

New potatoes can be put into a pan of boiling water and cooked for 15–20 minutes until tender. To crush boiled new potatoes, drain and allow to steam dry in the pan for 1–2 minutes. Crush gently with a potato masher, then drizzle with olive oil and add with fresh herbs and pepper.

Roast Parboil prepared maincrop potatoes for 10 minutes, then drain and allow to steam dry for 1–2 minutes. Shake to roughen the surface. Heat oil, goose fat or lard in a roasting tin at 220°C (200°C fan oven) mark 7 until very hot, add the potatoes, turn to coat, then roast, turning once or twice and basting with the fat, for 45 minutes–1 hour until golden.

Bake Scrub large potatoes well and pat dry. Prick with a fork, then bake at 200°C (180°C fan oven) mark 6 for 1–1½ hours until tender.

Deep-fry For chips, peel and cut into thick slices, then into sticks. Leave in a bowl of cold water for 30 minutes to remove excess starch, then drain and dry using a teatowel or kitchen paper. Heat the oil in a deep frying pan or deep-fryer to 190°C, or until one chip dropped in rises to the surface immediately, surrounded by bubbles. Quarter-fill the frying basket with chips, lower into the oil and cook for 6–7 minutes, until beginning to colour. Raise the basket to drain; repeat with the remaining potatoes. Fry all the chips for a second time, for 3 minutes or until golden and crisp.

Sauté Cut into slices. Coat the base of a heavy-based pan with oil and heat until medium-hot. Add the potatoes, and turn to coat with the oil. Season. cover the pan and cook for 5–8 minutes until they start to soften. Remove the lid and stir every minute or so while the potatoes cook.

Onions

Cut off the tip and base of the onion. Peel away the papery skin and any discoloured layers underneath. Put the onion cut side down on a chopping board then, using a sharp knife, cut the onion in half from tip to base. To slice an onion put one half on the board with the cut surface facing down, and slice across the onion. To chop an onion, put the flat sides down and make three horizontal cuts from the pointed end almost to the root. Cut along its length six or seven times. Now chop across the width, from pointed end to root, to make dice. Throw away the root.

Tomatoes

To skin tomatoes, plunge them into boiling water for 30 seconds, then refresh in cold water. Cut lightly into the skin then peel it away. To remove the seeds, halve the tomato and scoop out the seeds with a spoon or cut out with a small sharp knife.

For other vegetable preparation see the specific vegetable on the following pages.

Artichoke, Globe

Choose heavy heads with firm, tight leaves. Allow 1 per person if serving whole. Baby artichokes can be eaten whole. If only the hearts are being served, allow 2–3 per person. Cut off the stalks and snip off any leaf spikes. Cook in boiling salted water with a slice of lemon for 35–40 minutes or until you can pull out a leaf easily. Serve warm with melted butter or hollandaise, or cold with dressing. Pull off each leaf, dip in the dressing, then suck off the fleshy part. Slice off and discard the hairy choke and use a knife and fork to eat the delicate heart.

Artichoke, Jerusalem

Unrelated to the globe artichoke, this is a knobbly tuber with a nutty flavour. Choose the smoothest available as these will be easier to peel. Allow about 175g (6oz) per person. Scrub well and peel thinly. If they are very difficult to peel, cook first. They can be cubed, diced, sliced or cut into julienne. Cook in boiling salted water, acidulated with 1 tbsp lemon juice to prevent discoloration, for 10–15 minutes. Serve as an accompaniment, purée or make into a creamy soup.

Asparagus

Varieties include thick green, thin green, fine sprue and white. Choose fresh-looking bundles, with tight buds and smooth stems; avoid any wilted or coarse and woody stems. Allow 6–8 medium spears per person. Snap off the lower end of each stem – the point where it begins to toughen. Peel the ends of thicker stems. Stand the spears upright in a deep pan of gently simmering salted water, so that the tips steam while the stems cook in the water. Simmer for 3–5 minutes until tender. Serve hot with melted butter or hollandaise, or cold with mayonnaise or French dressing.

Aubergine

Available in various varieties. Choose aubergines that are firm and shiny. Allow about 175g (6oz) per person. Cut off the stem, trim the ends and halve or slice. Aubergines are less bitter nowadays, so it isn't usually necessary to dégorge them. Cook aubergine slices by sautéeing or grilling for 5–8 minutes, or in a moussaka. Bake aubergine halves, with or without stuffing and serve as a starter or main dish. Serve slices as an accompaniment; stuffed halves as a main dish or starter.

Avocado pear

Buy undamaged fruits that give slightly when gently squeezed in your palm; avoid very soft, overripe fruits. Ripen hard avocados at room temperature. The flesh is mild, buttery and smooth when ripe. To use, cut lengthways around the large, round stone in the centre; twist apart. Tap a sharp knife blade into the stone, then twist the blade to lift it out. Avocado flesh turns brown on exposure to air, so prepare just before use. Use sliced or chopped in salsas, dips and salads, as a container for prawn cocktail, or blend into soups or smoothies.

Bamboo shoot

Native to Asia, bamboo shoots are the conical-shaped shoots of the bamboo plant. They are sometimes obtainable fresh from Asian food stores. Buy canned ready-cooked bamboo shoots from supermarkets. Allow 50–75g (2–3oz) per person. Peel fresh bamboo shoots, then cook in boiling water for 40 minutes or until tender. Or par-boil and use in stir-fries.

Bean, broad

Choose small pods. Very young broad beans, less than 7.5cm (3in) long, can be cooked in their pods and eaten whole. Pod older beans and skin them to remove the outer coat, which toughens with age. To do this, slip the beans out of their skins after blanching. Allow about 250g (9oz) weight of whole beans in pods per person. Unless tiny, remove the beans from their pods. Cook in boiling salted water for 8–10 minutes until tender. Skin if necessary. Serve with melted butter and herbs. Older beans can be made into soup or puréed.

Bean, French (green bean), runner

Choose young, tender beans. Allow 125–50g (4–5oz) per person. Trim off the ends. Most varieties are stringless, otherwise remove the strings from the seams of the pods. Cut runner beans lengthways into fine slices using a bean slicer, or cut young beans into short lengths. Cook in boiling salted water or steam for 5–7 minutes until tender. Serve hot as an accompaniment. French beans can also be served cold as a salad tossed in a herb-flavoured vinaigrette.

Bean sprout

These are the crunchy-textured shoots of germinated dried beans, such as mung or aduki beans. Choose crisp, small, fresh shoots, or sprout your own, but be sure to buy beans or seeds which are specifically produced for sprouting – from a health-food shop or other reliable source. Mung beans take only five to six days to sprout. Allow about 125g (4oz) bean sprouts per person. Rinse bean sprouts thoroughly in cold water, then drain. Cook in boiling salted water or steam for 30 seconds, or stir-fry for 1–2 minutes.

Beetroot

Baby beetroot have a wonderful earthy flavour. Maincrop beetroot are often sold cooked, and vacuum packed or preserved in vinegar. Choose firm, smallish beetroot with crisp tops and skin that is intact. Allow 125–150g (4–5oz) per person. Cut off the leafy stalks about 2.5cm (1in) above the bulb. Wash the beetroot carefully. Cook in lightly salted boiling water for 30–40 minutes or until soft. Or roast at 180°C (160°C fan oven) mark 4 until tender – about 20 minutes for baby beets, up to 1 hour for larger beetroot. After cooking, peel, slice or dice.

Broccoli (calabrese)

There are two types of broccoli: the compact, dark-green headed calabrese and sprouting broccoli (see right). Choose firm, tightly packed heads with strong stalks. Allow 125–150g (4–5oz) per person. Trim the stalks. Halve the shoots if large. Cook upright in boiling salted water (to allow the heads to steam) for 5–6 minutes, or steam for 10–15 minutes. Or stir-fry small broccoli florets for 4–5 minutes.

Broccoli, purple sprouting

This purple-green variety of broccoli grows on shooting, fleshy stems rather than in a tightly packed head. It is most often served as an accompaniment with butter or oil and lemon, or as an appetiser drizzled with hollandaise sauce. Look for firm stems and fresh-looking heads and eat within a few days of purchase. To use, wash; trim the stalks, stripping away any thick skin; halve if large. Cook standing upright in water so that the stems are boiled and the heads steamed, until just tender.

Brussels sprout

Choose small round sprouts with tightly packed heads and no wilted leaves. Allow 125–175g (4–6oz) per person. Remove damaged or wilted leaves and cut off the stem. Cut a cross on the stump to help the thick part cook quickly. Cook in boiling salted water for 7–10 minutes or steam for 10–15 minutes. Serve hot as an accompaniment. Very young sprouts are also good shredded and served raw in salads.

Butternut squash

These range in size from around 15–30cm (6–12in) and may be pear- or club-shaped. The flesh is an intense orange colour with a firm texture. Look for firm squash with smooth, unblemished skin. Butternut squash is good halved, seeded and baked in its skin, with or without stuffing. To stuff, leave unpeeled, halve and scoop out the seeds. The flesh can also be chopped, sliced or diced and steamed, stir-fried, braised and added to stews and soups.

Cabbage

Spring, summer and winter cabbages are available. Savoy cabbage is considered one of the finest of the winter crops. Choose fresh-looking cabbage with firm leaves. Allow 175–225g (6–8oz) per person. Remove the coarse outer leaves, then cut in half and remove the centre stalk. Shred white or red cabbage for using raw in salads. Shred or cut into wedges and cook in boiling salted water or steam: 3–5 minutes if shredded; 10 minutes for wedges. Cabbage can also be braised or stir-fried. Blanched cabbage leaves can also be stuffed.

Carrot

Choose brightly coloured, firm carrots with smooth skins. Allow 125–175g (4–6oz) per person. Scrub small new carrots, leaving them whole with a tuft of green stalk. Peel older carrots and quarter lengthways or slice. Cook in boiling salted water for 10–15 minutes or steam for 12–18 minutes. Serve hot as an accompaniment or make into a purée or soup. Raw carrots, either grated or cut into julienne, are excellent in salads.

Cauliflower

Choose a cauliflower with a firm, compact creamy white head and fresh-looking green leaves. This vegetable is usually cooked, but can be eaten raw in salads. A medium cauliflower serves four to six people. Cut away the outer leaves, chop off the stem, and cut into florets. If cooking whole, cut a cross on the stump to help the thick part cook quickly. Steam or cook florets in boiling salted water for 5–8 minutes, keeping the heads out of the water, so that the florets steam. Allow about 15 minutes if cooking whole.

Celeriac

Celeriac has a pronounced celery flavour. Allow about 175g (6oz) per person. Choose small, firm heavy bulbs free from blemishes. Scrub well, cut off the roots and peel thickly. Grate or cut into julienne for salads; cut into slices or strips for cooking. Immerse in cold water with a little lemon juice to prevent discoloration before cooking. Cook in boiling salted water for 15–20 minutes, or steam allowing a little longer. Serve hot with butter, or mash with seasoning and butter or cream. Use blanched or raw in salads.

Celery

The intense flavour of celery makes it excellent for flavouring soups and stews, but it is also delicious served as a vegetable. Pale green celery is available all year; white (blanched) winter celery is available from October to January. Choose celery with firm, crisp sticks and fresh leafy tops. Allow 3–4 sticks per person. Trim off the base, separate the stalks and scrub well. Leave whole or slice. Braise in stock for 20 minutes, or stir-fry or steam until tender. Serve celery raw in salads or with cheese.

Chard, Swiss

Swiss chard is related to seakale beet and is grown mainly for its leaves, which resemble spinach. The prominent white central ribs are also eaten. Choose fresh-looking chard, with clean, unblemished ribs and crisp leaves. Allow 225g (8oz) leaves per person and 125–175g (4–6oz) ribs per person. Prepare and cook the leaves as for spinach (see page 282). Cook the ribs a minute or two longer, or they can be cooked for 20 minutes or more to reach a luxuriously melting softness.

Chicory

This compact, spear-shaped vegetable is grown in darkness to produce crisp white leaves. Choose chicory heads with crisp white leaves – too much green indicates a bitter flavour. Red-leafed chicory is also available. Allow ½ head per person in salads; one head if serving cooked. Trim off the root base and remove any damaged outer leaves. Leave whole, halve lengthways or slice. Blanch in boiling salted water for 3–4 minutes; or grill, braise or bake. Serve raw in salads.

Courgette

Most varieties of courgette are green, but you can also buy yellow. Baby courgettes are tender and delicately flavoured. Courgette flowers can also be eaten. Choose small, firm courgettes with smooth, shiny skins. Large ones often lack flavour and are best stuffed and baked. Allow 125–150g (4–5oz) per person. Trim off the ends, then slice or dice, or halve lengthways for stuffing. Cook baby courgettes whole. Cook in the minimum of boiling salted water for 3–5 minutes, or steam, microwave or sauté in butter. Serve topped with herbs or raw in salads.

Cucumber

Although usually a salad vegetable, cucumber can also be served hot. Choose small ones with blemish-free skins. Slice or dice. If required, seed by halving lengthways and scooping out the seeds using a teaspoon. Cook by steaming or sautéeing in butter. Toss with chervil, dill or fennel or serve raw in salads.

Fennel

Also known as Florence fennel or sweet fennel to distinguish it from the herb, this looks like a bulbous celery heart. It has a distinctive aniseed flavour. Choose well-rounded, white or pale green bulbs – a dark green indicates bitterness. Allow 125–150g (4–5oz) per person. Trim root and stalk ends, reserving the feathery leaves for garnish or to add to salads. Halve, quarter, slice or chop. Boil in salted water for 15 minutes, or steam, sauté in butter, braise or bake. Serve raw in salads.

Kale

Although from the same family as cabbage, kale has a more intense flavour. It has coarse-textured curly or flat leaves, dark green or sometimes purple in colour. Curly kale is the most common variety. Avoid kale that shows signs of wilting or yellowing. Allow 125–150g (4–5oz) per person. Trim tough stalks and tear leaves into pieces, or shred coarsely. Wash thoroughly. Boil in salted water, or steam, for 6–8 minutes until crisp-tender. Serve topped with a knob of butter. Or stir-fry finely sliced kale for 3 minutes.

Kohlrabi

An unusual looking white or purple-skinned vegetable, similar in size to a turnip and with a similar flavour. Kohlrabi is a swollen stalk with protruding leaves. Choose small fresh-looking kohlrabi, no more than 5cm (2in) in diameter, as larger ones can be tough. Allow 125–150g (4–5oz) per person. Trim the base, cut off the leaves and stalks, and peel thinly. Quarter or slice. Boil in salted water for 20–30 minutes, or steam for a little longer. Toss in butter or with a sauce. Or grate or slice very thinly and eat raw in salads.

Leek

Choose small, young firm leeks with white stalks and fresh green, blemish-free leaves. Trim the root and tops; discard the tough outer leaves. Slit leeks lengthways and rinse under cold running water to remove any grit from the layers. (If serving whole, slit the top only.) Allow 1–2 leeks per person. Boil in salted water for 8–10 minutes; steam for 12–15 minutes; braise in stock until tender; or sauté slices in butter until tender. Serve topped with herbs or a sauce. Or cool and serve with a herb dressing, or raw in salads. Good in soups.

Lettuce

Look for fresh, springy leaves when buying lettuce and avoid any that look limp, yellowing, bruised, or slimy. Store in the fridge and use within three days. To prepare, trim, then tear the leaves into pieces if necessary. Rinse in cold water and pat or spin dry. Dress just before serving. Although normally served raw in salads, lettuce can be cooked as a vegetable. Allow 1 small lettuce per person if cooked, less in salads. To cook, cut in quarters, and braise in stock for 10 minutes, or stir-fry. Lettuce also makes a good soup.

Marrow

Marrow has a delicate flavour when eaten young. Choose a firm marrow, 30.5cm (12in) or less, weighing 900g (2lb) or less. Larger ones tend to lack flavour. Allow about 175g (6oz) per person. Trim off the ends and cut into pieces. Peel larger marrow, halve lengthways and discard the seeds and fibres, then cut into pieces or rings and put into a colander. Sprinkle with salt and leave for 30 minutes to extract the bitter juices; rinse and pat dry. Boil in salted water for 5–10 minutes; steam for a little longer, sauté for 5 minutes or stuff and bake halves for 45 minutes.

Mushroom

Cultivated, oriental, dried and wild mushrooms are available. Gather wild mushrooms only if you are certain you can identify poisonous species. Use wild mushrooms soon after purchase because they deteriorate quickly. When reconstituted, 25g (1oz) dried mushrooms is equivalent to 150g (5oz) fresh. Soak dried mushrooms in warm water for 15–20 minutes before use. Fresh mushrooms should have firm caps and fresh stalks. Allow 125g (4oz) per person. Wipe with a clean, damp cloth or wash. Leave whole, halve, quarter or slice. Sauté, stir-fry, grill or bake.

Okra

Also known as ladies' fingers, these green tapering pods are used in Caribbean and Indian dishes. Choose firm, bright green pods, about 7.5cm (3in) long. Allow 125g (4oz) per person. Trim okra carefully, removing a tiny piece from each end without cutting into the seed pod, otherwise a sticky juice is released which lends a gelatinous texture. Boil in salted water for 5 minutes, or steam, sauté or stew with spices.

Onion

There are several varieties of onion. Brown-skinned are most commonly used. Spanish onions are larger and milder. Italian red onions have a mild, almost sweet flavour. White onions are mildly flavoured. Pickling onions are also referred to as button, pearl or silverskin onions. Allow 1 onion per person if serving as a vegetable. Trim root and top, then peel. Slice, chop or leave whole. Onions can be sautéed, fried, baked, braised, grilled, blanched (for 2–3 minutes prior to further cooking to reduce their pungency) or steamed. See also shallot and spring onion.

Pak choi

Also known as bok choy, the broad, thick, fleshy white stems gather in a bulbous base and are topped with firm, dark green leaves. Pak choi has a fresh taste, rather like spinach with a mildly peppery finish. Look for firm, unblemished stalks topped with fresh-looking leaves, and avoid any that are limp or wilted. Store in the fridge and use within a few days. To use, wash, trim the bases, then halve or quarter, and steam or quickly braise; slice the stems and leaves and stir-fry or add to Asian-style soups at the last minute.

Palm heart

The edible inner part of the palm tree shoot is the palm heart, which has firm, creamy-coloured flesh with a delicate flavour like artichoke or asparagus. They are rarely found fresh in the UK, but are sold pre-cooked and canned. Serve hot as a vegetable or add to salads.

Parsnip

The nutty, sweet flavour of parsnips improves if it is harvested after several frosts. Choose firm, small or medium parsnips without side shoots or brown marks. Allow 175g (6oz) per person. Scrub well, trim the top and base, and peel thinly. Leave young parsnips whole or slice. Quarter larger ones and remove the core. Steam, or add to cold salted water and boil for 10–15 minutes. Serve sprinkled with herbs, or mashed with butter and seasoning. Par-boil for 2 minutes, then roast around a joint of meat or sauté in butter or oil.

Pea

Fresh peas have a delicious sweet flavour. Tiny petits pois are particularly sweet and tender. Choose crisp, well-filled pods with some air space between the peas; very full pods are likely to contain tough peas. Allow 225g (8oz) in the pod, or 125g (4oz) shelled weight, per person. Shell the peas and discard any that are discoloured; rinse and cook immediately in the minimum amount of boiling salted water for 5–7 minutes. Toss with butter and mint. Very popular as a frozen vegetable.

VEGETABLES

Pepper, chilli

There are many different chillies, varying in appearance and potency, but they all have a hot, spicy flavour. Most start off green and ripen to red, but there are yellow and black ones too. Choose those free from wrinkles and brown patches. The volatile oils can cause skin irritation. Take care to avoid touching your eyes and wash hands immediately afterwards (see also Cook's Tips, page 69). Use chillies whole, or finely slice or dice, discarding the seeds if a less hot flavour is required. Cook in curries and stews as a spicy flavouring ingredient – use sparingly.

Pepper, sweet

The green pepper is the young fruit; it turns yellow, then orange and red as it matures. Red peppers are the sweetest and have the softest texture. Choose firm, shiny peppers. They can be eaten cooked or raw. Cut off the stalk end. If serving whole, scoop out the core and seeds; otherwise halve lengthways, core and seed. To skin peppers, grill skin side up, until charred, then cover with an upturned bowl; the steam will help to lift the skins. When cool enough to handle, peel away the skin. Slice or dice. Cook peppers by grilling, stir-frying or blanching, or stuff and bake whole.

Plantain

Although they taste slightly of banana, the taste is much less sweet. When cooked, the flesh is much firmer and more starchy than a banana, and similar to potato in texture. They can be baked, boiled, grilled, steamed, mashed, or dried and ground into flour. Never make the mistake of buying plantains when you want bananas; the two are completely different. Plantains are always cooked for use as a savoury ingredient, usually sliced, fried and served either as a snack, appetiser or accompaniment in place of rice or potatoes.

Potato

Potatoes vary in size, colour and texture and fall into two categories: new potatoes, which have a firm, waxy texture, and 'old potatoes', which have a floury texture that softens on cooking; Refer to pack instructions or ask your supplier for advice on which variety to use for which cooking method. Choose potatoes with smooth, firm skins and no green tinge, as these are unfit for eating. Buy new potatoes in small quantities and use them quickly. Allow 175–225g (6–8oz) per person. Bake, roast, boil, steam, mash or fry.

Pumpkin

Large squashes and pumpkins are often sold by the wedge. Choose firm pumpkins and, if the flesh is visible, check that it is not fibrous. Allow 175–225g (6–8oz) per person. Peel and halve squash, scoop out the seeds and cut into wedges. Chop into even-sized pieces. Steam rather than boil, which turns squash mushy. Or drizzle with olive oil and roast at 200°C (180°C fan oven) mark 6 for 30 minutes or until tender. Top with melted butter and herbs. Squash can also be stuffed and baked or used in soups or stews.

Radish

The familiar small, round red and white radish varieties are sold all year; these are typically eaten raw in salads. The white Japanese radish, known as mooli or daikon, is larger and elongated in shape. It is milder than the other types and is usually peeled, grated and used as a garnish, or pickled. The black-skinned round Spanish radish has a stronger flavour; after peeling it can be eaten raw or cooked. Choose radishes with fresh green tops or look for ones with firm bright skins. Allow 75–125g (3–4oz) per person.

Salsify and scorzonera

Salsify has a white skin and a flavour reminiscent of oysters – it is also known as vegetable oyster. Scorzonera – or black salsify – has a brownish black skin and a stronger flavour than salsify. Choose smooth, firm specimens. Allow 125–175g (4–6oz) per person. Top and tail, then scrub well under cold running water. Boil in salted water with a little lemon juice for 25–30 minutes until crisp-tender. Serve hot with lemon juice, melted butter and chopped herbs, or purée for soups; or use in casseroles or salads.

Shallot

There are various varieties of these small onions. Brown: use in dressings and sauces; roasted whole or caramelised. Pink: slice or finely chop and sauté; cook whole and use in tarts and salads. Red Thai: use raw in spice pastes and salads; slice and fry until brown and crisp for a garnish; pickle whole. Banana: slice or finely chop and use raw in salads and dressings; sauté in butter or olive oil.

Spinach

Choose bright green leaves; avoid any that are wilting or yellowing. Allow at least 225g (8oz) spinach per person. Wash thoroughly using several changes of water. Remove the tough stalks and central ribs from coarser spinach leaves. Young, tender leaves are excellent raw in salads. Steam larger leaves until just wilted. Cook in a covered pan with just the water that clings to the leaves after washing until just wilted. Drain well and press out the excess water from the leaves with the back of a wooden spoon.

Spring greens

An early variety of cabbage with tender, loose-packed leaves; it is harvested before it forms a heart. Spring greens were originally available only in spring but are now available most of the year. Look for fresh-looking heads and avoid any with wilting or flabby leaves. Store in the fridge and use within a few days. To use, wash well and shred. Boil or steam spring greens briefly to retain their sweet, fresh flavour and serve as an accompaniment topped with a knob of butter.

Spring onion

Also called salad onions, green onions or scallions, they vary in size from slender to bulbous. They have a mild, sweet flavour. Buy fresh-looking spring onions, store in a cool place or the fridge and use within a few days. Usually the green part is discarded (except in some Chinese dishes), but there is no reason not to use it as long as it is in good condition and well cleaned of grit. Trim off the root and any coarse leaves, then slice or use whole in salads and stir-fries, and as a garnish.

Swede

This heavy and coarse-skinned root vegetable has orange flesh and a strong flavour. Choose small swede, as large ones can be tough. Avoid those with damaged skins. Allow about 175g (6oz) per person. Peel thickly, then cut into chunks. Steam or add to cold salted water and boil for 15–20 minutes; drain well, return to the pan and dry over a low heat. Mash or purée with butter and seasoning. Or, par-boil, then sauté in butter, or roast chunks in hot fat around a joint of meat at 200°C (180°C fan oven) mark 6 for 1–1½ hours.

Sweetcorn

Sweetcorn is at its best just after picking. Choose whole cobs with a tightly fitting husk, enclosing plump, cream kernels. Baby corn is eaten whole. Allow one cob per person, or 75–125g (3–4oz) loose corn or baby corn. Remove the stem, leaves and silky fibres. To remove the kernels, hold the cob upright on a board and, working downwards with a sharp knife, cut off the kernels. Cook whole cobs in boiling water (without salt which toughens corn) for 5–15 minutes until a kernel comes away easily. Cook loose corn kernels in boiling water for 5–10 minutes.

Sweet potato

The sweet potato is not related to the common potato. Sweet potatoes are mostly elongated in shape, although some are round. The outer skin colour varies from tan to red, and the sweet flesh may be white or yellow. The red-skinned variety is most common in the UK. Choose small, firm sweet potatoes; large ones tend to be fibrous. Allow 225g (8oz) per person. Scrub well. If boiling, peel afterwards. Cook as for potatoes – boil, bake, fry or roast.

Tomato

Although strictly a fruit, the tomato is used as a vegetable and comes in many varieties. Cherry tomatoes (see below) and baby plum tomatoes are sweet and tasty. Beef tomatoes can weigh up to 450g (1lb) – stuff or use raw. Choose firm, unblemished tomatoes with a hint of fragrance. Allow 1–2 tomatoes per person if serving raw, 1 large tomato for stuffing. Slice or quarter tomatoes if using raw, and serve in salads. To stuff, cut a small sliver from the base, then cut off the top and scoop out the seeds and flesh. Serve hot or cold. Use overripe tomatoes in sauces.

Tomato, cherry

These have a much sweeter, more intense flavour than salad tomatoes. Their appealing size makes them good for salads, garnishes and canapés, but they are also good for quick-cook pasta sauces, because they do not require much cooking to achieve a sweet, rich flavour. They can also be threaded on to skewers and briefly barbecued, or stir-fried quickly with garlic as an accompaniment.

Turnip

Young turnips have a sweet flavour and are usually tender. Maincrop turnips have thicker skins and coarser flesh. Choose smooth, unblemished turnips. Allow 175g (6oz) per person. Peel young turnips thinly but older ones thickly, then slice or cut into chunks. Young turnips can be served raw, sliced thinly or grated into salads. Cook small young turnips whole; cut up older ones. Add to cold salted water and boil or steam for 20–30 minutes until tender. Serve older turnips sparingly in chunks or mashed.

Yam

A member of the tuber family, originating from Africa. Yams have a brownish-pink skin and white flesh. Allow 175g (6oz) per person. Wash and peel, then dice. Boil in salted water, with a little lemon juice, for 20 minutes or until tender; or steam. Yams can also be roasted, baked or fried.

SPRING VEGETABLE STEW

Serves 4
Preparation 20 minutes
Cooking time 30–35 minutes

225g (8oz) new potatoes, scrubbed and halved
75g (3oz) unsalted butter
4 shallots, blanched in boiling water, drained and thinly sliced
1 garlic clove, crushed
2 tsp freshly chopped thyme
1 tsp grated lime zest
6 baby leeks, trimmed and sliced into 5cm (2in) lengths
125g (4oz) baby carrots, scrubbed
125g (4oz) podded peas
125g (4oz) podded broad beans, skinned (see page 278)
300ml (½ pint) vegetable stock
1 Little Gem lettuce, shredded
4 tbsp freshly chopped herbs, such as chervil, chives,
    mint and parsley, plus extra chives to garnish
salt and ground black pepper

1 Put the potatoes into a pan of lightly salted water. Bring to the boil, cover and par-boil for 5 minutes. Drain and refresh under cold water.
2 Meanwhile, melt half the butter in a large sauté pan, add the shallots, garlic, thyme and lime zest and fry gently for 5 minutes or until softened and lightly golden. Add the leeks and carrots, and sauté for a further 5 minutes. Stir in the potatoes, peas and broad beans, then pour in the stock and bring to the boil. Reduce the heat, cover the pan and simmer gently for 10 minutes. Remove the lid and cook, uncovered, for a further 5–8 minutes until all the vegetables are tender.
3 Add the shredded lettuce to the stew with the chopped herbs and remaining butter. Heat through until the butter is melted. Check the seasoning and serve at once.

NUTRITION PER SERVING
270 cals | 17g fat (10g sats) | 23g carbs | 0.6g salt

VEGETABLE CURRY

Serves 4
Preparation 10 minutes
Cooking time 15 minutes

2–3 tbsp red Thai curry paste
(see Cook's Tip, page 260)
2.5cm (1in) piece fresh root ginger,
finely chopped
50g (2oz) cashew nuts
400ml can coconut milk
3 carrots, cut into thin batons
1 broccoli head, cut into florets
20g (³/₄oz) fresh coriander, roughly
chopped
zest and juice of 1 lime
2 large handfuls of spinach leaves
basmati rice to serve

1 Put the curry paste into a large
pan, add the ginger and cashew nuts,
and stir-fry over a medium heat for
2–3 minutes.

2 Add the coconut milk, cover and
bring to the boil. Stir the carrots into
the pan, then reduce the heat and
simmer for 5 minutes. Add the
broccoli florets and simmer for a
further 5 minutes or until tender.
3 Stir the coriander and lime zest
into the pan with the spinach. Squeeze
the lime juice over and serve with
basmati rice.

TRY SOMETHING DIFFERENT
Replace the carrots and/or broccoli
with alternative vegetables – try
baby sweetcorn, sugarsnap peas or
mangetouts and simmer for only
5 minutes or until tender.

NUTRITION PER SERVING 200 cals |
10g fat (2g sats) | 19g carbs | 0.7g salt Ⓥ

RATATOUILLE

Serves 6
Preparation 20 minutes
Cooking time about 45 minutes

4 tbsp olive oil
2 onions, thinly sliced
1 large garlic clove, crushed
350g (12oz) small aubergine, thinly
sliced
450g (1lb) small courgettes, thinly
sliced
450g (1lb) tomatoes, skinned, seeded
and roughly chopped
1 green and 1 red pepper, each cored,
seeded and sliced
1 tbsp freshly chopped basil
2 tsp freshly chopped thyme
2 tbsp freshly chopped flat-leafed
parsley
2 tbsp sun-dried tomato paste
salt and ground black pepper

1 Heat the olive oil in a large pan,
add the onions and garlic and fry
gently for 10 minutes or until softened
and golden.
2 Add the aubergine, courgettes,
tomatoes, sliced peppers, herbs, tomato
paste and seasoning. Fry, stirring, for
2–3 minutes.
3 Cover the pan tightly and simmer for
30 minutes or until all the vegetables
are just tender. If necessary, uncover
towards the end of the cooking time
to evaporate some of the liquid.
4 Taste and adjust the seasoning.
Serve the ratatouille hot or cold.

NUTRITION PER SERVING 150 cals |
10g fat (4g sats) | 12g carbs | 1.2g salt Ⓥ

GREEN BEANS AND FLAKED ALMONDS

Serves 4
Preparation 5 minutes
Cooking time 5–7 minutes

200g (7oz) green beans
1 tsp olive oil
25g (1oz) flaked almonds
$^1/_2$ lemon

1 Bring a large pan of water to the boil. Add the green beans and cook for 4–5 minutes. Drain.
2 Meanwhile, heat the oil in a large frying pan. Add the almonds and cook for 1–2 minutes until golden. Turn off the heat, add the drained beans to the frying pan and toss. Squeeze over a little lemon juice just before serving.

TRY SOMETHING DIFFERENT
- Use basil-infused oil and increase the amount of oil to 2 tbsp.
- Use pinenuts instead of almonds, drizzle with balsamic vinegar and scatter with basil leaves to serve.

NUTRITION PER SERVING 57 cals | 5g fat (trace sats) | 2g carbs | 0g salt **V**

BRAISED CHICORY IN WHITE WINE

Serves 6
Preparation 5 minutes
Cooking time about 1 hour

50g (2oz) butter, softened
6 heads of chicory, trimmed
100ml (3$^1/_2$ fl oz) white wine
salt and ground black pepper
snipped chives to serve

1 Preheat the oven to 190°C (170°C fan oven) mark 5. Grease a 1.7 litre (3 pint) ovenproof dish with 15g ($^1/_2$ oz) butter and lay the chicory in the dish.
2 Season to taste, add the wine and dot the remaining butter over the top. Cover with foil and cook in the oven for 1 hour or until soft. Scatter with chives to serve.

NUTRITION PER SERVING 80 cals | 7g fat (5g sats) | 3g carbs, | 0.1g salt **V**

HONEY-GLAZED SHALLOTS

Serves 4
Preparation 15 minutes, plus soaking
Cooking time 25 minutes

450g (1lb) shallots, halved
25g (1oz) butter
1 tbsp thin honey
juice of ½ lemon
1 tbsp Worcestershire sauce
1 tbsp balsamic vinegar
salt and ground black pepper

1 Put the shallots into a bowl, add cold water to cover and leave to soak for 20 minutes. Drain and peel away the skins.
2 Tip the shallots into a pan and add just enough cold water to cover. Bring to the boil, lower the heat and simmer for 5 minutes. Drain well and return the shallots to the pan.
3 Add all of the remaining ingredients and stir until the shallots are well coated with the glaze. Cover and cook gently, stirring occasionally, until the shallots are tender. Remove the lid and bubble for 2–3 minutes until the liquid is reduced and syrupy. Serve hot.

NUTRITION PER SERVING 100 cals |
5g fat (3g sats) | 14g carbs | 0.5g salt

CREAMED SPINACH

Serves 6
Preparation 15 minutes
Cooking time 5 minutes

900g (2lb) spinach leaves, stalks
    removed
4 tbsp crème fraîche
salt and ground black pepper

1 Cook the spinach with just the water clinging to the leaves in a covered pan for 3–4 minutes until just wilted.
2 Stir in the crème fraîche and season with salt and pepper to taste. Serve at once.

NUTRITION PER SERVING 80 cals |
5g fat (3g sats) | 3g carbs | 0.2g salt Ⓥ

STUFFED ROASTED PEPPERS

Serves 8
Preparation 20 minutes
Cooking time 45 minutes

40g (1½ oz) butter
4 Romano peppers, halved, with
    stalks on and seeded
3 tbsp olive oil
350g (12oz) chestnut mushrooms, roughly chopped
4 tbsp finely chopped fresh chives
100g (3½ oz) feta cheese (see page 228)
50g (2oz) fresh white breadcrumbs
25g (1oz) freshly grated Parmesan (see as above)
salt and ground black pepper

1 Preheat the oven to 180°C (160°C fan oven) mark 4.
Use a little of the butter to grease a shallow ovenproof dish
and put the peppers in it side by side, ready to be filled.
2 Heat the remaining butter and 1 tbsp oil in a pan. Add the
mushrooms and fry until they're golden and there's no excess
liquid left in the pan. Stir in the chives, then spoon the mixture
into the pepper halves.
3 Crumble the feta over the mushrooms. Mix the
breadcrumbs and Parmesan in a bowl, then sprinkle over the
peppers.
4 Season with salt and pepper and drizzle with the remaining
oil. Roast in the oven for 45 minutes or until golden and
tender. Serve warm.

GET AHEAD
- To prepare ahead, complete the recipe to the end of
  step 4, up to one day ahead. Cover and chill.
- To use, reheat under the grill for 5 minutes.

NUTRITION PER SERVING
189 cals | 14g fat (6g sats) | 11g carbs | 0.9g salt

PETITS POIS À LA FRANÇAISE

Serves 4
Preparation 5 minutes
Cooking time 15 minutes

1 firm-hearted lettuce
50g (2oz) butter
900g (2lb) young peas, shelled
12 spring onions, sliced
1 tsp sugar
150ml (¼ pint) chicken stock
salt and ground black pepper

1 Remove the outer leaves of the lettuce and cut the heart into quarters.
2 Melt the butter in a large pan, add the peas, spring onions, lettuce, sugar, seasoning and stock. Bring to the boil, cover and simmer for 15–20 minutes.

NUTRITION PER SERVING 297cals | 14g fat (7g sats) | 28g carbs | 0.7g salt

JERSEY ROYALS WITH MINT AND PETITS POIS

Serves 6
Preparation 15 minutes
Cooking time 30 minutes

3 tbsp olive oil
900g (2lb) Jersey Royals, scrubbed and thickly sliced
175g (6oz) frozen petits pois
3 tbsp chopped mint
salt and ground black pepper

1 Heat half the olive oil in a large non-stick frying pan, add half the potatoes and cook for 5 minutes, turning, until browned on both sides. Remove with a slotted spoon and set aside. Add the remaining oil to the pan, then brown the remaining potatoes in the same way.
2 Return all the potatoes to the pan and cook, partially covered, for a further 10–15 minutes.
3 Meanwhile, cook the petits pois in a pan of boiling water for 2 minutes, then drain well. Add them to the potatoes and cook through for 2–3 minutes.
4 Add the chopped mint, and salt and pepper to taste, then serve.

COOK'S TIP
Jersey Royal potatoes are highly regarded not just for their distinctively nutty flavour, waxy texture, yellow flesh and papery skin but for their true seasonality: they are at their best between April and June. When Jersey Royals are not in season use other new potatoes for this recipe.

NUTRITION PER SERVING 180 cals | 7g fat (1g sat) | 27g carbs | 0.2g salt Ⓥ

CRISPY ROAST POTATOES

Serves 8
Preparation 20 minutes
Cooking time 1 hour 50 minutes

1.8kg (4lb) potatoes, preferably King
    Edward, cut into two-bite pieces
2 tsp paprika
2–3 tbsp goose or white vegetable fat
salt

1 Put the potatoes in a pan of salted
cold water. Cover and bring to the boil.
Boil for 7 minutes, then drain well in
a colander.
2 Sprinkle the paprika over the
potatoes in the colander, then cover
and shake the potatoes roughly, so they
become fluffy around the edges.
3 Preheat the oven to 220°C (200°C
fan oven) mark 7. Heat the fat in a large
roasting tin on the hob. When it sizzles,
add the potatoes. Tilt the pan to coat,
taking care as the fat will splutter. Roast
in the oven for 1 hour.
4 Reduce the oven temperature to
200°C (180°C fan oven) mark 6 and
roast for a further 40 minutes. Shake
the potatoes only once or twice during
cooking, otherwise the edges won't
crisp and brown. Season with a little salt
before serving.

FREEZING TIP

➤ To freeze, complete the recipe to
   the end of step 2, then cool, seal in
   large freezer bags and freeze for up
   to one month.
➤ To use, cook from frozen, allowing
   an additional 15–20 minutes total
   cooking time.

NUTRITION PER SERVING 211 cals |
6g fat (3g sats) | 37g carbs | 0.1g salt

OVEN CHIPS

Serves 4
Preparation 10 minutes
Cooking time 40 minutes

900g (2lb) Desirée potatoes
2–3 tbsp olive oil
salt and sea salt flakes

1 Preheat the oven to 240°C (220°C
fan oven) mark 9. Peel the potatoes and
cut into chips. Add to a pan of boiling
salted water, cover and bring to the boil,
then boil for 2 minutes. Drain well, then
pat dry with kitchen paper.
2 Tip the par-boiled potatoes into a
large non-stick roasting tin, toss with the
olive oil and season with sea salt. Roast
for 40 minutes or until golden and
cooked, turning from time to time.
Drain on kitchen paper and serve.

NUTRITION PER SERVING 220 cals |
6g fat (1g sats) | 39g carbs | 0.3g salt **V**

POTATO CROQUETTES

Serves 6
Preparation 30 minutes, plus chilling
Cooking time 45 minutes

1kg (2¼ lb) Desirée potatoes, scrubbed
150g (5oz) fresh white breadcrumbs
50g (2oz) butter, softened, plus extra to grease
100g (3½ oz) Parmesan (see page 228),
    freshly grated
2 tbsp chopped flat-leafed parsley
freshly grated nutmeg, to taste
2 medium eggs, beaten
olive oil, to drizzle
salt and ground black pepper

1 Put the potatoes into a pan of cold salted water. Bring to the boil and simmer for about 20 minutes or until tender. Preheat the oven to 230°C (210°C fan oven) mark 8.
2 Meanwhile, spread the breadcrumbs on to a baking sheet and bake for 15 minutes or until golden. Tip on to a plate. Turn off the oven.
3 Drain the potatoes well, leave to cool for 5 minutes, then peel. Mash until smooth. Add the butter, Parmesan and parsley. Season well with nutmeg, salt and pepper, and mix thoroughly.
4 Put the beaten eggs into a shallow bowl. Take about 2 tbsp of the potato mixture and shape into a small sausage. Roll the croquette first in the beaten egg and then in the breadcrumbs to coat. Put into a greased roasting tin.
5 Repeat to use up all the potato mixture – you'll need two roasting tins. Cover with clingfilm and chill for 30 minutes. Preheat the oven to 230°C (210°C fan oven) mark 8.
6 Uncover the croquettes, drizzle with a little olive oil and bake for 25 minutes or until golden. Serve at once.

COOK'S TIP
Using a potato ricer insead of a masher gives them a lovely fluffy texture – make sure the potatoes are still hot when you begin to mash them.

NUTRITION PER SERVING
370 cals | 17g fat (8g sats) | 41g carbs | 1.4g salt **V**

GRATIN DAUPHINOIS

Serves 4–6
Preparation 10 minutes
Cooking time 50 minutes

900g (2lb) potatoes, cut into slices
1 garlic clove, crushed
a pinch of freshly grated nutmeg
150ml (¼ pint) single cream
75g (3oz) Gruyère cheese (see page
    228), grated
salt and ground black pepper

1 Preheat the oven to 180°C (160°C fan oven) mark 4. Cook the potatoes in boiling salted water for 5 minutes, then drain well. Turn into a greased 1.1 litre (2 pint) ovenproof dish.
2 Stir the seasoning, garlic and nutmeg into the single cream and pour over the potatoes.
3 Sprinkle with cheese, cover and cook in the oven for 45 minutes or until the potatoes are tender.
4 Uncover the dish and brown under a hot grill.

> NUTRITION PER SERVING 444 cals |
> 24g fat (11g sats) | 38g carbs | 1g salt **V**

RÖSTI POTATOES WITH FRIED EGGS

Serves 4
Preparation 20 minutes, plus cooling
Cooking time 20–25 minutes

900g (2lb) red potatoes, scrubbed
    and left whole
40g (1½ oz) butter
4 large eggs
salt and ground black pepper
sprigs of flat-leafed parsley to garnish

1 Put the potatoes into a pan of cold water. Cover, bring to the boil and parboil for 5–8 minutes. Drain and leave to cool for 15 minutes.
2 Preheat the oven to 150°C (130°C fan oven) mark 2. Put a baking tray inside to warm. Peel the potatoes and coarsely grate them lengthways into long strands. Divide into eight portions and shape into mounds.

3 Melt half the butter in a large non-stick frying pan. When it is beginning to brown, add four of the potato mounds, spacing them well apart, and flatten them a little. Fry slowly for 6–7 minutes until golden brown, then turn them and brown the other side for 6–7 minutes. Transfer to a warmed baking tray and keep warm in the oven while you fry the rest.
4 Just before serving, carefully break the eggs into the hot pan and fry for about 2 minutes or until the white is set and the yolk is still soft. Season with salt and pepper and serve at once, with the rösti. Garnish with sprigs of parsley.

> NUTRITION PER SERVING 324 cals |
> 16g fat (7g sats) | 36g carbs | 0.4g salt **V**

HASSELBACK POTATOES

Serves 4
Preparation 10 minutes
Cooking time 45 minutes

8 potatoes, weighing about 75g (3oz) each
vegetable oil for brushing
salt and ground black pepper

1 Preheat the oven to 220°C (200°C fan oven) mark 7.
Cut the potatoes across their width at 5mm (¼in) intervals
three-quarters of the way through.
2 Put in a single layer in an oiled baking tin. Brush with oil
and season. Roast, uncovered, for 45 minutes.

COOK'S TIP
To stop you from slicing all the way through
the potatoes, place them in the bowl of a wooden
spoon while you cut them.

NUTRITION PER SERVING
162 cals | 6g fat (1g sats) | 26g carbs | 0.3g salt ⓥ

BUBBLE AND SQUEAK CAKES

Makes 12
Preparation 15 minutes, plus cooling
Cooking time 45 minutes

550g (1¼ lb) old potatoes
125g (4oz) butter
175g (6oz) leeks, trimmed and finely
    shredded
175g (6oz) green cabbage, finely
    shredded
plain flour to dust
1 tbsp oil
salt and ground black pepper

1 Cook the potatoes in a large pan of lightly salted boiling water until tender, then drain and mash.
2 Heat 50g (2oz) butter in a large non-stick frying pan. Add the leeks and cabbage, and fry for 5 minutes, stirring, or until soft and beginning to colour. Combine the leeks and cabbage with the potatoes and season well with salt and pepper. Leave to cool. When cool enough to handle, mould into 12 cakes and dust with flour.
3 Heat the oil and remaining butter in a non-stick frying pan and cook the cakes for 4 minutes on each side or until they are golden, crisp and hot right through. Serve.

> NUTRITION PER CAKE 130 cals |
> 10g fat (6g sats) | 10g carbs | 0.2g salt ⓥ

SAVOY CABBAGE WITH CRÈME FRAÎCHE

Serves 6
Preparation 8 minutes
Cooking time 5 minutes

1 large Savoy cabbage, about 900g (2lb)
25g (1oz) butter
200ml crème fraîche
2 tbsp freshly chopped flat-leafed
    parsley
salt and ground black pepper

1 Cut the Savoy cabbage into large wedges. Bring a pan of salted water to the boil. Add the cabbage wedges, return to the boil and boil for 1–2 minutes only. Drain thoroughly.
2 Heat the butter in a large frying pan, add the cabbage and stir-fry for 3–4 minutes. Add the crème fraîche and chopped parsley, toss briefly and season with pepper to taste. Serve straight away.

> NUTRITION PER SERVING 200 cals |
> 17g fat (11g sats) | 6g carbs | 0.3g salt ⓥ

COLCANNON

Serves 4
Preparation 10 minutes
Cooking time 20 minutes

900g (2lb) potatoes, cut into
   even-sized chunks
50g (2oz) butter
1/4 Savoy cabbage, shredded
100ml (3 1/2 fl oz) semi-skimmed milk
salt and ground black pepper

1 Put the potatoes into a pan of cold salted water. Bring to the boil, then lower the heat and simmer, partially covered, for 15–20 minutes or until the potatoes are tender.
2 Meanwhile, melt the butter in a large frying pan. Add the cabbage and stir-fry for 3 minutes.

3 Drain the potatoes well, then tip back into the pan and put over a medium heat for 1 minute to drive off the excess moisture. Turn into a colander and cover to keep warm.
4 Pour the milk into the potato pan and bring to the boil, then take off the heat. Add the potatoes and mash well until smooth.
5 Add the cabbage and any butter from the pan and mix together. Season with salt and pepper to taste and serve.

NUTRITION PER SERVING 310 cals |
12g fat (7g sats) | 45g carbs | 0.5g salt **V**

NEEPS AND TATTIES

Serves 4
Preparation 15 minutes
Cooking time 25 minutes

250g (9oz) swede, cut into chunks
450g (1lb) potatoes, cut into chunks
50–100g (2–3 1/2 oz) butter
1 tbsp double cream (optional)
freshly grated nutmeg
salt and ground black pepper
haggis to serve

1 Bring a large pan of lightly salted water to the boil, add the swede and cook for 20–25 minutes until tender. Drain and steam dry for 2 minutes.
2 Bring another large pan of lightly salted water to the boil, add the potatoes and cook for 15–20 minutes until tender. Drain and steam dry for 2 minutes.
3 Mash each vegetable with half the butter until smooth, adding a splash of cream if you like. Season with nutmeg, salt and ground black pepper. Serve with haggis.

NUTRITION PER SERVING 276 cals |
20g fat (12g sats) | 23g carbs | 0.3g salt **V**

WHITE NUT ROAST

Serves 8
Preparation 20 minutes
Cooking time about 1 hour

40g (1½ oz) butter, plus extra to grease
1 onion, finely chopped
1 garlic clove, crushed
225g (8oz) mixed white nuts, such as Brazils, macadamias, pinenuts and whole almonds, ground in a food processor or nut mill
125g (4oz) fresh white breadcrumbs
grated zest and juice of ½ lemon
75g (3oz) sage Derby cheese or Parmesan (see page 228), grated
125g (4oz) cooked, peeled (or vacuum-packed) chestnuts, roughly chopped
½ × 400g can artichoke hearts, drained and roughly chopped
1 medium egg, lightly beaten
2 tsp each freshly chopped parsley, sage and thyme, plus extra sprigs to garnish (optional)
salt and ground black pepper

1 Preheat the oven to 200°C (180°C fan oven) mark 6. Melt the butter in a pan and cook the onion and garlic for 5 minutes or until soft. Put into a large bowl and set aside to cool.
2 Add the nuts, breadcrumbs, lemon zest and juice, cheese, chestnuts and artichokes. Season well and bind together with the egg. Stir in the herbs.
3 Put the mixture on to a large piece of buttered foil and shape into a fat sausage, packing tightly. Scatter with the extra herb sprigs and wrap in the foil.
4 Cook on a baking sheet for 35 minutes, then unwrap the foil slightly and cook for a further 15 minutes or until turning golden. Slice and serve garnished with her sprigs, if using.

FREEZING TIP

- To freeze, complete the recipe to the end of step 3, cool, cover and freeze for up to one month.
- To use, cook from frozen for 45 minutes, then unwrap the foil slightly and cook for a further 15 minutes or until turning golden.

NUTRITION PER SERVING
371 cals | 28g fat (9g sats) | 20g carbs | 0.8g salt (V)

CORN-ON-THE-COB WITH CHILLI LIME BUTTER

Serves 4
Preparation 15 minutes, plus chilling
Cooking time 6–8 minutes

4 corn-on-the-cobs

For the chilli lime butter
125g (4oz) unsalted butter, slightly softened
1 tbsp sweet chilli sauce
2 tbsp lime juice
salt and ground black pepper

1 First prepare the chilli lime butter. In a bowl, mix the butter with the chilli sauce and lime juice, then season with salt and pepper. Put on a piece of clingfilm, roll into a log, wrap well and chill to firm up.
2 Strip the outer husks from the corn cobs and trim the bases. Bring a large pan of water to the boil, add the corn cobs and cook for 6–8 minutes until tender. (Don't add salt to the cooking water, or it will toughen the corn.)
3 Drain the corn cobs and serve, topped with slices of chilli lime butter.

NUTRITION PER SERVING
360 cals | 28g fat (16g sats) | 23g carbs | 1.2g salt Ⓥ

BRAISED RED CABBAGE

Serves 6
Preparation 15 minutes
Cooking time about 50 minutes

1 tbsp olive oil
1 red onion, halved and sliced
2 garlic cloves, crushed
1 large red cabbage, about 1kg
   (2¼ lb), shredded
2 tbsp light muscovado sugar
2 tbsp red wine vinegar
8 juniper berries
¼ tsp ground allspice
300ml (½ pint) vegetable stock
2 pears, cored and sliced
salt and ground black pepper
fresh thyme sprigs to garnish

1 Heat the oil in a large pan, add the onion and fry for 5 minutes. Add the remaining ingredients, except the pears, and season with salt and pepper. Bring to the boil, then reduce the heat, cover and simmer for 30 minutes.
2 Add the pears and cook for a further 15 minutes or until nearly all the liquid has evaporated and the cabbage is tender. Serve hot, garnished with thyme.

> NUTRITION PER SERVING 63 cals |
> 1g fat (0g sats) | 12g carbs | 0.9g salt Ⓥ

SLOW-ROASTED TOMATOES

Serves 4
Preparation 10 minutes
Cooking time 2½–3 hours

12 large ripe tomatoes
2 garlic cloves, roughly chopped
2 thyme sprigs, bruised
a pinch of sugar
4 tbsp extra virgin olive oil
squeeze of lemon juice
basil leaves, to garnish
salt and ground black pepper

1 Preheat the oven to 150°C (130°C fan oven) mark 2. Halve the tomatoes and scoop out most of the seeds. Put the tomato halves into a baking dish in which they fit closely together and scatter over the garlic, thyme, sugar, salt and pepper.
2 Drizzle the olive oil over the tomatoes and add a good squeeze of lemon juice. Roast for 2½–3 hours until the tomatoes are shrivelled (but not as dried as sun-dried tomatoes). Allow to cool.
3 Scatter basil leaves over the tomatoes and serve, as an accompaniment to cold meats and cheese.

> NUTRITION PER SERVING 170 cals |
> 14g fat (2g sats) | 9g carbs | 0.3g salt Ⓥ

ROASTED ROOT VEGETABLES

Serves 4
Preparation 15 minutes
Cooking time 1 hour

1 large potato, cut into large chunks
1 large sweet potato, cut into large
    chunks
3 carrots, cut into large chunks
4 small parsnips, halved
1 small swede, cut into large chunks
3 tbsp olive oil
2 fresh rosemary and 2 fresh thyme
    sprigs
salt and ground black pepper

1 Preheat the oven to 200°C (180°C fan oven) mark 6. Put all the vegetables into a large roasting tin. Add the oil.
2 Use scissors to snip the herbs over the vegetables, then season with salt and and black pepper and toss everything together. Roast for 1 hour or until tender.

TRY SOMETHING DIFFERENT
Use other combinations of vegetables: try celeriac instead of parsnips, fennel instead of swede, peeled shallots instead of carrots.

NUTRITION PER SERVING 251 cals | 10g fat (1g sats) | 39g carbs | 0.2g salt **V**

BAKED BEETROOT

Serves 6
Preparation 15 minutes
Cooking time 1¼–1½ hours

1.25kg (2lb 12oz) beetroot
15g (½ oz) butter
salt and ground black pepper
freshly chopped parsley or chives, to
    garnish

TRY SOMETHING DIFFERENT
Use baby beetroot. Roast them whole as per the method, then in step 4 rub off the skins and halve or leave whole.

1 Preheat the oven to 200°C (180°C fan oven) mark 6. Trim the beetroot and carefully rinse in cold water, making sure you do not tear the skins.
2 Rub the butter over the middle of a large piece of foil. Put the beetroot on the buttered foil and season with salt and pepper. Bring the edges of the foil up over the beetroot and fold together to seal and form a parcel. Put on a baking sheet.
3 Bake for 1¼–1½ hours or until the beetroot are soft and the skin comes away easily.
4 Leave for a minute or two until cool enough to handle, then rub off the skins. and roughly chop, then scatter chopped parsley or chives over the beetroot to serve.

NUTRITION PER SERVING 90 cals | 2g fat (1g sats) | 15g carbs | 0.2g salt **V**

CRUNCHY PARSNIPS

Serves 8
Preparation 10 minutes
Cooking time 1 hour 10 minutes

4 tbsp goose fat or sunflower oil
8 parsnips, halved lengthways
2 tbsp semolina

1 Preheat the oven to 200°C (180°C fan) mark 6. Put the fat or oil into a roasting tin large enough for the parsnips to sit in one layer without touching each other. Heat up while the parsnips are parboiling.
2 Put the parsnips in a pan of cold, salted water and bring to the boil. Cook for 5 minutes. Drain and leave in the colander to steam for 2 minutes. Put the semolina on a plate and coat the parsnips, shaking off any excess.

3 Tip the parsnips into the roasting tin, tossing to coat in the hot fat. Roast for 45 minutes–1 hour, turning twice during cooking to re-coat, until the parsnips are crisp.

GET AHEAD
Prepare the parsnips up to step 2, up to 24 hours ahead. Chill in a sealed plastic bag. To use, complete the recipe.

NUTRITION PER SERVING 145 cals | 8g fat (2g sats) | 15g carbs | 1g salt

CREAMY LEEKS

Serves 8
Preparation 15 minutes, plus cooling
Cooking time 20 minutes

900g (2lb) trimmed leeks, cut into
   chunks
25g (1oz) butter
150ml (¼ pint) crème fraîche
freshly grated nutmeg, to taste
salt and ground black pepper

1 Cook the leeks in a pan of boiling salted water for 7–10 minutes until just tender. Drain and immediately plunge into a bowl of icy cold water to refresh. When cool, drain and pat dry with kitchen paper.
2 Roughly chop the leeks in a food processor. Take out half and set aside. Whiz the remainder until smooth.
3 Melt the butter in a frying pan, add the chopped and puréed leeks, and stir over a high heat for a minute or two. Add the crème fraîche, and season with salt and pepper. Stir over a medium heat until bubbling. Sprinkle with grated nutmeg to serve.

NUTRITION PER SERVING 120 cals | 11g fat (7 sats) | 3g carbs | 0.7g salt **V**

FENNEL GRATIN

Serves 6
Preparation 10 minutes
Cooking time 15–20 minutes

3 fennel bulbs, trimmed
300ml (½ pint) vegetable stock
25g (1oz) butter
1 garlic clove, crushed
1 bunch of spring onions, trimmed and
    finely chopped
2 tbsp chopped fennel fronds or dill
300ml (½ pint) double cream
50g (2oz) Cheddar cheese (see page
    228), grated
ground black pepper

1 Cut the fennel lengthways into 5mm
(¼in) thick slices and put into a large
shallow pan with the stock and half the
butter. Bring to the boil, lower the heat,
cover and simmer for 10–15 minutes
until just tender.

2 Meanwhile, melt the remaining
butter in another pan, add the garlic
and spring onions and fry gently for
5 minutes or until softened. Stir in the
chopped fennel fronds or dill.
3 Lift out the poached fennel with a
slotted spoon and put into a gratin dish.
Add 150ml (¼ pint) of the cooking
liquid to the spring onions. Pour in the
cream, bring to the boil and simmer
gently for 1 minute. Take off the heat
and stir in the cheese and pepper
to taste.
4 Pour the sauce over the fennel and
grill under a high heat for 1–2 minutes
until bubbling and golden.

> NUTRITION PER SERVING 310 cals |
> 31g fat (21g sats) | 4g carbs | 0.8g salt Ⓥ

CARAMELISED CARROTS

Serves 8
Preparation 15 minutes
Cooking time 10–15 minutes

700g (1½lb) baby carrots, scraped
50g (2oz) butter
50g (2oz) light muscovado sugar
300ml (½ pint) chicken or vegetable
    stock
2 tbsp balsamic vinegar
2 tbsp freshly chopped parsley,
    to serve
salt and ground black pepper

1 Thinly slice the carrots lengthways,
then put into a pan with the butter,
sugar and stock. Season with salt and
pepper, then cover and bring to the
boil. Reduce the heat and simmer for
5 minutes.
2 Remove the lid, add the balsamic
vinegar and cook for 5–10 minutes or
until the carrots are tender and the
liquid has reduced to form a glaze.
Scatter with the chopped parsley
to serve.

> NUTRITION PER SERVING 100 cals |
> 5g fat (3g sats) | 13g carbs | 0.8g salt Ⓥ

GRILLED MUSHROOMS WITH HERB AND GARLIC BUTTER

Serves 4
Preparation 10 minutes, plus chilling
Cooking time 10 minutes

125g (4oz) butter, softened
2 garlic cloves, crushed
2–3 tsp each freshly chopped chives and parsley
1 tsp grated lemon zest
12 field mushrooms, trimmed
1 tbsp olive oil
salt and ground black pepper

1 Cream the butter, garlic, herbs, lemon zest and a little salt and pepper together in a bowl. Cover and chill in the fridge for at least 30 minutes.
2 Brush the mushrooms with oil, lay gill-side down on a grill pan and grill under a high heat for 5 minutes. Meanwhile, cut the flavoured butter into pieces.
3 Turn the mushrooms gill-side up. Dot with the butter and grill for a further 4–5 minutes until tender and sizzling. Serve at once, as a starter or as an accompaniment to grilled meat or vegetables.

TRY SOMETHING DIFFERENT
Flavour the butter with chopped basil, garlic and chopped sun-dried tomatoes.

NUTRITION PER SERVING
300 cals | 30g fat (17g sats) | 0.8g carbs | 0.5g salt

SPICED OKRA WITH ONION AND TOMATO

Serves 4
Preparation 20 minutes
Cooking time 25 minutes

450g (1lb) okra
2.5cm (1in) piece fresh root ginger, peeled
1 onion, quartered
2 garlic cloves, roughly chopped
2 tsp ground coriander
1/2 tsp each ground cinnamon and turmeric
3 tbsp oil
3 tomatoes, skinned and chopped (see page 277)
2 tbsp thick yogurt
2 tbsp freshly chopped coriander
salt and ground black pepper

1 Trim the okra, removing a small piece from each end; don't cut into the flesh or the dish will acquire an unpleasant glutinous texture during cooking.
2 Roughly chop the ginger and put into a blender with the onion, garlic and 1 tbsp water. Process until smooth. Add the spices and process again.
3 Heat the oil in a large frying pan, add the spicy onion paste and stir-fry over a high heat for 2 minutes. Lower the heat and cook for 5 minutes or until the onion paste is golden brown and loses its raw aroma.
4 Add the chopped tomatoes and season with salt and pepper. Cook for 5 minutes or until the tomato has reduced, then add the okra and stir to coat in the mixture. Cover and simmer gently for 5 minutes or until the okra is just tender.
5 Stir in the yogurt, then add the chopped coriander and heat through gently. Serve straight away.

NUTRITION PER SERVING
150 cals | 12g fat (2g sats) | 8g carbs | 0.4g salt

BRUSSELS SPROUTS WITH CHESTNUTS AND SHALLOTS

Serves 8
Preparation 15 minutes
Cooking time 12 minutes

900g (2lb) small Brussels sprouts, trimmed
1 tbsp olive oil
8 shallots, finely chopped
200g pack peeled cooked chestnuts
15g (½oz) butter
pinch of freshly grated nutmeg
salt and ground black pepper

1 Add the sprouts to a large pan of boiling salted water, return to the boil and blanch for 2 minutes. Drain the sprouts and refresh with cold water.
2 Heat the olive oil in a wok or sauté pan. Add the shallots and stir-fry for 5 minutes or until almost tender.
3 Add the sprouts to the pan with the chestnuts and stir-fry for about 4 minutes to heat through.
4 Add the butter and nutmeg, and season generously with salt and pepper. Serve immediately.

COOK'S TIP
For convenience, blanch the Brussels sprouts ahead, then pan-fry just before serving. This helps to retain their colour and texture.

NUTRITION PER SERVING
140 cals | 5g fat (1g sats) | 8g carbs | 0.3g salt **V**

PEPERONATA

Serves 6
Preparation 15 minutes
Cooking time about 45 minutes

4 red peppers
3 orange peppers
1 green pepper
100ml (3½ fl oz) olive oil
2 garlic cloves, crushed
2 tbsp capers in brine, rinsed
18 black olives
1 tbsp freshly chopped flat-leafed parsley
salt and ground black pepper
crusty bread to serve

1 Halve the peppers through the core and remove the seeds. Heat the oil in a large pan, add the garlic and stir-fry over a medium heat for 1 minute.

2 Add the peppers, season well and toss to coat in the oil. Cover the pan with a lid and continue to cook over a low heat for 40 minutes.

3 Add the capers, olives and chopped parsley, and stir to mix. Either serve straightaway or cool and chill until required. Serve the Peperonata with warm crusty bread.

COOK'S TIP
This Italian sweet pepper stew is best made two to three days ahead to allow time for the flavours to develop. Cover and chill, but bring to room temperature to serve.

NUTRITION PER SERVING
180 cals | 16g fat (2g sats) | 0.8g carbs | 1.2g salt **V**

SALADS

SALADS

Endlessly versatile, quick and easy to prepare, as well as mouthwatering, salads may be served as starters, accompaniments, main courses, snacks, lunches or light suppers. A side salad needs to be carefully composed so that the colours, flavours and textures complement the main dish and don't overpower it. Substantial salads – served with some good bread – are excellent, healthy main dishes, especially in the summer. A satisfying complete meal salad is generally based around one or two high-protein foods with complementary flavouring ingredients, which offer a contrast in texture as well as taste. A tempting salad, served in moderate portions, is an ideal starter to stimulate the taste buds without taking the edge off the appetite. Warm salads, which are either tossed in a warm dressing or feature warm ingredients, are perfect starters.

SALAD LEAVES

The wonderful array of lettuces and other salad leaves on sale in most supermarkets, quality greengrocers and markets is inspiring. There are soft delicate leaves, such as the familiar round lettuce, lamb's lettuce (also known as corn salad and mâche), russet-coloured oak leaf and frilly-leafed lollo rosso. Crisper lettuces include cos, iceberg and little gem or, for a crunchy texture, buy Chinese leaves. In addition, there are deliciously bitter leaves such as dark red radicchio, peppery rocket, crisp chicory, watercress, frisée (curly endive) and tender baby spinach.

Ready-prepared bags of mixed salad leaves are a convenient way of buying salad leaves if you want a selection but only require a small quantity. Leaf salads are simple, refreshing and easily enhanced by the addition of fresh herbs or edible flowers.

When you are choosing lettuces, look for fresh, crisp leaves and a tightly packed head if appropriate. Avoid any with wilted or bruised leaves. Store loosely wrapped in the salad drawer of the fridge.

PREPARING SALAD LEAVES

Pull off and discard any coarse or damaged outer leaves. Tear the leaves into pieces, if necessary. Rinse in a bowl of cold water and pat or spin dry. Assemble and dress just before serving.

OTHER SALAD VEGETABLES

Beetroot, carrots, celery, courgettes, cucumber, fennel, mushrooms, peppers, radishes and salad onions are just a few of the many vegetables that are eaten raw in salads. Beans and peas, such as broad beans, French beans and mangetouts, are best blanched and refreshed first. Tomatoes and avocados are synonymous with salads, but they must be at their peak of ripeness and flavourful for optimum results. New potatoes are excellent in salads, especially if they are combined with the dressing while still warm.

SALAD HERBS

Fresh herbs will enhance most salads and it is well worth growing your own supply in the garden or in tubs or window boxes. The flowers from herbs such as borage, chives, fennel and thyme can also be added to salads. Not all herbs are good in raw salads, but most work well.

Basil is almost indispensable in tomato salads, and it complements leafy salads too. Chervil, chives and flat-leafed parsley will flatter most salads. Coriander is excellent with robust green leaves, bulgur wheat and couscous. Dill and fennel are particularly good in fish salads, while mint combines well with oranges and peas.

Oregano is a classic ingredient in traditional Greek salads and, like marjoram and thyme, it works well in cooked salads too. Strongly flavoured tarragon is great with chicken salads; it also enhances creamy salad dressings, particularly those containing mustard.

SALAD DRESSINGS

See pages 28–29.

TOMATO AND ONION SALAD

Serves 4
Preparation 15 minutes, plus standing

500g (1lb 2oz) baby plum tomatoes, halved
1 bunch of spring onions, sliced
500g (1lb 2oz) plum tomatoes, sliced lengthways
handful of fresh basil leaves, roughly torn, plus sprigs to
    garnish
2 beef tomatoes, about 450g (1lb) in total, sliced
100g (3½ oz) pinenuts, toasted (see Cook's Tip, page 312)
250g (9oz) medium tomatoes, cut into wedges
salt and ground black pepper

For the dressing
100ml (3½ fl oz) extra virgin olive oil
50ml (2fl oz) balsamic vinegar
pinch of golden caster sugar

1 First make the dressing. Put the olive oil, balsamic vinegar and sugar into a screw-topped jar, then season generously with salt and pepper. Shake well to combine.
2 Layer the baby plum tomatoes, spring onions, plum tomatoes, basil, beef tomatoes, pinenuts and finally the medium tomatoes in a shallow serving bowl, seasoning each layer with salt and pepper.
3 Drizzle the dressing over the salad and set aside to allow the flavours to mingle for 1 hour. Garnish with basil sprigs to serve.

TRY SOMETHING DIFFERENT
For a simple tomato and basil salad, omit the spring onions and pinenuts, and reduce the quantity of dressing by one-third.

NUTRITION PER SERVING
450 cals | 40g fat (4g sats) | 16g carbs | 0.3g salt **V**

MIXED LEAF SALAD

Serves 8
Preparation 10 minutes

3 round lettuce hearts, roughly
    shredded
100g (3¹/₂oz) watercress
2 ripe avocados, roughly chopped
1 box salad cress, chopped
100g (3¹/₂oz) sugarsnap peas,
    roughly sliced
4 tbsp French dressing (see page 29)

1 Put the lettuce hearts into a bowl
and add the watercress, avocados, salad
cress and sugarsnap peas.
2 Pour the dressing over the salad and
toss to mix. Serve immediately.

> **COOK'S TIP**
> Vary the salad leaves according
> to taste and availability. Try using
> treviso, red chicory and baby
> spinach leaves, for example.

> **NUTRITION PER SERVING** 90 cals |
> 9g fat (1g sats) | 1g carbs | 0.5g salt Ⓥ

BROAD BEAN AND FETA SALAD

Serves 2
Preparation 10 minutes
Cooking time 5 minutes

225g (8oz) podded broad beans
    (see Cook's Tip)
100g (3¹/₂oz) feta cheese (see page
    228), chopped
2 tbsp freshly chopped mint
2 tbsp extra virgin olive oil
a squeeze of lemon juice
lemon wedges to serve (optional)
salt and ground black pepper

1 Cook the beans in salted boiling
water for 3–5 minutes until tender.
Drain, then plunge into cold water and
drain again. Remove their skins if you
like (see page 278).

2 Tip the beans into a bowl, add the
feta, mint, olive oil and a squeeze of
lemon juice. Season well with salt and
pepper and toss together. Serve with
lemon wedges, if you like.

> **COOK'S TIP**
> For this quantity of broad beans,
> you will need to buy about
> 750g (1¹/₂lb) beans in pods.
> Choose small pods, as the
> beans will be young and
> will have a better flavour than
> bigger, older beans.

> **NUTRITION PER SERVING** 197 cals |
> 16g fat (4g sats) | 5g carbs | 1.3g salt Ⓥ

CLASSIC COLESLAW

Serves 6
Preparation 15 minutes

¹/₄ each medium red and white cabbage, shredded
1 carrot, grated
20g (³/₄ oz) flat-leafed parsley, finely chopped

For the dressing
1¹/₂ tbsp red wine vinegar
4 tbsp olive oil
¹/₂ tsp Dijon mustard
salt and ground black pepper

1 To make the dressing, put the vinegar into a small bowl, add the olive oil and mustard, season well with salt and pepper and mix well.
2 Put the cabbage and carrot into a large bowl and toss to mix well. Add the parsley.
3 Mix the dressing again, pour over the cabbage mixture and toss well to coat.

TRY SOMETHING DIFFERENT

Thai-style Coleslaw Replace the red cabbage with a good handful of fresh bean sprouts, the parsley with freshly chopped coriander, and add 1 seeded and finely chopped red chilli (see Cook's Tips, page 69). For the dressing, replace the vinegar with lime juice, the olive oil with toasted sesame oil and the mustard with soy sauce.

NUTRITION PER SERVING
92 cals | 8g fat (1g sats) | 5g carbs | 0.1g salt **V**

RED CABBAGE AND BEETROOT SALAD

Serves 8
Preparation 15 minutes

¹/₂ red cabbage, cored and finely sliced
500g (1lb 2oz) cooked beetroot
    (see Cook's Tips)
8 cornichons (baby gherkins), sliced
2 tbsp baby capers in vinegar, rinsed

For the dressing
6 tbsp extra virgin olive oil
2 tbsp sherry vinegar
3 tbsp freshly chopped dill
salt and ground black pepper

1 Put the red cabbage into a large bowl. Cut the beetroot into matchstick strips or grate coarsely and add to the cabbage with the cornichons and capers. Toss well to mix.

2 To make the dressing, put the olive oil, sherry vinegar and chopped dill into a small bowl. Season well with salt and pepper, then add a splash of cold water to help emulsify the dressing. Whisk together thoroughly.
3 Pour the dressing over the salad and toss everything together well.

COOK'S TIPS
— Buy vacuum-packed cooked beetroot or cook it yourself. Beetroot pickled in vinegar is not suitable.
— This salad is particularly good with baked ham.

NUTRITION PER SERVING 150 cals | 10g fat (1g sats) | 11g carbs | 0.3g salt Ⓥ

CHICORY, FENNEL AND ORANGE SALAD

Serves 4
Preparation 15 minutes
Cooking time 2–3 minutes

1 small fennel bulb, with fronds
2 chicory heads, divided into leaves,
    or ¹/₂ head Chinese leaf, shredded
2 oranges, peeled and cut into rounds,
    plus juice of ¹/₂ orange
25g (1oz) hazelnuts, chopped and
    toasted (see Cook's Tip)
2 tbsp hazelnut or walnut oil
salt and ground black pepper

1 Trim the fronds from the fennel, roughly chop them and put to one side. Finely slice the fennel bulb lengthways and put into a bowl with the chicory or Chinese leaves, the orange slices and toasted hazelnuts.
2 Put the orange juice, hazelnut or walnut oil and the reserved fennel fronds into a small bowl, season well with salt and pepper, and mix thoroughly. Pour over the salad and toss everything together.

COOK'S TIP
Put the nuts into a dry frying pan and toast over a medium heat, shaking the pan, until evenly toasted.

NUTRITION PER SERVING 127 cals | 10g fat (1g sats) | 9g carbs | trace salt Ⓥ

ROASTED TOMATO BULGUR SALAD

Serves 6
Preparation 10 minutes, plus soaking and standing
Cooking time 10–15 minutes

175g (6oz) bulgur wheat
700g (1½lb) cherry tomatoes
    or baby plum tomatoes
8 tbsp extra virgin olive oil
a handful each of mint and basil,
    roughly chopped, plus fresh basil
    sprigs to garnish
3–4 tbsp balsamic vinegar
1 bunch of spring onions, sliced
salt and ground black pepper

1 Put the bulgur wheat into a bowl and add boiling water to cover by 1cm (½in). Leave to soak for 30 minutes.
2 Preheat the oven to 220°C (200°C fan oven) mark 7. Put the tomatoes into a small roasting tin, drizzle with half the oil and add half the mint. Season with salt and pepper and roast for 10–15 minutes until beginning to soften.
3 Put the remaining oil and the vinegar into a large bowl. Add the warm pan juices from the roasted tomatoes and the soaked bulgur wheat.
4 Stir in the remaining chopped herbs and the spring onions and check the seasoning. You may need a little more vinegar depending on the sweetness of the tomatoes.
5 Add the tomatoes and carefully toss to combine, then serve garnished with basil sprigs.

NUTRITION PER SERVING 225 cals |
15g fat (2g sats) | 19g carbs | 0g salt (V)

POTATO SALAD WITH BASIL

Serves 4
Preparation 10 minutes
Cooking time 15 minutes,
plus cooling

700g (1½lb) firm waxy potatoes,
    scrubbed and cut into bite-sized
    pieces
90ml (3fl oz) extra virgin olive oil
1 garlic clove, crushed
grated zest of 1 lemon
2–3 tbsp chopped basil
1 tbsp sherry vinegar
4 spring onions, finely chopped
25g (1oz) pinenuts, toasted
    (see Cook's Tip page 312)
salt and ground black pepper

1 Put the potatoes into a pan, add cold salted water to cover, bring to the boil and cook for about 12–15 minutes until just tender.
2 Meanwhile, heat 2 tbsp of the olive oil in a large frying pan, add the garlic and lemon zest, and fry gently for 5 minutes or until soft but not golden.
3 In a bowl, whisk the remaining olive oil with the chopped basil, sherry vinegar and seasoning.
4 Drain the potatoes and shake off the excess water. Add to the frying pan and stir-fry for 1 minute. Stir in the basil mixture and remove from the heat. Set aside to cool to room temperature.
5 Just before serving, add the spring onions and pinenuts, and toss lightly; check the seasoning.

NUTRITION PER SERVING 350 cals |
24g fat (3g sats) | 31g carbs | 0.3g salt (V)

CHICKEN CAESAR SALAD

Serves 4
Preparation 15–20 minutes
Cooking time 12 minutes

2 tbsp olive oil
1 garlic clove, crushed
2 thick slices of country-style bread, cubed
6 tbsp freshly grated Parmesan
1 cos lettuce, washed, chilled and cut into bite-size pieces
700g (1½ lb) cooked chicken breast, sliced

For the dressing
4 tbsp mayonnaise (see page 29)
2 tbsp lemon juice
1 tsp Dijon mustard
2 anchovy fillets, very finely chopped
salt and ground black pepper

1 Preheat the oven to 180°C (160°C fan oven) mark 4. Put the olive oil, garlic and bread cubes in a bowl and toss well. Tip on to a baking sheet and bake in the oven for 10 minutes, turning halfway through.
2 Sprinkle the Parmesan over the croutons and bake for 2 minutes or until the cheese has melted and the bread is golden.
3 Put all the ingredients for the dressing in a bowl, season with salt and pepper and mix.
4 Put the lettuce and sliced chicken in a bowl, pour the dressing over and toss. Top with the cheese croutons.

> NUTRITION PER SERVING   482 cals |
> 27g fat (8g sats) | 8g carbs | 1.4g salt

TRADITIONAL GREEK SALAD

Serves 4
Preparation 15 minutes, plus standing

1 red onion, thinly sliced
½ cucumber, peeled and cut into chunks
1 green pepper, seeded and finely sliced
3 beef tomatoes, sliced
10 Kalamata olives packed in olive oil with oregano, drained
200g pack feta cheese (see page 228), chopped
juice of ½ lemon
4 tbsp extra virgin olive oil
salt and ground black pepper

1 Put the red onion, cucumber, green pepper, tomatoes, olives and feta cheese into a large bowl and toss to mix. Season very lightly with salt (as feta is quite salty) and generously with pepper.
2 Drizzle the lemon juice and olive oil over the salad and toss everything together. Leave to stand for about 10 minutes before serving to allow the flavours to mingle. Serve as a starter or light lunch.

TRY SOMETHING DIFFERENT
Use plain black olives and add 1–2 tbsp chopped oregano to the salad dressing.

> NUTRITION PER SERVING   280 cals |
> 24g fat (9g sats) | 6g carbs | 2.3g salt **V**

ROASTED VEGETABLE SALAD WITH MUSTARD MAYONNAISE

Serves 4
Preparation 15 minutes
Cooking time 40 minutes

900g (2lb) mixed vegetables, such as fennel,
    courgettes, leeks, aubergines, baby turnips,
    new potatoes and red onions
2 garlic cloves, unpeeled
4–5 fresh marjoram or rosemary sprigs
5 tbsp olive oil
1 tsp flaked sea salt
mixed crushed peppercorns to taste
4 tsp balsamic vinegar
warm crusty bread to serve

For the mustard mayonnaise
150ml (1/4 pint) mayonnaise (see page 29)
2 tbsp Dijon mustard
salt and ground black pepper

1 Preheat the oven to 220°C (200°C fan oven) mark 7.
For the vegetables, quarter the fennel, chop the courgettes,
leeks and aubergines, trim the turnips and cut the onions into
petals. Place the vegetables, garlic, marjoram or rosemary, the
olive oil, salt and peppercorns in a roasting tin and toss well
(see Cook's Tip).
2 Cook in the oven for 30–35 minutes or until the
vegetables are golden, tossing frequently. Sprinkle the balsamic
vinegar over and return to the oven for a further 5 minutes.
3 To make the mustard mayonnaise, mix together the
mayonnaise and mustard, then season with salt and pepper
and set aside.
4 Arrange the vegetable salad on a serving dish and serve
with the mustard mayonnaise and crusty bread.

COOK'S TIP
It's best to roast vegetables in a single layer as
otherwise they will steam and become soggy.
Use two tins if necessary.

NUTRITION PER SERVING
420 cals | 43g fat (6 sats) 5g carbs | 1g salt **V**

HALLOUMI AND AVOCADO SALAD

Serves 4
Preparation 10 minutes
Cooking time 2 minutes

250g (9oz) halloumi, sliced into eight (see Cook's Tip
    below and page 228)
1 tbsp flour, seasoned
2 tbsp olive oil
200g (7oz) mixed leaf salad
2 avocados, halved, stoned, peeled and sliced
fresh rocket leaves to garnish
lemon halves to serve

For the mint dressing
3 tbsp lemon juice
8 tbsp olive oil
3 tbsp freshly chopped mint
salt and ground black pepper

1 To make the dressing, whisk the lemon juice with the olive
oil and mint, then season with salt and pepper.
2 Coat the halloumi with the flour. Heat the oil in a large
frying pan and fry the cheese for 1 minute on each side or
until it forms a golden crust.
3 Meanwhile, in a large bowl, add half the dressing to the
salad leaves and avocado, and toss together. Arrange the
hot cheese on top and drizzle the remaining dressing over.
Garnish with rocket leaves and serve with lemon halves to
squeeze over.

COOK'S TIP
Halloumi is a firm cheese made from ewe's milk.
It is best used sliced and cooked.

NUTRITION PER SERVING
397 cals | 34g fat (13g sats) | 11g carbs | 2.3g salt Ⓥ

SALADE NIÇOISE

Serves 4
Preparation 40 minutes, plus marinating
Cooking time 30 minutes

450g (1lb) fresh tuna steaks (see Cook's Tip)
1 garlic clove, crushed
grated zest of 1/2 lemon
2 tbsp olive oil, plus extra to cook
1 fresh thyme sprig
2 small red peppers, halved and seeded
350g (12oz) vine-ripened tomatoes, peeled
    (see page 277)
2 large eggs
250g (9oz) podded broad beans
2 large fresh basil sprigs, leaves only
1/2 cucumber, seeded and cut into chunks
50g (2oz) small black olives
6 spring onions, trimmed and chopped
50g can anchovy fillets, drained and chopped
50g (2oz) rocket or other salad leaves
salt and ground black pepper

For the dressing
2 tbsp lemon juice
1 tsp Dijon mustard
6 tbsp extra virgin olive oil

1 Rub the tuna steaks with the garlic, lemon zest and pepper. Put into a dish, spoon over 2 tbsp oil, then cover and leave to marinate in a cool place for 3–4 hours.
2 Transfer the tuna to a small pan, add the thyme and enough oil to barely cover the tuna. Bring slowly to the boil, turn the tuna over and remove the pan from the heat. Leave to stand for 5 minutes, then remove the fish with a slotted spoon and leave until cool.
3 Grill the peppers, skin side up, under a hot grill until charred. Put in a bowl, cover with clingfilm and leave until cool. Thickly slice or quarter the tomatoes. Skin the peppers, cut into thick strips and put to one side.
4 Bring a small pan of water to the boil, add the eggs (making sure they're covered with water) and simmer for 8 minutes. Cool under cold running water, shell and quarter. Add the broad beans to a pan of boiling water and cook for 2–3 minutes. Drain and refresh in cold water, then slip off the skins.
5 To make the dressing, put all the ingredients into a screw-topped jar, season and shake well until combined.
6 Break the cooked tuna into large flakes. Pound the basil leaves with 1 tsp salt in a wide salad bowl to release their flavour. Add the peppers, tomatoes, eggs, cucumber, olives, spring onions, anchovies, tuna and broad beans. Add just enough dressing to moisten the salad and toss gently. Check the seasoning.
7 Serve on a bed of rocket or other leaves as a main course. Hand the remaining dressing separately.

TRY SOMETHING DIFFERENT
- Instead of fresh tuna, use 2 × 200g cans tuna steak in olive oil. Drain well and add at step 6.
- Add about 12 cooked small new potatoes at step 6.

NUTRITION PER SERVING
570 cals | 41g fat (6g sats) | 11g carbs | 2.8g salt

SALAD CAPRESE

Serves 4
Preparation 10 minutes

3 × 150g balls mozzarella di bufala
   (see page 228), drained
1kg (2¼lb) very ripe tomatoes, sliced
   into rounds
extra virgin olive oil for drizzling
small handful fresh basil leaves, roughly
   shredded
sea salt and ground black pepper

1 Slice the mozzarella into rounds and layer on a serving plate with the tomato slices.
2 Drizzle with the olive oil, season with sea salt and ground black pepper and scatter the basil over.

> NUTRITION PER SERVING 381 cals |
> 29g fat (17g sats) | 8g carbs | 1.5g salt Ⓥ

MIXED BEAN SALAD WITH LEMON VINAIGRETTE

Serves 6
Preparation 15 minutes

400g can mixed beans, drained and
   rinsed
400g can chickpeas, drained and rinsed
2 shallots, finely sliced
fresh mint sprigs and lemon zest to
   garnish

For the lemon vinaigrette
juice of 1 lemon
2 tsp clear honey
8 tbsp extra virgin olive oil
3 tbsp freshly chopped mint
4 tbsp roughly chopped flat-leafed
   parsley
salt and ground black pepper

1 Put the beans, chickpeas and shallots in a large bowl.
2 To make the lemon vinaigrette, whisk together the lemon juice, seasoning and honey. Gradually whisk in the olive oil and stir in the chopped herbs.
3 Pour the vinaigrette over the bean mixture, toss well, then garnish with the mint sprigs and lemon zest, and serve.

GET AHEAD
- Complete the recipe (but don't add the herbs or garnish), then cover and chill for up to two days.
- To use, remove from the fridge up to 1 hour before serving and add the herbs. Garnish.

> NUTRITION PER SERVING 265 cals |
> 16g fat (2g sats) | 22g carbs | 0.9g salt Ⓥ

WALDORF SALAD

Serves 4
Preparation 15 minutes, plus standing

450g (1lb) eating apples
juice of ½ lemon
1 tsp sugar
150ml (¼ pint) mayonnaise
    (see page 29)
1 lettuce
½ head of celery, sliced
50g (2oz) walnut pieces, chopped
a few walnut halves to garnish
    (optional)

1 Peel and core the apples, slice one and dice the rest. Dip the slices into lemon juice to prevent discoloration. Toss the diced apples in the lemon juice, the sugar and 1 tbsp mayonnaise and leave to stand for about 30 minutes.
2 Just before serving, line a salad bowl with lettuce leaves. Add the celery, walnuts and remaining mayonnaise to the diced apples and toss together. Spoon into the salad bowl and garnish with the apple slices and a few whole walnuts, if you like.

NUTRITION PER SERVING 413 cals | 38g fat (5g sats) | 16g carbs | 0.1g salt Ⓥ

ASPARAGUS, PEA AND MINT RICE SALAD

Serves 6
Preparation 10 minutes
Cooking time 20 minutes

175g (6oz) mixed basmati and
    wild rice
1 large shallot, finely sliced
grated zest and juice of 1 small lemon
2 tbsp sunflower oil
12 fresh mint leaves, roughly chopped,
    plus extra sprigs to garnish
150g (5oz) asparagus tips
75g (3oz) fresh or frozen peas
salt and ground black pepper
lemon zest to garnish

1 Put the rice in a pan with twice its volume of water and a pinch of salt. Cover and bring to the boil. Reduce the heat to very low and cook according to the pack instructions. Once cooked, tip the rice on to a baking sheet and spread out to cool quickly. When cool, spoon into a large bowl.
2 In a small bowl, mix the shallot with the lemon zest and juice, oil and chopped mint, then stir into the rice.
3 Bring a large pan of lightly salted water to the boil. Add the asparagus and peas, and cook for 3–4 minutes until tender. Drain and refresh in a bowl of cold water. Drain well and stir into the rice. Put into a serving dish and garnish with mint sprigs and lemon zest.

NUTRITION PER SERVING 157 cals | 4g fat (trace sats) | 26g carbs | trace salt Ⓥ

WARM GOAT'S CHEESE SALAD

Serves 4
Preparation 20 minutes
Cooking time 1–2 minutes

1 bunch of watercress
4 slices goat's cheese log (with rind)
   (see page 228)
1 quantity rocket pesto (see page 22)
50g (2oz) rocket leaves
40g (1½ oz) walnut halves, toasted
   (see Cook's Tip, page 312)

For the dressing
1 tbsp walnut oil
1 tbsp sunflower oil
1 tsp balsamic or sherry vinegar
salt and ground black pepper

1 To make the dressing, whisk the ingredients together in a bowl, seasoning with salt and pepper to taste.

2 Trim the watercress and discard the coarse stalks. Lay the goat's cheese slices on a foil-lined baking sheet. Put under the grill, as close to the heat as possible, for 1–2 minutes until browned.
3 Put a slice of goat's cheese on each plate and top with a spoonful of rocket pesto. Toss the rocket and watercress leaves with the dressing and then arrange around the goat's cheese. Scatter the walnuts over the salad and serve immediately.

TRY SOMETHING DIFFERENT
Use halved crottins de Chavignol (small hard goat's cheeses) instead of the log chèvre.

NUTRITION PER SERVING 520 cals | 46g fat (12g sats) | 2g carbs | 1.5g salt **V**

ASPARAGUS AND QUAIL EGG SALAD

Serves 8
Preparation 30 minutes
Cooking time 2 minutes

100g (3½ oz) watercress
24 quail's eggs
24 asparagus spears, trimmed
juice of ½ lemon
5 tbsp olive oil
4 large spring onions, finely sliced
a few fresh dill and tarragon sprigs
salt and ground black pepper

1 Trim the watercress and discard the coarse stalks, then chop roughly. Add the quail's eggs to a pan of boiling water and cook for 2 minutes, then drain and plunge into cold water. Cook the asparagus in lightly salted boiling water for 2 minutes or until just tender. Drain, plunge into cold water and leave to cool.
2 Whisk together the lemon juice, oil and seasoning. Stir in the spring onions and put to one side.
3 Peel the quail's eggs and cut in half. Put into a large bowl with the asparagus, watercress, dill and tarragon. Pour the dressing over and lightly toss all the ingredients together. Adjust the seasoning and serve.

NUTRITION PER SERVING 127 cals | 11g fat (2g sats) | 1g carbs | 0.1g salt **V**

BACON, AVOCADO AND PINENUT SALAD

Serves 4
Preparation 5 minutes
Cooking time 7 minutes

125g (4oz) streaky bacon rashers, rinded and cut into small, neat pieces (lardons)
1 shallot, finely chopped
120g bag mixed baby salad leaves
1 ripe avocado
50g (2oz) pinenuts
4 tbsp olive oil
4 tbsp red wine vinegar
salt and ground black pepper

1 Put the lardons into a frying pan over a medium heat for 1–2 minutes until the fat starts to run. Add the shallot and fry gently for about 5 minutes or until golden.

2 Meanwhile, divide the salad leaves among four serving plates. Halve, stone and peel the avocado, then slice the flesh. Arrange on the salad leaves.
3 Add the pinenuts, oil and vinegar to the frying pan and let it bubble for 1 minute. Season with salt and pepper.
4 Tip the bacon, pinenuts and dressing over the salad and serve at once, while still warm.

TRY SOMETHING DIFFERENT
Replace the pinenuts with walnuts.

NUTRITION PER SERVING 352 cals | 34g fat (6g sats) | 3g carbs | 1g salt

SMOKED MACKEREL SALAD

Serves 4
Preparation 15 minutes

250g (9oz) cooked (vacuum-packed without vinegar) beetroot, diced
1 tbsp olive oil
2 tsp white wine vinegar
350g (12oz) potato salad
1–2 tbsp lemon juice
4 peppered smoked mackerel fillets, skinned and flaked
2 tbsp freshly chopped chives, plus extra to garnish
salt and ground black pepper

1 Put the beetroot in a bowl. Sprinkle with the olive oil and vinegar. Season with salt and pepper, and toss together.
2 In a large bowl, mix the potato salad with the lemon juice to taste. Season with salt and pepper. Add the flaked mackerel and chopped chives, and toss together.
3 Just before serving, pile the mackerel mixture into four serving bowls. Sprinkle the beetroot over the top of the salad and garnish with chives.

NUTRITION PER SERVING 656 cals | 56g fat (10g sats) | 16g carbs | 2.4g salt

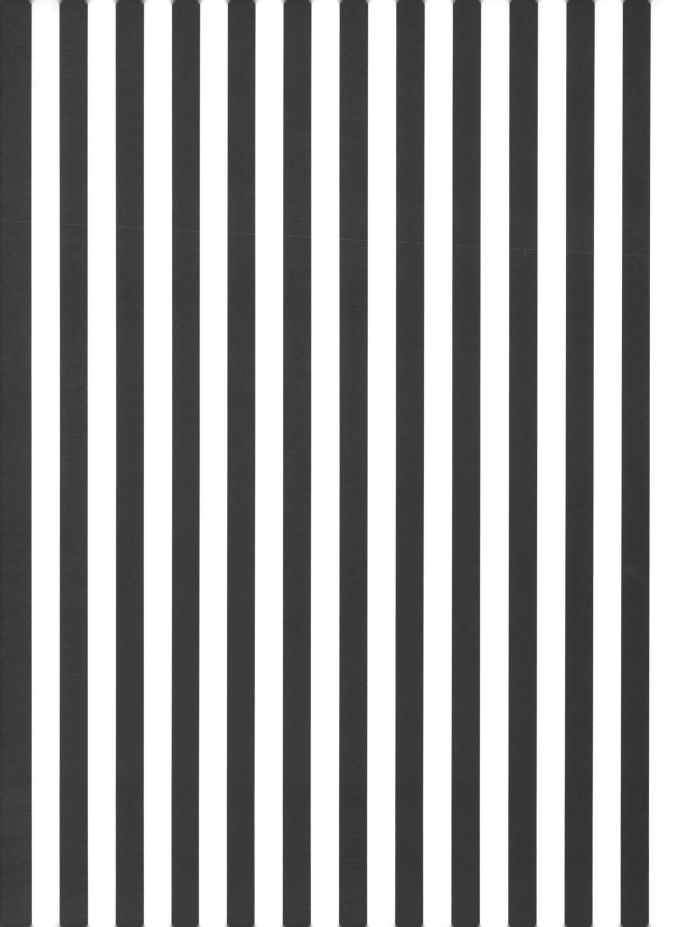

PASTRY

PASTRY

The art of successful pastry making lies in measuring the ingredients accurately, using the correct proportion of fat to flour and light, careful handling. With the exceptions of choux pastry and hot water crust pastry, everything needs to be kept cool when making pastry – the work surface, equipment, ingredients and your hands. It is also important to 'rest' pastry before baking, otherwise it is liable to shrink during cooking. Pastries which are handled a great deal, such as puff, must be rested before and after shaping. Most pastries are rested in the fridge and need to be well wrapped in clingfilm to prevent them from drying out.

The main types of pastry are short pastries, such as shortcrust, and flaked pastries, such as puff. Other pastries include hot water crust, suet crust, choux pastry and filo pastry. Sweetened short pastries can be used for sweet tarts. If you haven't the time or inclination to make your own pastry, buy a pack of ready-made chilled fresh or frozen pastry from the supermarket. Sweet shortcrust pastry is available as well as standard shortcrust. Ready-made puff pastry is so quick to use and successful that you may well prefer to buy it, as the alternative of making your own is very time-consuming.

Packets of ready-made filo sheets are widely available and give excellent results. Note that the size of filo sheets varies considerably between brands – check whether the recipe states a specific size before buying. It is essential to keep filo sheets covered as you work to prevent them from drying out and becoming brittle.

PASTRY INGREDIENTS

Flours For most pastries, plain flour works best, as it gives a light, crisp result. Self-raising flour would produce a soft, spongy pastry, although it can be used for suet crust, which needs a raising agent (see right). Wholemeal flour gives a heavier dough, which is more difficult to roll. For wholemeal pastry, it is therefore better to use half wholemeal and half white flour. Puff pastry is usually made with strong plain (bread) flour as this contains extra gluten to strengthen the dough, enabling it to withstand intensive rolling and folding. A little lemon juice is usually added to puff pastry to soften the gluten and make the dough more elastic. Strong plain flour is also used for making filo (strudel) pastry to allow it to be stretched out very thinly, although this is rarely made at home.

Fats Traditionally, shortcrust pastry is made with a mixture of lard (for shortness) and either butter or margarine (for flavour); however, it is now more often made with a mixture of white vegetable fat and butter or margarine, or all butter for a rich flavour. If you prefer to use margarine, it should be the hard, block type rather than soft tub margarine.

Suet crust, as the name suggests is made using suet, which is the fat around the kidneys, heart and liver of beef and mutton, and is sold shredded, although vegetarian suet is also available.

Liquids Care must be taken when adding the liquid to a pastry dough: too much will create a tough end result; too little will produce a crumbly pastry, which is difficult to handle. Use chilled water and add just enough to bind the dough. Egg yolks are often used to enrich pastry.

Raising agents Steam acts as the raising agent in flaked pastries in combination with the air enclosed in the layers of dough. In choux pastry the raising agents are eggs and steam. Unlike other pastries, suet crust needs a raising agent to lighten the dough. You can use either plain flour sifted with $2\frac{1}{2}$ tsp baking powder to each 225g (8oz) or self-raising flour can be used instead.

Salt The quantity of salt varies according to the type of pastry. Only a pinch is added to shortcrust pastry for flavour, but a measured quantity is added to flaked pastries and hot water crust to strengthen the gluten in the flour and, in the case of hot water crust, to allow for the amount of handling during shaping.

MIXING PASTRY BY HAND

Shortcrust and similar pastries involve rubbing the fat into the flour. To do this, cut the fat into small pieces, then add to the flour and salt, and mix briefly with a round-bladed knife, to coat the pieces with flour. Then, using your fingertips, pick up a small amount of the mixture at a time and rub the fat and flour together to break the fat down into tiny pieces. Do this as lightly and quickly as possible until the mixture resembles fine crumbs; avoid using the palm of your hands.

When you are ready to add the liquid, sprinkle this evenly over the surface; uneven addition may cause blistering once the pastry is cooked. Use a round-bladed knife to mix in the liquid. You may need a little more or less than the quantity stated in the recipe because the absorbency of flours varies. For this reason, don't add it all at once. Collect the dough with your hands and knead lightly for a few seconds until you have a smooth ball.

MIXING PASTRY IN A FOOD PROCESSOR

Short pastries can be made very successfully and quickly in a food processor. To ensure that the dough is not over-worked, use the pulse button or operate the processor in short bursts. Avoid making too large a quantity at one time or the result will be disappointing.

ROLLING OUT PASTRY

To reduce the risk of shrinkage during baking, wrap the pastry in clingfilm to prevent it drying out and rest in the fridge for 20 minutes before rolling out. Lightly dust the work surface and rolling pin – never the pastry – with flour to prevent sticking. Roll the dough lightly and evenly in one direction only – until thin. Always roll away from you, using light, firm strokes, and rotate the pastry frequently to keep an even shape and thickness.

Avoid over-rolling, pulling or stretching the dough as you roll it, otherwise it will shrink badly during cooking. The usual thickness for rolling out pastries is 3mm ($^1/_8$ in), although puff pastry is sometimes rolled out to a 5mm ($^1/_4$ in) thickness, depending on the use.

SHAPING AND GLAZING

Pastry is most often used to line tart tins and cover pies. It can also be folded around fillings to form pasties, or wrapped around whole boned fish or meat, as in salmon or beef en croûte.

To line a flan case, roll out the pastry thinly to a circle about 5cm (2in) wider than the flan ring. With a rolling pin, lift the pastry and lower it into the ring. Lift the edges and ease the pastry into the flan shape, lightly pressing the pastry against the edges. Turn any surplus pastry outwards over the rim and roll across the top with the rolling pin or use a knife to trim the edges.

To cover a pie dish, roll out the pastry to the required thickness and 5cm (2in) wider than the pie dish, using the inverted dish as a guide. Cut a 2.5cm (1in) wide strip from the outer edge and put it on the dampened rim of the dish. Seal the join and brush the strip with water. Lift the remaining pastry on the rolling pin and lay it over the pie dish. Press the lid lightly on to the pastry-lined rim to seal. Trim off any excess pastry.

Seal the edges firmly so that they do not open up during cooking, pressing a fork along the edge or pinching it between your thumb and finger. Cut a slit in the centre of the pie crust for the steam to escape.

For a double-crust pie, divide the pastry into two parts, one slightly larger than the other. Shape the larger piece into a ball and roll it out to about 2.5cm (1in) wider than the inverted pie plate. Lift the pastry using a rolling pin and unroll it over the pie dish. Press into the dish. Add the cold filling and then the lid as above.

To shape a large raised pie in a mould, make up 450g (1lb) Hot Water Crust Pastry (see page 329) and keep it warm. Grease a 1.7 litre (3 pint) hinged pie mould or use a loose-based round cake tin or loaf tin. Put the mould on a baking sheet. Roll out two-thirds of the pastry to 5mm ($^1/_4$ in) thick and use to line the tin. Fill and put on the lid as for a pie above.

To line a bowl with suet crust pastry, roll out a scant three-quarters of the dough (see page 329) on a lightly floured surface and use to line the pudding basin. Fill with the mixture. Brush the top edge of the pastry with water. Roll out the remainder to make a lid and lay over the pudding, pressing the edges together to seal. Cover the basin with a pleated, double layer of greaseproof paper, securing under the rim with string. Cover with foil.

Glazing

As well as giving pies an attractive sheen, glazing pastry seals the surface. Brush the pastry with egg glaze (egg yolk beaten with a little water), or with beaten whole egg. Alternatively, for a less shiny finish, brush with milk.

Part-baked pastry cases are sometimes glazed, then baked for a little longer to seal before filling. When adding cut-out decorations, use some glaze to position the decorations and then brush the whole surface of the pie.

READY-MADE PASTRY

When buying chilled or frozen ready-made pastry, it is important to note that the weight specified on the pack is the combined weight of the ingredients, not the flour weight. As a guide, a 375g (13oz) pack of ready-made shortcrust pastry is roughly equivalent to home-made pastry made with 225g (8oz) flour.

PASTRY QUANTITIES

Where a recipe specifies a weight of pastry, this generally refers to the weight of flour in the recipe rather than the combined weight of the ingredients; for example, if a pie or tart recipe calls for 225g (8oz) shortcrust pastry, you will need this amount of flour and 125g (4oz) fat, as the correct proportion of flour to fat is 2:1.

Recipes for the basic pastries are provided on the following pages. If your pie or tart requires more (or less) than the basic recipe quantity, just increase (or decrease) the pastry ingredients in proportion, remembering to adjust the liquid quantity accordingly.

QUANTITY GUIDE FOR TARTS

Tart tins, including individual ones, vary in depth and this obviously affects the quantity of pastry required to line them. Therefore the following chart is an approximate guide only. For a deep tart tin, allow extra pastry.

Tart tin size	Pastry
18cm (7in)	125g (4oz)
20.5cm (8in)	175g (6oz)
23cm (9in)	200g (7oz)
25.5cm (10in)	225g (8oz)

BAKING BLIND

If a recipe instructs you to 'bake blind', you need to bake or part-bake the pastry case without its filling. The pastry may be partially cooked before filling, or completely cooked if the filling does not require baking. Cooking the pastry before you add the filling gives a crisp result.

Preheat the oven according to the recipe. Prick the pastry base with a fork to prevent air bubbles forming. Cover with foil or greaseproof paper 8cm (3¼in) larger than the tin. Spread baking beans or dried pulses on top to weight the dough. Bake for 15 minutes or until the pastry looks set. Remove the foil or paper and beans and bake for 5–10 minutes until the base is firm to the touch and light golden; or a further 15 minutes until crisp and golden brown if the pastry case requires complete baking.

SPINACH AND FETA PIE

Serves 10
Preparation 40 minutes, plus cooling
Cooking time 45 minutes

1 tbsp vegetable oil
1 onion, peeled and finely chopped
1 garlic clove, peeled and crushed
1 tbsp cumin seeds
400g (14oz) baby leaf spinach
1.1kg (2½lb) waxy potatoes, such as Desirée, boiled in their
    skins until tender, cooled, peeled and sliced
2 × 200g packs feta cheese (see page 228), crumbled
2 medium eggs, beaten
50g (2oz) butter, melted, plus extra for greasing
200g pack filo pastry, thawed if frozen
salt and ground black pepper

1 Heat the oil in a large pan and cook the onion for
10 minutes or until soft. Add the garlic and cumin, and cook
for 1–2 minutes. Add the spinach, cover and cook until the
spinach has just wilted – 1–2 minutes. Tip into a bowl and
allow to cool. Add the potatoes, cheese and eggs. Season
and mix.
2 Preheat the oven to 200°C (180°C fan oven) mark 6.
Lightly butter a 28cm (11in) tart tin. Unroll the pastry and cut
the sheets lengthways into three. Work with one-third of the
strips at a time and cover the remainder with clingfilm.
Lay a strip on the tin, starting from the middle so that half
covers the tin and half hangs over the edge. Brush with
melted butter, then lay another strip next to it, slightly
overlapping, and brush again. Repeat, working quickly
around the tin in a cartwheel shape.
3 Add the filling and level the surface. Fold in the overhanging
pastry to cover the mixture, filling any gaps with leftover
pastry. Drizzle with the remaining melted butter, then cook for
45 minutes or until golden.

COOK'S TIP
If you don't eat all the pie, it's just as delicious cold the
next day or, if you prefer, warm it in the oven at
200°C (180°C fan oven) mark 6 for 15–20 minutes.
Cover with foil if it starts to over-brown.

NUTRITION PER SERVING
311 cals | 15g fat (9g sats) | 33g carbs | 1.7g salt

PISSALADIÈRE

Serves 6
Preparation 10 minutes
Cooking time 1 hour 5 minutes

4 tbsp olive oil
3 large Spanish onions, very finely sliced
1 garlic clove, crushed
375g pack ready-rolled puff pastry
125g (4oz) roasted red peppers in oil, drained and cut into
    thin strips
50g can anchovies in olive oil, drained
12 pitted black olives, halved
1 tsp mixed dried herbs
salt and ground black pepper

1 Preheat the oven to 220°C (200°C fan oven) mark 7. Heat the oil in a deep frying pan and stir in the onions and garlic. Season with salt and pepper. Cook, uncovered, over a gentle heat for 30–40 minutes, stirring occasionally to make sure the vegetables don't stick, until the onions are meltingly soft and pale golden.
2 While the onions are cooking, unroll the pastry, cut into six equal rectangles, then arrange on two small baking sheets.
3 Divide the cooked onion among the pastry bases and spread out evenly, leaving a 1cm (½in) gap around the edges. Arrange the red peppers in a diamond-shaped lattice pattern over the onions.
4 Cut the anchovies in half lengthways and arrange on top of the onions in swirls. Dot the olives over the top. Sprinkle over the dried herbs, then cook for 20–25 minutes until the pastry is golden and crisp.

NUTRITION PER SERVING
411 cals | 28g fat (2g sats) | 3.5g carbs | 1.8g salt

LEEK AND HAM GALETTE

Serves 4
Preparation 30 minutes, plus cooling and chilling
Cooking time 40 minutes

25g (1oz) butter, plus extra to grease
350g (12oz) medium leeks, trimmed and cut into
    2cm (³/₄ in) thick slices
25g (1oz) plain flour, plus extra to dust
50ml (2fl oz) milk
1 tbsp freshly chopped marjoram
50g (2oz) Gruyère cheese, cubed, plus 2 tbsp, grated
150g (5oz) cooked sliced ham, thickly shredded
225g (8oz) puff pastry, thawed if frozen
¹/₂ medium egg, beaten with a pinch of salt
salt and ground black pepper

1 Preheat the oven to 220°C (200°C fan oven) mark 7.
Grease a baking sheet. Cook the leeks in boiling salted water
for 2–3 minutes until just beginning to soften. Drain, keeping
the cooking liquid to one side. Plunge the leeks into cold
water, drain and dry well on kitchen paper.
2 Melt the butter in a pan, remove from the heat and mix in
the flour to form a smooth paste. Mix in 225ml (8fl oz) leek
water and the milk, stirring until smooth. Bring to the boil,
simmer for 1–2 minutes, then remove from the heat, cover
and cool for 20 minutes or until cold. Add the marjoram, leeks,
cubed cheese and ham, and season.
3 Roll out the pastry on a lightly floured surface to a
30.5 × 33cm (12 × 13in) rectangle. Cut into two rectangles,
one 15 × 30.5cm (6 × 12in) and the other 18 × 30.5cm
(7 × 12in). Put the smaller piece on to the baking sheet.
Spoon on the ham mixture, leaving a 2cm (³/₄ in) border all
the way around. Brush the border with beaten egg. Cover the
filling with the larger pastry rectangle and press the edges
together. Cut slashes in the top of the pastry to prevent the
filling seeping out. Crimp the edges to seal, then cover and
freeze for 20 minutes or until firm. Remove from the freezer,
brush again with the beaten egg and sprinkle with the grated
cheese. Bake for 20–30 minutes until brown and crisp. Serve
the galette hot.

NUTRITION PER SERVING
395 cals | 25g fat (6g sats) | 29g carbs | 2g salt

FREEZING TIP
➥ To freeze, cover the uncooked galette in clingfilm and
freeze on the baking sheet. When firm, remove from
the baking tray. Wrap in baking parchment, and then
in clingfilm.
➥ To use, thaw for 3 hours at cool room temperature on
baking parchment. Preheat the oven to 220°C (200°C fan
oven) mark 7 and put a baking tray in the oven to heat.
Brush the galette with beaten egg and sprinkle with
cheese. Put the galette on the hot tray (this will keep the
pastry base crisp) and bake for 40 minutes.

CHICKEN AND ARTICHOKE FILO PIE

Serves 4
Preparation 20 minutes
Cooking time 45 minutes

3 boneless, skinless chicken breasts, about 350g (12oz)
150ml (¼ pint) dry white wine
225g (8oz) reduced-fat soft cheese with garlic and herbs
400g can artichoke hearts, drained and quartered
4 sheets filo pastry, thawed if frozen
olive oil
1 tsp sesame seeds
salt and ground black pepper

1 Preheat the oven to 200°C (180°C fan oven) mark 6.
Put the chicken and wine in a pan and bring to the boil, then
cover and simmer for 10 minutes. Remove the chicken with a
slotted spoon and set aside. Add the cheese to the wine and
mix until smooth. Bring to the boil, then simmer the sauce
until thickened.
2 Cut the chicken into bite-size pieces, then add to the sauce
with the artichokes. Season and mix well.
3 Put the mixture in an ovenproof dish. Brush the pastry
lightly with oil, scrunch slightly and put on top of the chicken.
Sprinkle with sesame seeds, then cook for 30–35 minutes until
crisp. Serve hot.

TRY SOMETHING DIFFERENT
Replace the artichoke hearts with 225g (8oz) brown-cap
mushrooms, cooked in a little water with seasoning and
lemon juice.

NUTRITION PER SERVING
241 cals | 9g fat (5g sats) | 7g carbs | 0.2g salt

CHICKEN AND BACON PIE

Serves 4
Preparation 30 minutes, plus cooling
Cooking time about 55 minutes

1 tbsp olive oil
4 chicken breasts, cut into 2.5cm (1in) cubes
1 medium onion, peeled and sliced
1 carrot, peeled and roughly chopped
50g (2oz) smoked streaky bacon, chopped
1 tbsp flour
200ml (7fl oz) chicken stock
100ml (3½fl oz) double cream
25g (1oz) frozen peas
1½ tsp wholegrain mustard
1 tbsp freshly chopped tarragon
175g (6oz) puff pastry, thawed if frozen
plain flour to dust
1 medium egg, beaten
salt and ground black pepper

1 Heat half the oil in a large pan, then brown the chicken in batches. Remove from the pan and put to one side. Add the remaining oil and fry the onion and carrot for 10 minutes. Add the bacon and cook for 3 minutes.
2 Stir in the flour and cook for 1 minute. Gradually add the stock, stirring well. Add the cream and return the chicken and any juices to the pan. Simmer for 5 minutes or until the chicken is cooked.
3 Add the peas, mustard and tarragon, then check the seasoning. Leave to cool a little.
4 Preheat the oven to 200°C (180°C fan oven) mark 6. Put a pie funnel, if you have one, in the centre of a 1 litre (1¾ pint) pie dish or ovenproof casserole and tip in the filling. Roll out the pastry on a lightly floured surface to make a lid (make a slit for the pie funnel). Brush the pastry edges with the egg, then lay the pastry over the dish and trim with a sharp knife. Seal and brush with beaten egg and cook for 25–30 minutes until golden.

GET AHEAD
Assemble the pie, then cover and chill for up to two days. To use, brush with beaten egg and complete the recipe.

NUTRITION PER SERVING
554 cals | 34g fat (6g sats) | 24g carbs | 1.3g salt

STEAK AND KIDNEY PIE

Serves 6
Preparation 40 minutes, plus cooling
Cooking time about 1½ hours

700g (1½ lb) stewing steak, cubed and seasoned
2 tbsp plain flour, plus extra to dust
3 tbsp vegetable oil
25g (1oz) butter
1 small onion, peeled and finely chopped
175g (6oz) ox kidney, cut into small pieces
150g (5oz) flat mushrooms, cut into large chunks
small pinch of cayenne pepper
1 tsp anchovy essence
350g (12oz) puff pastry, thawed if frozen
1 large egg, beaten with pinch of salt, to glaze
salt and ground black pepper

1 Preheat the oven to 170°C (150°C fan oven) mark 3. Toss half the steak with half the flour. Heat the oil in a flameproof, non-stick casserole and add the butter. Fry the steak in batches until brown, remove and put to one side. Repeat with the remaining steak.
2 Add the onion and cook gently until soft. Return the steak to the casserole with 200ml (7fl oz) water, the kidney, mushrooms, cayenne and anchovy essence. Bring to the boil, then reduce the heat, cover and simmer for 5 minutes.
3 Transfer to the oven and cook for 1 hour or until tender. The sauce should be syrupy. If not, transfer the casserole to the hob, remove the lid, bring to the boil and bubble for 5 minutes to reduce the liquid. Leave the steak mixture to cool.
4 Preheat the oven to 200°C (180°C fan oven) mark 6. Put the steak and kidney mixture into a 900ml (1½ pint) pie dish. Pile it high to support the pastry.
5 Roll out the pastry on a lightly floured surface to 5mm (¼in) thick. Cut off four to six strips, 1cm (½in) wide. Dampen the edge of the dish with cold water, then press the pastry strips on to the edge. Dampen the pastry rim and lay the sheet of pastry on top. Press the surfaces together, trim the edge and press down with the back of a knife to seal. Brush the pastry with the glaze and score with the back of a knife. Put the pie dish on a baking sheet and cook for 30 minutes or until the pastry is golden brown and the filling is hot to the centre.

FREEZING TIP

- To freeze, complete the recipe but do not glaze or bake. Wrap the uncooked pie and freeze.
- To use, thaw at cool room temperature overnight. Glaze the pastry and add 5–10 minutes to the cooking time, covering the pie with foil if the top starts to turn too brown.

NUTRITION PER SERVING
565 cals | 36g fat (8g sats) | 26g carbs | 0.9g salt

RED ONION TARTE TATIN

Serves 12
Preparation 15 minutes
Cooking time 35–40 minutes

50g (2oz) butter
2 tbsp olive oil
1.1kg (2½lb) red onions, sliced into rounds
1 tbsp light muscovado sugar
175ml (6fl oz) white wine
4 tsp white wine vinegar
1 tbsp freshly chopped thyme, plus extra to garnish
    (optional)
450g (1lb) puff pastry
plain flour to dust
salt and ground black pepper

1 Lightly grease two 23cm (9in) non-stick sandwich tins with a little of the butter and set aside.
2 Melt the remaining butter with the oil in a large non-stick frying pan. Add the sliced onions and sugar, and fry for 10–15 minutes or until golden, keeping the onions in their rounds.
3 Preheat the oven to 220°C (200°C fan) mark 7. Add the wine, vinegar and thyme to the pan. Bring to the boil, and let it bubble until the liquid has evaporated. Season with salt and pepper, then divide the mixture between the tins and leave to cool.
4 Halve the pastry. On a lightly floured surface, roll out each piece thinly into a round shape just larger than the sandwich tin. Put one pastry round over the onion mixture in each tin and tuck in the edges. Prick the pastry dough all over with a fork.
5 Cook the tarts for 15–20 minutes or until the pastry is risen and golden. Take out of the oven and put a large warm plate over the pastry. Turn over and shake gently to release the tart, then remove the tin. Scatter with thyme, if you like, and cut into wedges to serve.

GET AHEAD
→ Complete the recipe to the end of step 4 up to one day in advance. Cover and keep in the fridge for up to 24 hours.
→ To use, complete the recipe.

> **NUTRITION PER SERVING**
> 235 cals | 15g fat (3g sats) | 23g carbs | 0.4g salt

WILD MUSHROOM PITHIVIERS

Serves 8
Preparation 1 hour, plus cooling and chilling
Cooking time about 1 hour

450g (1lb) wild mushrooms
300ml (½ pint) milk
200ml (7fl oz) double cream
2 garlic cloves, crushed
450g (1lb) floury potatoes, peeled and thinly sliced
freshly grated nutmeg
50g (2oz) butter
2 tsp freshly chopped thyme, plus fresh sprigs to garnish
2 × 500g packs puff pastry, thawed if frozen
plain flour to dust
1 large egg, beaten
salt and ground black pepper

1 Rinse the mushrooms in cold running water to remove any grit, then pat dry with kitchen paper. Roughly slice.
2 Pour the milk and cream into a large heavy-based pan and add the garlic. Bring to the boil, then add the potatoes. Bring back to the boil, then reduce the heat and simmer gently, stirring occasionally, for 15–20 minutes until the potatoes are tender. Season with salt, pepper and nutmeg. Leave to cool.
3 Melt the butter in a large frying pan. When it's sizzling, add the mushrooms and cook over a high heat, stirring all the time, for 5–10 minutes until the mushrooms are cooked and the juices have evaporated completely. Season. Stir in the chopped thyme, then set aside to cool.
4 Roll out the pastry thinly on a lightly floured surface. Cut into eight rounds, approximately 12.5cm (5in) in diameter, for the tops, and eight rounds, approximately 11.5cm (4½in) in diameter, for the bases. Put the smaller pastry rounds on baking sheets and brush the edges with beaten egg. Put a large spoonful of the cooled potato mixture in the centre of each round, leaving a 1cm (½in) border around the edge. Top with a spoonful of the mushroom mixture, then cover with the pastry tops. Press the edges together well to seal. Chill for 30 minutes–1 hour.
5 Meanwhile, preheat the oven to 220°C (200°C fan oven) mark 7 and put two baking sheets in to heat up. Use the back of a knife to scallop the edges of the pastry and brush the top with the remaining beaten egg. If you like, use a knife to decorate the tops of the pithiviers.
6 Put the pithiviers, on their baking sheets, on the preheated baking trays. Cook for 15–20 minutes until deep golden brown, swapping the trays around in the oven halfway through cooking. Serve immediately, garnished with thyme sprigs.

GET AHEAD

For convenience, complete the recipe to the end of step 4, then cover and chill overnight until ready to cook.

NUTRITION PER SERVING
710 cals | 51g fat (12g sats) | 58g carbs | 1.2g salt

CORNISH PASTIES

Serves 6
Preparation 30 minutes
Cooking time 1¹/₄ hours

450g (1lb) stewing steak, trimmed and cut into very small
    pieces
175g (6oz) potato, peeled and diced
175g (6oz) swede, peeled and diced
1 onion, peeled and chopped
1 tbsp freshly chopped thyme
1 tbsp freshly chopped parsley
1 tbsp Worcestershire sauce
shortcrust pastry (see page 327), made with
    500g (1lb 2oz) plain flour
plain flour to dust
25g (1oz) butter
1 medium egg, beaten, to glaze
salt and ground black pepper
salad to serve (optional)

1 Preheat the oven to 220°C (200°C fan oven) mark 7.
Put the meat into a bowl with the potato, swede and onion.
Add the chopped herbs, Worcestershire sauce and seasoning,
then mix well.
2 Divide the pastry into six and roll out each piece thinly on
a lightly floured surface to a 20.5cm (8in) round. Spoon the
filling on to one half of each round and top with a small knob
of butter.
3 Brush the edges of the pastry with water, then fold the
uncovered side over to make pasties. Press the edges firmly
together to seal and crimp them. Make a slit in the top of
each pasty. Put on a baking sheet.
4 Brush the pastry with beaten egg to glaze and bake the
pasties for 15 minutes. Reduce the oven setting to 170°C
(150°C fan oven) mark 3 and bake for a further 1 hour to
cook the filling. Serve the pasties warm or cold with salad,
if you like.

NUTRITION PER SERVING
756 cals | 42g fat (25g sats) | 74g carbs | 1.1g salt

QUICHE LORRAINE

Serves 8
Preparation 35 minutes, plus chilling
Cooking time 1 hour

shortcrust pastry (see page 327), made with 200g (7oz)
    plain flour, pinch of salt, 100g (3½oz) chilled butter
    plus 1 large egg
plain flour to dust

For the filling
5 large eggs
225g (8oz) unsmoked streaky bacon, rind removed
40g (1½oz) butter
125g (4oz) shallots, onions or spring onions, peeled and
    finely chopped
400g (14oz) crème fraîche
100g (3½oz) Gruyère cheese, grated
salt and ground black pepper
crispy bacon and fried spring onions to garnish

1 Preheat the oven to 200°C (180°C fan oven) mark 6.
Roll out the pastry thinly on a lightly floured surface and use
to line a 23cm (9in), 3cm (1¼in) deep, loose-based tart tin.
Bake the pastry case blind (see page 326). Meanwhile, lightly
whisk the eggs for the filling. Use a little to brush the inside of
the pastry case and return it to the oven for 5 minutes to seal
any cracks. Lower the oven setting to 190°C (170°C fan
oven) mark 5.
2 Cut the bacon into 5mm (¼in) strips. Put the bacon
in a pan of cold water and bring to the boil. Drain, refresh
under cold water and dry on kitchen paper.
3 Melt the butter in a frying pan, add the shallots or onions
and cook for 1 minute. Add the bacon and cook, stirring,
until brown.
4 Mix the eggs with the crème fraîche and cheese, and
season. Put the bacon mixture in the pastry case and spoon
the crème fraîche mixture on top (see Cook's Tip). Cook for
30–35 minutes until golden and just set. Cool for 10 minutes
before serving. Garnish with bacon and fried spring onions.

COOK'S TIP
Fill the pastry case as full as possible. You may find you
have a little mixture left, as flan tins vary in size.

NUTRITION PER SERVING
595 cals | 50g fat (29g sats) | 22g carbs | 1.5g salt

BROCCOLI, GORGONZOLA AND WALNUT QUICHE

Serves 6
Preparation 15 minutes, plus chilling
Cooking time about 1 hour

400g (14oz) shortcrust pastry
plain flour to dust
150g (5oz) broccoli florets
100g (3½ oz) gorgonzola (see page 228), crumbled
2 medium eggs plus 1 egg yolk
300ml (½ pint) double cream
25g (1oz) roughly chopped walnut halves
salt and freshly ground black pepper

1 Preheat the oven to 200°C (180°C fan oven) mark 6. Roll out the pastry on a lightly floured surface until the thickness of a £1 coin, then use to line a 23cm (9in) × 2.5cm (1in) deep fluted tart tin. Prick the base all over and chill for 15 minutes. Bake blind (see page 326) for 20 minutes then for 5 minutes. Lower the oven setting to 150°C (130°C fan oven) mark 2.

2 Cook the broccoli in boiling water for 3 minutes, then drain and dry on kitchen paper. Arrange the broccoli in the pastry case and dot with the gorgonzola. Whisk together the eggs and egg yolk, cream and seasoning, then pour into the case. Scatter the walnut halves over the surface.

3 Cook the quiche for 40 minutes or until the filling is set. Serve warm or at room temperature.

FREEZING TIP

➼ To freeze, complete the recipe up to one month in advance. Cool in the tin, then wrap in clingfilm and freeze.
➼ To use, thaw completely, then serve at room temperature, or gently reheat for 20 minutes in an oven preheated to 150°C (130°C fan oven) mark 2.

NUTRITION PER SERVING
683 cals | 57g fat (27g sats) | 33g carbs | 1g salt

PUDDINGS

BAKED APPLES

Serves 6
Preparation 5 minutes, plus soaking
Cooking time 15–20 minutes

125g (4oz) hazelnuts
125g (4oz) sultanas
2 tbsp brandy
6 large Bramley apples, cored
4 tbsp soft brown sugar
100ml (3¹/₂ fl oz) apple juice
thick cream to serve

1 Preheat the oven to 190°C (170°C fan oven) mark 5. Spread the hazelnuts over a baking sheet and toast under a hot grill until golden brown, turning them frequently. Put the hazelnuts in a clean teatowel and rub off the skins, then chop the nuts. Put to one side.

2 Soak the sultanas in the brandy and put to one side for 10 minutes. Using a small sharp knife, score around the middle of the apples to stop them from bursting, then stuff each apple with equal amounts of brandy-soaked sultanas. Put the apples in a roasting tin and sprinkle with the brown sugar and apple juice. Bake for 15–20 minutes until soft.

3 Serve the apples with the toasted hazelnuts and a dollop of cream.

NUTRITION PER SERVING 280 cals |
13g fat (1g sat) | 36g carbs | 0g salt Ⓥ

SPICED PEARS

Serves 4
Preparation 15 minutes
Cooking time 50 minutes

4 Williams or Comice pears
150g (5oz) granulated sugar
300ml (¹/₂ pint) red wine
150ml (¹/₄ pint) sloe gin
1 cinnamon stick
zest of 1 orange
6 star anise
Greek yogurt or whipped cream to
    serve (optional)

1 Peel the pears, cut out the calyx at the base of each and leave the stalks intact. Put the sugar, wine, sloe gin and 300ml (¹/₂ pint) water in a small pan and heat gently until the sugar dissolves.

2 Bring to the boil and add the cinnamon stick, orange zest and star anise. Add the pears, then cover and poach over a low heat for 30 minutes or until tender.

3 Remove the pears with a slotted spoon, then continue to heat the liquid until it has reduced to about 200ml (7fl oz) or until syrupy. Pour the syrup over the pears. Serve warm or chilled with Greek yogurt or whipped cream, if you like.

GET AHEAD

Complete the recipe, cool, cover and chill for up to three days.

NUTRITION PER SERVING 305 cals |
trace fat | 52g carbs | 0g salt Ⓥ

APPLE CRUMBLE

Serves 4
Preparation 15 minutes
Cooking time 45 minutes

125g (4oz) plain flour
50g (2oz) unsalted butter, cubed
50g (2oz) golden caster sugar
450g (1lb) apples, peeled, cored and sliced
custard or double cream to serve

1 Preheat the oven to 180°C (160°C fan oven) mark 4. Put the flour into a bowl, add the butter and rub in with your fingertips until the mixture resembles fine breadcrumbs. Stir in half the sugar. Put to one side.
2 Arrange half the apples in a 1.1 litre (2 pint) pie dish and sprinkle with the rest of the sugar. Add the remaining apple slices to the dish. Spoon the crumble mixture over the fruit.
3 Bake for 45 minutes or until the fruit is soft. Serve hot with custard or a drizzle of double cream.

NUTRITION PER SERVING
425 cals | 18g fat (7g sats) | 74g carbs | 0.3g salt **V**

BLACKBERRY AND APPLE CRUMBLE

Serves 6
Preparation 45 minutes
Cooking time 25 minutes

50g (2oz) plain white flour
25g (1oz) plain wholemeal flour
75g (3oz) light muscovado sugar
50g (2oz) ground almonds
50g (2oz) unsalted butter
custard, cream or ice cream to serve

For the filling
700g (1½ lb) eating apples
50g (2oz) unsalted butter
50g (2oz) golden caster sugar
225g (8oz) blackberries

1 Preheat the oven to 190°C (170°C fan oven) mark 5. Sift the flours into a bowl, then tip in any bran from the sieve. Stir in the sugar and ground almonds, then work in the butter, using your fingertips, to make a very crumbly mixture.

2 To make the filling, quarter the apples, then peel, core and cut into 2.5cm (1in) chunks. Melt the butter in a large frying pan. Add the apples with the sugar, and cook, stirring, over a high heat for 3–5 minutes until golden brown and tender. Transfer to a 1.7 litre (3 pint) pie dish. Scatter the blackberries on top.

3 Spoon over the crumble topping and bake for 25 minutes or until the topping is golden brown. Serve warm, with custard, cream or ice cream.

TRY SOMETHING DIFFERENT
Red Fruit Crumble Replace the blackberries with 225g (8oz) mixed summer fruits, such as red and blackcurrants, raspberries and pitted cherries.

NUTRITION PER SERVING
340 cals | 18g fat (9g sats) | 43g carbs | 0.3g salt 🅥

CHERRY CLAFOUTIS

Serves 6
Preparation 20 minutes, plus 1 hour soaking
Cooking time about 1 hour

350g (12oz) cherries, pitted
3 tbsp Kirsch
125g (4oz) golden caster sugar
4 large eggs
25g (1oz) plain flour, sifted
150ml (¼ pint) milk
150ml (¼ pint) double cream
1 tsp vanilla extract
a little butter to grease

1 Put the cherries into a bowl with the Kirsch and 1 tbsp sugar. Mix together, cover and set aside for 1 hour.
2 Meanwhile, whisk together the eggs, 100g (3½oz) of the sugar and the flour in a bowl. Put the milk and cream into a small pan and bring to the boil. Pour on to the egg mixture and whisk until combined. Stir in the vanilla extract, then strain into a bowl. Cover and set aside for 30 minutes. Preheat the oven to 180°C (160°C fan oven) mark 4.
3 Lightly butter a 1.7 litre (3 pint) shallow ovenproof dish and sprinkle with the remaining caster sugar. Spoon the Kirsch-soaked cherries into the dish. Whisk the batter again, then pour it over the cherries. Bake for 50 minutes–1 hour until golden and just set. Serve warm.

TRY SOMETHING DIFFERENT
For an autumnal clafoutis, replace the cherries with blackberries, the Kirsch with blackberry or blackcurrant liqueur and the vanilla with ¼ tsp ground cinnamon.

NUTRITION PER SERVING
326 cals | 18g fat (10g sats) | 33g carbs | 0.2g salt **V**

SYRUP SPONGE PUDDING

Serves 4
Preparation 15 minutes
Cooking time 1 1/2 hours

2 tbsp golden syrup
125g (4oz) butter
125g (4oz) caster sugar
2 medium eggs, beaten
a few drops of vanilla extract
175g (6oz) self-raising flour, sifted
a little milk to mix
Fresh Vanilla Custard (see page 24) to serve

1 Half-fill a steamer or large pan with water and put it on to boil. Grease a 900ml (1 1/2 pint) pudding basin and spoon the syrup into the base.
2 Cream together the butter and sugar until pale and fluffy. Add the beaten eggs and the vanilla, a little at a time, beating well after each addition.
3 Using a metal spoon, fold in half the sifted flour, then fold in the rest, with enough milk to give a dropping consistency.
4 Pour the mixture into the prepared basin, cover with greased greaseproof paper or foil and secure with string. Steam for 1 1/2 hours. Serve with custard.

TRY SOMETHING DIFFERENT

Steamed Jam Sponge Pudding Put 4 tbsp raspberry or blackberry jam into the base of the basin instead of the syrup.
Steamed Chocolate Sponge Pudding Omit the golden syrup. Blend 4 tbsp cocoa powder with 2 tbsp hot water, then gradually beat into the creamed mixture before adding the eggs.

NUTRITION PER SERVING
582 cals | 29 fat (17g sats) | 77g carbs | 1.1g salt **V**

SPOTTED DICK

Serves 4
Preparation 20 minutes
Cooking time 2 hours

125g (4oz) fresh breadcrumbs
75g (3oz) self-raising flour
75g (3oz) shredded suet
50g (2oz) caster sugar
175g (6oz) currants
finely grated zest of 1 lemon
5 tbsp milk
Fresh Vanilla Custard (see page 24) to serve

1 Half-fill a preserving pan or large pan with water and put on to boil.
2 Put the breadcrumbs, flour, suet, sugar, currants and lemon zest in a bowl and stir well until thoroughly mixed.
3 Pour in the milk and stir until well blended. Using one hand, bring the ingredients together to form a soft, slightly sticky dough.
4 Turn the dough on to a floured surface and knead gently until just smooth. Shape into a neat roll about 15cm (6in) in length.
5 Make a 5cm (2in) pleat across a clean teatowel or pudding cloth. Or pleat together sheets of greased greaseproof paper and strong foil. Encase the roll in the cloth or foil, pleating the open edges tightly together.
6 Tie the ends securely with string to form a cracker shape. Make a string handle across the top. Lower the suet roll into the pan of boiling water and boil for 2 hours.
7 Using the string handle, lift the Spotted Dick out of the water. Put on a wire rack standing over a plate and allow the excess moisture to drain off.
8 Snip the string and gently roll the pudding out of the cloth or foil on to a warmed serving plate. Serve sliced with custard.

NUTRITION PER SERVING
502 cals | 18g fat (10g sats) | 84g carbs | 0.8g salt

JAM ROLY-POLY

Serves 4
Preparation 15 minutes
Cooking time 1½–2 hours

175g (6oz) suet crust pastry (see
   page 329)
4–6 tbsp jam
a little milk
Fresh Vanilla Custard (see page 24)
   to serve

1 Half-fill a steamer with water and
put on to boil. Grease a piece of foil
23 × 33cm (9 × 13in).
2 Roll out the suet crust pastry on a
lightly floured surface to a rectangle
about 23 × 28cm (9 × 11in). Spread
the jam on the pastry, leaving 5mm
(¼in) clear along each edge. Brush the
edges with milk and roll up the pastry
evenly, starting from one short side.
3 Put the roll on the greased foil
and wrap the foil around it loosely, to
allow room for expansion, but seal the
edges well.
4 Steam for 1½–2 hours. Remove
from the foil and serve with custard.

NUTRITION PER SERVING 345 cals |
16g fat (9g sats) | 50g carbs | 0.6g salt

STICKY TOFFEE PUDDINGS

Serves 4
Preparation 20 minutes
Cooking time 25–30 minutes,
   plus 5 minutes resting

1 tbsp golden syrup
1 tbsp black treacle
150g (5oz) butter, softened
25g (1oz) pecan nuts or walnuts, finely
   ground
75g (3oz) self-raising flour
125g (4oz) caster sugar
2 large eggs, beaten
cream or custard to serve

1 Preheat the oven to 180°C (160°C
fan oven) mark 4. Put the syrup, treacle
and 25g (1oz) butter into a bowl and
beat until smooth. Divide the mixture
among four 150ml (¼pint) timbales
or ramekins and set aside.

2 Put the nuts into a bowl, sift in the
flour and mix together well.
3 Put the remaining butter and the
sugar into a food processor and blend
briefly. (Alternatively, use a hand-held
electric whisk.) Add the eggs and the
flour mixture and blend or mix again
for 30 seconds. Spoon the mixture into
the timbales or ramekins, covering the
syrup mixture on the base. Bake for
25–30 minutes until risen and golden.
4 Remove the puddings from the oven
and leave to rest for 5 minutes, then
unmould on to warmed plates. Serve
immediately with cream or custard.

NUTRITION PER SERVING 565 cals |
38g fat (21g sats) | 53g carbs | 0.9g salt Ⓥ

CRANBERRY CHRISTMAS PUDDING

Serves 12
Preparation 20 minutes, plus soaking
Cooking time 6 hours

200g (7oz) currants
200g (7oz) sultanas
200g (7oz) raisins
75g (3oz) dried cranberries or cherries
grated zest and juice of 1 orange
50ml (2fl oz) rum
50ml (2fl oz) brandy
1–2 tsp Angostura bitters
1 small apple, grated
1 carrot, grated
175g (6oz) fresh breadcrumbs
100g (3½ oz) plain flour, sifted
1 tsp mixed spice
175g (6oz) light vegetarian suet
100g (3½ oz) dark muscovado sugar
50g (2oz) blanched almonds, roughly chopped
2 medium eggs
butter to grease
Frosted cranberries and bay leaves (see Cook's Tip),
    and icing sugar to decorate
Brandy Butter (see page 27) to serve

1 Put the dried fruit, orange zest and juice in a large bowl. Pour over the rum, brandy and Angostura bitters. Cover and leave to soak in a cool place for at least 1 hour or overnight.
2 Add the apple, carrot, breadcrumbs, flour, mixed spice, suet, sugar, almonds and eggs to the bowl of soaked fruit. Use a wooden spoon to mix everything together well. Now's the time to make a wish!
3 Grease a 1.8 litre (3¼ pint) pudding basin and line with a 60cm (24in) square piece of muslin. Spoon the mixture into the pudding basin and flatten the surface. Gather the muslin up and over the top, then twist and secure with string.
4 Put the basin on an upturned heatproof saucer or trivet in the base of a large pan. Pour in enough boiling water to come halfway up the side of the basin. Cover with a tight-fitting lid and simmer for 6 hours. Keep the water topped up. Remove the basin from the pan and leave to cool. When the pudding is cold, remove it from the basin, then wrap it in clingfilm and a double layer of foil. Store in a cool, dry place for up to six months.
5 To reheat, steam for 2½ hours; check the water level every 40 minutes and top up if necessary. Leave the pudding in the pan, covered, to keep warm until needed. Decorate with cranberries and bay leaves, and dust with icing sugar. Serve with Brandy Butter.

COOK'S TIPS
Frosted Berries and Leaves Lightly beat 1 medium egg white and spread 25g (1oz) caster sugar out on a tray, making sure there are no lumps. Brush a few fresh cranberries and bay leaves with the beaten egg white. Dip the berries and leaves into the sugar, shake off any excess, then leave to dry on a tray lined with greaseproof paper or baking parchment for about 1 hour.

NUTRITION PER SERVING
448 cals | 17g fat (7g sats) | 68g carbs | 0.3g salt ⓥ

BREAD AND BUTTER PUDDING

Serves 4
Preparation 10 minutes, plus soaking
Cooking time 30–40 minutes

50g (2oz) butter, softened, plus extra
    to grease
275g (10oz) white farmhouse bread,
    cut into 1cm (½in) slices, crusts
    removed
50g (2oz) raisins or sultanas
3 medium eggs
450ml (¾ pint) milk
3 tbsp golden icing sugar, plus extra
    to dust

1 Lightly butter four 300ml (½ pint) gratin dishes or one 1.1 litre (2 pint) ovenproof dish. Butter the bread, then cut into quarters to make triangles. Arrange the bread in the dish(es) and sprinkle with the raisins or sultanas.
2 Beat the eggs, milk and sugar in a bowl. Pour the mixture over the bread and leave to soak for 10 minutes. Preheat the oven to 180°C (160°C fan oven) mark 4.
3 Put the pudding(s) in the oven and bake for 30–40 minutes. Dust with icing sugar to serve.

NUTRITION PER SERVING 450 cals | 13g fat (5g sats) | 70g carbs | 1.1g salt **V**

RICE PUDDING

Serves 6
Preparation 5 minutes
Cooking time 1½ hours

butter to grease
125g (4oz) short-grain pudding rice
1.1 litres (2 pints) milk
50g (2oz) golden caster sugar
1 tsp vanilla extract
grated zest of 1 orange (optional)
freshly grated nutmeg to taste

1 Preheat the oven to 170°C (150°C fan oven) mark 3. Lightly butter a 1.7 litre (3 pint) ovenproof dish.
2 Put the rice, milk, sugar, vanilla extract and orange zest, if using, into the dish and stir everything together. Grate the nutmeg over the top of the mixture.
3 Bake the pudding in the middle of the oven for 1½ hours or until the top is golden brown.

NUTRITION PER SERVING 239 cals | 8g fat (5g sats) | 34g carbs | 0.2g salt **V**

WARM CHOCOLATE FONDANTS

Serves 6
Preparation 25 minutes
Cooking time 10–12 minutes

150g (5oz) unsalted butter, plus extra
    to grease
3 medium eggs, plus 3 medium egg
    yolks
50g (2oz) golden caster sugar
175g (6oz) plain chocolate (at least
    70% cocoa solids), broken into
    pieces
50g (2oz) plain flour, sifted
6 chocolate truffles

1 Preheat the oven to 200°C (180°C
fan oven) mark 6. Lightly grease six
200ml (7fl oz) ramekins. Put the
whole eggs, egg yolks and sugar into a
large bowl and beat with a hand-held
electric whisk for 8–10 minutes until
pale and fluffy.

2 Meanwhile, melt the chocolate and
butter in a heatproof bowl set over a
pan of gently simmering water, making
sure the base of the bowl doesn't touch
the water, and stirring the chocolate
mixture occasionally.
3 Stir a spoonful of the melted
chocolate into the egg mixture, then
gently fold the remaining chocolate
mixture into the egg mixture. Fold in
the flour.
4 Put a large spoonful of mixture into
each ramekin. Put a chocolate truffle in
the centre of each, taking care not to
push it down. Divide the remainder of
the mixture among the ramekins to
cover the truffle; they should be
about three-quarters full. Bake for
10–12 minutes until the top is firm and
starting to rise and crack. Serve warm.

> NUTRITION PER SERVING 502 cals |
> 37g fat (21g sats) | 39g carbs | 0.5g salt **V**

QUEEN OF PUDDINGS

Serves 4
Preparation 20 minutes, plus standing
Cooking time about 1¼ hours

4 medium eggs
600ml (1 pint) milk
125g (4oz) fresh breadcrumbs
3–4 tbsp raspberry jam
75g (3oz) caster sugar

1 Separate 3 eggs and beat together
the 3 egg yolks and 1 whole egg. Add to
the milk and mix well. Stir in the
breadcrumbs.
2 Spread the jam on the base of a pie
dish. Pour in the milk mixture and leave
for 30 minutes. Preheat the oven to
150°C (130°C fan oven) mark 2.
3 Bake in the oven for 1 hour or until
set. Put the egg whites into a clean,
grease-free bowl and whisk until they
form stiff peaks. Fold in the sugar, then
pile on top of the custard and return to
the oven for a further 15–20 minutes
until the meringue is set.

> NUTRITION PER SERVING 387 cals |
> 9g fat (3g sats) | 65g carbs | 1g salt **V**

SUMMER PUDDING

Serves 8
Preparation 10 minutes, plus overnight chilling
Cooking time 10 minutes

800g (1lb 12oz) mixed summer berries, such as 250g (9oz) each redcurrants and blackcurrants and 300g (11oz) raspberries
125g (4oz) golden caster sugar
3 tbsp crème de cassis
9 thick slices slightly stale white bread, crusts removed
crème fraîche or clotted cream to serve

1 Put the redcurrants and blackcurrants into a medium pan. Add the sugar and cassis. Bring to a simmer and cook for 3–5 minutes until the sugar has dissolved. Add the raspberries and cook for 2 minutes. Once the fruit is cooked, taste it – there should be a good balance between tart and sweet.
2 Meanwhile, line a 1 litre (1¾ pint) bowl with clingfilm. Put the base of the bowl on one piece of bread and cut around it. Put the circle of bread in the base of the bowl.
3 Line the inside of the bowl with more slices of bread, slightly overlapping them to prevent any gaps. Spoon in the fruit, making sure the juice soaks into the bread. Keep back a few spoonfuls of juice in case the bread is unevenly soaked when you turn out the pudding.
4 Cut the remaining bread to fit the top of the pudding neatly, using a sharp knife to trim any excess bread from around the edges. Wrap in clingfilm, weigh down with a saucer and a can, and chill overnight.
5 To serve, unwrap the outer clingfilm, upturn the pudding on to a plate and remove the inner clingfilm. Drizzle with the reserved juice and serve with crème fraîche or clotted cream.

NUTRITION PER SERVING
173 cals | 1g fat (trace sats) | 38g carbs | 0.4g salt **V**

SUGAR-CRUSTED FRUIT PIE

Serves 4
Preparation 30 minutes, plus chilling
Cooking time about 40 minutes, plus cooling

75g (3oz) hazelnuts
350g (12oz) cherries, stoned
75g (3oz) caster sugar, plus 2 tbsp
175g (6oz) plain flour, plus extra
    to dust
125g (4oz) butter
275g (10oz) cooking apples, peeled,
    cored and quartered

1 Spread the hazelnuts over a baking sheet. Toast under a hot grill until golden brown, turning them frequently. Put the hazelnuts in a clean teatowel and rub off the skins. Leave to cool. Put the cherries into a bowl with 25g (1oz) caster sugar. Cover and set aside.

2 For the hazelnut pastry, put 50g (2oz) hazelnuts into a food processor with the flour and pulse to a powder. Remove and set aside. In the food processor, whiz the butter with 50g (2oz) sugar. Add the flour mixture and pulse until it forms a dough. Turn out on to a lightly floured surface and knead lightly, then wrap and chill for 30 minutes. If the pastry cracks, just work it together.

3 Preheat the oven to 180°C (160°C fan oven) mark 4. Cut the apples into small chunks and put into a 900ml (1½ pint) oval pie dish. Spoon the cherries on top. Roll out the pastry on a lightly floured surface to about 5mm (¼in) thick. Cut into 1cm (½in) strips. Dampen the edge of the pie dish with a little water and press a few of the strips on to the rim to cover it. Dampen the pastry rim. Put the remaining strips over the cherries to create a lattice pattern.

4 Brush the pastry with water and sprinkle with the extra sugar. Bake for 30–35 minutes until the pastry is golden. Leave to cool for 15 minutes.

5 Chop the remaining toasted hazelnuts and sprinkle over the tart. Serve warm.

NUTRITION PER SERVING
673 cals | 38g fat (17g sats) | 79g carbs | 0.5g salt

LEMON MERINGUE PIE

Serves 8
Preparation 30 minutes, plus 1 hour chilling
Cooking time about 1 hour, plus standing

sweet pastry (see page 327), made with
    225g (8oz) plain flour, pinch of salt, 2 tbsp caster sugar,
    150g (5oz) butter, cut into pieces, 1 medium egg yolk
    and 3 tbsp cold water
plain flour to dust
a little beaten egg

For the filling and topping
7 medium eggs, 4 separated, at room temperature
finely grated zest of 3 lemons
175ml (6fl oz) freshly squeezed lemon juice
    (about 4 lemons), strained
400g can condensed milk
150ml (¼ pint) double cream
225g (8oz) golden icing sugar

1 Roll out the pastry on a lightly floured surface and use to line a 23cm (9in), 4cm (1½in) deep, loose-based fluted tart tin. Prick the base with a fork and chill for 30 minutes. Meanwhile, preheat the oven to 190°C (170°C fan oven) mark 5.
2 Bake the pastry case blind (see page 326) for 10 minutes at each stage. Brush the inside with beaten egg and put back in the oven for 1 minute to seal. Increase the oven setting to 180°C (160°C fan oven) mark 4.
3 To make the filling, put 4 egg yolks into a bowl with the 3 whole eggs. Add the lemon zest and juice, and whisk lightly. Mix in the condensed milk and cream.
4 Pour the filling into the pastry case and bake for 30 minutes or until just set in the centre. Set aside to cool while you prepare the meringue. Increase the oven setting to 200°C (180°C fan oven) mark 6.
5 For the meringue, whisk the egg whites and icing sugar together in a heatproof bowl set over a pan of gently simmering water, using a hand-held electric whisk, for 10 minutes or until shiny and thick. Take off the heat and continue to whisk at low speed for 5–10 minutes until the bowl is cool. Pile the meringue on to the filling and swirl to form peaks. Bake for 5–10 minutes until the meringue is tinged brown. Leave to stand for about 1 hour, then serve.

TRY SOMETHING DIFFERENT
Use lime zest and juice instead of lemon.

NUTRITION PER SERVING
692 cals | 36g fat (21g sats) | 83g carbs | 0.6g salt **V**

BANOFFEE PIE

Serves 14
Preparation 15 minutes, plus chilling
Cooking time 2–3 minutes

100g (3¹/₂ oz) butter, melted, plus extra
   to grease
200g (7oz) digestive biscuits, roughly
   broken
2 small bananas, peeled and sliced
8 tbsp dulce de leche toffee sauce
284ml carton double cream
1 tbsp cocoa powder to dust

1   Grease the base and sides of a 23cm (9in) loose-based tart tin or dish. Whiz the biscuits in a food processor until they resemble breadcrumbs. Pour in the melted butter and whiz briefly to combine. Press the mixture into the prepared tart tin, using the back of a metal spoon to level the surface, and leave to chill for 2 hours.

2   Arrange the banana slices evenly over the biscuit base and spoon the dulce de leche on top. Whip the cream until thick and spread it over the top. Dust with a sprinkling of cocoa powder and serve.

TRY SOMETHING DIFFERENT
- Top with a handful of toasted flaked almonds instead of the cocoa powder.
- Whiz 25g (1oz) chopped pecan nuts into the biscuits with the butter.
- Scatter grated plain dark chocolate over the cream.

> NUTRITION PER SERVING   250 cals | 19g fat (10g sats) | 18g carbs | 0.4g salt Ⓥ

CLASSIC APPLE PIE

Serves 6
Preparation 20 minutes
Cooking time 35–40 minutes

900g (2lb) cooking apples, peeled,
   cored and sliced
50g (2oz) caster sugar, plus extra to
   sprinkle
sweet pastry (see page 327), made
   with
   225g (8oz) plain flour, a pinch of
   salt, 100g (3¹/₂ oz) chilled butter
   and 1 large egg
flour to dust
cream to serve

1   Preheat the oven to 190°C (170°C fan oven) mark 5.
2   Layer the apples and sugar in a 1.1 litre (2 pint) pie dish. Sprinkle with 1 tbsp water.
3   Roll out the pastry on a lightly floured worksurface to a round 2.5cm (1in) larger than the pie dish. Cut off a strip the width of the rim of the dish, dampen the rim of the dish and press on the strip. Dampen the pastry strip and cover with the pastry circle, pressing the edges together well. Decorate the edge of the pastry and make a slit in the centre to allow steam to escape.
4   Bake for 35–40 minutes until the pastry is lightly browned. Sprinkle with caster sugar before serving with cream.

> **COOK'S TIP**
> Apple pie is also great served cold, with Vanilla Ice Cream (see page 392).

> NUTRITION PER SERVING   268 cals | 11g fat (4g sats) | 43g carbs | 0.4g salt Ⓥ

MINCE PIES

Makes 24
Preparation 15 minutes, plus chilling
Cooking time 12–15 minutes

225g (8oz) plain flour, plus extra to dust
125g (4oz) unsalted butter, chilled and diced
100g (3½oz) cream cheese (see page 228)
1 egg yolk
finely grated zest of 1 orange
400g jar mincemeat (see below)
1 egg, beaten
icing sugar to dust

1 Put the flour in a food processor. Add the butter, cream cheese, egg yolk and orange zest, and whiz until the mixture just comes together. Tip the mixture into a large bowl and bring the dough together with your hands. Shape into a ball, wrap in clingfilm and put in the freezer for 5 minutes.
2 Preheat the oven to 220°C (200°C fan) mark 7. Cut off about one-third of the pastry dough and set aside. Roll out the remainder on a lightly floured surface to 5mm (¼in) thick. Stamp out circles with a 6.5cm (2½in) cutter to make 24 rounds, re-rolling the dough as necessary. Use the pastry circles to line two 12-cup patty tins. Roll out the reserved pastry and use a star cutter to stamp out the stars.
3 Put 1 tsp mincemeat into each pastry case, then top with pastry stars. Brush the tops with beaten egg, then bake for 12–15 minutes until golden. Remove from the tins and leave to cool on a wire rack. Serve warm or cold, dusted with icing sugar. Store in an airtight container for up to four days.

TRY SOMETHING DIFFERENT
Improve the flavour of a jar of bought mincemeat by adding 2 tbsp brandy, the grated zest of 1 lemon and 25g (1oz) pecan nuts, chopped. Or, instead of the nuts, try a piece of preserved stem ginger, chopped.

Luxury Mincemeat Put the following into a large mixing bowl and mix thoroughly to combine: 350g (12oz) each seedless raisins, currants, sultanas; 150g (5oz) candied peel, finely chopped; 250g pack shredded vegetable suet; 100g (3½oz) blanched almonds, finely chopped; 350g (12oz) demerara sugar; 125g (4oz) natural glacé cherries, chopped; 2 medium Bramley apples, peeled, cored and grated; 3 tsp ground mixed spice; grated zest and juice of 1 lemon and 1 orange; 150ml (¼ pint) each brandy and Drambuie. Cover and set aside in a cool place for 24 hours, stirring from time to time. Either use the mincemeat immediately or spoon into sterilised jars, cover and seal. Store in a cool, dark place and use within three months. Makes 2.6kg (5¾lb).

NUTRITION PER SERVING
150 cals | 8g fat (4g sats) | 17g carbs | 0.2g salt **V**

TREACLE TART

Cuts into 6 slices
Preparation 25 minutes, plus chilling
Cooking time 45–50 minutes, plus cooling

sweet pastry (see page 327), made with 225g (8oz) plain
    flour, 150g (5oz) unsalted butter, 15g (½oz) golden
    caster sugar and 1 medium egg yolk
plain flour to dust

For the filling
700g (1½lb) golden syrup
175g (6oz) fresh white breadcrumbs
grated zest of 3 lemons
2 medium eggs, lightly beaten

1 Preheat the oven to 180°C (160°C fan oven) mark 4.
Roll out the pastry on a lightly floured surface and use to
line a 25.5cm (10in), 4cm (1½in) deep, loose-based fluted tart
tin. Prick the base all over with a fork and chill for 30 minutes.
2 To make the filling, heat the syrup in a pan over a low heat
until thinner in consistency. Remove from the heat and mix in
the breadcrumbs and lemon zest. Stir in the beaten eggs.
3 Pour the filling into the pastry case and bake for
45–50 minutes until the filling is lightly set and golden.
Allow to cool slightly. Serve warm.

TRY SOMETHING DIFFERENT
For the pastry, replace half the plain flour with wholemeal
flour. For the filling, use fresh wholemeal breadcrumbs instead
of white.

NUTRITION PER SLICE
486 cals | 15g fat (8g sats) 88g carbs | 1.1g salt **V**

ALMOND BAKEWELL TARTS

Makes 6
Preparation 25 minutes, plus chilling
Cooking time 50 minutes, plus cooling

sweet pastry (see page 327), made with
200g (7oz) plain flour, 100g (3¹/₂ oz) unsalted butter,
75g (3oz) caster sugar, 3 large egg yolks and ¹/₂ tsp
vanilla extract
plain flour to dust
Plum Sauce (see Cook's Tip) to serve

For the filling
125g (4oz) unsalted butter, softened
125g (4oz) caster sugar
3 large eggs
125g (4oz) ground almonds
2–3 drops almond essence
6 tbsp redcurrant jelly

For the crumble topping
25g (1oz) unsalted butter
75g (3oz) plain flour
25g (1oz) caster sugar

1 Roll out the pastry thinly on a lightly floured surface and
line six 10cm (4in), 3cm (1¹/₄in) deep tartlet tins. Chill for 30
minutes. Preheat the oven to 190°C (170°C fan oven) mark 5.
2 Bake the tartlet cases blind (see page 326). Remove from
the oven and leave to cool.
3 To make the filling, beat the butter and sugar together
until light and fluffy. Gradually beat in 2 eggs, then beat in the
remaining egg with one-third of the ground almonds. Fold in
the remaining almonds and the almond essence.
4 Melt the redcurrant jelly in a small pan and brush over
the inside of each pastry case. Spoon in the almond filling.
Put the tarts on a baking sheet and bake for 20–25 minutes
until golden and just firm. Leave in the tins for 10 minutes,
then unmould on to a wire rack and leave to cool completely.
5 To make the crumble topping, rub the butter into the
flour and add the sugar. Spread evenly on a baking sheet and
grill until golden. Cool, then sprinkle over the tarts. Decorate
with plums (see right) and serve with Plum Sauce.

COOK'S TIP
Plum Sauce Put 450g (1lb) halved and stoned ripe
plums, 50–75g (2–3oz) soft brown sugar and 150ml
(¹/₄ pint) sweet white wine into a pan with 150ml (¹/₄ pint)
water. Bring to the boil, then simmer until tender.
Remove 3 plums to decorate; thickly slice and put to
one side. Cook the remaining plums for about 15 minutes
until very soft. Put into a food processor and whiz
until smooth. Sieve, if you like, adding more sugar to
taste. Leave to cool.

NUTRITION PER SERVING
931 cals | 52g fat (24g sats) | 104g carbs | 0.8g salt **V**

TARTE TATIN

Cuts into 6 slices
Preparation 30 minutes, plus chilling
Cooking time about 1 hour, plus cooling

sweet pastry (see page 327), made with 225g (8oz) plain
    flour, 1/4 tsp salt, 150g (5oz) unsalted butter, 50g (2oz)
    golden icing sugar in addition to the caster sugar,
    1 medium egg and 2–3 drops vanilla extract
plain flour to dust

For the filling
200g (7oz) golden caster sugar
125g (4oz) chilled unsalted butter
1.4–1.6kg (3–3½ lb) crisp dessert apples, peeled and cored
juice of ½ lemon

1 To make the filling, sprinkle the sugar over the base of a
20.5cm (8in) tarte tatin tin or ovenproof frying pan. Cut the
butter into slivers and arrange on the sugar. Halve the apples
and pack them tightly, cut-side up, on top of the butter.
2 Put the tin or pan on the hob and cook over a medium heat
for 30 minutes (making sure it doesn't bubble over or catch on
the bottom) or until the butter and sugar turn a dark golden
brown (see Cook's Tip). Sprinkle with the lemon juice, then
allow to cool for 15 minutes. Meanwhile, preheat the oven to
220°C (200°C fan oven) mark 7.
3 Put the pastry on a large sheet of lightly floured baking
parchment. Roll out the pastry to make a round 2.5cm
(1in) larger than the tin or pan. Prick several times with a fork.
Lay the pastry over the apples, tucking the edges down the
side of the tin. Bake for 25–30 minutes until golden brown.
Leave in the tin for 10 minutes, then carefully upturn on to a
serving plate. Serve warm.

COOK'S TIP
When caramelising the apples in step 2, be patient. Allow
the sauce to turn a dark golden brown – any paler and it
will be too sickly. Don't let it burn, though, as this will
make the caramel taste bitter.

NUTRITION PER SERVING
727 cals | 39g fat (24g sats) | 94g carbs | 0.7g salt

MAPLE PECAN TART

Serves 10
Preparation 40 minutes, plus chilling
Cooking time 1¼ hours

250g (9oz) plain flour, sifted
a large pinch of salt
225g (8oz) unsalted butter, cubed and chilled
100g (3½ oz) light muscovado sugar
125g (4oz) dates, stoned and roughly chopped
grated zest and juice of ½ lemon
100ml (3½ fl oz) maple syrup, plus 6 tbsp extra
1 tsp vanilla extract
4 medium eggs
300g (11oz) pecan nut halves
300ml (½ pint) double cream
2 tbsp bourbon whiskey

1 Put the flour and salt into a food processor. Add 125g
(4oz) of the butter and whiz to fine crumbs. (Alternatively,
rub the butter into the flour in a large bowl by hand or using
a pastry cutter.) Add 2 tbsp water and whiz, or stir, until the
mixture just comes together. Wrap in clingfilm and chill for
30 minutes. Use to line a 28 × 4cm (11 × 1½ in) loose-based
tart tin, then cover and chill for 30 minutes. Preheat the oven
to 200°C (180°C fan oven) mark 6.
2 Bake blind (see page 326) for 25 minutes, then for a
further 5 minutes or until the base is dry and light golden.
3 Meanwhile, whiz, or beat, the rest of the butter until soft.
Add the sugar and dates and whiz, or beat, to cream together.
Add the lemon zest and juice, 100ml (3½ fl oz) maple syrup,
the vanilla extract, eggs and 200g (7oz) nuts. Whiz until the
nuts are finely chopped – the mixture will look curdled. Pour
into the pastry case and top with the rest of the nuts.
4 Bake for 40–45 minutes until almost set in the middle.
Cover with greaseproof paper for the last 10 minutes if the
nuts turn very dark. Cool slightly before removing from the
tin, then brush with 4 tbsp maple syrup. Lightly whip the
cream with the whiskey and 2 tbsp maple syrup, then serve
with the pie.

TRY SOMETHING DIFFERENT
Replace the lemon with orange, the pecans with walnut halves
and the whiskey with Cointreau.

NUTRITION PER SERVING
748 cals | 57g fat (24g sats) | 51g carbs | 0.6g salt **V**

VANILLA EGG CUSTARD TART

Serves 6
Preparation 40 minutes, plus chilling
Cooking time 1 hour, plus cooling

sweet pastry (see page 327), made with
    175g (6oz) plain flour, 125g (4oz) unsalted butter,
    25g (1oz) vanilla sugar, 1 tsp grated orange zest and
    1 medium egg yolk
flour to dust
175g (6oz) raspberries (optional)
vanilla sugar to dust

For the vanilla custard
2 large eggs, plus 2 large egg yolks
40g (1¹/₂ oz) golden caster sugar
450ml (³/₄ pint) single cream
¹/₂ vanilla pod, split lengthways

1 Roll out the pastry on a lightly floured work surface and use to line a 20.5cm (8in), 4cm (1¹/₂ in) deep, loose-based fluted tart tin. Prick the base all over with a fork. Chill for 30 minutes.

2 Preheat the oven to 200°C (180°C fan oven) mark 6. Bake the pastry case blind (see page 326). Remove from the oven and leave to cool for 15 minutes. Reduce the oven temperature to 150°C (130°C fan oven) mark 2.

3 Meanwhile, make the vanilla custard. Put the whole eggs, egg yolks and sugar into a bowl and beat well. Put the cream and vanilla pod into a small pan over a very low heat until the cream is almost boiling. Pour on to the egg mixture, whisking constantly, then strain into the pastry case.

4 Put the tart back into the oven. Bake for 45 minutes or until the centre is softly set. Leave until cold, then carefully remove from the tin. Top with raspberries, if you like, and dust with vanilla sugar.

TRY SOMETHING DIFFERENT

Chocolate Custard Tart Replace 25g (1oz) of the flour with sifted cocoa powder. For the custard, omit the vanilla pod and heat 375ml (13fl oz) single cream with 100g (3¹/₂ oz) chopped plain chocolate (70% cocoa solids), until melted and just simmering.

NUTRITION PER SERVING
497 cals | 36g fat (21g sats) | 36g carbs | 0.4g salt **Ⓥ**

CHOCOLATE ORANGE TART

Serves 8
Preparation 30 minutes, plus chilling
Cooking time about 1 hour, plus cooling

sweet pastry (see page 327), made with 150g (5oz) plain
    flour, a pinch of salt, 75g (3oz) unsalted butter, 25g (1oz)
    golden icing sugar in addition to the caster sugar, grated
    zest of 1 orange and 2 large egg yolks
flour to dust
icing sugar to dust

For the filling
175g (6oz) plain chocolate (at least 50% cocoa solids),
    chopped
175ml (6fl oz) double cream
75g (3oz) light muscovado sugar
2 medium eggs
1 tbsp Grand Marnier or Cointreau

1 Roll out the pastry on a lightly floured work surface and
use to line a 20.5cm (8in) loose-based tart tin. Prick the base
all over with a fork, put the tin on a baking sheet and chill for
30 minutes. Preheat the oven to 190°C (170°C fan oven)
mark 5.
2 Bake the pastry case blind (see page 326). Remove from
the oven and put to one side. Reduce the oven temperature
to 170°C (150°C fan oven) mark 3.
3 To make the filling, melt the chocolate in a heatproof bowl
set over a pan of gently simmering water, making sure the
base of the bowl doesn't touch the water. Remove the bowl
from the pan and leave to cool for 10 minutes.
4 Put the cream, muscovado sugar, eggs and liqueur into
a bowl and stir, using a wooden spoon to mix thoroughly.
Gradually stir in the chocolate, then pour into the pastry
case and bake for 20 minutes or until just set.
5 Serve warm or cold, dusted liberally with icing sugar.

TRY SOMETHING DIFFERENT
Omit the orange zest and replace the Grand Marnier with
crème de menthe.

NUTRITION PER SERVING
441 cals | 28g fat (17g sats) | 42g carbs | 0.2g salt ⓥ

LEMON TART

Serves 8
Preparation 30 minutes, plus chilling
Cooking time 40–50 minutes

butter to grease
plain flour to dust
sweet pastry (see page 327), made with 150g (5oz) plain
    flour, 75g (3oz) unsalted butter, 50g (2oz) icing sugar
    and 2 large egg yolks
peach slices and fresh or frozen raspberries, thawed,
    to decorate
icing sugar to dust

For the filling
1 large egg, plus 4 large egg yolks
150g (5oz) caster sugar
grated zest of 4 lemons
150ml (¼ pint) freshly squeezed lemon juice (about 4
    medium lemons)
150ml (¼ pint) double cream

1 Grease and flour a 23cm (9in), 2.5cm (1in) deep,
loose-based flan tin. Roll out the pastry on a lightly floured
worksurface into a round – if the pastry sticks to the surface,
gently ease a palette knife under it to loosen. Line the tin with
the pastry and trim the excess. Prick the base all over with a
fork. Chill for 30 minutes.
2 Preheat the oven to 190°C (170°C fan oven) mark 5. Put
the tin on a baking sheet and bake the pastry case blind (see
page 326). Remove from the oven, leaving the flan tin on the
baking sheet. Reduce the oven temperature to 170°C (150°C
fan oven) mark 3.
3 Meanwhile, to make the filling, put the whole egg, egg
yolks and caster sugar into a bowl and beat together with
a wooden spoon or balloon whisk until smooth. Carefully
stir in the lemon zest, lemon juice and cream. Leave to stand
for 5 minutes.
4 Ladle three-quarters of the filling into the pastry case,
position the baking sheet on the oven shelf and ladle in the
remainder. Bake for 25–30 minutes until the filling bounces
back when touched lightly in the centre. Cool for 15 minutes
to serve warm, or cool completely and chill. Decorate with
peaches and raspberries and dust with icing sugar.

COOK'S TIPS
Remember that ovens vary, so check the tart after
15 minutes of cooking. Turn round if cooking unevenly,
otherwise the eggs might curdle.

NUTRITION PER SERVING
385 cals | 23g fat (13g sats) | 42g carbs | 0.2g salt

RASPBERRY MILLES FEUILLES

Serves 8
Preparation 40 minutes, plus chilling and standing
Cooking time 40 minutes, plus cooling

550g (1¼lb) puff pastry, thawed if frozen
plain flour to dust
25g (1oz) caster sugar, plus 3 tbsp
50g (2oz) hazelnuts, toasted and chopped
225g (8oz) raspberries
1 tbsp lemon juice
1 × quantity Confectioner's Custard (see Cook's Tip)
300ml (½ pint) double cream
50g (2oz) icing sugar, sifted

1 Cut the pastry into three and roll out each piece on a lightly floured surface into an 18 × 35.5cm (7 × 14in) rectangle. Put each on a baking sheet, prick and chill for 30 minutes.
2 Preheat the oven to 220°C (200°C fan oven) mark 7. Bake the pastry for 10 minutes, then turn the pieces over and cook for another 3 minutes. Sprinkle each sheet with 1 tbsp caster sugar and one-third of the nuts. Return to the oven for 8 minutes or until the sugar dissolves. Cool slightly, then transfer to wire racks to cool.
3 Sprinkle the raspberries with 25g (1oz) caster sugar and the lemon juice. Beat the custard until smooth and whip the cream until thick, then fold the cream into the custard with the raspberries and juices. Cover and chill.
4 Put the icing sugar into a bowl, then stir in 2 tbsp water. Trim each pastry sheet to 15 × 30.5cm (6 × 12in), then drizzle with the icing. Leave for 15 minutes.
5 Spoon half the custard over a sheet of pastry. Put another sheet on top and spoon on the remaining custard. Top with the final sheet and press down lightly. Leave for 30 minutes before slicing.

NUTRITION PER SERVING
828 cals | 57g fat (23g sats) | 65g carbs | 1.4g salt

PEAR AND CRANBERRY STRUDEL

Serves 8
Preparation 20 minutes
Cooking time 40–45 minutes

75g (3oz) butter, melted, plus extra to grease
125g (4oz) fresh cranberries
550g (1¼lb) Williams or Comice pears, cored and sliced
50g (2oz) Brazil nuts, chopped and toasted (see Cook's Tip, page 312)
grated zest and juice of 1 lemon
25g (1oz) golden caster sugar
1 tbsp fresh white breadcrumbs
1 tsp ground cinnamon
7 sheets filo pastry, thawed if frozen
icing sugar to dust

1 Preheat the oven to 190°C (170°C fan oven) mark 5. Grease a large baking sheet. Toss the cranberries with the pears, nuts and lemon juice. Mix the lemon zest with 1 tbsp caster sugar, the breadcrumbs and cinnamon, then combine with the cranberry mixture.

2 Lay a clean teatowel on a board and put three sheets of filo pastry on to it, each overlapping the other by 2.5cm (1in) to make a 56 × 48cm (22 × 19in) rectangle. Brush with melted butter, then put three more sheets on top and brush again.

3 Spoon the pear mixture on to the pastry and roll up from a long edge. Carefully lift on to the baking sheet, placing it seam side down. Cut the remaining filo pastry into strips, crumple and place on the strudel; brush with melted butter. Sprinkle the strudel with the remaining caster sugar and bake for 40–45 minutes, covering with foil if the top browns too quickly. Dust the strudel with icing sugar. Serve warm.

TRY SOMETHING DIFFERENT

Replace the lemon zest and juice with orange, the cranberries with blueberries and the Brazil nuts with hazelnuts.

NUTRITION PER SERVING
190 cals | 12g fat (6g sats) | 9g carbs | 0.2g salt **V**

PROFITEROLES

Serves 6
Preparation 25 minutes
Cooking time 30 minutes, plus cooling and chilling

65g (2½ oz) plain flour
a pinch of salt
50g (2oz) butter, diced
2 large eggs, lightly beaten
300ml (½ pint) double cream
a few drops of vanilla extract
1 tsp caster sugar

For the chocolate sauce
225g (8oz) plain chocolate (at least 70% cocoa solids),
    broken into pieces
140ml (4½ fl oz) double cream
1–2 tbsp Grand Marnier to taste (optional)
1–2 tsp golden caster sugar to taste (optional)

1 Preheat the oven to 220°C (200°C fan oven) mark 7. Sift the flour with the salt on to a sheet of greaseproof paper. Put the butter into a medium heavy-based pan with 150ml (¼ pint) water. Heat gently until the butter melts, then bring to a rapid boil. Take off the heat and immediately tip in all the flour and beat thoroughly with a wooden spoon until the mixture is smooth and forms a ball. Turn into a bowl and leave to cool for about 10 minutes.

2 Gradually add the eggs to the mixture, beating well after each addition. Ensure that the mixture becomes thick and shiny before adding any more egg – if added too quickly, the paste will become runny and the cooked buns will be flat.

3 Sprinkle a large baking sheet with a little water. Using two damp teaspoons, spoon about 18 small mounds of the choux paste on to the baking sheet, spacing well apart to allow room for them to expand. (Alternatively, spoon the choux paste into a piping bag fitted with a 1cm (½ in) plain nozzle and pipe mounds on to the baking sheet.)

4 Bake for 25 minutes or until well risen, crisp and golden brown. Make a small hole in the side of each bun to allow the steam to escape and then put back in the oven for a further 5 minutes or until thoroughly dried out. Slide on to a large wire rack and put to one side to cool.

5 To make the sauce, put the chocolate and cream in a medium pan with 4 tbsp water. Heat gently, stirring occasionally, until the chocolate melts to a smooth sauce; do not boil. Remove from the heat.

6 To assemble, lightly whip the cream with the vanilla extract and sugar until it just holds its shape. Pipe into the hole in each choux bun, or split the buns open and spoon in the cream. Chill for up to 2 hours.

7 Just before serving, gently reheat the chocolate sauce. Add Grand Marnier and sugar to taste, if you like. Divide the choux buns among serving bowls and pour the warm chocolate sauce over them. Serve immediately.

TRY SOMETHING DIFFERENT

Éclairs Put the choux pastry into a piping bag fitted with a medium plain nozzle and pipe 9cm (3½in) long fingers on to the baking sheet. Trim with a wet knife. Bake at 200°C (180°C fan oven) mark 6 for about 35 minutes until crisp and golden. Using a sharp, pointed knife, make a slit down the side of each bun to release the steam, then transfer to a wire rack and leave for 20–30 minutes to cool completely. Just before serving, whip 300ml (½ pint) double cream until stiff and use it to fill the éclairs. Break 125g (4oz) plain chocolate into a bowl set over a pan of simmering water, making sure the base of the bowl doesn't touch the water. Stir until melted. Pour into a wide shallow bowl and dip the top of each filled éclair into it, drawing each one across the surface of the chocolate. Leave to set. Makes 12.

NUTRITION PER SERVING
652 cals | 59g fat (33g sats) | 35g carbs | 0.3g salt Ⓥ

WARM GINGER RICOTTA CAKE

Serves 8
Preparation 25 minutes
Cooking time 1¼ hours, plus cooling

75g (3oz) unsalted butter, melted, plus extra to grease
225g (8oz) digestive biscuits
200g (7oz) cream cheese
225g (8oz) ricotta cheese (see page 228)
4 tbsp double cream
3 medium eggs, separated
1 tbsp cornflour
1 piece of preserved stem ginger in syrup, finely chopped,
    plus 1 tbsp syrup
125g (4oz) icing sugar
Ginger and Whisky Sauce to serve (optional, see
    Cook's Tips)

1 Preheat the oven to 200°C (180°C fan oven) mark 6.
Grease a 20.5cm (8in) springform cake tin. Whiz the biscuits
in a food processor until they resemble breadcrumbs.
(Alternatively, put them in a plastic bag and crush with a
rolling pin.) Put the biscuits into a bowl, add the melted butter
and mix to combine. Tip just over half the crumb mixture into
the prepared tin and press evenly into the base and up the
sides. Put to one side while you make the filling.
2 Beat together, or whiz in a food processor, the cheeses,
cream, egg yolks, cornflour, ginger and syrup. Transfer to
a bowl.
3 Put the egg whites into a clean, grease-free bowl and
whisk until soft peaks form. Gradually whisk in the icing sugar,
keeping the mixture stiff and shiny. Fold into the ginger
mixture. Spoon on to the biscuit base. Smooth the surface.
Sprinkle the top with the remaining crumbs.
4 Bake for 30 minutes. Reduce the oven temperature to
180°C (160°C fan oven) mark 4, cover the cake loosely with
foil and bake for a further 45 minutes. The cake should be just
set in the centre. Cool for 15 minutes on a wire rack.
5 Serve warm, with Ginger and Whisky Sauce, if you like.

COOK'S TIPS
➙ **Ginger and Whisky Sauce** Gently heat 300ml
(½ pint) single cream with 2 tsp preserved stem
ginger syrup and 1 tsp whisky. Serve just warm,
with the cake.
➙ The cake may also be served with sliced oranges
soaked in ginger syrup and Cointreau.

NUTRITION PER SERVING
494 cals | 36g fat (21g sats) | 38g carbs | 0.8g salt

CLASSIC BAKED CHEESECAKE

Cuts into 12 slices
Preparation 30 minutes, plus chilling
Cooking time 55 minutes, plus cooling and chilling

125g (4oz) unsalted butter, melted, plus extra to grease
250g pack digestive biscuits

For the filling
2 large lemons
2 × 250g cartons curd cheese (see page 228)
142ml carton soured cream
2 medium eggs
175g (6oz) golden caster sugar
1¹/₂ tsp vanilla extract
1 tbsp cornflour
50g (2oz) sultanas

1 Grease a 20.5cm (8in) springform cake tin. Whiz the biscuits in a food processor until they resemble breadcrumbs. (Alternatively, put them in a plastic bag and crush with a rolling pin.) Put the biscuit crumbs into a bowl, add the melted butter and mix until well combined. Tip the crumb mixture into the prepared tin and press evenly on to the base, using the back of a metal spoon to level the surface. Chill for 1 hour or until firm.

2 Preheat the oven to 180°C (160°C fan oven) mark 4. To make the filling, grate the zest from 1 of the lemons and set aside. Halve the same lemon and squeeze out the juice. Halve the other lemon and cut into very thin slices.

3 Put the lemon zest, lemon juice, curd cheese, soured cream, eggs, sugar, vanilla extract and cornflour into a large bowl. Using a hand-held electric whisk, beat together until thick and smooth, then fold in the sultanas. Pour the mixture into the tin and shake gently to level the surface.

4 Bake for 30 minutes. Put the lemon slices, overlapping, on top. Bake for a further 20–25 minutes until the cheesecake is just set and golden brown. Turn off the oven and leave the cheesecake inside, with the door ajar, until it is cool, then chill for at least 2 hours or overnight.

5 Remove the cheesecake from the fridge about 30 minutes before serving. Run a knife around the edge, release the clasp on the tin and remove the cake. Cut the cheesecake into slices to serve.

NUTRITION PER SLICE
340 cals | 19g fat (11g sats) | 36g carbs | 1g salt

PLAIN CRÊPES

Makes 8
Preparation 10 minutes, plus optional standing
Cooking time about 15 minutes

125g (4oz) plain flour
a pinch of salt
1 medium egg
300ml ($^1/_2$ pint) milk
a little oil, to fry
golden caster sugar and lemon juice to serve

1 Sift the flour and salt into a bowl and make a well in the centre. Add the egg and whisk well with a balloon whisk. Gradually beat in the milk, drawing in the flour from the sides to make a smooth batter. Cover and leave to stand, if possible, for 20 minutes.
2 Heat a few drops of oil in an 18cm (7in) heavy-based crêpe pan or non-stick frying pan. Pour in just enough batter to thinly coat the bottom of the pan. Cook over a medium-high heat for about 1 minute until golden brown. Turn or toss and cook the second side for $^1/_2$–1 minute until golden.
3 Transfer the crêpe to a plate and keep hot. Repeat to cook the remaining batter, stacking the cooked crêpes on top of each other with greaseproof paper in between; keep warm in the oven while cooking the remaining crêpes.
4 Serve as soon as the crêpes are all cooked, sprinkled with sugar and lemon juice.

TRY SOMETHING DIFFERENT
Buckwheat Crêpes Replace half the flour with buckwheat flour and add an extra egg white
Lemon, Orange or Lime Crêpes Add the finely grated zest of 1 lemon, $^1/_2$ orange or 1 lime, with the milk.
Chocolate Crêpes Replace 15g ($^1/_2$oz) of the flour with sifted cocoa powder.

NUTRITION PER CRÊPE
100 cals | 3g fat (1g sats) | 16g carbs | 0.2g salt **V**

CRÊPES SUZETTE

Serves 4
Preparation 20 minutes, plus standing
Cooking time 15 minutes

1 quantity crêpe batter (see opposite)
1 tsp golden icing sugar
grated zest of ½ orange
a knob of butter, plus extra to fry
2 tbsp brandy

For the orange sauce
50g (2oz) golden caster sugar
50g (2oz) butter
juice of 2 oranges
grated zest of 1 lemon
3 tbsp Cointreau

1 Flavour the crêpe batter with the icing sugar and orange zest, then leave to stand for 30 minutes. Just before cooking the crêpes, melt the knob of butter and stir it into the batter.
2 To cook the crêpes, heat a small amount of butter in a 15–18cm (6–7in) heavy-based frying pan. Pour in just enough batter to cover the base, swirling it to coat. Cook over a medium heat for about 1 minute or until the crêpe is golden underneath. Using a palette knife, flip it over and cook briefly on the other side. Lift on to a plate, cover with greaseproof paper and keep warm while you cook the others in the same way, interleaving each with a square of greaseproof paper to keep them separated.
3 To make the orange sauce, put the sugar into a large heavy-based frying pan and heat gently, shaking the pan occasionally, until the sugar has melted and turned golden brown. Remove from the heat and add the butter, orange juice and lemon zest. Return the pan to the heat, and stir the sauce until it begins to simmer. Add the Cointreau.
4 Fold each crêpe in half and then in half again. Put all the crêpes back into the pan and simmer for a few minutes to reheat, spooning the sauce over them.
5 To flambé, warm the brandy and pour it over the crêpes. Using a taper and standing well clear, ignite the brandy. When the flame dies down, serve at once.

NUTRITION PER SERVING
392 cals | 16g fat (9g sats) | 48g carbs | 0.7g salt Ⓥ

WAFFLES

Serves 4
Preparation 5 minutes
Cooking time 16 minutes

125g (4oz) self-raising flour
a pinch of salt
1 tbsp caster sugar
1 medium egg, separated
25g (1oz) butter, melted
150ml (¼ pint) milk
½ tsp vanilla flavouring (optional)
butter and golden or maple syrup to serve

1 Heat the waffle iron according to the manufacturer's instructions.
2 Mix the flour, salt and sugar together in a bowl. Add the egg yolk, melted butter, milk and flavouring, if using, and beat to give a smooth coating batter.
3 Put the egg white into a clean, grease-free bowl and whisk until it forms stiff peaks; fold into the batter. Pour just enough batter into the iron to run over the surface.
4 Close the iron and cook for 2–3 minutes, turning the iron if using a non-electric type. When the waffle is cooked, it should be golden brown and crisp and easily removed from the iron – if it sticks, cook for a minute longer. Cook the remainder in the same way.
5 Serve immediately with butter and golden or maple syrup. Alternatively, layer the waffles with whipped cream or vanilla ice cream and fresh fruit.

NUTRITION PER SERVING
207 cals | 8g fat (4g sats) | 31g carbs | 0.8g salt **V**

AMERICAN-STYLE PANCAKES

Makes 12
Preparation 10 minutes, plus standing
Cooking time about 15 minutes

175g (6oz) self-raising flour
1 tsp baking powder
1 tsp bicarbonate of soda
a pinch of salt
50g (2oz) caster sugar
1 large egg, beaten
300ml (½ pint) buttermilk
50g (2oz) butter, melted and cooled slightly,
    plus extra for frying
milk (optional)
crispy streaky bacon and maple syrup to serve

1 In a bowl, sift together the flour, baking powder and
bicarbonate of soda with a pinch of salt. Stir in the sugar.
2 Combine the egg, buttermilk and butter, and gradually
whisk into the flour to make a smooth batter – it should be
the consistency of thick double cream, so add a drop of milk
if necessary. Leave to stand for 5 minutes.
3 Put a large frying pan over a medium heat until hot. Brush
the surface with a little melted butter. Pour about 2 tbsp of
the mixture into the pan to form a 10cm (4in) circle – the
mixture should spread naturally to that size if it is the right
consistency. Cook for 2 minutes or until small holes appear on
the surface, then turn over and cook for another 1–2 minutes
or until golden and cooked through. Do this in batches,
depending on the size of your pan and regreasing the base
when necessary. Keep the pancakes warm in a low oven in
between sheets of greaseproof paper. Serve warm with plenty
of crispy streaky bacon and maple syrup.

NUTRITION PER SERVING
125 cals | 6g fat (3g sats) | 17g carbs | 0.7g salt

CRÈME BRÛLÉE

Serves 6
Preparation 15 minutes, plus infusing and chilling
Cooking time 30–35 minutes, plus cooling

600ml (1 pint) double cream
1 vanilla pod, split lengthways
4 large egg yolks
125g (4oz) golden caster sugar

1 Pour the cream into a pan, add the vanilla pod and bring slowly to the boil. Remove from the heat, cover and set aside to infuse for at least 30 minutes. Stand six ramekins in a roasting tin.
2 Beat the egg yolks with 1 tbsp caster sugar in a bowl. Pour in the vanilla-infused cream, stirring constantly. Strain into a jug, then pour into the ramekins. Surround with hand-hot water to come halfway up the sides of the ramekins. Bake at 150°C (130°C fan oven) mark 2 for 30–35 minutes. Cool, then chill for at least 4 hours or, even better, overnight.
3 Sprinkle the remaining sugar evenly on top of the custards to form a thin layer. Put under a very hot grill for 2–3 minutes until it caramelises. (Alternatively, you can wave a cook's blowtorch over the surface to caramelise the sugar.) Allow to cool for 1 hour, but do not chill – the caramel will form a crisp layer on the surface. Serve within 2–3 hours.

NUTRITION PER SERVING
580 cals | 52g fat (34g sats) | 25g carbs | 0.1g salt **V**

CRÈME CARAMEL

Serves 6
Preparation 15 minutes
Cooking time 20–30 minutes, plus cooling

175g (6oz) granulated sugar
600ml (1 pint) whole or semi-skimmed milk
1 vanilla pod, split lengthways, or a few drops of
    vanilla extract
4 large eggs, plus 4 egg yolks
50–65g (2–2½ oz) golden caster sugar, to taste

1 Warm six ramekins. To make the caramel, put the granulated sugar into a heavy-based pan and heat gently until melted, brushing any sugar down from the side of the pan. Increase the heat and boil rapidly for a few minutes until the syrup turns to a rich golden brown caramel, gently swirling the pan to ensure even browning. Immediately, dip the base of the pan into cool water to prevent further cooking.
2 Pour a little caramel into each of the warmed ramekins and quickly rotate to coat the base and part way up the sides. Leave to cool.
3 To make the custard, put the milk and vanilla pod in a pan and heat until almost boiling; if using vanilla extract, add after heating the milk.
4 Meanwhile, beat the eggs, egg yolks and caster sugar in a bowl until well mixed. Stir in the hot milk. Strain, then pour into the ramekins.
5 Stand the ramekins in a roasting tin containing enough hot water to come halfway up the sides. Bake at 170°C (150°C fan oven) mark 3 for 20–30 minutes until just set and a knife inserted into the centre comes out clean. Remove from the tin. Cool.
6 To turn out, free the edges by pressing with the fingertips then run a knife around the edge of each custard. Put a serving dish over the top, invert and lift off the ramekin; the caramel will have formed a sauce around the custard.

TRY SOMETHING DIFFERENT
Make one large crème caramel in a 15cm (6in) soufflé dish; bake as above for 1 hour or until just set. After cooling, chill for several hours. Transfer to room temperature 30 minutes before serving.

NUTRITION PER SERVING
300 cals | 10g fat (3g sats) | 45g carbs | 0.3g salt ✔

COFFEE BAVAROIS

Serves 6
Preparation 30 minutes, plus infusing
Cooking time 20 minutes, plus cooling and chilling

125g (4 oz) well-roasted coffee beans
900ml (1½ pints) milk
6 egg yolks
75g (3oz) caster sugar
4 tsp gelatine
300ml (½ pint) double cream
2 tbsp coffee-flavoured liqueur, such as Tia Maria (optional)
coffee dragées and grated chocolate, to decorate

1 Put the coffee beans in a pan and warm very gently over a low heat for 2–3 minutes, shaking the pan frequently. Remove from the heat, pour the milk into the pan, return to the heat and bring to the boil. Remove from the heat, cover and leave to infuse for 30 minutes.

2 Put the egg yolks and caster sugar in a deep mixing bowl and beat until the mixture is thick and light in colour. Strain the coffee infusion on to the egg yolks, then stir well. Return the custard mixture to the rinsed-out pan and cook very gently, stirring, until the custard thickens very slightly. Do not boil. Strain into a large bowl and cool.

3 In a small bowl, sprinkle the gelatine over 4 tbsp water. Place over a pan of hot water and stir until dissolved. Stir the gelatine into the cool custard. Stand the custard in a roasting tin of water and surround with ice cubes. Stir the custard frequently while it cools to setting point.

4 Meanwhile, lightly whip half the cream and grease a 1.4 litre (2½ pint) soufflé dish or mould.

5 When the custard is well chilled and beginning to thicken, fold in the whipped cream. Pour into the dish and chill until completely set.

6 With a dampened finger, gently ease the edges of the cream away from the dish. Invert on to a plate and shake gently. Ease off the dish and slide the cream into the centre of the plate.

7 Whisk the remaining cream until it holds its shape, then gradually whisk in the liqueur, if using. Serve the coffee cream separately, or spoon into a piping bag fitted with a 1cm (½in) star vegetable nozzle and pipe around the top edge in a shell pattern. Decorate with coffee dragées and grated chocolate.

TRY SOMETHING DIFFERENT

Chocolate Bavarois Omit the coffee beans, liqueur and coffee dragées. Melt 75g (3oz) plain chocolate in a little milk, whisk in the remaining milk. Complete as above.

NUTRITION PER SERVING
440 cals | 35g fat (20g sats) | 23g carbs | 0.2g salt

TIRAMISU

Serves 10
Preparation 20 minutes, plus chilling

200g carton mascarpone
1 vanilla pod, split lengthways
450ml (³/₄ pint) warm strong black coffee
4 medium egg yolks
75g (3oz) golden caster sugar
284ml carton double cream
100ml (3¹/₂ fl oz) grappa
200g pack savoiardi or sponge fingers
cocoa powder, to dust

1 Put the mascarpone into a bowl with the seeds from the vanilla pod.
2 Pour the coffee into a shallow dish, add the empty vanilla pod and set aside to infuse.
3 In a large bowl, whisk the egg yolks and sugar together until pale and thick, then whisk in the mascarpone until smooth.
4 Whip the cream in another bowl to soft peaks, then fold into the mascarpone mixture with the grappa.
5 Take half of the sponge fingers and dip each in turn into the coffee mixture, then arrange over the base of a 2.4 litre (4¹/₄ pint) shallow dish. Spread a layer of mascarpone mixture over the sponge fingers, then dip the remaining sponge fingers into the coffee and arrange on top. Finish with a top layer of mascarpone. Cover and chill for at least 2 hours.
6 Dust with cocoa and cut into portions with a sharp knife. Use a spatula to lift them neatly on to plates.

COOK'S TIP
For optimum flavour, prepare a day ahead.

NUTRITION PER SERVING
380 cals | 27g fat (16g sats) | 27g carbs | 0.1g salt

ILES FLOTTANTES

Serves 4
Preparation 30 minutes
Cooking time 18–20 minutes, plus cooling and chilling

2 large eggs, separated
150g (5oz) golden caster sugar
300ml (½ pint) single cream
300ml (½ pint) milk

For the praline
vegetable oil to grease
50g (2oz) unskinned pistachio nuts
50g (2oz) golden caster sugar

1 To make the praline, first oil a baking sheet. Put the pistachio nuts and sugar into a small heavy-based pan over a low heat and stir until the sugar melts and begins to caramelise. Cook to a deep brown colour, then immediately pour on to the oiled baking sheet. Leave to cool completely, then whiz to a coarse powder in a food processor.
2 Put the egg whites into a clean, grease-free bowl and whisk until they form soft peaks. Gradually whisk in 75g (3oz) caster sugar until the mixture is very stiff and shiny. Quickly and lightly fold in all but 2 tbsp of the praline.
3 Put the cream, milk and remaining sugar into a medium pan and bring to a gentle simmer. Spoon 5–6 small rounds of meringue mixture into the pan and cook gently for 2–3 minutes or until doubled in size and firm to the touch. Carefully remove with a slotted spoon and drain on kitchen paper. Repeat with the remaining mixture to make 12–18 poached meringues, depending on size.
4 Whisk the egg yolks into the poaching liquid. Heat gently, stirring all the time, until the custard thickens slightly to the consistency of double cream; do not boil.
5 Strain the custard into a serving dish, or individual dishes, and position the meringues on top. Cool, then chill for 30 minutes, or up to 2–3 hours.
6 Serve sprinkled with the reserved pistachio praline.

NUTRITION PER SERVING
500 cals | 25g fat (17g sats) | 61g carbs | 0.4g salt ♥

HOT ORANGE SOUFFLÉS

Serves 6
Preparation 20 minutes
Cooking time 25–30 minutes

65g (2½ oz) unsalted butter
2 tbsp dried breadcrumbs
40g (1½ oz) plain flour
grated zest and juice of 1 small
    (or ½ large) oranges
grated zest and juice of ½ lemon
75ml (2½ fl oz) milk
60g (2oz) golden caster sugar
2 tbsp Grand Marnier
2 egg yolks, 8 egg whites
icing sugar, to dust

1 Preheat the oven to 190°C (170°C fan oven) mark 5. Melt 15g (½ oz) of the butter and use to grease six ramekins. Coat them each with the breadcrumbs; set aside.
2 Melt the remaining butter in a pan, add the flour, orange and lemon zest, and cook for 30 seconds. Off the heat, gradually beat in the milk until smooth. Cook, stirring, over a low heat until the sauce is thickened and smooth. Continue to cook for a further 2 minutes.
3 Remove from the heat and stir in the sugar, orange and lemon juices and Grand Marnier, then beat in the egg yolks.
4 Put the egg whites into a clean, grease-free bowl and whisk until they form stiff peaks, then carefully fold into the sauce until evenly incorporated. Spoon into the soufflé dishes and run a knife around the outside of the mixture.
5 Immediately bake for 12–15 minutes until the soufflés are risen and golden. Dust with icing sugar and serve at once.

NUTRITION PER SERVING 310 cals | 14g fat (7g sats) | 38g carbs | 0.3g salt Ⓥ

CHOCOLATE MOUSSE

Serves 8
Preparation 20 minutes, plus chilling

350g (12oz) plain chocolate (at least
    70% cocoa solids), broken into
    pieces
6 tbsp rum, brandy or cold black
    coffee
6 large eggs, separated
a pinch of salt
chocolate curls to decorate (see
    Cook's Tip, page 379)

1 Put the chocolate with the rum, brandy or black coffee into a heatproof bowl set over a pan of gently simmering water, making sure the base of the bowl doesn't touch the water. Leave to melt, stirring occasionally. Take the bowl off the pan and leave to cool slightly for 3–4 minutes, stirring frequently.
2 Beat the egg yolks with 2 tbsp water, then beat into the chocolate mixture until evenly blended.
3 Put the egg whites and salt into a clean, grease-free bowl and whisk until they form firm peaks, then fold into the chocolate mixture.
4 Pour the mixture into a 1.4–1.7 litre (2½–3 pint) soufflé dish or divide among eight 150ml (¼ pint) cups or ramekins. Chill for at least 4 hours, or overnight, until set. Decorate with chocolate curls.

NUTRITION PER SERVING 309 cals | 17g fat (9g sats) | 28g carbs | 0.1g salt Ⓥ

COLD LEMON SOUFFLÉ

Serves 6
Preparation 1 hour, plus chilling
Cooking time 2 minutes

3 large lemons
2 tsp powdered gelatine
4 large eggs, separated
125g (4oz) golden caster sugar
300ml (½ pint) double cream
chopped pistachio nuts, toasted, and lemon zest to decorate

1 Prepare a 1.1 litre (2 pint) soufflé dish with a paper collar (see Cook's Tip).
2 Finely grate the zest of 2 lemons and squeeze the juice from all three; you need 125ml (4fl oz) juice. Spoon 3 tbsp cold water into a bowl, sprinkle on the gelatine and set aside to soften for 10 minutes.
3 Meanwhile, whisk the egg yolks and sugar together in a heatproof bowl set over a pan of hot water until the mixture is pale and thick enough to leave a trail when the beaters are lifted. Add the lemon juice and whisk for 2–3 minutes. Take off the heat and continue whisking from time to time until cool.
4 Stand the bowl of gelatine over a pan of simmering water until dissolved. Stir the dissolved gelatine into the lemon mixture. Lightly whip the cream in another bowl until it just holds its shape; set aside.
5 Stand the bowl of lemon mixture in a large bowl of ice-cold water. Stir very gently until it begins to thicken creamily. Lift the bowl out of the water and fold in the cream with the lemon zest, until just combined.
6 Put the egg whites into a clean, grease-free bowl and whisk until they form soft peaks. Stir a spoonful into the lemon mixture to loosen it, then gently fold in the remainder. Pour the mixture into the prepared soufflé dish. Chill for 2–3 hours or overnight until set.
7 To serve, remove the paper collar from the dish. Press the toasted nuts around the edge and scatter lemon zest over the top to decorate.

TRY SOMETHING DIFFERENT
Chilled Strawberry Soufflé Prepare a 900ml (1½ pint) soufflé dish as above. Whisk 125g (4oz) caster sugar and 4 medium egg yolks together over a pan of hot water until thick. (Reserve the egg whites.) Purée 350g (12oz) strawberries and fold into the egg mixture. Put 3 tbsp water in a small bowl and sprinkle 1 tbsp powdered gelatine over. Leave to soak. Put over a pan of simmering water and stir until dissolved. Fold into the soufflé mixture and chill. Lightly whip 300ml (½ pint) cream. Put the egg whites into a clean, grease-free bowl and whisk until they form stiff peaks. Fold half the cream into the soufflé, then the egg whites, until evenly blended. Pour into the soufflé dish and level the surface. Chill in the fridge for at least 4 hours or until set. Decorate the top of the soufflé with fresh strawberry slices and rosettes of piped cream.

COOK'S TIP
To make a paper collar for a chilled soufflé, wrap a double thickness of baking parchment around the outside of the soufflé dish, leaving a 4cm (2in) collar above the dish. Secure with string.

NUTRITION PER SERVING
390 cals | 30g fat (18g sats) | 24g carbs | 0.2g salt

TANGERINE JELLIES

Makes 12
Preparation 10 minutes
Cooking time about 3 minutes, plus
   chilling

5 gelatine leaves
12 tangerines, about 1kg (2¼lb)
150g (5oz) caster sugar
double cream to serve (optional)

1 Put the gelatine in a bowl and cover with cold water. Leave the gelatine to soak for 5 minutes. Meanwhile zest two tangerines and put the zest into a large pan. Squeeze the juice from the zested and whole tangerines and add to the pan with the sugar.

2 Lift the gelatine out of the water and discard the water. Add to the pan. Heat gently until the sugar dissolves. Strain the mixture into a large jug with a good pouring spout and make up to 1 litre (1¾ pints) with cold water. Pour the mixture into 12 small glasses and chill for at least 5 hours or, better still, overnight.
3 To serve, take out of the fridge 5 minutes before serving to allow them to soften slightly. Serve topped with double cream, if you like.

GET AHEAD
Make the jellies up to two days ahead.

NUTRITION PER JELLY (without cream)
73 cals | 0g fat (0g sats) | 18g carbs | 0g salt

KNICKERBOCKER GLORY

Serves 6
Preparation 15 minutes, plus chilling

¼ × 140g (4½ oz) pack raspberry or
   strawberry jelly
¼ × 140g (4½ oz) pack lemon jelly
200g (7oz) can peach slices, drained
   and chopped
200g (7oz) can pineapple chunks,
   drained
500ml (18fl oz) block of vanilla ice
   cream
150ml (¼ pint) double cream
6 glacé cherries
chocolate vermicelli to decorate

1 Make up the jellies as directed on the pack, allow to set and then chop them roughly.
2 Put small portions of the fruit into the base of six tall sundae glasses. Cover with a layer of red jelly. Put a scoop of ice cream on top and add a layer of yellow jelly.
3 Repeat the layering, finishing with a layer of cream and a cherry. Decorate with chocolate vermicelli.

NUTRITION PER SERVING 331 cals |
22g fat (13g sats) | 32g carbs | 0.2g salt

CLASSIC MERINGUES

Serves 6
Preparation 20 minutes
Cooking time 2–3 hours, plus cooling

3 medium egg whites, at room
    temperature
175g (6oz) golden caster sugar

To serve
200ml (7fl oz) double cream, whipped
icing sugar, to dust (optional)

1 Preheat the oven to 110°C (90°C
fan oven) mark ¼. Line two baking
sheets with baking parchment or a
Teflon non-stick liner. Put the egg whites
into a clean, grease-free bowl and whisk
using an electric whisk until they form
stiff peaks. Gradually add the caster
sugar, a tablespoonful at a time, whisking
well after each addition. Continue
whisking until the meringue is very
stiff and shiny.

2 Using two large spoons, shape the
meringue into 12–15 ovals or rounds,
spacing them well apart on the lined
baking sheets.
3 Bake for 2–3 hours until the
meringues are crisp and well-dried
out, but still pale; switch the baking
sheets around halfway through cooking.
Carefully peel the meringues off the
paper and transfer to a wire rack
to cool.
4 Sandwich the meringues together in
pairs with cream and serve, dusted with
icing sugar if you like.

NUTRITION PER SERVING 270 cals |
16g fat (11g sats) | 32g carbs | trace salt Ⓥ

ETON MESS

Serves 6
Preparation 10 minutes

200g (7oz) fromage frais, chilled
200g (7oz) low-fat Greek yogurt,
    chilled
1 tbsp golden caster sugar
2 tbsp strawberry liqueur
6 meringues, roughly crushed
350g (12oz) strawberries, hulled and
    halved

1 Put the fromage frais and yogurt into
a large bowl and stir to combine.
2 Add the sugar, strawberry liqueur,
meringues and strawberries. Mix
together gently and divide among
six dishes.

TRY SOMETHING DIFFERENT
Caribbean Crush Replace the sugar
and liqueur with dulce de leche toffee
sauce and the strawberries with sliced
bananas.

NUTRITION PER SERVING 198 cals |
5g fat (3g sats) | 33g carbs | 0.1g salt Ⓥ

STRAWBERRY PAVLOVA WITH ROSEWATER SYRUP

Serves 10
Preparation 20 minutes, plus cooling
Cooking time about 40 minutes

10 medium egg whites
600g (1lb 5oz) caster sugar
1³/₄ tbsp cornflour
1kg (2¹/₄ lb) strawberries, hulled
150ml (¹/₄ pint) dessert wine, such as Muscat de Beaumes
    de Venise
1 tsp rosewater
600ml (1 pint) double cream
3 tbsp icing sugar, sifted

1 Preheat the oven to 150°C (130°C fan oven) mark 2.
Line a large baking sheet with baking parchment. Use a pencil
to draw a 28cm (11 in) diameter circle on the parchment,
then flip it over so the pencil mark is underneath.
2 Using electric beaters, whisk the egg whites in a large,
grease-free bowl until stiff but not dry. Gradually add 550g
(1¹/₄ lb) caster sugar, whisking all the time, until the mixture is
stiff and glossy. Quickly beat in 1 tbsp cornflour.
3 Spoon the mixture on to the prepared baking tray within
the marked circle, pushing it into peaks at the edges of the
circle. Bake for 40 minutes or until the meringue is firm to the
touch and peels away from the parchment. Transfer to a rack
and leave to cool.
4 Meanwhile, put 200g (7oz) strawberries with the wine,
remaining caster sugar and the rosewater into a pan. Heat and
simmer gently for 5 minutes. Blend until smooth, then push
through a fine sieve, discarding the pips. Return the mixture to
the pan and whisk in the remaining cornflour. Heat gently for
3–4 minutes until the syrup thickens, whisking constantly to
remove any lumps. Take off the heat and leave to cool.
5 Transfer the cooled meringue to a serving plate. Gently
whip the cream with the icing sugar until it just holds its shape.
Dollop on top of the meringue, then pile on the remaining
strawberries. Drizzle the cooled syrup over and serve.

GET AHEAD
Cook the meringue, make the strawberry syrup and hull the
strawberries up to one day ahead. Cool the meringue on the
baking sheet, then cover with clingfilm and store at room
temperature. Cool the syrup, then cover and chill. Keep the
hulled strawberries covered in the fridge. Whip the cream
mixture up to 2 hours ahead, then chill. To serve, bring the
syrup, strawberries and cream up to room temperature, then
complete the recipe.

NUTRITION PER SERVING
614 cals | 32g fat (20g sats) | 78g carbs | trace salt Ⓥ

BAKED ALASKA

Serves 8
Preparation 30 minutes, plus freezing
Cooking time 3–4 minutes

1 large sponge flan case, 25.5cm (10in) diameter
5 tbsp orange juice
7 tbsp jam – any kind
1.5 litre tub vanilla ice cream
6 large egg whites
pinch of cream of tartar
pinch of salt
275g (10oz) golden caster sugar

1 Put the flan case on an ovenproof plate. Spoon the orange juice over the sponge, then spread with the jam. Scoop the ice cream on top of the jam, then put in the freezer for at least 30 minutes.
2 Put the egg whites into a large, clean, grease-free bowl and whisk until stiff. Beat in the cream of tartar and salt. Using a large spoon, fold in the sugar, 1 tbsp at a time, then whisk until very thick and shiny.
3 Spoon the meringue over the ice cream to cover, making sure that the meringue is sealed to the flan case edge all the way round. Freeze for at least 1 hour or overnight.
4 Preheat the oven to 230°C (210°C fan oven) mark 8. Bake for 3–4 minutes until the meringue is tinged golden brown. Serve immediately. If the Baked Alaska has been in the freezer overnight, bake and leave to stand for about 15 minutes before serving.

NUTRITION PER SERVING
659 cals | 30g fat (17g sats) | 91g carbs | 0.5g salt 🅥

VANILLA ICE CREAM

Serves 4
Preparation 20 minutes, plus infusing and freezing
Cooking time 15 minutes

300ml (¹/₂ pint) milk
1 vanilla pod, split lengthways
3 medium egg yolks
50–75g (2–3oz) golden caster sugar
300ml (¹/₂ pint) double cream

1 Pour the milk into a heavy-based pan, add the vanilla pod and heat slowly until almost boiling. Take off the heat and leave to infuse for about 20 minutes. Remove the vanilla pod.
2 Whisk the egg yolks and sugar together in a bowl until thick and creamy. Gradually whisk in the hot milk, then strain back into the pan. Cook over a low heat, stirring constantly, until the custard has thickened enough to coat the back of the wooden spoon; do not boil. Pour into a chilled bowl and allow to cool.
3 Whisk the double cream into the cold custard until evenly blended.
4 Pour the mixture into an ice-cream maker and churn until frozen. (Alternatively, freeze in a shallow container, whisking two or three times during freezing to break down the ice crystals and ensure an even-textured result.)
5 Allow the ice cream to soften slightly at cool room temperature before serving. Scoop into balls and serve in individual bowls.

TRY SOMETHING DIFFERENT

Strawberry Ice Cream Omit the vanilla pod. Sweeten 300ml (¹/₂ pint) strawberry purée with sugar to taste, then add the cooled custard. (Other fruit ice creams can be made in the same way.)
Chocolate Ice Cream Omit the vanilla pod. Add 125g (4oz) plain dark chocolate to the milk and heat gently until melted, then bring almost to the boil and continue as above.
Coffee Ice Cream Omit the vanilla pod. Add 150ml (¹/₄ pint) freshly made strong cooled coffee to the cooled custard, or 2 tsp instant coffee granules to the hot milk, stirring to dissolve.
Rum and Raisin Ice Cream Put 250g (9oz) large raisins into a pan, add 100ml (3¹/₂ fl oz) dark rum and bring to the boil. Turn off the heat and leave to soak. Whip 600ml (1 pint) double cream until it just holds its shape. Put 4 large egg yolks, 3 tbsp golden syrup and 1 tbsp black treacle into another bowl. Whisk for 2–3 minutes until mousselike. Pour into the cream and whisk for a further 3–4 minutes until thick. Set the freezer to fast freeze. Pour the ice cream mixture into a 2 litre (3¹/₂ pint) roasting tin and freeze for 45 minutes–1 hour until it begins to harden around the edges. Add the soaked fruit and any liquid to the ice cream and mix well. Freeze for 45 minutes. Spoon into a 1.7 litre (3 pint) sealable container and freeze for at least 2 hours.
Instant Banana Ice Cream Peel 6 ripe bananas, about 700g (1¹/₂ lb), slice and spread on a large non-stick baking tray. Put into the freezer for 30 minutes or until frozen. Let the frozen banana slices stand at room temperature for 2–3 minutes. Put the still frozen pieces in a food processor or blender with 1 tbsp fromage frais, 1 tbsp orange juice, 1 tsp vanilla extract and a splash of rum or Cointreau, if you like. Whiz until smooth, scraping down the sides of the bowl and adding more fromage frais and orange juice as necessary to give a creamy consistency. Add lime juice to taste and serve or turn into a freezerproof container and freeze for up to one month.

> NUTRITION PER SERVING
> 480 cals | 41g fat (27g sats) | 22g carbs | 0.1g salt

LEMON SORBET

Serves 4
Preparation 10 minutes, plus chilling and freezing
Cooking time 15 minutes

3 juicy lemons
125g (4oz) golden caster sugar
1 large egg white

1 Finely pare the lemon zest, using a zester, then squeeze
the juice. Put the zest into a pan with the sugar and 350ml
(12fl oz) water and heat gently until the sugar has dissolved.
Increase the heat and boil for 10 minutes. Leave to cool.
2 Stir the lemon juice into the cooled sugar syrup. Cover
and chill in the fridge for 30 minutes.
3 Strain the syrup through a fine sieve into a bowl. In another
bowl, beat the egg white until just frothy, then whisk into the
lemon mixture.
4 For best results, freeze in an ice-cream maker. Otherwise,
pour into a shallow freezerproof container and freeze until
almost frozen; mash well with a fork and freeze until solid.
Transfer the sorbet to the fridge 30 minutes before serving
to soften slightly.

TRY SOMETHING DIFFERENT
Orange Sorbet Replace two of the lemons with oranges.
Lime Sorbet Replace two of the lemons with four limes.
Mango Sorbet Make the sugar syrup as directed, but using
the zest of 1 lime instead of the lemons. Blend the flesh
of two ripe mangos with the juice of the lime until smooth
and then stir in the cooled sugar syrup. Complete the recipe
from step 4.

NUTRITION PER SERVING
130 cals | 0g fat (0g sats) | 33g carbs | trace salt

CHOCOLATE GINGER REFRIGERATOR CAKE

Makes 36 squares
Preparation 15 minutes
Cooking time 10 minutes, plus chilling

a little oil to grease
350g (12oz) plain chocolate, chopped
150g (5oz) unsalted butter
75g (3oz) golden syrup
300g (11oz) crunchy ginger biscuits, roughly crushed
75g (3oz) flaked almonds
75g (3oz) dried cranberries
50g (2oz) white chocolate, roughly chopped

1 Lightly oil a deep 23cm (9in) square tin and line the base and sides with greaseproof paper.
2 Put the plain chocolate, butter and syrup into a heatproof bowl set over a pan of gently simmering water, making sure the base of the bowl doesn't touch the water. Leave for 5–10 minutes, without stirring, until melted, then stir everything to combine. Set aside to cool slightly.
3 Put the ginger biscuits into a large bowl with the almonds and cranberries. Pour the chocolate mixture into the bowl and stir well. Spoon into the prepared tin and level the surface.
4 Melt the white chocolate in a small heatproof bowl set over a pan of gently simmering water, making sure the base of the bowl doesn't touch the water, then drizzle over the top of the chocolate and biscuit mixture. Use a skewer to swirl the chocolate and create a marbled effect. Cover the tin with clingfilm, making sure it doesn't touch the chocolate. Chill for at least 4 hours or overnight.
5 Cut into squares to serve.

TO STORE
Cover and store in the fridge. It will keep for up to three weeks.

> NUTRITION PER SQUARE
> 152 cals | 9g fat (5g sats) | 17g carbs | 0.2g salt

CAKES AND BAKES

MADELEINES

Makes 24
Preparation 20 minutes, plus chilling
Cooking time 10–12 minutes, plus cooling

125g (4oz) unsalted butter, melted and cooled until tepid
125g (4oz) plain flour, plus extra to dust
4 medium eggs
125g (4oz) golden caster sugar
finely grated zest of 1 lemon
1 tsp baking powder
a pinch of salt
icing sugar, to dust

1 Brush two Madeleine trays with a little of the melted butter. Allow to set, then dust with flour, shaking out any excess.
2 Whisk the eggs, sugar and lemon zest together in a bowl, using an electric whisk, until the mixture is pale, creamy and thick enough to leave a trail when the whisk is lifted.
3 Sift in half the flour, together with the baking powder and salt. Carefully pour in half the melted butter around the edge of the bowl and gently fold in until evenly incorporated. Repeat with the remaining flour and butter. Cover and chill the mixture in the fridge for 45 minutes. Preheat the oven to 220°C (200°C fan oven) mark 7.
4 Two-thirds fill the Madeleine moulds with the mixture and bake for 10–12 minutes or until well risen and golden. Ease out of the tins and cool on a wire rack. Serve dusted with icing sugar.

COOK'S TIPS
— Resting the sponge mixture before baking gives the Madeleines their characteristic dense texture.
— If you have only one Madeleine tray, bake the cakes in two batches.

NUTRITION PER CAKE
90 cals | 5g fat (3g sats) | 10g carbs | 0.2g salt **V**

FAIRY CAKES

Makes 18
Preparation 20 minutes
Cooking time 10–15 minutes, plus cooling and setting

125g (4oz) self-raising flour, sifted
1 tsp baking powder
125g (4oz) caster sugar
125g (4oz) unsalted butter, very soft
2 medium eggs
1 tbsp milk

For the icing and decoration
225g (8oz) icing sugar, sifted
assorted food colourings (optional)
sweets, sprinkles or coloured sugar

1 Preheat the oven to 200°C (180°C fan oven) mark 6.
Put paper cases into 18 of the cups in two bun tins.
2 Put the flour, baking powder, sugar, butter, eggs and milk
into a mixing bowl and beat with a hand-held electric whisk
for 2 minutes or until the mixture is pale and very soft.
Half-fill each paper case with the mixture.
3 Bake for 10–15 minutes until golden brown. Transfer
to a wire rack and leave to cool completely.
4 Put the icing sugar into a bowl and gradually blend
in 2–3 tbsp warm water until the icing is fairly stiff, but
spreadable. Add a couple of drops of food colouring,
if you like.
5 When the cakes are cold, spread the tops with the
icing and decorate.

TO STORE
Store in an airtight container. The cakes will keep for
three to five days.

FREEZING TIP
- To freeze, complete the recipe to the end of step 3.
  Open-freeze, then wrap and freeze.
- To use, thaw for about 1 hour, then complete the recipe.

TRY SOMETHING DIFFERENT
Chocolate Fairy Cakes Replace 2 tbsp of the flour with
the same amount of cocoa powder. Stir 50g (2oz) chocolate
drops, sultanas or chopped dried apricots into the mixture at
the end of step 2. Complete the recipe.

NUTRITION PER CAKE
160 cals | 6g fat (4g sats) | 26g carbs | 0.2g salt Ⓥ

RASPBERRY RIPPLE CUPCAKES

Makes 9
Preparation 30 minutes
Cooking time 20 minutes, plus cooling

50g (2oz) seedless raspberry jam
50g (2oz) fresh raspberries
125g (4oz) unsalted butter, softened
100g (3½oz) caster sugar
2 medium eggs
1 tbsp milk
150g (5oz) self-raising flour, sifted

For the topping and decoration
150g (5oz) fresh raspberries
300ml (½ pint) whipping cream
50g (2oz) icing sugar, sifted

1 Preheat the oven to 190°C (170°C fan oven), mark 5. Line a 9 cups of a bun tin or muffin pan with paper muffin cases.
2 Mix the raspberry jam with the raspberries, lightly crushing the raspberries. Set aside.
3 Using a hand-held electric whisk, whisk the butter and caster sugar in a bowl, or beat with a wooden spoon, until pale and creamy. Gradually whisk in the eggs and milk until just combined. Using a metal spoon, fold in the flour until just combined, then carefully fold in the raspberry jam mixture until just marbled, being careful not to over-mix. Divide the mixture equally among the paper cases.
4 Bake for 20 minutes or until golden and risen. Leave to cool in the tin for 5 minutes, then transfer to a wire rack to cool completely.
5 For the decoration, keep to one side 9 raspberries. Mash the remaining raspberries in a bowl with a fork. Pass through a sieve into a bowl to remove the seeds. Using a hand-held electric whisk, whisk the cream and icing sugar together until stiff peaks form. Mix the raspberry purée into the cream until combined.
6 Insert a star nozzle into a piping bag, then fill the bag with the cream and pipe a swirl on to the top of each cake. Decorate each with a raspberry.

> **NUTRITION PER CUPCAKE**
> 385 cals | 26g fat (16g sats) | 36g carbs | 0.5g salt Ⓥ

TO STORE
Store in an airtight container in the fridge. They will keep for up to two days.

FREEZING TIP
→ To freeze, complete the recipe to the end of step 4. Open-freeze, then wrap and freeze.
→ To use, thaw for about 1 hour, then complete the recipe.

TRY SOMETHING DIFFERENT
Orange and Poppy Seed Cupcakes Whisk 175g (6oz) softened unsalted butter and 175g (6oz) caster sugar until pale and creamy. Gradually whisk in 3 medium eggs until just combined. Fold in 175g (6oz) self-raising flour, grated zest and juice of 1 large orange, 2 tbsp poppy seeds and 1 tsp baking powder until combined. Divide between the paper cases. Bake as above. Cool. Topping: put 125g (4oz) softened unsalted butter into a bowl and whisk until fluffy. Gradually add 250g (9oz) icing sugar and 1 tbsp orange flower water and whisk until light and fluffy. Pipe a swirl of the topping on to each cake.
Chocolate Cupcakes Line a 12-cup and a 6-cup bun tin or muffin tin with paper muffin cases. Whisk the butter with 125g (4oz) light muscovado sugar. Beat in the eggs. Sift 15g (½oz) cocoa powder with 100g (3½oz) self-raising flour and fold into the mixture with 100g (3½oz) chopped plain chocolate (70% cocoa solids). Divide among the paper cases. Bake and cool. Topping: put 150ml (¼ pint) double cream and 100g (3½oz) plain chocolate into a heavy-based pan over a low heat and heat until melted, then allow to cool and thicken slightly. Spoon on to the cakes, then leave to set.

BLUEBERRY MUFFINS

Makes 12
Preparation 10 minutes
Cooking time 20–25 minutes, plus cooling

2 medium eggs
250ml (9fl oz) semi-skimmed milk
250g (9oz) golden granulated sugar
2 tsp vanilla extract
350g (12oz) plain flour
4 tsp baking powder
250g (9oz) blueberries, frozen
finely grated zest of 2 lemons

1 Preheat the oven to 200°C (180°C fan oven) mark 6. Line a 12-cup bun tin or muffin pan with paper muffin cases.
2 Put the eggs, milk, sugar and vanilla extract into a bowl and mix well.
3 In another bowl, sift the flour and baking powder together, then add the blueberries and lemon zest. Toss together and make a well in the centre.
4 Pour the egg mixture into the flour and blueberries, and mix in gently – over-beating will make the muffins tough. Divide the mixture equally among the paper cases.
5 Bake for 20–25 minutes until risen and just firm. Transfer to a wire rack and leave to cool completely. These are best eaten on the day they are made.

FREEZING TIP
⁓ To freeze, complete the recipe. Once the muffins are cold, pack, seal and freeze.
⁓ To use, thaw at cool room temperature.

TRY SOMETHING DIFFERENT
Double Chocolate Chip Muffins Omit the blueberries and lemon zest. Replace 40g (1½oz) of the flour with cocoa powder, then add 150g (5oz) chopped dark chocolate to the dry ingredients in step 3.
Honey and Yogurt Muffins Sift 225g (8oz) plain flour, 1½ tsp baking powder, 1 tsp bicarbonate of soda, ½ tsp each ground mixed spice and grated nutmeg and a pinch of salt into a bowl. Stir in 50g (2oz) ground oatmeal and 50g (2oz) light muscovado sugar. Mix 225g (8oz) Greek yogurt with 125ml (4fl oz) milk in a bowl, then beat in 1 medium egg, 50g (2oz) butter, melted and cooled, and 4 tbsp clear honey. Pour on to the dry ingredients and stir in quickly until just blended. Divide among the paper cases. Bake for 17–20 minutes until the muffins are well risen and just firm. Cool in the tin for 5 minutes, then transfer to a wire rack.

Cranberry Muffins Sift 300g (11oz) plain flour and 2 tsp baking powder into a bowl. Stir in 150g (5oz) caster sugar, the finely grated zest of 1 lemon and 125g (4oz) dried cranberries. Put 1 medium egg, 1 tsp vanilla extract, 225ml (8fl oz) milk and 50g (2oz) melted butter into a jug and mix with a fork. Pour into the dry ingredients and lightly fold together – don't over-mix. Spoon into 10 muffin cases to three-quarters fill them. Bake as main recipe. Cool slightly, then dust with icing sugar.

NUTRITION PER MUFFIN
218 cals | 2g fat (trace sats) | 49g carbs | 0.5g salt Ⓥ

ECCLES CAKES

Makes 8
Preparation 10 minutes, plus resting
Cooking time 15 minutes, plus cooling

212g (7½ oz) packet frozen puff pastry,
    thawed
plain flour to dust
25g (1oz) butter, softened
25g (1oz) dark brown soft sugar
25g (1oz) fine chopped mixed peel
50g (2oz) currants
caster sugar to sprinkle

1 Roll out the pastry on a lightly
floured surface and cut into 9cm
(3½in) rounds.
2 For the filling, mix the butter, sugar,
mixed peel and currants in a bowl.

3 Put 1 tsp of the fruit and butter
mixture in the centre of each pastry
round. Draw up the edges of each
pastry round to enclose the filling and
then reshape. Turn each round over and
roll lightly until the currants just show
through. Prick the top of each with a
fork. Leave to rest for about 10 minutes
in a cool place. Preheat the oven to
230°C (210°C fan oven) mark 8.
4 Put the pastry rounds on a damp
baking sheet and bake for about
15 minutes until golden. Transfer to a
wire rack and leave to cool for 30
minutes. Sprinkle with caster sugar while
still warm.

NUTRITION PER CAKE 158 cals |
9g fat (2g sats) | 19g carbs | 0.3g salt Ⓥ

ROCK BUNS

Makes 12
Preparation 5 minutes
Cooking time 20 minutes, plus cooling

125g (4oz) butter or margarine, plus
    extra to grease
225g (8oz) plain flour
pinch of salt
2 tsp baking powder
75g (3oz) demerara sugar
75g (3oz) mixed dried fruit
zest of ½ lemon
1 medium egg
milk

1 Preheat the oven to 200°C (180°C
fan oven) mark 6. Lightly grease two
baking sheets.
2 Sift together the flour, salt and baking
powder. Rub in the butter until the
mixture resembles fine breadcrumbs.
Add the sugar, fruit and lemon zest,
and mix together thoroughly.
3 Using a fork, mix to a moist but
stiff dough with the beaten egg and a
little milk.
4 Using two forks, shape into really
rocky heaps on the baking sheets. Bake
for about 20 minutes or until golden
brown. Transfer to a wire rack and leave
to cool. Rock buns are best eaten on
the day they are made.

NUTRITION PER BUN 192 cals |
9g fat (6g sats) | 26g carbs | 0.5g salt Ⓥ

OVEN SCONES

Makes 8
Preparation 15 minutes
Cooking time 10 minutes, plus cooling

225g (8oz) self-raising flour, plus extra to dust
pinch of salt
1 tsp baking powder
40g (1¹/₂oz) butter, diced, plus extra to grease
about 150ml (¹/₄ pint) milk
beaten egg or milk, to glaze
whipped cream, or butter and jam, to serve

1 Preheat the oven to 220°C (200°C fan oven) mark 7.
Grease a baking sheet. Sift the flour, salt and baking powder
together into a bowl. Rub in the butter until the mixture
resembles fine breadcrumbs. Using a knife to stir it in, add
enough milk to give a fairly soft dough.
2 Gently roll or pat out the dough on a lightly floured
surface to a 2cm (³/₄in) thickness and then, using a 6.5cm
(2¹/₂in) plain cutter, cut out rounds.
3 Put on the baking sheet and brush the tops with beaten
egg or milk. Bake for 10 minutes or until golden brown and
well risen. Transfer to a wire rack and leave to cool.
4 Serve warm, split and filled with cream, or butter and jam.

TRY SOMETHING DIFFERENT
Wholemeal Scones Replace half the white flour with
wholemeal flour.
Fruit Scones Add 50g (2oz) currants, sultanas, raisins or
chopped dates (or a mixture) to the dry ingredients.
Buttermilk Scones Increase the flour to 300g (11oz) and
the butter to 50g (2oz). Replace the milk with 284ml carton
buttermilk and add 25g (1oz) golden caster sugar. Bake for
12–15 minutes, then cool a little. Beat 250g (9oz) mascarpone
in a bowl to soften. Add the seeds from 1 vanilla pod and
beat well to combine. Serve the warm scones split and
sandwiched together with the vanilla mascarpone and
blueberry jam.
Cheese and Herb Scones Sift 1 tsp mustard powder
with the dry ingredients. Stir 50g (2oz) finely grated Cheddar
cheese into the mixture before adding the milk. After glazing,
sprinkle the tops with a little cheese.

COOK'S TIP
To ensure a good rise, avoid heavy handling
and make sure the rolled-out dough is at
least 2cm (³/₄in) thick.

NUTRITION PER SCONE
140 cals | 5g fat (3g sats) | 22g carbs | 0.7g salt **V**

DROP SCONES (SCOTCH PANCAKES)

Makes 15
Preparation 10 minutes
Cooking time 12–18 minutes

125g (4oz) self-raising flour
2 tbsp caster sugar
1 medium egg, beaten
150ml (¼ pint) milk
vegetable oil to grease
butter, or whipped cream and jam,
    to serve

1 Mix the flour and sugar together in a bowl. Make a well in the centre and mix in the egg, with enough of the milk to make a batter the consistency of thick cream – working as quickly and lightly as possible.

2 Cook the mixture in batches: drop spoonfuls on to an oiled hot griddle or heavy-based frying pan. Keep the griddle at a steady heat and when bubbles rise to the surface of the scone and burst, after 2–3 minutes, turn over with a palette knife.
3 Cook for a further 2–3 minutes until golden brown on the other side.
4 Put the cooked drop scones on a clean teatowel and cover with another teatowel to keep them moist. Serve warm, with butter, or cream and jam.

NUTRITION PER SCONE 50 cals | 1g fat (0.2g sats) | 9g carbs | 0.1g salt **V**

WELSH CAKES

Makes about 16
Preparation 10 minutes
Cooking time 3 minutes per batch, plus
    cooling

50g (2oz) butter or margarine, plus
    extra to grease
225g (8oz) plain flour, plus extra to dust
1 tsp baking powder
pinch of salt
50g (2oz) lard
75g (3oz) caster sugar
50g (2oz) currants
1 medium egg, beaten
about 2 tbsp milk

1 Grease a griddle or heavy frying pan. Sift together the flour, baking powder and salt. Rub in the fats until the mixture resembles fine breadcrumbs. Add the sugar and currants.
3 Make a well in the centre, then add the egg and enough milk to make a stiff paste similar to shortcrust pastry.

4 Roll out on a lightly floured surface until 5mm (¼ in) thick and then, using a 7.5cm (3in) cutter, cut into rounds.
5 Cook the cakes slowly on the medium-hot griddle for 3 minutes on each side or until golden brown. Cool on a wire rack. Eat on the day they are made.

TRY SOMETHING DIFFERENT
Griddle Scones Use self-raising flour instead of plain, with 1 tsp baking powder, a pinch of salt and ½ tsp grated nutmeg. Omit the lard. Use 50g (2oz) golden caster sugar. Omit the currants. You may need 3–4 tbsp milk. Roll out to 1cm (½ in) thick and cut into triangles. Cook for 5 minutes on each side. Serve warm, split and buttered.

NUTRITION PER CAKE 123 cals | 6g fat (3g sats) | 18g carbs | 0.2g salt

BANANA AND BUTTERSCOTCH LOAF

Makes 1 loaf (15 slices)
Preparation 20 minutes
Cooking time 1 hour, plus cooling

butter to grease
175g (6oz) plain flour, sifted
2 tsp baking powder
$^1/_2$ tsp bicarbonate of soda
$^1/_2$ tsp salt
175g (6oz) light muscovado sugar
2 large eggs
3 medium-size ripe bananas, mashed
150g carton natural yogurt
150g bar butterscotch chocolate, roughly chopped
100g (3$^1/_2$oz) pecan nuts, chopped
1–2 tbsp demerara sugar

1 Preheat the oven to 170°C (150°C fan oven) mark 3.
Grease a 1.4kg (3lb) loaf tin and line with greaseproof paper.
2 Put the flour, baking powder, bicarbonate of soda and salt
into a large bowl and mix together.
3 In a separate bowl, beat the muscovado sugar and eggs
together with a hand-held electric whisk until pale and fluffy.
Carefully stir in the bananas, yogurt, chocolate and 50g (2oz)
pecan nuts, followed by the flour mixture.
4 Spoon the mixture into the prepared tin and level the
surface. Sprinkle with the remaining chopped pecan nuts and
the demerara sugar. Bake for 1 hour or until a skewer inserted
into the centre comes out clean. Leave to cool in the tin on a
wire rack, then turn out and slice.

TO STORE
Store in an airtight container. It will keep for up to
two days.

TRY SOMETHING DIFFERENT
If you can't find butterscotch chocolate, use a bar of plain dark
chocolate instead.

> NUTRITION PER SLICE
> 221 cals | 9g fat (2g sats) | 34g carbs | 0.2g salt Ⓥ

GINGER AND FRUIT TEABREAD

Cuts into 12 slices
Preparation 15 minutes, plus soaking
Cooking time 1 hour, plus cooling

125g (4oz) each dried apricots, apples and pitted prunes,
    chopped
300ml (½ pint) strong fruit tea
a little butter to grease
25g (1oz) preserved stem ginger in syrup, chopped
225g (8oz) wholemeal flour
2 tsp baking powder
125g (4oz) dark muscovado sugar
1 medium egg, beaten

1 Put the dried fruit into a large bowl, add the tea and leave
to soak for 2 hours.
2 Preheat the oven to 180°C (160°C fan oven) mark 4.
Grease a 900g (2lb) loaf tin and base-line with baking
parchment.
3 Add the remaining ingredients to the soaked fruit and mix
thoroughly. Spoon into the prepared tin and brush with 2 tbsp
cold water. Bake for 1 hour or until a skewer inserted into the
centre comes out clean.
4 Cool in the tin for 10–15 minutes, then turn out on to a
wire rack and leave to cool completely.

TO STORE
Wrap the teabread in clingfilm and store in an airtight
container. It will keep for up to three days.

NUTRITION PER SLICE
145 cals | 1g fat (trace sats) | 33g carbs | 0g salt

CHOCOLATE FUDGE BROWNIES

Makes 12 brownies
Preparation 20 minutes
Cooking time 1 hour, plus cooling

butter to grease
125g (4oz) milk chocolate, broken into pieces
9 ready-to-eat prunes
200g (7oz) light muscovado sugar
3 large egg whites
1 tsp vanilla extract
75g (3oz) plain flour, sifted
50g (2oz) white chocolate, chopped
icing sugar to dust

1 Preheat the oven to 180°C (160°C fan oven) mark 4.
Grease and baseline a 15cm (6in) square shallow cake tin.
Melt the milk chocolate in a heatproof bowl over a pan of
gently simmering water, making sure the base of the bowl
doesn't touch the water. Remove from the heat and leave
to cool slightly.
2 Put the prunes in a food processor or blender with
100ml (3½ fl oz) water and whiz for 2–3 minutes to make
a purée. Add the muscovado sugar and whiz briefly to mix.
3 In a clean, grease-free bowl, whisk the egg whites until
they form soft peaks.
4 Add the vanilla extract, prune mixture, flour, white
chocolate and egg whites to the bowl of melted chocolate.
Fold everything together gently. Pour the mixture into the
prepared tin and bake for 1 hour or until firm to the touch.
5 Leave to cool in the tin. Turn out, dust with icing sugar
and cut into 12 squares.

TO STORE
Store in an airtight container. They will keep for up to
two days.

> NUTRITION PER BROWNIE
> 174 cals | 5g fat (3g sats) | 33g carbs | 0.1g salt **V**

STICKY GINGERBREAD

Cuts into 10 slices
Preparation 15 minutes, plus cooling
Cooking time 1 hour 10 minutes, plus cooling

125g (4oz) unsalted butter, plus extra to grease
125g (4oz) light muscovado sugar
75g (3oz) black treacle
200g (7oz) golden syrup
250g (9oz) plain flour
2 tsp ground mixed spice
65g (2$^1/_2$ oz) preserved stem ginger, finely chopped
2 large eggs
100ml (3$^1/_2$ fl oz) milk
1 tsp bicarbonate of soda
extra treacle or golden syrup to glaze (optional)

1   Put the butter, sugar, treacle and golden syrup in a pan
and heat gently until the butter has melted. Leave to cool
for 5 minutes. Grease and line the bread maker bucket
with baking parchment, if specified in the manual.
2   Sift the flour and mixed spice together into a bowl.
Add the syrup mixture, chopped ginger, eggs and milk,
and stir well until combined.
3   In a cup, mix the bicarbonate of soda with 2 tbsp hot
water, then add to the bowl. Stir the mixture well and pour
into the bread maker bucket.
4   Fit the bucket into the bread maker and set to the Cake
or Bake-only programme. Select 1 hour 10 minutes on the
timer and choose a light crust. Press start.
5   To check whether the cake is done, pierce the centre with
a skewer; it should come out fairly clean. If necessary, re-set
the timer for a little longer.
6   Remove the bucket from the machine, leave the cake in
the bucket for 5 minutes, then turn out on to a wire rack.
Brush the top of the cake with the treacle or syrup to glaze,
if you like, and leave to cool.

TO STORE

Wrap and store in an airtight container. It will keep for up to
one week.

NUTRITION PER SLICE
341 cals | 12g fat (7g sats) | 58g carbs | 0.7g salt Ⓥ

APRICOT AND ALMOND TRAYBAKE

Cuts into 18 bars
Preparation 20 minutes
Cooking time 30–40 minutes, plus cooling

250g (9oz) unsalted butter, softened, plus extra to grease
225g (8oz) golden caster sugar
275g (10oz) self-raising flour, sifted
2 tsp baking powder
finely grated zest of 1 orange and 2 tbsp orange juice
75g (3oz) ground almonds
5 medium eggs, lightly beaten
225g (8oz) ready-to-eat dried apricots, roughly chopped
25g (1oz) flaked almonds
icing sugar to dust (optional)

1 Preheat the oven to 180°C (160°C fan oven) mark 4. Grease a 33 × 20.5cm (13 × 8in) baking tin and base-line with baking parchment.
2 Put the butter, caster sugar, flour, baking powder, orange zest and juice, ground almonds and eggs into the bowl of a large freestanding mixer. Mix on a low setting for 30 seconds, then increase the speed and mix for 1 minute or until thoroughly combined. (Alternatively, mix well, using a wooden spoon.)
3 Remove the bowl from the mixer. Using a large metal spoon, fold in the apricots. Spoon the mixture into the prepared tin, level the surface and sprinkle the flaked almonds over the top.
4 Bake for 30–40 minutes until risen and golden brown and a skewer inserted into the centre comes out clean. Leave to cool in the tin.
5 Cut into 18 bars. Dust with icing sugar, if you like.

TO STORE
Wrap in clingfilm and store in an airtight container. They will keep for up to three days.

NUTRITION PER BAR
277 cals | 16g fat (8g sats) | 30g carbs | 0.4g salt **V**

BLACKBERRY TRAYBAKE

Cuts into 24 squares
Preparation 20 minutes
Cooking time about 45 minutes, plus cooling and setting

275g (10oz) unsalted butter, softened, plus extra to grease
275g (10oz) golden caster sugar
400g (14oz) self-raising flour
1½ tsp baking powder
5 medium eggs, beaten
finely grated zest of 1 large orange
1 tbsp vanilla extract
4–5 tbsp milk
250g (9oz) blackberries
40g (1½oz) flaked almonds

For the icing
150g (5oz) icing sugar
1 tsp vanilla extract
about 2 tbsp orange juice

1 Preheat the oven to 190°C (170°C fan oven) mark 5. Grease a shallow 30.5 x 20.5cm (12 x 8in) baking tin and line with greaseproof paper.
2 Put the butter and caster sugar into a large bowl. Sift in the flour and baking powder, then add the eggs, orange zest, vanilla extract and milk, and beat together until light and fluffy.
3 Using a metal spoon, fold in the blackberries. Spoon into the prepared tin and dot with the almonds.
4 Bake for 40–45 minutes until springy to the touch. Cool in the tin for 5 minutes, then turn out on to a wire rack and leave to cool completely.
5 When the cake is cool, make the icing. Sift the icing sugar into a bowl, then add the vanilla extract and orange juice, mixing as you go, until smooth and runny. Drizzle over the cake and leave for 30 minutes to set. Cut into 24 squares to serve.

TO STORE
Wrap in clingfilm and store in an airtight container. It will keep for up to four days.

FREEZING TIP
— To freeze, complete the recipe to the end of step 4. Cool completely, keeping the cake in its greaseproof paper, then wrap in clingfilm. Freeze for up to one month.
— To use, thaw overnight at cool room temperature. Complete the recipe.

NUTRITION PER SQUARE
239 cals | 12g fat (7g sats) | 32g carbs | 0.4g salt **V**

VICTORIA SPONGE

Cuts into 10 slices
Preparation 30 minutes
Cooking time about 25 minutes, plus cooling

175g (6oz) unsalted butter at room temperature,
    plus extra to grease
175g (6oz) golden caster sugar
3 medium eggs
175g (6oz) self-raising flour, sifted
3–4 tbsp jam
a little icing sugar to dust

1 Grease two 18cm (7in) sandwich tins and base-line with
greaseproof paper. Preheat the oven to 190°C (170°C fan
oven) mark 5.
2 Put the butter and caster sugar into a large bowl and, using
a hand-held electric whisk, beat together until pale and fluffy.
Add the eggs, one at a time, beating well after each addition
and adding a spoonful of flour to the mixture if it looks as if
it's about to curdle. Using a large metal spoon, fold in the
remaining flour.
3 Divide the mixture evenly between the prepared tins and
level the surface with a palette knife. Bake in the centre of the
oven for 20–25 minutes until the cakes are well risen and
spring back when lightly pressed in the centre. Loosen the
edges with a palette knife and leave in the tins for 5 minutes.
4 Turn out, remove the lining paper and leave to cool on a
wire rack. Sandwich the two cakes together with jam and dust
icing sugar over the top. Slice and serve.

TO STORE
Store in an airtight container. It will keep for up to
three days. If stored in the fridge it will keep for up
to one week.

NUTRITION PER SLICE
445 cals | 21g fat (11g sats) | 30g carbs | 0.8g salt Ⓥ

CARROT CAKE

Cuts into 12 slices
Preparation 15 minutes
Cooking time 40 minutes, plus cooling

250ml (9fl oz) sunflower oil, plus extra to grease
225g (8oz) light muscovado sugar
3 large eggs
225g (8oz) self-raising flour
large pinch of salt
$1/2$ tsp each ground mixed spice, ground nutmeg
    and ground cinnamon
250g (9oz) carrots, peeled and coarsely grated

For the frosting
50g (2oz) butter, preferably unsalted, at room temperature
225g pack cream cheese
25g (1oz) golden icing sugar
$1/2$ tsp vanilla extract
8 pecan halves, roughly chopped

1 Preheat the oven to 180°C (160°C fan oven) mark 4.
Grease two 18cm (7in) sandwich tins and base-line with
greaseproof paper.
2 Using a hand-held electric whisk, whisk the oil and
muscovado sugar together to combine, then whisk in the eggs,
one at a time.
3 Sift the flour, salt and spices together over the mixture,
then gently fold in, using a large metal spoon. Tip the carrots
into the bowl and fold in.
4 Divide the cake mixture between the prepared tins and
bake for 30–40 minutes until golden and a skewer inserted
into the centre comes out clean. Remove from the oven and
leave in the tins for 10 minutes, then turn out on to a wire
rack and leave to cool completely.
5 To make the frosting, beat the butter and cream cheese
together in a bowl until light and fluffy. Sift in the icing sugar,
add the vanilla extract and beat well until smooth. Spread
one-third of the frosting over one cake and sandwich together
with the other cake. Spread the remaining frosting on top and
sprinkle with the pecan halves.

TO STORE

Store in an airtight container. Eat within two days. Alternatively,
the cake will keep for up to one week in an airtight container
if it is stored before the frosting is applied.

NUTRITION PER SLICE
383 cals | 32g fat (10g sats) | 24g carbs | 0.3g salt Ⓥ

BLACK FOREST GATEAU

Serves 12
Preparation 30 minutes, plus cooling
Cooking time about 50 minutes

125g (4oz) unsalted butter, melted
200g (7oz) plain flour
50g (2oz) cornflour
50g (2oz) cocoa powder, plus extra to dust
2 tsp espresso instant coffee powder
1 tsp baking powder
4 large eggs, separated
300g (11oz) golden caster sugar
2 × 300g jars morello cherries in syrup
2 tbsp Kirsch
200ml (7fl oz) double cream
2 tbsp icing sugar, sifted
fresh cherries and chocolate curls (see Cook's Tip,
    page 379) to decorate

1 Preheat the oven to 180°C (160°C fan oven) mark 4.
Brush a little of the melted butter over the base and sides
of a 20.5cm (8in) round × 9cm (3½ in) deep cake tin. Line the
base and sides with baking parchment.
2 Sift the flour, cornflour, cocoa powder, coffee powder and
baking powder together three times – this helps to add air
and makes sure the ingredients are well mixed.
3 Put the egg yolks, caster sugar and 100ml (3½ fl oz) cold
water into a freestanding mixer and whisk for 8 minutes
until the mixture leaves a trail for 3 seconds when the whisk
is lifted.
4 Add the rest of the melted butter, pouring it around the
edge of the bowl so that the mixture doesn't lose any air,
then quickly fold it in, followed by the sifted flour mixture in
two batches.
5 In another bowl, whisk the egg whites until stiff peaks form,
then fold a spoonful into the cake mixture to loosen. Carefully
fold in the rest of the egg whites, making sure there are no
white blobs left. Pour into the prepared tin and bake in the
oven for 45–50 minutes until a skewer inserted into the
centre comes out clean. Leave in the tin for 10 minutes, then
turn out on to a wire rack to cool completely.
6 When the cake is cold, trim the top to make a flat surface.
Turn the cake over so that the top becomes the base. Using a
long serrated bread knife, carefully cut horizontally into three.
Drain the cherries, reserving 250ml (9fl oz) of the syrup. Put
the syrup into a pan and simmer to reduce by half. Stir in the
Kirsch. Brush the hot syrup on to each layer of the cake –
including the top – using up all the liquid.

7 Lightly whip the cream with the icing sugar. Spread one-
third over the bottom layer of cake and cover with half the
cherries. Top with the next cake layer and repeat with
another third of the cream and the remaining cherries. Top
with the final cake layer and spread the remaining cream over.
Decorate with fresh cherries, chocolate curls and a dusting of
cocoa powder.

GET AHEAD
Make the gateau up to 2 hours ahead to allow the flavours to
mingle and the syrup to moisten the cake.

NUTRITION PER SERVING
440 cals | 22g fat (12g sats) | 59g carbs | 0.8g salt 🅥

ONE-STAGE FRUIT CAKE

Serves 12
Preparation 10 minutes
Cooking time 1³/₄ hours, plus cooling

125g (4oz) soft tub margarine, plus
  extra to grease
225g (8oz) self-raising flour
2 tsp mixed spice
1 tsp baking powder
125g (4oz) soft brown sugar
225g (8oz) mixed dried fruit
2 medium eggs, beaten
2 tbsp milk

1 Preheat the oven to 170°C (150°C fan oven) mark 3. Grease and base line an 18cm (7in) round cake tin with greaseproof paper. Sift the flour, spice and baking powder into a large bowl, add the remaining ingredients and beat until thoroughly combined.
2 Turn the mixture into the tin and bake for 1³/₄ hours or until a fine warmed skewer inserted into the centre comes out clean. Turn out and cool on a wire rack.

NUTRITION PER SERVING 245 cals | 10g fat (2g sats) | 38g carbs | 0.3g salt **V**

MADEIRA CAKE

Cuts into 12 slices
Preparation 20 minutes
Cooking time 50 minutes, plus cooling

175g (6oz) butter, softened, plus extra
  to grease
125g (4oz) plain flour
125g (4oz) self-raising flour
175g (6oz) golden caster sugar
1 tsp vanilla extract
3 large eggs, beaten
1–2 tbsp milk (optional)
2–3 thin slices citron peel

1 Preheat the oven to 180°C (160°C fan oven) mark 4. Grease and line a deep 18cm (7in) round cake tin. Sift the plain and self-raising flours together.
2 Cream the butter and sugar together in a bowl until pale and fluffy, then beat in the vanilla extract. Add the eggs, a little at a time, beating well after each addition.

3 Using a metal spoon, fold in the sifted flours, adding a little milk if necessary to give a dropping consistency.
4 Spoon the mixture into the prepared tin and level the surface. Bake for 20 minutes. Lay the citron peel on the cake and bake for a further 30 minutes or until a skewer inserted into the centre comes out clean. Turn out on to a wire rack and leave to cool.

TRY SOMETHING DIFFERENT

Add the grated zest of 1 lemon at step 2. Add the juice of the lemon instead of the milk at step 3.

NUTRITION PER SLICE 260 cals | 14g fat (8g sats) | 31g carbs | 0.4g salt **V**

BATTENBURG CAKE

Makes about 10 slices
Preparation 40 minutes, plus cooling
Cooking time 40 minutes

350g (12oz) butter or margarine, plus extra for greasing
350g (12oz) caster sugar
vanilla flavouring
6 eggs, beaten
350g (12oz) self-raising flour
pink food colouring
milk
apricot jam
400g (14oz) white marzipan or almond paste (see page 436)
icing sugar to dust

1 Preheat the oven to 190°C (170°C fan oven) mark 5. Grease and line a Swiss roll tin measuring 30.5 x 20.5 x 4cm (12 x 8 x 1½ in) and divide it lengthways with a 'wall' of greaseproof paper or kitchen foil.
2 Cream the butter and sugar together until light and fluffy. Add a few drops of vanilla flavouring then gradually add the eggs a little at a time, beating well after each addition. When all the egg has been added, lightly fold in the flour, using a metal spoon.
3 Turn half the mixture into one side of the tin. Fold two drops of pink food colouring into the other half with a little milk and spoon this mixture into the second side of the tin.
4 Bake for 40–45 minutes until well risen and firm to the touch. Turn out and cool on a wire rack.
5 When the cake is cold, cut each half in half lengthways and then carefully cut away all the brown surfaces. Spread all the sides of the strips with jam and stick each yellow strip to a pink strip. Then stick one double strip on top of the other, so that the colours alternate. Press the pieces well together.
6 Roll out the marzipan thinly on a work surface dusted with a little icing sugar, into a rectangle measuring about 35.5 x 25.5 cm (14 x 10in). Wrap completely around the cake. Press firmly against the sides and trim the edges. Crimp along the outer edges and score the top of the cake with a sharp knife to give a criss-cross pattern.

TRY SOMETHING DIFFERENT
To make a chocolate Battenburg, omit the pink food colouring and add 15g (½oz) cocoa powder to the coloured half of the cake mixture.

NUTRITION PER SLICE
450 cals | 26g fat (11g sats) | 42g carbs | 0.5g salt Ⓥ

CHOCOLATE ROULADE

Serves 8
Preparation 25 minutes
Cooking time about 15 minutes

150g (5oz) dark chocolate (at least 70% cocoa solids),
    broken into pieces
5 large eggs, separated
150g (5oz) caster sugar
1 tbsp cornflour
cocoa powder to dust

For the topping
125ml (4fl oz) double cream
75g (3oz) dark chocolate, finely chopped
2 tbsp golden syrup
silver and gold balls, plus edible glitter, to decorate

For the filling
150ml (¼ pint) double cream
1 tbsp icing sugar

1 Preheat the oven to 180°C (160°C fan) mark 4. Line a 33 × 23cm (13 × 9in) shallow baking tin with baking parchment. Melt the chocolate in a heatproof bowl over a pan of gently simmering water, making sure the base of the bowl doesn't touch the water. Leave to cool.
2 In a large bowl beat together the egg yolks and caster sugar using an electric hand whisk for about 5 minutes or until pale and thick. Fold in the cooled chocolate. Put the egg whites into a clean, grease-free bowl and whisk (using clean beaters) until they form soft peaks. Use a large metal spoon to fold the whites into the chocolate mixture – be careful not to knock out too much air.
3 Spoon the mixture into the prepared tin and level the surface. Bake for 12–15 minutes, then take out of the oven and cover with a damp teatowel. Leave to cool.
4 Meanwhile, to make the topping, put the cream into a pan and bring just to the boil, then take off the heat and stir in the 75g (3oz) chocolate until melted. Stir in the golden syrup and leave to cool.
5 Make the filling by lightly whipping the cream and icing sugar in a bowl until the cream just holds its shape. Dust a rectangle of greaseproof paper, a little larger than the baking tin, with cocoa powder, then invert the cake on to the paper.

6 Remove the tin and peel off the paper. Spread the cream mixture over the cooled cake. Roll up the cake from the short edge, using the paper underneath it to help you. Transfer to a serving plate. Dust with icing sugar.

NUTRITION PER SERVING
480 cals | 31g (18g sats) | 45g carbs | 0.5g salt (V)

ALMOND AND ORANGE TORTE

Cuts into 12
Preparation 30 minutes
Cooking time 1 hour 50 minutes, plus cooling

oil to grease
plain flour to dust
1 medium orange
3 medium eggs
225g (8oz) golden caster sugar
250g (9oz) ground almonds
$^{1}/_{2}$ tsp baking powder
icing sugar to dust
crème fraîche to serve

1 Grease and line with greaseproof paper, then oil and flour
a 20.5cm (8in) springform cake tin. Put the whole orange into
a small pan and cover with water. Bring to the boil, then cover
and simmer for at least 1 hour or until tender (see Cook's
Tip). Remove from the water and leave to cool.
2 Cut the orange in half and remove the pips. Whiz in a
food processor or blender to make a smooth purée.
3 Preheat the oven to 180°C (160°C fan oven) mark 4.
Put the eggs and caster sugar into a bowl and whisk together
until thick and pale. Fold in the almonds, baking powder and
orange purée. Pour the mixture into the prepared tin.
4 Bake for 40–50 minutes until a skewer inserted into the
centre comes out clean. Leave to cool in the tin.
5 Release the clasp on the tin and remove the cake. Carefully
peel off the lining paper and put the cake on a serving plate.
Dust with icing sugar, then cut into 12 wedges. Serve with
crème fraîche.

TO STORE
Store in an airtight container. It will keep for up to three days.

COOK'S TIP
To save time, you can microwave the orange.
Put it into a small heatproof bowl, cover with 100ml
(3$^{1}/_{2}$ fl oz) water and cook in a 900W microwave oven
on full power for 10–12 minutes until soft.

NUTRITION PER SERVING
223 cals | 13g fat (1g sats) | 22g carbs | 0.1g salt **V**

WHITE CHOCOLATE TORTE

Serves 16
Preparation about 50 minutes, plus chilling and freezing
Cooking time about 2 minutes, plus cooling

125g (4oz) unsalted butter
225g (8oz) ginger snaps or digestive biscuits, roughly broken
750g (1lb 11oz) white chocolate
568ml carton double cream
white Maltesers to decorate

1 Line the base and sides of a 20.5 × 6.5cm (8 × 2½in) springform tin with non-stick baking parchment or greaseproof paper. Melt the butter in a pan. Whiz the biscuits in a food processor until finely crushed. Tip the crumbs into a bowl and stir in the melted butter. Spread evenly over the base of the prepared tin and press down. Chill for 15 minutes to set.

2 Chop 700g (1½lb) chocolate and combine with half the cream in a bowl set over a pan of barely simmering water, making sure the base of the bowl doesn't touch the water. Leave the chocolate to melt, but don't stir it – this might take as long as 30 minutes. Once melted, remove from the heat and stir until smooth, then leave to cool for 15 minutes or until just beginning to thicken, stirring occasionally. Don't allow it to cool completely or the cream won't fold in evenly.

3 In a separate bowl, whip the remaining cream until soft peaks form, then fold into the chocolate mixture. Pour over the biscuit base and chill for 3 hours.

4 Pull a vegetable peeler across the remaining white chocolate to make rough curls and scatter them over the torte, then arrange the Maltesers on top. Freeze for 15 minutes, then remove from the tin and serve.

FREEZING TIP
To freeze, complete the recipe up to one month ahead, then freeze the torte in its tin. When frozen, remove the torte from the tin and carefully wrap in clingfilm before returning to the freezer. To use, thaw overnight in the fridge, then put back in the freezer for 15 minutes before serving to make sure it's chilled.

NUTRITION PER SERVING
563 cals | 44g fat (26g sats) | 40g carbs | 0.5g salt Ⓥ

DUNDEE CAKE

Cuts into 16 slices
Preparation 20 minutes
Cooking time about 2 hours, plus cooling

225g (8oz) butter or margarine, softened, plus extra
 to grease
125g (4oz) currants
125g (4oz) raisins
50g (2oz) blanched almonds, chopped
125g (4oz) chopped mixed candied peel
300g (11oz) plain flour
225g (8oz) light muscovado sugar
finely grated zest of 1 lemon
4 large eggs, beaten
75g (3oz) split almonds, to finish

1 Preheat the oven to 170°C (150°C fan oven) mark 3.
Grease and line a deep 20cm (8in) round cake tin. Wrap a
double thickness of brown paper around the outside and
secure with string.
2 Combine the dried fruit, chopped nuts and peel in a bowl.
Sift in a little flour and stir to coat the fruit.
3 Cream the butter and sugar together in a bowl until pale
and fluffy, then beat in the lemon zest. Add the eggs a little at
a time, beating well after each addition.
4 Sift in the remaining flour and fold in lightly, using a metal
spoon, then fold in the fruit and nut mixture.
5 Turn the mixture into the prepared tin and, using the back
of a metal spoon, make a slight hollow in the centre. Arrange
the split almonds on top.
6 Bake on the centre shelf of the oven for 2 hours or until
a skewer inserted into the centre comes out clean. Loosely
cover the top of the cake with foil if it appears to be
browning too quickly. Leave in the tin for 15 minutes, then
turn out on to a wire rack and leave to cool completely.
Wrap in greaseproof paper and foil and leave to mature
for at least a week before cutting.

NUTRITION PER SLICE
350 cals | 18g fat (8g sats) | 45g carbs | 0.4g salt **V**

SACHERTORTE

Cuts into 12 slices
Preparation 35 minutes
Cooking time 45–55 minutes, plus cooling and setting

175g (6oz) unsalted butter, at room temperature,
    plus extra to grease
225g (8oz) plain chocolate (at least 70% cocoa solids),
    broken into pieces
175g (6oz) golden caster sugar
5 medium eggs, lightly beaten
3 tbsp cocoa powder
125g (4oz) self-raising flour
4 tbsp brandy
1 × quantity warm Chocolate Ganache (see page 436)
12 lilac sugar-coated almonds, or 50g (2oz) milk chocolate,
    melted

1   Preheat the oven to 190°C (170°C fan oven) mark 5.
Grease a 20.5cm (8in) springform cake tin and line with
baking parchment.
2   Melt the chocolate in a heatproof bowl over a pan of
gently simmering water, making sure the base of the bowl
doesn't touch the water. Cool for 5 minutes. Cream together
the butter and sugar until pale and fluffy. Gradually beat in
two-thirds of the beaten eggs – don't worry if the mixture
curdles. Sift in the cocoa powder and 3 tbsp flour, then
gradually beat in the remaining eggs. Fold in the remaining
flour. Fold in the melted chocolate until evenly incorporated.
Stir in 2 tbsp brandy. Pour the mixture into the prepared tin.
3   Bake for 45 minutes. If necessary, loosely cover the top
of the cake with foil if it appears to be browning too quickly.
To test if done, insert a skewer into the centre of the cake –
it should come out clean. Cool in the tin for 30 minutes, then
turn out on to a wire rack and leave to cool completely.
4   Drizzle with the remaining brandy, then position the wire
rack over a tray. Ladle the ganache over the top of the cake,
letting it trickle down the sides. Using a palette knife, spread it
evenly over the cake. Decorate with almonds or melted milk
chocolate and leave for about 1 hour to set.

NUTRITION PER SLICE
496 cals | 33g fat (20g sats) | 45g carbs | 0.7g salt 🅥

SIMNEL CAKE

Cuts into 12 slices
Preparation 1½ hours, plus setting
Cooking time 2¾ hours, plus cooling

250g (9oz) unsalted butter, softened, plus extra to grease
grated zest of 2 unwaxed lemons
250g (9oz) golden caster sugar
4 large eggs, beaten
250g (9oz) plain flour
½ tsp ground mixed spice
75g (3oz) ground almonds
50g (2oz) mixed candied peel, finely chopped
150g (5oz) currants
300g (11oz) sultanas
75g (3oz) natural glacé cherries, halved
600g (1lb 5oz) almond paste (see page 436) or ready-made
    white marzipan
100g (3½ oz) icing sugar, plus extra to dust
2 tbsp thin honey, warmed
1 medium egg, beaten, to glaze

NUTRITION PER SLICE
750 cals | 36g fat (12g sats) | 104g carbs | 0.5g salt Ⓥ

1 Preheat the oven to 170°C (150°C fan oven) mark 3. Grease a 20cm (8in) round, 7.5cm (3in) deep cake tin and line with greaseproof paper.

2 Using a free-standing mixer or hand-held electric whisk, beat the butter and lemon zest together until very soft. Gradually add the sugar and continue beating until light and fluffy. Slowly beat in the eggs until evenly incorporated.

3 Sift in the flour with the mixed spice, then add the ground almonds, candied peel, currants, sultanas and glacé cherries. Using a large metal spoon, fold the ingredients together, until evenly combined. Set aside.

4 Spoon just over half of the cake mixture into the prepared tin and smooth the surface. Roll out 200g (7oz) almond paste on a surface lightly dusted with icing sugar to an 18cm (7in) round.

5 Put the almond paste round on top of the mixture in the tin, then cover with the remaining cake mixture. Smooth the surface and make a slight hollow in the centre, then brush lightly with cold water. Wrap a double layer of brown paper around the outside of the tin and secure with string. Bake for 1¼ hours. Cover with greaseproof paper, lower the oven setting to 150°C (130°C fan oven) mark 2 and bake for a further 1½ hours or until cooked to the centre.

6 Cool in the tin for 1 hour, then turn out on to a wire rack and leave to cool completely. Wrap in greaseproof paper and foil and store in an airtight container for up to two weeks.

7 When ready to decorate, roll out 200g (7oz) almond paste to a 20.5cm (8in) round. Cut a 7.5cm (3in) round from the centre and add this piece to the remaining almond paste. Brush the top of the cake with honey, cover with the almond paste ring and press down. Crimp the edge with your fingers.

8 Divide the rest of the almond paste into 11 or 12 pieces (see Cook's Tip) and shape into oval balls. Brush the ring with the beaten egg, position the balls on top and brush them with egg. Put a disc of foil over the exposed centre of the cake, then put under a hot grill for 1–2 minutes to brown the almond paste.

9 Mix the icing sugar with 2–3 tbsp warm water to make a smooth icing. Remove the foil disc, then pour the icing on to the exposed centre and smooth it with a palette knife. Leave the icing to set. To finish, secure a yellow ribbon around the side of the cake.

COOK'S TIP
Simnel cake is the classic Easter celebration cake, its marzipan balls representing the disciples – either 11 or 12 – depending on whether you think Judas should be included.

RICH FRUIT CAKE

Cuts into 16 slices
Preparation 30 minutes
Cooking time 4 hours, plus cooling

625g (1lb 6oz) currants
225g (8oz) each sultanas and raisins
175g (6oz) glacé cherries
125g (4oz) each mixed peel and flaked almonds
400g (14oz) plain flour
1 tsp each cinnamon and mixed spice
350g (12oz) butter, softened
350g (12oz) muscovado sugar
zest of ¼ lemon
6 medium eggs, beaten
4–5 tbsp brandy

1 Preheat the oven to 150°C (130°C fan oven) mark 2. Grease and line a 20.5cm (8in) cake tin using a double thickness of greaseproof paper. Tie a double band of brown paper around the outside and secure with string. Stand the tin on a baking sheet, double lined with brown paper.
2 Put the dried fruit, glacé cherries, peel and almonds into a large bowl. Stir, then cover the bowl with clingfilm. Leave for several hours.
3 Sift the flour and spices together into another bowl. Put the butter, muscovado sugar and lemon zest into another bowl and cream together until pale and fluffy. Add the beaten eggs gradually, beating well after each addition.
4 Gradually fold the flour into the creamed mixture, then fold in 2 tablespoons brandy. Finally fold in the fruit and nuts.
5 Spoon the mixture into the tin and spread evenly. Tap the tin sharply on the worksurface to remove any air pockets. Smooth the surface with the back of a metal spoon, making a slight depression in the centre.
6 Bake for 4 hours. Test the cake to see if it is cooked 15 minutes before the end of the baking time. It should feel firm and a skewer inserted into the centre should come out clean. If necessary, return the cake to the oven, and re-test at 15-minute intervals. Cool in the tin.
7 Turn out the cake with its lining paper. Prick the top all over with a skewer and spoon 2 tablespoons of brandy over. Wrap in a double thickness of foil.
8 Store the cake in a cool dry place for 1 week. Unwrap and spoon over another tablespoon of brandy, if you like. Re-wrap and store upside down to keep the top flat.

TO STORE
Store in an airtight container for up to three months.

ICING THE CAKE

Makes enough to cover a 20.5cm (8in) cake
Preparation: 30 minutes, plus drying and cooling

4 tbsp apricot jam
1 fruit cake (see opposite)
sifted icing sugar to dust
450g almond paste (see page 436)
vegetable oil to grease
150g (5oz) glacier mint sweets
500g packet royal icing sugar
75 x 2cm (30 x ¾in) silver ribbon
silver candles

1 Gently heat the jam in a pan with 1 tbsp water until softened, then press through a sieve into a bowl to make a smooth glaze. Put the cake on a board and brush over the top and sides with the glaze.
2 Dust a rolling pin and work surface with a little icing sugar and roll out the marzipan to a round about 15cm (6in) larger than the cake. Position over the cake and ease to fit around the sides, pressing out any creases. Trim off the excess around the base. Leave to dry for 24 hours.
3 Preheat the oven to 180°C (160°C fan oven) mark 4. Line a baking sheet with foil and brush lightly with oil. Unwrap the mints and put pairs of sweets on the baking sheet about 1cm (½in) apart, leaving 5cm (2in) of space between each pair, to allow room for them to spread as they melt. Cook for 3–4 minutes until the sweets have melted and are just starting to bubble around the edges. Leave to cool on the foil for 3–4 minutes until firm enough to be lifted off. Use kitchen scissors to snip the pieces into large slivers and shards.
4 Wrap the ribbon around the edge of the cake. Put the icing sugar in a bowl and make up according to the pack instructions. Using a small palette knife, spread the icing over the top of the cake, flicking it into small peaks as you go. Then tease the edges of the icing down the sides of the cake to form icicles.
5 While the icing is still soft, push the mint shards into the top of the cake and insert the silver candles. Leave the cake to dry. Light the candles and serve.

TO STORE
Once cut into, store the cake in a container in a cool, dry place. It will keep for up to two weeks.

NUTRITION PER SLICE (CAKE AND ICING)
569 cals | 17g fat (6g sats) | 100g carbs | 0.2g salt Ⓥ

RICH FRUIT CAKE CHART

QUANTITIES AND SIZES FOR RICH FRUIT CAKES

(See previous pages for recipe method.)
To make a formal cake for a birthday, wedding or anniversary, the following chart will show you the quantity of ingredients required to fill the chosen cake tin or tins, whether round or square.

Note: When baking large cakes, 25.5cm (10in) and upwards, it is advisable to reduce the oven temperature to 130°C (110°C fan) mark ½ after two-thirds of the cooking time.

The amounts of almond paste quoted in this chart will give a thin covering. The quantities of Royal Icing should be enough for two coats. If using ready-to-roll fondant icing, use the quantities suggested for Royal Icing as a rough guide.

Size	Square tin	Round tin	Cooking time	Weight when cooked	Ingredients
1	12.5cm (5in)	15cm (6in)	2½–3 hours	1.1kg (2½lb)	225g (8oz) currants, 125g (4oz) each sultanas and raisins, 50g (2oz) glacé cherries, 25g (1oz) each mixed peel and flaked almonds, a little lemon zest, 175g (6oz) plain flour, 4 tsp each mixed spice and cinnamon, 150g (5oz) each softened butter and soft brown sugar, 2½ medium eggs, beaten, 2–3 tbsp brandy. Almond paste: 350g (12oz) Royal icing: 450g (1lb)
2	15cm (6in)	18cm (7in)	3 hours	1.6kg (3½lb)	350g (12oz) currants, 125g (4oz) each sultanas and raisins, 75g (3oz) glacé cherries, 50g (2oz) each mixed peel and flaked almonds, a little lemon zest, 200g (7oz) plain flour, ½ tsp each mixed spice and cinnamon, 175g (6oz) each softened butter and soft brown sugar, 3 medium eggs, beaten, 2–3 tbsp brandy. Almond paste: 450g (1lb) Royal icing: 550g (1¼lb)
3	20.5cm (8in)	23cm (9in)	4 hours	2.7kg (6lb)	625g (1lb 6oz) currants, 225g (8oz) each sultanas and raisins, 175g (6oz) glacé cherries, 125g (4oz) each mixed peel and flaked almonds, zest of ¼ lemon, 400g (14oz) plain flour, 1 tsp each cinnamon and mixed spice, 350g (12oz) each softened butter and soft brown sugar, 6 medium eggs, beaten, 4–5 tbsp brandy. Almond paste: 800g (1¾lb) Royal icing: 900g (2lb)
4	23cm (9in)	25.5cm (10in)	6 hours	4kg (8lb 13oz)	800g (1¾lb) currants, 375g (13oz) each sultanas and raisins, 250g (9oz) glacé cherries, 150g (5oz) each mixed peel and flaked almonds, zest of ¼–½ lemon, 600g (1lb 5oz) plain flour, 1 tsp each mixed spice and cinnamon, 500g (1lb 2oz) each softened butter and soft brown sugar, 9 medium eggs, beaten, 5–6 tbsp brandy. Almond paste: 900g (2lb) Royal icing: 1kg (2¼lb)
5	28cm (11in)	30.5cm (12in)	8 hours	6.7kg (14¾lb)	1.5kg (3lb 4oz) currants, 525g (1lb 3oz) each sultanas and raisins, 350g (12oz) glacé cherries, 250g (9oz) each mixed peel and flaked almonds, zest of ½ lemon, 825g (1lb 13oz) plain flour, 2½ tsp each mixed spice and cinnamon, 800g (1¾lb) each softened butter and soft brown sugar, 14 medium eggs, beaten, 7–8 tbsp brandy. Almond paste: 1.1kg (2½lb) Royal icing: 1.4kg (3lb)
6	30.5cm (12in)	33cm (13in)	8½ hours	7.7kg (17lb)	1.7kg (3lb 12oz) currants, 625g (1lb 6oz) each sultanas and raisins, 425g (15oz) glacé cherries, 275g (10oz) each mixed peel and flaked almonds, zest of 1 lemon, 1kg (2¼lb) plain flour, 2½ tsp each mixed spice and cinnamon, 950g (2lb 2oz) each softened butter and soft brown sugar, 17 medium eggs, beaten, 8–9 tbsp brandy. Almond paste: 1.4kg (3lb) Royal icing: 1.6kg (3½lb)

EASTER FUDGE CHOCOLATE CAKE

Cuts into 12 slices
Preparation 30 minutes, plus cooling
Cooking time about 50 minutes

175g (6oz) unsalted butter, softened, plus extra to grease
150g (5oz) plain flour
50g (2oz) cocoa powder
1 tsp baking powder
pinch of salt
150g (5oz) light muscovado sugar
3 medium eggs, beaten
250ml (9fl oz) soured cream
1 tsp vanilla extract

For the icing and decoration
100g (3¹/₂oz) plain chocolate, finely chopped
150g (5oz) unsalted butter, softened
125g (4oz) cream cheese
175g (6oz) icing sugar, sifted
50g (2oz) chocolate curls (see page 379), lightly crushed
foil-covered chocolate eggs

1 Preheat the oven to 180°C (160°C fan oven) mark 4.
Grease and line a 20.5cm (8in) springform tin. Sift the flour,
cocoa powder, baking powder and salt into a bowl.
2 Using an electric mixer or electric beaters, mix the butter
and muscovado sugar in a separate bowl until pale and fluffy –
about 5 minutes. Gradually add the beaten eggs, mixing well
after each addition. Add a little of the flour mixture if the
butter mixture looks like curdling. In one go, add the remaining
flour mixture, the soured cream and vanilla extract, then fold
everything together gently with a metal spoon. Spoon into the
prepared tin and bake for 40–50 minutes until a skewer
inserted into centre comes out clean. Cool in the tin.
3 To make the icing, melt the chocolate in a heatproof bowl
set over a pan of barely simmering water, making sure the
base of the bowl doesn't touch the water. Leave to cool for
15 minutes. In a separate bowl, beat the butter and cream
cheese with a wooden spoon until combined. Beat in the icing
sugar, then the cooled chocolate. Take care not to over-beat
the mixture – it should be fudgey, not stiff.
4 Remove the cake from the tin, cut in half horizontally
and use some icing to sandwich the layers together.
Transfer to a cake stand, then ice the top and sides, smoothing
with a palette knife. Decorate with crushed curls and
chocolate eggs.

NUTRITION PER SLICE
590 cals | 42g fat (25g sats) | 0g carbs | 0.1g salt Ⓥ

ROYAL ICING

Makes 450g (1lb), enough to cover the top and sides of a
20.5cm (8in) cake
Preparation 20 minutes

2 large egg whites, or 1 tbsp egg albumen powder
2 tsp liquid glycerine (optional, see Cook's Tips)
450g (1lb) icing sugar, sifted

1 If using the egg whites and the glycerine, put them in a
bowl and stir just enough to break up the egg whites. If using
albumen powder, mix according to the pack instructions.
2 Add a little icing sugar and mix gently with a wooden
spoon to incorporate as little air as possible.
3 Add a little more icing sugar as the mixture becomes
lighter. Continue to add the icing sugar, stirring gently but
thoroughly until the mixture is stiff and stands in soft peaks.
For coating it should form soft peaks; for piping it should be
a little stiffer.
4 Transfer to an airtight container, cover the surface closely
with clingfilm to prevent it drying out, then seal. When
required, stir the icing slowly.

COOK'S TIPS

— Glycerine keeps the icing from becoming hard.
Omit it if the icing is required to cover a tiered
cake, as a very hard surface is required to support
the tiers.
— It is better not to make up more than 900g (2lb)
at a time.

NUTRITION PER 25G (1OZ)
100 cals | 0g fat (0g sats) | 26g carbs | trace salt Ⓥ

EASIEST ICING

Makes 675g (1lb 7oz), enough to cover a 20.5cm (8in) almond
paste-covered cake
Preparation 20 minutes, plus drying

3 medium egg whites
2 tbsp lemon juice
2 tsp glycerine
675g (1lb 7oz) icing sugar, sifted

1 Put the egg whites into a large bowl and whisk until frothy.
There should be just a layer of bubbles across the top. Add
the lemon juice, glycerine and 2 tbsp icing sugar, and whisk
until smooth.
2 Whisk in the rest of the sugar, a little at a time, until the
mixture is smooth, thick and forming soft peaks.
3 Using a palette knife, smooth half the icing over the top
and sides of the cake, then repeat using the remaining icing to
cover. Run the knife around the sides to neaten, then use the
tip to make peaks all over the top. Leave to dry in a cool
place for at least 48 hours.

NUTRITION PER 25G (1OZ)
84 cals | 0g fat (0g sats) | 22g carbs | trace salt Ⓥ

READY-TO-ROLL (FONDANT) ICING

Ready-to-roll icing is pliable and can be used to cover cakes
or moulded into decorative shapes. Blocks of ready-to-roll
icing (fondant or sugar paste) are available in a variety of
colours from supermarkets and specialist cake decorating
shops. A 450g (1lb) pack will cover an 18cm (7in) cake.
Wrap any unused icing in clingfilm to stop it drying out and
store in a cool, dry place.

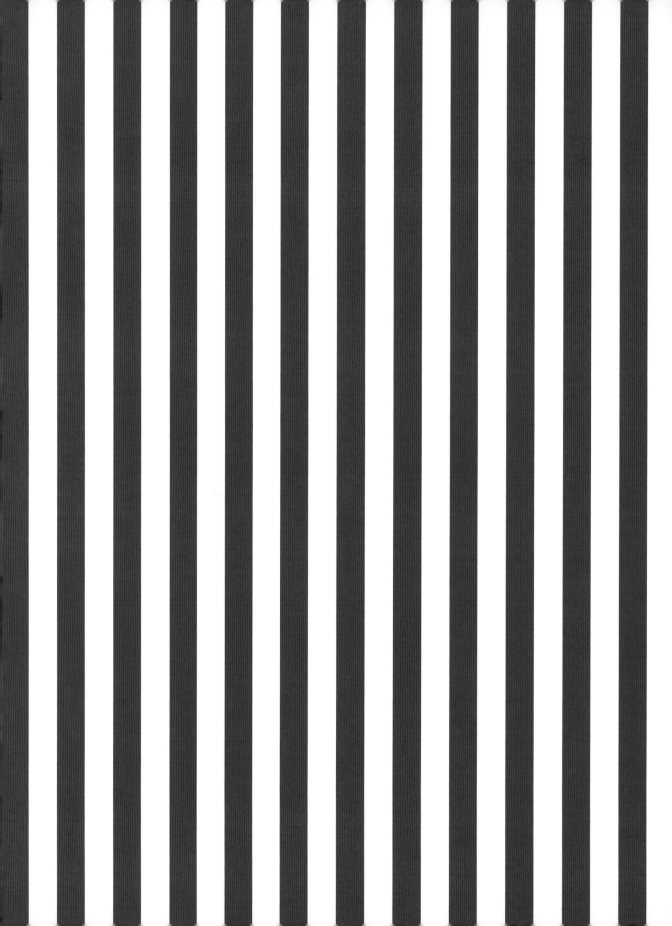

BISCUITS

SHORTBREAD

Makes 18
Preparation 20 minutes, plus chilling
Cooking time 15–20 minutes, plus cooling

225g (8oz) butter, at room temperature
125g (4oz) golden caster sugar
225g (8oz) plain flour
125g (4oz) rice flour
pinch of salt
golden or coloured granulated sugar to coat
caster sugar to sprinkle

1 Cream the butter and sugar together in a bowl until pale and fluffy. Sift the flours and salt together on to the creamed mixture and stir in, using a wooden spoon, until the mixture resembles breadcrumbs.
2 Gather the dough together with your hand and turn on to a clean surface. Knead very lightly until it forms a ball, then lightly roll into a sausage, about 5cm (2in) thick. Wrap in clingfilm and chill in the fridge until firm.
3 Preheat the oven to 190°C (170°C fan oven) mark 5. Line two baking sheets with greaseproof paper. Remove the clingfilm and slice the dough into discs, 7–10mm ($^1/_3$–$^1/_2$in) thick. Pour some granulated sugar on to a plate and roll the edge of each disc in the sugar. Put the shortbread, cut-side up, on the baking sheets.
4 Bake the shortbread for 15–20 minutes, depending on thickness, until very pale golden. On removing from the oven, sprinkle with caster sugar. Leave on the baking sheets for 10 minutes, then transfer to a wire rack and leave to cool.

TO STORE
Store in an airtight container. They will keep for up to two weeks.

NUTRITION PER PIECE
190 cals | 10g fat (7g sats) 23g carbs | 0.3 g salt

THE ULTIMATE CHOCOLATE CHIP COOKIE

Makes about 25 cookies
Preparation 15 minutes
Cooking time about 12 minutes

225g (8oz) unsalted butter, very soft
125g (4oz) caster sugar
150g (5oz) light muscovado sugar
1¹/₂ tbsp golden syrup
1 tsp vanilla extract
2 large eggs, beaten
375g (13oz) plain flour
1 tsp bicarbonate of soda
¹/₄ tsp salt
350g (12oz) milk chocolate, cut into large chunks

1 Preheat the oven to 200°C (180°C fan oven) mark 6.
Line three baking sheets with baking parchment.
2 Put the butter, caster and muscovado sugars, golden syrup
and vanilla extract into a bowl and, using a hand-held electric
whisk or freestanding mixer, beat until pale and fluffy – this
should take about 5 minutes.
3 Gradually beat in the eggs, adding 2 tbsp flour if the
mixture looks as if it's about to curdle. Sift in the remaining
flour, the bicarbonate of soda and salt all at once and beat in
quickly for a few seconds. Using a large metal spoon, mix in
the milk chocolate chunks.
4 Spoon heaped teaspoonfuls of the mixture on to the
baking sheets, spacing them well apart. Don't press the
mixture down – the mounds will spread during baking. For a
chewy biscuit, bake for 10 minutes until pale and golden; for a
crisper version, bake for 12 minutes. Transfer from the trays
on to wire racks and leave to cool.

TO STORE
Store in an airtight container. They will keep for up to
one week.

NUTRITION PER COOKIE
223 cals | 11g fat (7g sats) | 28g carbs | 0.9g salt

SULTANA AND PECAN COOKIES

Makes 20
Preparation 15 minutes
Cooking time 12–15 minutes, plus cooling

225g (8oz) unsalted butter, at room temperature,
    plus extra to grease
175g (6oz) light muscovado sugar
2 medium eggs, lightly beaten
225g (8oz) pecan nut halves
300g (11oz) self-raising flour, sifted
1/4 tsp baking powder
125g (4oz) sultanas
2 tbsp maple syrup

1 Preheat the oven to 190°C (170°C fan oven) mark 5.
Lightly grease four baking sheets.
2 Cream the butter and sugar together until the mixture is
pale and fluffy. Gradually beat in the eggs until thoroughly
combined.
3 Put 20 pecan nut halves to one side, then roughly chop the
rest and fold into the mixture with the flour, baking powder,
sultanas and syrup.
4 Roll the mixture into 20 balls and place them, spaced well
apart, on the prepared baking sheets. Using a dampened
palette knife, flatten the cookies and top each with a piece of
pecan nut.
5 Bake for 12–15 minutes until pale golden. Leave on the
baking sheets for 5 minutes, then transfer to a wire rack and
leave to cool completely.

TO STORE
Store in an airtight container. They will keep for up to
one week.

FREEZING TIP
➥ To freeze, complete the recipe to the end of step 4, then
    open-freeze a tray of unbaked cookies. When frozen,
    pack into bags or containers.
➥ To use, cook from frozen for 18–20 minutes.

NUTRITION PER COOKIE
276 cals | 18g fat (7g sats) | 27g carbs | 0.2g salt

CHRISTMAS COOKIES

Makes about 22
Preparation 25 minutes, plus chilling
Cooking time about 15 minutes, plus cooling

75g (3oz) unsalted butter, softened
100g (3 1/2 oz) caster sugar
1 medium egg
1/2 tsp vanilla extract
250g (9oz) plain flour, plus extra to dust
1/2 tsp baking powder
a selection of coloured ready-to-roll fondant icings,
    royal icing (see page 437), food colourings and
    edible decorations

1 Using a wooden spoon, cream the butter and sugar together in a large bowl until smooth. Beat in the egg and vanilla extract. Sift the flour and baking powder into the bowl and stir until combined. Tip out on to a lightly floured surface and knead gently to make a soft dough. Shape into a disc and wrap in clingfilm, then chill for 1 hour until firm.
2 Preheat the oven to 180°C (160°C fan oven) mark 4. Roll out the dough on a lightly floured surface until 5mm (1/4 in) thick. Using Christmas cookie cutters, stamp out shapes, re-rolling the trimmings if necessary. If the cookies are to be hung as decorations, use a skewer to make a 5mm (1/4 in) hole in each one. Place on two non-stick baking trays and bake for 10–15 minutes until pale golden and risen. Leave to cool on the sheets for 3 minutes to harden, then transfer to a wire rack to cool completely.
3 When the cookies are completely cool, decorate with coloured fondant icings or royal icing and edible decorations.

TO STORE
Store in an airtight container. They will keep for up to two weeks.

> NUTRITION PER COOKIE
> 94 cals | 3g fat (2g sats) | 16.5g carbs | 0.1g salt

GINGER BISCUITS

Makes 24
Preparation 15 minutes
Cooking time about 12 minutes, plus
cooling

50g (2oz) butter, plus extra to grease
125g (4oz) golden syrup
50g (2oz) dark muscovado sugar
finely grated zest of 1 orange
2 tbsp orange juice
175g (6oz) self-raising flour
1 tsp ground ginger

1 Preheat the oven to 180°C (160°C
fan oven) mark 4. Lightly grease two
large baking sheets.
2 Put the butter, golden syrup, sugar,
orange zest and juice into a heavy-
based pan and heat very gently until
melted and evenly blended.

3 Leave the mixture to cool slightly,
then sift in the flour with the ginger. Mix
thoroughly until smooth. Put small
spoonfuls of the mixture on the baking
sheets, spacing them well apart to allow
room for spreading.
4 Bake for 12 minutes or until the
biscuits are golden brown. Leave on the
baking sheets for 1 minute, then
carefully transfer to a wire rack and
leave to cool.

TO STORE
Store in an airtight container. They will
keep for up to five days.

> **NUTRITION PER BISCUIT** 55 cals |
> 2g fat (1g sats) | 10g carbs | 0.1g salt **V**

ALMOND MACAROONS

Makes 22
Preparation 10 minutes
Cooking time 12–15 minutes, plus cooling

2 medium egg whites
125g (4oz) caster sugar
125g (4oz) ground almonds
1/4 tsp almond extract
22 blanched almonds

1 Preheat the oven to 180°C (fan
oven 160°C) mark 4. Line two baking
sheets with baking parchment.
2 Whisk the egg whites in a clean,
grease-free bowl until stiff peaks form.
Gradually whisk in the sugar, a little at
a time, until thick and glossy. Gently
stir in the ground almonds and
almond extract.

3 Spoon teaspoonfuls of the mixture
on to the prepared baking sheets,
spacing them slightly apart. Press an
almond into the centre of each one and
bake in the oven for 12–15 minutes
until just golden and firm to the touch.
4 Leave on the baking sheets for
10 minutes, then transfer to a wire
rack and leave to cool completely. On
cooling, these biscuits have a soft, chewy
centre; they harden up after a few days.

TO STORE
Store in airtight containers. They will
keep for up to one week.

> **NUTRITION PER MACAROON** 86 cals |
> 6g fat (1g sats) | 7g carbs | 0g salt **V**

FLORENTINES

Makes 18
Preparation 15 minutes
Cooking time 16–20 minutes, plus cooling

65g (2¹/₂ oz) unsalted butter, plus extra to grease
50g (2oz) golden caster sugar
2 tbsp double cream
25g (1oz) sunflower seeds
20g (³/₄ oz) chopped mixed candied peel
20g (³/₄ oz) sultanas
25g (1oz) natural glacé cherries, roughly chopped
40g (1¹/₂ oz) flaked almonds, lightly crushed
15g (¹/₂ oz) plain flour
125g (4oz) plain chocolate (at least 70% cocoa solids),
    broken into pieces

1 Preheat the oven to 180°C (160°C fan oven) mark 4.
Lightly grease two large baking sheets.
2 Melt the butter in a small heavy-based pan. Add the sugar
and heat gently until dissolved, then bring to the boil. Take off
the heat and stir in the cream, seeds, peel, sultanas, cherries,
almonds and flour. Mix until evenly combined. Put heaped
teaspoonfuls on to the prepared baking sheets, spaced well
apart to allow for spreading.
3 Bake one sheet at a time, for 6–8 minutes, until the biscuits
have spread considerably and the edges are golden brown.
Using a large plain metal biscuit cutter, push the edges into the
centre to create neat rounds. Bake for a further 2 minutes or
until deep golden. Leave on the baking sheet for 2 minutes,
then transfer to a wire rack and leave to cool completely.
4 Melt the chocolate in a heatproof bowl set over a pan of
gently simmering water, making sure the base of the bowl
doesn't touch the water, stirring occasionally. Spread on the
underside of each Florentine and mark wavy lines with a fork.
Put, chocolate-side up, on a sheet of baking parchment and
leave to set.

TO STORE
Store in an airtight container. They will keep for up to
two weeks.

NUTRITION PER BISCUIT
115 cals | 8g fat (4g sats) | 11g carbs | 0.1g salt

CHOCOLATE VIENNESE FINGERS

Makes 20
Preparation 15 minutes
Cooking time 15–20 minutes, plus cooling

125g (4oz) butter, softened, plus extra to grease
25g (1oz) icing sugar
125g (4oz) plain flour
¼ tsp baking powder
a few drops of vanilla extract
50g (2oz) plain chocolate or plain chocolate-flavour
    cake covering, broken into pieces
icing sugar, to decorate (optional)

1 Preheat the oven to 190°C (170°C fan oven) mark 5 and grease two baking sheets. Beat the butter until smooth, then beat in the icing sugar until pale and fluffy.
2 Sift in the flour and baking powder. Beat well, adding the vanilla extract.
3 Put into a piping bag fitted with a medium star nozzle. Pipe out finger shapes, about 7.5cm (3in) long, on to the baking sheets, spacing them well apart.
4 Bake for 15–20 minutes. Cool on a wire rack.
5 Melt the chocolate in a heatproof bowl over a pan of gently simmering water. Dip the ends of each Viennese Finger into the melted chocolate. Leave to set on the wire rack. Dredge with icing sugar, if you like.

TO STORE
Store in an airtight container. They will keep for up to one week.

NUTRITION PER BISCUIT
86 cals | 6g fat (4g sats) | 8g carbs | 0.1g salt

HAZELNUT AND CHOCOLATE BISCOTTI

Makes about 28
Preparation 10 minutes
Cooking time 35–40 minutes, plus cooling

125g (4oz) plain flour, sifted, plus extra to dust
75g (3oz) golden caster sugar
¼ tsp baking powder
pinch of cinnamon
pinch of salt
1 large egg, beaten
1 tbsp milk
¼ tsp vanilla extract
25g (1oz) hazelnuts
25g (1oz) plain chocolate chips

1 Preheat the oven to 200°C (180°C fan oven) mark 6.
Put the flour into a large bowl. Stir in the sugar, baking
powder, cinnamon and salt. Make a well in the centre and,
using a fork, stir in the beaten egg, milk, vanilla extract,
hazelnuts and chocolate chips to form a sticky dough.
2 Turn out the dough on to a lightly floured surface and
gently knead into a ball. Roll into a 28cm (11in) log shape.
Put on a non-stick baking sheet and flatten slightly. Bake
for 20–25 minutes until pale golden.
3 Lower the oven setting to 150°C (130°C fan oven) mark
2. Transfer the biscotti log on to a chopping board and slice
diagonally with a bread knife at 1cm (½in) intervals. Arrange
the slices on the baking sheet and put back into the oven for
15 minutes or until golden and dry. Transfer to a wire rack and
leave to cool completely.

TO STORE
Store in an airtight container. They will keep for up to
one month.

NOTES
➥ To enjoy Italian-style, dunk in coffee or dessert wine.
➥ To make as gifts, divide the biscuits among four large
squares of cellophane, then draw up the edges and tie
with ribbon. Label the packages with storage information
and an eat-by date.

NUTRITION PER BISCUIT
50 cals | 1g fat (trace sats) | 9g carbs | 0g salt **V**

MILLIONAIRE'S SHORTBREAD

Makes 20 squares
Preparation 30 minutes
Cooking time 20 minutes, plus cooling

175g (6oz) unsalted butter, at room temperature, diced,
    plus extra to grease
250g (9oz) plain flour, plus extra to dust
75g (3oz) golden caster sugar

For the topping
2 × 397g cans sweetened condensed milk
100g (3¹/₂ oz) light muscovado sugar
100g (3¹/₂ oz) butter
250g (9oz) plain chocolate (at least 70% cocoa solids),
    broken into pieces

1 Preheat the oven to 180°C (160°C fan oven) mark 4.
Grease a 33 × 23cm (13 × 9in) Swiss roll tin and line with
baking parchment. Put the flour, caster sugar and butter into
a food processor and blend until the mixture forms crumbs,
then pulse a little more until it forms a ball. (Alternatively, rub
the butter into the flour and sugar in a large bowl by hand, or
using a pastry cutter, until it resembles fine crumbs. Gather
together into a ball.) Turn out on to a lightly floured surface
and knead lightly to combine.
2 Press the mixture into the prepared tin and bake for
20 minutes or until firm to the touch and a very pale brown.
3 To make the topping, put the condensed milk, muscovado
sugar and butter into a non-stick pan and cook over a
medium heat, stirring continuously until a fudge-like
consistency. (Alternatively, put into a heatproof bowl and
microwave on full power for 12 minutes – based on a 900W
oven – or until the mixture is thick and fudgy, beating with a
whisk every 2–3 minutes.) Spoon the caramel on to the
shortbread, smooth over and allow to cool.
4 To finish, melt the chocolate in a heatproof bowl set over
a pan of gently simmering water, making sure the base of the
bowl doesn't touch the water, then pour over the caramel
layer. Leave to set at room temperature, then cut into
20 squares to serve.

TO STORE
Store in an airtight container. They will keep for up to
one week.

NUTRITION PER SQUARE
369 cals | 19g fat (12g sats) | 48g carbs | 0.4g salt

TRADITIONAL FLAPJACKS

Makes 12 squares
Preparation 10 minutes
Cooking time 17 minutes, plus cooling

200g (7oz) butter, plus extra to grease
150g (5oz) demerara sugar
4 tbsp golden syrup
1 tsp ground cinnamon
finely grated zest of $^1/_2$–1 orange
400g (14oz) jumbo oats
100g (3$^1/_2$oz) raisins or sultanas

1 Preheat the oven to 190°C (170°C fan) mark 5. Grease
and line a 20.5cm (8in) square baking tin with baking
parchment. Melt the butter in a large pan and add the
sugar, syrup, cinnamon and orange zest. Heat gently until
the sugar dissolves.
2 Remove the pan from the heat and stir in the oats and
raisins or sultanas. Press the mixture into the prepared tin
and bake for 17–20 minutes until lightly golden. Cool before
cutting into squares.

TO STORE
Store the flapjacks in an airtight container for up to three days.

NUTRITION PER SQUARE
354 cals | 17g fat (9g sats) | 50g carbs | 0.4g salt

BREADS, PIZZAS AND PASTRIES

WHITE FARMHOUSE LOAF

Cuts into about 12 slices
Preparation 10 minutes, plus machine dough-making and rising
Cooking time 30–35 minutes, plus cooling

1 tsp easy-blend dried yeast
500g (1lb 2oz) strong white bread flour, plus extra
    to sprinkle
1 tbsp caster sugar
2 tbsp milk powder
1½ tsp salt
25g (1oz) butter
350ml (12fl oz) water

1 Put the ingredients into the bread maker bucket, following
the order and method specified in the manual.
2 Fit the bucket into the bread maker and set to the Basic
programme with a crust of your choice. Press start.
3 Just before baking starts, brush the top of the dough with
water and sprinkle with flour. If preferred, slash the top of the
bread lengthways with a sharp knife, taking care not to scratch
the bucket.
4 After baking, remove the bread from the machine and
shake out on to a wire rack to cool.

NUTRITION PER SLICE
180 cals | 3g fat (1g sats) | 34g carbs | 0.9g salt **V**

WHOLEMEAL LOAF

Cuts into 16 slices
Preparation 15 minutes, plus rising
Cooking time 30–35 minutes, plus cooling

225g (8oz) strong white bread flour, plus extra to dust
450g (1lb) strong wholemeal bread flour
2 tsp salt
1 tsp golden caster sugar
2 tsp easy-blend dried yeast (see Cook's Tip)
vegetable oil to grease

1 Sift the white flour into a large bowl and stir in the wholemeal flour, salt, sugar and yeast. Make a well in the centre and add about 450ml (¾ pint) warm water. Work to a smooth, soft dough, adding a little extra water if necessary.
2 Knead for 10 minutes or until smooth, then shape the dough into a ball and put into an oiled bowl. Cover and leave to rise in a warm place for 2 hours or until doubled in size.
3 Knock back the dough on a lightly floured surface and shape into a rectangle. Press into an oiled 900g (2lb) loaf tin, cover and leave to rise for a further 30 minutes.
4 Preheat the oven to 230°C (210°C fan oven) mark 8. Bake the loaf for 15 minutes. Lower the oven setting to 200°C (180°C fan oven) mark 6 and bake for a further 15–20 minutes until the bread is risen and sounds hollow when tapped underneath. Leave in the tin for 10 minutes, then turn out on to a wire rack and leave to cool.

COOK'S TIP
If available, use 40g (1½oz) fresh yeast instead of dried. Blend the yeast and sugar and leave for 15 minutes to froth, then add to the flour and salt.

NUTRITION PER SLICE
140 cals | 1g fat (0.1g sats) | 29g carbs | 0.6g salt Ⓥ

GRANARY BREAD

Cuts into 16 slices
Preparation 20 minutes, plus rising
Cooking time 30–35 minutes, plus cooling

125g (4oz) strong wholemeal bread flour, plus extra to dust
450g (1lb) malted strong Granary flour
2 tsp salt
15g (½ oz) butter, diced
125g (4oz) rolled oats, plus extra to dust
2 tsp easy-blend dried yeast
150ml (¼ pint) warm milk
1 tbsp malt extract
vegetable oil to grease

1 Put the flours into a bowl and stir in the salt. Rub in the butter, then stir in the rolled oats and yeast. Make a well in the centre and add the warm milk, malt extract and 300ml (½ pint) warm water. Work to a smooth soft dough, adding a little extra water if necessary.

2 Knead for 10 minutes or until smooth, then shape the dough into a ball and put into an oiled bowl. Cover and leave to rise in a warm place for 1–2 hours until doubled in size.
3 Knock back the dough on a lightly floured surface and shape into a large round. Put on a baking sheet, cover and leave to rise for a further 30 minutes.
4 Preheat the oven to 230°C (210°C fan oven) mark 8. Using a sharp knife, cut a cross on the top of the loaf and sprinkle a few more oats over. Bake for 15 minutes. Lower the oven setting to 200°C (180°C fan oven) mark 6 and bake for a further 15–20 minutes until the bread is risen and sounds hollow when tapped underneath. Transfer to a wire rack and leave to cool.

NUTRITION PER SLICE 160 cals | 2g fat (0.7g sats) | 30g carbs | 0.6g salt Ⓥ

FLOURY BAPS

Makes 8 rolls
Preparation 10 minutes, plus machine dough-making and rising
Cooking time 18–20 minutes, plus cooling

1 tsp easy-blend dried yeast
450g (1lb) strong white bread flour, plus extra to dust
1 tsp salt
1 tsp golden caster sugar
15g (½ oz) butter
150ml (¼ pint) milk, plus extra to brush
125ml (4fl oz) water

1 Put the ingredients into the bread maker bucket, following the order and method specified in the manual.
2 Fit the bucket into the bread maker and set to the Dough programme. Lightly grease a large baking sheet.

3 Once the dough is ready, turn it out on to a lightly floured surface and punch it down to deflate. Divide into eight even-sized pieces. Shape each piece into a round and flatten with the palm of your hand until about 10cm (4in) in diameter. Space slightly apart on a baking sheet and brush lightly with milk. Sprinkle generously with flour, cover loosely with a cloth and leave to rise for 30–40 minutes until doubled in size.
4 Preheat the oven to 200°C (180°C fan oven) mark 6. Make a deep impression in the centre of each bap with your thumb. Dust with a little more flour and bake for 18–20 minutes until risen and pale golden around the edges. Eat warm or transfer to a wire rack to cool.

NUTRITION PER ROLL 220 cals | 3g fat (1g sats) | 45g carbs | 0.7g salt Ⓥ

DARK RYE BREAD

Makes cuts into 16 slices
Preparation 20 minutes, plus rising
Cooking time about 50 minutes, plus cooling

350g (12oz) rye flour, plus extra to dust
50g (2oz) strong wholemeal bread flour
zest of 1 lemon
1 tsp salt
25g (1oz) butter
1 tsp caraway seeds, lightly crushed (optional)
125g (4oz) cool mashed potato
15g (^{1}/$_2$oz) fresh yeast or 1^1/$_2$ tsp dried yeast and 1 tsp sugar
1 tsp sugar
50g (2oz) molasses or black treacle
oil to grease

1 Mix together the flours, lemon zest and salt. Rub in the butter, caraway seeds, if you like, and mashed potato.
2 Blend the fresh yeast with 150ml (^{1}/$_4$ pint) tepid water. If using dried yeast, sprinkle it into the water with 1 tsp sugar and leave in a warm place for 15 minutes or until frothy. Heat the other 1 tsp sugar, molasses and 2 tbsp water together. Cool until tepid.
3 Pour the yeast liquid and molasses mixture on to the dry ingredients and beat well to form a firm dough. Knead on a lightly floured surface for 10 minutes or until smooth and no longer sticky. Place in an oiled bowl, cover with oiled clingfilm and leave to rise in a warm place for about 1^1/$_2$ hours or until doubled in size.
4 Knead again for 5 minutes, then shape into a large round, about 18cm (7in) in diameter. Place on a baking sheet. Cut a criss-cross pattern on the surface of the loaf to a depth of 5mm (^{1}/$_4$ in). Dust with a little more flour. Leave to rise in a warm place for 10–15 minutes. Preheat the oven to 200°C (180°C fan oven) mark 6.
5 Bake the loaf in the oven for about 50 minutes. Turn on to a wire rack and leave to cool completely.

NUTRITION PER SLICE
112 cals | 2g fat (1g sats) 22g carbs | 0.4g salt ⓥ

CORNBREAD

Serves 8
Preparation 5 minutes
Cooking time 25–30 minutes, plus
    resting

oil to grease
125g (4oz) plain flour
175g (6oz) dried polenta or cornmeal
1 tbsp baking powder
1 tbsp caster sugar
1/2 tsp salt
300ml (1/2 pint) buttermilk, or equal
    quantities of natural yogurt and
    milk, mixed together
2 medium eggs
4 tbsp extra virgin olive oil

1 Preheat the oven to 200°C (180°C fan oven) mark 6. Generously grease a 20.5cm (8in) square shallow tin.
2 Put the flour into a large bowl, then add the polenta or cornmeal, the baking powder, sugar and salt. Make a well in the centre and pour in the buttermilk or yogurt and milk mixture. Add the eggs and olive oil, and stir together until evenly mixed.
3 Pour the mixure into the tin and bake for 25–30 minutes until firm to the touch. Insert a skewer into the centre – if should come out clean.
4 Leave the cornbread to rest in the tin for 5 minutes, then turn out and cut into chunky triangles. Serve warm with butter.

NUTRITION PER SERVING 229 cals |
8g fat (1g sats) | 33g carbs | 1.3g salt Ⓥ

OATMEAL SODA BREAD

Cuts into about 10 slices
Preparation 10 minutes
Cooking time 25 minutes

25g (1oz) butter, plus extra to grease
275g (10oz) plain wholemeal flour
175g (6oz) coarse oatmeal
2 tsp cream of tartar
1 tsp salt
about 300ml (1/2 pint) milk and water,
    mixed

1 Preheat the oven to 220°C (200°C fan oven) mark 7. Grease and base-line a 900g (2lb) loaf tin.
2 Mix together all the dry ingredients in a bowl. Rub in the butter, then add the milk and water to bind to a soft dough. Spoon into the prepared tin.
3 Bake in the oven for 25 minutes or until golden brown and well risen. Turn out on to a wire rack and leave to cool slightly. The bread is best eaten on the day it is made.

NUTRITION PER SLICE 183 cals |
4g fat (2g sats) | 31g carbs | 0.6g salt Ⓥ

FOCACCIA

Serves 8
Preparation 5 minutes, plus machine dough-making and rising
Cooking time 20 minutes, plus cooling

1 tsp easy-blend dried yeast
475g (1lb 1oz) strong white bread flour, plus extra to dust
1¹/₂ tsp salt
3 tbsp olive oil, plus extra for greasing
300ml (¹/₂ pint) water

For the topping
fresh rosemary sprigs
2 tbsp olive oil
sea salt flakes

1 Put the dough ingredients into the bread maker bucket, following the order and method specified in the manual.
2 Fit the bucket into the bread maker and set to the Dough programme. Press start. Grease a 28cm (11in) metal flan ring and place on a greased baking sheet.
3 Once the dough is ready, turn it out on to a floured surface and punch it down to deflate. Roll out to a 25.5cm (10in) round and lay inside the flan ring, pushing the dough to the edges with your fingertips. (Don't worry if it shrinks back, the dough will expand to fill the ring as it proves.) Cover loosely with oiled clingfilm and leave to rise in a warm place for 30 minutes.
4 Using fingertips dipped in flour, make deep dimples all over the dough. Scatter with small rosemary sprigs, drizzle with the olive oil and sprinkle generously with sea salt flakes. Re-cover with oiled clingfilm and leave for a further 10 minutes, as the dough might have shrunk back when dimpled. Preheat the oven to 200°C (fan oven 180°C) mark 6.
5 Drizzle the dough with water. (This is not essential but helps the crust to stay soft during baking.) Bake for 20–25 minutes until just firm and pale golden. Transfer to a wire rack and leave to cool.

> **COOK'S TIP**
> The flan ring helps the bread to rise and bake in a perfect round, but don't worry if you haven't got one, just lay the dough, pizza style, on the baking sheet.

NUTRITION PER SERVING
264 cals | 8g fat (1g sats) | 45g carbs | 1.2g salt **V**

CRUMPETS

Makes about 24
Preparation 20 minutes, plus rising
Cooking time about 35 minutes

350g (12oz) strong plain white flour
¹/₂ tsp salt
¹/₂ tsp bicarbonate of soda
1¹/₂ tsp easy-blend dried yeast
250ml (9fl oz) warm milk
a little vegetable oil to fry
butter to serve

1 Sift the flour, salt and bicarbonate of soda into a large bowl and stir in the yeast. Make a well in the centre, then pour in 300ml (¹/₂ pint) warm water and the milk. Mix to a thick batter.

2 Using a wooden spoon, beat the batter vigorously for about 5 minutes. Cover and leave in a warm place for about 1 hour until sponge-like in texture. Beat the batter for a further 2 minutes, then transfer to a jug.

3 Put a large non-stick frying pan over a high heat and brush a little oil over the surface. Oil the insides of four crumpet rings or 7.5cm (3in) plain metal cutters. Put the rings, blunt-edge down, on to the hot pan surface and leave for about 2 minutes until very hot.

4 Pour a little batter into each ring to a depth of 1cm (¹/₂in). Cook the crumpets for 5–7 minutes until the surface is set and appears honeycombed with holes.

5 Carefully remove each metal ring. Flip the crumpets over and cook the other side for 1 minute only. Transfer to a wire rack. Repeat to use all of the batter.

6 To serve, toast the crumpets on both sides and serve with butter.

COOK'S TIP
The pan and metal rings must be well oiled each time, and heated between frying each batch.

NUTRITION PER CRUMPET
60 cals | 1g fat (0.1g sats) | 12g carbs | 0.2g salt Ⓥ

PISTACHIO AND ROSEWATER STOLLEN

Makes 10 thick slices
Preparation 20 minutes, plus machine dough-making and rising
Cooking time 20, plus cooling

1¼ tsp easy-blend dried yeast
350g (12oz) strong white bread flour
½ tsp salt
1 tsp ground mixed spice
25g (1oz) golden caster sugar
50g (2oz) butter, melted
150ml (¼ pint) milk
3 tbsp rosewater
75g (3oz) sultanas
50g (2oz) pistachio nuts
50g (2oz) candied peel, chopped
icing sugar to dust

For the marzipan
150g (5oz) pistachio nuts, skinned (see Cook's Tip)
40g (1½oz) golden caster sugar
40g (1½oz) golden icing sugar
2 egg yolks

1 Put all the dough ingredients except the sultanas, pistachio nuts, candied peel and icing sugar into the bread maker bucket, following the order and method specified in the manual.

2 Fit the bucket into the bread maker and set to the Dough programme with Raisin setting, if applicable. Press start. Add the sultanas, pistachio nuts and candied peel when the machine beeps, or halfway through the kneading cycle.

3 Meanwhile, make the marzipan. Put the pistachio nuts into a food processor and blend until finely ground. Add the sugars and egg yolks, and blend to a paste. Turn out on to the work surface and shape into a log, 24cm (9½in) long. Grease a large baking sheet.

4 Once the dough is ready, turn out on to a floured surface and punch it down to deflate. Roll out to a rectangle, 28cm (11in) long and 15cm (6in) wide. Lay the marzipan on the dough, slightly to one side of the centre. Brush the long edges of the dough with water then fold the wider piece of dough over the paste, sealing well.

5 Transfer to the baking sheet, cover loosely with oiled clingfilm and leave in a warm place for 40 minutes or until doubled in size. Preheat the oven to 200°C (fan oven 180°C) mark 6.

6 Bake for 20–25 minutes until risen and golden. Transfer to a wire rack to cool. Serve generously dusted with icing sugar.

COOK'S TIP
For a vibrantly coloured marzipan it's best to skin the pistachio nuts first. Soak them in boiling water for a couple of minutes then rub them between pieces of kitchen paper to remove the skins.

NUTRITION PER SLICE
380 cals | 17g fat (5g sats) | 51g carbs | 0.7g salt **V**

HOT CROSS BUNS

Makes 15 buns
Preparation 30 minutes, plus rising
Cooking time 15–18 minutes, plus cooling

100ml (3½ fl oz) warm milk, plus extra to glaze
15g (½ oz) fresh yeast or 7g sachet (2 tsp)
    dried yeast
50g (2oz) golden caster sugar, plus extra to glaze
350g (12oz) strong plain white flour, sifted, plus extra
    to dust
pinch of salt
pinch of ground cinnamon
pinch of freshly grated nutmeg
25g (1oz) chopped mixed candied peel
125g (4oz) mixed raisins, sultanas and currants
25g (1oz) butter, melted and cooled until tepid
1 medium egg, beaten
vegetable oil to grease

1 Mix the warm milk with an equal quantity of warm water.
Put the yeast into a small bowl with 1 tbsp of the warm liquid
and 1 tsp sugar, and set aside for 5 minutes.
2 Put 225g (8oz) flour and the salt into a large bowl, make a
well in the centre and pour in the yeast mixture. Cover with
a clean teatowel and leave in a warm place for 20 minutes
until frothy.
3 Mix the remaining flour and sugar together with the spices,
peel and dried fruit. Add to the yeast mixture with the melted
butter and egg. Mix thoroughly to form a soft dough, adding a
little more liquid if needed. Put the dough into a lightly oiled
bowl, cover and leave to rise in a warm place for 1–1½ hours
or until doubled in size.
4 Knock back the dough and knead lightly on a lightly floured
surface for 1–2 minutes. Divide the dough into 15 equal-sized
pieces and shape into buns. Put well apart on a large oiled
baking sheet. Make a deep cross on the top of each one with
a sharp knife, then cover with a teatowel and leave in a warm
place for 30 minutes or until doubled in size.
5 Preheat the oven to 220°C (200°C fan oven) mark 7.
Brush the buns with milk and sprinkle with sugar, then bake
for 15–18 minutes until they sound hollow when tapped
underneath. Transfer to a wire rack and leave to cool.
Serve warm.

TRY SOMETHING DIFFERENT
Rather than mark crosses on the buns, brush with beaten egg
to glaze, then top each with a pastry cross and glaze again.
Bake as above.

NUTRITION PER BUN
140 cals | 2g fat (1g sats) | 28g carbs | 0.2g salt **V**

BRIOCHE

Serves 10
Preparation 20 minutes, plus rising
Cooking time 15–20 minutes, plus cooling

15g (¹/₂ oz) fresh yeast or 1¹/₂ tsp easy-blend dried yeast
225g (8oz) strong plain white flour, plus extra to dust
pinch of salt
1 tbsp golden caster sugar
2 extra large eggs, beaten
50g (2oz) butter, melted and cooled until tepid
vegetable oil to grease
beaten egg to glaze

1 If using fresh yeast, blend with 2 tbsp tepid water. Mix the flour, salt and sugar together in a large bowl. (Stir in easy-blend dried yeast if using.)

2 Make a well in the centre and pour in the yeast liquid (or 2 tbsp tepid water if using easy-blend dried yeast) plus the eggs and melted butter. Work the ingredients together to a soft dough.

3 Turn out on to a lightly floured surface and knead for about 5 minutes until smooth and elastic. Put the dough into a large oiled bowl, cover and leave in a warm place for about 1 hour until doubled in size.

4 Knock back the dough on a lightly floured surface. Shape three-quarters of it into a ball and put into an oiled 1.1 litre (2 pint) brioche mould. Press a hole through the centre. Shape the remaining dough into a round, put on top of the brioche and press down lightly. Cover and leave in a warm place until the dough is puffy and nearly risen to the top of the mould.

5 Preheat the oven to 230°C (210°C fan oven) mark 8. Brush the brioche dough lightly with beaten egg and bake for 15–20 minutes until golden.

6 Turn out on to a wire rack and leave to cool. Serve warm or cold.

COOK'S TIP
For individual brioches, divide the dough into 10 pieces. Shape as above. Bake in individual tins, for 10 minutes..

NUTRITION PER SERVING
140 cals | 6g fat (3g sats) | 19g carbs | 0.2g salt ⓥ

DANISH PASTRIES

Makes 16
Preparation 1 hour, plus rising and resting
Cooking time 15 minutes

25g (1oz) fresh yeast or 1 tbsp dried yeast and 1 tsp sugar
150ml (¼ pint) tepid water
450g (1lb) plain white flour, plus extra to dust
1 tsp salt
50g (2oz) lard
2 tbsp sugar
2 medium eggs, beaten
275g (10oz) butter, softened
1 medium egg, beaten, to glaze
glacé icing (see page 434) and flaked almonds, to decorate

For the almond paste
15g (½ oz) butter
75g (3oz) caster sugar
75g (3oz) ground almonds
1 medium egg, beaten

For the cinnamon butter
50g (2oz) butter
50g (2oz) caster sugar
2 tsp ground cinnamon

1 Blend the fresh yeast with the water. If using dried yeast, sprinkle it into the water with the 1 tsp sugar and leave in a warm place for 15 minutes or until frothy.
2 Mix the flour and salt, rub in the lard and stir in the 2 tbsp sugar. Add the yeast liquid and beaten eggs and mix to an elastic dough, adding a little more water if necessary. Knead well for 5 minutes on a lightly floured surface, until smooth. Return the dough to the rinsed-out bowl, cover with a clean teatowel and leave to rest in the fridge for 10 minutes.
3 Shape the butter into a rectangle. Roll out the dough on a floured board to a rectangle about three times as wide as the butter. Put the butter in the centre of the dough and fold the sides of the dough over the butter. Press the edges to seal.
4 With the folds at the sides, roll the dough into a strip three times as long as it is wide; fold the bottom third up, and the top third down, cover and leave to rest for 10 minutes. Turn and repeat the rolling, folding and resting twice more.
5 To make the almond paste, cream the butter and sugar, stir in the almonds and add enough egg to make a soft and pliable consistency. Make the cinnamon butter by creaming the butter and sugar and beating in the cinnamon.
6 Roll out the dough into the required shapes (see below) and fill with almond paste or cinnamon butter. Cover the pastries with a clean teatowel and leave to rise in a warm place for 20–30 minutes until doubled in size. Preheat the oven to 220°C (200°C fan oven) mark 7. Brush the pastries with beaten egg. Bake for 15 minutes or until golden. While hot, brush with thin glacé icing and sprinkle with flaked almonds.

TO SHAPE THE PASTRIES

Imperial stars Cut into 7.5cm (3in) squares. Make diagonal cuts from each corner to within 1cm (½in) of the centre. Put a piece of almond paste in the centre. Fold one corner of each cut section down to the centre, secure the tips with beaten egg.
Foldovers and cushions Cut into 7.5cm (3in) squares and put a little almond paste in the centre. Fold over two opposite corners to the centre. Make a cushion by folding over all four corners, securing the tips with beaten egg.
Twists Cut into 25.5 x 10cm (10 x 4in) rectangles. Cut each rectangle lengthways to give four pieces. Spread with cinnamon butter and fold the bottom third of each up and the top third down; seal and cut each across into thin slices. Form into twists.

> NUTRITION PER DANISH
> 376 cals | 25g fat (14g sats) | 35g carbs | 0.7g salt Ⓥ

PIZZA BASE DOUGH

Makes 1 large or 2 small pizza bases
Preparation 5 minutes, plus rising

225g (8oz) strong white bread flour, plus extra to dust
1/2 tsp sea salt
1/2 tsp easy-blend dried yeast
1 tbsp extra virgin olive oil, plus extra to oil

1 Sift the flour and salt into a bowl and stir in the dried yeast. Make a well in the centre and gradually work in 150ml (1/4 pint) warm water and the olive oil to form a soft dough.
2 Turn the pizza dough on to a lightly floured worksurface and knead well for 8–10 minutes until smooth and elastic. (Alternatively, knead the dough in a large food mixer fitted with a dough hook.)
3 Put into an oiled bowl, turn the dough once to coat the surface with oil and cover the bowl with clingfilm. Leave to rise in a warm place for 1 hour or until doubled in size.
4 Knock back the dough and shape as required.

TOPPINGS

Top the pizza with a thin layer of tomato purée, then scatter one or two of the following on top and finish with grated cheese or slices of mozzarella:
- Bacon or pancetta bits, or slices of prosciutto
- Rocket leaves
- Dried chilli flakes
- Capers
- Sliced sun-dried tomatoes
- Pepperoni slices
- Roasted peppers
- Artichoke hearts, drained and quartered
- Sliced mushrooms

Cook the topped pizzas on baking sheets in an oven preheated to 200°C (180°C fan oven) mark 6 for 15–18 minutes until golden.

COOK'S TIP
If you like, use 15g (1/2oz) fresh yeast instead of easy-blend dried yeast. Mix with 2 tbsp of the flour, a pinch of sugar and the warm water. Leave in a warm place for 10 minutes or until frothy, then add to the rest of the flour and salt. Mix to a dough and continue as above.

NUTRITION PER 25G (1OZ)
60 cals | 1g fat (0.1g sats) | 11g carbs | 0.2g salt (V)

MOZZARELLA, PARMA HAM AND ROCKET PIZZA

Serves 4
Preparation 10 minutes
Cooking time 15–18 minutes

a little plain flour to dust
290g pack pizza base mix
350g (12oz) fresh tomato and chilli
    pasta sauce
250g (9oz) buffalo mozzarella cheese,
    drained and roughly chopped
6 slices Parma ham (see Cook's Tip,
    page 65), torn into strips
50g (2oz) rocket
a little extra virgin olive oil to drizzle
salt and ground black pepper

1 Preheat the oven to 200°C (180°C fan oven) mark 6 and lightly flour two large baking sheets. Mix the pizza base dough according to the instructions on the pack. Divide the dough into two and knead each ball on a lightly floured surface for about 5 minutes, then roll them out to make two 23cm (9in) rounds. Put one on each of the prepared baking sheets.
2 Divide the tomato sauce between the pizza bases and spread it over, leaving a small border around each edge. Scatter on the mozzarella pieces, then scatter with ham. Season well with salt and pepper.
3 Cook the pizzas for 15–18 minutes until golden. Slide on to a wooden board, top with rocket leaves and drizzle with oil. Cut in half to serve.

> **COOK'S TIP**
> If you're short of time, buy two ready-made pizza bases.

NUTRITION PER SERVING 508 cals |
19g fat (11g sats) | 64g carbs | 1.9g salt

TUNA MELT PIZZA

Serves 4
Preparation 5 minutes
Cooking time 10–12 minutes

2 large pizza bases, ready made, or
    make your own (see left)
4 tbsp sun-dried tomato pesto
2 × 185g cans tuna, drained
50g can anchovies, drained and
    chopped
125g (4oz) mature Cheddar cheese,
    grated
rocket to serve

1 Preheat the oven to 220°C (200°C fan oven) mark 7. Spread each pizza base with 2 tbsp sun-dried tomato pesto. Top each with half the tuna, half the anchovies and half the grated cheese.
2 Put on a baking sheet and cook in the oven for 10–12 minutes until the cheese has melted. Sprinkle with rocket to serve.

TRY SOMETHING DIFFERENT
Mozzarella and Tomato Pizza
Spread the pizza bases with 4 tbsp pesto and top with 125g (4oz) chopped sunblush tomatoes and 2 × 125g sliced mozzarella balls. Cook, then serve topped with a handful of baby spinach leaves.
Ham and Pineapple Pizza
Spread the pizza bases with 4 tbsp Fresh Tomato Sauce (see page 20). Top with a 225g can drained unsweetened pineapple chunks, 125g (4oz) diced ham and 125g (4oz) grated Gruyère.

NUTRITION PER SERVING 688 cals |
26g fat (9g sats) | 72g carbs | 3.5g salt

SWEETS

PEPPERMINT CREAMS

Makes 50
Preparation 45 minutes

450g (1lb) icing sugar, sifted, plus extra to dust
$^1\!/_2$ tsp cream of tartar
4–5 tbsp evaporated milk
2 tsp peppermint essence
red food colouring

1 Put the icing sugar and cream of tartar into a bowl.
Add the evaporated milk and peppermint essence, and stir
together until evenly combined. Use your hands to bring the
mixture together into a ball.
2 Knead on a surface dusted with icing sugar to make a
smooth fondant. Cut the fondant in half; wrap one piece in
clingfilm and set aside.
3 Dust the surface with more icing sugar. Roll out the other
half of the fondant to a round, about 5mm ($^1\!/_4$ in) thick. Stamp
out 4cm (1$^1\!/_2$ in) rounds, with a plain cutter. Transfer the
fondant discs to a tray lined with baking parchment.
4 Unwrap the other portion of fondant. Dip a skewer into
the food colouring, press on to the fondant to apply a little
colouring, then knead until it is evenly pink in colour. Roll out
to a 5mm ($^1\!/_4$ in) thickness, stamp out 4cm (1$^1\!/_2$ in) rounds and
then put on a lined tray, as above. Cover the mints loosely
with baking parchment and leave to dry overnight.
5 Store in airtight containers for up to three weeks and
serve as after-dinner mints, or put into paper sweet cases and
pack into boxes to offer as a gift.

NUTRITION PER PEPPERMINT CREAM
40 cals | trace fat | (0g sats) | 12g carbs | trace salt

BUTTERSCOTCH

Makes about 450g (1lb)
Preparation 15 minutes
Cooking time about 15 minutes, plus cooling

450g (1lb) demerara sugar
50–75g (2–3oz) unsalted butter
vegetable oil to grease

1 Put the sugar and 150ml (¼ pint) water in a heavy-based pan and heat gently until dissolved.
2 Bring to the boil and boil steadily until the syrup registers 138°C on a sugar thermometer (the medium crack stage – when a little of the mixture dropped into a cup of cold water separates into hard, but not brittle threads). While the syrup is boiling, brush down the sides of the pan occasionally with a damp pastry brush.
3 Add the butter, a little at a time, stirring until each addition is incorporated before adding more. Pour the mixture into a lightly oiled 15cm (6in) shallow square tin. Leave until almost set, then mark into pieces.
4 Leave until completely cold, then break into pieces. Store in an airtight container.

> **NUTRITION PER 25G (1OZ)**
> 120 cals | 3g fat (2g sats) | 26g carbs | trace salt

CLOTTED CREAM VANILLA FUDGE

Makes 700g (1½ lb)
Preparation 15 minutes, plus overnight chilling
Cooking time 20–30 minutes, plus cooling

50g (2oz) butter, plus extra to grease
450g (1lb) granulated sugar
170g can evaporated milk
113g carton clotted cream
1 tsp vanilla extract

1 Lightly grease a shallow 18cm (7in) square tin. Put the sugar, evaporated milk, clotted cream and butter into a large heavy-based pan and heat gently to dissolve the sugar.
2 Bring to the boil and boil steadily, stirring frequently to prevent sticking. The mixture is ready when it registers 115°C on a sugar thermometer (the soft ball stage: in cold water it forms a soft ball which you can easily squash between your finger and thumb). Immediately plunge the base of the pan into a sink of cold water to stop the cooking process, then remove.
3 Add the vanilla extract and beat with a hand-held electric whisk, scraping down the sides from time to time, until the mixture is thick, paste-like and no longer glossy; this will take about 5 minutes.

4 Pour the fudge into the prepared tin, patting it into the corners with the back of a spoon. Cover and chill overnight until completely set.
5 Cut into squares and pack into boxes, or store in an airtight container in the fridge for up to two weeks.

TRY SOMETHING DIFFERENT
Ginger Fudge Add 75g (3oz) chopped stem ginger (drained of syrup) at the end of step 3.
Coffee and Pecan Fudge Add 3–4 tbsp coffee essence in step 1 and 75g (3oz) chopped pecan nuts at the end of step 3. Omit the vanilla extract.

> **NUTRITION PER 25G (1OZ)**
> 120 cals | 4g fat (2g sats) | 20g carbs | 0.1g salt

CHOCOLATE FUDGE

Makes 675g (1lb 7oz)
Preparation 15 minutes
Cooking time 6–8 minutes, plus cooling

50g (2oz) unsalted butter, plus extra
    to grease
225g (8oz) granulated sugar
397g can sweetened condensed milk
1 tbsp clear honey
1 tsp vanilla extract
100g (3½oz) plain chocolate (at least 70% cocoa
    solids), grated

1 Grease a 20.5cm (8in) square cake tin and line the base
and 2.5cm (1in) up the sides with baking parchment. Put the
sugar in a medium heavy-based pan and add the butter,
condensed milk, honey and vanilla extract. Heat gently until
the sugar dissolves. Bring to the boil, stirring, and boil for
6–8 minutes, stirring frequently to prevent sticking. The
mixture is ready when it reaches 115°C on a sugar
thermometer (the soft ball stage: in cold water it forms a
soft ball which you can easily squash between your finger
and thumb).
2 Remove the pan from the heat, add the grated chocolate
and beat until the mixture is smooth and glossy. Pour the
fudge into the prepared tin, spreading it into the corners.
Leave for 2 hours or until completely set.
3 Remove the fudge from the tin and peel away the lining
paper. Cut into squares. Store in an airtight container.

NUTRITION PER 25G (1OZ)
99 cals | 3g fat (2g sats) | 17g carbs | 0.1g salt **V**

TURKISH DELIGHT

Makes 49 squares
Preparation 15 minutes, plus soaking and setting
Cooking time 30 minutes, plus overnight setting

25g (1oz) gelatine
450g (1lb) granulated sugar
$^1/_4$ tsp citric acid
a few drops of red food colouring
a few drops of rosewater
oil to grease

For the sherbet mix
50g (2oz) icing sugar
$^1/_2$ tsp bicarbonate of soda
$^1/_4$ tsp citric acid

1 Pour 300ml ($^1/_2$ pint) water into a heavy-based pan. Sprinkle over the gelatine. Stir gently to ensure that all the grains are covered. Leave to soak for 10 minutes or until the gelatine is spongelike.
2 Over a very gentle heat, slowly dissolve the gelatine. When clear and liquid, add the sugar and citric acid. Stir gently until the sugar dissolves. (Take care not to splash the sugar up the sides of the pan, as this may cause the mixture to crystallise.)
3 Bring the contents of the pan to the boil and boil over a medium heat for 20 minutes or until the mixture is syrupy and a pale straw colour (do not stir the mixture, or the scum which appears on the surface will then be distributed through it and make a cloudy jelly).

4 Remove the pan from the heat, let the bubbles subside, then skim any scum from the surface of the mixture. Leave the mixture to stand for 25 minutes or until cool, thick and almost set. Stir in sufficient red food colouring to give a pale pink colour and add rosewater to taste.
5 Base line an 18cm (7in) square tin. Oil the base and sides well. Carefully pour in the Turkish Delight mixture. Leave until completely cold, then put in the fridge and leave overnight to set.
6 Meanwhile, sieve together the icing sugar, bicarbonate of soda and citric acid for the sherbet coating. Store in a polythene bag.
7 The next day, sprinkle half the quantity of sherbet mix on to a sheet of greaseproof paper. Put the Turkish Delight on to the sherbet layer. Peel off the lining paper, then turn the Turkish Delight over to coat the other side.
8 Rinse a large sharp knife in cold running water, then use to cut the Turkish Delight into 2.5cm (1in) squares. Put in a bowl, shake over the remaining sherbet mix until completely coated.
9 To store, line an airtight container with greaseproof paper, put in the Turkish Delight squares and sprinkle over any remaining sherbet.

NUTRITION PER SQUARE
40 cals | 0g fat (0g sats) | 11g carbs | trace salt

COCONUT ICE BARS

Makes about 550g (1¼ lb), about 21 squares
Preparation 10 minutes
Cooking time 15 minutes, plus cooling

oil to grease
450g (1lb) granulated sugar
150ml (¼ pint) milk
150g (5oz) desiccated coconut
a few drops of red food colouring

1 Lightly oil an 18cm (7in) shallow square tin.
2 Put the sugar and the milk in a heavy-based pan and heat gently until the sugar has dissolved. Bring to the boil and boil gently for 10 minutes or until 115°C (soft-ball stage, see opposite) is reached.
3 Remove from the heat and stir in the coconut.
4 Pour half the mixture quickly into the prepared tin. Add a few drops of food colouring to the second half and pour quickly over the first layer.
5 Leave until half set, mark into bars and cut or break when cold.

SUGAR STAGES

There are five stages in syrup-making. You can test using with a sugar thermometer or by dropping a little of the syrup into cold water.
Thread stage Temperature 110°C; in cold water the syrup forms a fine, soft thread.
Soft-ball stage Temperature 115°C; in cold water the syrup forms a soft ball that you can easily squash between your finger and thumb.
Hard-ball stage Temperature 120°C; in cold water the syrup forms a firmer but still pliable ball.
Soft-crack stage Temperature 125°C; in cold water the syrup forms thick threads which bend a little but then break up.
Hard-crack stage Temperature 145°C; in cold water the syrup forms thick, brittle threads which break immediately when you bend them.

> **NUTRITION PER 25G (1OZ)**
> 92 cals | 3g fat (3g sats) | 16g carbs | trace salt **V**

PECAN PRALINE

Makes about 450g (1lb)
Preparation 10 minutes
Cooking time 15 minutes, plus cooling

50g (2oz) unsalted butter, plus extra to grease
200g (7oz) granulated sugar
125ml (4fl oz) golden syrup
150g (5oz) pecan halves
½ tsp vanilla extract
¾ tsp bicarbonate of soda
a pinch of salt

1 Grease a large baking sheet. Put the sugar and golden syrup into a large heavy-based pan and heat gently, stirring constantly until the sugar dissolves in the syrup.
2 Increase the heat and boil until the syrup registers 110°C on a sugar thermometer (in cold water it forms a fine, soft thread).

3 Add the pecan halves to the pan and continue to boil until the mixture reaches 140–150°C (in cold water it forms thick, brittle threads which break immediately when you bend them). Immediately remove the pan from the heat and stir in the vanilla extract, butter, bicarbonate of soda and salt. Make sure the ingredients are thoroughly combined.
4 Tip the mixture on to the prepared baking sheet, spreading it thinly. Set aside until completely cooled and hardened.
5 Break the pecan praline into pieces and store in an airtight container, layered between baking parchment, for up to ten days, or gift wrap in cellophane.

> **NUTRITION PER 25G (1OZ)**
> 140 cals | 8g fat (5g sats) | 18g carbs | 0.2g salt

NUTTY CHOCOLATE TRUFFLES

Makes 30
Preparation 20 minutes, plus chilling
Cooking time 12 minutes

100g (3¹/₂oz) hazelnuts
200g (7oz) plain chocolate (at least 50% cocoa solids),
    broken into pieces
25g (1oz) butter
150ml (¹/₄ pint) double cream
3 tbsp cocoa powder, sifted
3 tbsp golden icing sugar, sifted

1 Put the hazelnuts in a frying pan and heat gently for
3–4 minutes, shaking the pan occasionally, until toasted all
over. Put 30 nuts in a bowl and leave to cool. Whiz the
remaining nuts in a food processor until finely chopped.
Put the chopped nuts in a shallow dish.
2 Melt the chocolate in a heatproof bowl over a pan of
gently simmering water, taking care not to let the bowl
touch the water. In a separate pan, melt the butter and
cream. Bring just to the boil, then remove from the heat.
Carefully stir into the chocolate. Whisk until cool and thick,
then chill for 1–2 hours.
3 Put the cocoa powder and icing sugar in separate shallow
dishes. Scoop up a teaspoonful of the chilled truffle mixture
and push a hazelnut into the centre. Working quickly, shape
into a ball, then roll in cocoa powder, icing sugar or chopped
nuts. Repeat with the remaining truffle mixture, then chill until
ready to serve.

GET AHEAD
Store the truffles in an airtight container in the fridge for up
to two weeks.

NUTRITION PER TRUFFLE
96 cals | 8g fat (4g sats) | 6g carbs | 0.1g salt

PRESERVES

JAMS

Jams are basically a cooked mixture of fruit and sugar. The high concentration of sugar used effectively preserves the fruit and retards the growth of micro-organisms, allowing the jam to be kept in a cool place for many months without deterioration. Home-made jams taste infinitely better than commercially produced ones.

CHOOSING FRUIT

Fruit for jam should be sound – poor quality fruit will not have as much flavour – and either just ripe or slightly underripe. The jam will set only if there are sufficient quantities of pectin, acid and sugar present. Some fruits are naturally rich in pectin (see the chart opposite) and give a good set, whereas others do not contain as much and may need to have it boosted with added pectin. Lemon juice is most often used for this purpose, since it aids the set and often brings out the flavour of the fruit. Allow 2 tbsp lemon juice to 2kg (4½ lb) of a fruit with poor setting properties. Alternatively, you can buy bottled pectin – follow the manufacturer's instructions for how much to use. Sometimes, only an acid is added, such as citric or tartaric acid. These contain no pectin but help to extract the natural pectin from the fruit and improve the flavour of fruits lacking in acid. Allow ½ tsp acid for 2kg (4½ lb) of a fruit with poor setting properties.

HOMEMADE PECTIN EXTRACTS

A pectin extract can be made from sour cooking apples, crab apples or apple peelings, cores and windfalls.

Wash 1kg (2¼ lb) fruit and chop roughly without peeling or coring. Cover with 600–900ml (1–1½ pints) water and stew gently for about 45 minutes or until well pulped. Strain through a jelly bag or muslin cloth, then carry out a pectin test to ensure that there is sufficient pectin present. Allow 150–300ml (¼–½ pint) of this extract to 2kg (4½ lb) of fruit which is low in pectin. Pectin extract can also be made using the same method from fresh gooseberries and redcurrants.

SUGAR

Sugar acts as a preservative in jam and also affects its setting quality. The exact amount of sugar needed depends on the pectin strength of the fruit, so it is essential to use the amount specified in a recipe. Too little sugar produces a poor set and the jam may go mouldy when stored. Too much sugar makes a dark sticky jam, overpowers the fruit flavour and may crystallise.

Granulated sugar is the most economical for jam making, although less foamy scum is formed on the surface of the jam when lump or preserving sugar is used; however, these are more expensive and the only real benefit is that the end product is slightly clearer than when granulated sugar is used. Caster sugar can be used, but again is more expensive; brown sugar can also be used but will produce a darker jam and will affect flavour.

You can make your own reduced-sugar jams similar to those on the market. Don't reduce sugar content by more than 20 per cent or the jam will be runny. As it doesn't keep well, make it in small batches and store in the fridge (for up to six weeks) or a cool place (three to four weeks).

TESTING FOR PECTIN CONTENT

The chart opposite shows the pectin content of fruits and vegetables used in preserving. If you are not sure of your fruit setting qualities, carry out this test:

When the fruit has been cooked until soft, but before you add sugar, take 1 tsp juice, put it in a glass and, when cool, add 1 tbsp methylated spirit. Shake the glass and leave for 1 minute. If the mixture forms a jelly-like clot, the fruit has a good pectin content. If it does not form a single firm clot, the pectin content is too low and you will need extra.

TESTING FOR A SET

Thermometer test Dip a sugar thermometer into the pan away from the base and side. Leave it for a few moments. Jams and jellies set when the temperatures reach 105°C.

Saucer test Chill two or thee saucers in the freezer. When the preserve is nearly ready, take the pan off the heat and spoon a blob of preserve on to a plate and chill for a few minutes. When the preserve has cooled, push the surface with your finger; it is set if it wrinkles and doesn't break to reveal liquid.

Flake test Using a wooden spoon, lift a little of the preserve out of the pan. Let it cool slightly, then tip the spoon so that the preserve drops back into the pan. If it is set, it will run together along the edge of the spoon and form flakes that will break off.

THE PECTIN CONTENT OF FRUITS AND VEGETABLES

Good	Medium	Poor
Cooking apples	Apricots	Bananas
Crab apples	Bilberries	Cherries
Cranberries	Blackberries	Elderberries
Currants (red and black)	Cranberries	Figs
Damsons	Dessert apples	Grapes
Gooseberries	Greengages	Japonica
Lemons	Loganberries	Marrows
Limes	Mulberries	Medlars
Quinces	Plums	Melons
Seville oranges	Raspberries	Nectarines
		Peaches
		Pineapples
		Rhubarb
		Strawberries

POTTING, COVERING AND STORING

All preserves must be potted in scrupulously clean, sterilised containers. Wash the jars or bottles in very hot soapy water, rinse thoroughly, then put upturned on a baking sheet in the oven at 140°C (120°C fan oven) mark 1 for 10–15 minutes until completely dry. Stand the jars upside down on a clean tea-towel until the preserve is ready.

As soon as a set has been reached, immediately remove the pan from the heat and, with a slotted spoon, skim off any scum. Don't pot strawberry and other whole-fruit jams immediately or all the fruit will rise to the top. Leave them in the pan for 15–20 minutes before potting. Spoon the jam into the warm jars, filling them right to the top.

Wipe the outside of the jars with a damp cloth while they are still warm, and immediately put wax discs, wax side down, on the surface of the jam, making sure they lie flat. Either cover immediately with a dampened round of cellophane and secure with a rubber band or string, or leave the jam until quite cold before doing this. Label the jars and store in a cool, dry, dark place. Most jams keep well for about a year after which their flavour starts to deteriorate.

WATCHPOINTS

Problems with jam making can be eliminated if the following simple tips are followed:

- Mould growth usually occurs because the jam has not been covered with a wax disc while still hot. Alternatively, the pots were not cleaned properly or may have been stored in a place where they picked up bacteria. Other possible causes are insufficient evaporation of water while the fruit was being cooked before sugar was added and/or too short a boiling time after the sugar was added. It is important not to eat jam that has mould growth on it, as it produces toxins. Throw away the whole jar if you find any mould on the top surface.
- Bubbles in jam indicate fermentation, which is usually because not enough sugar has been used or because the jam was not reduced sufficiently. Fermented jam can be boiled up again and repotted but thereafter should only be used for cooking.
- Crystallisation is usually caused by lack of enough acid or by under- or over-boiling the jam after the sugar has been added.
- Shrinkage of jam in pots is caused by inadequate covering or failure to store the jam in a cool, dark, dry place.

STRAWBERRY JAM

Makes about 1.8kg (4lb)
Preparation 10 minutes, plus standing
Cooking time about 10 minutes

900g (2lb) strawberries, hulled
1kg (2¼lb) 'sugar with pectin'
juice of ½ lemon

1 Put the strawberries into a preserving pan with the sugar and lemon juice. Heat gently, stirring until the sugar has dissolved.
2 Bring to the boil and boil steadily for 4 minutes or until setting point is reached (see page 475).
3 Take the pan off the heat and remove any scum from the surface with a slotted spoon. Leave to stand for 15–20 minutes. Stir the jam gently, then pot and cover in the usual way (see page 476).

NUTRITION PER TABLESPOON
35 cals | 0g fat (0g sats) | 9g carbs | trace salt

RASPBERRY JAM

Makes about 2.6kg (5¾lb)
Preparation 10 minutes, plus standing
Cooking time about 45 minutes

1.8kg (4lb) raspberries
1.8kg (4lb) golden caster sugar
knob of butter

1 Put the raspberries into a preserving pan and simmer very gently in their own juice for 15–20 minutes, stirring carefully from time to time, until soft.
2 Remove the pan from the heat and add the sugar, stirring until dissolved, then add the butter and boil rapidly for 20 minutes or until setting point is reached (see page 475).
3 Take the pan off the heat, remove any scum with a slotted spoon, then leave to stand for 15 minutes. Pot and cover in the usual way (see page 476).

NUTRITION PER TABLESPOON
50 cals | trace fat (0 sats) | 12g carbs | trace salt

UNCOOKED FREEZER JAM

Makes about 3.2kg (7lb)
Preparation 15 minutes, plus overnight standing

1.4kg (3lb) raspberries or strawberries, hulled
1.8kg (4lb) golden caster sugar
4 tbsp lemon juice
225ml (8 fl oz) commercial pectin

1 Put the fruit into a large bowl and very lightly mash with a fork. Stir in the sugar and lemon juice, and leave at room temperature, stirring occasionally, for about 1 hour until the sugar has dissolved.
2 Gently stir in the pectin and continue stirring for a further 2 minutes.
3 Pour the jam into small freezerproof containers, leaving a little space at the top to allow for expansion. Cover and leave at room temperature for a further 24 hours.
4 Label and freeze for up to six months.
5 To serve, thaw the jam at room temperature for 1 hour.

NUTRITION PER TABLESPOON
35 cals | 0g fat (0g sats) | 9g carbs | trace salt

BLACKCURRANT JAM

Makes about 4.5kg (10lb)
Preparation 10 minutes, plus standing
Cooking time 55 minutes

1.8kg (4lb) blackcurrants
2.7kg (6lb) sugar
knob of butter

1 Put the blackcurrants into a preserving pan with 1.7 litres (3 pints) water. Simmer gently for 45 minutes or until the fruit is soft and the liquid is well reduced, stirring from time to time to prevent sticking.
2 Remove the pan from the heat, add the sugar, stir until dissolved, then add the knob of butter. Bring to the boil and boil rapidly for 10 minutes, stirring frequently, or until setting point is reached (see page 475).
3 Take the pan off the heat, remove any scum with a slotted spoon, then leave to stand for 15 minutes. Pot and cover in the usual way (see page 476).

NUTRITION PER TABLESPOON
40 cals | trace fat (0g sats) | 10g carbs | trace salt

RHUBARB GINGER JAM

Makes about 2kg (4¹/₂ lb)
Preparation 20 minutes, plus overnight standing
Cooking time 20 minutes

1.1kg (2¹/₂ lb) rhubarb (prepared weight), chopped
1.1kg (2¹/₂ lb) sugar
juice of 2 lemons
25g (1oz) root ginger
125g (4oz) stem or crystallised ginger, chopped

1 Put the rhubarb in a large bowl in alternate layers with the sugar and lemon juice, cover and leave overnight.
2 Next day, peel and bruise the root ginger slightly, using a weight or rolling pin, and tie it in a piece of muslin. Put the rhubarb mixture in a preserving pan with the muslin bag, bring to the boil and boil rapidly for 15 minutes, stirring frequently.
3 Remove the muslin bag, add the stem or crystallised ginger and boil for a further 5 minutes.
4 Test for a set and, when setting point is reached (see page 475), take the pan off the heat and remove any scum with a slotted spoon. Pot and cover in the usual way (see page 476).

NUTRITION PER TABLESPOON
20 cals | 0g fat (0g sats) | 5g carbs | trace salt Ⓥ

APRICOT JAM

Makes about 3kg (6¹/₂ lb)
Preparation 20 minutes, plus standing
Cooking time about 40 minutes

1.8kg (4lb) apricots, halved and stoned
juice of 1 lemon
1.8kg (4lb) sugar
knob of butter

1 Crack a few of the apricot stones with a nutcracker; take out the kernels and blanch them in boiling water for 1 minute; drain.
2 Put the apricots, lemon juice, apricot kernels and 450ml (³/₄ pint) water into a preserving pan and simmer for about 15 minutes or until well reduced and the fruit is soft.
3 Off the heat, add the sugar and stir until dissolved. Add the butter and boil rapidly for 15 minutes or until setting point is reached (see page 475).
4 Take the pan off the heat, remove any scum with a slotted spoon, then leave to stand for 15 minutes. Pot and cover in the usual way (see page 476).

NUTRITION PER TABLESPOON
40 cals | trace fat (0g sats) | 10g carbs | 0.1g salt Ⓥ

PLUM JAM

Makes about 4.5kg (10lb)
Preparation 15 minutes, plus standing
Cooking time 50 minutes

2.7kg (6lb) plums
2.7kg (6lb) sugar
knob of butter

TRY SOMETHING DIFFERENT

Greengage Jam Use greengages instead of plums and reduce the water to 600ml (1 pint).
Damson Jam Use 2.3kg (5lb) damsons instead of plums. After adding sugar, boil for 10 minutes only.

1 Put the plums and 900ml (1¹/₂ pints) water into a preserving pan. Bring to the boil, then simmer gently for 30 minutes or until well reduced and the fruit is very soft.
2 Remove the pan from the heat, add the sugar, stirring until dissolved, then add the knob of butter. Bring to the boil and boil rapidly for 10–15 minutes or until setting point is reached (see page 475), stirring frequently.
3 Take the pan off the heat. Using a slotted spoon, remove the plum stones and skim off any scum from the surface of the jam, then leave to stand for about 15 minutes. Pot and cover in the usual way (see page 476).

COOK'S TIP
If dessert plums are used rather than a cooking variety, add the juice of 1 large lemon.

NUTRITION PER TABLESPOON
40 cals | trace fat (0g sats) | 10g carbs | trace salt

JELLIES, CURDS AND MARMALADES

Jellies differ from jams in that only the juice from the fruit is used in the end product. They are a little more difficult to make and the yield is not as high, but they taste delicious and are well worth the effort. Homemade jellies can be served with roast meats to counteract the richness, used as a glaze for flans, and spread on scones or bread in the same way as jam. It isn't practicable to state the exact yield in jelly recipes because the ripeness of the fruit and time allowed for dripping both affect the quantity of juice obtained. As a rough guide, for each 450g (1lb) sugar added, a yield of about 700g (1½ lb) will result. It is also difficult to give precise nutritional information for the same reasons, but you can assume that for each of the following recipes 1 tbsp jelly provides roughly 40 calories.

Made with eggs and butter as well as sugar and fruit, curds are not true 'preserves' as they do not keep for long, but they are eaten in the same way as jams and are well worth making. All fruit curds should be made in small quantities, kept in the fridge and eaten within two weeks.

Seville or bitter oranges make the best marmalade, with a good flavour and a clear set, although other citrus fruits, such as limes and grapefruit, can be used. The best time to make marmalade is during January and February when Seville oranges are in season. Buy unwaxed fruit if you possibly can, otherwise wash thoroughly in water with a little washing-up liquid added, then rinse well.

REDCURRANT JELLY

Makes 1.3kg (3lb)
Preparation 30 minutes, plus standing
Cooking time about 1 hour

1.4kg (3lb) redcurrants
sugar (see method)
3 tbsp port (optional)

1 Put the redcurrants into a preserving pan with 600ml (1 pint) water and simmer gently for 30 minutes or until the fruit is very soft and pulpy, stirring from time to time to prevent sticking.
2 Spoon the fruit pulp into a jelly bag suspended over a large bowl and leave to drip through for at least 12 hours.
3 Discard the pulp remaining in the jelly bag. Measure the juice extract and return it to the pan, adding 450g (1lb) sugar for each 600ml (1 pint) extract.
4 Heat gently, stirring, until the sugar has dissolved, then bring to the boil and boil rapidly for 15 minutes or until setting point is reached (see page 475).
5 Take the pan off the heat and remove any scum with a slotted spoon. Stir in the port if using. Pot and cover in the usual way (see page 476).

TRY SOMETHING DIFFERENT

Bramble Jelly Follow the above using 1.8kg (4lb) slightly under-ripe blackberries with the juice of 2 lemons and 450ml (¾ pint) water.

QUINCE JELLY

Makes about 1.8kg (4lb)
Preparation 30 minutes, plus standing
Cooking time about 2 hours

1.8kg (4lb) quinces, washed and roughly chopped
grated rind and juice of 3 lemons
sugar (see method)

1 Put the fruit in a preserving pan with 2.3 litres (4 pints) water and the lemon zest and juice.
2 Cover with foil or a baking sheet and simmer for 1 hour or until the fruit is tender. Stir occasionally to prevent sticking.
3 Spoon the fruit pulp into a jelly bag or cloth attached to the legs of an upturned stool, and leave to strain into a large bowl for at least 12 hours.
4 Return the pulp in the jelly bag to the pan and add 1.1 litres (2 pints) water. Bring to the boil, simmer gently for 30 minutes, then strain again through a jelly bag or cloth for at least 12 hours.
5 Discard the pulp remaining in the jelly bag. Combine the two lots of juice extract and measure. Return to the pan with 450g (1lb) sugar for each 600ml (1 pint) extract. Heat gently, stirring, until the sugar has dissolved, then bring to the boil and boil rapidly for about 10 minutes.
6 Test for a set (see page 475) and, when setting point is reached, take the pan off the heat and remove any scum with a slotted spoon. Pot and cover in the usual way (see page 476).

NUTRITION PER TABLESPOON
39 cals | 0g fat (0g sats) | 10g carbs | trace salt

NUTRITION PER TABLESPOON
37 cals | 0g fat (0g sats) | 10g carbs | trace salt

APPLE AND MINT JELLY

Makes about 1.8kg (4lb)
Preparation 30 minutes, plus standing
Cooking time about 1¼ hours

2.3kg (5lb) cooking apples, such as Bramleys
a few large mint sprigs
1.1 litres (2 pints) distilled white vinegar
sugar (see method)
6–8 tbsp freshly chopped mint
a few drops of green food colouring (optional)

1 Remove any bruised parts from the apples, then cut into chunks without peeling or coring. Put the apples into a preserving pan with 1.1 litres (2 pints) water and the mint sprigs.
2 Bring to the boil, then simmer gently for 45 minutes or until soft and pulpy, stirring from time to time to prevent sticking. Add the vinegar and boil for a further 5 minutes.
3 Spoon the pulp into a jelly bag suspended over a large bowl. Leave to drip through for at least 12 hours.
4 Discard the pulp left in the jelly bag. Measure the extract and return to the preserving pan, adding 450g (1lb) sugar for each 600ml (1 pint) extract.
5 Heat gently, stirring, until the sugar has dissolved, then bring to the boil and boil rapidly for 10 minutes or until setting point is reached (see page 475).
6 Take off the heat and remove any scum with a slotted spoon. Stir in the chopped mint and colouring, if using. Cool slightly, stir well to distribute the mint, then pot and cover in the usual way (see page 476).

NUTRITION PER TABLESPOON
30 cals | 0g fat (0g sats) | 8g carbs | trace salt

LEMON CURD

Makes about 700g (1½ lb)
Preparation 20 minutes
Cooking time about 25 minutes

grated zest and juice of 4 medium ripe, juicy lemons
4 medium eggs, beaten
125g (4oz) butter, cut into small pieces
350g (12oz) golden caster sugar

1 Put all the ingredients into a double boiler or a large heatproof bowl set over a pan of simmering water. Stir the mixture until the sugar has dissolved. Continue to heat gently, stirring frequently, for about 20 minutes or until thick enough to coat the back of the spoon; do not allow to boil or it will curdle.
2 Strain the lemon curd through a fine sieve. Pot and cover in the usual way (see page 476). Store in the fridge and use within two weeks.

TRY SOMETHING DIFFERENT
Lime Curd Replace the lemons with the grated zest and juice of 5 large ripe, juicy limes.

NUTRITION PER TABLESPOON
60 cals | 3g fat (2g sats) | 8g carbs | 0.1g salt

MIXED FRUIT MARMALADE

Makes about 4kg (8lb 13oz)
Preparation 30 minutes, plus standing
Cooking time about 2¼ hours

2 Seville oranges
2 yellow grapefruit
2 limes
4 large unwaxed lemons
3kg (6½ lb) sugar, warmed

1 Wash any unwaxed fruit thoroughly, rinse well and dry. Weigh the fruit – you need around 1.6kg (3½ lb) in total. Cut in half and squeeze to extract as much juice as possible, then pour through a sieve into a jug, reserving any pips in the sieve.
2 Cut the spent fruit halves into quarters. Cut away the membrane and a thin layer of pith and tie these and the pips in a piece of muslin.
3 Cut the peel into thin strips and tip into a preserving pan.
4 Add all of the citrus fruit juices to the preserving pan, together with 3 litres (5¼ pints) cold water and the muslin bag. Bring to the boil, then simmer for 2 hours or until the peel is very, very tender and the liquid has reduced by about half. Skim off any scum during cooking and discard.
5 Remove the muslin bag from the pan, squeezing well and allowing the juice to run back into the pan. Add the warmed sugar to the pan and stir until dissolved. Bring to the boil, then reduce the heat and bubble until the temperature registers 104°C on a sugar thermometer. Cook at this temperature for about 10 minutes or until setting point is reached. Use the saucer test (see page 475).
6 Take the pan off the heat and remove any scum with a slotted spoon. Leave to stand for 15 minutes, then stir to distribute the peel. Pot and cover in the usual way (see page 476).

> NUTRITION PER TABLESPOON
> 45 cals | 0g fat (0g sats) | 12g carbs | trace salt

LEMON SHRED MARMALADE

Makes 2.3kg (5lb)
Preparation 25 minutes, plus standing
Cooking time 2¾ hours, plus standing

900g (2lb) lemons, washed
juice of 2 lemons
2.6 litres (4½ pints) water
1.4kg (3lb) sugar

1 Peel off enough rind from the lemons, avoiding the pith, to weigh 125g (4oz). Cut the rind into thin strips. Cut up the rest of the fruit and simmer it in a covered preserving pan with the lemon juice and 1.4 litres (2½ pints) water for 2 hours or until the fruit is very soft.
2 Put the shredded rind in another pan with 600ml (1 pint) water, cover and simmer gently until this also is very soft.
3 Drain off the liquid from the shreds and put the shreds to one side.
4 Pour the contents of the pan into a jelly bag or cloth attached to the legs of an upturned stool and leave to drip into a large bowl for 15 minutes.
5 Return the pulp remaining in the jelly bag to the pan with 600ml (1 pint) water, simmer for a further 20 minutes, then pour into the jelly bag again and leave to drip for several hours.
6 Combine the two lots of extract and test for pectin (see page 475). If the liquid does not clot, reduce it slightly by rapid boiling, then test again. Add the sugar and stir until it has dissolved. Add the reserved lemon peel shreds and boil rapidly for about 15 minutes.
7 Test for a set and, when setting point is reached, take the pan off the heat and remove any scum with a slotted spoon. Leave the marmalade to stand for about 15 minutes, then stir to distribute the peel. Pot and cover in the usual way (see page 476).

> NUTRITION PER TABLESPOON
> 35 cals | 0g fat (0g sats) | 90g carbs | trace salt V

SEVILLE ORANGE MARMALADE

Makes about 4.5kg (10lb)
Preparation 30 minutes, plus standing
Cooking time about 2½ hours

1.4kg (3lb) Seville oranges
juice of 2 lemons
2.7kg (6lb) sugar, warmed

1 Halve the oranges and squeeze out the juice and pips. Tie the pips, and any membrane that has come away during squeezing, in a piece of muslin. Slice the orange peel thinly or thickly, as preferred, and put it into a preserving pan with the orange and lemon juices, muslin bag and 3.4 litres (6 pints) water.
2 Simmer gently for about 2 hours or until the peel is very soft and the liquid has reduced by about half.
3 Remove the muslin bag, squeezing it well and allowing the juice to run back into the pan. Add the sugar and heat gently,

stirring until it has dissolved. Bring to the boil and boil rapidly for 15 minutes or until setting point is reached (see page 475). Use the saucer test.
4 Take the pan off the heat and remove any scum with a slotted spoon. Leave to stand for 15 minutes, then stir to distribute the peel. Pot and cover in the usual way (see page 476).

COOK'S TIP
It is important to add all the pips and excess pith to the muslin bag as they contain pectin, which helps to set the marmalade.

NUTRITION PER TABLESPOON
40 cals | 0g fat (0g sats) | 10g carbs | trace salt

PICKLES

Pickles are a traditional way of preserving fruit and vegetables with vinegar, spices and flavourings. They can be either sweet or sharp, or an interesting blend of both. Fruits for pickling are usually lightly cooked first. For sharp pickles, the vegetables are generally brined first in a salt solution for up to 24 hours, or sometimes longer.

Large, wide-necked bottles are recommended for pickling, although smaller jam jars can be used. Screw-topped jars with tops that have plastic-coated linings, such as those used for coffee jars and bought pickles, are ideal. Metal tops should not be placed in direct contact with the pickle because the vinegar will react with the metal.

PICKLED ONIONS

Makes 1.8kg (4lb)
Preparation 25 minutes, plus 2 days marinating and maturing

1.8kg (4lb) pickling onions, unpeeled
450g (1lb) salt

For the spiced vinegar
1.1 litres (2 pints) distilled vinegar
2–3 mace blades
1 tbsp whole allspice
1 tbsp cloves
2 cinnamon sticks
6 black peppercorns
1 bay leaf

NUTRITION PER 25g (1oz)
10 cals | 0g fat (0g sats) | 1g carbs | 0.3g salt

---

1 To make the spiced vinegar, put the vinegar, spices and bay leaf into a pan, bring to the boil, then allow to cool. Cover and leave to marinate for about 2 hours. Strain the vinegar through a muslin-lined sieve into a jug. Pour into sterilised bottles and seal with airtight and vinegar-proof tops until ready to use.
2 Put the onions in a large bowl. Dissolve half the salt in 2.3 litres (4 pints) water. Pour this brine solution over the onions and leave to marinate for 12 hours.
3 Drain the onions, peel away the skins, then put in a clean bowl. Dissolve the rest of the salt in 2.3 litres (4 pints) water. Pour this fresh brine over the peeled onions and leave for a further 24–36 hours.
4 Drain the onions and rinse well, then pack into sterilised jars. Pour enough spiced vinegar over the onions to cover them completely. Cover with vinegar-proof tops. Store in a cool, dark place for at least one month before using.

PICKLED RED CABBAGE

Makes about 1.4kg (3lb)
Preparation 20 minutes, plus overnight standing

1.4kg (3lb) firm red cabbage, cored and finely shredded
2 large onions, peeled and sliced
4 tbsp salt
2.3 litres (4 pints) spiced vinegar (see pickled onions, opposite)
1 tbsp light muscovado sugar

1 Layer the red cabbage and onions in a large bowl, sprinkling each layer with salt, then cover and leave to stand overnight.
2 The following day, drain the cabbage and onions, rinse off the surplus salt and drain thoroughly.
3 Pack the cabbage mixture into sterilised jars. Pour the spiced vinegar into a pan and heat gently. Add the sugar and stir until dissolved. Leave to cool.
4 Pour the cooled vinegar over the cabbage and onion and cover immediately with vinegar-proof tops. Use within two to three weeks; thereafter the cabbage tends to lose its crispness.

NUTRITION PER TABLESPOON
10 cals | trace fat (0g sats) | 1g carbs | 0g salt **V**

PICCALILLI

Makes 1.8kg (4lb)
Preparation 25 minutes, plus standing and maturing
Cooking time 25 minutes

1.8kg (4lb) mixed marrow, cucumber, French beans, small onions and cauliflower (prepared weight, see recipe)
225g (8oz) salt
175g (6oz) sugar
2 tsp mustard powder
1 tsp ground ginger
2 garlic cloves, peeled and crushed
1 litre (1³/₄ pints) distilled vinegar
25g (1oz) plain flour
4 tsp ground turmeric

1 Deseed and finely dice the marrow and cucumber; top, tail and slice the French beans; peel and halve the onions; divide the cauliflower into florets.
2 Layer the vegetables in a large bowl, sprinkling each layer with salt. Add 2.4 litres (4¹/₄ pints) water, cover and leave to stand for 24 hours.
3 The following day, drain the vegetables, rinse well and drain thoroughly.
4 Combine the sugar, mustard powder, ginger, garlic and 900ml (1¹/₂ pints) of the vinegar in a preserving pan. Add the vegetables, bring to the boil, lower the heat and simmer, uncovered, for 20 minutes or until the vegetables are cooked but still crisp.
5 Blend the flour and turmeric with the remaining vinegar and stir into the vegetables. Bring to the boil and cook for 2 minutes.
6 Spoon into sterilised jars, then cover and seal in the usual way (see page 476) with vinegar-proof tops. Store in a cool, dark place for at least one month before using.

NUTRITION PER TABLESPOON
10 cals | trace fat (0g sats) | 2g carbs | 0.7g salt

CHUTNEYS

Chutneys are easy to make – you simply put all the ingredients into a large pan and cook until thick. The fruit and/or vegetables are first chopped or sliced, then cooked slowly for several hours with vinegar and spices to produce a sweet–sour mixture, with the texture of a chunky jam. Never leave chutney unattended while it is simmering, as it can easily burn, especially towards the end of cooking. The flavour of chutney improves with keeping.

APPLE CHUTNEY

Makes 2.7kg (6lb)
Preparation 30 minutes
Cooking time 3¼ hours

1.4kg (3lb) cooking apples, peeled, cored and diced
1.4kg (3lb) onions, chopped
450g (1lb) sultanas or seedless raisins
grated zest and juice of 2 lemons
700g (1½ lb) demerara sugar
600ml (1 pint) malt vinegar

1 Put the apples, onions, sultanas or raisins, lemon zest and juice, sugar and vinegar in a preserving pan.
2 Bring to the boil, then reduce the heat and simmer, uncovered, stirring occasionally, for 3 hours or until the mixture is of a thick consistency with no excess liquid remaining.
3 Spoon the chutney into prepared jars and cover immediately with airtight and vinegar-proof tops.

TRY SOMETHING DIFFERENT
Smooth Apple Chutney A blender or food processor can be used to produce a smoother texture, if you like. In this case, bring all the ingredients, except the sultanas or raisins, to the boil and simmer until really soft. Allow to cool slightly, then whiz in a blender or processor, a little at a time, until smooth. Return to the pan with the sultanas or raisins and cook for a further 15 minutes or until thick. Pot and cover in the usual way.
Gooseberry Chutney Follow the recipe above, replacing the apples with 1.4kg (3lb) prepared gooseberries.

> NUTRITION PER TABLESPOON
> 28 cals | 0g fat (0g sats) | 7g carbs | trace salt 🅥

TOMATO RELISH

Makes 1.4kg (3lb)
Preparation 30 minutes, plus overnight salting
Cooking time 1 hour

1.4kg (3lb) tomatoes, peeled and sliced (see page 277)
450g (1lb) cucumber or marrow, peeled, seeded and
    roughly chopped
50g (2oz) salt
2 garlic cloves, finely chopped
1 large red pepper, seeded and roughly chopped
450ml (¾ pint) malt vinegar
1 tbsp mustard powder
½ tsp ground allspice
½ tsp mustard seeds

1 Layer the tomatoes and cucumber or marrow in a bowl, sprinkling each layer with salt. Cover and leave overnight.
2 Next day, drain and rinse well and put in a large pan. Add the garlic and pepper.
3 Blend the vinegar with the dry ingredients and stir into the pan. Bring slowly to the boil then reduce the heat and simmer gently, uncovered, for about 1 hour, stirring occasionally, until the mixture is soft.
4 Spoon the relish into prepared jars and cover immediately with airtight and vinegar-proof tops

> NUTRITION PER TABLESPOON
> 5 cals | 0g fat (0g sats) | 1g carbs | 0.1g salt

SWEET MANGO CHUTNEY

Makes 2kg (4¹/₂ lb)
Preparation 30 minutes
Cooking time about 1¹/₂ hours

1.8kg (4lb) ripe yellow mangoes
2 small cooking apples
2 onions, peeled and chopped
125g (4oz) seedless raisins
600ml (1 pint) distilled malt vinegar
350g (12oz) demerara sugar
1 tbsp ground ginger
3 garlic cloves, peeled and crushed
1 tsp freshly grated nutmeg
¹/₂ tsp salt

1 Halve, peel and thinly slice the mangoes, cutting the flesh away from the stone. Peel, quarter, core and chop the apples. Put the fruits into a preserving pan together with all the remaining ingredients.
2 Bring to the boil, then reduce the heat and simmer gently, uncovered, stirring occasionally, for about 1¹/₂ hours or until no excess liquid remains and the mixture is thick and pulpy.
3 Spoon the chutney into warmed sterilised jars and allow to cool. Cover and seal with vinegar-proof tops. Once opened, store in the fridge and use within one month. Serve with curries, cheese and cold meats.

> **NUTRITION PER TABLESPOON**
> 20 cals | trace fat (0g sats) | 6g carbs | 0.1g salt

CHILLI JAM

Makes 900g (2 lb)
Preparation 25 minutes
Cooking time 55 minutes

550g (1¹/₄ lb) caster sugar
200ml (7fl oz) red wine vinegar
900g (2lb) very ripe tomatoes, skinned and
    roughly chopped (see page 277)
8 medium red chillies (see Cook's Tip, page 69),
    seeded and finely chopped
6 garlic cloves, crushed
5cm (2in) fresh root ginger, grated
6 whole cloves
6 black peppercorns
4 whole allspice berries

1 Put the sugar and vinegar into a large pan. Heat gently to dissolve the sugar.
2 Add the tomatoes, chillies, garlic and ginger, and the spices tied in a muslin bag. Bring to the boil, then cook very gently for 45–50 minutes until the mixture is thickened. To test, draw a wooden spoon across the base of the pan – it should stay clear for 3 seconds.
3 Pour into sterilised jars and cover with vinegar-proof tops. Store in a cool, dark place for one month before eating.

> **NUTRITION PER TABLESPOON**
> 29 cals | 0g fat (0g sats) | 7g carbs | trace salt

RHUBARB AND GINGER CHUTNEY

Makes about 1.6kg (3¹/₂lb)
Preparation 15 minutes, plus 12 hours standing
Cooking time 1¹/₄ hours

1kg (2¹/₄lb) thick rhubarb stems, trimmed and cut
    into 5cm (2in) pieces
4 tsp salt
225g (8oz) red onions, cut into thick slices
700g (1¹/₂lb 9oz) dark muscovado sugar
450ml (³/₄ pint) white wine vinegar
25g (1oz) fresh root ginger, peeled and coarsely grated
¹/₄ tsp ground allspice
125g (4oz) raisins

1 Put the rhubarb in a non-metallic bowl, mix with 1 tsp salt, then cover and leave in a cool place for 12 hours.
2 Drain and rinse the rhubarb, then put in a preserving pan with all the other ingredients except the raisins. Cook over a gentle heat until the sugar has dissolved, then increase the heat and bubble for 45 minutes–1 hour until well reduced and pulpy. Add the raisins and bubble for 5 minutes.
3 Pot while hot or cool (not warm), then cover with vinegar-proof tops. Store in a cool, dark place for up to six months.

> **COOK'S TIP**
> This spiced chutney is a useful preserve to have in the store-cupboard and tastes especially good with mature cheeses and cold meats.

> **NUTRITION PER TABLESPOON**
> 10 cals | 0g fat (0g sats) | 3g carbs | 0.1g salt

DRINKS

ALCOHOLIC DRINKS

BRANDY ALEXANDER

Serves 1
Preparation 2 minutes

25ml (1fl oz) brandy
25ml (1fl oz) crème de caçao
25ml (1fl oz) double cream
a pinch of grated nutmeg

1 Mix together the brandy, crème de caçao and cream, and shake well.
2 Dust with a little nutmeg and serve.

TRY SOMETHING DIFFERENT
Gin Alexander Replace the brandy with gin.

NUTRITION PER SERVING
245 cals | 13g fat (8g sats) | 9g carbs | trace salt Ⓥ

DRY MARTINI

Serves 1
Preparation 2 minutes

50ml (2fl oz) French vermouth
25ml (1fl oz) dry gin
crushed ice
1 stuffed olive or lemon zest curl

1 Shake the vermouth and gin together with some crushed ice in a shaker.
2 Pour into a glass and float an olive or a lemon zest curl on top. The proportions of a martini are a matter of personal taste; some people prefer 50ml (2fl oz) gin to 25ml (1fl oz) vermouth, others equal quantities of gin and vermouth.

TRY SOMETHING DIFFERENT
Sweet Martini Cocktail Follow the recipe above, but use sweet vermouth and decorate with a cocktail cherry.

NUTRITION PER SERVING
110 cals | 0g fat (0g sats) | 2g carbs | trace salt

WHISKY SOUR

Serves 1
Preparation 2 minutes

juice of ½ lemon
1 tsp sugar
25ml (1fl oz) rye whisky
crushed ice

1 Mix together the lemon juice, sugar and whisky, and shake well with the ice.
2 Serve in a whisky tumbler.

NUTRITION PER SERVING
71 cals | 0g fat (0g sats) | 5g carbs | trace salt Ⓥ

BLOODY MARY

Serves 4
Preparation 2 minutes

1 tbsp Worcestershire sauce
1 dash Tabasco sauce
25ml (1fl oz) vodka, chilled
150ml (¼ pint) tomato juice, chilled
ice cubes
lemon juice to taste
celery salt to taste
1 celery stick, with the leaves left on, to serve

1 Pour the Worcestershire sauce, Tabasco sauce, vodka and tomato juice into a tall glass and stir.
2 Add ice cubes and the lemon juice and celery salt to taste. Put the celery stick in the glass and serve.

TRY SOMETHING DIFFERENT
Virgin Mary Omit the vodka for a non-alcoholic cocktail.

NUTRITION PER SERVING
96 cals | 0g fat | 9g carbs | 1.8g salt

PINK GIN

Serves 1
Preparation 2 minutes

2–3 drops Angostura bitters • 25ml (1fl oz) gin
50–75ml (2–2¹/₂fl oz) iced water

1 Put the bitters into a glass and turn it until the side is well coated.
2 Add the gin and top up with iced water to taste.

NUTRITION PER SERVING
51 cals | 0g fat (0g sats) | 0g carbs | 0g salt

KIR

Serves 1
Preparation 2 minutes

25ml (1fl oz) crème di cassis
150ml (¹/₄ pint) white wine

1 Pour the crème di cassis and white wine into a glass and serve.

TRY SOMETHING DIFFERENT
For a Kir Royale, use 150ml (¹/₄ pint) Champagne or sparking white wine.

NUTRITION PER SERVING
165 cals | 0g fat (0g sats) | 9g carbs | 0g salt

BUCK'S FIZZ

Serves 1
Preparation 2 minutes

juice from one small orange
150ml (¹/₄ pint) champagne

1 Strain the orange juice into a champagne flute and top up with chilled champagne. Serve at once.

NUTRITION PER SERVING
132 cals | 0g fat (0g sats) | 7g carbs | 0g salt

DAIQUIRI

Serves 1
Preparation 2 minutes

juice of ¹/₂ lime or ¹/₄ lemon • 1 tsp sugar
25ml (1fl oz) white rum • crushed ice
extra fruit juice and caster sugar for frosting

1 Mix the fruit juice, sugar and rum and shake well with the crushed ice in a shaker.
2 Dip the edges of the glass in a little more fruit juice and then into caster sugar to frost the rim before filling.

NUTRITION PER SERVING
72 cals | 0g fat (0g sats) | 5g carbs | 0g salt

MARGARITA

Serves 1
Preparation 2 minutes

lemon juice • salt • 125ml (4fl oz) tequila
25ml (1fl oz) curaçao • 25ml (1fl oz) lemon or lime juice

1 Dip the edges of a chilled glass into lemon juice and then salt.
2 In a shaker, mix the tequila, curaçao and lemon juice.
3 Strain into the chilled glass and serve immediately.

NUTRITION PER SERVING
342 cals | 0g fat (0g sats) | 39g carbs | 0g salt

PINA COLADA

Serves 1
Preparation 2 minutes

85ml (3fl oz) white rum • 125ml (4fl oz) pineapple juice
50ml (2fl oz) coconut cream • crushed ice
1 pineapple slice and 1 cherry to decorate

1 Blend together the rum, pineapple juice, coconut cream and crushed ice.
2 Pour into a large goblet or a hollowed-out pineapple half.
3 Decorate with a slice of pineapple and a cherry. Serve with straws.

NUTRITION PER SERVING
382 cals | 17g fat (15g sats) | 13g carbs | trace salt

IRISH OR GAELIC COFFEE

Serves 1
Preparation 5 minutes, plus standing

25ml (1fl oz) Irish whiskey
1 tsp brown sugar
85–125ml (3–4fl oz) hot double-strength coffee
1–2 tbsp double cream, chilled

1 Gently warm a glass, pour in the whiskey and add the brown sugar.
2 Pour in black coffee to within 2.5cm (1in) of the brim and stir to dissolve the sugar.
3 Fill to the brim with cream, poured over the back of a spoon, and allow to stand for a few minutes.

TRY SOMETHING DIFFERENT
Liqueur Coffee Around the World The following are made as for Irish Coffee. Allow 25ml (1fl oz) of the liqueur or spirit to 125ml (4fl oz) of double-strength black coffee, with sugar to taste – usually about 1 tsp – and some thick double cream to pour on top; these quantities will make 1 glassful:
- Cointreau Coffee (made with Cointreau)
- Caribbean Coffee (made with rum)
- German Coffee (made with Kirsch)
- Normandy Coffee (made with Calvados)
- Russian Coffee (made with vodka)
- Calypso Coffee (made with Tia Maria)
- Witch's Coffee (made with strega; sprinkle a little grated lemon zest on top)
- Curaçao Coffee (made with curaçao; stir with a stick of cinnamon)

NUTRITION PER SERVING
218 cals | 16g fat (10g sats) | 6g carbs | trace salt

EGG NOG
Serves 1
Preparation 5 minutes
Cooking time 3 minutes

1 medium egg
1 tbsp sugar
50ml (2fl oz) sherry or brandy
300ml (1/2 pint) milk

1 Whisk the egg and sugar and add the sherry or brandy.
2 Heat the milk without boiling and pour it over the egg mixture. Stir well and serve hot in a glass.

NUTRITION PER SERVING
356 cals | 11g fat (5g sats) | 38g carbs | 0.5g salt

MULLED WINE

Serves 6
Preparation 10 minutes, plus infusing
Cooking time 10–15 minutes

2 oranges
6 cloves
75cl bottle fruity red wine
50ml (2fl oz) brandy or Cointreau
1 cinnamon stick, broken, plus extra to garnish
1/2 tsp mixed spice
2 tbsp golden granulated sugar

1 Cut one of the oranges into six wedges and push a clove into each wedge. Using a vegetable peeler, carefully pare the zest of the other orange into strips.
2 Put the clove-studded orange wedges into a stainless-steel pan, along with the red wine, brandy or Cointreau, cinnamon stick, mixed spice and sugar. Warm gently over a low heat for 10–15 minutes, then remove the pan from the heat and set aside for 10 minutes to let the flavours infuse.
3 Strain the wine into a serving jug through a non-metallic sieve to remove the orange wedges and the cinnamon. Serve in heatproof glasses with a strip of orange zest draped over a broken cinnamon stick.

COOK'S TIPS
Choose a bold, fruity red – nothing too oaky – such as Bordeaux or another wine made from Cabernet Sauvignon or Merlot.

NUTRITION PER SERVING
120 cals | 0g fat (0g sats) | 5g carbs | trace salt

ALCOHOLIC DRINKS AND VEGETARIANS
Animal-derived ingredients, such as gelatine (from cattle) and isinglass (from fish) are often used as fining agents in wine, sherry, port, beer and cider. For this reason some vegetarians prefer to drink only vegetarian alternatives. You can find these in supermarkets and online. Spirits (apart from some malt whiskies, which have been matured in sherry casks) and many liqueurs are generally acceptable to vegetarians.

NON-ALCOHOLIC DRINKS

'STILL' LEMONADE

Serves 6
Makes about 1.1 litres (2 pints)
Preparation 10 minutes

3 lemons
175g (6oz) sugar

1 Remove the lemon zest thinly with a potato peeler.
2 Put the zest and sugar into a bowl or large jug and pour on 900ml (1½ pints) boiling water. Cover and leave to cool, stirring occasionally.
3 Add the juice of the lemons and strain the lemonade. Serve chilled.

NUTRITION PER SERVING
116 cals | 0g fat (0g sats) | 31g carbs | 0g salt **V**

WARMING GINGER SODA

Serves 6
Preparation 5 minutes
Cooking time 10–15 minutes, plus cooling

300g (11oz) unpeeled fresh root ginger, finely sliced
225g (8oz) caster sugar
the zest and juice of 1½ lemons
1 litre (1¾ pints) soda water

1 Put the root ginger into a pan with the sugar and lemon zest and juice. Add about 600ml (1 pint) cold water to cover. Heat gently to dissolve the sugar, then turn up the heat and simmer for 10 minutes.
2 Strain through a fine sieve into a jug. Allow to cool for at least 10 minutes, then top up with soda water.

GET AHEAD
Make syrup up to three days ahead. Chill. Add soda to serve.

NUTRITION PER SERVING
148 cals | 0g fat (0g sats) | 39g carbs | trace salt **V**

ELDERFLOWER CORDIAL

Serves about 30
Makes about 1.1 litres (2 pints)
Preparation 5 minutes

2kg (4½lb) golden granulated sugar
80g (just over 3oz) citric acid
2 medium lemons, sliced
20 large young elderflower heads
   (shake to release any insects)

1 Bring 1.1 litres (2 pints) water to the boil, add the sugar and stir until dissolved.
2 Add the citric acid and lemon slices. Stir in the flower heads. Leave overnight, covered.
3 In the morning sieve. If you want it clearer, strain again through muslin or a coffee filter. Bottle, give some away and keep the rest in the fridge – it will last for months!

TRY SOMETHING DIFFERENT
Try this cocktail (everything must be ice cold): put a dribble of elderflower cordial into a champagne glass, followed by a shot of vodka and a splash of rosewater. Finally, top up with prosecco or cava.

NUTRITION PER SERVING
263 cals | 0g fat (0g sats) | 70g carbs | 0g salt **V**

SUMMER BERRY SMOOTHIE

Serves 6
Preparation 10 minutes

2 large, ripe bananas, about 450g (1lb)
150g (5oz) natural yogurt
500g (1lb 2oz) fresh or frozen summer berries

1 Peel and chop the bananas, then put into a blender. Add the yogurt and 150ml (¼ pint) water, then whiz until smooth. Add the berries and whiz to a purée.
2 Sieve the mixture into a large jug, using the back of a ladle to press it through the sieve. Pour into six glasses and serve.

TRY SOMETHING DIFFERENT
Six ripe apricots or 16 ready-to-eat dried apricots or 400g (14oz) canned apricots in natural juice can be used instead of the berries.

NUTRITION PER SERVING
108 cals | 0.6g fat (trace sats) | 24.3g carbs | 0.1g salt

MANGO AND PASSION FRUIT SMOOTHIE

Serves 2
Preparation 5 minutes

1 small mango
1 passion fruit
150g (5oz) natural yogurt
ice to serve
orange juice (optional)

1 Peel the mango and slice off the flesh from the central stone. Roughly chop. Halve the passion fruit and scoop out the flesh. Rub through a sieve to extract the juice, reserving some of the seeds for decoration, if you like.
2 Put the mango flesh and passion fruit juice into a blender with the yogurt. Whiz until smooth, then serve at once over ice garnished with the passion fruit seeds, if you like. Pour in a little fresh orange juice, if you prefer a thinner smoothie.

NUTRITION PER SERVING
73 cals | 1g fat (1g sats) | 13g carbs | 0.1g salt V

CREAMY OAT AND RASPBERRY COOLER

Serves 2
Preparation 5 minutes

175g (6oz) raspberries, thawed if frozen, juices reserved
100ml (3½ fl oz) freshly squeezed orange juice or 1 large orange, juiced
100ml (3½ fl oz) oat milk, well chilled
100ml (3½ fl oz) low-fat natural or soya yogurt, well chilled
40g (1½ oz) fine oatmeal
2 tsp wheat bran
2 tsp clear honey (optional)

1 If using fresh raspberries, remove the hulls, then wash and pat the fruit dry with kitchen paper. Put into a blender. If the fruit has been frozen, add the juices as well.
2 Pour in the orange juice and oat milk, and spoon in the yogurt. Add the oatmeal and 1 tsp wheat bran. Blend until smooth.
3 Taste and sweeten with honey if necessary. Pour into two glasses, sprinkle with the remaining wheat bran and serve.

TRY SOMETHING DIFFERENT
Use blackberries or strawberries instead of raspberries.

NUTRITION PER SERVING
82 cals | 3.8g fat (0.6g sats) | 29.4g carbs | 0.2g salt

ENTERTAINING, FOOD STORAGE AND HYGIENE

ENTERTAINING

Plan ahead and you are more likely to enjoy the occasion. Avoid planning a meal that is too complicated, and don't tackle a recipe that is totally unfamiliar – or have a practice run first. When deciding on a menu, keep it as well balanced as possible. Think about the colours, flavours and textures of the foods – rich and light, sweet and savoury, crunchy and smooth, hot and cold. Don't have cream or fruit featuring in all the courses; avoid an all-brown menu.

Select produce in season, for the best flavour and value for money. Check whether any of your guests have special dietary needs and plan appropriately. Try to cook an entirely meatless meal even if there is going to be just one vegetarian – it's not as difficult as it sounds, and rarely does anybody notice!

It is worthwhile choosing dishes that can be prepared well ahead of time or prepared up to a certain point, only needing a little last-minute finishing in the kitchen.

PLANNING THE EVENT

Make a master shopping list and separate lists of dishes to be prepared ahead, with a note of when to make them. Plan fridge and freezer space; for a large party, you may need to make different arrangements such as asking your neighbour to keep some foods in their fridge, or putting bulky items into cool boxes. Check that you have candles if you plan to use them.

Make invitations to a dinner party over the phone about 10–12 days in advance. Mention whether it's a formal or informal occsion, the date and time, address if necessary, and say if there are any special dress requirements to avoid embarrassing situations! If you are sending written invitations, post them two to three weeks in advance.

Check that table linen is laundered and ironed in advance, and that glasses and cutlery are clean. Clean the house a day or two beforehand. Buy or order wine and drinks in advance and avoid doing all the shopping at once.

COOKING IN QUANTITY

Decide on the type of party you want to have. A buffet party is ideal if you are entertaining a large number and wish to serve a full meal; make sure that starters and main courses can be eaten with a fork. Choose some recipes that can be prepared and frozen ahead. Many of the recipes in this book can be doubled up easily; however, it isn't usually feasible to prepare a quantity that will serve more than 12 people in one go. So, make up the dishes in batches. On the day, allow plenty of time to reheat dishes and/or arrange serving dishes of cold food. Make sure you have enough people to pass food around – at least one per 20 guests.

HANDY HINTS FOR ENTERTAINING

- Try to strike a balance between hot and cold items, light and substantial ones.
- Most supermarkets have a good selection of ready-to-eat or cook appetisers, if you haven't time to make some. You can also use good-quality bought ingredients, such as mayonnaise and fresh sauces, to save time.
- A freezer is invaluable when entertaining whether on a grand scale or just dinner for two.
- Keep a supply of ready-to-bake bread in the fridge or freezer for quick fresh bread. Freeze packs of half-baked breads to pop in the oven as and when needed.
- Keep a supply of luxury ice cream in the freezer.
- Remember to unwrap cheeses and bring them to room temperature at least an hour before serving, keeping them lightly covered, to prevent drying out, until the last minute.
- Make ice well in advance, and see page 497 for advice on chilling drinks.
- During the winter, if you run out of fridge space, use a greenhouse or garage to keep drinks and other perishables cold.
- Use the microwave to reheat pre-cooked vegetables, sauces and gravy.
- Decide in advance where you are going to stack dirty plates. A kitchen overflowing with washing-up looks unsightly, so consider paying someone to do this for you on the day.

CATERING QUANTITIES

Approximate quantities to serve 12 people. For 25, multiply the quantities by 2.
For 50, multiply by 4. For 75, multiply by 5¹/₂. For 100, multiply by 7.

Starters

Soups	2.6 litres (4¹/₂ pints)
Pâtés	1.1kg (2¹/₂ lb)
Smoked salmon	900g (2lb)
Prawns	900g (2lb)

Main dishes

Boneless chicken or turkey	1.8kg (4lb)
Whole chicken	three 1.4kg (3lb) oven-ready birds
Turkey	one 5.4kg (12lb) oven-ready bird
Lamb/beef/pork	
Boneless	2–2.3kg (4¹/₂–5lb)
On the bone	3.2–3.6kg (7–8lb)
Mince	2kg (4¹/₂ lb)
Fish	
Whole with head	2.3kg (5lb)
Steaks	twelve 175g (6oz) steaks
Fillets	2kg (4¹/₂ lb)
Prawns (main course)	1.4kg (3lb)

Turkey

6–10 people	2.3–3.6kg (5–8lb)
10–15	3.6–5kg (8–11lb)
15–20	5–6.8kg (11–15lb)
20–30	6.8–9kg (15–20lb)

Accompaniments

Roast and mashed potatoes	2kg (4¹/₂ lb)
New potatoes	1.8kg (4lb)
Rice and pasta	700g (1¹/₂ lb)
Green vegetables	1.4kg (3lb)
Fresh spinach	3.6kg (8lb)

Salads

Tomatoes	700g (1¹/₂ lb)
Salad leaves	2 medium heads
Cucumber	1 large
French dressing	175ml (6fl oz)
Mayonnaise	300ml (¹/₂ pint)

Bread

Fresh uncut bread	1 large loaf
Medium sliced loaf	1 large (approximately 24 slices)

Cheese

For a cheese and wine party	1.4kg (3lb)
To serve at the end of a meal	700g (1¹/₂ b)

Butter

To serve with bread or biscuits and cheese	225g (8oz)
To serve with bread and biscuits and cheese	350g (12oz)
For sandwiches	175g (6oz) softened butter for 12 rounds

Cream

For pudding	600ml (1 pint) single cream
For coffee	300ml (¹/₂ pint)

Coffee and tea

Ground coffee	125g (4oz) for 12 medium cups
Instant	75g (3oz) for 12 large cups
Milk	allow 450ml (³/₄ pint) for 12 cups of tea

APPROXIMATE COFFEE AND TEA QUANTITIES

		1 Serving	24–26 Servings	Notes
Coffee	ground	200ml (7fl oz)	250–275g (9–10oz) coffee 3.4 litres (6 pints) water 1.7 litres (3 pints) milk 450g (1lb) sugar	If you make the coffee in advance, strain it after infusion. Reheat without boiling.
Tea	Indian	200ml (7fl oz)	50g (2oz) tea 4.5 litres (8 pints) water 900ml (1¹/₂ pints) milk 450g (1lb) sugar	It is better to make tea in several pots rather than in one outsized one.
	China	200ml (7fl oz)	50g (2oz) tea 5.1 litres (9 pints) water 2–3 lemons 450g (1lb) sugar	Infuse China tea for 2–3 minutes only. Put a thin lemon slice in each cup before pouring. Serve sugar separately.

APPROXIMATE QUANTITIES FOR BUFFET PARTIES

	Ingredients	Portions	Notes
STARTERS			
Fish cocktail	50g (2oz) peeled shrimps, prawns, crab or lobster meat, 2 lettuce leaves, about 40ml (1¹/₂fl oz) sauce	1	Serve in stemmed glasses, garnished with a shrimp or prawn Serve with lemon wedges.
	700g (1¹/₂lb) fish (as above), 1 large lettuce, 450ml (³/₄ pint) sauce	12	
Pâtés – allow 3 half slices hot toast per person to serve with the pâté	75–125g (3–4oz)	1	
	1.1kg (2¹/₂lb)	12	
Smoked salmon (serve with toast as above or brown bread)	40–50g (1¹/₂–2oz)	1	
	550g (1¹/₄lb)	12	
	1.1kg (2¹/₂lb)	25	
Other smoked fish, such as smoked trout, mackerel	125g (4oz)	1	
	1.1kg (2¹/₂lb)	12	
	2–2.5kg (4¹/₂–5¹/₂lb)	25	
Soups – cream, clear or iced	150–200ml (5–7fl oz)	1	
	2.3 litres (4 pints)	12	
	4.5 litres (8 pints)	25	
MAIN DISHES			
Delicatessen meats – ham, tongue, salami	75–125g (3–4oz)	1	
	1kg (2¹/₄lb)	12	
	2.3kg (5lb)	25	
Salmon	125–175g (4–6oz)	1	
	1.4–1.8kg (3–4lb)	12	
Roast turkey	3.6–5kg (8–11lb)	10–15	
	6.8–9kg (15–20lb)	20–30	
Chicken – whole	Three 2.7kg (6lb) birds	24–26	Serve hot or cold
– joint	150–225g (5–8oz)	1	
SALAD VEGETABLES			
Carrots	900g (2lb), grated	12	
	1.8kg (4lb), grated	25	
Celery	2–3 heads	12	
	5 heads	25	
Cucumbers	1–1¹/₂ cucumbers	12	
	2–3 cucumbers	25	
Lettuce	2–3 lettuces	12	Dress at last minute
	5–6 lettuces	25	
Boiled potatoes	700g (1¹/₂lb)	12	For potato salads
	1.4kg (3lb)	25	
Tomatoes	700g (1¹/₂lb)	12	
	1.4kg (3lb)	25	
DRESSINGS			
French Dressing	300ml (¹/₂ pint)	12	
	450–600ml (³/₄–1 pint)	25	
Mayonnaise	600ml (1 pint)	12	
	900ml–1 litre (1¹/₂–1³/₄ pints)	25	

APPROXIMATE QUANTITIES FOR BUFFET PARTIES

	Ingredients	Portions	Notes
DESSERTS			
Meringues	6 egg whites, 350g (12oz) caster sugar, 600ml (1pint) whipped cream	40 (small) meringue halves	Sandwich meringue halves together with the whipped cream not more than 2 hours before serving
Trifle	Old-English Trifle	6	
	Old-English Trifle x 2	15	
Profiteroles	1 quantity of Choux Pastry, 150ml (¼ pint) whipped cream, 1 quantity of Rich Chocolate Sauce	6	Fill the profiteroles with the whipped cream not more than 2 hours before serving
	2 quantities of Choux Pastry, 300ml (¼ pint) whipped cream, 2 quantities of Chocolate Sauce	12–15	
Lemon Syllabub	Lemon Syllabub x 4	16	
Ice cream (bought or homemade)	1 litre (1¾ pints)	12	Transfer from the freezer to the fridge 30 minutes before serving
	2.3 litres (4 pints)	25–30	
SAVOURIES			
Cheese Straws	Cheese Straws x 2	48	
Sausage Rolls	Sausage Rolls x 4	64	
Tangy Chicken Bites	Tangy Chicken Bites	48	
Red Pepper Pesto Croutes	Red Pepper Pesto Croutes x 2	48	
Mozzarella Nibbles	Mozzarella Nibbles x 2	60	
Cocktail sausages	450g (1lb)	32	
Quiche	20.5cm (8in) quiche	6–8	
BREAD, CRACKERS AND SANDWICHES			
Bread loaves	1 large loaf, about 800g (1lb 12oz)	20–24 slices	
	1 small loaf, about 400g (14oz)	10–12 slices	
	1 long sandwich loaf, 1.4kg (3lb)	50 slices	
Slices of bread	1–1½ slices	1	Cut into triangles when serving with a meal
French bread	1 large loaf	12–15	
	1 small loaf	6–8	
Cheese biscuits or crackers	3 biscuits	1	
	60 biscuits	30	
BUTTER			
	15–25g (½–1oz) butter	1	If bread is served with the meal
	25–40g (1–1½oz) butter	1	If serving cheese as a course
	About 125g (4oz) butter	spreads 10–12 sandwiches	
	About 125g (4oz) butter	spreads 10–12 bread rolls	
CHEESE			
Cheese (for biscuits)	25–40g (1–1½oz)	1	Serve a selection of at least four types
	700–900g (1½–2lb)	25	
Cheese (for wine and cheese parties)	75g (3oz)	1	
	2–2.3kg (4½–5lb)	25	

WINES AND OTHER PARTY DRINKS

For large gatherings, offer one white and one red wine, sticking to around 12.5 per cent alcohol, and have plenty of different soft drinks. Provide beer and lager if you like, but avoid spirits. Wines, sparkling wines, and hot or cold punches are ideal party drinks.

For very large numbers, buy wines and champagne on a sale-or-return basis from a wine merchant. Mineral water, fruit juices and soft drinks can also be bought in this way. Most supermarkets will also allow this, provided the returned bottles are undamaged – check first.

Wine boxes are good value and it is worth asking your local wine merchant for their advice – some are better than others. If you prefer to serve wine from the bottle, look at the cost-saving potential of buying by the case.

When it comes to choosing wine it makes sense to find a supplier you can trust, whether it be a supermarket, wine merchant or warehouse. If you opt for something different, just buy one bottle and see if you enjoy it.

Generally, red wine goes best with red meats, and white wine is the better complement to fish, chicken and light meats, but there really are no longer any hard-and-fast rules.

For an aperitif, it is nice to serve a glass of chilled champagne or sparkling wine, or perhaps dry sherry. Avoid sweet drinks, or spirits with a high alcohol content, as these tend to take the edge off the appetite, rather than stimulating it. Wine or sherry can be served with a soup course. A full-bodied red wine is an excellent accompaniment to the cheeseboard, although some people prefer to drink port with their cheese. You may wish to serve a dessert wine, such as Sauternes, or a glass of fruity demi-sec champagne. Coffee follows, with brandy and liqueurs if you like.

How much to buy?

If you allow one 75cl bottle of wine per head you should have more than enough. One standard 75cl bottle of wine, champagne or sparkling wine will give six glasses. A litre bottle will provide eight glasses. For a dinner party, allow one or two glasses of wine as an aperitif, one or two glasses with the first course, two glasses with the main course and another with the dessert or cheese.

Remember to buy plenty of mineral water – sparkling and still – and fresh fruit juices. For every ten guests, buy two 1.5 litre bottles of sparkling water and three similar-sized bottles of still water.

Serving wine

Warm white wine and champagne is inexcusable, and chilled red wine (unless young and intended for serving cold) is not at all pleasant. The ideal temperature for red wine is around 15–18°C, with the more tannic wines benefiting from the higher temperature. On a warm day,

a brief spell in the fridge will help red wine. For whites, the more powerful wines, like Chardonnay, should be served cool rather than cold, at around 11–15°C, while other whites should be properly cold, at around 6–10°C. Party food will probably take up your available fridge space, so you will need plenty of ice to keep drinks cool.

If you have a lot of wine to chill, use the bath, or a large deep sink if you have one. About an hour before the party, half-fill the bath with ice, pour in some cold water and stand the bottles upright, making sure the ice and water come up to their necks. Alternatively, use a clean plastic dustbin or cool boxes as containers. (Some hire companies will loan special plastic bins for cooling wines.)

A large block of ice added to chilled water is a good idea. Make this by filling a large strong plastic bag with water, seal securely and place in the freezer until frozen.

Wine and party drink checklist

- ❏ Champagne and sparkling wine
- ❏ Red wine
- ❏ White wine
- ❏ Beer and lager
- ❏ Mineral water, sparkling and natural
- ❏ Real fruit juices
- ❏ Other soft drinks and squashes
- ❏ Dessert wine or sweet sparkling wine
- ❏ Low-alcohol/alcohol-free wines, beer and lager
- ❏ Liqueurs, brandies etc., for cocktails
- ❏ Mixers
- ❏ Fail-safe corkscrews and wine-bottle stoppers – to 're-cork' opened wine bottles
- ❏ Plenty of ice and reusable ice packs.

QUANTITY GUIDE: DRINKS TO THE BOTTLE

(using a standard size 100ml (3½ fl oz) wine glass)

Sherry, port, vermouth	12 glasses
Single measure of spirits	30
'Split' – 200ml (7fl oz) soda, tonic, ginger ale	2–3
Table wine (75cl)	6
Table wine (1 litre)	8
Fruit juices – 600ml (1 pint)	4–6
Fruit cordial – 1 litre (1¾ pints) bottle diluted with 4 litres (7 pints) water	20–26
Punch – 1.7 litres (3 pints)	6–8

FOOD STORAGE AND HYGIENE

Storing food correctly and preparing food in a hygienic way is important to ensure that it remains nutritious and as flavourful as possible, and to reduce the risk of food poisoning. When you are preparing food, always wash your hands thoroughly before and after handling it, particularly raw and cooked meat and poultry. Keep work surfaces clean and kitchen utensils washed in between preparing raw and cooked foods. Keep raw and cooked foods separate, especially meat, fish and poultry. Never put cooked or ready-to-eat foods directly on to a surface that has just had raw fish, meat or poultry on it. To ensure food safety, remember that foods with a longer shelf life have a 'best-before' date; more perishable items have a 'use-by' date. Make sure items are within either date. When supermarket shopping, pack frozen and chilled items in an insulated cool bag and put them away as soon as you get home.

STORAGE IN THE FRIDGE

Store day-to-day perishable items, such as opened jams, mayonnaise and bottled sauces, in the fridge along with eggs and dairy products, fruit juices, bacon, fresh and cooked meat (on separate shelves), and salads and vegetables (except potatoes which don't like the cold). The fridge should be kept at 4–5°C. For safe food storage:

- Ensure that all items are well wrapped, and that meat and poultry cannot drip on to other foods.
- Never put hot food into the fridge, as this will raise the temperature.
- To keep the fridge cold, don't leave the door open any longer than necessary, and don't overfill.
- Clean the fridge regularly using a proprietary cleaner or a solution of 1 tbsp bicarbonate of soda to 1 litre (1³/₄ pints) water.
- Thaw the fridge regularly.

STORAGE IN THE FREEZER

Freezing is an excellent way of preserving food. As well as storing bought frozen items, you can cook meals in bulk and freeze portions to be eaten later. You can also freeze concentrated reduced fresh stock. The following prepared items freeze well: bread and scones; pastries and part-baked bread from the supermarket; soups and pizzas. The correct operating temperature for a freezer is -18°C. The following guidelines apply:

- Only freeze food that is very fresh.
- Never put any foods that are still slightly warm into the freezer, or freeze more than one-tenth of your freezer's capacity in any 24 hours, as these will cause a rise in temperature.
- When freezing large quantities, use 'fast-freeze'.
- Pack and seal items well before freezing to avoid moisture or cold air coming into contact with the food,

MAXIMUM FRIDGE STORAGE TIMES

For pre-packed foods, adhere to the 'use-by' date. For other foods the following storage times should apply:

Raw fish and meat		Cooked meat		Vegetables and fruit	
fish	1 day	joints	3 days	salad leaves	2–3 days
shellfish	1 day	casseroles/stews	2 days	green vegetables	3–4 days
joints	3 days	pies	2 days	soft fruit	1–2 days
poultry	2 days	sliced meat	2 days	hard and stone fruit	3–7 days
game	2 days	ham	2 days		
raw sliced meat	2 days	vacuum-packed 1–2 weeks (or according to pack instructions)		**Dairy food**	
minced meat	1 day			milk	4–5 days
offal	1 day			cheese, soft	2–3 days
sausages	3 days			cheese, hard	1 week
bacon	7 days			eggs	1 week

MAXIMUM FREEZER STORAGE TIMES

Follow the manufacturer's instructions or use the following recommended times:

Vegetables		Meat and poultry		Prepared foods	
blanched vegetables	10–12 months	beef and veal	4–6 months	soups and sauces	3 months
unblanched vegetables	3–4 weeks	lamb	4–6 months	stocks	6 months
tomatoes	6–8 months	pork	4–6 months	prepared meals	4–6 months
vegetable purées	6–8 months	offal	3–4 months	cakes	4–6 months
		sliced bacon	2–3 months	bread	2–3 months
Fruit		cured meat	2–3 months	sandwiches	2–3 months
fruit in syrup	9–12 months	ham/bacon joints	3–4 months	bread dough	2–3 months
open frozen fruit	6–8 months	chicken/turkey	4–6 months	pastries	3–4 months
fruit purées	6–8 months	duck and goose	4–6 months		
fruit juice	4–6 months	venison	4–6 months	**Dairy produce**	
		rabbit	4–6 months	butter, salted	3–4 months
Fish		sausages	2–3 months	butter, unsalted	6–8 months
white fish	6–8 months	minced beef	3–4 months	ice cream	3–4 months
oily fish	3–4 months				
fish portions	3–4 months				
shellfish	2–3 months				

or cross-flavouring occurring. Wrap awkward-shaped items in foil or freezer film (ordinary clingfilm is not suitable), then seal in a bag. Freezer film can also be used as a lining for acidic foods. Label and date.

- Use square containers to store food, as they stack well and take up less space.
- Interleave items of food that might stick together with greaseproof paper, polythene, foil or freezer film.
- Don't fill containers too full with liquids, allow room for expansion.
- Do not re-freeze food once it has thawed.
- Keep your freezer as full as possible. Empty spaces require more energy to keep cool.

FREEZING VEGETABLES AND FRUIT

If you have your own vegetable garden or local farm shop, freezing is the ideal way to preserve vegetables and fruit in peak condition. Most vegetables keep better for longer if they are blanched before freezing although those that will be eaten within a few weeks of freezing do not need to be blanched. Prepare the vegetable as appropriate, then weigh and divide into 450g (1lb) quantities. Blanch by putting the prepared vegetable in a basket and lowering into a large pan of fast-boiling water. Bring to the boil and time 1 minute for most varieties; 2–3 minutes for hard vegetables (carrots and corn-on-the-cob); and 10 seconds for soft vegetables

(courgettes, mangetouts and spinach). Plunge the basket straight into a bowl of ice-cold water, drain and pack.

Not all seasonal fruits freeze well; most berry fruits lose some quality of texture; use fruit that is perfectly ripe and in very good condition. Open-freeze small berry fruits, such as raspberries, blackcurrants and redcurrants. Spread them out on a tray lined with baking parchment and freeze until solid, then pack. Fruits that don't freeze well because their texture is spoiled – strawberries, for example – are only suitable for freezing as a purée. Fruits that need to be cooked before eating, such as blackcurrants and gooseberries, should be cooked first. Purée the fresh or cooked fruit, then sieve. Sweeten with sugar to taste if necessary, then pack.

Apricots, damsons, greengages, plums, cooking apples and rhubarb are best frozen in sugar syrup with lemon to avoid discoloration. Dissolve 450g (1lb) sugar in 1 litre (1³/₄ pints) water over a low heat. Boil for 1 minute, then cool. Add the juice of 1 lemon. Pack the halved or sliced fruit in plastic containers, add sufficient sugar syrup to cover, leaving room for expansion, then seal.

THAWING FROZEN FOOD

Never leave food to thaw in a warm place but thaw it gradually in the fridge or a cool larder. Cover loosely while thawing and ensure it is thoroughly thawed before cooking. Cook food soon after thawing.

THE STORECUPBOARD

Having a storecupboard well stocked with the basic essentials will save repeated visits to the shops to pick up missing items. Correct storage is important:

- Always check packaging for storage advice; storage requirements may change if additives, sugar or salt have been reduced.
- Never keep storecupboard foods beyond their 'use-by' date.
- Keep all food cupboards scrupulously clean.
- Once canned foods are opened, transfer the contents to a clean container, cover and keep in the fridge.
- Transfer dry goods such as sugar, rice and pasta to moisture-proof containers. When supplies are used up, wash out and thoroughly dry containers before refilling with fresh stock.

THE WELL-STOCKED STORECUPBOARD

Tailor the following guidelines to your own needs and likes:

Cans, bottles and condiments The following items are most useful: canned tomatoes, cartons of passata, tomato paste and sun-dried tomatoes in oil; jars of pesto; canned coconut milk; tomato ketchup, English, wholegrain and Dijon mustard; Worcestershire sauce, Tabasco, chilli, hoisin, oyster and soy sauces; cans of fruits in natural juice; cartons or cans of ready-made custard; canned chickpeas, red kidney beans and haricot beans; and, of course, baked beans.

Rice, grains and pulses Keep a stock of the following: long-grain rice, pudding rice, mixed wild rice, brown rice and Arborio rice for creamy risottos; couscous, bulgur wheat, rolled oats, oatmeal and polenta; dried kidney beans, haricot beans and flageolets; red, green and Puy lentils.

Pasta Keep at least one long dried pasta such as spaghetti, a box of dried ribbon pasta like tagliatelle, several dried pasta shapes, such as penne, spirals and macaroni, plus a box of lasagne sheets. A bag of tiny soup pasta is also useful.

Dried fruit and nuts Store them in airtight containers in a cool, dry cupboard. Nuts stale quickly if they are kept in a humid atmosphere. Vacuum-packed chestnuts are a handy time-saver; shelled walnuts, hazelnuts, almonds (and ground almonds), pistachio nuts and pinenuts are worth buying; currants, raisins, sultanas, dried apricots and prunes are useful for winter fruit compotes, cakes and biscuits.

Dried mushrooms There are several different varieties of dried wild mushrooms, including ceps, porcini and morels.

Oils are best stored in a dark cupboard away from any heat source, as heat and light can make them turn rancid and affect the colour. Buy olive oil in dark green bottles. Keep a stock of the following: vegetable oil for deep-frying; sunflower oil for frying and salads; light olive oil for cooking; extra virgin olive oil for salad dressings; sesame oil for Chinese cooking; walnut or hazelnut oil for dressings. Vinegars must be kept cool or they can turn bad. Stock up with white and red wine vinegars; balsamic and sherry vinegars for sauces and dressings; cider vinegar and flavoured vinegars for dressings and mayonnaise; distilled malt vinegar for pickles and chutneys; malt vinegar for traditional fish 'n' chips.

Dried herbs, spices and flavourings Stock a good selection from those detailed on pages 32–38. Whole spices keep their flavour better than ready-ground, but all need to be replaced after a while, as they lose their pungency. Store them in a cool, dark cupboard or in dark jars. Stock up with sea salt, black and green peppercorns; Indian curry and tandoori pastes; Thai green and red curry pastes; vanilla and almond extracts; vanilla pods, whole nutmegs, cloves and cinnamon sticks.

Baking ingredients Baking powder, bicarbonate of soda and cream of tartar; thin honey and golden syrup; gelatine; easy-blend dried yeast; cocoa powder; instant coffee granules; chocolate with at least 70% cocoa solids (keep wrapped and cool); UHT or dried milk (in case you run out of fresh milk).

Flours, sugars etc. should be stored in airtight containers that are easy to access with a spoon or measure. Stock up with plain white flour; self-raising white flour; wholemeal flour; cornflour; golden caster sugar; unrefined granulated sugar; light and dark muscovado sugars and white and golden icing sugar.

Other ingredients can be bought as required in small quantities.

GLOSSARY

Acidulated water Water to which lemon juice or vinegar has been added in which fruit or vegetables, such as pears or Jerusalem artichokes, are immersed to prevent discoloration.

Al dente Italian term commonly used to describe food, especially pasta and vegetables, which are cooked until tender but still firm to the bite.

Antipasto Italian selection of cold meats, fish, salads, etc., served as a starter.

Au gratin Describes a dish that has been coated with sauce, sprinkled with breadcrumbs or cheese and browned under the grill or in the oven. Low-sided gratin dishes are used.

Bain-marie Literally, a water bath, used to keep foods, such as delicate custards and sauces, at a constant low temperature during cooking. On the hob a double pan or bowl over a pan of simmering water is used; for oven cooking, the baking dish(es) are placed in a roasting tin containing enough hot water to come halfway up the sides.

Baking blind Pre-baking a pastry case before filling. The pastry case is lined with greaseproof paper and weighted down with dried beans or ceramic baking beans.

Baking powder A raising agent consisting of an acid, usually cream of tartar and an alkali, such as bicarbonate of soda, which react to produce carbon dioxide. This expands during baking and makes cakes and breads rise.

Bard To cover the breast of game birds or poultry, or lean meat with fat to prevent the meat from drying out during roasting.

Baste To spoon the juices and melted fat over meat, poultry, game or vegetables during roasting to keep them moist. The term is also used to describe spooning over a marinade.

Beat To incorporate air into an ingredient or mixture by agitating it vigorously with a spoon, fork, whisk or electric mixer. The technique is also used to soften ingredients.

Béchamel Classic French white sauce, used as the basis for other sauces and savoury dishes.

Beurre manié Equal parts of flour and butter kneaded together to make a paste. Used to thicken soups, stews and casseroles. It is whisked into the hot liquid a little at a time at the end of cooking.

Bind To mix beaten egg or other liquid into a dry mixture to hold it together.

Blanch To immerse food briefly in fast-boiling water to loosen skins, such as peaches or tomatoes, or to remove bitterness, or to destroy enzymes and preserve the colour, flavour and texture of vegetables (especially prior to freezing).

Bone To remove the bones from meat, poultry, game or fish, so that it can be stuffed or simply rolled before cooking.

Bottle To preserve fruit, jams, pickles or other preserves in sterile glass jars.

Bouquet garni Small bunch of herbs – usually a mixture of parsley stems, thyme and a bay leaf – tied in muslin and used to flavour stocks, soups and stews.

Braise To cook meat, poultry, game or vegetables slowly in a small amount of liquid in a pan or casserole with a tight-fitting lid. The food is usually first browned in oil or fat.

Brochette Food cooked on a skewer or spit.

Brûlée A French term, literally meaning 'burnt' used to refer to a dish with a crisp coating of caramelised sugar.

Butterfly To split a food, such as a large prawn or poussin, almost in half and open out flat, so that it will cook more quickly.

Calorie Strictly a kilocalorie, this is used in dietetics to measure the energy value of foods.

Canapé Small appetiser, served with drinks.

Candying Method of preserving fruit or peel by impregnating with sugar.

Caramelise To heat sugar or sugar syrup slowly until it is brown in colour; ie forms a caramel.

Carbonade Rich stew or braise of meat, which includes beer.

Casserole A dish with a tight-fitting lid used for slow-cooking meat, poultry and vegetables, now used to describe food cooked in this way.

Charcuterie French term for cooked pork products, including hams, sausages and terrines.

Chill To cool food in the fridge.

Chine To sever the rib bones from the backbone, close to the spine. This is done to meat joints, such as loin of pork or lamb, to make them easier to carve into chops after cooking.

Clarify To remove sediment or impurities from a liquid. Stock is clarified by heating with egg white, while butter is clarified by melting and skimming. Butter that has been clarified will withstand a higher frying temperature. To clarify butter, heat until melted and all bubbling stops. Take off the heat and let it stand until the sediment has sunk to the bottom, then gently pour off the fat, straining it through muslin.

Compote Mixture of fresh or dried fruit stewed in sugar syrup. Served hot or cold.

Concassé Diced fresh ingredient, used as a garnish. The term is most often applied to skinned, deseeded tomatoes.

Coulis A smooth fruit or vegetable purée, thinned if necessary to a pouring consistency.

Court bouillon Aromatic cooking liquid containing wine, vinegar or lemon juice, used for poaching delicate fish, poultry or vegetables.

Consistency Term used to describe the texture of a mixture, eg firm, dropping or soft.

Cream To beat together fat and sugar until the mixture is pale and fluffy, and resembles whipped cream in texture and colour. The method is used in cakes and puddings which contain a high proportion of fat and require the incorporation of a lot of air.

Crêpe French term for a pancake.

Crimp To decorate the edge of a pie, tart or shortbread by pinching it at regular intervals to give a fluted effect.

Croquette Seasoned mixture of cooked potato and fish, meat, poultry or vegetables shaped into a small roll, coated with egg and breadcrumbs and shallow-fried.

Croûte Circle or other shaped piece of fried bread, typically used as a base for serving small game birds.

Croûtons Small pieces of fried or toasted bread, served with soups and salads.

Crudités Raw vegetables, usually cut into slices or sticks, typically served with a dipping sauce as an appetiser.

Crystallise To preserve fruit in sugar syrup.

Curdle To cause sauces or creamed mixtures to separate once the egg is added, usually by overheating or over-beating.

Cure To preserve fish, meat or poultry by smoking, drying or salting.

Daube Braising meat and vegetables with stock, often with wine and herbs added.

Deglaze To heat stock, wine or other liquid with the cooking juices left in the pan after roasting or sautéeing, scraping and stirring vigorously to dissolve the sediment on the bottom of the pan.

Dégorge To draw out moisture from a food, eg salting aubergines to remove bitter juices.

Dice To cut food into small cubes.

Draw To remove the entrails from poultry or game.

Dredge To sprinkle food generously with flour, sugar, icing sugar and so on.

Dress To pluck, draw and truss poultry or game. The term is also used to describe tossing a salad in vinaigrette or other dressing.

Dry To preserve food, such as fruit, vegetables, pasta and pulses by dehydration.

Dust To sprinkle lightly with flour, cornflour, icing sugar etc.

Emulsion A mixture of two liquids, which do not dissolve into one another, such as oil and vinegar. Vigorous shaking or heating will emulsify them, as for a vinaigrette.

En croûte Term used to describe food that is wrapped in pastry before cooking.

En papillote Term used to describe food that is baked in a greaseproof paper or baking parchment parcel and served from the paper.

Enzyme Organic substance in food that causes chemical changes. Enzymes are a complex group. Their action is usually halted during cooking.

Escalope Thin slice of meat, such as pork, veal or turkey, from the top of the leg, usually pan-fried.

Extract Concentrated flavouring, which is used in small quantities, eg yeast extract, vanilla extract.

Ferment Chemical change deliberately or accidentally brought about by fermenting agents, such as yeast or bacteria. Fermentation is utilised for making bread, yogurt, beer and wine.

Fillet Term used to describe boned breasts of birds, boned sides of fish, and the undercut of a loin of beef, lamb, pork or veal.

Flake To separate food, such as cooked fish, into natural pieces.

Flambé Flavouring a dish with alcohol, usually brandy or rum, which is then ignited so that the actual alcohol content is burned off.

Folding in Method of combining a whisked or creamed mixture with other ingredients by cutting and folding so that it retains its lightness. A large metal spoon or plastic-bladed spatula is used.

Frosting To coat leaves and flowers with a fine layer of sugar to use as a decoration. Also an American term for icing cakes.

Fry To cook food in hot fat or oil. There are various methods: shallow-frying in a little fat in a shallow pan; deep-frying where the food is totally immersed in oil; dry-frying in which fatty foods are cooked in a non-stick pan without extra fat; see also Stir-fry.

Galette Cooked savoury or sweet mixture shaped into a round.

Garnish A decoration, usually edible, such as parsley or lemon, which is used to enhance the appearance of a savoury dish.

Glaze A glossy coating given to sweet and savoury dishes to improve their appearance and sometimes flavour. Ingredients for glazes include beaten egg, egg white, milk and syrup.

Gluten A protein constituent of grains, such as wheat and rye, which develops when the flour is mixed with water to give the dough elasticity.

Grate To shred hard food, such as cheese and carrots, with a grater or food processor attachment.

Griddle A flat, heavy, metal plate used on the hob for cooking scones or for searing savoury ingredients.

Grind To reduce foods such as coffee beans, nuts and whole spices to small particles using a food mill, pestle and mortar, electric grinder or food processor.

Gut To clean out the entrails from fish.

Hang To suspend meat or game in a cool, dry place for a number of days to tenderise the flesh and develop flavour.

Hull To remove the stalk and calyx from soft fruits, such as strawberries.

Infuse To immerse flavourings, such as aromatic vegetables, herbs, spices and vanilla, in a liquid to impart flavour. Usually the infused liquid is brought to the boil, then left to stand.

Julienne Fine 'matchstick' strips of vegetables or citrus zest, sometimes used as a garnish.

Knead To work dough by pummelling with the heel of the hand.

Knock back To knead a yeast dough for a second time after rising, to ensure an even texture.

Lard To insert small strips of fat or streaky bacon into the flesh of game birds and dry meat before cooking. A special larding needle is used.

Liaison A thickening or binding agent based on a combination of ingredients, such as flour and water, or oil and egg.

Macerate To soften and flavour raw or dried foods by soaking in a liquid, eg soaking fruit in alcohol.

Mandolin A flat wooden or metal frame with adjustable cutting blades for slicing vegetables.

Marinate To soak raw meat, poultry or game – usually in a mixture of oil, wine, vinegar and flavourings – to soften and impart flavour. The mixture, which is known as a marinade, may also be used to baste the food during cooking.

Medallion Small round piece of meat, usually beef or veal.

Mince To cut food into very fine pieces, using a mincer, food processor or knife.

Mocha Term which has come to mean a blend of chocolate and coffee.

Parboil To boil a vegetable or other food for part of its cooking time before finishing it by another method.

Pare To finely peel the skin or zest from vegetables or fruit.

Pâte The French word for pastry, familiar in pâte sucrée, a sweet flan pastry.

Pâté A savoury mixture of finely chopped or minced meat, fish and/or vegetables, usually served as a starter with bread or toast.

Patty tin Tray of cup-shaped moulds for cooking small cakes and deep tartlets. Also called a bun tin.

Pectin A naturally occurring substance found in most varieties of fruit and some vegetables, which is necessary for setting jams and jellies. Commercial pectin and sugar with pectin are also available for preserve-making.

Pickle To preserve meat or vegetables in brine or vinegar.

Pith The bitter white skin under the thin zest of citrus fruit.

Pluck To remove the feathers from poultry and game birds.

Poach To cook food gently in liquid at simmering point; the surface should be just trembling.

Pot roast To cook meat in a covered pan with some fat and a little liquid.

Prove To leave bread dough to rise (usually for a second time) after shaping.

Purée To pound, sieve or liquidise vegetables, fish or fruit to a smooth pulp. Purées often form the basis for soups and sauces.

Reduce To fast-boil stock or other liquid in an uncovered pan to evaporate water and concentrate the flavour.

Refresh To cool hot vegetables very quickly by plunging into ice-cold water or holding under cold running water in order to stop the cooking process and preserve the colour.

Render To melt fat slowly to a liquid, either by heating meat trimmings, or to release the fat from fatty meat, such as duck or goose, during roasting.

Rennet An animal-derived enzyme used to coagulate milk in cheese-making. A vegetarian alternative is available.

Roast To cook meat by dry heat in the oven.

Roulade Soufflé or sponge mixture rolled around a savoury or sweet filling.

Roux A mixture of equal quantities of butter (or other fat) and flour cooked together to form the basis of many sauces.

Rub-in Method of incorporating fat into flour by rubbing between the fingertips, used when a short texture is required. Used for pastry, cakes, scones and biscuits.

Salsa Piquant sauce made from chopped fresh vegetables and sometimes fruit.

Sauté To cook food in a small quantity of fat over a high heat, shaking the pan constantly – usually in a sauté pan (a frying pan with straight sides and a wide base).

Scald To pour boiling water over food to clean it, or loosen skin, eg tomatoes. Also used to describe heating milk to just below boiling point.

Score To cut parallel lines in the surface of food, such as fish (or the fat layer on meat), to improve its appearance or help it cook more quickly.

Sear To brown meat quickly in a little hot fat before grilling or roasting.

Seasoned flour Flour mixed with a little salt and pepper, used for dusting meat, fish etc., before frying.

Shred To grate cheese or slice vegetables into very fine pieces or strips.

Sieve To press food through a perforated sieve to obtain a smooth texture.

Sift To shake dry ingredients through a sieve to remove lumps.

Simmer To keep a liquid just below boiling point.

Skim To remove froth, scum or fat from the surface of stock, gravy, stews, jam etc. Use either a skimmer, a spoon or kitchen paper.

Smoke To cure meat, poultry and fish by exposing it to wood smoke.

Souse To pickle food, especially fish, in vinegar flavoured with spices.

Steam To cook food in steam, usually in a steamer over rapidly boiling water.

Steep To immerse food in warm or cold liquid to soften it, and sometimes to draw out strong flavours.

Sterilise To destroy bacteria in foods by heating.

Stew To cook food, such as tougher cuts of meat, in flavoured liquid which is kept at simmering point.

Stir-fry To cook small even-sized pieces of food rapidly in a little fat, tossing constantly over a high heat, usually in a wok.

Suet Hard fat of animal origin used in pastry and steamed puddings. A vegetarian alternative is readily available.

Sugar syrup A concentrated solution of sugar in water used to poach fruit and make sorbets, granitas, fruit juices etc.

Sweat To cook chopped or sliced vegetables in a little fat without liquid in a covered pan over a low heat to soften.

Tepid The term used to describe temperature at approximately blood heat, ie 37°C (98.7°F).

Thermometer, sugar/fat Used for accurately checking the temperature of boiling sugar syrups, and fat for deep-frying respectively. Dual-purpose thermometers are obtainable.

Truss To tie or skewer poultry or game into shape prior to roasting.

Unleavened Flat bread, such as pitta, made without using a raising agent.

Vanilla sugar Sugar in which a vanilla pod has been stored to impart its flavour.

Whipping (whisking) Beating air rapidly into a mixture either with a manual or electric whisk. Whipping usually refers to cream.

Zest The thin coloured outer layer of citrus fruit, which can be removed in fine strips with a zester.

INDEX